THE
RISE OF MODERN
MYTHOLOGY

THE

RISE OF MODERN

MYTHOLOGY

1680-1860

BURTON FELDMAN

AND

ROBERT D. RICHARDSON

Indiana University Press

BLOOMINGTON / LONDON

For permission to quote from copyrighted material, we wish to thank the following:

The Bobbs-Merrill Company, Inc., for material from Novalis, *Hymns to the Night,* translated by Charles E. Passage, copyright © 1960 by The Bobbs-Merrill Company, Inc.;

Cambridge University Press, for material from *J. G. Herder on Social and Political Culture,* translated and edited by F. M. Barnard, copyright © 1969 by Cambridge University Press;

Cornell University Press, for material from *The New Science of Giambattista Vico,* Abridged Translation of the Third Edition (1744), by Thomas Goddard Bergin and Max Harold Fisch, copyright © 1970 by Cornell University; copyright © 1961 by Thomas Goddard Bergin and Max Harold Fisch; copyright 1948 by Cornell University;

Doubleday & Company, Inc., for material from *Writings of the Young Marx on Philosophy and Society,* by Loyd D. Easton and Kurt H. Guddat, copyright © 1967 by Loyd D. Easton and Kurt H. Guddat; and for material from *The Poetry and Prose of William Blake,* edited by David V. Erdman, copyright © 1965 by David V. Erdman and Harold Bloom;

Dover Publications, Inc., for material from Arthur Schopenhauer, *The World as Will and Representation,* translated by E. J. Payne, 1958;

Angel Flores, for material from *An Anthology of French Poetry from Nerval to Valery in English Translation,* edited by Angel Flores and published by Doubleday & Company, Inc., 1958;

Harvard University Press, for material from *The Early Lectures of Ralph Waldo Emerson,* Volume I, edited by S. E. Whicher and R. E. Spiller, copyright © 1959 by Harvard University Press;

The Pennsylvania State University Press, for material from Friedrich Schlegel, *Dialogue on Poetry and Literary Aphorisms,* translated, introduced, and annotated by Ernst Behler and Roman Struc, copyright © 1968 by The Pennsylvania State University Press;

Random House, Inc. (Modern Library), for material from A. Hofstadter and R. Kuhns, *Philosophies of Art and Beauty,* copyright © 1964 by Random House, Inc.;

The University of Michigan Press, for material from Friedrich Hölderlin, *Poems and Fragments,* translated by Michael Hamburger, copyright © 1967 by Michael Hamburger.

For her gracious permission to use Professor J.-R. Carré's edition of Fontenelle's *De l'origine des fables* as the basis of our translation, we wish to thank Mme. Carré, Directrice honoraire de Lycée in Bordeaux, France.

Published in Canada by Fitzhenry & Whiteside Limited, Don Mills, Ontario

Library of Congress catalog card number: 71–135005

ISBN: 0–253–35012–3

Manufactured in the United States of America

For Peggy and for Elizabeth

CONTENTS

PART TWO / *The Later Eighteenth Century*

PART THREE / *The Nineteenth Century to 1860*

Contents

FOREWORD

ONE IS GRATEFUL TO PROFESSOR BURTON FELDMAN AND PROFESSOR Robert Richardson for reading so many thousands of pages of both illustrious and half-forgotten authors, and for selecting, presenting, and competently annotating the texts of this rich and illuminating anthology. Such a source book on eighteenth- and nineteenth-century myth exegesis and historiography has not existed until now; one may be confident that it will not be equalled for a long period of time.

It was to be expected that the interest in myth and mythical thought, which has expanded spectacularly in recent decades, would incite more adequate investigation into the myth historiography of the past. Understandably, attention has been concentrated on nineteenth- and twentieth-century authors: that is to say, on those authors who, following the example of Max Müller, claimed a "scientific" approach to the study of myth. (Strangely enough, we do not as yet have at our disposal a comprehensive source book of this period.)

But a great surprise awaits the reader of the present anthology. He will discover that many of the rather "modern" post-Müllerian interpretations of myth prolong, although in a different perspective, some of the theses popular in the seventeenth and eighteenth centuries. It seems as if certain approaches and methodological presuppositions—for instance, the "naturalistic" or "astral," the psychological or historical, and specifically the "diffusionist" interpretations—periodically regain a more or less durable authority or, in some cases, even an unexpected vogue. Authors denouncing myth and mythical thinking as "irrational" abound in the seventeenth and eighteenth centuries as well as in modern times (for example, Andrew Lang, Wilhelm Schmidt, Émile Durkheim, Freud, and others). Likewise, the old and venerable opinion that the myths contain noble and elevated ideas or conceal scientifically correct descriptions of cosmic structures and norms is periodically reformulated. Thus, for example, at the beginning of our century E. Siecke and E. Stucken enthusiastically reactualized the central interpretation of the world mythologies. Siecke protested against the "rationalistic" depreciation of myth. Against E. B. Tylor, he emphatically stated that myths do not reflect animistic experiences and conceptions; they have nothing to do with belief in the soul, or with dreams and nightmares. Myths, argued Siecke, must be understood literally, because their contents always refer to specific celestial phenomena.

Stucken went even further. In his three-volume work, *Astralmythen* (Leipzig, 1896–1907), he tried to prove the direct or indirect Mesopotamian origin of all the mythologies of the world. For Stucken, as for the majority of pan-Babylonianists, all myths are concerned with the movements of the sun, the moon, and the planet Venus. Celestial revolutions were regarded by the Mesopotamians as the expression of the power, will, and intelligence of the deities. As early as 3000 B.C. this system had been completely developed in Mesopotamia, from which it was then diffused over the whole earth, being found even today in the myths of the "primitives." The pan-Babylonianists saw evidence of this diffusion in the astronomical knowledge implied in every mythological system. Such scientific observations, they argued, were certainly impossible for archaic peoples.

Thus, Siecke, Stucken, and the pan-Babylonianists linked the *naturalistic* origin of myths with their *historical* diffusion. Against the supporters of animism and of the theory of "elementary ideas" of Bastian, who explained the similarity of myths by the basic unity of the human mind, the pan-Babylonianists emphasized the highly elevated, "scientific" origin of mythology and its diffusion even among the most primitive tribes. One recognizes in this theory the prolongation of the astral interpretations of myths proposed by such men as Abbé Pluche (*Histoire du Ciel,* Paris, 1739) and Dupuis (*Mémoire sur l'origine des constellations et sur l'explication de la fable par le moyen de l'astronomie,* Paris, 1777–81). But, of course, these eighteenth-century authors were, in their turn, only correcting and improving the Neoplatonic exegesis of late antiquity.

But the interest of the texts collected in the present anthology is not limited to such examples of "continuity and change" in the understanding of mythology and mythical thinking. A close reading of these seventeenth- to nineteenth-century writers is revealing for the history of the Western mind. As has been abundantly illustrated in the present century, the evaluation of myth goes together with a specific understanding of religion and, accordingly, with a specific conception of man. After the collapse of Max Müller's solar mythology and of his *nomina-numina* theory, that is, of his explanation of myth as a "disease of language," most of the scholars writing between 1880 and 1920 considered myth as a secondary product, namely, as a verbal explication and justification of ritual. As Jane Harrison stated with regard to the ancient Greeks, *mythos* was primarily "just a thing spoken, uttered by the *mouth*"; its correlative was "the thing done, enacted, the *ergon* or work." Thirty years earlier, while investigating the origin and growth of Semitic religion, W. Robertson Smith had emphatically declared that "the myth was derived from the ritual, and not the ritual from the myth."

But proclaiming the myth "secondary" was not without consequences for the general evaluation of religion. All these authors tacitly took for granted that the primary and fundamental element of religion, and hence of human culture, is the *act* done by man, not the *story* of divine activity. Freud accepted these presuppositions, but he decided to push them much further: he identified in the "primeval murder" the primordial unique *act* which established the human condition, and consequently opened the way to religious and mythical creations.

The priority of ritual is no longer unanimously accepted today, and we witness again a stimulating tension between the partisans of "in the beginning was the *word*" and those who hold that "in the beginning" was the *act*. It would be a fascinating inquiry to decipher and investigate corresponding analogous tensions among the authors presented in this anthology. Of course, one can easily distinguish the "rationalists" and agnostics (Voltaire, Bayle, etc.) from the "illuminists," "occultists," and romantics (Pernety, Novalis, Schelling, etc.): the first group disparaging, the second group exalting the myth and mythical thought. But all these writers were nevertheless the heirs of the Greek and Judaeo-Christian understanding of *mythos* as fable or fiction, opposed to both *logos* and *historia*. Accordingly, Swedenborgians, illuminists, and occultists alike tried valiantly to defend the value of myth by elucidating its secret allegories and disclosing its profound symbolic meaning. It was only recently that, thanks to the work of three generations of anthropologists, the Western world has discovered that in archaic and traditional cultures the myth represents a sacred and *true* story, and constitutes the exemplary model for all significant human activities. Thus, only recently has one been able to speak of the *truth* of myth, that is, of its meaning, function, and power, while acknowledging its fictional character on the plane of cosmic or historical realities.

Consequently, it is no wonder that both the "rationalists" and the "illuminists" and romantics paid almost no attention to a number of supposedly well-known historical facts. Indeed, some of the rationalists and skeptics, like Voltaire and Bayle, went very far in their criticism of religion in general and Judaeo-Christianity in particular; but none of them suspected the mythical structure of other, more recent phenomena. Among these were many powerful and highly significant collective movements, popular enthusiasms, and millenaristic and apocalyptic systems, such as the doctrine of Antichrist and the Last Emperor, the eschatological theology of history of Gioacchino di Fiore and his prophecy of the imminent third *regnum,* the Angelic Pope and the *Renovatio mundi,* the Children's Crusade, the mythology of Frederick II, cosmocrator and cosmic Messiah who was supposed to bind the elements of the universe together, or even the esoteric mythology provoked by the rediscovery of the *Corpus hermeticum,* the millenarian implications of Giordano Bruno's heliocentrism, and the mystico-political prophecies of Campanella and Guillaume Postel. How important these messianic and prophetic movements were for the mediaeval and Renaissance Western world, how powerful their appeal was for all social classes, and how superbly *mythical* their structures were—we now begin to realize after the researches of K. Burdach, E. Kantorowicz, E. Buonaiuti, A. Dupront, and many others; it suffices to recall such books as *The Pursuit of the Millennium* (1957) by Norman Cohn, *Concordia Mundi* (1957) by W. Bousma, *Giordano Bruno and the Hermetic Tradition* (1964) by Frances A. Yates, or *The Influence of Prophecy in the Later Middle Ages: A Study of Joachimism* (1969) by Marjorie Reeves.

We would like to know how our "rationalist" and "illuminist" or "occultist" authors would have judged the value and meaning of myth if they could have investigated *these* mediaeval and Renaissance mythologies. But, of course, they were trained to consider all such material as being simply popular superstitions, heresies, or, worse, fanatical, and thus spiritually irrelevant, movements. When they analyzed and discussed the "myths," our authors opened their Homer and Ossian; or they enthusiastically devoured the memoirs of travelers and missionaries, or the newly discovered (and badly translated) Asiatic texts, or the remains of Teutonic mythology.

But, in spite of their limitations, how refreshing and illuminating are their writings! The compilers of the present anthology are to be congratulated for bringing them again to light.

MIRCEA ELIADE

ACKNOWLEDGMENTS

IN THE COURSE OF COMPLETING THIS STUDY, WE HAVE INCURRED innumerable debts of assistance and encouragement. We wish to thank the University of Denver, and especially Deans Nathaniel Evers and Edward Lindell and Vice Chancellor Wilbur Miller for faculty research grants that had wonderfully flexible time limits. We are greatly indebted to Professor Mircea Eliade for his bracing confidence that some such study as this was needed, and for his friendliness in contributing the Foreword to this volume. Professors Walter Jackson Bate and Gerald W. Chapman adjudged our aims and efforts with a kindliness and perspicuity one would have expected. Professor Robert Ackerman's erudite and astute comments on our manuscript have sustained (and sometimes chastened) us. We were fortunate to have the help of energetic, skillful librarians, especially Mrs. Gail Dow, and also Mr. Dennis North and Mr. Leo Nathanson. Miss Theresa Pearson must surely be one of the world's better typists, and her virtuosity saved us endless time; Mrs. Kathy Seaman Twain and Mr. Ray Fritts helped considerably. We are grateful for help with translations from Professor Raymond Tripp and Mrs. Karen Boklund Coffer. We relied heavily on the collections and services of the Widener Library at Harvard, the British Museum, and the Boston Athenaeum. Obviously, we owe debts of every kind to books and authors, but one at least ought to be acknowledged: the catalytic effect on our study of Professor Frank Manuel's brilliant *The Eighteenth Century Confronts the Gods*. Finally, we wish to thank Indiana University Press for their interest and most generous backing of this long study: most of all, Miss Nancy Ann Miller, who as an editor has all the skill that we desperately needed, superb tact and taste, and an unflagging enthusiasm that we sometimes felt was more than we deserved.

INTRODUCTION

THIS BOOK IS A CRITICAL HISTORY, WITH EXTENSIVE DOCUMENTA-
tion, of the rise and development of interest in myth from the early eighteenth
century through the middle of the nineteenth century. What prompts such
a volume is our sense that a reassessment of this period's contribution to the
study of myth is long overdue—both for its intrinsic worth and for its decisive
part in shaping twentieth-century views of myth. We hope to make clear
that our own century's fascination with myth is part of a broader movement
which spreads and intensifies from post-Renaissance times to our own. And, if
only implicitly, we wish to suggest that the remarkable impact of such modern
mythologists as Tylor or Frazer, Freud or Jung, Malinowski or Cassirer
or others has partly contributed to but also importantly derived from the relative
neglect of what has been said and thought about myth in the century and a
half after 1700. One of our aims here is to redress this neglect, and to show
that contemporary mythologizing is an indivisible part of a tradition—one
that has become increasingly obscured. But our main interest is to try to
demonstrate that this early modern work on myth is worth studying for its own
sake: that from around 1700 to around 1860, theorists, scholars, and artists
formulated and elaborated ideas that constitute a watershed in which radically
new views of myth emerged and continue to emerge. And these may help to
illuminate—from an unusual but nonetheless central viewpoint—some of the
much-debated shifts in taste and thought described under such rubrics as the
movement from neoclassic to romantic, or some of the problems involving,
for example, primitivism, nationalism, or historicism. To remedy neglect, but
convinced too that this early modern mythology can still show itself directly
persuasive and interesting, we have given over a sizable part of this volume to
documents. No comparable collection of texts on myth from this period exists;
several of these texts have not appeared before in English, and even in the
original languages and editions many of these are available only in very large
or specialized libraries. Many of these texts are indeed widely and easily
available, but their original concern with and importance for mythology is
often overlooked: it is not usually remembered that Hume or Isaac Newton
or Marx were also mythologists.

    Some of the main reasons for reopening the study of early modern mythology
begin with the recognition that the current study of myth seems unfortunately

fragmented. Literary people will be more likely to know about Sir James Frazer, Jesse Weston, and Northrop Frye than to value or be intimately acquainted with Bronislaw Malinowski, Lucien Lévy-Bruhl, or Claude Levi-Strauss. Psychological approaches to myth, such as those of Sigmund Freud or Carl Jung, remain apart from the symbolic-linguistic approaches of Ernst Cassirer or Suzanne Langer. The folklorist, such as Stith Thompson or Richard Dorson, shares material or approaches only in very small part with the historian of religion, such as Mircea Eliade; and a comparative mythologist, such as Joseph Campbell, will not necessarily share the same ground with a theologian, such as Rudolph Bultmann.

Existing histories of the study of myth reflect this fragmentation or specialization. Richard Chase's *The Quest for Myth* operates upon literary assumptions; Jan de Vries's *The Study of Religion* and his *Forschungsgeschichte der Mythologie* consider myth a subject for the historian of religion, as does Pinard de la Boullaye's *L'Étude comparée des Religions;* while Frank Manuel's *The Eighteenth Century Confronts the Gods* relates myth to broader eighteenth-century ideas about religion. Two recent symposia, Henry Murray's *Myth and Mythmaking* and Thomas Sebeok's *Myth: a Symposium,* have amply shown the range and diversity of modern approaches to myth, but offer no compelling reasons for preferring some theories to others.

One might conclude from this that myth is not a coherent subject; or that myth is in fact susceptible of several, perhaps many, approaches, even contradictory ones; or that there is a certain amount of confusion in the current study of myth. Since it is clear that myth is important to our century, and has been important for quite some time, we decided to examine the rise of the modern interest in myth, starting as far back as seemed necessary and proceeding on the assumption that no single theory or approach or definition or even attitude would be favored over any other. The period from 1680 to 1860 is, as we hope to show, the crucial one for an understanding of modern thought on myth; and this volume will try to show that almost every major theory about myth has roots and counterparts in that period. Indeed, we will suggest—indirectly, but with a sense of challenge—that almost every major approach to myth now in use was either originated, developed, or strongly foreshadowed during the eighteenth century and the first half of the nineteenth century.

The period from 1680 to 1860 is central to the study of modern myth for a variety of reasons. The end of the seventeenth century and the beginning of the eighteenth saw the rise and triumph of a rational spirit of inquiry, produced a flood of travel narratives revealing new customs and manners and myths, and saw the rise of deism and natural religion and the related attack on Christianity via the attack on pagan myth. It also witnessed the rise of the historical spirit and the rise of the comparative method of inquiry. All these factors encouraged and even demanded a complete reinvestigation of pagan myth, for it appeared to be related to religious truth, prehistory, current savage ideas and practices, and philosophical and artistic expression of contemporaneous ideas. Later, from the middle of the eighteenth century on, myth became increasingly caught up in the movement usually characterized as romanticism. Myth was restudied, radically revalued, and widely applied to practical ends in art, religion, history, and social theory. The revival of interest in the folk, the primitive, the archaic, and the heroic all fed the interest in myth. Then too, myth often became, for the nineteenth-century artist, a great source of new energy and power.

Around 1700, the term *myth* meant mainly the inherited body of myths, principally Greek and Roman; but this was gradually enlarged to include Indic, Nordic, African, and indeed all mythologies, ancient and modern. Secondly, myth was often associated during this period with pagan religious beliefs and was contrasted with Christian religious belief; a most interesting shift took place as the nineteenth century came to respect or approve the nature-based polytheism of the now noble Greeks instead of treating it as "heathen idolatry." Myth also meant—or involved—the study of myth, or mythography. And increasingly during the first half of the nineteenth century, myth came to take on two additional meanings. Myth came to be thought of as a creative process, a mode of the imagination usually expressed via art or literature. Myth also came to have a religious quality. No longer simply derogated as pagan and therefore false, myth came to be seen as the inner vivifying principle in all religion, and that inner life became, happily, accessible to art again for perhaps the first time since the Renaissance. Myth even became a new way of redeeming modern man by seeking to restore him to his original oneness with nature and by reacquainting him with that oneness, with his own best self, or with divinity.

Indeed, one way to characterize this whole period is to say that before about 1700 myth was largely confined to ancient pagan mythologies and was a subordinate or secondary study, rarely studied for itself and not considered important in its own right. It might seem that the opposite has been true of the scholarly study of myth from the mid-nineteenth century to the present: myth has formed part of the modern fields of anthropology, literary criticism, folklore, psychology, and history of religion. And yet in our time myth has less and less been treated as a subject in itself. But from the Enlightenment down through the first half of the nineteenth century, myth was widely and increasingly thought of as a primary subject, even a synoptic one, a master field of the first importance. Myth was taken up because it was thought of as a key, variously, to history, to linguistics and philology, to religion, to art, to the primitive mind, and to the creative imagination. Rather than claiming, as we tend to do now, that one's own field or discipline can illuminate mythology, scholars during the period from 1680 to 1860 tended to think, or to hope, that mythology would illuminate other fields around it. In various ways, Vico, Herder, Creuzer, K. O. Müller, and F. Max Müller share this point of view.

From 1680 to 1860, mythology grew from a concern with Greek, Roman, and at times, Egyptian myth into a concern with all myth. New mythologies were found in India, in China, in Persia, in Scandinavia, in Germany, in Africa, and in the New World. From bodies of myth, the writers and scholars of the time went on to consider the myth-making mind and to seek for the principles governing myths. As myth came to be considered more and more as a mode of thought or imagination and less and less as merely a body of knowledge about old stories, it was eagerly taken up by romantic writers in England, Germany, France, America, and elsewhere. By the mid-nineteenth century, the triumph of what might be called romantic conceptions of myth was notable in literature, religion, language study, and historical study.

Perhaps its very range, its interdisciplinary spread, as we would call it, led to the fragmentation of myth study by the third quarter of the nineteenth century. Myth had become important to a number of rapidly growing and increasingly narrow fields; but as a serious subject, myth had been unintentionally discredited by such puerile but popular compilations as Bulfinch's *The Age of Fable* and by the many books and essays of the widely esteemed F. Max Müller and his numerous followers. Thus mythology disappeared as the central or synoptic study that it had been with, say, Karl Otfried Müller, and became only a branch of each of half a dozen different academic fields. But within these fields, from the mid-nineteenth century on, myth study has continued at an ever-accelerating pace; and while the developments have not always kept track of each other, the major work is all easily available and need not take up space in this work.

Another reason for concentrating on the period from 1680 to 1860 is, as noted, that all the important modern approaches to myth may fairly seem to have been anticipated in one way or another during that time. The folklore approaches to myth may be seen in the work of the brothers Grimm, and in England, in the books of Thomas Keightley. Linguistic approaches to myth have a longer history, going back to the seventeenth-century etymological researches of Kircher, Bochart, and Fourmont, and coming down through students of language, such as Sir William Jones and Robert Lowth, to scholarly philologians, such as Heyne and F. Max Müller. The existential approach to myth was prefigured in Schelling; the racist use of myth, in Gobineau. Archetype criticism appears to have an early analogue, if not source, in biblical typology, and it can be seen reaching into myth study in our period in the works of Andrew Ramsay and George Faber. Symbolism as an approach to myth can be seen in the works of Herder, Goethe, Moritz, Creuzer, and the latter's followers. The modern myth work of biblical criticism and theology was prefigured and prepared by Lowth, by Eichhorn, and by D. F. Strauss. An interest in

myth as an aid to historical study, and even as history itself, can be traced in
Vico, in Fréret, in Gibbon, in Karl Otfried Müller, in Michelet, and in Quinet.
Early monomythographers or monomythologists include such Christian apolo-
gists as Fourmont and Faber, as well as such non-Christian synthesizers as
Charles Dupuis and F. Max Müller. Psychological theories of myth may be seen
in Fontenelle, Trenchard, Hume, and in many of the German romantics.
Anthropological approaches were anticipated by Lafitau, De Brosses, and
R. P. Knight.

The recent study of myth, then, is perhaps less novel than it sometimes
appears. And it is one object of this work to show that a wider acquaintance
with earlier thought on myth will substantially illuminate our own modern
concern with the subject.

The importance of, yet difficulty of access to, this material has in large part
dictated our approach in this volume. Originally, a critical anthology had been
projected: representative readings, with minimum notes. But the nature of
our subject forced us to recast this plan, and to expand the critical and
historical material radically. For one thing, the interest in myth in the period
considered here spreads over every and any area, scholarly, religious, philosophical, anthropological, artistic. It was as enthusiastically taken up in England
or Germany or France or America; it had many famous and also many quite
obscure devotees; it often exhibited the less familiar side of famous minds
(Isaac Newton or Gibbon, for example), or showed otherwise marginal figures
participating genuinely in a mainstream of thought. This ferment and diversity
of interest in myth is stimulated by, moves through, and cuts across almost
every climate and movement of thought in the hundred and fifty or so years here
considered. Although deep affinities or cores of agreement exist, the fluidity,
flexibility, and eclecticism frustrate any effort to extract very neat positions or
programs. This period's interest in myth offers almost a surfeit of riches. Thus,
the texts given seemed to demand a substantial amount of preparatory historical comment and continuity; and yet the natural evolution of the subject
had to be sustained. Our solution has been to give as much background and
interpretation as seemed useful, whether biographical, historical, or philosophical, but placed as closely as possible to the actual texts.

Such an organization has the advantage of imposing and intruding our own
biases or shortsightedness on any figure as little as possible. On the other
hand, of course, to proceed from figure to figure means that a continuous
narrative thread of history and description cannot be maintained. The advantages of the former seemed to us to far outweigh the disadvantages of the
latter. One more disadvantage: the figures we take up are obviously likely to
have been those who mainly wrote, theorized, or created, rather than those who
explored or did important practical work: thus, our study scants archaeologists,
field anthropologists, or philologists. But we must plead that this is a study of

attitudes, interest in and thought about myth in this period. In another way, this volume might have been called a study of the rise of modern mythography, that is, the historiography of mythology. But the term mythography is not sufficiently inclusive. It does not, for example, cover the *uses* of myth, such as the interest a poet takes in myth when he tries to turn ancient or received myths to new poetic account or when he seeks to grasp the inner principles or crucial experiences of myth itself, and so create new myth. Nor is mythography usually thought to include the interest in myth shown by theology, philology, anthropology, history, and classics. If myth and mythology are somewhat looser terms, they are also more inclusive; and one of the key aspects of interest taken in myth by the eighteenth and nineteenth centuries is the comprehensiveness and many-sidedness of myth.

T. S. Eliot once said that his study of Indian religion had brought him only to a state of enlightened ignorance. We may claim as much here. Our efforts to find in contemporary mythology a confident angle of departure or vision from which to synthesize our findings about myth soon foundered. The various and alluring mythologic persuasions of our own time—psychological, anthropological, literary, structuralist, history of religions, each sometimes derogatory of myth, sometimes nothing less than chthonic—are likely to send the unwary researcher back only to some eighteenth- or nineteenth-century version or root of a current position. We hoped to avoid this, and also to avoid here that too familiar phenomenon of contemporary interest in myth, that passionate and even learned bias toward some facet or other of myth as the true key or royal road. Certainly, as much was often true of the *philosophes* or romantics with their various certainties and enthusiasms. But even though alert to the dangers of such bias, our enlightened perplexity was only compounded since, as we moved back a century or so, we found all the same positions seemingly reappearing, if in different guise and with different data. The problem confronting the student of myth in the face of the richness and confusion of our time turns out to be the same problem found during the Enlightenment and romantic period. All the possible positions seem already there, only some dominant, some subdued: Blackwell was at the same time a "scientific" historian, a promoter of a sociologic view of myth, and a dedicated Orphist; that urbane *philosophe,* Fontenelle, very early saw most of the possible questions mythic interpretation might pose, including some arch-romantic ones, though he would not stay for an answer; Herder had much of the deist in his ardencies about the *Volk,* and even Marx occasionally sounded like Schelling or Friedrich Schlegel. If there is a conclusion to be reached here, it might be a quite tentative yet difficult one: that modern mythology—recent and earlier—is in urgent need of radical philosophic and historical examination of its own tradition, accomplishments, and presuppositions.

Inevitably, there have been omissions here, some deliberate, some unnoticed or undreamt. This study deliberately stops short of the recent modern period, which we set as beginning around 1860; the sufficient reason, we hope, is that the excited and many-sided mythologizing of our own period would require a companion volume, but is probably familiar enough to need no such exhumation of texts as attempted here. Within our period, for example, Swedenborg might have been included on his own merit and as an influence on Blake, Emerson, and others. Besides Marx, Comte or Saint-Simon or Bakunin or Bruno Bauer deserve extended attention. Certainly more could have been said about Hegel's view of myth, and particularly his interest in Creuzer's theories. Thomas Taylor, the influential Neoplatonist and translator of Plato, also merits much more examination. As much is true of Wilhelm von Humboldt and especially Alexander von Humboldt. If we were redoing this book, we would explore much more extensively the mythologic theories of the Illuminists, the alchemists, and the near-mythopoetic "cult of Reason" which flourished during the French Revolution. As much is true of lesser figures such as Lobeck, the great opponent of Creuzer, or Champollion and his work on hieroglyphs, or Émeric-David, the French eclectic. Or Hans Christian Andersen. Considering the omission of these and many others—in music, in painting and sculpture, in the mythology of the Far East—we can only argue that we had to stop somewhere, hoping for the best that our selections were most representative or important or both.

SECONDARY SOURCES

The following works have been found especially helpful for the study of myth as treated in our period. The list, confined to books published since 1860, is a brief selection of modern scholarship which can provide an initial yet broad survey of the subject. The bibliographies in these works also provide a starting point for further introduction into the proliferation of modern research and thought on myth. For texts from the period 1680 to 1860, see our primary bibliography; for works relating to specific topics or figures, see our separate bibliographical entries to each section.

Pinard de la Boullaye, S. J., *L'Étude comparée des Religions,* 2 vols. (Paris: G. Beauchesne, 1922) compactly and extensively provides a history of research and theorizing on religion and myth. Douglas Bush, *Mythology and the Romantic Tradition in English Poetry* (Cambridge: Harvard University Press, 1937) gives a most detailed account of English poetic use of Greek and Roman mythic themes, but restricts itself to this. Richard Chase, *Quest for Myth* (Baton Rouge: Louisiana State University Press, 1949) is a brief, enthusiastic but partisan account of some main mythologic positions, arguing for a view of myth as literature. Jan de Vries, *Forschungsgeschichte der Mythologie* (Freiburg and Munich: Verlag Karl Alber, 1961) surveys mythology from ancient times to the present, gives descriptions and brief texts, and is openly sympathetic with certain romantic viewpoints; the rationalist period is somewhat scanted. Richard M. Dorson, *The British Folklorists. A History* (Chicago: The University of Chicago Press, 1968) offers a rich sampling of texts from early folklorists.

Otto Gruppe, *Geschichte der klassischen Mythologie und Religionsgeschichte während des Mittelalters im Abendland und während der Neuzeit* (Supplement to *Ausführliches Lexikon der Griechischen und Römischen Mythologie,* ed. W. H. Roscher) (Leipzig, 1921): a monument of historical scholarship, with brief accounts and bibliographies of hundreds of mythologists from classical times to date of writing, and the single most useful reference work for the study of myth. Gruppe, however, excludes all mythic thought not primarily scholarly or theoretical. Christian Hartlich and Walter Sachs, *Der Ursprung des Mythosbegriffes in der Modernen Bibelwissenschaft* (Tübingen: Mohr, 1952) is the best account of how modern "demythologizing" descends from eighteenth-century mythology and Bible criticism. M. J. and F. S. Herskovits, "Introduction" in *Dahomean Narrative* (Evanston: Northwestern University Press, 1958) gives a condensed but wide survey of thinking about myth with anthropological study in mind. Erik Iversen, *The Myth of Egypt and its Hieroglyphs* (Copenhagen, 1961) for a sweeping history of mythologic interest in Egypt, and especially good on the Egyptology of such seventeenth-century figures as Kircher.

Frank Manuel, *The Eighteenth Century Confronts the Gods* (Cambridge: Harvard University Press, 1959) views the Enlightenment from the perspective of its absorbed interest in myth and religion, from Fontenelle through the earliest work of Herder. Arnaldo Momigliano, *Studies in Historiography* (London: Weidenfeld and Nicolson, 1966), especially the first chapter distinguishing between *érudit* and *philosophe* mentality and approach to myth. Martin Nilsson, *Geschichte der Griechischen Religion,* 2 vols. (Munich, 1941), a standard work. R. Pettazoni, *Svolgimento e carattere della storia delle religioni* (Bari: Laterza, 1924), a classic work in history of religion. Charles Picard, *Les religions préhistoriques* (Paris, 1948). P. D. Chantepie de la Saussaye, *Lehrbuch der Religionsgeschichte,* 2 vols. (Freiburg, 1887), especially Volume I on mythology; trans. English, 1891. Raymond Schwab, *La Renaissance orientale* (Paris: Payot, 1950), an indispensable survey of European interest in India and Persia during the eighteenth and nineteenth centuries. Fritz Strich, *Die Mythologie in der deutschen Literatur von Klopstock bis Wagner,* 2 vols. (Halle, 1910): German literary interest in myth, wide coverage but poorly bibliographed. A. Leslie Willson, *A Mythical Image: The ideal of India in German Romanticism* (Durham: Duke University Press, 1964), especially good for an account of the impact of newly discovered mythology on an important literary movement.

   Standard modern reference and dictionary works are excluded here; besides
being readily available, most of these scant or ignore the scholarship of our
earlier period. For this reason, acquaintance with such great older standard
reference works as those of Charles Anthon, *A Classical Dictionary* (1841) or
of Sir William Smith, *Dictionary of Greek and Roman Biography and
Mythology* (1844–1849) are preferable to most current examples. Attention
should be directed to an exemplary modern work dealing with our subject and
period: Herbert Hunger, *Lexikon der Griechischen und Römischen Mythologie*
(Vienna: Verlag Brüder Hollinek, 1959) which is at once an encyclopedia of
classical myths but also of the detailed use of these from ancient to modern
times in literature, theater, music, painting, opera, and sculpture.

THE
RISE OF MODERN
MYTHOLOGY

PART ONE

The Earlier Eighteenth Century

FROM 1700 TO 1750—USING THESE DATES ONLY AS A CONVENIENT but imprecise set of brackets for what might otherwise be called the Enlightenment—most thinking about myth may be described as subscribing to the orthodox Christian view of myth, the deist view of myth, or the rationalist view of myth. The Christians, as Henry Murray has reminded us, drove home the notion that *myth* meant pagan fables and pagan religion and was therefore, as a word, exactly equal to *false,* while *gospel,* meaning Christian religious stories, was exactly equal to *true*. To Christian thinkers in the eighteenth century, such as Samuel Shuckford, the Abbé Fourmont, or Bishop Warburton, Greek or Roman or Egyptian myth meant only a collection of false gods and grotesque tales that needed to be explained away or reconciled with Scripture. Pagan myth could be interpreted as an invention of the devil, or the gods could be identified as the fallen angels; but the usual interpretation was to consider pagan fable a degenerate version of biblical truth. The deists, among them John Toland and John Trenchard, believed in a primitive natural monotheistic religion, and they were apt to argue that Christian belief and ritual and pagan myth and custom alike represented corruptions of the simple primal religion. And such rationalists as Fontenelle, Bayle, Voltaire, and Hume tended to approach myth as something savage or foolish, at best a memorial of primitive man's erroneous attempts to explain his world. Most enlightenment thought, then, did not admire myth, did not seek to enter into its spirit or spell, and in fact sought ways to disarm and denature it, to undercut its popularity with artists and writers, and to belittle or deny its curious and long-lived hold on the imagination.

But while rationalist disparagement of myth was the rule, there were important exceptions. Poets and dramatists, essay writers and painters, and most of the educated people of the day knew and made familiar use of mythology, usually Greek and Roman; and writers such as Alexander Pope kept alive the attractive and entertaining aspect of myth, free of heavy theorizing. Secondly, there was a surprising number of thinkers who admired or respected or were moved by myth; who were, to some degree, imaginatively in sympathy with myth; or who were becoming interested in recalling the nobly heroic and early ages of man. Vico, Andrew Ramsay, Nicolas Fréret, Joseph Spence, Mark Akenside, Thomas Blackwell, and Robert Lowth all had impulses in this direction, and it is from this aspect of eighteenth-century myth study that one can most clearly forecast the later romantic revival of myth.

Within these broad groupings and these different attitudes, the period witnessed a wide variety of particular theories, individual emphases, new ideas, and new applications of both old and new materials. Fontenelle's essay on fables is neither Christian nor deist, and it not only avoids narrowness and polemic but also sketches or entertains a surprising number of sensible and still defensible approaches to myth. Fontenelle suggested, among other things, that myths arise from psychological causes (fear or wonder in a savage mind), from primitive philosophizing, and from the successive exaggerations of generations of story tellers. Pierre Bayle made constant use of pagan myth, which he seemed to despise, but which was really enhanced by his sharp, witty writing. Whether one approves of his attitude or not—and he is hard to pin down—mythology is, in his hands, highly detailed, wonderfully scandalous, and utterly fascinating. His treatment of pagan myth also has a way of seeming applicable to the Bible and to Christianity; can one afford to smile at pagan monogenesis in the story of Athene but look with reverent awe upon its Christian equivalent in the story of Christ? John Toland, a deist, attacked Christianity and pagan myth alike as corruptions of a natural primal monotheism. Toland argued that polytheism was a cynical invention of the priests. This is the "two-religion theory," which posits one high religion for the wise and the initiated and one vulgar, priest-ridden, ritual-laden, superstition-filled religion for the herd. John Trenchard, also a deist, spoke to the irrational element in myth, in his *The Natural History of Superstition,* arguing that the myth-making impulse is the same as the religious impulse and that both tend to progress naturally from faith to fervor to fanaticism; only a thoroughly rational religion could avoid the pitfall. Richard Blome, Willem Bosman, and Père Joseph Lafitau all left accounts of contemporary savage peoples, that illustrate in various ways the range and the impact of new knowledge about the savage mind and about primitive myth

and religion. One reason that enlightenment thinking about myth is as suggestive as it is, is that theorists of myth and religion could rely, if they wished,
not on Greek and Roman writers alone, but on the new and exciting discoveries made by the travelers, merchants, and missionaries of the time.

Vico's profound and original approach to myth emphasized the idea that
myth came—and legitimately so—from man's own inner nature. Thus, for
Vico myth was not mere error, or degenerate truth, or the result of misunderstood or misexplained natural events. Vico's effort, which was not appreciated
widely until a hundred years later, paves the way for an acceptance of myth
as an early, necessary, and even an admirable phase in the development of
civilized man. Andrew Ramsay, a little known Scot, put forward in *The
Travels of Cyrus* a remarkable essay on mythology which uses comparative
and structural criticism to locate the major archetypal patterns behind several
major religious systems, an approach that tacitly recognized these religions and
was therefore not as well received by Christian thinkers as the greatly inferior
but widely known works of Samuel Shuckford. Shuckford wrote a chronology
of early history which took the Bible to be literally true and which pushed all
other early narratives into an enforced harmony with the biblical account.
Procrustean and rigid as this work is, it nevertheless treats myth as at least an
historical record, however warped and bungled. This approach to myth as
history, most ably championed by the Abbé Banier, interprets gods as deified
mortal heroes, is called Euhemerism, and is a common feature of eighteenth-
century thought on myth. Another French *érudit,* the Abbé Fourmont, is an
example of how etymological "research" could be used to make all heathen
deities mere linguistic variations on biblical names.

The article from Ephraim Chambers's *Cyclopedia* is included to show the
various concepts of fable during the period. Chambers shows how one could
connect Aesopian apologue with Homeric myth, and also shows that plot or
action is central to the idea of myth. The Abbé Fréret, a controversial figure
in French scholarly circles, wrote as sensibly on myth as any eighteenth-
century scholar. He emphasized, refreshingly, the complexities of myth, where
so many writers worked only to narrow and simplify. A brilliant example of
this single-minded reductionism is Bishop Warburton's ponderous work on
The Divine Legation of Moses, which refers myth back to early sun or star
worship, as does the work of the Abbé Pluche. The strangely unbalanced tone
of these last two should not obscure the fact that they were early adherents of
the solar theory of myth, a theory that is not dead.

With Thomas Blackwell and Robert Lowth, one begins to see how myth,
considered as the literary record or religious beliefs or social code of early
heroic societies (Greek or Hebrew), begins to stir serious interest in itself as
something true and valuable. No longer interested in debunking myth as
savagery in order to exalt reason and civilization, these writers began to look

to myth for the simple and sublime values, pure religion, and honest emotions that decline as society advances. This approach took root most strongly in Germany, but emerged all over Europe as the romantic tide advanced. But one still finds, around the middle of the eighteenth century, such men as Joseph Spence treating mythology as a polite and elegant branch of the fine arts, even though poets, such as Akenside, are beginning to try to get not only elegance but also some sort of climate of emotional acceptance of myth into their poetry; and William Stukeley's interest in Druids and in primitive and heroic British society before the Romans shows how myth study could run in the narrow channel of antiquarian nationalism. Hume and Voltaire, both well known for their views about religion, also had views about mythology, and have been included to show that however one may see the stirrings of a romantic revaluation of myth, the enlightenment rationalist distrust of myth was still a powerful force and was still being given eloquent expression at mid-century in essays that command respect today.

R.R.

Bernard Fontenelle

[1657–1757]

FONTENELLE'S ESSAY *Of the Origin of Fables* marks a turning point in the study of mythology. Polyhistors and etymologizers, such as Bochart, Vossius, and Kircher, had typified the seventeenth-century approach to myth; with Fontenelle and Bayle, the new tone of enlightened rational criticism becomes the dominant, perhaps the exclusive force. In his purposeful insistence on the primitive mentality, his assumption of a universal human nature, and his sophisticated awareness of psychology, Fontenelle brings new ideas to the familiar subject of Greek mythology. His essay's reliance on historical perspective and his brilliant, although sketchy, use of comparative techniques are evidence of the new methods and approaches that were coming into use toward the end of the seventeenth century. Though the essay was not printed until 1724, it had been written much earlier: Fontenelle's biographer, Trublet, thought the essay was actually composed during the sixteen nineties. The short essay *De l'origine des fables* grew out of a larger essay on history, and is also related to Fontenelle's well-known redaction of Antonius Van Dale's *De Oraculis.* Van Dale had written, in 1683, a knotty and polylingual treatise that by attacking miracles, magic, and superstition in pagan and even in Jewish religion, was actually attacking the same elements in Christianity. Fontenelle's witty and readable *Histoire des oracles* (1686) maintained this covert attack and sought to sap the still current belief in demons, but was ostensibly only a plea for rationalism. The piece became popular, even notorious, and has been at least as influential as the essay on fables. Indeed, the Abbé Banier, in his *La mythologie et les fables expliquées par l'histoire,* records his debt to the former work, rather than to the latter and more relevant essay:

M. Fontenelle, than whom none was more proper to throw out all the stiff pedantry of Greek and Latin, which makes Van Dale's Treatise but dry, and only fit for the learned, has put it into a genteeler dress, and adapted it to the capacity of every reader, but this work has already made so much noise, that I shall easily be forgiven, though I say no more of it. (Book IV, Chap. 1)

Fontenelle's influence on later studies of myth is wide, various, and unusually hard to specify. Professor Manuel has noted David Hume's debt, and both Andrew Lang and Levy-Bruhl have spoken of the work on fables as a pioneer effort. Lang even wrote an appendix for his *Myth, Ritual, and Religion,* called "Fontenelle's Forgotten Common Sense," in which he wrote:

Why did the ancient peoples—above all the Greeks—tell such extremely gross and irrational stories about their Gods and heroes? That is the riddle of the mythological Sphinx. It was answered briefly, wittily and correctly by Fontenelle; and the answer was neglected, and half a dozen learned but impossible theories have since come in and out of fashion.

Only within the last ten years has Fontenelle's idea been, not resuscitated, but rediscovered; the followers of Mr. E. B. Tylor, Mannhardt, Gaidoz, and the rest do not seem to be aware that they are only repeating the notions of the nephew of Corneille.

Indeed, from the early eighteenth century on, Fontenelle was steadily acknowledged, but always lightly; continually praised, but always quickly; generally deferred to, but generally with a touch of patronage. The blunt truth seems to be that Fontenelle's brilliant, many-sided, and suggestive essay was something of an embarrassment, even a thunder-stealer, for many students of myth, for there is scarcely a single important attitude toward myth that was not taken up, developed, or implied in this remarkable short essay.

At a time when most writers on mythology thought of their subject either as the problem of heathen idolatry or as the explication of rather silly artistic embellishments, Fontenelle had the sense and insight to focus on the fables or myths themselves. He thus avoided the polemical tone so common to the sort of eighteenth-century myth study that is essentially religious debate, John Toland being a good example. Furthermore, the essay's clear interest in origins, in transmission, and in the persistence of mythological thinking lends the piece coherence and logic, for the origins of mythology reveal for Fontenelle the nature, the function, and finally the meaning of mythology.

Initial emphasis is on the psychological origins of myth. Using the analogies of savages and children, Fontenelle constructs a typical savage mind: weak, credulous, imaginative, given to self-magnification, and in love with marvels—in short, rather prone to invent and to embellish wonders in a gentle and harmless fashion. Fontenelle's generalizations about the primitive mentality are not based on what we call field work; he

comes to his point by analogies, fed in turn by his wide reading, particularly in contemporaneous travel literature. His description of the myth-making mind seems quite close to the early eighteenth-century attitude that regarded fancy as an essentially misleading although pleasant sort of imaginative activity.

Fontenelle quickly balances such psychologizing by arguing that in some cases fables were the physics of the ancients, which is to say that myths came about as answers to the questions about the world posed by primitive thinkers. These "just-so stories" were, of course, silly and wrong; but Fontenelle's instinct is more for urbane condescension than for sneering, and he quickly goes on to say that the method involved in this early "philosophy," as he calls it, is exactly the same method as that of modern thinkers in that both try to explain the unknown by means of the known. The only advantage the moderns have is that of superior premises. Here and elsewhere, Fontenelle comes back again and again to the point that the human mind is essentially the same, not only in widely separated cultures but even at different levels of cultural development. And this assumption of a universal human nature is one of the reasons for the essay's remarkable modernity of tone. By insisting that myths have their origin in mental processes that would be the same in any time or climate, Fontenelle prefigured such later thinkers as Jung. He also, for his own time, struck at the popular diffusion theory, which, as the religionists generally held it, argued that everything in the world, including the Greek myths, had to be either a pure or an impure descendant of what we are given in Genesis. But Fontenelle avoided any direct reference to these religious controversies. One reason, of course, was the then fierce censorship and the very real threat of the Bastille; another is that a great ironist need not attack openly. What would a thoughtful Christian have made of Fontenelle's comment that "some extraordinary happening may have led people to believe that a god had had an affair with a woman"? The Immaculate Conception is not mentioned, and the writer could quickly claim to be speaking of pagan notions only. By the time one sees blood, the knife has passed on.

Fontenelle's restless and imaginative eclecticism led him to a new and highly suggestive version of the older fear-theory that interpreted mythology as a concrete expression of man's fascination with power. In trying to account for the violence and irrationalism of the Greek myths, Fontenelle argued that these were due to the fact that all the pagan deities have the attributes of power, bodily strength, and physical domination uppermost in them and that this, in turn, was due to the high value placed on these qualities in the primitive societies in which the myths were formed.

Since he sought universal explanations for origins and for the transmission of myths, Fontenelle was continually groping for general principles. Thus, for example, he came to consider how it was that the imaginative and fanciful stories about the gods were passed from one generation to the next uncritically and without question, and he concluded that what began as novelty must have quickly become convention. He followed this with a precise and thoughtful estimate of the nature and force of literary convention as it applies to myth.

Of all the techniques and approaches that Fontenelle's work made fashionable, none has had a greater or more lasting effect than his apparently casual comparison between the classical Greeks and the Indians of South America. From similarities between the Orpheus and the Manco Capac stories, Fontenelle argued that when the Orpheus stories were formed, the Greeks were, therefore, on the same cultural level as the Peruvians.

This sort of juxtaposition is the start of the modern comparative method, which has been used so successfully in mythology, anthropology, religion, and literature. But Fontenelle's comparative method should not be regarded as the modern scholarly technique it has become. It is, rather, a secularization of the study of the conformities between Christian and pagan history, religion, customs, and manners which was to remain a staple of eighteenth-century religious scholarship. Then too, Fontenelle's sympathy with the Moderns in the quarrel between the Ancients and the Moderns relieved him of any obligatory veneration for the Greeks, which might have stood in the way of his comparing them to a rough tribe of South American Indians.

Of the Origin of Fables never bogs down; with ease and skill, Fontenelle picked up idea after idea, turning his subject this way and that in an effort to see all sides of it. He remarked that "with most peoples, fables changed into religion, but among the Greeks they changed, so to speak, into the fine arts." He hinted that this is due to the myths' embodying "the sort of imagination most common among men," and if this is not a full explanation, it at least recognizes that for the study of myth we must be prepared to cope with a confluence of religion and art. In like manner, Fontenelle touched suggestively upon the idea that some myths are due to the debasement or degeneration that occurs when they are transmitted from one people to another. He set out the idea that some myths came from the Greeks' having misunderstood certain words or having forgotten the meanings of certain others, a notion later to be celebrated as the "disease of language" theory and to be associated with F. Max Müller. After shrewdly observing that the advent of writing both facilitated transmission and fixed the previously fluid texts, thus putting a date to the mythopoeic era, Fontenelle brought the essay to a close maintaining, by way of logical conclusion, that the myths are not at all allegories of a higher wisdom. They are at last errors, and the sometimes charming results of other errors, made by uncultivated minds.

Fontenelle was the most imaginative of those who deprecate myth. But although he found the stories absurd, he at least addressed the problems with a variety of approaches and with an imaginative sympathy that often seems to counterbalance his settled distrust. And between this famous and typical thinker of the Enlightenment and many modern theorists of myth there is only one crucial difference, though it is a crucial difference; modern theorists of myth, using most of Fontenelle's techniques, give full assent and approval to myths, praise the mythopoeic age, and deplore the rational, non-mythic age Fontenelle thought so highly of.

R.R.

REFERENCES The text is our translation, based on J. R. Carré, *De l'origine des fables* (Paris: Félix Alcan, 1932). This is a critical edition, with notes, and is now standard. Other works of Fontenelle bearing directly on myth include *Sur l'histoire*, in *Oeuvres* (Paris, 1825), and *Histoire des oracles,* ed. Louis Maigron (Paris, 1908). This redaction of Van Dale's *De Oraculis* was translated into English by Aphra Behn in 1688 as *History of Oracles.*

There is no full-length assessment of Fontenelle's contributions to the study of myth, but see Andrew Lang, *Myth, Ritual, and Religion* (London, 1887); Richard Chase, *The Quest for Myth* (Baton Rouge: Louisiana State University Press, 1949); and Frank Manuel, *The Eighteenth Century Confronts the Gods* (Cambridge: Harvard University Press, 1959). Also useful are the Abbé Trublet's *Mémoires pour servir à l'histoire de la vie et des ouvrages de M. de Fontenelle,* 2d ed. (1758), J. R. Carré's *La Philosophie de Fontenelle ou le sourire de la raison* (1932), Henry Vyverberg, *Historical Pessimism in the French Enlightenment* (Cambridge: Harvard University Press, 1958), J. H. Brumfitt, *Voltaire Historian* (Oxford: Oxford University Press, 1958), and H. L. Edsall, *The Idea of History and Progress in Fontenelle and Voltaire* (New Haven: Yale University Press, 1941).

FONTENELLE

Of the Origin of Fables

DURING our childhood we become so very accustomed to the fables of the Greeks that when we are able to reason we no longer find them as astonishing as they are. But if one eventually rids himself of the customary way of seeing things, it is impossible not to be appalled at seeing the entire ancient literature of a people nothing but a pile of chimeras, dreams, and absurdities. Would it be possible for anyone to give all that out as true? To what purpose would anyone have given it out as false? What was that love of man for manifest and ridiculous falsehoods and why didn't it persist? For the fables of the Greeks were not like our novels, which are given us for what they are and not for history; there are no other ancient stories except the fables.* Let us clear up this matter, if it is possible; let us study the human mind in one of its strangest productions, for often enough, it is just there that it can be best understood.

In the first centuries of the world, and among the nations who had never heard of or who had not preserved the traditions of the family of Seth, ignorance and barbarism must have existed to a degree which we are now hardly able to imagine. Consider the Kafirs, the Laplanders, or the Iroquois; but even this must be done with caution, since these peoples are already ancient and must have come to a degree of knowledge and manners that the earliest men did not have.

The more ignorant one is and the less experience one has, the more miracles one will see. The first men saw plenty of them, and naturally, as the fathers told their children what they had seen and what they had done, there were nothing but prodigies in the tales of those times.

When we tell about some surprising thing, our imagination gets heated up with its subject and begins of itself to enlarge the subject and to add to it whatever may be lacking to make it altogether marvelous, as though regretting to leave a good thing imperfect. Moreover, one is flattered by the surprise and admiration one causes in his audience and is quite happy to augment it further, since something in this seems to please our vanity. These two reasons, taken together, make it possible for a man, who had no intention of lying when he began to tell a story that was a little unusual, to catch himself starting to lie despite precautions; thence it comes that it takes a considerable effort and a particular attentiveness to keep from telling things that are not strictly true. How easy,

* Fontenelle uses *histoire* to mean both "story" and "history" throughout the essay.—Ed.

given this, would it be for those who naturally love to invent and to impose on others?

The tales that the first men told their children were, then, often false in themselves, because they were made up by people inclined to a great many things that weren't there; and beyond that, having been exaggerated either in good faith, as we just explained, or in bad, it is clear that they were already considerably altered from their source. But assuredly it would get worse when they passed from mouth to mouth; each one would forget some little scrap of the truth and would put in a false bit—principally a miraculous bit, which is the most agreeable kind—and perhaps it would happen that after a century or two, not only would nothing at all of the small amount of original truth remain but also practically nothing of the original falsehood.

Can one believe what I am saying? There had been philosophy even in those rude times, and it did considerable service in the birth of fables. Those men who had a bit more talent than others were naturally moved to look for the causes of the things they saw. From whence could come this river which always flowed, a thinker of those ages must have asked. A strange sort of philosopher, but he would have been a Descartes in his time. After a long meditation, he discovered with great joy that there was someone who had charge of always pouring this water from a pitcher. But who furnished the water in the first place? The thinker did not go that far.

It is necessary to note that these ideas, which might be called the philosophic systems of those times, were always copied after the best-known things. One had often seen water poured out of a pitcher. One could then imagine with ease how a god could pour out the water of a river; and by the same facility one had in imagining it, one was completely moved to believe it. Thus, to give a reason for thunder and lightning, one could willingly picture to oneself a god in human form throwing arrows of fire at us—ideas manifestly taken from very familiar objects.

This philosophy of the first ages worked on a principle so natural that even today our philosophy has no other; that is, we explain the unknown things in nature in terms of those we have before our eyes, and we carry over into natural philosophy ideas supplied us by experience. We have discovered by usage, and not by divination, how weights, springs, and levers work; we cannot imagine nature working except by levers, weights, and springs. These poor savages, who were the first to live in the world, either did not know these things at all or paid them little attention. They could only explain the effects of nature by grosser and more palpable things with which they were familiar. And have we not done the same? We are always representing the unknown by analogies with what is known to us, but, happily, there is all the reason in the world to believe that the unknown cannot but resemble what we presently know.

From this crude philosophy, which necessarily ruled in the early ages, were born the gods and goddesses. It is quite curious to see how the human imagination has given birth to false divinities. Men saw many things that they were unable to do: throwing lightning, stirring winds, raising the waves of the sea; all these were well beyond their powers. They imagined beings more powerful than themselves, and able to produce these grand effects. It was of course necessary that these beings be made like men. What other form could they have? From the moment they had human figures, imagination naturally attributed to

them everything human; and there they were, men in all respects, except that they were always just a little stronger than men.

Thence comes something we have not yet reflected on; and that is, in all the divinities that the pagans imagined, the idea of power was made dominant, and hardly any consideration was given to wisdom, justice, and all the other attributes that pertain to the divine nature. Nothing could more effectively prove that these divinities are very old, and nothing could better mark the road taken by the imagination in forming them. The first men were utterly unaware of any better quality than bodily strength. Wisdom and justice did not even have names in ancient languages, nor have they today among the barbarians of America. Moreover, the first idea that men had of some superior being was based on extraordinary effects, and not on the regulated order of the universe, which they were incapable of recognizing or admiring. Thus they imagined the gods in a time when they had nothing finer to give them than power, and they imagined them according to things that bore the mark of power and not according to things that had the stamp of wisdom. It is therefore not surprising that they imagined many gods, often opposed to one another, cruel, bizarre, unjust, and ignorant, all of which is not the least contrary to the idea of force and power, which is the sole idea they had used. It was of course necessary that these gods be perceived in terms both of the time they were first made and of the occasion that first produced them. Yet what a miserable sort of power was given them. Mars, the god of war, is wounded in a fight with a mortal, which undermines his dignity a good deal; but as he retires, he raises a cry such that ten thousand men together could not have equalled it; it is by this vigorous cry that Mars excels

Diomedes, and it is enough, according to the judicious Homer, to save the god's honor. From the way the imagination is constructed, it is content with little things, and it will always recognize for a god whatever has a bit more power than a man.

Cicero has said somewhere that he would have preferred it if Homer had endowed men with the qualities of gods rather than, as he did, endow the gods with the qualities of men. But Cicero was asking too much; what he called in his own time the qualities of gods were unknown in the time of Homer. The pagans had always copied their divinities after themselves; thus to the extent that men became more perfect, the gods became so as well. The first men were indeed brutal, and they yielded everything to force; the gods became nearly as brutal, and only a bit more powerful, and thus one gets the gods of the time of Homer. Men began to have ideas of wisdom and justice; the gods picked them up; they began to be wise and just, and became more and more so in proportion to the extent to which these ideas developed among men; and thus one gets the gods of the time of Cicero, and they are preferable to those of Homer's time because better philosophies had had a hand in the business.

So far, the first men had given birth to fables more or less innocently. One is ignorant, consequently one sees numerous prodigies, and naturally one exaggerates the surprising things in narrating them. They continue to collect diverse falsehoods as they pass through many mouths. Some very crude and absurd sorts of systems of philosophy become established, but no others could be built on such a basis. Upon these foundations, we shall now see that men have, in some manner, taken pleasure in deceiving themselves.

What we are calling the philosophy of

the first ages found it quite natural to ally itself with historical fact. A young man fell into a river and no one could recover the body. What happened? The philosophy of the time teaches that there are in the river young girls who rule it. The girls have carried off the young man—as is very natural—and one needs no proofs in order to believe it. A man, of whose birth one knows nothing at all, has some remarkable talent. There are gods made very much like men; so one looks no further for his parents; he is the son of one of those gods. When one considers attentively the majority of fables, one finds that they are only a mixture of fact with the philosophy of the time, which explains quite easily why the facts have, naturally, the tinge of the marvelous. It was simply that gods and goddesses, who resembled us completely, were mingling with men on earth.

As these true stories, mixed together with false imaginings, had a good deal of currency, people began to make up others without any basis; or at least one no longer told about mildly remarkable things without reclothing them with elaborations that one knew were bound to please. These elaborations were false; sometimes perhaps they were intended to be taken as false; and yet the stories did not pass as fabulous. This can be understood by a comparison between our modern histories and the ancient.

In the times when the intellect was most vigorous, as in the era of Augustus and in the present century, we have enjoyed reasoning about the actions of men, penetrating into motive, and knowing character. Historians of these times accommodate themselves to this taste. They take care not to write bare dry facts; they accompany them with motives and mix in portraits of their personages. Do we believe that these portraits and motives are precisely true? Do we have the same faith in them as we have in the facts? No, we know perfectly well that the historians have guessed at them as well as they were able and that it is nearly impossible that they have guessed altogether accurately. However, we do not complain that the historians have worked up this embellishment, which appears quite realistic, and it is on account of this verisimilitude that the mixture of falsehoods that we realize are in our histories does not make us regard the histories as fables.

Similarly, after the ancients had acquired a taste for stories (in ways of which we have spoken) in which gods, goddesses, and the marvelous in general played a part, they no longer retailed stories that were not elaborated with these. They knew that it could not be true, but in those times it was probable and that was enough to preserve for the fables the quality of histories.

Even today, the Arabs fill their histories with prodigies and miracles, most often ridiculous and grotesque. Doubtless they are taken by them only as ornaments; and they do not have to guard against deception, since it is with them a sort of convention to write thus. But when this sort of history reaches other peoples who have the taste to want to write the exact truth about things, they are believed in the literal sense, or at least people persuade themselves that the events were considered true by those who published them and by those who received them without contradiction. Certainly the misunderstanding is considerable. When I said that the lies in these histories were recognized for what they were, I intended to speak of people a little more enlightened than the majority, who are destined to be the dupes of everyone.

In the early ages, one not only explained via a chimerical philosophy whatever was

surprising in the stories, but it was the nature of the philosophy of that time to explain it by a story invented to please. One saw in the northern skies two constellations, called the two bears, that appeared all the time, not setting like the others. One did not hesitate to imagine that they were raised to the pole star for the consideration of the spectators; one did not know much about it. One imagined that, of the two bears, one was formerly a mistress and the other a son of Jupiter; that when these two persons had been changed into constellations, the jealous Juno had asked Ocean not to allow them to descend to his domain like the others and rest there. All metamorphoses are the physics of the early ages. Mulberries are red because they were dyed in the blood of lovers; the partridge flies close to the ground because Daedalus, who was changed into a partridge, remembered the bad fortune of his son, who had flown too high, and so forth. I have never forgotten that when I was a child they told me that the elder tree had once had grapes as fine as those of the vine, but that when the traitor Judas hanged himself from this tree, its fruits had become as bad as they are now. This fable could only have been born since Christianity, and it is precisely of the same order as those ancient metamorphoses Ovid collected; that is to say, man has always had an inclination for this sort of story. They are doubly pleasing, both in striking the fancy [*esprit*] by some marvel and in satisfying our curiosity by the apparent reasons they give for some natural and well-known phenomenon.

Beyond these particular principles of the birth of fables, there are two other more general ones that have helped them considerably. The first is the right one has to invent things similar to familiar matters, or to extend them by drawing out consequences. Some extraordinary happening may have led people to believe that a god had had an affair with a woman. At once all the stories will be full only of amorous gods. You already believe the one, why not the other as well? If the gods have children, they love them and they employ all their power for them upon occasion; and thus one has an inexhaustible source of prodigies that one cannot call absurd.

The second principle that leads us into plentiful mistakes is our blind respect for antiquity. Our fathers believed it, and do we pretend to be wiser than they? These two principles, taken together, work wonders. The one, upon the slightest foundation that the feebleness of human nature allows, extends a stupidity to infinity, and the other preserves it forever because it has been committed. The first, because we are already in error, leads us to become more so, and the second prevents us from extricating ourselves because we have been stuck for some time.

And so there, to all appearances, is what has elevated the fables to the high degree of absurdity at which they have arrived, and is what keeps them there; for what nature has directly supplied was neither so completely ridiculous nor in such quantity, and men are far from being so mad that they could have, all of a sudden, given birth to such reveries, added faith to them, and spent such a very long time in trying to get rid of them unless it was all compounded by the two things we have been discussing.

Looking at the errors of these times, we find that the same things established them, extended them, and preserved them. It is true that we have arrived at no absurdity as considerable as the ancient fables of the Greeks; but that is because we have not had so foolish a point of departure. We know as well as they did how to extend and preserve our mistakes; but happily they are not so great, because we are enlightened by the true religion and, as I believe, by some rays of true philosophy.

People ordinarily attribute the origin of fables to the lively imagination of the Eastern peoples [*Orientaux*]; for myself, I attribute it to the ignorance of the first men. Put a new people near the north pole, their first histories will be fables; and in effect, are not the earlier stories of the northern skies full of them? They are nothing but giants and magicians. I do not say that a live and very hot sun could not yet give the mind a final boiling that would perfect the disposition they have to revel in fables, but all men have talents for that revelling, quite independent of the sun. Also, in all that I have been saying, I have only supposed in men qualities common to all and qualities that must operate in the glacial zones as well as in the torrid zones.

I could perhaps show, if it were necessary, an astonishing conformity between the fables of the Americans and those of the Greeks. The Americans send the souls of those who have lived badly to certain muddy and disagreeable lakes, as the Greeks sent them to the edges of their rivers Styx and Acheron. The Americans believe that the rain comes because a girl in the clouds is playing with her little brother, who breaks her jug of water; does that not strongly resemble those fountain nymphs who pour out water from their urns? According to the traditions of Peru, the Inca Manco Guyna Capac, child of the sun, found it possible by his eloquence to recall from the depths of the forests the inhabitants of the country, who lived there after the fashion of animals, and to make them live under rational laws. Orpheus did as much for the Greeks, and he was also a child of the sun. This shows that the

Greeks were, for a while, savages, just as much as were the Americans, that they were lifted from barbarism by the same means, and that the imagination of these two peoples, so far apart, agree in believing that those who have extraordinary talents are children of the sun. Since the Greeks, with all their intelligence [*esprit*], when they were still a young people thought not at all more rationally than the barbarians of America, who were, to all appearances, quite a young people when they were discovered by the Spaniards, there is reason to believe that the Americans would have come eventually to think as rationally as the Greeks, if they had had the time.

The method the Greeks had of inventing stories to supply reasons for natural events can also be found among the ancient Chinese. Whence came the ebbing and flooding of the tide? You can well imagine that they did not think of the pressure of the moon upon the earth. They thought that there was a princess who had a hundred children; fifty lived on the shores of the ocean, the other fifty in the mountains. From them came two great peoples, who often warred together. When those who lived on the shore got the advantage on those of the mountains and pushed them back, it was flood tide. When they were repelled and they fled from the mountains toward the shore, it was the ebb. This manner of philosophizing bears a resemblance to that of Ovid's *Metamorphoses*; so true is it that the same ignorance has produced more or less the same effects among all peoples.

It is for this reason that there are no peoples whose history does not begin in fables, except the chosen people, among whom a particular care on the part of providence has preserved the truth. With what prodigious slowness men arrived at

something rational, however simple! To preserve the memory of facts just as they have been, that is not a great marvel; and yet many centuries passed before anyone was capable of doing it. And until then, the events of which one kept a memory were only visions and dreams. One would make a great mistake, after that, to be surprised that philosophy and reasoning had been for a great number of centuries in a very gross and imperfect state, and that even today progress should be so slow.

Among most peoples, fables change into religion; but among the Greeks, they changed, so to speak, into the fine arts [*en agrément*]. As they furnished ideas only in conformity with the sort of imagination most common among men, poetry and painting accommodated themselves to the fables perfectly well—and everyone knows the passion the Greeks had for those fine arts. Divinities of all sorts, lavished everywhere, making everything alive and animated, interested in everything, and what is more important, divinities who often acted in surprising ways, could hardly fail to make a pleasant impression, be it in poems or in pictures, where it was only a matter of seducing the imagination by presenting to it objects that it could easily grasp and that at the same time would be striking and impressive. And why should the fables not impress the imagination, since it was from thence that they were born? When poetry or painting actualized them in order to present the spectacle of them to the imagination, they only gave back to the imagination its own productions.

Mistakes, once established among men, have a way of taking deep root and of clinging to the various things that support them. Religion and good sense have disabused us of the fables of the Greeks, but they still maintain themselves among us through poetry and painting, to which it seems the fables have found the trick of making themselves indispensable. Although we are incomparably more enlightened than those whose crude mentality invented the fables in all good faith, we easily recover the same outlook that made these fables so agreeable to them. They glutted themselves on them because they believed them, and we indulge ourselves in them with just as much pleasure but without believing in them; and nothing could better prove that imagination and reason rarely have any dealing with one another, and that things concerning which reason is fully disabused lose nothing of their appeal to the imagination.

So far, we have only gone into the history of the origin of fables insofar as it comes from the depth of human nature, and to be sure, that is the dominant thread. But it is connected to some strange things, to which we cannot refuse a place here. For example, since the Phoenicians and the Egyptians were older peoples than the Greeks, their fables passed to the Greeks and were debased in so passing, so that even their truest histories became fables in Greece. The Phoenician language, and perhaps also the Egyptian, was full of ambiguous words; moreover the Greeks scarcely understood either language, and there one has a marvelous source of mistakes. Two Egyptian women whose proper name meant "dove" came to live in the forest of Dodona to tell fortunes; the Greeks understood that there were two doves who prophesied perched in the trees; and presently it was the trees themselves that prophesied. The rudder of a boat has a Phoenician name which also means "talking"; the Greeks, in the story of the ship *Argo,* thought that it had a talking rudder. The learned men of recent times have found a thousand other examples in which one can see clearly that the origin of many fables is what we loosely call confusions or mistaking the word, and that the Greeks were quite subject to such misreading of Phoenician or Egyptian. I myself find that the Greeks, who had so much intelligence [*esprit*] and curiosity, lacked something of one or the other in not taking it upon themselves either to learn these languages perfectly or else to neglect them altogether. Did they not know perfectly well that almost all their towns had been Egyptian or Phoenician colonies and that the majority of their old stories came from these lands? The origins of their language and the antiquities of their country, did they not depend on these two languages? But they were barbarian languages, harsh and disagreeable. What ridiculous delicacy!

When the art of writing was invented, it helped greatly to disseminate the fables and to enrich one people with all the stupidities of another; but one gained from it in that the shifting traditions became more or less fixed, and the bulk of the fables, remaining pretty much in the state in which the invention of writing found them, degenerated no further.

Ignorance diminished bit by bit, and as a result, one saw fewer prodigies and invented fewer false systems of philosophy, and stories became less fabulous—for all these are interconnected. Until recently, no one took any pains to remember things past, except out of pure curiosity; but then people perceived that it could be useful to remember, whether it be to preserve the things that nations prided themselves on, or to sort out the differences that can arise among peoples, or to furnish examples of virtue; and I believe that this last is the most recent that has been thought of, though it is the one that we make the most of. All of this required that history be true; I mean true as opposed to ancient histories, which were solely made up of absurdities. So people began, in various countries, to write histories in a more reasonable manner and generally with more verisimilitude.

So no new fables appear; people are satisfied with preserving the old ones. But can this ever stop those who are infatuated with antiquity? They imagine to themselves that under the fables are hidden secrets of the physical and moral world.

Could it have been possible for the ancients to have produced such reveries without intending some subtle meanings? The name of the ancients is an imposing one, but it is certain that those who made the fables were not the men to understand moral and physical nature, let alone discover the art of disguising such knowledge under borrowed images.

So let us not look for anything in the fables except the history of the errors of the human mind. It is less capable of error when it knows to what extent it is subject to error. For it is not a science to cause one's head to be filled with all the extravagances of the Phoenicians and the Greeks, but it is a science to know what led the Phoenicians and the Greeks into these extravagances. All men are so much alike that there is no people whose folly shouldn't make us tremble.

PIERRE BAYLE

[1647-1706]

BAYLE'S encyclopedic *Historical and Critical Dictionary* pervades and provokes the eighteenth century with information and skepticism, is cited, defended, and refuted everywhere, is famously rebutted by Leibniz in the *Theodicy,* and is admiringly borrowed by Mandeville, Voltaire, Diderot, and Hume among countless others. In eighteenth-century libraries in France, according to Mornet, the *Dictionary* appeared almost twice as often as that other influential book, Locke's *Essay Concerning Human Understanding.* Bayle's notoriety as a destructive skeptic is familiar enough but perhaps finally misleading. He remained a loyal member of the French Reformed Church much of his life and professed to die a Christian philosopher, even though as Karl C. Sandberg says in his volume of Bayle selections, *The Great Contest of Faith and Reason,* "The defenders of the faith nonetheless felt that his arguments supported Christianity as a rope supports a hanged man." The growing conflict between orthodox Christianity and the new rational spirit is at the heart of his thought, but it is difficult to decide whether Bayle's skepticism is aimed against faith as such, or only against the pretensions and errors of theology and religion. Certainly as regards myth, his work turned out to be unexpectedly "constructive," an early example of how arguments about myth set moving in one direction could end up, surprisingly, elsewhere. Here at least, Bayle's view appears unambiguous: myths are without intrinsic dignity or interest; they are merely foolish, lewd, and vicious fables to be dismissed contemptuously. In Jupiter, the greatest pagan god, for example, Bayle apparently saw little else than farcicality and cruelty and a career of crime, incest, debauchery, and deceit. But it is also true that no eighteenth-century writing on mythology is more influential than Bayle's in finally elevating myth as a subject of the most serious intellectual interest.

For one thing, as much as any single work in the eighteenth century, the *Dictionary* rescued mythology from dull, learned obscurity and poetic trivializing. What matters most here is not how often Bayle took up pagan fable as such, but what he emphasized when he did. With tireless satirical delight, Bayle set out to expose the worst scandals in pagan myth. In doing this, he dramatized these myths as being nothing less than the deadly enemy of reason and truth, and indeed of everything humanly worthy. Thus, however much Bayle wished to destroy these myths, his daring approach had the ironic effect of flattering them with new excitement and attention. The more savagely and triumphantly Bayle attacked the absurdities of myth, the more prominently and dramatically myth rose to sight. The rationalist rejection of myth in the seventeenth century was already well established by Spinoza and Hobbes, and with far greater philosophic penetration than by Bayle. But Bayle's literary brilliance, his ability to polemicize, popularize, and even theatricalize myth as something shockingly irrational and often dangerous, is historically an important new change in the fortunes of myth. When Bayle's attacks on paganism moved on thereafter to implicate the Bible and Christianity, myth could assume a new seriousness not easy to ignore.

Left at this, however, Bayle's treatment of myth or the Bible might be said to have gone beyond Spinoza and Hobbes only in polemical lack of restraint. In a sense, compared to these predecessors Bayle seems less an innovator than a popularizer. His tactic (though not perhaps his final purpose) is that of Spinoza and Hobbes: to criticize pagan religion and the Bible and Christianity from the viewpoint of a religiously neutral, "higher" criterion—to "write a new kind of commentary" on Scripture, as Bayle said, based on the "principles of natural light." Religion must submit itself to judgment by "natural morality": the pagan gods will thus be unveiled as real criminals or poetic fancies, and will be condemned either way. Even a sacred figure such as David, the ancestor of the Messiah, will be shown as he was historically: David was murderous, adulterous, and treasonous, compelling the question why he should have been chosen as a divine instrument by a wise and good God. But while continuing such a rational critique of religion, Bayle changed the emphasis enough to emerge as something of an innovator in his own right. Spinoza and Hobbes revalued religion in terms of natural passions such as fear and violence, and by appealing from theory to "experience," but they also supported their insights with systems worked out on the model of mathematical rigor. Bayle dissolves these rational systems into a most unsystematic flood of historical detail. He goes so far in this direction that it becomes difficult to formulate his final position with any confidence. But he gained

in two important ways. First, his lack of systematic approach, his ironies and ambiguities, made him more, rather than less, influential to those after him. Thinkers of all persuasions—atheist, deist, fideist—could find him sympathetic. Especially important next is that he gains enormously in richness of historical detail and immediacy.

Perhaps it can be argued that Bayle's specific views on myth matter less than this new emphasis on the *historical* side of myth, and that this—however onesidedly presented and with whatever motives—is Bayle's greatest contribution to the modern interest in mythology. His *Dictionary,* so saturated in historical fact, so fascinated, amused, and outraged by the concrete absurdities of human history, must be contrasted with the most prominent academic interpretations of myth in the seventeenth century. Such men as Athanasius Kircher, Samuel Bochart, or John Spencer were perhaps as learned as Bayle, but their approach to myth is by comparison remarkably scholastic, obsessed with etymologizing or with collating and re-collating scriptural and classical citation to obtain new "proofs." As is clear, Bayle's own roots are in the seventeenth-century revolt against such academicism and scholasticism and his particular approach is a more extreme but inevitable outcome of that revolt. Thus, Bayle depends most of all on Descartes's earlier effort to reject tradition. But where Descartes sets out methodically to doubt all traditionally "certain" ideas, Bayle sets out methodically to doubt all traditionally "certain" historical fact. He will accept nothing as historically true on the authority of tradition, pagan or Christian. Or rather, he will subject every tradition to "historical criticism." In this spirit, he uses the new travel and anthropological literature coming in from Africa, America, and the East, for he can pit such contemporary, verifiable historical data against the distortions of tradition. The

Greeks lose their distance and awesomeness when shown to be much like the African fetishists, for example.

As an historian and moralist, Bayle mediates between a rationalist insistence on universal moral and natural standards and a newly emphasized relativism. In the same way, his view of myth moves unsteadily between a distinctly older view and a recognizably newer one. On the one hand, myth for Bayle still narrowly embraces pagan fable, savage superstition, or any magic, idolatry, or polytheism. None of this deserves more than scornful rejection: it is either untrue or immoral. On the other hand, if the "minds of men are unstable" and if men are as prone to absurdity as Bayle suggests, then myth reveals something profoundly true about mankind. Bayle's writing always stresses how susceptible the human mind and heart are to error, folly, and darkness, mostly through gullibility and self-deception. In a crucial way, all religion, as well as all myth, originates from and feeds on human credulousness. Myth for Bayle may finally mean a religion that has yielded itself uncritically to credulity. Greek polytheism, for example, is a ridiculous popular belief credulously built on ridiculous poetic inventions. Greek philosophers and theologians compound the error by trying to find rational justification for such absurd beliefs; and historians perpetuate the mass of error. Similarly, Bayle rejects any effort to interpret myth allegorically. For allegory, applied ingeniously or stupidly enough, can finally justify and dignify any scandalous event or ignorant belief. Jupiter's monstrous incest can be perfectly explained away and even ennobled allegorically as signifying cosmic harmony. Nor will Bayle accept myth as expressing poetic truths about natural forces. If Juno is nothing but the air, it is ridiculous to worship her; indeed, such worship is either only "material atheism" or "self-delusion."

Admired though he was by all sides of the Enlightenment, Bayle still stands apart. He sees no evidence for natural religion or for natural monotheism; he declares instead that early societies were probably nonreligious or even atheist. He avoids any fervent optimism about human reason or progress, insisting that confidence in reason is usually misplaced. The grand, clear design of Newtonian order failed to tempt Bayle out of his Pyrrhonic skepticism. Skepticism as Bayle practices it is a two-edged sword, cutting toward classical rationalism as well as toward orthodox faith. It was a position ideally suited to opening new possibilities and reopening old ones, and to holding all ambiguities in fruitful tension; this is also a description of the change and tentative advance of mythology in Bayle's work.

B.F.

REFERENCES *Dictionaire historique et critique* (Rotterdam, 1697); 2d ed., 1702. An English translation appeared in 1710; another, *The Dictionary Historical and Critical,* 2d ed., 5 vols. (London, 1734–1738), is used for our selection; and *A General Dictionary, Historical and Critical,* 10 vols. (London, 1734–1741). For works other than *The Dictionary,* see: *Oeuvres diverses,* 4 vols. (The Hague and Rotterdam, 1727–1731).

Among the voluminous criticism on Bayle, the following may be useful: Howard Robinson, *Bayle the Sceptic* (New York: Columbia University Press, 1931), includes a comprehensive bibliography of works by and on Bayle; Jean Delvolvé, *Religion, critique et philosophie positive chez Pierre Bayle* (Paris, 1906), inaugurates modern study of Bayle; Léo Courtines, *Bayle's Relations with England and the English* (New York: Columbia University Press, 1938); Frank E. Manuel, *The Eighteenth Century Confronts the Gods* (Cambridge: Harvard University Press, 1959), most directly and helpfully views Bayle against the mythological interests of his age; H. T. Mason, *Pierre Bayle and Voltaire*

(London: Oxford University Press, 1963), esp. Chaps. II and IV; Walter Rex, *Essays on Pierre Bayle and Religious Controversy* (The Hague: Nijhoff, 1967); Elisabeth Labrousse, *Pierre Bayle: Vol. 1. Du Pays de Foix à la* *cité d'Erasme; Vol. 2. Hétérodoxie et rigorisme* (The Hague: Nijhoff, 1966); Henri Margival, *Essai sur Richard Simon et la critique biblique au XVIIe siècle* (Paris: Maillet, 1900).

BAYLE

FROM *The Dictionary Historical and Critical*

"Jupiter"

JUPITER, the greatest of all the Heathen gods, was the son of Saturn and Cybele. There is no crime, but what he was defiled with; for besides that he dethroned his own father, that he castrated him, and bound him in chains in the deepest hell, he committed incest with his sisters, daughters, and aunts, and even attempted to ravish his mother. He debauched a great number of maids and wives; and to compass his designs, he borrowed the shapes of all sorts of beasts. He was guilty of the unnatural sin; for he stole away the beautiful Ganymede, and preferred him to the office of cupbearer to the gods, that he might have him at hand, as often as his heart desired. Treacheries and perjuries, and in general, all actions that are punishable by the laws, were familiar to him. They had gone so far, as to say, that he devoured one of his wives; and therefore nothing can be more monstrous, than the religion of the Pagans, who looked upon such a God, as the supreme governour of the world, and suited to that notion, the religious worship that was paid him. The fathers of the church have laid a great stress upon this argument, to prove the falsehood of the Pagan religion; and it may be said, that this system was very proper to corrupt morality (D). I shall say nothing about the fables, that concern the birth or education of Jupiter. Moreri has mentioned something of it; and this is to be found in a great many books, which school-boys have daily in their hands. I shall only speak of the eagle that brought him Nectar. This particular is not so commonly known.

What the Heathens have said of Jupiter's original, seemed to me for a long time so unaccountable, that the more I thought on it, the more monstrous it appeared to me, and such, in a word, as I could not apprehend how the Philosophers could maintain it; but I have at last discovered, that they might be led into that error, by a sort of reasoning (G), the weakness whereof it was no easy thing for them to find out. They did not believe, that any thing could be created, and acknowledged no substances wholly distinct from extension. Now when once these two hypotheses are laid down, it is almost as easy to imagine, that a subtilized matter might become a god, as to believe the soul of man to be material, as most Philosophers believed. See the remark (G). There was in Arcadia a temple of God the Good. Pausanias conjectures that it was consecrated to Jupiter: his reason is because that epithet ought to belong by way of pre-eminence to the greatest of the gods. It is certain that Jupiter's goodness was denoted by several names, under which he was adored. But he was likewise adored, under several names, which shewed how terrible he was. Nay, his quality of thunderer was denoted by the bare idea of his descent upon earth. There were some places, where they said he required human sacrifices. I shall say in another place, that the book intituled *Cymbalum Mundi* contains several jests upon Jupiter's actions; but I question whether it is possible to go farther than Arnobius on such a subject. The vivacity of his imagination flows like a torrent, and as he had lately been a professed Rhetorician, there are no colours nor figures but what he animates his stile with. I relate in several places in this Dictionary some of his thoughts, and I have mentioned in one of them his jest upon the great Jupiter for spending nine nights in getting a boy, who wanted only one night to get fifty maids with child. There is some probability that his memory failed him, and that he confounded things. He had read that Jupiter spent nine nights in the production of the Muses, and he applied this to a quite different subject, I mean, to the adventures of Alcmena. Authors, who have a quick and lively fancy, are subject to the like mistakes. Jupiter made love both in heaven and upon earth, he took all that came, whether goddesses or women; it was all one to him. Arnobius did not forget this, and observed that the bodies of mortal women, though transparent with

respect to Jupiter, had yet sufficient charms to inspire him with a leud passion. It is not improper to observe, that the ridiculous stories which the poets had vented concerning that God, served as a foundation for the Pagan religion, and that some grave men endeavoured to explain them either by allegories or by the principles of Natural Philosophy; but their labour was as ridiculous as that of the poets, and terminated very often in serious impieties. See the remark, where I shall speak of those who said that Juno was the air, and Jupiter the Æther.

NOTES

In the interest of easier access to the text, Bayle's extraordinarily frequent, lengthy, and often digressive footnotes have not been given. The footnote citations in the text have been omitted as well, for the same reason. The footnotes given here are selected as bearing most directly on the problem of myth.—Ed.

(D) *The System of the Pagan religion was very proper to corrupt morality.* Christian authors have drawn potent arguments from these infamous actions of Jupiter, to convict the Heathens of the falsity of their gods; as may be seen in many places of Lactantius, Tertullian, Clemens Alexandrinus, Arnobius, and several others. For besides that such horrid crimes are inconsistent with the deity, the Gentiles might thence take a just pretext for giving themselves up to all sorts of wickedness · · · not believing themselves criminal, whilst they imitated their gods. This is what Ion means in a tragedy by Euripides, that bears his name.

Blame not the wretch, who imitates the gods,
But charge the crime on those, who set th' example.

Meziriac makes this reflexion upon a passage of Ovid, where Phaedra observes, that incest was scrupled in the rustical time of Saturn, but that under the reign of his successor, a woman might be permitted to lie with her son-in-law. Jupiter, says she, authorises all by his marriage with his sister. . . . Ovid falls here into a very gross mistake since it is certain that Saturn was married to his sister, just as Jupiter was to his. One might add to the passage of Euripides, quoted by Meziriac, a hundred others of the same force. Nothing is more common in the antient poets, that to see people, in order to excuse their crimes, maintain, that they have only imitated the gods, or that the gods have instigated them to do evil. But not to dissemble the truth, it must be said to the glory of the Heathens, that they did not live according to their principles. It is true, that the corruption of manners was very great among the Heathens; but many of them did not follow the example of their false gods, and preferred the ideas of virtue before so great an authority. What is strange is, that the Christians, whose system is so pure, come but a little short of the Heathens in their vices. It is a mistake to believe, that the morals of a religion answer the doctrines of the articles of faith.

(G) . . . Lastly, we all spring from celestial seed:
The universal father be, from whom
When mother earth receives the watry drops,

She teems with shining fruits, and flow'ring herbs,
Gives birth to men and beasts, and food prepares,
By which they live, and propagate their race.
Hence does she justly claim a parent's name.

We may infer from all this that there is nothing more dangerous or contagious, than to lay down a false principle. It is a bad leaven, which though it be but small, may spoil the whole lump. One absurdity once laid down, draws after it many others. If you only err concerning the nature of the human soul; if you falsly think that it is not a substance distinct from matter; that falsity will lead you to believe that there are gods, who at first were born from fermentation, and afterwards multiplied by marriage. I cannot conclude, without observing a thing at which I am amazed. Nothing appears to me grounded upon clearer and more distinct ideas than the immateriality of every thinking being, and yet some Christian Philosophers maintain, that matter is capable of thinking; and they are Philosophers of great parts, and of a most profound meditation. Can we depend after this on the clearness of ideas?

JOHN TOLAND

[1670–1722]

MORE often than not in the early eighteenth century, an interest in what we would call myth occurs only in connection with what were then thought to be religious matters; myths were treated as a branch of theology, and rites and rituals were taken up in discussions of ecclesiastical polity. Religious attitudes still latent or implicit in modern myth study were dominant in the early eighteenth century, and then as now, a division can be perceived between monists and pluralists, between believers and skeptics.

The English deists, represented here by John Toland, had little interest in myth as such, but their great impact on later thought in France, Germany, and England included important, although hard to trace, influences on the then rising interest in myth. Toland himself stands, as Leslie Stephen has noted, as "a follower of Locke, and in the path which leads to the purely sceptical solution of Hume." Toland's best-known book, *Christianity not Mysterious,* was, in 1696, an early popular statement of the current idea that "there is nothing in the Gospel contrary to reason nor above it." Toland set out to show, in blunt and simple language, "how so divine an institution [primitive rational monotheism] did, through the Craft and Ambition of Priests and Philosophers degenerate into mere paganism."

The third of the *Letters to Serena,* on "The Origin of Idolatry, and Reasons of Heathenism," shows Toland's deist stance as clearly as one could wish. Myth for Toland was a collection of stupidities that only served to show how far the original rational monotheism had been corrupted. His opening section airily assumes monotheism to have been the earliest and best form of religion; this is a common deist starting point. In the same fashion, Toland takes Euhemerism for granted. Having thus excluded all the possible ways of interpreting myths except the simplest, Toland finally descends to argument only for a secondary point: the assertion of the Egyptian origins of fables. Section two completes Toland's initial sweep, describing the original monotheistic religion as natural, rational, and simple, and insisting that the fall from this lofty and prehistoric deism into idolatry and paganism was due principally to a conspiracy. The argument, turning on a fairly crude psychological idea, is that the wiser ancients inherited and preserved a rational monotheism, but in order to retain political power they instituted a popular polytheism full of ritual and nonsense for the people. "Without question," Toland writes in section seven of the *Letter,* "when wise and good Men perceiv'd that the People wou'd needs have a plurality of Gods, and Temples dedicated to them, they, to comply with their Weakness, and at the same time to bring 'em as much as they cou'd to better and nobler Thoughts, deify'd such Things" as virtue, honor, etc. This is one version of the widespread two-religion theory, which has been well treated recently by Frank Manuel in *The Eighteenth Century Confronts the Gods*. One religion was for the wise, usually a simple monotheism, and one religion was for the people, usually gaudy, elaborate, and irrational congeries of superstition, Euhemerized men, and queer rituals.

Section three adds only a negative point; Toland argues against the idea that worship may have originated in man's awe of the ordered stars and the orderly universe. But, unable to deny the impressiveness of such order, Toland adds that this explanation was later given by men who were ignorant or ashamed of the real origins of religion. Sections sixteen and seventeen are Toland's central discussion of the major Greek deities, a discussion interesting only for the outrageous wholesale dismissal and glib unimaginative contempt that the rational English pamphleteer brings to the subject. Section nineteen continues the line of argument commenced in section three: that of discrediting interpretations of myth other than Euhemerist. Toland here attacks the idea that the myths are allegories, claiming that this interpretation too was tacked on later. The sections that follow take up contemporaneous savage nations and compare them with the Greeks in an effort to show the universality of Euhemerism. Toland, with many of the deists, puts little emphasis on historical perspective, and his equation of his own rational deism with primitive religion and with Christianity shows little historical imagination. The letter closes with verses emphasizing once more the conspiracy theory. It is still a long way to Coleridge's "fair humanities of old religion."

The deists in general and John Toland in particular show the reductionist temperament at its most abrupt. The harsh and scornful rationalism discredits itself by its rhetorical strategies, its tricky logic, and its intemperate unreasonableness; and even if Toland's range was a bit wider than has been suggested—he had read Bayle, he wrote on Druids, and he did a pamphlet on Giordano Bruno—it is still arguable that in utterly and contemptuously dismissing the old myths, he helped discredit such dismissals. In another sense, deistic criticism of myth is an early step in the long process of replacing revealed religion with natural religion. Deism scorned revelation and Greek mythology alike, but in its fervent assent to reasonable worship, one might almost say it made a myth of natural religion and showed the way for later and more successful attempts to create new myths. This may seem to be stretching a point, though, and on balance it is clear that the main thrust of deism was to debase the study of myth to the lowest point it has reached in three hundred years.

R.R.

REFERENCES Our text is from Letter III in *Letters to Serena* (London: B. Lintot, 1704), published in facsimile (Stuttgart-Bad Cannstatt, 1964). Toland's best-known work is *Christianity not Mysterious* (London, 1696). See also his "Life of Milton" in *A Complete Collection . . . of the Works of John Milton* (London, 1698), and his *Pantheisticon* (1720).

A standard account of Toland's thought is in Sir Leslie Stephen's *History of English Thought in the Eighteenth Century* (London: Smith, Elder & Co., 1876), vol. 1. See also G. V. Lechler, *Geschichte des Englischen Deismus* (Stuttgart, 1841); R. N. Stromberg, *Religious Liberalism in Eighteenth-century England* (London: Oxford University Press, 1954); and Basil Willey, *The Eighteenth Century Background* (New York: Columbia University Press, 1941).

TOLAND

FROM *Letters to Serena*

The Origin of Idolatry, and Reasons of Heathenism

1. I AM under a double Obligation, MADAM, to impart my Thoughts to you about the *Origin of Idolatry,* both from the Promise I made you by word of mouth, and by what I have since written to you in the Letter concerning *the Soul's Immortality among the Heathens.* But you are not to expect an account of all the antient Superstitions, which wou'd require many Volumes, nor of any one Religion whatsoever. I shall only endeavour to show by what means the Reason of men became so deprav'd, as to think of subordinate Deitys, how the Worship of many Gods was first introduc'd into the world, and what induc'd Men to pay Divine Honors to their Fellow-Creatures, whether on Earth or in the Heavens: then I shall explain the Fables of the Heathens by general and certain Principles, giving the occasion of their Temples, Priests, and Altars; of their Images and Statues; their Oracles, Sacrifices, Feasts, Expiations, Judiciary Astrology, Ghosts, and Specters; of the tutelary Powers of several Countrys; of Peoples thinking that Heaven is over us, that Hell is under us, and such other things as commonly occur in the Greek and Roman Authors. Tho with very small pains I could manifestly prove that in Egypt *Men had first, long before others, arriv'd at the various beginnings of Religions* (as AMMIANUS MARCELLINUS speaks) *and that they preserv'd the first occasions of Sacred Rites conceal'd in their secret Writings;* yet I shall not trouble you with repeating the Arguments I have already produc'd to this purpose in *the History of the Soul's Immortality,* from the Authority of HERODOTUS, DIODORUS SICULUS, LUCIAN, DION CASSIUS, MACROBIUS, and others: nor will I urge that, by Examples and Laws from the Pentateuch, it clearly appears that Magick, the Interpretation of Dreams, Astrology, and Necromancy, were long us'd in Egypt before they were known in Chaldaea or any other place.

2. The most antient Egyptians, Persians, and Romans, the first Patriarchs of the Hebrews, with several other Nations and Sects, had no sacred Images or Statues, no peculiar Places or costly Fashions of Worship; the plain Easiness of their Religion being most agreeable to the Simplicity of the Divine Nature, as indifference of Place or Time were the best Expressions of infinite Power and Omnipresence. But tho *God did thus make Men upright, yet they found out* (says the wisest King of Israel) *many inventions.* And certainly when once a Man suffers himself to be led into precarious or arbi-

trary Practices, he cannot stop for any Reason, but what, if it be good, must conclude with equal Force against all. I believe I may without much difficulty prove, that such as first entertain'd Designs against the Liberty of Mankind, were also the first Depravers of their Reason. For none, in his right senses, can ever be persuaded voluntarily to part with his Freedom; and he that makes use of Force to deprive him of it, must have brib'd or deluded very many beforehand to support his unjust Pretensions, by which accession of strength he cou'd seduce, frighten, or subdue others. It will not therefore appear unlikely that Men very early learnt to have the same Conception of God himself, which they had before of their earthly Princes: and after thus fancying him mutable, jealous, revengeful, and arbitrary, they next endeavour'd to procure his Favor much after the same manner that they made their court to those who pretended to be his Representatives or Lieutenants, nay to be Gods themselves, or to be descended of heavenly Parentage, as the antient Monarchs us'd to do.

3. It seems evident from the remotest Monuments of Learning, that all Superstition originally related to the Worship of the Dead, being principally deriv'd from Funeral Rites, tho the first occasion might be very innocent or laudable, and was no other than Orations wherein they were sometimes personally addrest (such as the Panegyricks of the Egyptians) or Statues dedicated with many Ceremonys to their Memory. But the Flatterers of great Men in the Person of their Predecessors, the excessive Affection of Friends or Relations, and the Advantage which the Heathen Priests drew from the Credulity of the simple, carry'd this matter a great deal further. Not only Kings and Queens, great Generals and Legislators, the Patrons of

Learning, Promoters of curious Arts, and Authors of useful Inventions, partook of this Honor; but also such private Persons, as by their virtuous Actions had distinguish'd themselves from others, were often consecrated to pious and eternal Memory by their Country or their Kindred, as reputable to the Dead, and exemplary to the Living. This is the true reason (as we shall shew in its proper place) of all Nations having their proper tutelary Gods; and hence are deriv'd the peculiar Religions of particular Familys. PLINY, in the second Book of his *Natural History,* says, That *the most antient way of Mens paying their Acknowledgments to their Benefactors, was by deifying of them after their Decease* (which was affirm'd by CICERO with several others before him) *and that the several Appellations of the Gods and of the Stars are deriv'd from the meritorious Actions of Men.* The first Idolatry therefore did not proceed (as 'tis commonly suppos'd) from the Beauty, or Order, or Influence of the Stars: but Men, as I told you in *the History of the Soul's Immortality,* observing Books to perish by Fire, Worms or Rottenness; and Iron, Brass, or Marble not less subject to violent Hands or the Injurys of the Weather, they Impos'd on the Stars (as the only everlasting Monuments) the proper Names of their Heroes, or of something memorable in their History. ERATOSTHENES the Cyrenean, a very antient Philosopher of prodigious Knowledge in all the Sciences, wrote a Book (yet extant) *of the Constellations,* wherein he delivers the Reasons of their Names, which are perpetual Allusions to antient History, tho wonderfully disguiz'd by Time, and for the most part mere Fables. The most learned Monsieur LE CLERC, when he wrote an Extract of ERATOSTHENES, among some other Mythological Tracts in the eighth Volume of *the*

Universal and Historical Library, made the following Epigram.

Antiquity, b'ing sure that Nature's Force
Wou'd Brass and Marble Monuments con-
    sume,
Did wisely its own History transmit
To future Times by Heav'ns eternal Fires.

In other places he declares himself to be of the same opinion concerning the Appellations of the Stars, and in that very Journal explains some Fables upon this Principle. As divers Nations learnt this Custom one of another, so they accordingly chang'd their Spheres, each imposing on the heavenly bodys the Names and Actions belonging to their own country. This is manifest in the Spheres of the Greeks and Barbarians, and for this reason the Cretans maintain'd that, *most of the Gods were born among them, being Men, who, for their Benefits to the Publick, had obtain'd Immortal Honors:* for they believ'd the Grecian Gods to be those of all Mankind, and knew not that in other places this way of naming the Constellations and deifying deserving Men, was long in use before they had practis'd it. Nor was there wanting one among the Christians, who, approving this Method, endeavour'd to abolish those Heathen Names, as not understood, or of no concern to us; and to impose on the Stars new Names in their stead, containing the History of the Old and New Testament. But since he cou'd not prevail with the Astronomers, let's not digress. At last such as were ignorant or asham'd of the true Reasons of these things, wou'd justify their Worship (tho, as I shall evince, by weak Arguments) from the endless and orderly Revolution, the admirable Lustre, and general Usefulness of the Sun, Moon, and other Planets and Stars. This did likewise give the Philosophers a handle to explain the Motions of the Planets by certain Intelligences fixt and inhabiting in their Orbs, which they perpetually guided in their Courses; and hence the Bodys of the Sun and Moon are painted like a Face with Eyes, Nose, and a Mouth.

16. Let's now return, if you please, to the higher Powers; for as in Life so after Death they were of several Orders, Gods of the upper, and Gods of the lower Form, the Nobility and Commons, as also intermediate, inferior, and vagabond Daemons (originally from the Supposition of departed Souls) who had no certain Habitation, but wander'd in the Air, and were constantly sent on Errands, either to carry the Prayers of Men to their Superiors, or to acquaint the World with the Wrath or Favor of the Gods, whereof they were commonly thought to be the Ministers and Executioners, for those Princes had their Armys in Heaven as well as on Earth. But as the Heathens sent the best of their Gods to Heaven, so they recall'd 'em again at their Pleasure, confining their Presence to some small Chappel, or to the poor Idol within that: for they imagin'd that many of them liv'd in Tombs or wander'd in the Air, before they help'd 'em to those Accommodations, where the Desires of their Petitioners were more agreeably heard than in any other place. They often fell down before the Work of their own Hands, which, had it Life or Reflection, ought rather to worship them from whose Skill all its Excellency had bin deriv'd: but the wiser Mice, Swallows, and Spiders made very bold with their Statues, notwithstanding the virtue of Consecration, while silly Men were forc'd themselves to protect what they fear'd and ador'd. These very Statues are an Argument of their human Figure and Original, and we know the respect that was paid to the Statues, even

of living Princes. Their Shrines were often visited by the most ignorant and devout, who also hung the Temples round with Offerings and rich Presents, consulted the Oracles in all dubious Events, bound themselves by Vows in their Distress, believ'd their very Dreams to be divinely inspir'd, and made their Religion in every respect as troublesom to others as to themselves. From what they practis'd on Earth, there was not a darling Passion or Game of their great Men (such as drinking, wenching, or hunting) but the like were ascrib'd to the Gods. Wherefore we often read of their Amours, Marriages, Rapes and Adulterys; their Dissensions, Revellings, Quarrels, and Wounds; their Revenges and Thefts; their Complaints and manifold Distresses, being sometimes expos'd, at other times imprison'd, and once fairly beaten out of their Cittadel in Heaven by the Giants, to seek in a pitiful manner for shelter on Earth; all which things demonstrate their Earthly Original. We need not wonder after this to find, that they are always represented in the State wherein they dy'd, and with all the distinguishing Marks in which they liv'd. Thus are some of 'em ever old, and others ever young; Parents, Children, and Relations; some lame and blind, of different Colours and Appetites; some cloven-footed (whence the present vulgar notion of the Devil) some furnish'd with Wings, or arm'd with Swords, Spears, Helmets, Clubs, Forks and Bows; or drawn in their Chariots by Lions, Tygers, Horses, Sea-calfs, Peacocks, and Doves. Now all these things were partly borrow'd from their true History, and are partly allegorical, poetical, and fabulous Disguises of what is no longer perfectly known nor understood.

17. AENOMAUS, EUHEMERUS, LUCIAN, and many other Persons who made use of their Reason, did fearlessly mock the

Deitys for being naturaliz'd of this or that Place, where they exercis'd every one the Trade wherein he excell'd. Thus APOLLO had an Office of Intelligence, and told Fortunes at Delphos; ESCULAPIUS set up an Apothecary's shop at Pergamus; VENUS kept a noted Baudyhouse at Paphos; VULCAN had a Blacksmith's Forge in Lemnos; some were Midwives, some Huntresses, and all of them traffick'd where they cou'd: for they us'd, like us Mortals, such as they had formerly bin, when they did not thrive in one place, to remove into some other more convenient for their Business. As all Events were believ'd to be the Effects of their Love or Displeasure, so Men found out several Methods to thank or appease them; and particularly gave 'em (by way of acknowledgment for the rest) the First-Fruits of all Productions, whether of Animals or Vegetables, with Tythes and other Offerings which they were bound to pay to their Living Princes. Nor was there any thing almost that came amiss in their Sacrifices; for what was the aversion of one prov'd the delight of another, and some of 'em would be content with nothing under human Victims, an argument of their bloody Disposition in this World. We often find them highly resenting the Affront (as Princes and Great Men use to do) when their Altars were neglected, especially if the People feasted other Gods; and Men have not less frequently in their Turns reproach'd the Divine Powers with Ingratitude, and even outrag'd their Statues (being sometimes inclin'd to Rebellion) when they thought themselves not sufficiently requited for the rich Presents or Bribes which they gave them.

19. To be short, MADAM, the Religion of the Gentiles (as contrary or superadded to the Light of Reason) is such as cou'd not influence Virtue or Morality very much

in this Life, nor afford any certain Hopes or Security against the Terror of Death. 'Tis true, there were many among the Heathens, who, loath to believe their Religion so groundless and ridiculous as it seem'd to appear, especially from the Descriptions of the Poets, wou'd have their numberless Gods to be nothing else but the various Appellations, Attributes, or Provinces of some one Being, whether it were the Sun, or BACCHUS, or any God besides, of whom they had a better Opinion. Legislators did put the best face they cou'd upon the matter, and, without anxious Inquiry into the Truth or Falsehood of things, they approv'd of all that contributed to keep Mankind in order, that excited 'em to Virtue by Example and Rewards, that deter'd 'em from Vice by Punishments and Disgrace. But others, as the well-meaning Philosophers, allegoriz'd all their Doctrins into mere natural things, wherein the Deity manifests his Efficacy, Bounty, or Goodness; from which threefold Consideration proceeded the famous Distinction of their Poetical, Political, and Philosophical Theology. Yet the more discerning Persons laught at these shifts, well knowing that it was impossible to make any tolerable Apology for most of their Fables. CICERO therefore condemns the Stoicks for pretending that all the Greek Theology was mysterious. *First* ZENO, *says he, after him* CLEANTHES, *and then* CHRYSIPPUS *were at great pains to no purpose, to give a reasonable Explication of commentitious Fables, and to account for the Etymology of the very Names of every God: which proceeding plainly shows that they believe not the Truth of these things in the literal sense.* However, to give a Specimen of their Allegorys, they made JUPITER and JUNO, to signify the Air and Clouds; NEPTUNE and THETIS, the Sea and Flouds; CERES and BACCHUS, the Earth

and all its Productions, MERCURY and MINERVA the ingenious Talents of the Mind, as Learning, Merchandize, Arts, or the like; CUPID and VENUS, our earnest Desires and amorous Inclinations; MARS and BELLONA, Dissensions and Wars; PLUTO and PROSERPINA, Mines, Treasures, and whatever lies conceal'd under ground. So they proceeded to explain away the rest of the Gods; and, as Allegorys are as fruitful as our Imaginations, scarce any two Authors cou'd wholly agree in their Opinions. But supposing the Truth of the matter had bin as any or all of 'em wou'd have it, yet their Religion was not a whit the better, and deserv'd to be abolish'd; since, whatever were the Speculations of a few among the Learned, 'tis evident that the Vulgar took all these to be very real Gods, of whom they stood in mighty fear, and to whom they paid Divine Adoration: not to insist on the Trouble and Expensiveness of their Rites, or the Cheats and Dominion of the Priests. This was clearly perceiv'd by CICERO, who, enumerating the several kinds of the Heathen Gods, *From another Reason,* says he, *and indeed a physical one, has proceeded a great multitude of Gods, which, being introduc'd under human Shape, have supply'd the Poets with Fables, but at the same time have fill'd the Life of Men with all sorts of Superstition.* The same may be as truly said of the modern Saints and Images: for notwithstanding the nice Distinctions of supreme and absolute, of inferior and relative Worship; all the common People are downright gross Idolaters; and as to the multitude of their Observations, the Impostures or Power of their Clergy in the places where this Worship is establish'd, the Superstitions of the whole World put together wou'd, in respect of them, make a very easy and tolerable Religion. Nor ought we to forget that this new Idolatry of the Christians is altogether grounded, as that of the antient Heathens, on the excessive Veneration of dead Men and Women; but improv'd by degrees to such a pitch by the Artifices of the Priests, who allure others by this example to follow their Directions, which always tend to the Increase of their own Glory, Power, and Profit.

20. The present Heathens, who inhabit the greatest part of Africa, vast Tracts of Asia, almost all America, and some few Corners of Europe, agree very much with the Antients in their Opinions, which is the reason that I have hitherto omitted some things I mention under this Head, to avoid Repetition. But they disagree among themselves in different places, as the Antients did. They have their several Cosmogonias, or Accounts of the Creation of the World; and their Theogonias, or Genealogys of the Gods, whom some hold to be coequal, others subordinate, some to be all good, others again to be all bad: and many that there are two sovereign Principles of Good and Ill, such as the OROMAZES and ARIMANES of the old Chaldeans: nor are there wanting who maintain the Divine Unity, sometimes with, and sometimes without inferior Ministers; as there be who assert the Eternity and Immensity of the Universe, and that all things happen by an irresistible Decree of Fate. Their Sentiments are as different about Providence, the Duration of the World, and a future State; whether the Soul be immortal, is confin'd after Death to any certain Mansions, or transmigrates out of one Body into another, this last being the most prevailing Opinion. They diversify their Sacrifices with numberless Rites and Ceremonys, one Nation worshipping that Animal whereof another makes an Offering to its God; and one Man religiously using that Gesture or Garb,

which another rejects as unbecoming and profane: for as JUVENAL observes of the old Egyptians,

Such is the Madness of the thoughtless Mob,
Each place abhors the Deitys of others,
And own no Gods but what themselves adore.

They perform Divine Service on the Tops of Hills, in the open Air, or in Temples, and Groves, or Caves. They believe good and bad Daemons, and guardian Powers of Places and Men. They have several subordinate Degrees of Priests and Priestesses, Colleges in many parts for their Education, and religious Houses for their Maintenance. They have their sacred Books, Traditions, and Images; pretended Miracles, Prophecys, Revelations and Oracles; Sorcerys, Augurys, Sortileges, Omens, and all sorts of Divination. As they have their Merry-meetings where they eat and drink, sing and dance before their Gods; so they have their more melancholy Seasons, when they not only mortify themselves with strange Austeritys of Fasting, Abstinence from Women, coarse Habits, long Pilgrimages, or other laborious Penances: but they also burn and whip, and cut and slash their Bodys in a most cruel manner; vainly imagining to honor or please the Deity by such things as do themselves real hurt and no body else any good. When the Unintelligibleness or Absurdity of any of their Practices or Doctrins is objected to them, they presently tell you that nothing is impossible to the higher Powers, and that these are Mysterys neither to be fathom'd or examin'd by the finite Understanding of Man; as may be read in almost all the Travels of all Nations.

21. Having given this summary Account; SERENA, of antient and modern Heathenism, we may remark that almost every Point of those superstitious and idolatrous Religions are in these or grosser

Circumstances reviv'd by many Christians in our Western Parts of the World, and by all the Oriental Sects: as Sacrifices, Incense, Lights, Images, Lustrations, Feasts, Musick, Altars, Pilgrimages, Fastings, religious Celibacy and Habits, Consecrations, Divinations, Sorcerys, Omens, Presages, Charms, the Worship of dead Men and Women, a continual Canonization of more, Mediators between God and Men, good and evil Daemons, guardian Genius's, Male and Female tutelar Powers to whom they dedicate Temples, appoint Feasts and peculiar Modes of Worship, not only cantoning all Places among 'em, but likewise the Cure of Diseases, and the disposal of every thing which Men are glad to want or enjoy. These things, I confess, are not observ'd in all places alike; yet more or less in every place, and rivetted by Education where they are not establish'd by Law. But how little right these have to the Denomination of Christians, who defend the very things which JESUS CHRIST went about to destroy, is evident to all them who don't consider Christianity as a politick Faction or a bare Sound; but as an Institution design'd to rectify our Morals, to give us just Ideas of the Divinity, and consequently to extirpate all superstitious Opinions and Practices. In plain and proper Terms this is Antichristianism, nothing being more diametrically repugnant to the Doctrin of CHRIST; and as far as any is tinctur'd with it, so far he is a Heathen or a Jew, but no Christian.

22. This Reflection is a Tribute due to Religion and Truth; nor, in my opinion, is the gratifying of mens Curiosity a sufficient Recommendation to any Disquisitions, without some general Instruction naturally conducing to Wisdom or Virtue. And indeed this whole Dissertation, MADAM, is a memorable Proof and Instance to what an astonishing degree of Extravagance human Nature is capable of arriving; and that in all times Superstition is the same, however the Names of it may vary, or that it may have different Objects, or be greater or less in degrees, as any Country has more or less Liberty of Conscience and free Speech. But if any shou'd wonder how Men cou'd leave the direct and easy Path of Reason to wander in such inextricable Mazes, let him but consider how in very many and considerable Regions the plain Institution of JESUS CHRIST cou'd degenerate into the most absurd Doctrins, unintelligible Jargon, ridiculous Practices, and inexplicable Mysterys: and how almost in every corner of the world Religion and Truth cou'd be chang'd into Superstition and Priestcraft. In a word, the Subject of this long Letter is elegantly comprehended in those four lines which are in every body's mouth:

Natural Religion was easy first and plain,
Tales made it Mystery, Offrings made it Gain;
Sacrifices and Shows were at length prepar'd,
The Priests ate Roast-meat, and the People star'd.

I am afraid, by the time you come thus far, you'l be as weary of reading as I am now of writing; and therefore, MADAM, for both our Ease I shall add no more on this occasion, but that I shall continue all my Life your most sincere and obedient Servant.

JOHN TRENCHARD

[1662–1723]

JOHN TRENCHARD, a little-known deist and Whig Member of Parliament best known in his own time for his attacks on the idea of a standing army, published in 1709 a treatise on the psychopathology of religion that stands halfway between Robert Burton's *Anatomy of Melancholy* and David Hume's *Natural History of Religion. The Natural History of Superstition,* which could be subtitled a rational account of the psychological causes of religious beliefs (assent, faith, fervor, and fanaticism being for Trenchard just gradations of superstition), is a lively and adroit pamphlet that influenced Hume, was reprinted in 1751, and was translated into French by Holbach in 1767. The essay is nowhere explicitly anti-Christian or anti-Church of England, and although it was generally taken as a deist document, it seems now as though its main point is Trenchard's strongly felt and warmly expressed fear of fanaticism. Indeed, the essay is a darkly eloquent denunciation of what has recently been called the passionate state of mind. Fontenelle had concentrated on the primitive mind, but had thought of it mainly as being in the past; Trenchard's focus is clearly the primitive or even savage mentality of his own day as it had surfaced menacingly in witchcraft and in the sort of fanaticism the period called enthusiasm.

In the closing paragraphs of the essay, Trenchard makes a final ringing summary of his leading ideas. He goes back to the Greek myths, giving his own version of their origin. He argues that men have always tended to find deity in "whatever is unusually great or vehement," a common enough argument at first, but Trenchard quickly moves this "myth-making" tendency into the present, and argues that the same instinct makes a melancholy man mistake an "impetuous Transport" for a "divine Inspiration." Trenchard argues that the myth-making impulse is the same as the religious impulse. Further, his argument clearly implies that all religiosity tends naturally toward exclusiveness, intolerance, and self-righteousness, thence into delusion, fanaticism, rabid proselytizing, and acrid persecution, finally to erupt as a roaring passion for the bloody extirpation of error and enemy alike.

What Trenchard obviously perceived and was frightened by was the demonic or Dionysian element, so often described as lying near the heart of both myth and religion. But Trenchard found no positive value in this element, no "Eros, builder of cities." Myth for Trenchard suggested a kind of mentality preset for fanaticism, because it involved and encouraged private emotionalism unchecked by reason. The problem of the irrational element in myth has been a continual concern since the early eighteenth century, but it has taken different forms. Not to catalogue the various shades of attitude, it may suf-

fice to say that the two main positions—
that the irrational in myth is a powerful,
regenerative, upwelling of vital energies,
or that the irrational in myth is a dark,
blind force apt to break out horribly in
certain religious and political forms—still
exist, and it is clear that John Trenchard's
is the second and currently less popular of
these positions. For his main argument is
that when one once begins, in all innocence, to make myth, there is then nothing
to prevent one becoming, by slow and in-
sidious gradations, a believer, an enthusiast, a receiver of visions and revelations,
a bigot, and, at last, a fanatic.

R.R.

REFERENCES Our text is from *The Natural
History of Superstition* (London, 1709),
printed in John Trenchard, *A Collection of
Tracts* (London: F. Cogan, 1751), pp. 378–
403. There is very little commentary on
Trenchard, an exception being that of Frank
Manuel in *The Eighteenth Century Confronts
the Gods* (Cambridge: Harvard University
Press, 1959).

TRENCHARD

FROM *The Natural History of Superstition*

"Atheism *leaves Men to Sense, to Philosophy, to Laws, to Reputation, all which may
be Guides to moral Virtue, tho' Religion
were not; but Superstition dismounts all
these, and erects an absolute Monarchy in
the Minds of Men: Therefore,* Atheism *did
never perturb States; but Superstition hath
been the Confusion of many. The Causes
of Superstition are pleasing and sensual
Rites and Ceremonies, Excess of Pharisai-
cal and outside Holiness, Reverence to
Traditions, and the Stratagems of Prelates
for their own Ambition and Lucre.*
                                    —LORD BACON

IF ANY Man surveys and contemplates
the visible World, the Great and glorious
Body of the Sun, many thousand times
bigger than the Earth, its immense Distance
from us, this Globe on which we live, and
numerous other Planets moving about it,
and receiving vital Warmth and Nourishment from its Beams; if he pursues and
aggrandizes this Idea, by considering the
much greater Distance and Magnitude of
the fixt Stars, in all probability so many
Suns, with each their particular System of
Worlds, and Inhabitants, and the frequent
Discovery of new Ones, by the Invention
of better Glasses and Telescopes; how
must he admire and adore the Power of
God, who has given Being and Motion to
such vast Machines, created them of such
Figure and Magnitude, disposed them in
such Order, placed them at such Distances,
gave them such proper and suitable Motions as oblige them to perform the regular
and ordinary Purposes of his Providence,
without the constant and momentary Inter-
position of his Power.

Nor is it less conspicuous in the Formation of inferior Animals, in this little Part

of the World in which we live, whose Parts are so adapted, and disposed by his all wise Providence, as by the Necessity of their own Natures to perform the Functions and Operations of their Beings: Hence we see that universal Harmony in all Creatures of the same Species. . . .

But we have ample amends made us in the Faculties of our Souls which makes it evident we were designed for nobler Uses; for whereas other Animals appear to have no Thoughts or Desires above their quotidian Food, Ease, Diversions or Lusts; Men have visibly larger and more extensive Views, as not only from the ordinary and regular System of the Universe, to carry their Minds to their great Creator, but to infer from thence the Duty and Obedience owing to him, and the Justice, Compassion, Love and Assistance owing to one another. And since the Defect and Narrowness of our natural Capacities has left us in the Dark about a future State, his abundant Goodness has amply supplied the Shortness of our Knowledge with divine Revelation, and has discovered and annexed a State of immortal Happiness to the natural Rewards attending a Just and virtuous Life.

But as there is no Perfection in this frail State, nor any Excellency without some Defect accompanying it, so these noble Faculties of the Mind have misled and betrayed us into Superstition, as appears in that, notwithstanding we are abundantly cautioned not to mistake the Impostures of pretended Prophets, the Frauds of Priests, and the Dreams and Visions of Enthusiasts for heavenly Revelations, and our own Infirmities and panic Fears for divine Impulses, yet the Fables of the Heathens, the Alcoran of *Mahomet,* the more gross and impious Forgeries of the Papists, and the Frauds and Follies of some who call themselves Protestants, have so far pre-

vailed over genuine Christianity, that the Righteous and Faithful are but like *the Gold to the Earth,* which could not have thus happened in all Ages, unless something innate in our Constitution made us easily to be susceptible of wrong Impressions, subject to panic Fears, and prone to Superstition and Error, and therefore it is incumbent upon us, first of all to examine into the Frame and Constitutions of our own Bodies, and search into the Causes of our Passions and Infirmities, for till we know from what Source or Principle we are so apt to be deceived by others, and by ourselves, we can never be capable of true Knowledge, much less of true Religion, which is the Perfection of it.

I take this wholly to proceed from our Ignorance of Causes, and yet Curiosity, to know them, it being impossible for any Man so far to divest himself of Concern for his own Happiness, as not to endeavour to promote it, and consequently to avoid what he thinks may hurt him; and since there must be Causes in Nature for every Thing that does or will happen, either here or hereafter, it is hard to avoid Sollicitude till we think we know them, and therefore since the divine Providence has for the most Part hid the Causes of Things which chiefly concern us from our View, we must either entirely abandon the Enquiry, or substitute such in their Room, as our own Imaginations or Prejudices suggest to us, or take the Words of others, whom we think wiser than ourselves, and as we believe have no intent to deceive us.

To these Weaknesses of our own, and Frauds of others, we owe the heathen Gods and Goddesses, Oracles and Prophets, Nymphs and Satyrs, Fawns and Tritons, Furies and Demons, most of the Stories of Conjurers and Witches, Spirits and Apparitions, Fairies and Hobgoblins, the Doctrine of Prognostics, the numerous Ways

of Divination, viz. Oniromancy, Sider-
omancy, Tephranomancy, Botonomancy,
Crommyomancy, Cleromancy, Acromancy,
Onomatomancy, Arithmomancy, Geo-
mancy, Alectryomancy, Cephalomancy,
Axinomancy, Coscinomancy, Hydro-
mancy, Onychomancy, Dactlyomancy,
Christallomancy, Cataptromancy, Gastro-
mancy, Lecanomancy, Alphitomancy, Chi-
romancy, Orneomancy and Necromancy,
Horoscopy, Astrology and Augury Meto-
poscopy and Palmistry, the Fear of
Eclipses, Comets, Meteors, Earthquakes,
Inundations, and any uncommon Appearances, though ever so much depending
upon natural and necessary Causes, nor are
there wanting People otherwise of good
Understanding, who are affected with the
falling of Salt-celler, crossing of a Hare,
croaking of a Raven, howling of Dogs,
screaching of Owls, the Motion of Worms
in a Bedstead, mistaken for Death-Watches,
and other as senseless and trifling Accidents.

It is this Ignorance of Causes, &c. subjects us to mistake the Phantasms and
Images of our own Brains (which have no
Existence any where else) for real Beings,
and subsisting without us, as in Dreams
where we see Persons and Things, feel Pain
and Pleasure, form Designs, hear and make
Discourses, and sometimes the Objects are
represented so lively to our Fancies, and
the Impression so strong, that it would be
hard to distinguish them from Realities, if
we did not find ourselves in Bed.

But if a melancholy Man, sitting by himself in a doleful Mood, with his Brains
brooding upon Visions and Revelations;
should carelessly nod himself half a Sleep,
and his Imagination having received a
vigorous Representation of an Angel delivering a Message to him, should wake
in a surprize, without having observed his
own Sleeping (as often happens) I can-

not see how he should distinguish it from
a divine Vision.

There have been surprizing Instances of
this Kind, in extatic Fits and Trances,
which are but sounder Sleeps, that cause
more lively and intense Dreams: Some in
these Delirium's have fancied their Souls
to have been transported to Heaven or
Hell, to have had personal Communication
with God and the holy Trinity, have given
Descriptions of the Angels and their
Habitations, and brought back Messages,
Prophecies and Instructions to Mankind,
which Phoenomena's however strange at
first Sight, are easily to be accounted for
by natural Causes, for the Ideas and Operations of our Minds being evidently produced, by the Agitations and Motions of
the internal Parts of our own Bodies, and
Impressions heretofore made on them, as
well as the Actions of Objects without us
(which will be made appear in the Sequel
of this Discourse.) It must necessarily happen when the Organs of Sense (which are
the Avenues and Doors to let in external
Objects) are shut and locked up by Sleep,
Distempers, or strong Prejudices, that
the Imaginations produced from inward
Causes, must reign without any Rival, for
the Images within us striking strongly
upon, and affecting the Brain, Spirits, or
Organ, where the imaginative Faculty resides, and all Objects from without, being
wholly, or in a great Measure shut out and
excluded, so as to give no Information or
Assistance we must unavoidably submit to
an Evidence which meets with no Contradiction, and takes things to be as they
appear.

I conceive that *Ignis Fatuus* of the Mind,
which the Visionaries in all Ages, have
called the inward Light and leads all that
have followed it into Pools and Ditches,
to be like what is before described: For by
their own Description it is only to be at-

tained by renouncing the Senses, and all the intellectual Faculties, and wholly sequestring their Thoughts from worldly and material Objects, by which Elevation of Mind, they arrive to a more close and intimate Union with God, have internal Communication with him, and by immediate Motions and Inspirations learn all Truths, and whatever is necessary to be done. This is what Men of vulgar Notions, call *sending their Wits for a Venture,* and indeed is but a waking Dream, for they alike lock up all their outward Senses, which are the only Conduits of Knowledge, and deliver themselves up to the Guidance of wild Fancy, and consequently must be actuated wholly by their several Complexions, Constitutions and Distempers, which often make them *ixion*-like, embrace their own Clouds and Fogs for Deities. . . .

(pp. 378–383)

Mankind in their Ignorance of Causes, have been always prone to believe some special Presence of God, or a Supernatural Power, to be in whatever is unusually great or vehement. This made the Ancients ascribe Thunder and Lightning to *Jupiter,* Wisdom to *Pallas,* Craft to *Mercury,* the lively Thoughts produced by Wine to *Bacchus,* Storms and Tempests to *Aeolus,* the Rapsodies of Poetry to the Muses, Courage to *Mars,* Rage and Madness to the *Eumenides* or *Furies,* the Passions of Love to *Cupid,* the Productions of the Earth to *Ceres,* and Things seemingly accidental to *Fortune;* to these Idols of their own Fancies, they built magnificent Temples, endowed them with Priests, Lands, Officers and Revenues; and worshipped them with Oblations, Prayers and Thanks; this Disposition gave Rise to the worshipping of Heroes, Legislators and Founders of new Sects and Opinions; for the People perceiving uncommon Wisdom, Eloquence, Res-

olution and Success to attend all their Words and Actions, believed them to be inspired and assisted by some superior Power, and so intirely abandoned themselves to their Conduct whilst living, and adored them when dead.

It is this makes a melancholy Man mistake the impetuous Transport, whereby he is fervently and zealously carried in Matters of Religion, for divine Inspiration, and the Power of God in him; for feeling a Storm of Devotion coming upon him, his Heart full of godly Affection, his Head in his own Opinion pregnant with clear and sensible Representations, his Mouth flowing with powerful Eloquence, and not being able to observe from what Conduct of Reason, or other Causes in Nature this sudden Change proceeds, immediately concludes it to be the Power of God, working supernaturally in him; he thinks every sudden Help or Evasion, every lucky Hint to avoid Dangers or compass Deliverances, to proceed immediately from God; every imagined Discovery of an Error held by others, to be a supernatural Revelation; every fine and curious Thought that steals into his Mind, a Pledge of the divine Favour, and a singular Illumination; every staring and rampant Fancy, every unbridled, bold and confident Obstruction of his own uncouth and supine Invention to be a special Truth, and the Power and Presence of God in his Soul: He esteems his Pride and Tumour of Mind, his stiff, inflexible and unyielding Temper, his steady and obstinate Resolution to admit no Demonstrations against his Opinions, and to suffer Torture or Martyrdom, to be the special Support and divine Assistance of God, and his ardent Zeal, and implacable Desire of Revenge towards all who oppose him, to be the more than ordinary Influence and Impulse of the Holy Ghost, for the Extirpation of Heresy; whereas the

Enthusiast is only intoxicated with Vapours ascending from the lower Regions of his Body, as the *Pythian* Prophetess of old, in her prophetic Trances, was by the Power of certain Exhalations breathing from subterranean Caverns; for all these Appearances are easily resolvable into the Power of Melancholy, which is but a sort of natural Inebriation, the same Effects being produced often by Wine; and it is observable that such high-flown and bloated Expressions, Rapsodies of slight and lofty Words, and rolling and streaming Tautologies, which fall from Enthusiasts, generally happen to Persons before they are stark Mad.

The particular Disposition of the Blood, which produces this Temper of the Mind, seems to be the Predominance of adust Melancholy, well impregnated with Gall; the first gives presumptuous Confidence, and the latter Insolence and Impatience of Contradiction; which if it prevails so much in speculative Questions, which regard no Man's Profit or Power, and that both sides agree, are to be determined by the Rules of Reason (insomuch, that People of this Complexion, can converse with none but of their own Opinions) what Havock must it make in Matters of Religion? Upon which Subject almost all Mankind seem to have agreed by universal Consent to talk unintelligibly, and by that Means have endeavoured to destroy or take away the only Criterion between Truth and Falsehood, Religion and Superstition; every side pretends to Visions, Revelations, Miracles and Mysteries, expect to be believed upon their own Authority, and pursue all who dare oppose them, with Vengeance and Destruction, as perverse Unbelievers, Heretics, Deists and Atheists; which charitable and polite Language is promiscuously given by and to all Parties and Factions in Religion.

Though at first Sight it appears very absurd, that all Mankind should be concerned in the Visions and Revelations of two or three Men, when few of the same Nation or District can know their Persons, fewer their Sincerity, and whether they are inspired by God, are deceived themselves, or intend to deceive others; it must be more so, to expect Nations distant in Situation, Language and Customs, to leave their Affairs and Habitations to hunt after Prophets, Miracles, and Revelation Mongers, or give Credit to the fabulous or uncertain Stories or Legends of People they know nothing of, when we can hardly believe anything said, to be done in the same Town or Neighbourhood, and scarce in the same House, or tell a Story of ever so simple Particulars, that we can know again when we hear it; it is yet more ridiculous to oblige all the World to rake into the Rubbish of Antiquity, to learn all Languages, examine all Systems, and thereby discover all Impostures, Forgeries, Interpolations, Errors and Mistakes, or else submit to the Guidance of others, who are neither honester nor wiser than themselves, and besides have an Interest to deceive them; yet the true Enthusiast sees none of these Difficulties, starts at no Absurdities; is very sure that he has received frequent Revelations, is thoroughly satisfied of his own Inspiration and Mission, and expects all Mankind, both now and hereafter to be so too; he has given them sufficient Notice, by promulgating his Doctrine amongst a few that he can persuade to hear him, and condemns all the rest as obstinate contumacious Heretics, and wilful Transgressors against Demonstration and evident Light: Aversion, Pride and Fury in the Shape of Zeal, like a mighty Storm ruffles his Mind into beating Billows, and boisterous Fluctuations; at last he is all in a Rage, and no Church-Buckets to quench his fiery Religion, Religion and the Glory of God drives him on: The holy Enthusiastic longs to feast and riot upon human Sacrifices, turn Cities and Nations into Shambles, and destroy with Fire and Sword such who dare thwart his Frenzy, and all the while like another *Nero,* plays upon his Harp and sings *Te Deum* at the Conflagration.   (pp. 400–403)

RICHARD BLOME [d. 1705]

WILLEM BOSMAN [b. 1672]

PÈRE JOSEPH LAFITAU [1670–1740]

EARLY eighteenth-century myth study profited greatly from the great mass of new, firsthand information that was being published by travelers, missionaries, and merchants. Fontenelle made use of material from travel literature on South America, and Bayle drew upon Bosman's account of fetishism, to mention only two instances. This new knowledge came from observation, not from previous books, and while one can see many of the preoccupations of the age in the set of mind of a Blome or a Lafitau, the actual information provided by them (as well as by La Créquinière, Le Gobien, and many others) was indeed novel and interesting, and much of it was to prove profoundly unsettling. Further, there is discernible in merchants and travelers such as Bosman and Blome a new spirit of inquiry. Never fearful or timid, hardly bookish, difficult to shock, and interested in everything, there is a certain zest in the way these men enthusiastically describe what was new and strange; they show the Monday morning side of the Enlightenment in their cheerful, practical openness.

The influence of their usually unpretentious writings was often far out of proportion to their intrinsic and intended value. These men helped shape the new view of old pagan religion as similar to contemporary savagery, they fed the study of comparative religion, and they weakened, without ever intending to do so, the idea of Revelation. (In the case of Père Lafitau this effect of his well-meant volume amounts to a spectacular backfiring of his all-embracing but off-balance piety.) Finally, having provided the flood of new material, these travelers laid the groundwork for what was later to be called the anthropological approach to myth.

Richard Blome's volume is a report on English territories in America and is intended for the information of colonists. He gives brief accounts of the religious beliefs and practices of the natives of St. Vincent, of Maryland, New York, New England, and Newfoundland, but he is not much interested in religion, nor does he seem very clear on some points of doctrine. Blome's frame of reference, as he looks at the Indians, is of course Christianity, but he seems familiar with the fear-theory of myth, and he exhibits a tart anticlericalism. Blome makes few direct comparisons between pagan and savage religion, but his account, even when represented by snippets, shows the sort of material from which such comparisons came.

Willem Bosman's *A New and Accurate Description of the Coast of Guinea*, published—in Dutch—in 1704, had been through four editions in Dutch by 1737, and had been translated into French, English, and German. It was translated into Italian in 1752 and has had two more English editions in our own century. Bosman was chief factor for the Dutch at the Fort of Elmira, and is said to have been the second most important Dutch official on the coast of Guinea from about 1688 to 1702. Bosman devotes a whole section of his account to religion; his comments are those of a shrewd, alert, and intelligent—and quite skeptical—observer. He is alive both to differences and to similarities between what he sees and what he knows. He distinguishes quickly between private worship which he finds to vary widely, and public worship which is standardized. He notes that such monotheism as the Africans have is the result of their European overlay, while the real native religion is fetishism, an observation that undercuts not only Christianity but deism as well, since it ignores and even refutes the idea of natural monotheism. Bosman's brief piece on fetishism proved useful to Bayle and later to Charles de Brosses, whose *Du culte des dieux fétiches* set forth the idea that all religion began in fetishism, and the line from de Brosses's emphasis on ritual origins to modern anthropological thought is not obscure.

Père Joseph Lafitau, Jesuit missionary to the Canadian Indians, published in 1724 a large volume that became for a time the best-known and most widely-cited book of its kind. *Moeurs des Sauvages Amériquains comparées aux moeurs des premiers temps* is a sort of eighteenth-century *Golden Bough*. It was novel, prestigious, and composed of a relatively simple and not altogether new thesis backed up by an avalanche of documentation that often proves more interesting than the overruling theory. It was based on the comparative method, and aimed at explaining how the savage mind works.

Lafitau's argument springs from the elaborate comparison of the customs of the modern Indians with what is recorded of antiquity. The similarities lead to the idea that the Indians are somehow descended from the ancients, and yet further to the idea that both ancient paganism and modern savagery are degenerated offshoots of a pure primitive religion; the former are, in fact, Christianity muddled and barbarized, only retaining—like man after the Fall—a glimmer of former purity. One of Lafitau's avowed purposes was to confute the atheists "by showing the unanimous consent among people as regards a Superior Being." However bizarre a religion might be, Lafitau could find a scrap of monotheistic thought in it. But to many, it was the parade of strange, colorful savage rites and customs that was impressive, while the "proofs" of monotheism seemed so thin as to virtually demonstrate the opposite. In trying to straightjacket diversity into unity, Lafitau only showed more impressively than ever how very diverse men's religions were. And as a source book for future myth study, Lafitau's work helped underpin pluralist and skeptical accounts just as much as monist and Christian work.

R.R.

REFERENCES Our texts are from Richard Blome, *The Present State of His Majesties Isles and Territories in America* (London: H. Clark, 1687); Willem Bosman, *A New and Accurate Description of the Coast of Guinea* (New York: Barnes and Noble, 1967), a reprint of the 1705 edition; Père Joseph Lafitau, *Moeurs des Sauvages Amériquains comparées aux moeurs des premiers temps* (Paris, 1724), our translation.

These writers and others like them are treated—if at all—by historians of anthropology. For Lafitau, especially, see Margaret T. Hodgen, *Early Anthropology in the Sixteenth and Seventeenth Centuries* (Philadelphia: University of Pennsylvania Press, 1964), and Marvin Harris, *The Rise of Anthropolog-*

ical Theory (New York: Thomas Y. Crowell Co., 1968). For a survey and bibliography of the entire contribution of travelers and missionaries to the study of religions in the early eighteenth century, see H. Pinard de la Boullaye, *L'Étude comparée des Religions* (Paris: G. Beauchesne, 1922), tome I, pp. 177–189. Among the best known are La Créquinière,

The Agreement of the Customs of the East-Indians with those of the Jews . . . , tr. John Toland (London, 1705) and Le Gobien, *Lettres édifiantes et curieuses écrits des missions étrangères,* 8 vols. (Paris, 1703–1708). C. Meiners' *Allgemeine Kritische Geschichte der Religionen* (Hanover, 1806–1807) lists over three hundred such books.

Blome

from *The Present State of His Majesties Isles and Territories in America*

[The natives of Newfoundland]

THEY believe in one God, who created all things, but have many whimsical Notions, and ridiculous Opinions, for they say *That after God had made all things, he took a number of arrows, and struck them in the ground from whence Men and Women first sprung up, and have multiplied ever since. A Sagamore or Governour* being asked concerning the Trinity, answered *There was only one God, one Son, one Mother and the Sun, which were four, yet God was above all.* Being questioned if they or their Ancestors had heard that God was come into the World, he said, *That he had not seen him.* (p. 241)

[The Indians of New England]

When they design to make War they first consult with their Priests and Conjurors, no People being so Barbarous almost, but they have their Gods, Priests and Religion:

They adore as it were all things that they think may unavoidably hurt them, as *Fire, Water, Lightning, Thunder,* our Great *Guns, Muskets* and *Horses:* yea, some of them once seeing an *English boar,* were struck with some terror, because he bristled up his Hairs and gnashed his Teeth, believing him to be the God of the *Swine,* who was offended with them. The Chief God they worship is the Devil, which they call *Okee;* They have conference with him, and fashion themselves into his shape: In their Temple they have his Image ill-favouredly Carved, Painted and Adorned with Chains, Copper and Beads and covered with a skin. (pp. 212–213)

[The Indians of New York]

They observe several Ceremonies in their Religious Rites and are said to Worship the Devil, which usually they perform once or twice a Year, unless upon some extraordinary occasion, as the making of War, or the like, when their *Corn* is ripe, which is usually about *Michaelmas:* The day being appointed by the Chief Priest or *Pawaw,* most of them go a Hunting for *Venison:* when they are all assembled, if the Priest wants Money, he then tells them, their God will accept no offering, but Money, which the People believing, every one gives according to his ability: the Priest takes the Money and putting it into some Dishes, sets them on the top of their low, flat-roofed Houses, and so falls a calling upon their God. . . .   (p. 205)

BOSMAN

FROM *Description of Guinea*

Letter X

SIR,

My last was very long; and if I treat the Subject largely, this will not be much shorter; For the Religion of the *Negroes,* of which I design to speak, will afford Matter enough for a Book alone, by reason of the numerous and different sorts of it: For there is no Village or Town, nay, I had almost said, no private Family which doth not differ from another on this Head: But not thinking it worth while to recount all the various Opinions, I shall therefore pass them over, and only speak of their publick Religion and Worship; in which they almost all agree.

Almost all the Coast *Negroes* believe in one true God, to whom they attribute the Creation of the World, and all things in it, though in a crude indigested Manner, they not being able to form a just idea of a Deity. They are not obliged to themselves nor the Tradition of their Ancestors for their Opinion, rude as it is, but to their daily Conversation with the *Europeans,* who from time to time have continually endeavoured to emplant this Notion in them. There are two Reasons which confirm me in this Sentiment: First, that they never make any Offerings to God, nor call upon him in time of need; but in all their Difficulties, they apply themselves to their *Fetiche* (of which more hereafter) and pray to him for Success in their Undertakings: The Second is, the different Opinions of some of them concerning the Creation; for a great part of the *Negroes* believe that man was made by *Anansie,* that is, a great Spider: the rest attribute the Creation of Man to God, which they assert to have happened in the following manner: They tell us, that in the beginning God created Black as well as White Men; thereby not only hinting but endeavouring to prove that their race was as soon in the World as ours; and to bestow a yet greater Honour on themselves, they tell us that God having created these two sorts of Men, offered two sorts of Gifts, *viz,* Gold, and the

Knowledge or Arts of Reading and Writing, giving the Blacks, the first Election, who chose Gold, and left the Knowledge of Letters to the White. God granted their Request, but being incensed at their Avarice, resolved that the Whites should for ever be their Masters, and they obliged to wait on them as their Slaves. Others again affirm, that Man at his first Creation was not shaped as at present; but that those parts which serve for the distinction of Sexes in Men and Women, were placed more in view for the convenience of Propagation: What think you, Sir, is not this a ridiculous Notion? would it not be very obliging to the *Turks* to sometimes gratify their Bestial Appetites with Women in an Unnatural Manner, not to mention their *Sodomy* with Men.

I have found very few *Negroes* of this sentiment; but having asked those who are its Assertors, when the shape of Man was alter'd to its present State: they replied, that God had done it out of respect to Modesty when the World became so well Peopled that the Shape was sufficient to preserve the Race of Mankind. Others on the Gold Coast would perswade us, that the first Men came out of Holes and Pits, like that at present in a great Rock on the Sea, near our Fort of *Acra*. But 'tis time to stop my Hand; for if I should particularize all their Notions concerning the Creation, the Moon and Stars, instead of being short, I should grow insupportable tedious. I shall only tell you, that Father *Kirchen* [sic] would not find it very difficult to perswade them that the Planets are Peopled, or at least the Moon: for they have already discovered a Fellow beating a Drum in her.

I promised just now to explain the Word *Fetiche,* which is used in various Senses. *Fetiche* or *Bossum* in the *Negro* Language, derives its self from their False God, which they call *Bossum*. Are they enclined to make Offerings to their idols, or desire to be informed of something by them? they cry out, Let us make *Fetiche;* by which they express as much, as let us perform our Religious Worship, and see or hear what our God saith. In like manner, if they are injured by another they make *Fetiche* to destroy him in the following manner: they cause some Victuals and Drink to be Exorcised by their *Feticheer* or Priest, and scatter it in some place which their Enemy is accustomed to pass; firmly believing, that he who comes to touch this conjured Stuff shall certainly dye soon after. Those who are afraid of this coming to such places, cause themselves to be carried over them; for 'tis the wonderful Nature of this Exorcised Trash, that then it does not in the least affect the Person, nor can it at all affect those who carry him, or any Body else besides him. So that tho' the Art of poisoning is a Favourite peculiar to the *Italians,* yet they have always found themselves obliged to endanger the innocent to come at the Guilty, and never yet could hit on so distinguishing and discreet a Poison as this of our *Negroes;* though I must confess I like that of the *Italians* so little, that I had rather walk over all that the *Negroes* can lay for me, than have any thing to do with theirs. . . .

(pp. 145–148)

Each Priest or *Feticheer* hath his peculiar Idol, prepared and adjusted in a particular and different manner, but most of them like the following Description. They have a great Wooden Pipe filled with Earth, Oil, Blood, the Bones of dead Men and Beasts, Feathers, Hair; and, to be short, all sorts of Excrementitious and filthy Trash, which they do not endeavour to mould into any Shape, but lay it in a confused heap in the Pipe. The *Negroe* who is to take an Oath before this Idol, is placed directly opposite to it, and asks the Priest the Name of his Idol (each having a particular one;) of which being informed, he calls the *Fetiche* by its Name, and recites at large the Contents of what he designs to bind by an Oath, and makes it his Petitionary Request that the Idol may punish him with Death if he swears falsly; then he goes round the Pipe and stands still and swears a second time in the same place and manner as before, and so a third time likewise: after which the Priest takes some of the mentioned Ingredients out of the Pipe; with which he touches the Swearer's Head, Arms, Belly and Legs, and holding it above his Head, turns it three times round; then he cuts off a bit of the Nail of one Finger in each Hand, of one Toe of each Foot and some of the Hair of his Head, which he throws into the Pipe where the Idol is loged; all which done the Oath is firmly Obligatory. But to turn to another Subject.

When the *Negroes* design to begin a War, to drive a Bargain, to Travel or attempt any thing of Importance; their first Business is to consult their False God by the Priest, concerning the Event of their Undertaking, who very seldom Prophesies Ill, but generally encourages them to hope for prosperous Success; which they take on his Word, not doubting the Issue in the least, and obsequiously perform all the Priest's Commands; which generally oblige them to offer up Sheep, Hogs, Fowls, Dogs and Cats to their Idol; or at other times perhaps, Cloaths, Wine and Gold; by which the Priest is sure to be the greatest Gainer, for he sweeps all to himself,

only presenting Garbage and the Excrements of the slaughtered Sacrifice to his God to divert himself withal: And thus, besides the Money given him, he makes a shift to pay himself very well out of the Offerings for his small trouble. . . .

(pp. 150–151)

If it was possible to convert the *Negroes* to the Christian Religion, the *Roman*-Catholicks would succeed better than we should, because they already agree in several particulars, especially in their ridiculous Ceremonies; for do the *Romanists* abstain one or two Days weekly from Flesh; these have also their Days when they forbear Wine; which considering they are very great lovers of it, is somewhat severe. The *Romanists* have their allotted times for eating peculiar sorts of Food, or perhaps wholly abstaining from it, in which the *Negroes* out-do them; for each Person here is forbidden the eating of one sort of Flesh or other; one eats no Mutton, another no Goats-Flesh, Beef, Swines-Flesh, Wild-Fowl, Cocks, with white Feathers, &c. This Restraint is not laid upon them for a limited time, but for their whole Lives: And if the *Romanists* brag of the Antiquities of their Ecclesiastical Commands; so if you ask the *Negroes* why they do this, they will readily tell you, because their Ancestors did so from the beginning of the World, and it hath been handed down from one Age to another by Tradition. The Son never eats what the Father is restrained from, as the Daughter herein follows the Mother's Example; and this Rule is so strictly observed amongst them, that 'tis impossible to perswade them to the contrary. (pp. 154–155)

LAFITAU

FROM *The Customs of the American Savages Compared
to the Customs of the First Ages*

IT IS not then a vain curiosity and a sterile knowledge that voyagers who give accounts of their travels to the public, and those who read them, should have in mind. One should study manners only to form manners, and he will find everywhere something from which to draw advantage.

The religious zeal that obliges a missionary to cross the seas should also serve as his motive and guide his pen, when in his leisure he works to reveal the discoveries he has made and the knowledge he has acquired. That is the goal of an Evangelical worker, and is also the goal I have tried to reach in all my study and all my work.

I have become painfully aware that, in the majority of accounts, those who have written of the manners of barbarous people have painted them for us as people having no sentiment of religion, no knowledge of divinity, no object to whom they render any worship; as people who have neither laws, nor any sort of civil order, nor any form of government; in a word, as men who have almost nothing of Man except the form. It is a fault which missionaries themselves and honest people have committed, who have written on the one hand with too great haste of things they knew insufficiently, and who, on the other hand, were unaware of the unfortunate consequences that could be drawn from a senti-

ment so unfavorable to Religion. These authors, however, may contradict themselves in their works, and at the same time that they say that these barbarians have neither worship nor gods, they say also things which suppose a divinity and a regulated worship, as M. Bayle himself has observed. Nevertheless the result is that one sees at first only that initial proposition, and thus one gets used to forming an idea of savages and barbarians which scarcely distinguishes them from animals.

But what an argument does one not thereby furnish to the Atheists? One of the strongest proofs that we have against them of the necessity and existence of a religion is the unanimous consent of all peoples in recognizing a superior Being and of honoring him in some fashion that shows how they feel his superiority and the need one has to turn to him. But this argument falls, if it is true that there is a multitude of diverse nations brutalized to the point that they have no idea of a God, nor any established way of rendering him the worship due him, for from these the Atheist seems to reason justly in concluding that if there is almost a whole world of nations that have no religion at all, the religion that one finds among other nations is the work of human prudence, and a creation of legislators who have invented it to lead people by fear, the mother of superstition.

To render then to religion all the advantage it ought to draw from a proof as strong as that of the unanimous consent of all people, and to deny the Atheist all means of attacking by this entrance, it is necessary to destroy the false idea that these authors have given of the savages, since this idea alone is the basis of so disadvantageous a prejudice.

I know that latterly people have wished to weaken this proof of the unanimous consent of peoples in recognizing a divinity, as if this unanimous consent could be susceptible of error, but the sophistries and subtleties of some particular person who has no religion, or whose religion is strongly suspect, cannot shake a truth that has been recognized even by the Pagans, that has been received in all times without contradiction, and that we can assume as a principle.

It is only then a question of proving this unanimity of sentiment in all nations in showing that in effect there is none so barbarous but that it has religion and manners. But I flatter myself that I will make the thing so clear that one cannot doubt it, unless one wishes to close one's eyes against the light.

Not only do the people we call barbarians have a religion, but this religion has affinities of so great a conformity with that of the earliest time, with what was called in antiquity the orgies of Bacchus and of the mother of the Gods, the mysteries of Isis and Osiris, that one thinks at first of these resemblances that they are everywhere and share the same principles and the same bases.

In the matter of Religion we have nothing in profane antiquity more ancient than these mysteries and these orgies that compose all the religion of the Phrygians, of the Egyptians, and of the first Cretans, who regarded themselves as the first people of the world and the first authors of the worship of the Gods, who from among them passed to all nations and spread out throughout the universe.

But as several centuries of shadow and obscurity passed between the authors of this religion and those who wrote about it, and as these writers did not appear until the time of religion's corruption, after it had been altered by an innumerable multitude of fables, it was impossible for them to show exactly the time of its origin. Those commentators have interpreted Isis and Osiris, Bacchus and Ceres and a number of others, as particular lawgivers for whom they have fixed dates as they pleased, and these dates, as generally accepted, are not only much later than the creation of the world, but even later than the deluge.

As the idea of this religion has only come to us since the time of its corruption, it has never appeared other than a monstrous religion. In effect it is enveloped with all the shadows of idolatry and all the horrors of magic, fecund source of the greatest crimes, of the most pitiable errors of the mind, and of the greatest disorders of the heart.

This corruption, however, no matter how enormous it was, is not so general that one cannot find in the depths of this corrupted Religion principles contradictorily opposed to the corruption, principles of a strict morality that calls for an austere virtue, that is an enemy to disorder, and that supposes a religion holy in its origin and holy before it was corrupted. For it is not natural to think that purity of morals can be born from corruption and vice, while it is only too natural to see vice and corruption ravage and alter the most holy things.

Moreover there is to be found in this

religion of the first Gentiles so great a resemblance between several points of belief that faith informs us of, and which suppose a revelation, and such a conformity in worship with that of true religion, that it seems that nearly all the essential points come from the same foundations.

One cannot deny this resemblance and this conformity. One finds, for example, vestiges of the mystery of the most holy Trinity in the mysteries of Isis, in the works of Plato, and in the religions of the Indies, of Japan, and of the Mexicans. One discovers many other similar traits in the pagan mythology, as I will show in what follows.   (from Chapter 1, "The Design and Plan of the Work")

GIAMBATTISTA VICO

[1668–1744]

VICO's interpretation of myth is in many ways the most profound of his century; it is certainly the most original. Although rooted in a seventeenth-century rationalism, his thought anticipates much nineteenth- and twentieth-century interest in poetry and myth and in history and philosophy of history; his admirers include Michelet, Coleridge, Croce, James Joyce, and W. B. Yeats. Vico's *New Science* appeared in 1725 (second edition, 1730; third edition, 1744). As might be expected, his full influence was delayed, his larger reputation rising only with Michelet's abridged French translation of 1827. By then, Vico's insights could be appreciated, as Michelet summarized them in 1831: Vico's priority in seeing "Homer" as the work of a whole people, not a single poet, a theory later made famous by F. A. Wolf; his anticipation of the symbolic theories of romantics such as Görres and Creuzer, of the kinship between law and custom in Montesquieu, of the study of earliest Roman history by Barthold Niebuhr, of philosophies of history in Herder, Hegel, and others. A later assessment would add his presaging of Marx's stress on understanding history through class struggles, of the romantic effort to revitalize poetry by cultivating unsophisticated wisdom, and of new theories of grammar and etymology such as those advanced by Grimm. Aside from its originality, Vico's work is also the most striking early instance of how myth ceases to be only a familiar but degraded chapter in the history of Christianity or reason, and begins to gain autonomy and approval for itself. Vico's achievement is perhaps best seen as it emerges from his fundamental assumptions and ambitions.

Vico's great fame begins with the romantic period. And while myth was often enough taken up in romantic and modern times with antirationalist or antiscientific motives, myth preoccupies Vico —and emerges finally as his "master key" —precisely because he has vast rationalist ambitions to construct a new science. He shares, with certain other rationalists, the hopes of finding the true "principles of humanity," the undeniable axioms and certain method revealing the necessary rationale underlying what Vico called the "common nature of nations." The laws and findings of this science would unify and explain nothing less than social and political man as he is found everywhere, under whatever different kinds of civil laws, institutions, languages, and religion. But myth was, as Vico saw, a great stumbling block to the accomplishment of such a science of man: for myth concerned the origins of every side of human life, but seemed to make all beginnings "incomplete, obscure, unreasonable, incredible, and without hope of reduction to scientific principles."

Where Vico now proposed to work his way through this formidable obstacle, the usual course had been to ignore or to reject looking to myth for much help. By proposing now that myth could yield true "principles," Vico stands against the orthodox Christian claim that only Revelation could adequately explain the origins and history of the "gentile" nations. And Vico's confidence in myth as a source of knowledge sets him against the "official" rationalist position, which held the savage and dark world of mythic customs and beliefs to be absurd, monstrous, or even disgusting. Vico gets around the orthodox Christian claim by insisting he is treating only those peoples outside the Biblical-Christian dispensation, that is, the "gentiles," who exist in a kind of state of nature. Vico's collision with the rationalists is more direct. The irrational, primitive, barbarous mythic realm, after all, was hardly assimilable to any rationalist or deist appeal to natural law, natural reason, or natural religion. And yet, as Vico knew, the most impressive recent attempts at sciences of human society were in terms of nature and natural law, especially as reinterpreted in terms of those "new sciences" which had revolutionized the study of the natural world on new principles, such as Bacon's *Novum Organum,* the new *Method* of Descartes, and Galileo's *Dialogue on the New Sciences.* The explicit words "New Science" in the title of Vico's greatest book show clearly that Vico had those other sciences in mind as he formed his own ambitious design.

But by proposing to be scientifically rational about myth—or by claiming that myth correctly understood can yield true rational principles—Vico could seem to be yoking two incompatibles. His originality lies precisely in this seemingly paradoxical enterprise. Vico argues that any true science of man must be able to explain mythic origins, or else admit its incompetency. For Vico, no true human science is possible or worthy unless it can account for why human society *necessarily* involved myth, and this neither the natural law rationalists nor the Christians

could do. Guided by a view of nature as uniform and clear, natural law theorists (like Grotius or Hobbes) mistakenly think that a "developed human reason" is "current by nature through all times in all nations." Similarly, as the story of Adam shows, Christianity also views man as created from the start in full rationality, in full humanity. Holding such views, when faced with the polytheism, savagery, and bizarre details of myth, rationalists and Christians alike tended to reject myth altogether or else to "adjust" it to piety or reasonableness. Thus, they often saw myth as only a corrupted version of revealed truth, or as horrifying fables that really concealed enlightened wisdom in allegoric form. But to argue like this, Vico claims, is only to read one's own civilized, sophisticated views back into quite different beginnings.

Vico now proposes an entirely new approach to the study of myth. But it is important to note at once that he arrives at this daring step because he affirms what scientific rationalists such as Descartes claimed. Descartes saw nature as a separate realm, different from the spiritual or "human" realm. Such an insistence on nature having its own laws often had antireligious motives or uses, as in Hobbes or Spinoza. But Vico turns this separation of physical and spiritual or human worlds to the advantage of myth as a most important subject. Physical nature may be different from the human, but obviously the reverse is true as well: the spiritual or human can now be seen as free from rigid obedience to nature's laws, and thus the human realm becomes unusually autonomous, with its own autonomous principles of development. "Humanity" needs to be explored then in terms of how it necessarily develops ideas, expresses them, and perpetuates them. Vico shifts from thinking of myth as caused externally to myth as caused immanently: it is not satanic demons, wicked priests, or confusing natural events that cause myths to appear, but the deepest inner nature of man himself.

Not reason but imagination must thus be the key to myth; and human history is where one must look, not to "nature" or some permanently ordered ideal law or realm. The immediate effect of this is that Vico can bring into his "science" what before seemed unreasonable, morally outrageous, or impious. A crucial axiom of the *New Science* declares that a science "must begin where its subject matter begins." The true science of humanity does not begin with men more or less rational, but with mythic men as they in fact were—as Vico says, with men before they became "human" or humanized, with "stupid, insensate and horrible beasts."

Vico claims to have spent twenty years learning to "descend from these human and refined natures of ours to those quite wild and savage natures, which we cannot at all imagine and can comprehend only with great difficulty." But what in fact can we comprehend or imagine of these seemingly incomprehensible "first men" poised on that primal step between bestiality and humanity? We can understand why and how these first men entered what we know as the human world. Our whole civilized and rational world indeed springs from that first step forward, and by grasping what caused this first all-important event, we can grasp the principle by which humanity in general begins and develops. Myth is the key here. Vico starts with the traditional Christian division of all men into those covered by Revelation and those outside it. The "gentiles" obviously and utterly lack knowledge of the revealed truths God gave the Hebrews. Vico describes the bestial semi-men as impious descendents of Noah who dispersed after the Flood, wandered, and finally became wholly degraded, reduced to inner darkness. Never does God intervene directly or miraculously in their affairs. Thus, these first gentile men, com-

pletely abandoned to their own devices, may indeed be said to have created their own laws, institutions, and civil societies. Vico's point is made clear by turning to the Bible: the Jews could not claim to have "created" their own laws and institutions; they received them. No historian who accepts Scripture as divinely given could claim to have more than a limited, external knowledge of the causes involved in the Jews' history; God alone knows these causes finally. But a historian can gain reliable knowledge of why and how gentile civilization arose. Again, this is possible because the first gentile men, bereft of revealed guidance, created their own laws and societies, and, quite necessarily, recorded and interpreted as best they could what had happened, in poetic or mythic language.

To discover what happened in the beginnings, then, one must study myth; and one can study myth confident that it will yield true principles, if read rightly. Thus, for example, from the seemingly universal fact (as Vico claims) that "every gentile nation had its Jove," its thunderbolt hurler, Vico can unfold an historical meaning and a metaphysical meaning. He reimagines the life of the first men, bestial, shameless, fearless, quite possibly copulating animally and out in the open with captive women. But as myths tell us: "Jove hurls his thunderbolts": that is, these bestial men, giants in size and strength, could be frightened only by something overwhelmingly strong and awesome, such as lightning. For the first time they meet a power never before met; astonished, they raise their eyes to the sky, and "began to think humanly." What human thought could such creatures be capable of? Obviously nothing "abstract, refined or spiritualized," says Vico in an obvious thrust at rationalists; but some "thought" strangely sensual, passionate, even physical. But the clue that "the first divine fable, the greatest" ever created by pagans, involved Jove's thunderbolts helps us see what bestial man "thought": "some notion of God such as even the most savage, wild monstrous men do not lack." That is, bestial, primal man awakened to the divine, in fear and trembling.

Vico's point here is that the world of humanity begins in religion. These giants, now afraid and ashamed for the first time, carried off their women to caves, there to settle, to "marry," to divide the land, and to bury their dead (from *humare,* to bury the dead, Vico derives *humanitas*). Later, other wandering giants seek protection from those who have already settled, and civil society has begun. If gentile humanity begins with religion, however, that gentile religion itself begins in fear—not fear of other men (as Hobbes might say), but fear of the divine. In contrast, the Hebrew religion begins with the Covenant, an act of promise and trust. But gentile or mythic man becomes aware of the divine in the only way possible to such a degraded creature: by having his "nature" overawed by the divine. Since "fear created the gods in the world," and since men everywhere see the world in terms of themselves, they pictured the sky as a great, animated, strong body, and called it "Jove."

Mythic man is here not "projecting" his fear illusorily into the sky. Vico reverses the familiar rationalist scorn of poetry as lacking truth. Poetry *does* lack reasoning power, but this is precisely its strength. Vico describes the proper material of poetry as the "credible impossibility." Poetry or myth expresses the 'hidden sense" such men had in God's omnipotence. They knew, and knew not what they knew; alone, in despair, they desired something superior to the wild, savage nature they had been. God's revelation guided the Jews, but divine providence guided the bestial gentiles. Working indirectly, even obliquely, divine providence "permitted them to be deceived into fearing the false divinity of Jove." Idolatry is thus really the "true falsehood" out of

which ultimate truth comes. Poetry or divination is born with idolatry. Poets are *mystae,* "interpreters of the gods." Vico insists, however, that all primal men were poets or diviners, since all animated the sky, all grasped the divine power above them, all "created" the gods. Where the God of the Hebrews revealed truth in a mysterious but direct way to the Hebrews, mythic peoples reveal truth in a mysterious, indirect way to themselves. Where God reveals truth out of His omniscience, mythic peoples discover truth out of their ignorance. God created by pure intelligence, but poetry creates from corporeal imagination, with marvelous sublimity. Myth thus stands to the first age of man as God stands to the Chosen People and then to the Christians. Myths are "poetic truths," and this poetic truth is always "metaphysical truth" or divination; "fables are ideal truths," but fitted to those who hear and tell them. Poetry or myth is thus the "master key" to the origins of humanity.

The richness of Vico's work precludes even a minimal mention of the insights and conclusions he draws from such fundamental assumptions as briefly touched on above. Moderns are perhaps most familiar with his view of history as a cyclical movement through three stages, theological, heroic, and human, with a *recorso*. In the theological age, man sees all in terms of the gods; in the next age, he sees himself as the son of the gods, a mixed god-human, a hero; and finally, as human alone. Vico uses this to clarify when the mythic age properly occurred, and pushes "ancient" back far beyond most traditional accounts. He opposes such views as Francis Bacon's allegorical explanation of myth as representing the "matchless wisdom of the ancients"—Bacon's "ancients" were in fact only late, sophisticated poets and thinkers. In this way, Vico gives an original interpretation of Homer, who now becomes a late poet: the first mythic poets were themselves "heroes"; the next poets sang of the heroes, but were already altering and corrupting the fables; and the Homeric age received these fables in corrupted form. By Homer's time, all has shrunk, diminished, and the great gods in the *Iliad* are close to human dimension. On similar grounds, Vico argues that "Homer" was "composed and compiled by various hands through successive ages"—for his poems embrace such discordant views of gods and men. But though far from his predecessors, Homer is still much closer to them than, say, Dante; thus Dante can never equal "Homer," since Dante is too "philosophic," too full of the spirit of a later, less poetic age. But it is also true that in Vico's grand historical scheme, all ages tend to parallel each other, since the whole spiralling cycle comes round again: and thus Dante's age is parallel to Homer's, both "feudal" ages.

Only the most extensive commentary could cover Vico's rich and ingenious uses of etymology to locate mythic meaning; his explanation of how one name covers similar types, such as "Hercules"; his distinction between fable and myth, which analyzes allegory and genres of meaning and levels of truth; his analysis of Roman history in terms of class struggle, with Roman mythology as the key; his view of history as a continuous, evolving organic whole. He may be said to have redeemed myth from its own darkness, and from the patronizing treatments accorded myth by rationalists and orthodox religionists. He did his work thoroughly and brilliantly, but not a little obscurely, so that his effect on his age and after was hardly what it might have been. Fisch and Bergin, in their edition of Vico's *Autobiography,* have recounted the impressive history of Vico's influence or affinities: among those who admired or used him were Hamann, Herder, Goethe, Heyne, Savigny, Hume, Guizot, Michelet, Quinet, Ballanche, Comte, and Coleridge

(who most influentially introduced him into English thought).

Vico clearly anticipates the romantic affirmation of myth as primal wisdom in poetic form, and in another way presages Herderian and other views that myth is a key to history as a secular or indirect working of divine purpose. But he remains independent. By insisting that myth is a key to those peoples outside the Bible, Vico diminishes the authority of biblical explanations of myth. On the other side, by rejecting "physical" nature as the main criterion by which to understand humanity and human history, Vico attacks the authority of the new science and rationalism. By insisting that providence guides the history of man, Vico stands apart as well from later radically secular views that "man makes his own history."

Vico wishes to preserve myth's claim to teach divine wisdom. Here though, too, by insisting that myth is a key to what he called a "rational civil theology" of humanity's development, Vico stands apart from efforts (mainly romantic) to make myth too singly a science of the "divine" or transcendent: Vico's mythology is firmly seated in prosaic historical events and institutions.

B.F.

REFERENCES Our text is from *The New Science of Giambattista Vico,* translated from the third edition (1744) and abridged by T. G. Bergin and M. H. Fisch (New York, 1961). Vico's work in a standard edition is *Opere,* 8 vols., ed. F. Nicolini (Bari, 1911–1941). A complete English translation is *The New Science of Giambattista Vico,* translated by T. G. Bergin and M. H. Fisch (Ithaca: Cornell University Press, 1948). See also the complete English translation, *The Autobiography of Giambattista Vico* (Ithaca: Cornell University Press, 1944) which gives a long, valuable introduction covering Vico's life, the background for his works, and an account of his reputation and influence. For bibliographical information: B. Croce, *Bibliografia vi-chiana,* accresiuta e rielaborata da F. Nicolini, 2 vols. (Naples, 1947).

For useful commentary: B. Croce, *La filosofia di Giambattista Vico* (Bari, 1911), which is translated into English by R. G. Collingwood, *The Philosophy of Giambattista Vico* (London, 1913); F. Nicolini, *Commento storico alla seconda Scienza nuova,* 2 vols. (Rome, 1949–1950); Karl Löwith, *Meaning in History* (Chicago: University of Chicago Press, 1949), ch. 6; Michelet, *Principes de la philosophie de l'histoire, traduits de la Sci-enza nuova* (Paris, 1827), "Discours sur la système et la vie de l'auteur," i–xlvii. Frank E. Manuel, *The Eighteenth Century Confronts the Gods* (Cambridge: Harvard University Press, 1959), for a succinct, vivid exposition; *Giambattista Vico, An International Symposium,* ed. Giorgio Tagliacozzo (Baltimore: The Johns Hopkins Press, 1969), for a rich variety of essays on every side of Vico's achievement and influence, with a useful bibliography covering the last fifty years, and see esp. David Bidney, "Vico's New Science of Myth," pp. 259–78.

VICO

FROM *The New Science**

144 UNIFORM ideas originating among entire peoples unknown to each other must have a common ground of truth.   145 This axiom is a great principle which establishes the common sense of the human race as the criterion taught to the nations by divine providence to define what is certain in the natural law of the gentes. And the nations reach this certainty by recognizing the underlying agreements which, despite variations in detail, obtain among them all in respect of this law. Thence issues the mental dictionary for assigning origins to all the divers articulated languages. It is by means of this dictionary that the ideal eternal history is conceived, which gives us the histories in time of all nations. . . .   146 This same axiom does away with all the ideas hitherto held concerning the natural law of the gentes, which has been thought to have come out of one first nation and to have been received from it by the others. This error was encouraged by the bad example of the Egyptians and Greeks in vainly boasting that they gave rise to the fiction that the Law of the Twelve Tables came to Rome from Greece. If that had been the case, it would have been a civil law communicated to other peoples by human provision, and not a law which divine providence instituted naturally in all nations along with human customs themselves. On the contrary, as it will be one of our constant labors throughout this book to demonstrate, the natural law of the gentes had separate origins among the several peoples, each in ignorance of the others, and it was only subsequently, as a result

* We retain the paragraph numbers used by Nicolini in his edition of the *New Science* (Bari, 1928), and followed by Bergin and Fisch in their (1949) translation.—Ed.

of wars, embassies, alliances, and commerce, that it came to be recognized as common to the entire human race.

167   The Hebrew religion was founded by the true God on the prohibition of the divination on which all the gentile nations arose.   168 This axiom is one of the principal reasons for the division of the entire world of the ancient nations into Hebrews and gentiles.

184   Wonder is the daughter of ignorance; and the greater the object of wonder, the more the wonder grows.

187   This philologico-philosophical axiom proves to us that in the world's childhood men were by nature sublime poets.

196   Every gentile nation had its Hercules, who was the son of Jove; and Varro, the most learned of antiquarians, numbered as many as forty of them.   197 This axiom marks the beginning, among the first peoples, of heroism, which was born of the false opinion that the heroes were of divine origin.   198 This same axiom and the preceding one, giving us so many Joves and then so many Herculeses among the gentile nations, together show us that these nations could not have been founded without religion and could not grow without valor. Moreover, since in their beginnings these nations were forest-bred and shut off from any knowledge of each other, and since uniform ideas, born among peoples unknown to each other, must have a common ground of truth, these axioms give us this great principle as well: that the first fables must have contained civil truths, and must therefore have been the histories of the first peoples.

199   The first sages of the Greek world were the theological poets, who undoubtedly flourished before the heroic poets, just as Jove was the father of Hercules.

220   Whatever appertains to men but is doubtful or obscure, they naturally interpret according to their own natures and the passions and customs springing from them.   221 This axiom is a great canon of our mythology. According to it, the fables originating among the first savage and crude men were very severe, as suited the founding of nations emerging from a fierce bestial freedom. Then, with the long passage of years and change of customs, they lost their original meanings and were altered and obscured in the dissolute and corrupt times [beginning] even before Homer. Because religion was important to them, the men of Greece, lest the gods should oppose their desires as well as their customs, imputed these customs to the gods, and gave improper, ugly, and obscene meanings to the fables.

238   The order of ideas must follow the order of institutions.

239   This was the order of human institutions: first the forests, after that the huts, then the villages, next the cities, and finally the academies.   240 This axiom is a great principle of etymology, for this sequence of human institutions sets the pattern for the histories of words in the various native languages. Thus we observe in the Latin language that almost the whole corpus of its words had sylvan or rustic origins. For example, *lex*. First it must have meant a collection of acorns. Thence we believe is derived *ilex*, as it were *illex*, the oak (as certainly *aquilex* means collector of waters); for the oak produces the acorns by which the swine are drawn together. *Lex* was next a collection of vegetables, from which the latter were called *legumina*. Later on, at a time when vulgar letters had not yet been invented for writing down the laws, *lex* by a necessity of civil nature must have meant a collection of citizens, or the public parliament; so that the presence of the people was the *lex*, or "law," that solemnized the wills

that were made *calatis comitiis,* in the presence of the assembled *comitia.* Finally, collecting letters, and making, as it were, a sheaf of them for each word, was called *legere,* reading.

330 . . . For on the one hand the conceit of the nations, each believing itself to have been the first in the world, leaves us no hope of getting the principles of our Science from the philologians. And on the other hand the conceit of the scholars, who will have it that what they know must have been eminently understood from the beginning of the world, makes us despair of getting them from the philosophers. So, for purposes of this inquiry, we must reckon as if there were no books in the world.   331 But in the night of thick darkness enveloping the earliest antiquity, so remote from ourselves, there shines the eternal and never failing light of a truth beyond all question: that the world of civil society has certainly been made by men, and that its principles are therefore to be found within the modifications of our own human mind. Whoever reflects on this cannot but marvel that the philosophers should have bent all their energies to the study of the world of nature, which, since God made it, He alone knows; and that they should have neglected the study of the world of nations, or civil world, which, since men had made it, men could come to know. This aberration was a consequence of that infirmity of the human mind which, immersed and buried in the body, it naturally inclines to take notice of bodily things, and finds the effort to attend to itself too laborious; just as the bodily eye sees all objects outside itself but needs a mirror to see itself.

333 We observe that all nations, barbarous as well as civilized, though separately founded because remote from each other in time and space, keep these three

human customs: all have some religion, all contract solemn marriages, all bury their dead. And in no nation, however savage and crude, are any human actions performed with more elaborate ceremonies and more sacred solemnity than the rites of religion, marriage, and burial. For, by the axiom that "uniform ideas, born among peoples unknown to each other, must have a common ground of truth," it must have been dictated to all nations that from these three institutions humanity began among them all, and therefore they must be most devoutly guarded by them all, so that the world should not again become a bestial wilderness. For this reason we have taken these three eternal and universal customs as three first principles of this Science.

338 To complete the establishment of the principles which have been adopted for this Science, it remains in this first book to discuss the method which it should follow. It must begin where its subject matter began, as we said in the Axioms. We must therefore go back with the philologians and fetch it from the stones of Deucalion and Pyrrha, from the rocks of Amphion, from the men who sprang from the furrows of Cadmus or the hard oak of Vergil. With the philosophers we must fetch it from the frogs of Epicurus, from the cicadas of Hobbes, from the simpletons of Grotius; from the men cast into this world without care or aid of God, of whom Pufendorf speaks, as clumsy and wild as the giants called "Big Feet," who are said to be found near the Strait of Magellan; which is as much as to say from the cyclopes of Homer, in whom Plato recognizes the first fathers in the state of the families. (This is the science the philologians and philosophers have given us of the principles of humanity!) Our treatment of it must take its start from the time these creatures began to think humanly. In their monstrous

savagery and unbridled bestial freedom
there was no means to tame the former or
bridle the latter but the frightful thought of
some divinity, the fear of whom is the only
powerful means of reducing to duty a
liberty gone wild. To discover the way
in which this first human thinking arose
in the gentile world, we encountered ex-
asperating difficulties which have cost us
the research of a good twenty years. [We
had] to descend from these human and
refined natures of ours to those quite wild
and savage natures, which we cannot at
all imagine and can comprehend only
with great effort.   339 By reason of all
this, we must start from some notion of
God such as even the most savage, wild,
and monstrous men do not lack. That
notion we show to be this: that man, fallen
into despair of all the succors of nature,
desires something superior to save him. But
something superior to nature is God, and
this is the light that God has shed on all
men. Confirmation may be found in a
common human custom: that libertines
grown old, feeling their natural forces
fail, turn naturally to religion.

360   From all that has been set forth
in general concerning the establishment
of the principles of this Science, we conclude that, since its principles are (1) divine providence, (2) marriage and therewith moderation of the passions, and (3)
burial and therewith immortality of human souls; and since the criterion it uses
is that what is felt to be just by all men
or by the majority must be the rule of
social life (and on these principles and
this criterion there is agreement between
the vulgar wisdom of all lawgivers and the
esoteric wisdom of the philosophers of
greatest repute)—these must be the bounds
of human reason. And let him who would
transgress them beware lest he transgress
all humanity.

374   From these first men, stupid, insensate, and horrible beasts, all the philosophers and philologians should have
begun their investigations of the wisdom
of the ancient gentiles; that is, from the
giants in the proper sense in which we have
just taken them. . . . And they should
have begun with metaphysics, which seeks
its proofs not in the external world but
within the modifications of the mind of
him who meditates it. For since this world
of nations has certainly been made by men,
it is within these modifications that its
principles should have been sought. And
human nature, so far as it is like that of
animals, carries with it this property, that
the senses are its sole way of knowing
things.

375   Hence poetic wisdom, the first
wisdom of the gentile world, must have
begun with a metaphysics not rational and
abstract like that of learned men now, but
felt and imagined as that of these first
men must have been, who, without power
of ratiocination, were all robust sense and
vigorous imagination. This metaphysics
was their poetry, a faculty born with them
(for they were furnished by nature with
these senses and imaginations); born of
their ignorance of causes, for ignorance,
the mother of wonder, made everything
wonderful to men who were ignorant of
everything. Their poetry was at first divine,
because they imagined the causes of the
things they felt and wondered at to be
gods. (This is now confirmed by the American Indians, who call gods all the things
that surpass their small understanding. We
may add the ancient Germans dwelling
about the Arctic Ocean, of whom Tacitus
tells that they spoke of hearing the sun
pass at night from west to east through the
sea, and affirmed that they saw the gods.
These very rude and simple nations help
us to a much better understanding of the

founders of the gentile world with whom we are now concerned.) At the same time they gave the things they wondered at substantial being after their own ideas, just as children do, whom we see take inanimate things in their hands and play with them and talk to them as though they were living persons.

378   But the nature of our civilized minds is so detached from the senses, even in the vulgar, by abstractions corresponding to all the abstract terms our languages abound in, and so refined by the art of writing, and as it were spiritualized by the use of numbers, because even the vulgar know how to count and reckon, that it is naturally beyond our power to form the vast image of this mistress called "Sympathetic Nature." Men shape the phrase with their lips but have nothing in their minds; for what they have in mind is falsehood, which is nothing; and their imagination no longer avails to form a vast false image. It is equally beyond our power to enter into the vast imagination of those first men, whose minds were not in the least abstract, refined, or spiritualized, because they were entirely immersed in the senses, buffeted by the passions, buried in the body. That is why we said above that we can scarcely understand, still less imagine, how those first men thought who founded gentile humanity.

379   In this fashion the first theological poets created the first divine fable, the greatest they ever created: that of Jove, king and father of men and gods, in the act of hurling the lightning bolt; an image so popular, disturbing, and instructive that its creators themselves believed in it, and feared, revered, and worshipped it in frightful religions. Whatever these men saw, imagined, or even made or did themselves they believed to be Jove; and to all of the universe that came within

their scope, and to all its parts, they gave the being of animate substance. This is the civil history of the expression "All things are full of Jove" (*Iovis omnia plena*)[1] . . . But for the theological poets Jove was no higher than the mountain peaks. The first men, who spoke by signs, naturally believed that lightning bolts and thunderclaps were signs made to them by Jove; whence from *nuo,* to make a sign, came *numen,* the divine will, by an idea more than sublime and worthy to express the divine majesty. They believed that Jove commanded by signs, that such signs were real words, and that nature was the language of Jove. The science of this language the gentiles universally believed to be divination, which by the Greeks was called theology, meaning the science of the language of the gods. . . .

382   All the things here discussed agree with that golden passage on the origins of idolatry: that the first people, simple and rough, invented the gods "from terror of present power." Thus it was fear which created gods in the world; not fear awakened in men by other men, but fear awakened in men by themselves. Along with this origin of idolatry is demonstrated likewise the origin of divination which was brought into the world at the same birth. The origins of these two were followed by that of the sacrifices made to procure or rightly understand the auspices.

383   That such was the origin of poetry is finally confirmed by this eternal property of it: that its proper material is the credible impossibility. It is impossible that bodies should be minds, yet it was believed that the thundering sky was Jove. And nothing is dearer to poets than singing the marvels wrought by sorceresses by means of incantations. All this is to be explained by a hidden sense the nations have of the omnipotence of God. From

this sense springs another by which all peoples are naturally led to do infinite honors to divinity. In this manner the poets founded religions among the gentiles.

401   . . . Similarly, *mythos* came to be defined for us as *vera narratio,* or true speech, the natural speech which first Plato and then Iamblichus said had been spoken in the world at one time. But this was mere conjecture on their part, and Plato's effort to recover this speech in the *Cratylus* was therefore vain, and he was criticized for it by Aristotle and Galen. For that first language, spoken by the theological poets, was not a language in accord with the nature of the things it dealt with (as must have been the sacred language invented by Adam, to whom God granted divine onomathesia, the giving of names to things according to the nature of each), but was a fantastic speech making use of physical substances endowed with life and most of them imagined to be divine.

402   This is the way in which the theological poets apprehended Jove, Cybele or Berecynthia, and Neptune, for example, and, at first mutely pointing, explained them as substances of the sky, the earth, and the sea, which they imagined to be animate divinities and were therefore true to their senses in believing them to be gods. By means of these three divinities, in accordance with what we have said above concerning poetic characters, they explained everything appertaining to the sky, the earth, and the sea. And similarly by means of the other divinities they signified the other kinds of things appertaining to each, denoting all flowers, for instance, by Flora, and all fruits by Pomona. We nowadays reverse this practice in respect of spiritual things, such as the faculties of the human mind, the passions, virtues, vices, sciences, and arts; for the most part the ideas we form of them are so many feminine personifications, to which we refer all the causes, properties, and effects that severally appertain to them. For when we wish to give utterance to our understanding of spiritual things, we must seek aid from our imagination to explain them and, like painters, form human images of them. But these theological poets, unable to make use of the understanding, did the opposite and more sublime thing: they attributed the senses and passions, as we saw not long since, to bodies, and to bodies as vast as sky, sea, and earth. Later, as these vast imaginations shrank and the power of abstraction grew, the personifications were reduced to diminutive signs. Metonymy drew a cloak of learning over the prevailing ignorance of these origins of human institutions, which have remained buried until now. Jove becomes so small and light that he is flown about by an eagle. Neptune rides the waves in a fragile chariot. And Cybele rides seated on a lion.

403   Thus the mythologies, as their name indicates, must have been the proper languages of the fables; the fables being imaginative class concepts, as we have shown, the mythologies must have been the allegories corresponding to them.

460   From all this it appears to have been demonstrated that, by a necessity of human nature, poetic style arose before prose style; just as, by the same necessity, the fables, or imaginative universals, arose before the rational or philosophic universals, which were formed through the medium of prose speech. For after the poets had formed poetic speech by associating particular ideas, as we have fully shown, the peoples went on to form prose speech by contracting into a single word, as into a genus, the parts which poetic speech had associated.

498   Providence gave good guidance to human affairs when it aroused human

minds first to topics rather than to criticism, for acquaintance with things must come before judgment of them. Topics has the function of making minds inventive, as criticism has that of making them exact. And in those first times all things necessary to human life had to be invented, and invention is the property of genius. In fact, whoever gives the matter some thought will observe that not only the necessaries of life but the useful, comfortable, pleasing, and even luxurious and superfluous had already been invented in Greece before the advent of the philosophers. On this point we have set forth an axiom above: namely, that "children are extraordinarily gifted in imitation," that "poetry is nothing but imitation," and that "the arts are only imitations of nature and consequently in a certain sense real poetry." Thus the first peoples, who were the children of the human race, founded the first world of the arts; then the philosophers, who came a long time afterward and so may be regarded as the old men of the nations, founded the world of the sciences, thereby making humanity complete.

499   This history of human ideas is strikingly confirmed by the history of philosophy itself. . . .

1. Virgil: *Bucolics* 3.60.

ANDREW RAMSAY

[1686–1743]

ANDREW RAMSAY, sometimes called the Chevalier Ramsay or even de Ramsai, came from a Scotch Presbyterian background, became a deist after a stay at the University of Edinburgh, went to France in 1710 to study with Fénelon, and was converted by the controversial archbishop and author of *Télémaque*. Ramsay's fitful and eclectic temper included a mystical streak, and even a marked enthusiasm for Newton's thought; but despite the apparent fashionableness of his intellectual style or styles, his influence, at least upon the study of myth, appears to have been small. Hume derided one of his arguments; Nicholas Fréret, the permanent secretary of the French *Académie des Inscriptions,* applauded the careful observance of chronology in Ramsay's *Travels of Cyrus*; and, as late as 1826, the Rev. Jerome Alley, author of a volume called *Vindiciae Christianiae,* mentions with respect Ramsay's detection "in a multiplicity of heathen deities, a celestial triad of wisdom, of goodness, and of power."

The Travels of Cyrus is a moral-historical romance halfway between *Télémaque* and *Rasselas.* Conceived in vague emulation of Homer and written to conform to the ideal of instructing by pleasing—with the emphasis on instructing—the book is a fictional account of Cyrus's early years and possible travels. It is more a historical novel than a romance, however, and in a sense, it is a small step, though an unconscious one, toward the idea that perhaps the moderns too could create myth. It is, for example, suggestive that Fénelon himself wrote Aesop-like fables for instructional purposes and that Ramsay did so as well in *The Travels of Cyrus.* At any rate, mythology was of considerable importance to Ramsay, and he appended two long essays to the book, one on the theology of the ancients and the second on their mythology. Ramsay was one of the first to try to make a clear distinction between theology and mythology. His essay on the former undertakes to show that all the nations of antiquity show traces of a belief in a single all-powerful deity; the second essay, on mythology, demonstrates, in Ramsay's words, that "there are Traces of the principle Doctrines of revealed Religion with regard to the three States of Nature to be found in the Mythology of all Nations." Thus the essay is ultimately Christian, at least in intent, but its tone, its mode of argument, its comparative approach, and its chief findings all suggest that Ramsay approached the subject with a clear and open mind. There is, in the essay, no insistent pietism, no polemic, no heat of belief; all is laid out and commented upon in a scholarly spirit of free inquiry.

Starting from the problem of evil and the need for some sort of explanation for evil, Ramsay argues that the mythologies of Greece, Egypt, Persia, India, China, and ancient Israel all approach the problem similarly, and all exhibit four common features. Each mythology, as Ramsay interprets it, posits a "State before Good and Evil were blended and confounded together." Each also speaks of a second "State after they were so blended and confounded," and each looks forward to a third period "when Evil shall be entirely destroyed." Lastly, Ramsay notes, each national mythology has "a middle God between the good and evil Principle."

Commencing with the Greeks, Ramsay goes for his mythology to the philosophers, rather than poets. In preferring Plato and Pythagoras to Homer, Ramsay is simply showing that he takes mythology quite seriously and is looking for the best authorities. Going on through the then little-known mythologies of Persia, India, and China, Ramsay finds the same basic structure in each. There is a blessed time, then a fall, then a promise of a restoration, and, presiding over man's fate, there is an interceding deity. Summing up, he treats his findings in a calm, thoughtful, and detached manner:

It looks as if the Source of all these Allegories was only an Antient Tradition common to all Nations, that the Middle God, to whom they all give the Name of *Sotor* or *Saviour,* was to put an end to Crimes by his great Sufferings. But I do not lay a Stress upon this Notion, my Design being only to speak of the Traces that appear in all Religions of a Nature *exalted, fallen* and *to be repaired* again by a Divine Hero.

The tone here is oddly modern; it is the language of a professional historian of religions; it is anything but special pleading.

In Ramsay's little-known essay can be seen a number of ideas and attitudes that were later to have considerable importance. He distinguished carefully between theology and mythology, the former having to do with deity, the latter with stories of all sorts from various lands. He further distinguishes mythology from mere fable,

the latter being only idle invention, while the former conveys serious and important concepts having to do with sacred subjects. In setting out his essay on mythology, Ramsay uses what can only be described as a structural approach: he looks for similar structures in apparently dissimilar bodies of myth. Finally, Ramsay's unimpassioned emphasis on the three sequential ages and on the divine intercessor to be found in all mythologies clearly foreshadows modern archetype criticism. Probably derived from the branch of theology known as typology —in which the Gospel narratives provide archetypes and the rest of the Bible, including the Old Testament, provide types (thus Isaac is a type of the archetype Christ)—Ramsay carried the idea beyond the Bible into what we would call comparative religions or comparative mythology. Ramsay's essay thus has, in common with some modern archetype criticism, the idea that certain unchanging structures lie behind observable phenomena. And whether one's archetype theory is theologically derived or psychologically derived, it tends to work in much the same way: to connect and unify, to value the non-rational and the pre-rational very highly, and to want to simplify and classify its material. It is hard to determine whether Ramsay is in some way ahead of his time, or merely apart from it. At any rate, his ideas about myth were hardly the sort that the first half of the eighteenth century could deal with easily. In his search for structures and patterns, and above all in his essentially serious acceptance of myth, Ramsay is, in a small way, a glimpse of what is to come in the romantic era's involvement with myth, and in our more recent interest in comparative and structural myth criticism.

R.R.

REFERENCES   Our text is from Andrew Ramsay, *The Travels of Cyrus* (London: T. Woodward, 1728), 2d ed., "Of the Mythology of the Antients." For commentary, see J. M. Robertson, *A History of Freethought* (London: Watts and Co., 1936), 4th ed., Vol. II, p. 805; A. J. Matter, *Le mysticism en France en temps de Fénelon* (Paris, 1865), pp. 352 ff.; E. K. Sanders, *Fénelon, his Friends and his Enemies* (London: Longmans and Co., 1901), p. 327. For the place of Fénelon and his followers in the revival of classical antiquity, see A. Lombard, *Fénelon et le retour à l'antique au xviii* siècle* (Neuchâtel, 1954).

RAMSAY

FROM *The Travels of Cyrus*

"Of the Mythology of the Antients"

MEN left to the Light of their Reason alone, have always looked upon moral and physical Evil, as a shocking Phaenomenon in the Work of a Being infinitely wise, good, and powerful. To account for it, the Philosophers have had recourse to several Hypotheses.

Reason told them all, that what is supremely good could never produce any thing that was wicked or miserable. From hence they concluded that Souls are not now what they were at first; that they are degraded from some Fault committed by them in a former State; that this Life is a Place of Exile and Expiation; and in a Word, that all Beings are to be restored to their proper Order.

These philosophical Notions, however, had another Original. Tradition struck in with Reason to gain them a Reception, and that Tradition had spread over all Nations certain Opinions which they held in common, with regard to the three States of the World, as I shall shew in this second Part, which will be a sort of Abridgment of the traditional Doctrine of the Ancients.

I begin with the Mythology of the *Greeks* and *Romans*. All the Poets speaking of the Golden Age or Reign of *Saturn,* describe it to us as an happy State, where there were neither Calamities, nor Crimes, nor Labour, nor Pains, nor Diseases, nor Death.

They represent to us on the contrary, the Iron Age, as the time when physical and moral Evil first appeared; when Vices, Sufferings, and all manner of Evils came forth of *Pandora's* fatal Box, and overflowed the Face of the Earth.

They speak to us of the Golden Age revived, as of a time when *Astraea* was to return upon Earth; when Justice, Peace and Innocence were to flourish again with their original Lustre; and when every thing was to be restored to its primitive Perfection.

In a Word, they sing on all Occasions the Exploits of a Son of *Jupiter,* who was to quit his heavenly Abode and live among Men. They give him different Names, according to his different Functions; sometimes he is *Apollo* fighting against *Python* and the *Titans*. Sometimes he is *Hercules* destroying Monsters and Giants, and purging the Earth of their Enormities and Crimes. One while he is *Mercury,* or the Messenger of *Jove,* flying about every where to execute his Decrees; and another while he is *Perseus* delivering *Andromeda* or human Nature, from the Monster that rose out of the great Deep to devour her. He is always some Son of *Jupiter* giving Battles and gaining Victories.

I lay no great Stress upon those poetical Descriptions, because they may perhaps be looked upon as meer Fictions, and a Machinery introduc'd to embellish a Poem and amuse the Mind. Allegorical Explications are liable to Uncertainty and Mistake. So that I shall pass directly to represent the Doctrine of the Philosophers, particularly that of *Plato;* who is the Source from whence *Plotinus, Proclus,* and the *Platonists* of the third Century drew their principal Notions.

To begin with the Dialogue of *Phaedo,* or of Immortality, and give a short Analysis of it. *Phaedo* gives his Friends an Account of the Condition that he saw *Socrates* in at the time of his Death. 'He quitted Life, (says he) with a peaceable Joy, and a noble Intrepidity.' His Friends asking him the Reason of it, 'I hope, (says *Socrates* in his Answer) to be reunited to the good and perfect Gods, and to be associated with better Men than those I leave upon Earth.'

When *Cebes* objects to him, that the Soul vanished after Death, like a Smoke, and was entirely annihilated, *Socrates* sets himself to refute that Opinion, and endeavours to prove that the Soul had a real Existence in an happy State, before it informed an human Body.

This Doctrine he ascribes to *Orpheus.* 'The Disciples of *Orpheus,* (says he) called the Body a Prison, because the Soul is here in a State of Punishment till it has expiated the Faults that it committed in Heaven.'

'Souls (continues *Plato*) that are too much given to bodily Pleasures, and are in a manner besotted, wander upon the Earth, and are put into new Bodies. For all Sensuality and Passion bind the Soul more closely to Bodies, make her fancy that she is of the same Nature, and render her in a manner corporeal. So that she contracts an Incapacity of flying away into another Life, and being oppressed with the Weight of her Impurity and Corruption, sinks deeper into Matter, and becomes thereby disabled to re-mount towards the Regions of Purity, and attain to a Reunion with her Principle.'

Upon this Foundation is built the Doctrine of the Transmigration of Souls, which *Plato* represents in his *Timaeus Locrus* as an Allegory, and at other times as a real State, where Souls that have made themselves unworthy of the supreme Beatitude, sojourn and suffer successively in the Bodies of different Animals, till they are purged at last of their Crimes by the Pains they undergo. This hath made some Philosophers believe that the Souls of Beasts are degraded Spirits.

'Pure Souls,' adds *Plato,* 'that have exerted themselves here below to get the better of all Corruption, and free themselves from the Impurities of their terrestrial Prison, retire after Death into an invisible Place, unknown to us, where the pure unites with the pure, the good cleaves to its like, and our immortal Essence is united to the divine.'

He calls this Place the first Earth, where Souls made their Abode before their Degradation. 'The Earth,' says he, 'is immense; we know and we inhabit only a small Corner of it. The ethereal Earth, the antient Abode of Souls, is placed in the pure Regions of Heaven, where the fixed Stars are seated. We that live in this low Abyss, are apt enough to fancy that we are in an high Place, and we call the Air the Heavens; just like a Man that from the Bottom of the Sea should view the Sun and Stars through the Water, and fancy the Ocean to be the Firmament it self. But if we had Wings to mount on high, we should see that *there* is the true Heaven, the true Light, and the true Earth. As in the Sea every thing is changed, and disfigured by the Salts that abound in it; so in our present Earth every thing is deformed, corrupted, and in a ruinous Condition, if compared with the primitive Earth.'

Plato gives afterwards a pompous Description of that aethereal Earth, of which ours is only a shattered Crust. He says, 'every thing there was beautiful, harmonious and transparent; Fruits of an exquisite Taste grew there naturally, and it was watered with Rivers of Nectar. They breathed there the Light as here we breathe the Air, and they drank Waters that were purer than Air it self.'

This Notion in *Plato* agrees in a great Measure with that of *Des Cartes,* about the Nature of the Planets. This modern Philosopher thinks that they were at first Suns, which contracted afterwards a thick and opake Crust; but he does not enter into the moral Reasons of this Change, his View being only to consider the World as a natural Philosopher. . . .

(pp. 81–91)

'Tis therefore evidently the Doctrine of the most famous *Greek* Philosophers, 1st, That Souls had a Pre-existence in Heaven. 2dly, That the *Jupiter* who marched at the Head of Souls before the Loss of their Wings; and he to whom *Saturn* gave the

Reins of his Empire after the Origin of Evil is a distinct Being from the supreme Essence, and is very like the *Mythras* of the *Persians,* and the *Orus* of the *Egyptians.* 3dly, That Souls lost their Wings, and were thrust down into mortal Bodies, because that instead of following *Jupiter's* Chariot, they gave themselves too much up to the Enjoyment of lower Pleasures. 4thly, That at the end of a certain Period of time, the Wings of the Soul shall grow again, and *Saturn* shall resume the Reins of his Empire in order to restore the Universe to its original Perfection.

Let us now examine the *Egyptian* Mythology, the Source from whence that of the *Greeks* was derived. I shall not offer to maintain the mystical Explications that *Kircher* gives of the famous Table of *Isis,* or of the *Obelisks* that are to be seen at *Rome:* I confine my self to *Plutarch,* who has preserved us an admirable Monument of that Mythology. To represent it in its real Beauties, it will be proper to give a short and clear Analysis of his treatise on *Isis* and *Osiris,* which is a Letter written to *Clea,* Priestess of *Isis.*

'The *Egyptian* Mythology,' says *Plutarch,* 'has two Senses, the one sacred and sublime, the other sensible and *palpable.* 'Tis for this Reason that the *Egyptians* put *Sphinxes* before the Door of their Temples; designing thereby to signify to us that their Theology contains the Secrets of Wisdom under enigmatical Words. This is also the Sense of the Inscription upon a Statue of *Pallas* or *Isis* at *Sais, I am all that is, has been, and shall be, and no Mortal has ever yet removed the Veil that covers me.'

He afterwards relates the *Egyptian* Fable of *Isis* and *Osiris.* They were both born of *Rhea* and the *Sun:* Whilst they were still in their Mother's Womb, they copulated and ingendered the God *Orus,* the living Image of their Substance. *Ty-phon* was not born, but burst violently through the Ribs of *Rhea*. He afterwards revolted against *Osiris,* filled the Universe with his Rage and Violence, tore the Body of his Brother in Pieces, mangled his Limbs, and scattered them about. Ever since that time *Isis* goes wandring about the Earth, to gather up the scattered Limbs of her Brother and Husband. The eternal and immortal Soul of *Osiris* led his Son *Orus* to the Shades below, where he gave him Instructions how to fight, and beat *Typhon*. *Orus* returned upon Earth, fought and defeated *Typhon* but did not kill him. All that he did was to bind him, and take away his Power of doing Mischief. The wicked one made his Escape afterwards, and was going to renew his Malice: But *Orus* fought him in two bloody Battles, and destroyed him entirely.

Plutarch goes on thus; 'Whoever applieth these Allegories to the blessed immortal Divine Nature, deserves to be treated with Contempt. We must not however believe that they are mere Fables without any meaning, like those of the Poets. They represent to us things that really happened.'

'It would be likewise a dangerous Error, and manifest Impiety to interpret what is said of the Gods, as *Euemerus* the *Messenian* did, and apply it to the antient Kings and great Generals. This would in the end serve to destroy Religion, and estrange Men from the Deity.'

'There are others,' adds he, 'much juster in their Notions, who have wrote, that whatever is related of *Typhon, Osiris, Isis,* and *Orus* must be understood of *Genii* and *Daemons*. This was the Opinion of *Pythagoras, Plato, Xenocrates,* and *Chrysippus,* who followed the antient Theologists in this Notion. All those great

Men maintained that these *Genii* were very powerful, and far superior to Mortals. They did not however partake of the Deity in a pure and simple manner, but were composed of a Spiritual and corporeal Nature; and consequently capable of Pleasures and Pains, Passions and Changes; for there are Virtues and Vices among the *Genii* as well as among Men. Hence come the Fables of the *Greeks* about the *Titans* and the Giants, the Engagements of *Python* against *Apollo,* the Furies and Extravagance of *Bacchus,* and several Fictions like those of *Osiris* and *Typhon*. Hence is it that *Homer* speaks of good and evil *Daemons*. *Plato* calls the first *Tutelary-Deities,* because they are Mediators between God and Man, and carry up the Prayers of Mortals to Heaven, and bring us from thence the Knowledge and Revelation of secret and future Things.'

'*Empedocles,*' continues he, 'says, that the evil *Daemons* are punished for the Faults they have committed. The Sun precipitates them at first into the Air, the Air casts them into the deep Sea. The Sea vomits them upon the Land, and from the Earth they are raised up at last towards Heaven. Thus are they transported from one Place to another; till being in the End punished and purified, they return to the Place adapted to their Nature.'

Plutarch, after having given such a Theological Explanation of the *Egyptian* Allegories, gives likewise the physical Explications thereof; but he rejects them all, and returns to his first Doctrine. '*Osiris* is neither the Sun, nor the Water, nor the Earth, nor the Heaven; but whatever there is in Nature well disposed, well regulated, good and perfect, all *that* is the Image of *Osiris*. *Typhon* is neither scorching Heat, nor the Fire, nor the Sea; but whatever is hurtful, inconstant and irregular. . . .'

(pp. 103–116)

Let us pass next into *Persia,* to consult the Mythology of the Orientals. The nearer we approach the first Origin of Nations, the clearer shall we find their Theology.

'*Zoroaster,*' says *Plutarch,* 'taught that there are two Gods contrary to each other in their Operations, the one the Author of all the Good, the other of all the Evil in Nature. The good Principle he calls *Oromazes,* the other the Daemon *Arimanius.* He says that the one resembles Light and Truth, the other Darkness and Ignorance. There is likewise a middle God between these two, named *Mythras,* whom the *Persians* call the Intercessor or Mediator, The *Magi* add, that *Oromazes* is born of the purest Light, and *Arimanius* of Darkness; that they make War upon one another, and that *Oromazes* made six *Genii,* Goodness, Truth, Justice, Wisdom, Plenty and Joy; and *Arimanius* made six others to oppose them, Malice, Falsehood, Injustice, Folly, Want and Sadness. *Oromazes* having withdrawn himself to as great a Distance from the Sphere of *Arimanius,* as the Sun is from the Earth, beautified the Heavens with Stars and Constellations. He created afterwards four and twenty other *Genii,* and put them into an Egg; (*by which the Ancients mean the Earth*) but *Arimanius* and his *Genii* pierced through this shining Egg, and immediately Evil was blended and confounded with Good. But there will come a Time appointed by Fate, when *Arimanius* shall be entirely destroyed and extirpated; the Earth shall change its Form, and become plain and even; and happy Men shall have only one and the same Life, Language and Government.'

'*Theopompus* writes also, that according to the Doctrine of the *Magi,* these Gods must make War for nine thousand Years, the one destroying the other's Work, till

at last Hell shall be taken away. Then Men shall be happy, and their Bodies become transparent. The God who was the Author of their Being keeps himself retired till that time, an Interval not too long for a God, but rather like a Moment of Sleep.'

We have lost the ancient Books of the first *Persians;* so that in order to judge of their Mythology, we must have recourse to the oriental Philosophers of our own time, and see if there be still left among the Disciples of *Zoroaster* any Traces of the antient Doctrine of their Master. The famous Dr. *Hyde,* a Divine of the Church of *England,* who had traveled into the East, and perfectly understood the Language of the Country, has translated the following Passages out of *Sharisthani,* an *Arabian* Philosopher of the fifteenth Century. 'The first *Magi* did not look upon the two Principles as coeternal, but believed that the Light was eternal, and that the Darkness was produced in time; and the Origin of this evil Principle they account for in this Manner. Light can produce nothing but Light, and can never be the Origin of Evil; how then was Evil produced, since there was nothing coequal or like the Light in its eternal Production? Light, say they, produced several Beings, all of them spiritual, luminous and powerful. But their Chief, whose Name was *Ahriman* or *Arimanius,* had an evil Thought contrary to the Light. He doubted, and by that Doubt he became dark. Hence arose all the Evils, the Dissention, the Malice, and every thing else of a contrary Nature to the Light. These two Principles made War upon one another, till at last Peace was made, upon Condition that the lower World should be in subjection to *Arimanius* for seven Thousand Years; after which space of Time, he is to surrender back the World to the Light.'

Here we see the four Notions that I speak of in the foregoing Work: 1. A State before Good and Evil were blended and confounded together. 2. A State after they were so blended and confounded. 3. A State when Evil shall be entirely destroyed. 4. A middle God between the good and the evil Principle.

As the Doctrine of the *Persian Magi* is a Sequel of the Doctrine of the *Indian Brachmans,* we must consult the one to put the other in a clear Light. We have but few Traces left of the antient Theology of the *Gymnosophists,* yet those which *Strabo* has preserved, suppose the three different States of the World.

After that Historian has described the Life and Manners of the *Brachmans,* he adds, 'Those Philosophers look upon the State of Men in this Life, to be like that of Children in their Mother's Womb; Death according to their Notion being a Birth to a true and an happy Life. They believe that whatever happens to Mortals here, does not deserve the Name either of *good or evil*. Agreeable to the *Greeks* in several Things, they think that the World had a Beginning, and that it will have an End; that God who made it, and who governs it, is every where present to his Work.'

The same Author goes on in this Manner; '*Onesecritus* being sent by *Alexander* the Great to learn the Life, the Manners, and the Doctrine of those Philosophers, found a *Brachman* named *Calanus,* who taught him the following Principles. (1) Formerly, Plenty reigned over all Nature; Milk, Wine, Honey and Oil, flowed in a continual Stream from Fountains. (2) But Men having made an ill use of this Felicity, *Jupiter* deprived them of it, and condemned them to labour for the Sus-

tenance of their Lives. (3) When Temperance and the rest of the Virtues shall return upon Earth, then the antient Plenty shall be restored.'

For forming a better Judgment of the Doctrine of the antient *Gymnosophists* I have consulted what has been translated of the *Vedam,* which is the sacred Book of the modern *Bramins.* Though its Antiquity is not perhaps so great as they affirm it to be, yet there is no denying but it contains the ancient Traditions of those People, and of their Philosophers.

'Tis plain by this Book, 'That the *Bramins* acknowledge one sole and supreme God, whom they call *Vistnou.* That his first and most antient Production was a secondary God, named *Brama,* whom the supreme God formed out of a Flower that floated upon the Surface of the great Deep before the Creation of the World; and that *Vistnou* afterwards, on account of *Brama's* Virtue, Gratitude and Fidelity, gave him Power to create the Universe.'

They believe moreover, 'That Souls are eternal Emanations of the Divine Essence, or at least that they were produced long before the Creation of the World; that they were originally in a State of Purity, but sinned, and have been ever since thrown down into the Bodies of Men and Beasts, according to their several Demerits; so that the Body, where the Soul resides, is a sort of Dungeon or Prison.'

In a Word, they hold that, 'after a certain Number of Transmigrations, all Souls shall be re-united to their Origin, shall be re-admitted into the Company of the Gods, and shall at last be deified.'

I should hardly have thought these Traditions authentick, or have brought my self to trust to the Translators of the *Vedam,* if this Doctrine had not been perfectly agreeable to that of *Pythagoras,* which I gave an Account of a little before. This Philosopher taught the *Greeks* nothing but what he had learned from the *Gymnosophists*. . . . (pp. 116–126)

The *Chinese* Books speak likewise of the Sufferings and Conflicts of *Kiuntse*, just as the *Syrians* do of the Death of *Adonis*, who was to rise again to make Men happy, and as the *Greeks* do of the Labours and painful Exploits of the Son of *Jupiter* who was to come down upon Earth. It looks as if the Source of all these Allegories was only an antient Tradition common to all Nations, that the Middle God, to whom they all give the Name of *Soter* or *Saviour*, was to put an end to Crimes by his great Sufferings. But I do not lay a Stress upon this Notion, my Design being only to speak of the Traces that appear in all Religions of a Nature *exalted, fallen,* and *to be repaired* again by a Divine Hero.

These Truths run equally throughout the Mythologies of the *Greeks,* the *Egyptians,* the *Persians,* the *Indians,* and the *Chinese.* 'Tis time to come at last to the *Jewish* Mythology.

I mean by it the Rabbinism or Philosophy of the *Jewish* Doctors, and particularly of the *Essenes.* These Philosophers asserted, according to the Testimony of *Philo* and *Josephus,* 'That the literal Sense of the sacred Text was only an Image of hidden Truths. They changed the Words and Precepts of Wisdom into Allegories, after the Custom of their Ancestors, who had left them several Books for their Instruction in this Science.'

'Twas the universal Taste of the *Orientals* to make use of corporeal Images to represent the Properties and Operations of Spirits.

This symbolical Stile seems in a great Measure authorized by the sacred Writers. The Prophet *Daniel* represents God to us under the Image of the *Antient of Days.* The *Hebrew* Mythologists and Cabbalists, who are a Succession of the School of *Essenes,* took occasion from thence to explain the Divine Attributes, as Members of the Body of the *Antient of Days.* We see this Allegory carried to an Extravagance in the Books of the Rabbins. They speak there of the Dew that distilled from the Brain of the *Antient of Days,* from his Skull, his Hair, his Forehead, his Eyes, and especially from his wonderful Beard.

These Comparisons are undoubtedly absurd, and unbecoming the Majesty of God: But the Cabbalistical Philosophers pretend to authorize them by some very metaphysical Notions.

The Creation, according to them, is a Picture of the Divine Perfections. All created Beings are consequently Images of the supreme Being, more or less perfect in proportion as they have more or less Conformity with their Original.

Hence it follows that all Creatures are in some Respect like one another, and that Man, or the *Microcosm,* resembles the great World or *Macrocosm;* the material World resembles the intelligible World, as the intelligible World does the Archetype, which is God. . . .

(pp. 132–136)

SAMUEL SHUCKFORD

[c. 1694–1754]

IN THE work of Samuel Shuckford can be seen the eighteenth century's interest in chronology, its penchant for making connections and showing conformities between the non-Christian and the Christian worlds—normally to the advantage of the latter—and the chief means of showing such conformities, a kind of applied Euhemerism which assumed that myth is coded history. Chronology was important then as now as the backbone of ancient history, but for the early eighteenth century it had another more urgent importance. For by manipulating chronology one could conceivably reconcile all non-biblical dates, figures, and stories with the fairly strict chronology set forth in the Bible.

With the work of Scaliger, Marsham, Ussher, and many others, there was, around 1700, general agreement on the chronology of the ancient world. And in all the systems, persons from the Bible, from the Greek and Roman historians, and from myth and legend were all treated alike and uncritically as actual historical figures. Myth and Scripture were both made to serve not so much a new sense of history as a renewed zeal for system. Even the great Isaac Newton became involved, spent much time on chronology, and produced numerous manuscripts, and his radical emendation of the standard chronology caused a small sensation when published (without Newton's consent). Newton based his dating on the movement of the equinoxes,

he ignored many early texts, and he cut hundreds of years off the accepted chronology. A furor ensued. Newton was attacked from both England and France, and in the end seems to have gotten the worst of it. The interest of this quarrel for the study of myth is that it shows that an uncritical Euhemerism was the standard attitude of the early eighteenth century toward myth—so standard that a mind like Newton's could pick it up and pursue it. The chronologers, including Newton, utilized an utterly naive historicism, treated all sources as equally valid, and adopted a uniform style—literalism. One can hardly help seeing behind most of their work a grim determination to vindicate the Bible at all cost. The chronologers had, however, great prestige, and this prestige may help explain why the relatively simple Euhemerist ideas about myth dominated the time as they did.

Samuel Shuckford's *The Sacred and Profane History of the World Connected from the Creation of the World to the Dissolution of the Assyrian Empire at the Death of Sardanapalus, and to the Declension of the Kingdoms of Judah and Israel Under the Reigns of Ahaz and Pekah,* usually referred to as Shuckford's *Connections,* appeared in two volumes in 1728 and went through at least eight editions in England and America, the last being in 1858. The work was conceived as a complement to Dean Humphrey Prideaux's *The Old and New Testament*

Connected, in the History of the Jews and Neighboring Nations, published in 1724. Prideaux's work was straight history, carefully and soberly done; he undertook, as his preface tells us, "the clearing of the sacred history by the profane, the connecting of the Old Testament by the New, by an account of the time intervening and the explaining of the prophecies that were fulfilled in them." Prideaux began his account with B.C. 742 and the reign of Ahaz—Shuckford's terminal point— and it is worth noting that Prideaux's work went through at least twenty editions and was still considered valuable by Henry Preserved Smith in 1903. Prideaux, of course, was dealing with historical times, while Shuckford, in deciding to fill in from Creation to Prideaux, was committed to prehistory—and to the murky realm of myth. (For the sake of completeness, it should be noted that in 1827 the Reverend Michael Russell carried the labor one step further in his *A Connection of Sacred and Profane History from the Death of Joshua to the Decline of the Kingdoms of Israel and Judah.*)

Of these three works, only Shuckford's deals with myth, and Shuckford is a good and a sobering example of the literalist mentality. His aim—that of any orthodox Christian chronologer—was to reconcile all non-biblical material to the account of the world given in the Bible. The tone and style of his approach may be gathered from his opening sentence: "Whatever may have been the opinions of philosophers, or the fables of poets, about the origin of mankind, we are sufficiently informed from history, that we are descended from two persons, Adam and Eve." Shuckford was untroubled by the conflict of history and Revelation, since they were for him identical. Whatever did not agree with Scripture was wrong.

An example of Shuckford's method is his approach to the various accounts of creation. Unaware of conflicts and discrepancies in *Genesis* itself, Shuckford quickly surveys the few cosmogonies he knows for their resemblance to *Genesis,* and his conclusion that "Moses is the only writer whose accounts are liable to no exception" hardly comes as a surprise to the reader. An extreme example of the higher bias of the lower criticism, though not in this case original with Shuckford, is his treatment of the old Egyptian chronology. The problem here is that if one takes due account of the long lists of Egyptian rulers one ends up with more years—more elapsed time—than *Genesis* allows. Rather than entertain the possibility that the Egyptian records are older than the Hebrew, Shuckford, following John Marsham, treats one group of eight rulers as contemporaries and another group of fifteen rulers as contemporaries, thus telescoping Egyptian history into the space spared for it in the Mosaic account.

Here as elsewhere Shuckford and others like him simply dismiss everything outside the Bible under an elaborate show of scholarship. There is a quiet but cold-eyed fanaticism in his relentless one-dimensional mentality. The worlds of myth and Scripture are alike treated without warmth, interest, or imagination. Shuckford is a great example of the absence of a sense of history. For all the orthodox and pious expressions of faith, the work itself exhibits a case of rational backlash; not only myth, but religion itself loses its awe, and its wonder, to become only a rather dull matter of dates.

R.R.

REFERENCES   Our text is from Samuel Shuckford, *The Sacred and Profane History of the World Connected . . . ,* 2 vols. (Philadelphia, 1824), and has been collated with the first edition, (London: R. Knaplock and J. Tonson, 1728), 2 vols. Further information on the use of myth in establishing chronology or in "connecting" sacred with profane history may be sought in Humphrey Prideaux, *The Old and*

New Testament Connected in the History of the Jews and Neighboring Nations (London, 1716–1718), 2 vols.; and in Isaac Newton, The Chronology of Ancient Kingdoms Amended (London, 1728). An important modern account is Frank Manuel, Isaac Newton, Historian (Cambridge: Harvard University Press, 1963), which gives an extensive bibliography on the chronologers. William Hales, A

New Analysis of Chronology and Geography, History and Prophecy, 2d ed., 4 vols. (London, 1830), gives a useful summary of the principal chronologic systems of the two centuries before his writing. See also H. Meyer, The age of the world: a chapter in the history of the Enlightenment (Allentown, Pennsylvania: multigraphed at Muhlenberg College, 1951).

SHUCKFORD

FROM *Sacred and Profane History Connected*

I SHALL very probably be thought to have taken great liberty in the accounts I have given of the most ancient profane history; particularly in that which is antediluvian, and which I have reduced to an agreement with the history of Moses. It will be said, "take it altogether, as it lies in the authors from whom we have it, that it has no such harmony with the sacred writer; and to make a harmony by taking part of what is represented, and such part only as you please, everything, or any thing, may be made to agree in this manner; but such an agreement will not be much regarded by the unbiassed." To this I answer: the heathen accounts, which we have of these early ages, were taken from the records of either Thyoth the Egyptian or Sanchoniathon of Berytus; and whatever the original memoirs of these men were, we are sure the accounts were, some time after their decease, corrupted with fable and mystical philosophy. Philo of Biblos in one place seems to think, that Taautus himself wrote his Sacra, and his theology, in a way above the under-

standing of the common people, in order to create reverence and respect to the subject of which he treated; and that Surmubelus and Theuro, some ages after, endeavoured to explain his works, by stripping them of the allegory, and giving them their true meaning. But I cannot think a writer so ancient as Athothes wrote in fable or allegory; the first memoirs or histories were without doubt short and plain, and men afterwards embellished them with false learning, and in time endeavoured to correct that, and arrive at the true. All therefore that I can collect from this passage of Philo Biblius is this, that Thyoth's memoirs did not continue such as he left them. Surmubelus and Theuro in some time altered them, and I fear, whoever they were, they altered them for the worse; for such were the alterations which succeeding generations made in the records of their ancestors, as appears from what the same writer farther offers. "When Saturnus," says he (now I think Saturnus to be only another name for Mizraim,) "went to the South," (*i. e.*

when he removed from the Lower Egypt into Thebais, which I have taken notice of in its place,) "he made Taautus king of all Egypt, and the Cabiri" (who were the sons of Mizraim) "made memoirs of these transactions." Such were the first writings of mankind; short hints or records of what they did, and where they settled: "but the son of Thabio, one of the first interpreters of the Sacra of the Phoenicians, by his comments and interpretations filled these records full of allegory, and mixed his physiological philosophy with them, and so left them to the priests, and they to their successors. With these additions and mixtures they came into the hands of the Greeks, who were men of an abounding fancy, and who, by new applications, and by increasing the number and the extravagancy of the fable, did in time leave but little appearance of any thing like truth in them." We have much the same account of the writings of Sanchoniathon. "Sanchoniathon of Berytus," we are told, "wrote his history of the Jewish antiquities with the greatest care and fidelity, having received his facts from Hierombalus, a priest; and having a mind to write a universal history of all nations from the beginning, he took the greatest pains in searching the records of Taautus. But some later writers (probably the persons before-mentioned) had corrupted his remains by their allegorical interpretations, and physical additions; for (says Philo) the more modern *hierologoi*, priests, or explainers of the Sacra, had omitted to relate the true facts as they were recorded, instead of which, they had obscured them by invented accounts and mysterious fictions, drawn from their notions of the nature of the universe; so that it was not easy for one to distinguish the real facts which Taautus had recorded, from the fictions superadded to them.

But he (*i. e.* Sanchoniathon) finding some of the books of the Ammonei, which were kept in the libraries or registries of the temples, examined every thing with the greatest care; and rejecting the allegories and fables, which at first sight offered themselves, he at length brought his work to perfection. But the priests, who lived after him, adding their comments and explications to his work, in some time brought all back to mythology again." This, I think, is a just account of what has been the fate of the ancient heathen remains; they were clear and true, when left by their authors, but after-writers corrupted them by the addition of fable and false philosophy. Therefore, whoever would endeavour to give a probable account of things from the remains of Thyoth, or Sanchoniathon, must set aside what he finds to be allegory and fable, as the surest way to come at the true remains of these ancient authors. This I have endeavoured to do in my accounts of the Phoenician and Egyptian antiquities. I have added nothing to their history, and if their ancient remains be carefully examined, the nature of what I have omitted will justify my omitting it; and what I have taken from them, will, I believe, satisfy the judicious reader, that these ancient authors, before their writings were corrupted, left accounts very agreeable to that of Moses. (pp. 12–15)

As the works of Taautus and Sanchoniathon were corrupted, by the fables of authors who wrote after them, so probably the Chaldean records suffered alterations from the fancies of those who in after ages copied them; and from hence the the reigns (or lives) of Berosus's Antediluvian Kings (or rather men) came to be extended to so incredible a length. The lives of men, in these times, were extraordinary, as Moses hath represented them; but the profane historians, fond of the marvellous, have far exceeded the truth in their relations. Berosus computes their lives by a term of years called *sarus;* each sarus, he says, is six hundred and three years, and he thinks that some of them lived ten, twelve, thirteen, and eighteen sari, *i. e.* six thousand and thirty, seven thousand two hundred and thirty-six, seven thousand eight hundred and thirty-nine, and ten thousand eight hundred and fifty-four years; but mistakes of this sort have happened with writers of a much later date. Diodorus, and other writers, represent the armies of Semiramis, and her buildings at Babylon, more numerous and magnificent than can be conceived by any one who considers the infant state kingdoms were in when she reigned. Abraham, with a family of between three and four hundred persons, made the figure of a mighty prince in these early times, for the earth was not full of people: and if we come down to the times of the Trojan War, we do not find reason to imagine, that those countries of which the heathen writers treated, were more potent or populous than their contemporaries, of whom we have accounts in the sacred pages; but the heathen historians, hearing that Semiramis, or other ancient princes, did what were wonders in their age, took care to tell them in a way and manner, that should make them wonders in their own. In a word, Moses is the only writer whose accounts are liable to no exception.   (pp. 15–16)

Now, in order to explain what is meant by the number of years in these reigns, I would observe, that perhaps Egypt was peopled no more than six hundred and sixty years before the Flood; which may be true, though we suppose an elder son of Adam to have brought a colony thither. Seth was born in the one hundred and thirtieth year of Adam's life, and Seth lived until within six hundred and fourteen years of the Flood; and therefore a son of Adam, but a century younger than Seth (and Adam lived eight hundred years after the birth of Seth, and begat sons and daughters,) might plant Egypt, and live one hundred and fifty years at the head of his plantation: or if we suppose it first planted by some children of Adam, two or three centuries younger, they might come to Egypt in the flower of their days.

It must, indeed, be allowed, that the eight demi-gods, and the fifteen heroes, cannot be a series of kings succeeding one another; for seven generations, in such a succession, would take up very near the number of years allotted to all of them, as may be seen by looking into the lives of Adam's descendants, set down by Moses. If we begin forty-six years before the death of Seth, we may see that Enos lived ninety-eight years after Seth, Cainan ninety-five years after Enos, Mahalaleel fifty-five years after Cainan, Jared one hundred and thirty-two years after Mahalaleel; Enoch was translated before his father's death; Methuselah died two hundred and thirty-four years after Jared, and in the year of the Flood, and Lamech died before Methuselah; the succession of these men, and there are but seven of them, and a short piece of Seth's life, took up six hundred and sixty years; and therefore if the lives of the other branches of Adam's family were of the same length with these, and it is probable they were, eight demi-gods and fifteen heroes (twenty-three persons) could not succeed one another in so few years. In this point, therefore, the Egyptian writers make great difficulties, by supposing these demi-gods and heroes to reign one after another, when it is impossible to find a good account of the times of such successive reigns, or to bring the whole series of them within the compass of time allotted to them; but we may make this difficulty easy, if we suppose the eight demi-gods to be contemporaries, persons of great eminence and figure in the age they lived in, and the fifteen heroes, who lived after these demi-gods, contemporaries of one another; and I think their different titles, as well as what we find about them in the historians, lead us to this notion of them. If these persons were a successive number of kings, from the first of them to the Flood, why should eight of them be called demi-gods, and the rest but heroes? The superior appellation of the first eight, looks as if they stood upon an equal ground with one another, but something higher than those who came after them. And perhaps they were eight children of Adam, and he had certainly enough to spare many times eight to people the several parts of the world. These came together with their families into Egypt, lived all within the compass of two hundred and seventeen years; (which is an easy supposition,) and being all the heads of the families that came with them, and were descended from them, they might be so revered by their posterity, as to have a title superior to what their descendants attained to. And it is observable that the historians, who mention them, give them names very favourable to this account of them, the demi-gods, according to Diodorus, were Sol, Saturnus, Rhea, Jupiter, Juno, Vulcanus, Vesta, Mercurius; and these are the names of persons, not of different, but of the same descent; brothers and sisters, some of whom, according to what was the early custom in Adam's family, married one another. In like manner, if we look among their heroes, we shall find them of the same sort: Osiris

and Isis, Typhon, and Apollo, and Venus, are all said to be children of the same family; they taught agriculture and other useful arts, and thereby made themselves famous, and we are told that several of them went up and down together, and were therefore contemporaries; and it is easy to suppose fifteen of them, the number which the old Chronicon mentions, to flourish within the space of four hundred and forty-three years. And thus it will appear, that the reigns of the demi-gods and heroes reach up to the very first peopling of Egypt, and therefore what they offer about a race of gods, superior to and before these, must belong to ages before the creation of the world.

It was a usual and customary thing, for the ancient writers to begin their antiquities with some account of the origin of things, and the creation of the world. Moses did so in his book of Genesis: Sanchoniathon's Phoenician history began in the same manner, and it appears from Diodorus that the Egyptian antiquities did so too. Their accounts began with speculations about the origin of things, and the nature of the gods; then follows an account of their demi-gods and terrestrial deities, after them come their heroes, or first rank of men; and last of all their kings. Now if their kings began from the Flood; if their heroes and demi-gods reached up to the beginning of the world; then the account they give of the reigns of gods before these, can be only their theological speculations put into such order as they thought most truly philosophical.

The first and most ancient gods of the Egyptians, and of all other heathen nations, after they had departed from the worship of the true GOD, were the luminaries of heaven; and it is very probable, that what they took to be the period or time, in which any of these deities finished its course, that they might call the time of its reign; thus a perfect and complete revolution of any star which they worshipped, was the reign of that star; and though it might be tedious to trace too far into their antiquated philosophy, in order to find out how they came to imagine that the revolutions of the several heavenly bodies answered to such a number of years, as they ascribed to the respective reigns; yet it is remarkable that a whole entire revolution of the heavens took up, according to their computations, exactly the number of years ascribed by them to all their gods. A period of 36,525 years, is what they call an entire *mundane* revolution, and brings on the *apochatasasis cosmike:* in this passage of time, they say, the several heavenly bodies do exactly go through all the relations which they can have in their motions to one another, and come round to the same point from which all their courses began. These heavenly bodies therefore being their gods, such a perfect and entire revolution of them is a complete reign of all the gods, and contained 36,525 years.

But to the first of their gods, called here Vulcan, they assign no time; his reign is unlimited. I suppose they meant hereby to intimate that the supreme GOD was eternal, his power infinite, his reign not confined to any one, or any number of ages, but extending itself through all: and such high notions the Egyptians certainly had of the supreme Deity, though they had also buried them in heaps of the grossest errors. This I take to be a true account of the Egyptian dynasties; and if it be so, their history is not so extravagant as has been imagined. The substance of what they offer is, that the supreme GOD is eternal—to his reign they assign no time; that the sun, moon, and stars ran their courses thousands of years before

man was upon the Earth; into this notion they were led by their astronomy; that Egypt was peopled six hundred and sixty years before the Flood; and very probably it might not be peopled sooner, considering that mankind began in Chaldea, and that first the plantation went eastward with Cain, and that Seth and his family settled near home. Amongst these first inhabitants of Egypt there were eight demigods, and fifteen heroes, *i. e.* three and twenty persons illustrious and eminent in their generations. After the Flood reigned Menes, whom Moses called Mizraim, and after Mizraim, a succession of kings down to Nectanebus.

Manetho wrote his history by order of Ptolemy Philadelphus, some time after the Septuagint translation was made. When the Hebrew antiquities were published to the world, the Egyptians grew jealous of the honour of their nation, and were willing to show that they could trace up their memoirs, even higher than Moses could carry those of the Israelites; for this end Manetho made his collection; it was his design to make the Egyptian antiquities reach as far backwards as he could, and therefore as many kings' names as he could find in their records, so many successive monarchs he determined them to have had; not considering that Egypt was at first divided into three, and afterwards into four sovereignties for some time, so that three or four of his kings many times reigned together. When he got up to Menes, then he set down the names of such persons as had been famous before the times of this their first king; and then, it being a point of his religion that their gods had reigned on earth, and their astronomy teaching that the reigns of the gods took up the space of 36,525 years; he added these also, and by this management his antiquities seem to reach higher than the accounts of Moses: when in reality, if rightly interpreted, they fall short of Moses, by such a number of years, as we may fairly suppose might pass be- fore mankind could be so increased as to people the Earth, from Chaldea, the place where Adam and Eve lived, unto Egypt.

(pp. 44–48)

EPHRAIM CHAMBERS

[d.1740]

EPHRAIM CHAMBERS's *Cyclopedia,* or *Universal Dictionary of Arts and Sciences,* was first published in 1728, reached a seventh edition in 1751–1752, was reissued, expanded, and excerpted all through the eighteenth century, and was translated into Italian and into French, the latter translation leading directly to Diderot's great *Encyclopédie.* It is still a useful index to the received opinions of the eighteenth century. Mythology is defined in a single sentence as "the History of the fabulous Gods, and heroes of Antiquity: and the explanation of their Mysteries, of their Religion, their Fables, and Metamorphoses," but there is a long article on fable which draws heavily on de la Motte and Bossu as well as Aristotle.

Fable is taken up under two headings and is first dealt with as "instruction disguised under the allegory of an action" and it is clear that the writer has Aesop and La Fontaine in mind. It is claimed that fable is the most ancient form of teaching, that it embodies the allegorical mode so natural to the ancients and so antipathetical to the moderns, and it is further claimed that the divine nature and theology generally were originally described via fable, either to aid the mind in grasping such difficult concepts, or to conceal such concepts from unworthy minds. Gradually, these theological stories or fables came to include philosophy and general morality. Soon all subjects were expressible via fables, and thus arose poetry or what we would call imaginative literature. The article goes on to link fables with epic poems, arguing that fables and epic poems are essentially or structurally the same, different only in the extent to which the basic idea is elaborated.

Under Chambers's second general heading, fable is considered in its Aristotelian sense as the plot or action of a piece of literature. This notion of fable also has two aspects: there must be some truth as the foundation for the fable, and there must be a fiction that clothes or disguises the truth and gives it a form. The truth involved is often a moral truth, while the fiction is the surface action or story line.

Chambers goes on to illustrate this dual nature of fable and to illustrate at the same time the earlier claim that fable is always the same, whether its form be that of a short apologue or of an epic poem. To this end, Chambers, following Bossu, compares the *Iliad* with a fable of Aesop's: each, he claims, has at its center the truth that "the misunderstandings of princes ruin their states." Homer has provided a very elaborate surface action to carry this truth, while the Aesopian fable provides only a brief animal story to carry the same point. This is, in fact, a species of structural criticism, an attempt to find the common central structure of several apparently dissimilar works.

Chambers's article is finally interesting for its effort to link fable considered as plot or story with fable considered as higher truth. His work also illustrates an approach to myth often found in formal literary criticism of the eighteenth century, an interest in fable as plot, rather than as a Greco-Roman ornament.

R.R.

REFERENCES Our text is from Ephraim Chambers, *Cyclopedia or Universal Dictionary of Arts and Sciences,* 7th edition (London, 1751), which reprints the original 1728 article in unchanged form. Discussions of fable in the sense of plot can be found in virtually all eighteenth-century criticism. Aesopian fables or apologues were written by Charles Perrault, La Fontaine, Fénelon, and many others. See the recent *Fable* by Erwin Leibfried (Stuttgart, 1967) for historical survey of the fable in this period and extensive bibliography. Other eighteenth century dictionary articles of interest include those in the first three editions of the *Encyclopedia Britannica* (1771, 1777–84, 1788–97), in the French translation of Chambers's *Cyclopedia* (1743–45), and of course, in Diderot's *Encyclopédie*. See also our introduction to Fréret.

CHAMBERS

FROM *Cyclopedia*

FABLE, a tale, or feigned narration, designed either to instruct or divert: or, as Mons. de la Motte defines it, an instruction disguised under the allegory of an action.

Fable seems to be the most antient way of teaching: the principal difference between the eloquence of the antients, and that of the moderns, consists, according to Père Bossu, in this, that our manner of speaking is simple and proper; and theirs full of mysteries and allegories. With them, the truth was usually disguised under those ingenious inventions, called, by way of excellence, *mythoi, fabulae, fables,* that is, words; as intimating that there was the same difference between these *fabulous* discourses of the learned, and the common language of the people, as between the words of men, and the voices of beasts. At first, *fables* were only employed in speaking of the divine nature, as then conceived: whence the antient theology was all *fable.* The divine attributes were separated as into so many persons; and all the oeconomy of the godhead laid down in the feigned relations and actions thereof; either by reason the human mind could not conceive so much power and action in a single and indivisible being; or, perhaps, because they thought such things too great and high for the knowledge of the vulgar. And as they could not well speak of the operations of this almighty cause, without speaking likewise of its effects; natural philosophy, and at length human nature, and morality itself, came thus to be veiled under the same *fabulous* allegoric expression; and hence was the origin of poetry, and particularly of epic poetry.

The critics, after Aphthonius and Theon, reckon three kinds of *fables,* rational, moral, and mixed.

Rational FABLES, are called also parables: these are relations of things supposed to have been said and done by men; and which might possibly have been said and done, though in reality they were not.—Such, in the sacred writings, as those of the ten virgins; of Dives and Lazarus; the prodigal son, etc. . . .

Moral FABLES, called also apologues, are those wherein beasts are introduced as the actors, speakers, etc. These are also called Aesopic *fables.* . . . In this kind, not only beasts, but even sometimes trees, instruments, etc. are supposed to speak.

The *rational* differs from the *moral fable* in this; that the former, though it be feigned, might be true: but the latter is impossible; as it is impossible for brutes or stocks to speak.

Mixed FABLES are those composed of both sorts, rational and moral; or wherein men and brutes are introduced conversing together. . . .

M. de la Motte has some fine remarks on the subject of *fables,* at the beginning of his *fables nouvelles, dediées au roi,* 1719. A *fable,* according to this polite writer, is a little epic poem; differing in nothing from the great one, but in extent, and in that being less confined as to the choice of its persons, it may take in all sorts at pleasure, as gods, men, beasts, or genii; or even, if occasion be, create persons, *i. e.* personify virtues, vices, rivers, trees, etc. Thus M. de la Motte very happily introduces virtue, talent, and reputation, as persons making a voyage together. . . .

The *fable* must always imply or convey some truth: in other works, delight alone may suffice; but the *fable* must instruct. Its essence is to be a symbol, and of consequence to signify somewhat more than is expressed by the letter. This truth should for the generality be a moral one; and a series of fictions conceived and composed in this view, would form a treatise of morality preferable to any more direct and methodical treatise: accordingly, Socrates, we are told, had a design to compose a course of morality in this way. This truth should be concealed under the allegory; and in strictness, it ought not to be explained either at the beginning or end. The truth, or idea intended, should arise up in the reader's mind from the fable itself. However, for the conveniency of the less discerning readers, it may be a good way to point out the truth or moral in preciser terms. To have the moral at the end of the *fable,* seems much better than at the beginning: the mind is apt to be forestalled in the latter case; I carry the key all along with me, so that there is no room to exercise my mind, in finding anything myself. . . .

FABLE is also used for the plot of an epic, or dramatic poem, or the action which makes the subject of such poem, or romance. The *fable,* according to Aristotle, is the principal part, and as it were the soul, of a poem. It must be considered as the first foundation of the composition; or the principle, which gives life and motion to all the parts.— In this sense, the *fable* is defined, "A discourse invented with art, to form the manners by instructions disguised under the allegory of an action."

The epic *fable,* according to Bossu, is confined to the rational kind; *i. e.,* the actors and persons are to be gods and men. And yet it admits of a deal of latitude: it may be either grave, illustrious, and important; or low, and popular; either whole, or defective; in verse, or in prose; much episodified, or brief; rehearsed by an author, or represented actors on the scene: all which are only so many circumstances, which do not make any alteration in the nature and essence of the *fable*.

The characters that specify the epic *fable* are these: it is rational and probable; it imitates a whole, and an important action; and it is long, and related in verse. None of which properties affect the nature of the *fable;* or make it less a *fable* than those of Aesop. The *fable,* according to Aristotle, consists of two essential parts; *viz.* truth, as its foundation; and fiction, which disguises the truth, and gives it the form of *fable*. The truth is the point of morality intended to be inculcated; the fiction is the action, or words the instruction is covered under.

ÉTIENNE FOURMONT

[1683–1745]

ÉTIENNE FOURMONT, another member of the *Académie des Inscriptions,* was an early orientalist who published a *Meditationes Sinicae* in 1737 and a *Linguae Sinarum . . . grammatica* in 1742; he was Professor of Arabic in the Collège de France; he also knew Hebrew, Chaldean, Chinese, and even Tibetan, and when he put his mind to the problem of mythology, the result, his *Réflexions critiques sur les histoires des anciens peuples, Chaldéens, Hébreux, Phéniciens, Égyptiens, Grecs etc, jusqu'au temps de Cyrus* (1735), was a forbiddingly erudite reduction of myth to biblical history, held together by the idea of connecting sacred and profane history, and using etymology as the principal method of demonstration.

Fourmont's preface argues that one of the great problems in our knowledge of ancient history is that of idolatry. He finds the purely psychological and moral explanations of idolatry or paganism insufficient—clearly he had the deists in mind here—and he goes on to assert that Sanchoniathon (the Phoenician historian of whose work fragments are preserved in Eusebius) has given the true, the historical explanation of the heathen gods. Fourmont first presents Sanchoniathon's own work, then applies it to the job of connecting Greek deities and Hebrew history.

According to Fourmont, the Phoenicians deified the Hebrew Patriarchs, the Egyptians then picked up the habit from the Phoenicians, the Greeks took their deities from the Egyptian-Phoenician-Hebrew conglomerate, and the Romans took their gods from the Greeks. Fourmont tries to demonstrate this with unsparing detail, taking it name by name, and deity by deity; nor is he above multiple proofs of a single proposition. A sample of the etymological technique by means of which Fourmont can sound so authoritative, and which makes him at the same time very hard to refute, is his simple assertion that "Lot, en Phénicien *Lota,* est Tholas où Atlas." A sample of what this freewheeling etymologizing can produce is Fourmont's contention that Abraham in the Bible is the same person as Kronus, also known as Saturn, who is in turn Ilus, which is the root for Elohim, which is Hebrew for "the gods." Thus Sadid, who is the son of Saturn, and Jupiter, who is the son of Kronus, and Isaac, who is the son of Abraham, are all, therefore, the same person; Zeus equals Isaac. It is all "clair comme le jour," as Fourmont complacently notes.

Fourmont's use of inexact etymology, slender comparisons, and reckless genealogies to support what is essentially a very conventional argument, nevertheless looks both backward and forward. Vossius, Kircher, and Bochart had made the etymological method famous during the seventeenth century. Scholars like Fourmont carried it on. Etymology changed into philology toward the end of the eighteenth century, and although it became a more respectable study, it still maintained a close connection with myth studies: F. Max Müller is a later example of the combination of comparative mythology and philology. In his own obscure fashion, then, Fourmont is part of a long line of students of myth who began with simple verbal resemblances and eventually found and refined the connections between language, linguistics, and myth, which are even today an unexhausted field. Fourmont's actual contribution is minimal however, since his learning outran his perception and his knowledge of exotic languages served a pedestrian imagination; he remains at last a curiosity, an eighteenth-century scholar whose seventeenth-century methods foreshadowed nineteenth-century conclusions.

R.R.

REFERENCES   The text is our translation from Étienne Fourmont, *Réflexions critiques sur les histoires des anciens peuples* . . . (Paris: Musier père, 1735), 2 vols. The edition of the *Réflexions* published in 1747 contains a list of Fourmont's works and a life of him by his students deGuignes and Deshautesrayes. Views similar to Fourmont's can be found in deGuignes, *Mémoire dans lequel on prouve que les Chinois sont une colonie Égyptienne* (Paris, 1795) and in D. de Mairan, *Lettres de M de Mairan au R. P. Parreain* (Paris, 1759). See also the summary of Fourmont's ideas in J. H. Brumfitt, *Voltaire Historian* (Oxford, 1958), and W. Engemann, *Voltaire and China* (Leipzig, 1933).

FOURMONT

FROM *Critical Reflections on the Accounts of Ancient Peoples*

BOOK II, SECTION 3, CHAPTER 11

Continuation on the family of Uranus and of Kronos, New Proof that Isaac is Sadid, and Sadid is Σδευς or Zeus.

THROUGHOUT this discourse we have seen that Abraham was Saturn, that Issac was Ζευς or *Jupiter,* and Ishmael *Dis* or *Pluto.* This second part of the proposition is proven; the first is also, in some manner. But one can object, what connection is there between the Isaac of Moses and the Sadid of Sanchoniathon; between the *Sadid* of the Phenicien author and the Zeus or Jupiter of the Greek and Latin poets?

This connection is great, and will become evident. The ancients ordinarily had several names, the birth name and the accidental or acquired names: nothing more frequent among all peoples. *Isaak* was the birth name for the son of Abraham; the smile of Sara had occasioned it, and from this several authors have said that Abraham had had a son named γελως, which is the translation of Isaac; but at the time when Abraham had wanted to sacrifice his son, the story having gotten around the country, he called him *Sadid*, in Arab and in Phenicien *ligatus;* nothing could be more accurate than this name; but Zeus, is he Sadid? yes, and this becomes a most embarrassing denouement for the history of the world.

Up to now, we have taken Zeus from ζεω *bouillir,* or from ζωω *vivre;* the ζαν ζανσς from which would appear to have been formed Ζανω *Juno,* seemed to confirm the last of these etymologies. We thought Ηρη formed from Αηρ Air.

But at last there remained a doubt about Zeus, the ancients said also Σδευς or even Δευς; and this δευς could come equally from δεω *ligo, lier.* A mark such as ζεω in the first ages of Greece signified *lier* as well as δεω, and from this obsolete word, which is however the parent of several other words, was derived the diminutive ζωω, from which ζωνη, ζωννυω *ceindre,* in Latin *zona.* It is then as clear as day that δευς signified *ligatus, constrictus.*

ANTOINE BANIER

[1675–1741]

OF THE writers who interpreted myth as gilded history, the Abbé Antoine Banier was probably the best-known, the most widely cited, and the least controversial. Much quoted and much deferred to, Banier's ideas and phrases show up everywhere: Fourmont and many others rest their arguments on his, and the articles on *Mythologie* and *Fable* in Diderot's *Encyclopédie* made heavy and not always acknowledged use of his writings. Indeed, one finds Banier's name in nearly every eighteenth-century account of mythology, where he is always referred to as a leading Euhemerist and as an anti-allegorist. His work on myth began with the publication in 1711 of the two-volume *Explication historique des fables où l'on découvre leur origine et leur conformité avec l'histoire ancienne*. Banier put out a new edition in 1715, casting it in dialogue form. The third and best version was the thoroughly reworked three-volume edition that appeared in 1738–1740, and was at once translated into English as *The Mythology and Fables of the Ancients explain'd from history*.

Banier defined mythology in his preface as the "knowledge of Fable and at the same time of the Pagan religion, its mysteries, Ceremonies, and the Worship paid to its false divinities." As the definition goes on to suggest, his essentially Christian viewpoint is muted and counterweighted by his assumption that myth has as much to do with *belles lettres* as with "false" religion. Banier's tone is

calm and reasonable; he is not principally interested in advancing the faith. And while the title of his earliest work suggests that he was not perhaps so far from the "conformities" approach of Shuckford or Lafitau, Banier is not a polemicist for the faith. Neither is he particularly interested in new science, in astronomical dating (he was one of Newton's attackers), nor in the primitive mind. He approached myth essentially as a branch of history, and he considered history itself a branch of *belles lettres*. He is said to have become involved in myth when reading ancient poetry with a student, and his belletristic leanings are clear in his description of fables as "beautiful Veils under which the Truths of ancient History are concealed."

His general thesis is presented in his second chapter. Myths are not usually, in Banier's view, allegories; he does not find it credible that the conflict of the gods in Homer "signifies no more than the struggle of our passions." Banier argues that "mere fables" would attract little attention, would last only a short while, and would achieve no reputation. Therefore there must be something substantial in the old stories, and the substantial something, Banier thought, must be historical fact. The bulk of his work labors to provide the facts behind the veils of myth.

But even if Banier tended towards Euhemerist interpretation, he nevertheless goes out of his way to acknowledge a wide variety of other approaches to myth; and throughout his work, one is aware that the Abbé is always alert to matters of method and approach. This sophistication about technique can be seen in his third chapter, a careful break-down of myths into six main types. In subsequent chapters, he goes even further in this effort to be open-minded about all possibilities and he lists some sixteen different origins of myth. With the eclecticism that marks the best French work on myth during this time, Banier considers vanity, monuments or memorial traditions, the eloquence of inventive orators, and travelers' tales all as possible origins; he lumps together poets, painters, and the stage, and mentions the plurality or unity of names and the ignorance in philosophy (as Fontenelle had). The processes of colonization, the ascent from barbarism, the wish to have gods for ancestors, the misreading of sacred scriptures, and ignorance of ancient history, of languages, and of geography are listed as other possible sources for fables. Banier ends, after noting the Egyptian origins of many Greek fables, by observing gravely that some fables probably owe their origin to a need to save a lady's reputation. A mismanaged liaison could always be explained as a visit from Zeus. The list is interesting for its range, for what it leaves out—genuine if primitive thought about nature and personification of natural forces, for example—for its lack of emphasis on revealed religion, and for its urbane concessions to variety.

One of the great ironies about the widespread eighteenth-century application of Euhemerus's reductionist theory of myth is that while Euhemerus himself had been an atheist and his work apparently had been intended to mock and debase Greek religion, those same ideas were used by eighteenth-century defenders of Christianity, who were quick to seize anything that would downgrade paganism but slow to see that what undermined one religion might undermine another. Banier had been trained by the Jesuits, and while his work is free of open apologetic, he retained a Christian outlook alongside his short-sighted and eventually self-confounding Euhemerist approach. For this reason, and also perhaps because he was aware of the irrationalism and the violence behind archaic Greek religion, Banier felt obliged to attack Homer and Virgil for presenting deity as they did. Perhaps at bottom, Banier was afraid of the barbarous and unenlightened qualities in the Homeric epics. Whatever the exact mixture of motives, Banier spends considerable time trying to discredit Virgil and Homer, principally because of their treatment of deity, but also because of what he considers their scandalous and unscrupulous willingness to just invent things out of whole cloth. Banier's naiveté about the literary as well as the mythical imagination was not unique—such attacks are common during this period—but a radical revaluation of Homer, of primitivism, of archaic religion, and of the primitive spirit was just around the corner. And as Homer's subject matter was reviewed and reconsidered, so too the role of the poet, so foolishly simplified and ignored by Banier and others like him, began to appear in a new, less frivolous, and much more interesting light. Banier at last furnishes the necessary introduction to the whole revival of Homer in the middle and later eighteenth century. Homer will shortly be praised for precisely the qualities Banier objects to. Banier assumes the inherent wrongness and degeneracy of Greek religion; but that same religion will begin to seem noble, simple, powerful, and affecting to other eighteenth-century minds. And with a shift in attitude toward Homer's subject will come a new view of the nature of poetry, of the poet, of his role, and of his connection with religion.

R.R.

REFERENCES Our text is from Antoine Banier, *The Mythology and Fables of the Ancients explain'd from history* (London: A. Millor, 1739). For commentary, see the entries by Weiss in *Biographie Universelle* (Paris, 1843) and by Roman D'Amat in *Dictionnaire de Biographie Française* (Paris, 1951); see also Frank Manuel, *The Eighteenth Century Confronts the Gods* (Cambridge: Harvard University Press, 1959), and the introduction to Fréret in this volume.

BANIER

FROM *The Mythology and Fables of the Ancients explain'd from history*

THOUGH 'tis our happiness not to live in one of those Ages, when almost the whole World was plunged in an Abyss of Idolatry, yet 'tis far from being unnecessary to know the History of the Pagan Gods and Fables; Mythology, which teaches us to be acquainted with those Gods and Fables, makes so considerable a Part of the *Belles-Lettres*, that it cannot well be neglected. And indeed, we are daily conversant in the Works of *Greeks* and *Romans,* in those of their Poets, especially, which we should often be at a loss to understand, were we not acquainted with the Fables to which they are eternally alluding.

Besides, every thing concurs to remind us of those ancient Fictions; such as Statues, Bas-Reliefs, Monuments of all sorts; and to be short, what do the Books of the Antiquaries, and the Cabinets of the Curious contain, but Figures of the Pagan Divinities, Instruments used in their sacrifices, and what other Remains we have of the Pagan Superstition? Our Galleries, our Ceilings, our Pictures, our Statues are continually representing to us the same Objects: and as if History, sacred and profane, did not furnish out to us a sufficient number of important Facts, and such as are capable of inspiring us with virtuous Sentiments, we borrow our Arguments from *Fable,* in our Dramatick Poetry especially.

Our Theatres are every day resounding with the Complaints of *Iphigenia* and *Andromache,* the Outrages of *Orestes,* the Wrath of *Achilles,* and the unbridled Lust of *Clytemnestra;* nor are we ashamed to own, that we see those Heroes and Heroines daily upon our Stage, with new delight, while we can hardly bear a Representation of other Personages, that are more proper to awaken in us a noble Emulation.

Thus the Knowledge of Mythology is useful, and in some sort necessary, insomuch that one cannot be ignorant of it, but he must pass for a Man of narrow Education, deficient in the more essential Branches of polite Learning. But what makes Mythology still of greater Importance, and at the same time gives it a juster Claim to be the Object of our

Curiosity, is to consider, that Fables are not mere Fictions, as I prove in the Introduction to this Work, but that they have a real Connection with the History of the first Ages, comprehend some of their considerable Transactions, and that most of the Gods had been Men, whose History makes a part of that of the particular Nations, from whom they had divine Honour. . . .   (from Preface, pp. v–vi)

In which 'tis proved that Fables
are not mere Allegories, but
comprehend several ancient Facts.

Fables are to be no otherwise accounted of than so many beautiful Veils, under which the Truths of ancient History are concealed; and however they may be disguised by the great number of Ornaments mixed with them, it is not absolutely impossible to unfold the historical Facts they contain. I grant there are some Circumstances, in the Fables which were merely of Poetical Invention; but there is a deal of Probability that they had a true Foundation: and tho' we are not to take all that they have said of their Gods and Heroes in the literal Sense, yet it would be as wrong to reject it altogether, and the rather that they frequently speak of Persons whose Deeds we have recorded in History; which gives *Pausanias* occasion to say, "In every Period of time, singular and extraordinary Events, in proportion as they were remote from the Memory of Men, so much the less did they retain the air of Credibility, thro' their fault who built Fables upon the foundation of Truth."

I know the Poets have sometimes gone the length even of inventing the Personages they describe; but it is easy to discover these, and to be sure no reasonable man judges of *Saturn* or *Neptune,* as he does of *Fortune* and of *Destiny.* There is no impossibility to distinguish amongst all these Poetical Personages, the real from the figurative or allegorical. Learned Men have done it before me, nor did *St. Augustine, Lactantius,* and *Arnobius* judge this Article unworthy their Consideration, believing they did no small service to Religion, by shewing to the World that the ancient Pagan Divinities had been no other than Men. I own, for my part, if there was nothing in all the Fables of the Poets but some Allegories, I don't see what great value we ought to have for their Works: nothing to me would appear more insipid. Whereas, if it is true that they comprize ancient Facts, their making use of such numbers of Fables has nothing at all surprizing; it gives us even a better opinion of the Genius of the *Greeks,* since we see that in spight of their invincible byass towards Fictions they did not however feed themselves with Tales of mere Invention;[1] and tho' they have embellished their Narratives, yet we know at least that they contain several Truths of Importance. Accordingly it is certain that the greatest Men of Antiquity, have always had a high Idea of the Poets, whom they looked upon as the earliest Historians. *Strabo* says, the Historians came nearer to the Character of *Homer,* in proportion as they were more ancient: which makes *Casaubon* say,[2] that in reading *Herodotus,* he thought he was reading *Homer* himself. . . . Nor are we ignorant that *Titus Livius,* in the Fables that relate to the Antiquity of *Rome,* brings back the Gods to Men, as in that about the Birth of *Romulus,* his Education, &c. Does he not reduce to History the Voyages of *Antenor* and *Aeneas,* the Wars and Victories of the last, and his Apotheosis? Is not the Subject of the *Aeneid* considered by him in the same light as *Polybius* and *Strabo* had done the *Iliad* and *Odyssey*? When *Cicero* is enumerating the Sages, does he not bring in *Nestor* and *Ulysses*? would he have given mere Phantoms a place among them? Has he not explained the Fables of *Atlas, Cepheus,* and *Prometheus*? Are we not taught by him, that what gave occasion to feign that the one supported the Heavens on his Shoulders, and the other was chained to Mount *Caucasus* was their indefatigable Application to contemplate the Heavenly Bodies? I might bring in here the Authority of most of the Ancients: I might produce that of the primitive Fathers of the Church, *Arnobius, Lactantius,* and several others, who looked upon Fables to be founded on true Histories; and I might finish this List with the Names of the most Illustrious of our Moderns, who have traced out in ancient Fictions, so many Remains of the Tradition of the primitive Ages.

But, say you, would not this be granting enough, to allow Fables to comprehend the Philosophy and Religion of the Ancients? I grant we have some Allegories mixed with them, which point that way; but still it was the primary Intention of the Poets, to comprize in these Fables the History of their Heroes; and we wander from their true Scope, when we confine our Views entirely to the Allegory. Is it really credible, that when they tell us *Bacchus* was clapped into *Jupiter's* Thigh, they only meant to let us know, that Wine, of which that God is a Symbol, must, in order to ripen, have a moderate Heat, as there is in that part of the Body? That the Combat of the Gods in *Homer* signifies no more than the Struggle of our Passions, or the Conjunction of the Planets in the same Point of the Zodiac, according to the Reveries of some Scholiasts? That *Vulcan* is only represented lame, because Fire

without Fewel, goes out, *Deficit, claudi-cat?* [3] Is it to be thought, that when they tell us how *Jupiter* decreed upon *Pluto's* carrying off *Proserpina,* that she should be six Months in Hell, and six Months with her Mother *Ceres,* they designed only to inform us that the Grain is lodged six Months in the Earth, and six Months out of it? [4] That they have made up a match between *Jupiter* and *Juno,* only because *Jupiter* is the Air, and *Juno* the Earth; and *Jupiter* by sending Showers upon the Earth, makes it fertile? That the bad understanding betwixt this married Couple, and the Jealousies of *Juno,* teach us nothing else, but that the Air put into commotion raises Storms which work such havock upon the Earth? [5] For my part, it is what I shall never be persuaded of, and I doubt not but *Homer* would not be a little surprized, was he to come into the World and know all that is attributed to him; in truth, would he cry out in the Words of the ingenious Author of *The Dialogues of the Dead* [6] I was suspicious enough that some People of wonderful Penetration, would discover things that never came into my head: As it requires no great Cunning to make a Prophecy which some time or other shall hit on an Event, so it is a mighty easy thing to make a Fable that may chance to be turned to an ingenious Allegory. And if he should be ask'd, whether it was really so that he had wrapped up deep Mysteries in his Works, he would ingenuously acknowledge, he had not thought upon it; but, that knowing there was a strong Sympathy between Truth and Falshood, and that the Mind of Man does not always seek after Truth, he thought fit to borrow the Disguise of Fiction, to make Truth be the more relished. It is no new thing to make Authors speak what they never thought; and if we must have recourse to Allegories, all we shall learn from it is, according to the Remark of a learned Modern,[7] that the first Inhabitants of *Greece* made their whole Wisdom consist in expressing trivial things in a very obscure manner. Who knows not that Rain makes the Earth prolifick? And yet according to Patrons of Allegory, they could not tell us this, till of the Earth and Air they had made their *Jupiter* and *Juno,* whom they afterwards came to worship as Gods. The Ancients proceeded in a way of honest Simplicity; as they knew little about Virtue and Vice, when they reckoned their first Kings among their Gods, they recorded their Actions good or bad, as formerly; and after representing *Jupiter* striking the *Titans* with Thunder, they transformed him to a Goat, or a Satyr, to ensnare simple Shepherdesses.

(from Book I, Chap. 2, pp. 20–24)

Division of the Fables

I find among the Poets six kinds of Fables;[8] Historical, Philosophical, Allegorical, Moral, Mix'd, or invented merely for the sake of the Fable.

The first are ancient Histories, mix'd with several Fictions; such are those which speak of *Hercules, Jason,* &c. instead of telling us in the simple way, that the latter went to recover the Treasures which *Phrixus* had carried to *Colchis,* they have given us the Fable of the Golden Fleece.

The Philosophical Fables are those which the Ancients invented as apt Parables to wrap up the Mysteries of their Philosophy; as when the Ocean is said to be the Father of the Rivers; the Moon to have married the Air, and become the Mother of the Dew.

The allegorical were likewise Parables where some Mystical Sense lay concealed, as that in *Plato* about *Porus* and *Penia,* or Riches and Poverty, whose Offspring was Pleasure.

The Moral Fables are those they have contrived for the conveyance of some Precepts of Morality, as that which tells us[9] *Jupiter* sends the Stars upon this Earth in the day-time, to take notice of the Actions of Men: so the Fables of *Aesop,* and in general all Apologues.

There are also mix'd Fables, which are made up of Allegory and Morality, but have nothing Historical, such is the Fable of *Até,* related by *Homer.*[10] *Até,* according to this Poet, was *Jupiter's* Daughter; her Name marks her Character, and her Inclinations; accordingly she thought upon nothing but doing mischief. Odious as she was to Gods and Men, *Jupiter* seized her by the Hair of the Head, and threw her down head-long from the height of Heaven, whither he made an Oath she should never enter more.

'Tis easy to see the Poet, under this Fable, design'd to represent the proneness we have to Evil, or Evil itself, under an Allegorical Figure; for having describ'd this mischievous Imp, who, according to him, traverses the whole Earth, with an incredible Celerity, doing all the mischief in her power; he adds that her Sisters, likewise *Jupiter's* Daughters, whom he calls *litai, Prayers,* come always after her to repair, as far as lies in their power, the Evil done by her; but being lame, they move far slower than their Sister: as much as to say, Men are always more forward to sin, and more in earnest, than when they exercise Repentance, and make Reparation.

The Fables invented merely for the sake of Fable, have no other end, but to divert, as that of *Psyche*[11] and what we call the *Milesian* Tales, and those of the *Sybarites.*

Fables of the Historical kind, are easily distinguished, because mention is made in them of People we know elsewhere. Such as are composed for Amusement are likewise easy to be discovered, by the ridiculous Stories they tell of unknown Persons. The Sense of the Moral and Allegorical Fables is obvious; as for the Philosophical ones, they are full of Prosopopoeias that animate Nature: There Earth and Air are hid under the borrowed Names of *Jupiter* and *Juno.*

Generally speaking there are very few Fables in the ancient Poets, but contain some Passages of History; it is only they that came after that have added to them Circumstances of pure Invention. When *Homer,* for example, says,[12] *Aeolus* gave *Ulysses* the Winds shut up in a Bag, whence his Companions let them out; this is a cover'd Piece of History, which informs us that this Prince foretold *Ulysses* what Wind was to blow for some days, and that the Shipwreck he suffer'd, was owing entirely to his neglecting to follow his Counsel. But when *Virgil* adds,[13] that the same *Aeolus,* at *Juno's* Request, raised a terrible Storm, which drove *Aeneas's* fleet upon the Coast of *Africa,* it is a mere Fable founded upon the Opinion of *Aeolus's* being God of the Winds. Those

Fables too which we have called Philosophical were at first Historical, and it was after their invention they were join'd with the Idea of natural Things: Hence those mix'd Fables, if we may so call them, comprehending an Historical Fact, and a Piece of Natural Philosophy, like that of *Myrrha* and *Leucothoe,* changed into the Tree that bears Frankincense, and that of *Clytia* into the *Heliotrope.* . . .

(from Book I, Chap. 3, pp. 30–32)

NOTES

Some of Banier's footnotes give Latin quotations to reinforce points in the text, or give the Latin which the text translates: these notes have not been included. The following are Banier's reference notes.—Ed.

1. See M. le Clerc Bibl. chois. Tom. 2.
2. Notae in Strabon lib. 1.
3. St. Augustin, after the ancient Poets.
4. Sallust. L. de Diis & Mundo.
5. Eusebius after Plutarch explains it in this manner.
6. Dialogue of Homer and Es.
7. M. le Clerc.
8. The word for Fable in Greek is *mythos,* as much as to say, Discourse by way of Eminence.
9. Plaut. Prol. de Rud.
10. Iliad. 19.
11. See Apuleius's *Golden Ass.*
12. Odys. 1. 10.
13. Aen. 1. 1.

NICOLAS FRÉRET

[1688–1749]

NICOLAS FRÉRET, the eminent scholar and perpetual secretary of the *Académie des Inscriptions et Belles-Lettres* from 1742 until his death in 1749, was a man of considerable reputation in his own time. He openly challenged Newton's revision of chronology, he dominated French antiquarian scholarship during the first half of the eighteenth century, and Frank Manuel has called him "by far the most sophisticated mythologist" of the same period. Fréret came early to myth studies; at the age of sixteen he was compiling a mythological dictionary for his own use; at nineteen he was preparing discourses on topics in Greek mythology and religion. Admitted to the *Académie* in 1714, he was almost at once committed to the Bastille for reading a paper containing unorthodox opinions of the French people. Incredible as it now sounds, Fréret was jailed for arguing that the French were originally a league of south German tribes and not a nation of free men derived from Greece or Troy. After his release, while taking care to avoid a repetition of this incident, he produced a remarkable amount of work during a long life of active scholarship. Almost all his work was done for, presented to, and printed by the *Académie*, which enjoyed during the first half of the century a widely recognized eminence in mythological scholarship. Fontenelle, Fourmont, Banier, and Pluche also belonged to the *Académie* and its

characteristic tone was one of urbane, learned, and Christian Euhemerism.

Fréret himself had broader interests than most of his colleagues, writing a great many dissertations on chronology, on grammar, on philosophy, on history, on religion, on mythology, and on geography. (His interest in the last of these produced some thirteen hundred and fifty-seven maps found among his papers.) In chronology, he refuted Newton, he upheld the Mosaic time scheme, and he reconciled Chinese history to the biblical account. Well-known and highly esteemed during his lifetime, Fréret yet left remarkably little impress on later scholarship. For one thing, his work, with the exception of the *Défense de la chronologie . . . contre le système chronologique de M. Newton,* and with the further exception noted before, was printed only in the *Recueil de l'Académie des Inscriptions et Belles-Lettres,* and much of it, even there, was imperfectly edited. Moreover, after Fréret's death, Holbach and his friends wrote and circulated under Fréret's name quite a few clever and subtle antireligious and atheist works, among them the *Lettre de Thrasibule à Leucippe, La Moïsade,* and the *Examen critique des apologistes de la religion chrétienne*—all of which, along with others, were printed and reprinted as the *Oeuvres philosophiques de Fréret.* Later editions of Fréret's real works did little to restore his reputation, and the clever

forgeries of the atheists were more admired than the sober and scholarly work
of the academician. Fréret has thus never
had the place he deserves in assessments
of early eighteenth-century thought.

In one regard, however, Fréret's sane
eclectic ideas about myth and his sober
assessment of the historical and scholarly
problems involved have had great influence, though not under Fréret's name.
For if Holbach and others used Fréret's
name for their own work, the Chevalier
de Jaucourt used his own name for
Fréret's work. Jaucourt simply took the
opening of Fréret's essay on "Mythology,
or the Religion of the Greeks," which we
reprint below, and printed it as the article
on "Mythologie" in Diderot's famous and
vastly influential *Encyclopédie.*

As it appears in the *Encyclopédie,* the
article commences with a few brief remarks that define mythology as a branch
of history, of religion, and of literature,
and that claim that a knowledge of mythology is part of any "common education." The article then reprints Fréret's
general essay on mythology in exactly
the same form as it appears in the
Septchênes edition of Fréret's works (and
as printed below). Jaucourt finished by
appending a few remarks, presumably
his own, directed against mythographers
of narrow persuasions; Pluche is named
and Fourmont is referred to but not
named. The article concludes with a
paragraph, lifted from the Abbé Banier's
work, about how each specialist finds
myth centrally involved in that very
specialty. The last sentence refers the
reader to Banier's ideas as set forth in
the article "Fable" and to Fréret's "more
profound" works in the *Recueil de
l'Académie des Inscriptions et Belles-
Lettres.* The wide influence enjoyed by
the *Encyclopédie* during the second half
of the eighteenth century, especially in
liberal circles, means that Fréret's per-
ceptive and broad-minded approach, his
scholarly sanity, reached, finally, the

whole generation after him, even if
Fréret himself was never given the credit.

In the fields of religion, myth, and
chronology, Fréret wrote on Bellerophon,
on the Cyclops, on Bacchus, and on
Ceres, as well as writing more general
pieces, such as his *Réflexions générales
sur l'étude de l'ancienne histoire.* Fréret
is sometimes thought of as a subtle and
broad-minded Euhemerist, and his *Sur
les fondemens historiques de la fable de
Bellerophon,* for example, bears this out.
Fréret is also, however, reckoned among
the anti-Euhemerists, not because he espoused allegorism or some other clear-cut
alternative doctrine, but because he was
so fully aware of the magnitude and complexity of the problems presented by Euhemerists and by other simplistic interpretations. Indeed, Fréret's ideas seem
to have changed during his career, and
one can cite him either for or against
Euhemerism. The piece reprinted here—
which Jaucourt had the good taste to
select—emphasizes quite frankly the
second of these positions: it shows Fréret
clearly skeptical of Euhemerizing, and
trying to broaden it or even replace it
with what for his time was a remarkably
advanced idea—that myth considered in
its largest sense is indeed a kind of history of human culture.

Thus Fréret acknowledges the charm
of myth, he is willing to concede that it
is a "world" and that it entices or even
compels belief, and he is far from the
scornful attitude of the deists or the
skepticism of the Encyclopedists. Fréret
finds myth attractive, and thus is no
longer compelled to reduce its stories or
to historicize its heroes. Indeed Fréret is
keenly and overtly aware of the limitations of Euhemerism, a method that he
castigates by name and that he sees clearly
to be the prevailing trend of his times.
His own concept of myth emerges as he
speaks about the function of myth criticism. Rather than seeking a narrow or
even a specific base for each fable or

myth, Fréret argues that fable or my-thology as a whole should be approached as an introduction to ancient history, broadly conceived.

Fréret thus hopes to find in myth the temper of the Greek mind, and it is im-portant that he is more interested in the Greek mind than in modern primitive mentality. Fréret is in fact interested in myth for its own sake, and thus is not obliged to cut it to suit Christianity, deism, atheism, or any rigid point of view. Indeed Fréret's hope that fable will lead us into what is best in Greek thought and culture sounds oddly modern, not only in its humanistic breadth of outlook but also in its insistence on a sense of the past, an insistence not often found in eighteenth-century studies of myth.

Fréret describes myth finally as "a formless irregular body" of stories, a mix-ture of "the dreams, of the imagination, the visions of philosophy, and the debris of ancient history," and he is one of the first modern students of myth to fully grasp the enormous range of problems that beset the mythologist. In long cata-logues, he recites the difficulties, the forces that work against clarity and order in myths, and he is alert to historical complexity as he is to the complexity of the human mind and the vagaries of scholarship. Here, at least, Fréret ex-hibits just the opposite of the reductionist mentality, and if the great French scholar offers no clear and simple solution to the vast problems of myth, he at least faces the subject squarely, takes full account of the problems, and entertains the whole spectrum of possible approaches and in-terpretations. No better proof could be brought forward to show that along with an enlightenment tendency to simplify and to reduce, some men were beginning to realize the tremendous importance of religious and mythic subjects and were beginning to face them solidly. After Fréret, it becomes much more difficult for the serious theorist of myth to advance a simple solution. Little remembered and less honored, Fréret's assessment of the problem forms an important part of the base of modern work on myth.

R.R.

REFERENCES   The text is our translation from *Oeuvres Complètes de Fréret,* ed. de Sept-chênes (Paris, 1796), 20 vols. There is much confusion in textual and bibliographic matters relating to Fréret. During his lifetime, his work appeared only in the *Recueil de l'Académie des Inscriptions,* often in reported form (phrases such as "M. Fréret nous a dit" appear frequently). Jaucourt presumably worked from the *Recueil.* The one-volume *Oeuvres philosophiques de Fréret,* containing the *Let-tre de Thrasibule à Leucippe,* the *Examen critique des apologistes de la religion chré-tienne, La Moïsade,* etc., appears to be wholly spurious, the pieces having been written by Holbach, Levesque de Burigny, and others. The Septchênes edition is apparently defective, and was to be replaced by a new edition by Champollion-Figeac, but only one volume of this appeared in 1825.

A recent and very helpful study is Renée Simon, *Nicolas Fréret Académicien* (Geneva: Institute et Musée Voltaire, 1961). See also Otto Gruppe, *Geschichte der klassischen My-thologie und Religionsgeschichte* (Leipzig: Teubner, 1921), pp. 69–72, and Frank Manuel, *Isaac Newton Historian* (Cambridge: Harvard University Press, 1963), p. 286.

FRÉRET

FROM *Mythology; or the Religion of the Greeks*

THE STUDY of Greek mythology and at least a superficial knowledge of its innumerable fictions, which are taken to be the history of heroic times, are necessary to poets, to painters, and generally to all those whose object is to embellish nature and to please the imagination. Fable is the patrimony of the arts; it is an inexhaustible source of ingenious ideas, pleasing images, interesting subjects, allegories, and emblems, and the more or less happy use of these depends upon taste and genius. Everything moves, everything breathes in this enchanted world, where intellectual beings have bodies, where material things are animated, where the fields, the forests, the rivers, the elements, all have their particular divinities. These are chimerical personages indeed, but the role they play in the works of the ancient poets and in the frequent allusions of modern poets has made them almost real to us. We take them so much for granted that we can hardly regard them as imaginary beings. We persuade ourselves that their history is the distorted picture of the events of the first age. We try to find in it a continuity, a connection, a truth that it doesn't have. Criticism thinks it enough to strip facts of this sort of their often absurd and miraculous air, and to sacrifice details to preserve the foundation. Having reduced the gods to

the simple rank of heroes and the heroes to the rank of men, criticism thinks itself entitled to maintain their historical existence although it is easy to prove that of all the gods of paganism, Hercules, Castor, and Pollux are the only ones who were truly men. Euhemerus, author of this hypothesis which saps the foundations of popular religion while seeming to explain it, had even in antiquity a great number of partisans, and the great majority of the moderns has ranged itself with his opinion. Almost all our mythologists, scarcely in agreement with one another as regards the explication of detail, are united in favor of a principle which the majority suppose is incontestable. It is the common point from which they depart, and their systems, despite the differences which separate them, are all edifices built on the same base with the same materials differently combined. Everywhere we see Euhemerism dominant, expatiated upon in a more or less plausible manner.

We must admit that this reduction of the marvelous to the natural is one of the keys of Greek mythology, but this key is neither the only one nor the most important. The Greeks, says Strabo (X, 474), were in the habit of proposing ideas that they had, not only on physics and on other objects related to nature and to philosophy but also on the facts of their former history, under the veil of fables and allegories.

This passage indicates one essential difference among the diverse sorts of fictions that form the body of fable. It follows from this that some have a connection with the general physical world, that others express metaphysical ideas by sensible images; that, finally, several preserve some traces of early traditions. Those of this third class were the only historical ones, and they are the only ones that sane criticism should be allowed to link with the known facts of earlier times. Criticism can and must reestablish order in this field, seek in it a strict connection conforming to what we know for certain or in all likelihood about the origins and mingling of peoples; and disentangle the essence from foreign circumstances which have tainted it from age to age, and, in a word, see it as an introduction to the history of antiquity. The stories of this class have their own character, which distinguishes them from those whose basis is mystagogic or philosophical. The latter, a confused assemblage of marvels and absurdities, should be relegated to the chaos from which the spirit of system has tried vainly to retrieve them. These can, from there, furnish images and allegories to the poets. Moreover, the spectacle that they offer to our reflections, bizarre though it be, instructs us even by its strangeness. We can follow in them the progress of the human spirit; we discover the temper of the national genius of the Greeks. They possessed the art of imagining, the talent for painting, and the good fortune of being able to feel, but through a deranged love of themselves and of the marvelous, they abused these happy gifts of nature. Vain, indulgent, voluptuous, and credulous, they

accepted at the expense of morality and reason all that would authorize license, flatter pride, and let loose metaphysical speculations. The nature of polytheism, tolerant in its essence, permitted the introduction of foreign cults, and soon these cults, naturalized in Greece, were incorporated into the old rites. Their dogmas and practices, confused with each other, formed a whole whose parts, originally in little agreement, could be reconciled only through explanations and alterations on both sides. Their combinations, everywhere arbitrary and subject to innumerable variations, took various forms, multiplied endlessly according to place, circumstances, and interests. The successive revolutions in the different provinces of Greece, the mingling of the population, the diversity of their origins, their trade with foreign nations, the ignorance of the people, the fanaticism and foolishness of the priests, the subtlety of the metaphysicians, the caprice of the poets, the mistakes of the etymologists, the hyperbole so frequent among enthusiasts of all sorts, the singularity of ceremonies, the secrecy of the mysteries, the illusion of enchantment, all had a detrimental influence on the core, on the form, on all the branches of mythology. It was an indefinite but immense and fertile field, open to all, and claimed by everyone, where everyone leapt into action at will with no subordination, with no harmony, with none of the mutual understanding that produces uniformity. Each country, each province had its gods, its errors, its religious practices, as it had its own laws and customs. The same god changed names, attributes, and functions in changing temples; he lost in one city what he had usurped in another. So many diverse opinions, circulating from place to place, perpetuating themselves from century to century, collided, mingled, separated to reunite later on; and sometimes in agreement and sometimes opposed, they arranged themselves interchangeably in thousands upon thousands of different ways; just as the multitude of atoms that are spread out in the void distribute themselves, according to Epicurus, in all kinds of bodies to be composed, organized, and destroyed by chance.

This picture, in which every line could easily be justified by a multitude of examples, is sufficient to show that one must not treat mythology too closely as history; that to attempt to find facts everywhere in it, and facts connected and surrounded by probable circumstances, would be to substitute a new historical system for the one transmitted to us from the earliest age of Greece, by writers such as Herodotus and Thucydides, witnesses who when they set down the antiquities of their nations are more trustworthy than modern mythologists, who are uncritical and tasteless compilers on the one hand, and on the other, poets whose privilege it is to pretend without intending to deceive.

Mythology is not in the least a whole composed of corresponding parts; it is a formless irregular body, but pleasing in its details; it is the confused mixture of the dreams of the imagination, the visions of philosophy, and the debris of ancient history. Analysis of it is impossible; at least one will never arrive at a sufficiently skilful dissection as to be in a position to lay bare the origin of each legend, still less the origin of all the details of which each legend is an assemblage. The Theogony of Hesiod and Homer is the basis on which the theologians of paganism, that is, the priests, poets, and philosophers, have always worked. But by overweighting the foundation, and disfiguring it even in embellishing it, they have rendered it unrecognizable; and as with all monuments, we cannot determine with precision what Fable owes to this or that poet particularly, what of it belongs to such or such a people, such or such an age.

THOMAS BLACKWELL

[1701–1757]

DURING the early eighteenth century the historical and imaginative image of myth remained decisively confined to classical antiquity. Outside sacred history, earliest history itself necessarily meant mainly classical sources. And what was known "historically" about classical myth funneled completely backward, not to living rites or cults of Greek or Egyptian religion, long vanished, but rather to what was preserved about mythic beliefs and practices in certain Greek texts. Traditionally, the oldest of these was Homer. Pope expressed merely a prevalent view when he declared Homer the "oldest writer in the world except Moses," the emphasis here falling on "writer." Any change therefore in the view of Homer, the ultimate recorded cornerstone of the mythic tradition, implied the most serious change for all mythology, past and present. Indeed, the oldest major rationalist interpretations of myth—such as the Euhemerist or allegorical interpretations —arose from an awareness that Homer's gods and heroes could hardly be taken at face value. In the early eighteenth century, the Homeric problem again becomes urgent; and like the attack on the authority of the Bible, a similar "higher criticism" is launched against Homer. The most radical and influential revaluation of Homer emerges first in Thomas Blackwell's *An Enquiry into the Life and Writings of Homer* (1735).

In Blackwell's achievement, a whole series of related eighteenth-century prob-lems receives comprehensive treatment and solution. The initial question Blackwell sets as the theme of his Homer book is nothing less than a resume of a whole literary and philosophic dispute of the time: How does it happen that "none have equalled him [Homer] in Epic-Poetry for two thousand seven hundred years, the Time since he wrote; Nor any, that we know, ever surpassed him before"? By the late seventeenth century, there was a growing sense that Homer was perhaps alien to the modern scientific, rational—not to mention Christian —spirit. The question was much argued, particularly in the famous Ancients and Moderns quarrel, whether Homer was a poet of genuinely universal qualities or mainly reflected a distant, rude, dawning, even savage age. In part, the issue was of vulgarity versus refinement, or more seriously, of civilization versus barbarism, or more seriously still, of whether modernity might claim superiority over antiquity in the largest sense—in refinement of civilization, progress of moral life, and advancement of knowledge. The modern claim could be supported in two ways: first, by positive achievement undeniably surpassing that of the ancients, exemplified in Galileo and Newton; or second, by a negative critique of antiquity, aimed at undermining its claims to universal significance. This latter approach had already been launched against Christianity, emphasizing the narrowness and merely "local" truths of the Bible, or the dependence on a special historical moment and special revelation. But Christian and even Scriptural history was more accessible than that of the earliest times; and a successful historical critique of Homer required more accurate knowledge of antiquity than the eighteenth century in fact commanded. By Blackwell's time, classical philology—indispensable to a correct view of Homer—was hardly founded: Richard Bentley had indeed discovered the existence of the Greek digamma, which (in J. L. Myres's words) was "the first direct proof that within the limits of the literary tradition the Greek language had been undergoing change, and had in fact an historical perspective." But Bentley's discoveries remained unfruitful until taken up by German philology more than fifty years later. Before 1735, the English especially had been avid but amateur collectors of classical specimens; there were numerous travel reports from the East, Near East, Greece, and Egypt; the French *Académie des Inscriptions et Belles-Lettres* was a center for classical and oriental studies; only in 1734 was the Society of Dilettanti organized in England to support travel, scholarly exploration, and publication; and the first modern excavations began at Herculaneum in 1738 and in Pompeii in 1748.

To the historical inquiry into classical antiquity Blackwell brought remarkable philological gifts: by the age of twenty-three, he had been appointed a Professor of classics in the University of Aberdeen. Beyond this, he possessed a philologic rigor missing in the Ancients-Moderns dispute, in the speculations of Fontenelle, or in the Pyrrhonic erudition of Bayle. Blackwell's approach to Homer, as he summarizes it in his *Letters concerning Mythology* (1748), is also a model of the new analytic-rationalist method: to understand, one must analyze back to the "first beginnings" or causes or origins, and then scientifically reconstruct the chain of causes and effects. Blackwell im-

mediately sets aside any "supernatural" explanation for Homer's greatness (as, say, the Muses), which the ancients believed, "tho' *We* do not." Then, he analyzes the art of poetry itself into its constituent parts—into language, manners, religion, rhythm, or history. Having established the basic elements, his next move is to see how all these elements combined in Greece during Homer's time and in Homer himself.

It would be misleading to think that Blackwell's book is as dry as his method here reported: he is remarkably lively, insightful, polemic, and even witty. But in pursuing this method, Blackwell may seem entirely a champion of the modernist assault on Homer, for much of the modern denigration of Homer had also emphasized the historical "particulars" in his poems, all detracting from his universality. Blackwell's Homer is an unsurpassed epic poet precisely because of a singular concatenation of fortunate particulars hardly ever likely to be repeated. Homer appeared during that exact moment in Greek history when the older heroic ways had not yet disappeared, and before debilitating decline had set in—a moment poised between the simplicity of the past and the sophistication and decline pressing in later on Greek life. Homer's life thus coincided with an age of variety and excitement, where violence, heroism, and isolation still mingled with peace, civil order, domestic virtue, and freedom. Moreover, in his personal life Homer combined just the right elements: literary genius; poverty, which forced him to travel widely as a bard; travel, by which he came to know life most extensively; and an education in composition and entertaining, useful for a bard. (Blackwell can often sound like a romantic exhorting the artist to seek life as widely, as intensely, and as nakedly as possible.)

The result of his portrait is to deny that another epic poet can arise to surpass Homer, since poets are tied to their ages, and the Homeric age cannot again appear. The growth and decline of poetry is tied strictly to the growth and decline of the poet's nation. Greece passed, in turn, from savagery to an era filled with labor, commerce, and civility, but also still with piracy and violence; thence to Periclean glory, and finally to decline. The Greek language follows the same progress: from monosyllables uttered out of strong passion, to a refined flexible speech, to effeteness; while manners similarly move from brutishness to usefulness to refinement and then overrefinement. Homer was probably born toward the end of the second of these stages, able to look back to the not-yet vanished beginnings of the world but also forward to high sophistication—without the disadvantage of either alone. Since Homer's time, however, civilization has risen decisively. And the same country cannot be civilized and still furnish adequate subjects for great poetry: ". . . a People's Felicity clips the Wings of their Verse." Milton succeeded best in *Paradise Lost*: he had the good luck (as an epic poet) to live through the Civil War, and he had the genius to ignore over-polished modern manners.

Left at this, however, Blackwell can seem primarily a superb critic unusually sensitive to the infinity of causes—historical, biographical, psychological, natural, political, and accidental—comprising a great poet or poetic age. But he may also seem to end up devastating any claim that poetry is timeless. And Blackwell's admirers have often enough suggested that his originality of insight lies in a critical analysis pushed almost to outright historical relativism.

But it may fairly be argued that to see Blackwell as reducing all literary universality to a flux of historical particulars utterly distorts his own intentions. His own purpose seems just the opposite: to combat the kind of narrow rationalist reductionism he finds so popular in his age.

He is a remorseless and open antagonist of almost every famous rationalist mythologist in his time. All Euhemerists, such as Banier or Fourmont, who reduce the gods to mere men deified, are deemed foolishly complacent; Christian apologists, such as Bossuet, who affirm Euhemerism, are misguided or worse; the same holds for Bayle, who thinks he can dismiss myth by recounting its scandals. Against all materialists, skeptics, Cartesians, or Hobbists, Blackwell argues that mythology is a "vast and various Compound; a Labyrinth through whose Windings no one Thread can conduct us."

And yet, did not Blackwell do the same when he analyzed all poetry and Homer's age, life, and work back to their original causes in order to find the key to "Homer"? The fact is that Blackwell is an allegorical sheep in rationalist wolf's clothing: he uses rationalist methods, but not for rationalist purposes: he seeks to defend myth, not to demolish it. His chief aim is to redeem ancient myth from being thought "merely" historical: ". . . the early Fables were framed to convey a Doctrine which is not a mere Conjecture of the Moderns" nor of the ancients. Thus, Blackwell rejects Euhemerism precisely because it reduces myth to being only *"historical."* If Blackwell also uses the historical method, his tactic is to push the historical analysis as far as it will go in order to find out what in Homer is irreducibly universal and supra-historical. History can reveal the truth by showing what is false, but it can also bring us back to what is oldest, thus truest, holiest, and wisest. Thus, Blackwell insists that mythic wisdom comes earlier than mythic corruption. "Homer's Mythology is but little understood," he says, for few "consider his Divine Persons (i. e., Gods) in any other light, than as so many *groundless Fictions*." But the true old meaning of fable has been lost. To refute the narrow rationalistic view of myth as fiction, Blackwell praises Homer for imitating

"Nature." Nature here means two things: the immediate social, historical events and people before Homer's eyes; but also what is metaphysically true—that is, Nature in the divine sense. To see Homer as a narrow "realist" is absurd, and to search after naturalistic origins for his greatness is as absurd. When Blackwell talks of tracing what Homer knew back to the "beginnings," he means what Homer knew of the true beginnings of the cosmos, which means the theogony taught by the first poet, Orpheus. Homer is a disciple of Orpheus; and though he wrote later, Homer's allegories preserve an Orphism that is "the noblest and oldest remain of the pure Grecian liturgy." Indeed, all true poets are "Great Masters of Science," and are the true teachers and founders of politics, history, and philosophy. Poets are the teachers of mankind: their mythology helps tame and restrain men, permitting them to live together. Orpheus sang; and music soothes wild breasts. So poetry in its noblest form—that is, the allegories of mythology—will always have to lie, but nobly.

If poetry is conditioned by its age, the epic may no longer be possible. But Blackwell does not equate all poetry with mythology. Poetry may indeed be historically conditioned; but mythic poetry deals with what is ever unchanging and unchanged: "the primary *great Gods*" represent the "Natural Powers of the Universe." Blackwell reveals himself thus a Platonist, but a most balanced one. He warns against the "madness" that allegorists are prone to, like the Neoplatonists Iamblichus or Porphyry who fantasize about gaining magic or doing miracles, or those who, like Thomas Burnet, madly systematize similarities. Unlike other Platonists, too, Blackwell does not see mythology finally as a kind of prephilosophic raw material: he rejects Varro and Plutarch as too rationalistic and thus as missing the true heights of mythic wisdom.

What Blackwell is after would likely seem more familiar to those who come after him than to his contemporaries. Blackwell finally praises Homer for his great language and imagination, at once "simple and comprehensive." Homer is the master of the metaphor at its philosophic-poetic best: "A Metaphor is a general Pattern, which may be applied to many particulars: It is susceptible of an infinite number of Meanings; and reaches far, because of its Ambiguity." In such passages, Blackwell seems to presage what later minds, such as Coleridge, will say about poetry's reconciling of the abstract and concrete or the particular and universal. He divides mythologic thinking into two kinds—first, that which is artificial, rational, cool, scientific; and the other, "sudden and flashy; rapid Feelings, and Starts of Passion not in our power." The first can be taught, the other is a gift —but both may be improved by culture. Blackwell seeks to keep mythology from becoming only one or the other extreme. The true power of mythology demands reason and "starts of passion."

Blackwell's influence was great, as much on the German as on the English preromantics. He was admired by Robert Wood, Heyne, and Herder. Robert Chambers, Gerard, and James Beattie studied with him. William Duff, John Ogilvie, and James Macpherson knew him as students. Lord Monboddo admired him greatly. Blackwell's prestige as the foremost Homeric critic was finally rivalled or surpassed by Wood, and then by F. A. Wolf; but by then, Blackwell's larger critical position had helped form the climate for his successors.

B.F.

REFERENCES   Our texts are from *An Enquiry into the Life and Writings of Homer* (London, 1735); and, *Letters concerning Mythology* (London, 1748) (this work is by Blackwell and an unknown continuator). For commentary, see: Donald Foerster, *Homer in English Criticism: the Historical Approach in the Eighteenth Century* (New Haven: Yale University Press, 1947), for best general study. Lois Whitney, "Eighteenth-Century Primitivistic Theories of the Epic," MP, XXI (1924). Ernest Tuveson, *Millennium and Utopia: a study in the background of the idea of prog-* *ress* (Berkeley: University of California Press, 1949). Gerald W. Chapman, ed., *Literary Criticism in England 1660–1800* (New York: Knopf, 1966), p. 265 for Blackwell as literary critic. Rene Wellek, *Rise of English Literary History* (Chapel Hill: University of North Carolina Press, 1941), for Blackwell and other Scotch critics.

BLACKWELL

FROM *An Enquiry into the Life and Writings of Homer*

I SHALL soon have occasion to make a stricter Enquiry into the Origin both of the *Grecian Religion* and *Learning.* At present it is sufficient to say, that they came from the great Parent of *Sacred* and *Civil* Institutions, the Kingdom of *Egypt.* That wise People seem to have early observed the Curbs of the human Passions, and the Methods of governing a large Society. They saw the general Bent of Mankind, *to admire what they do not understand,* and to stand in awe of unknown Powers, which they fancy capable to do them great good or ill: They adapted their religious Belief and solemn Ceremonies, to this Disposition; made their Rites *mysterious,* and delivered their allegorical Doctrines under great Ties of profound and pious Secrecy. . . .

Hence the Number of monstrous Stories concerning their Gods, which the first *Grecian* Sages that travell'd into *Egypt* certainly understood, and explained to their Adepts, among whom, after some Descents, I reckon *Hesiod* and *Homer:* But falling afterwards into the hands of Men of warm Fancies, who thought they might *invent* as well as their Masters, there were many traditional Stories tacked to the former; sometimes untowardly enough, and sometimes so as to make a tolerable Piece of the *literal* Relation, but confounding when applied to the *Allegory.* These are all the *Hieroi Logoi* (*sacred Traditions*) mentioned so often by *Herodotus,* with a Declaration that he will not venture to publish them; and of the same kind is the *Theos Logos* (*the divine Tradition*) recommended by *Orpheus* to his favourite Scholar, and quoted by a primitive Father for another purpose.

This Allegorical Religion having been transplanted into *Greece,* found it a very proper Soil for such a Plantation. It took deep root in the Minds of the *Greeks,* who were grossly ignorant, and prepossessed with no rival Opinions: They made Additions to it of their own, and in a few Ages it was incorporated with their *Manners,* mixed itself with their Language, and gained *universal Belief.* "Such was its Condition when *Homer* made his Appearance in the World: It had attained its Vigour, and had not lost the Grace of *Novelty* and *Youth*." . . . (pp. 50–51)

In the early Ages of the *Grecian* State, the wild and barbarous Inhabitants wanted the Assistance of the Muses to soften and tame them. They stood in need of being impressed with an Awe of superior and irresistible Powers, and a liking to *social* Life. They wanted a *Mythology* to lead them by *Fear* and *Dread* (the only Holds to be taken of a rude Multitude) into a Feeling of *natural Causes,* and their *Influence* upon our Lives and Actions. The *Wise* and *Good* among the Ancients saw this Necessity, and supplied it. . . . They had *Religion* for their Theme and the *Service* of Mankind for the End of their Song. . . .

But the first Men of Science in *Greece,* better instructed in Human Nature, and knowing the Advantages of national Rites, wrote in a different Strain: The Formation of *Things,* the Birth of the *Gods,* their Properties and Exploits, first informed their Numbers: Next were celebrated the Heroes, who had extirpated *Tyrants,* destroyed *Monsters,* and subdued *Robbers.* They sung the Flood of *Deucalion,* and Reparation of *Mankind;* and Wars of the *Centaurs,* and the Fate of the *Giants.* . . .
(pp. 78–79)

While the *Policies* of *Greece* were yet but forming, *Assyria, Phoenicia,* and *Egypt* were mighty Kingdoms, flourishing under regular Governments, and happy in the Richness of their Soil, and their Methods of improving it. In a course of Years, the long Peace they enjoyed, and the *Arts* which such Times produce, having brought a great part of the Administration into the hands of the *Sacred Order,* they took all possible Methods to keep up their *Authority,* and aimed at nothing more than the raising their Reputation for Wisdom and Knowledge. *This* render'd them first envious of their *Discoveries,* and then at pains to find out Methods, "How to transmit them to their *Descendants,* without imparting them to the *Vulgar*." Here was the Origin of *Allegory* and *Parable;* and the Foundation of the received Saying among the Ancients. . . . *To allegorize is an* Egyptian *invention.* (p. 84)

These are some of the Men in whose hands the ancient *Mythology* and *Poetry* grew together. When I review them, I think it happy that *Hesiod's* noble Work has reached our Times. We should scarcely know else what to make of so many THE-OGONIAS, KOSMOPOIIAS, KOSMOGONIAS as we have enumerated: But from it we know, that the *Birth of the Gods,* the *Rise of Things,* and the *Creation of the World* are but reciprocal Terms, and in the ancient Stile stand for just the same thing. They were the common Theme of the first *Poets* and *Lawgivers,* (the earliest Philosophers) who by their several Improvements and Additions enabled *Hesiod* and *Homer,* their Successors, to give their Theology a *Body,* and reduce it to a Standard, that flourished while *Greece* was a free Country, and lasted some time after their Liberty was gone. . . .

Whoever knows any thing of the *Nature* of that kind of Writing, needs make but one Reflection, to be convinced that a THEOGONY is a Piece of *deep Learning,* and vast *Labour.* "It is *a System of the Universe, digested and wrought into an Allegory:* It is a Composition, made up of infinite Parts, each of which has been a Discovery by itself, and delivered as a *Mystery* to the initiated." The contriving and putting them together has been a Work of some Ages, and is a conjunct Effort of *Politicks* and *Philosophy.*

Neither, on the other hand, were *Hesiod* and *Homer* the *first* who learned Religion in *Egypt,* and brought it over Sea to *Greece.* A small Acquaintance with their Writings will convince any Man of Taste that they wrote from *Life;* and describe the Exercise of a Worship long since established in their Country. . . .

(pp. 97–98–99)

. . . *what kind* of Knowledge it was possible in *Homer's* days to acquire? It was wholly *fabulous* and *allegorical.* "The Powers of Nature, and Human Passions were the Subject; and they described their various Effects with some Analogy and Resemblance to *Human Actions.* They began with the *Rise* of Things, their Vicissitudes and Transformations, defined their Nature and Influence; and, in their metaphorical Stile, gave to each a *Person,* a *Speech,* and *Method* of *Operation,* conformable to their fancied *Qualities.*" This they called a *History of the Birth of the Gods;* of the *Heaven,* to wit, the *Earth, Air,* and *Sea;* of the *Sun, Moon,* and Divisions of the *Stars;* of the *Rivers, Woods, Rocks, Fountains,* and the other constituent Parts of the Universe.[1] They related their Loves and Hatreds; their Marriages, Disasters, Seditions, and Wars; or in other Terms, the *Struggles* of their opposite Natures, and the *Concord* arising from their *Equilibrium.* . . .

Such was the Science of the early Ancients; Nor is there any other kind of Learning to be met with in Homer. . . .

(p. 102)

. . . tho' it be very pleasant to trace the Likeness between the Customs of one Country, and those of another derived from them; to search into the Origin of the borrowed Rites, and the *natural* Foundation of the new *Mythology;* yet their Connexion is delicate, and the Perception of it generally *too fine,* to be turned into a direct Proof: It cannot be felt at all, without a nice Knowledge of the Mother-Country and of its Manners, as well as of their *moral Progeny.* . . . (p. 136)

I am very sensible, that *Homer's Mythology* is but little understood; or, to express it better, is *little felt:* and for this reason, the Effects of his *Egyptian* Education are lost upon the greater part of his Readers. There are but few who consider his *Divine Persons* in any other Light, than as so many *groundless Fictions,* which he made at pleasure, and might employ indifferently; giving to *Neptune,* for instance, the Work done by *Apollo,* and introducing *Venus* to perform what he now ascribes to *Minerva.* But it is mere want of Perception. His Gods are *all natural Feelings of the several Powers of the Universe:* or, as the Bishop of *Thessalonica* calls them . . . "*Shadowings, or Wrappers of noble Sentiments.*" They are not a Bundle of extravagant Stories; but the most delicate, and, at the same time, the most *majestick Method* of expressing the Effects of those natural Powers, which have the greatest Influence upon *our Bodies* and *Minds.* (p. 148)

Mythology, taken in the largest Sense, must be distinguished into two sorts: the one *abstracted* and *cool;* the Result of great Search and Science: "Being a Comparison of the Harmony and Discord, the Resemblance and Dissimilitude of the Powers and Parts of the *Universe.*" It often consists of their finest *Proportions* and hidden *Aptitudes* set together, and personated by a *Being* acting like a *Mortal.* "The other, sudden and flashy; rapid Feelings, and Starts of a Passion not in our power." The first of these may be called *artificial,* and the second *natural* Mythology; the one is a Science, and may be learned; and other is the Faculty that for the most part, if not always, invents and expresses it. This last cannot be learned; but like other natural Powers, admits of *Culture* and *Improvement*. "The Use I would make of such a Division is to observe, That *Homer* had the happiest Opportunities the World could give, to *acquire* the one, and *improve* the other."

It is but calling to mind his Climate and Parentage, his Education and Business, to be persuaded of the fair Chance he had for a *noble Capacity* and a proportioned *Culture*. They conspired to bless him with so powerful an Influence, that the sagacious *Democritus,* struck with admiration of his *Genius,* and its Effects, said in a happily invented word, *That it approached to Divinity.* And as for *acquired* Knowledge in the *mythological* way, had he been to range over the Globe, He could have pitched upon no Country, in any Age before or since, so proper for his Instruction as the *then Kingdom of* Egypt.

In Egypt he might learn their Doctrine concerning the *Origin* of Things; he wou'd be informed of the *Antiquity of* Pan and the *Inventions of* Thoth: He wou'd hear their Statute-Songs and legal Hymns, handed down for thousands of Years, and containing the Principles of their primitive *Theology:* The Nature of the *Elements,* the Influences of the *Planets,* the Course of the *Year,* and the Instincts of *Animals.* How attentively would he listen to the *Songs* of their *Goddess?*—the Compositions of the beneficent Isis,[2] who, while on Earth, condescended thus to employ the *Muses,* and prescribe the *Form* in which she would be worshipped after she was gone? These he would imbibe; and like some young *Druid* come over from *Gaul* to study under the *British Priests,* the senior Doctors of their oral Mysteries, He wou'd return to his Country *fully instruc-*

ted, and a Master in their *emblematical Mythology.*

Never was there a People so addicted to *Metaphor* and *Allusion:* Their very *Method of Writing* or *Sacred Sculpture,* was a complete and standing System of *Natural Simile's.*   (pp. 167–169)

The *Veil of Fable* is of such surprising Virtue, that it *magnifies* the Objects which it covers: It shows them in a grander Light, and invites the Eye to contemplate them more eagerly than if they were open and undisguised. To *Vulgar* Eyes it is dark and impenetrable, while it speaks plainly to the *Wise,* yet sometimes amends is made even where it *hides;* for if you see not the real Object, it presents you with some *Species* or *Appearance* in its stead, which, tho' not so instructive, is perhaps as entertaining as the Reality. Homer came into the World at a proper *distance of Time,* after the Expedition which he sung; not too near it, when *naked Truth,* and the severe Appearance of known Facts, might quash Enthusiasm, and render Ornaments ridiculous; but when the Circumstances of the Story had sufficient time to *ripen into Fable,* or at least be susceptible of it, from a skilful hand.

His *Manner* of writing must therefore be taken into the Account. A *Metaphor* is a *general Pattern,* which may be applied to many Particulars: It is susceptible of an infinite number of Meanings; and reaches far, because of its Ambiguity. It leads, as we found before, even to *Madness;* and wantonly ranges the Corners of the World for Comparisons to fit its fancied Properties. This way of treating a Subject must render it still more general, and when joined with the Truth of *Description,* will account for the Mysteries in *Homer's* Writings.

But how wonderful a thing is it to be able to *join* these Extremes? To speak in the simplest and most *comprehensive* manner: To soar so high, and stoop so low, as to follow Nature minutely, and at the same time fill the Images with *Expression* and *Majesty*. And yet the greatest Objections against our Poet, arise from the *too* *great Truth* of his Descriptions; and from his representing his Heroes in those *natural Lights* which we think below the Politeness of our Manners. They have been frequently answered; and here, their very *Foundation* turns out to the Honour of the Poet, and proves the grand Ornament of his Performance. . . .   (pp. 326–328)

FROM *Letters concerning Mythology*

THE WHOLE Book [i. e., his *Enquiry into the Life and Writings of Homer*] therefore is an Attempt to resolve this Single Question, *"By what means did* Homer *become a greater Poet, than either anyone, known to us, ever was before him, or than any who has appeared since his Time?* Or in other Words, *Why no Poem either formerly heard of, or now extant, was or is comparable to the* Iliad *and* Odyssey?"

In order to resolve it, you must either ascribe his Superiority to a supernatural divine Assistance, which many of the Ancients firmly believed, tho' *We* do not; or, allowing him to have been an ordinary Man, you must enquire into every *Cause*, natural or accidental, that can possibly have Influence upon the human Mind, towards forming it to Poetry and Verse. You must consider the Influence of Education, of Example, of Fortune public and private upon the Soul of Man, and as you go along you must always compare their different Kinds, and apply them to the various corresponding Branches of Poetry. You must trace that Art from its earliest Beginnings; separate its constituent Parts, *Language, Manners, Religion, Fable, History, Characters, Rythmus, Measure,* and proper *Mythology.* You must view and ascertain the abstract Nature of each of these Parts, then trace its Progress, and compare that again with the Age of *Homer,* and enquire How *He* came to excel in it, and in what respects he does so. To bring all these together, and make them bear upon a *single Point,* was a Task inseparable from the *Answer* of the Question. A Question which you see must necessarily include a surprizing number of different Researches into the Nature and Origin of *Fiction,* and its Connexion with the various, indeed almost infinite Turns of Life and Learning. . . .   (pp. 36–37)

You ask first, whether the Meanings we ascribe to ancient Fables, be not for the most part *Conjectures* of the Moderns, who admire every thing that is ancient, merely because it is so, and torture their Brains to find out Meanings and Mysteries which the Authors or their Contemporaries never thought of? Let me answer you by another Question, *Can you now believe it?* Can you read a Fable of *Aesop,* and imagine it means nothing? No more can you now read one of the old Fictions, without looking for the moral or natural Lesson latent in the wondrous Tale. Take our great Lord *Bacon's* little Book *De*

Sapientia Veterum, read it coolly, and disbelieve if you can. But to answer more directly; I say they are not mere modern Inventions, but what a very learned Writer[1] wou'd fain persuade us of Tradition, "That by its means *a Body of Religion* is preserved in the holy Catholic Church independent of written Records," holds true in the learned World; a Body of mythological Doctrine having been preserved from the earliest Ages until now, and handed down from Generation to Generation, varied indeed like its Betters, according to the Run of the Times, but still retaining enough of its original Purity to free it from the Suspicion of a Counterfeit. . . .

(pp. 186–187)

. . . *That the early Fables were framed to convey a Doctrine which is not a mere Conjecture of the Moderns.*

You ask next, Whether there be not many of the ancient Fictions we do not now understand at all? Some I believe there are into whose Meaning we have not yet penetrated—; not very many; owing in the first place to the *Corruption* of the pure genuine Mythology, which stript it of all Meaning, and of which you are now sufficiently apprised; and next, to the Secret Rites at *Initiations,* so carefully kept from unhallowed Eyes, but which yet daily clear up. There remain but few Parts of Antiquity upon which the Sagacity and Labours of the Learned have not poured new Light: Rites and Doctrines before unintelligible are by degrees explained; and lately, a very learned and lively Writer, in attempting to demonstrate the divine Legation of *Moses*[2] from an uncommon Topic, has taught us, *en passant,* how the Ancients veiled their solemn Lessons of Immortality and a future State. It is certain that Mythology, as it now stands, is not to be understood without a wide and accurate Knowledge of the *religious Rites* of the several Nations from whom the *Greeks* received their Gods; because upon some significant Ceremony concerning the Nature, or traditional Tale concerning the Exploits of the Divinity depends the Key to the Legend, and sometimes the very *Name* of the God himself. As the early *Egyptian* Rites were all established by Law, were all recorded, were all typical and symbolical, the Type or Symbol came by an easy Transition, not only to signify obscurely, but directly to express the Thing typified: a grand Source of Error and Incertainty in the Foundation of the Allegory! . . . (pp. 189–190)

. . . But we cou'd never have been thoroughly satisfied of the real Rise of that Rite without the *original Tradition.* There are many Customs both in sacred and civil matters, now prevailing over the World that are upon the same uncertain Footing. Mankind in this respect are excessively docile, shall I say, or stupid. A Rite once received is carefully kept up, and even spreads, when the Reasons of its Institution have been long forgot, or are quite unknown. . . . (p. 195)

When therefore nothing but the *Rite* remains, whether preserved by stupid Practice, or barely recorded in History, and the Tradition is lost, that shou'd explain it, no wonder the Allegory shou'd be dark, and continue a proper Subject for critical Conjectures. But this, as I said, is not often the Case: Symbols carry natural Marks that strike a sagacious Mind, and lead it by degrees to their real Meaning. A Hint in one Author brightens the Obscurities in many others; as one single Observation of *Macrobius* proved the Clew to *Abbé Pluche,* how justly I say not, to unravel the whole Mystery of the *Egyptian, Assyrian* and *Grecian* Gods: Nay, the very

Ruin of the ancient Rites has contributed not a little to their Illustration. How little soever it may seem plausible at first view, it is very certain that the *Roman Constitution,* for instance, cou'd never have been so accurately learned from *Roman* Authors, (who took no care to explain what everybody knew as well as themselves) as from the knowing polite *Foreigners,* who lived at *Rome,* and wrote, not for *Romans,* but for the Instruction of their own ingenious Country-men that knew little about *Rome,* but its Conquest's and Power. Much in the same way, it is not from the Votaries of the several Religions into which the ancient Devotion had split, that we are to learn the Detail and Intention of their Ceremonies: it is rather from Foreigners, or even from *Enemies,* who pry'd into their Mysteries in order to expose them. . . .

(pp. 203–204)

That the primitive Philosophy, upon which the several Religions of the Ancients were originally grafted, was soon corrupted, appears already pretty evident: that it was so by the Introduction of *human Persons* into it as Gods, appears in part from the same Reasoning: But as many of the Fathers, and several learned Men of late, for whose Memory and Character I have a real regard, have revived the Opinion of *Euhemerus,* it becomes worth while to review that Hypothesis, and consider, whether it be well founded?

It is past doubt that many of the Gods, and especially of the Heroes worshipp'd in *Greece,* had been mortal Men: as mortal as *Pater Quirinus,* or *Divus Julius,* or any of their infamous Successors, who had Priests, and Shrines, and Sacrifices decreed to them after Death. The Question regards neither the later *Grecian*

nor *Roman* Deities, but the primary great Gods of *Assyria* and *Egypt,* the immediate Offspring of Chaos, and Progeny of *Oceanus* and *Tethys;* whether *these* were meer Men deified by Superstition and Ignorance, or contrived Types and Representations of the Rise, Progress, and Powers of the Universe? . . .

(pp. 208–209)

. . . But *their* ill Success, in reducing the ancient Fictions to modern Refinements, concludes nothing against the Doctrine of the primary Gods having been originally intended and contrived to express the Parts and Powers of Nature. . . .

(p. 210)

. . . Nor can any unbiassed Mind peruse *Hesiod's* Theogony, and not perceive that he intends and plainly *professes* to describe the Origin, and represent the Government of the World: And that the Plan of his Work, tho' interwove with many a disjointed Tale, is substantially the same with *Orpheus's* Hieros Logos or Holy Word, in which we are told that the great Theologue of the *Greeks,* and Pattern of pious Poets explained Points of no less Importance than *the Births of the Gods, the Creation of the World and Formation of Man.* 'Tis plain therefore, the Allegory *did not come too late:* It was not framed after the Fable, like modern Predictions, after the Event: It was understood and receiv'd from the Beginning. . . .

(pp. 212–213)

You are not therefore to expect poetical Entertainment from an Author[3] who writes upon this Plan, nor to have the fair side of Mythology set in an advantageous Light: Not a word of the Wisdom of the Ancients, the Depth of their Conceptions, Strength of their Fancies, or Services in civilizing the Savage Tribes of Men. On the contrary, whether from a proper Deference to his Profession, or from some other View, he is constantly endeavouring to render the ancient Mythology *odious,* and with superfluous Pains confuting strenuously what no body now believes. . . .

(p. 218)

But why then does both he[4] and the greater part of the Fathers favour the mortalizing Scheme introduced by *Euhemerus;* that all the Gods of the Ancients were once Men? For two Reasons: First it was a cheap and ready Method of Confutation, that rid them of all the Gods at once, like L[eland's] *Shortest Way with the Dissenters:* Next it was the most *odious* Light in which they cou'd represent them. . . .   (p. 230)

. . . Under this Prepossession many learned Moderns have gone upon various Scents in quest of the human Origin of the ancient Gods. Their several Attempts resemble the different Systems of Philosophy contrived to account for the Phaenomena of Nature. The Authors of these Systems are commonly so full and fond of one Principle of their own Invention, or at least of their own Applying, that by *it's* sole means they must needs explain the Structure, and unravel the Mysteries of the Creation. This *Gilbert* attempted by Magnetism, Dr. *More* by his *hylarchic* or Matter-ruling Genius, and M. *des Cartes* by *Matter* and *Motion.*

In the very same manner, the excellent Abbé *Pluche,* whose Works I read with real delight, reduces the whole Gods of Antiquity to certain Statues or emblematical Figures set up in public Places in *Egypt* by way of Almanach, to warn the People of Seed-time and Harvest, or like Heralds to proclaim Peace and War: . . . The Abbé *Banier* to real historical Persons, or dead Men deified; and the

greatest part, *Vossius, Bochart, Huet,* and of late *M. Fourmont,* will have the Gods to be *Scripture Worthies,* and their Legends to be *hebrew Tales* misunderstood.

But Mythology is a vast and various Compound; a Labyrinth thro' whose Windings no *one* Thread can conduct us; "since all the Powers of Heaven and Earth, whatever is, whatever acts, whatever changes, whatever remains the same, is by some congruent Image to its peculiar Nature, variously painted in this mimic Mirror of the Universe." The primary *great Gods* represent its principal Parts and Powers, the numerous *inferior* Train exhibit either the under-parts of the World and their Influences, or they belong to human Passions and human Transactions as connected with them: The rest are *Men* adopted into the number of Gods, and frequently *blended* with the original Deities—To imagine all *these* can be reduced to *one* Class, and their infinite Relations, Applications and Misapplications, through succeeding Ages of different Taste, and distant Nations of different Manners, can be traced and laid open by any *one* however ingenious System, is believing an Impossibility. It is like seeking a full View of the World with the Light of a Taper; and an Attempt to subject the Vagaries of heated Fancy on such Subjects as Religion and Philosophy to a simple Uniformity. It may shew great Acuteness, and greater Learning, as indeed it has done; but turns out at best a pretty ingenious Hypothesis, like *des Cartes' Vortices* or *Epicurus' Atoms;* a Fiction in the main with some mixture of Truth. . . .

(pp. 231–233)

But after wandering thro' so many different Schemes, wou'd you be content to have all the various Gods of the Ancients ranged, and set before you in one comprehensive View? They fall naturally into *three* Classes, and had Worshippers suited to them of *three* different Characters. I. The Parts and natural Powers of the Universe, called out of *Chaos,* said the Poets; formed in *Chaos,* said the Philosophers, by an all-wise Mind that first regulated and still keeps them in order. II. Genii, or spiritual abstract Substances, supposed to exist in, or preside over these Powers; and III. Human Creatures deified. The Worshippers of the *first* were the wise and knowing *Few,* who believed in one supreme God, governing all the subordinate Powers of the World. The Worshippers of the *second* were the middle sort of People, of good Sense in the Affairs of Life; but who had no Leisure nor Inclination to question the received Religion. The Worshippers of the *last,* and of every thing that had the Name of a God, were the unthinking Multitude, standing in awe of their Statues, and swallowing the literal Legend. . . .

(pp. 246–247)

NOTES

For the sake of keeping the text uncluttered, most of Blackwell's extensive (and often only indirectly supporting) footnotes have been omitted. His characteristic spelling and italicizing have been kept, to preserve his emphases.—Ed.

Enquiry into the Life and Writings of Homer
  1. Vergil, Aeneid, VII.
  2. Plato, Laws, B.

Letters concerning Mythology
  1. Père Simon, *Histoire critique du vieux Testament.*
  2. Warburton, *Divine Legation of Moses.*—Ed.
  3. Banier.—Ed.
  4. Bossuet.—Ed.

WILLIAM WARBURTON

[1698–1779]

WILLIAM WARBURTON, perhaps chiefly remembered now as editor and friend of Alexander Pope, was in his own time the famous Bishop of Gloucester and author of that formidable theologico-historical book, *The Divine Legation of Moses Demonstrated* (1737–1741). It is not at first easy to see why the work caused such a remarkable stir, for the book's aim was to "prove" once more that Israel was directly and divinely founded. What helped make the book exciting was that in an atmosphere increasingly charged with freethinking, Warburton's "proof" took the form of a daring paradox: he defends Christian orthodoxy, but on deist (or as he said, "infidel") premises. Freethinkers had often argued that civil society needed religion, that is, some promise of future rewards and punishments, to enforce human law; and they frequently went on to imply that religion was perhaps meaningful only as a lever of political power. Warburton admitted all this, and then triumphantly showed that thus the Hebrew theocracy must be directly supported by God—since Moses did not mention future rewards or penalties and since no other reason could be found. If all societies need the "corrective" of divine judgment in the afterlife, but Israel does not, then God must have set up Israel directly. Thus, this "simple, plain and convincing" argument "demonstrated" Moses' divine legation, and convicts free thought by its own premises. What matters here is that Warburton moves naturally into arguing about mythology to argue his case for Christianity. His book is an encyclopedic survey of mythic learning up to his own time, and it is proof that myth has become an historical ground important for corroborating the claims of either Christianity or free thought.

Warburton's self-proving, self-congratulating paradoxes made him a splendid target. He was also a wonderfully rancorous personality, as injured and insulted readers testify then and now. Hume on the Warburtonians: "illiberal petulance, arrogance, and scurrility"; Leslie Stephen: "Warburton led the life of a terrier in a rat-pit, worrying all theological vermin." But Dr. Johnson said Warburton had "genius and learning"—high praise. Lowth's description of Warburton as "proud, pragmatical and insolent" balances the description nicely. Warburton does explain religion almost always pragmatically and politically; religion preserves civil society, and should, in all times. Indeed, myth itself turns out to be a pragmatic device for teaching one thing publically and believing another thing privately. The elite are monotheistic (in a pagan way) and the multitude polytheistic; and Mysteries (the pagan equivalent of biblical prophecy) likewise have two faces, esoteric and exoteric. What is commonly called myth or fables is only the ignorant side, first taught by malicious priests who knew better, and then preserved by stupid poets and scholiasts who did not. This is true both in Greece and in Egypt, says Warburton, for Greek religion simply borrowed from Egypt, adopting the names of gods, rites, ceremonies, hero-worship, and the use of Mysteries. Warburton makes myth allegoric and monotheistic on its higher side, and literal on its crude side. Egyptian religion was first "pure" (as it was in paganism); that is, sun or star worship. Esoterically, this led to astronomy, as in the Pythagoreans; on the vulgar side, to sun idolatry. Animal worship similarly began as the recording of deeds of kings and heroes, in hieroglyphic form, using animal images; but the vulgar mistook the sign for the thing, and began to worship the depicted animals.

Warburton's mythologic theories were provocative and influential: his hieroglyphic explanations moved into the *Encyclopédie,* for example; his view of the Mysteries as allegoric teachings about monotheism and immortality of soul was widely taken up, lasting as scholarship until the crucial quarrel in Germany between Creuzer's symbolist-allegoric mythology and the historical rebuttal by Lobeck and others in the early nineteenth century.

B.F.

REFERENCES   Our text is from *The Divine Legation of Moses Demonstrated, on the Principles of a Religious Deist, From the Omission of a Future State of Reward and Punishment in the Jewish Dispensation,* 2 vols. (London, 1737–41). For commentary see: Sainte-Croix, *Récherches historiques et critiques sur les mystères du paganisme* (Paris: Bures Frères, 1817, orig. pub. 1784), esp. vol. 1, pp. 438–449, for survey of mythic theorizing about Mysteries and a rebuttal of Warburton's allegorism; Arthur William Evans, *Warburton and the Warburtonians; a Study in some 18th Century Controversies* (London, 1932). Frank Manuel, *Isaac Newton Historian* (Cambridge: Harvard University Press, 1963), p. 300, n. 52 and n. 55 for Warburton's hieroglyphic theories, and influence on Fréret and *Encyclopédie.*

WARBURTON

FROM *The Divine Legation of Moses Demonstrated*

LET US next enquire how HIEROGLYPHICS came to be employed for the *vehicle of mystery.*

I. The Egyptians, in the beginnings of their monarchy, wrote like all other infant nations, in a kind of universal character by picture; of which rude original essays, we have yet some traces remaining amongst the *hieroglyphics of Horapollo;* who tells us, that the ancient Egyptians painted a *man's two feet in water* to signify a *fuller,*[1] and *smoke ascending upwards* to denote *fire.*[2] But to render this rude invention less incommodious, they soon devised the more artful way of putting one single figure for the mark or representative of several things; and thus made their picture an HIEROGLYPHIC.

This was the first improvement of that rude and barbarous way of recording men's ideas; and was practised in a two-fold manner; the one more simple, by putting the principal part for the whole; the other more artificial, by putting one thing, of resembling qualities, for another.

(II, Book iv, Sect. iv)

II. Thus far went the two species, of the *proper* Hieroglyphic; which, in its last stage of the tropical,* touched upon SYM-BOLS (of which we are now to speak) they having this in common, that each *represented one thing by another;* in this they differed, that the *tropical Hieroglyphic* was employed to divulge; the *tropical Symbol,* to secrete: for all the several modes of writing by THINGS having had their progressive state, from less to more perfection, they easily fell into one another; so that there was but little difference between the *proper* Hieroglyphic in its last state, and the *symbolic* in its first. For this method of contriving *tropical hieroglyphic,* by similar properties, would of itself produce refinement and nice enquiry into the more hidden and abstruse qualities of things; which meeting at the same time with a temper now much turned to speculation[3] on matters of theology and philosophy, would as naturally introduce a new species of zoographic writing, called by the ancients SYMBOLIC, and employed for SECRECY; which the high speculations, conveyed in it, required; and for which it was well fitted by the enigmatic quaint-ness of its representations.

(II, Book iv, Sect. iv)

My second argument for this antiquity is deduced from the true original of AN-IMAL-WORSHIP; and stands thus: We have observed, that in those improved hiero-glyphics, called *Symbols* (in which, it is

* i.e., refers to trope or figure—Ed.

confessed, the ancient Egyptian learning was contained) the less obvious properties of animals occasioned their becoming marks, by analogical adaption, for very different ideas, whether of substances or modes; which plainly intimates that phys-ical knowledge had been long cultivated. Now these symbols I hold to be the true original of ANIMAL-WORSHIP in Egypt. But animal-worship was the *established worship* in the time of Moses, as is evi-dent from the book of *Exodus:* Therefore the Egyptian learning was of this high antiquity. The only proposition, in this argument, that needs any proof, is the first. The reasons therefore which induce me to think *symbolic writing* to be the sole origin of *Animal-worship* are these:

1. This kind of idolatry was peculiar to the *Egyptian* superstition; and almost un-known to all the Casts of paganism, but such as were evidently copied from that original:[4] Moses treats it as their distin-guishing superstition:[5] The Greeks and Romans, though at a loss for its original, yet speak of it as the peculiar extrava-gance of *Egypt:* And the most intelligent of the moderns consider it in the very same light.[6]

2. The *Egyptians* not only worshipped *Animals,* but PLANTS; and, in a word, every kind of being that had qualities re-markably singular or efficacious; because all these had found their place in sym-bolic writing: For, as hath been shewn, when Hieroglyphics came to be employed for mystery, no sooner was one symbol grown common and vulgar, that another was invented of a more recondite meaning: so that the animal, vegetable, and mineral kingdoms would be all explored to paint the histories of their Gods.

3. Besides the adoration of almost every thing existing, the *Egyptians* worshipped a thousand Chimeras of their own creation:

Some with human bodies, and the head or feet of brutes; others with brutal bodies, and the heads or feet of men; while others again were a fantastic compound of the several parts of beasts, birds, and reptiles, terrestrial and aquatic: for besides the simpler method, in hieroglyphic writing, of expressing their hero-gods by an intire plant or animal, there were two others which the more circumstantial history of those deities brought in use. Thus when the subject was only one single quality of a god or hero, the human shape was only partially deformed; as with the head of a dog, hawk, or ram, to denote fidelity, vigilance, or strength; with the feet and thighs of a goat, to represent rusticity, agility, or lust; and this gave Being to their Anubis, Pan, and Jupiter Ammon: But where the subject required a fuller catalogue of the hero's virtues or useful qualities, there they employed an assemblage of the several parts of various animals: each of which, in hieroglyphic writing, was significative of a distinct property: in which assemblage, that animal, more peculiarly representative of the God, was most conspicuous. . . . The sun was generally expressed by a *hawk;* but this *symbolic hawk,* under various considerations, had the various parts of other animals added to it.

4. That animal which was worshipped in one city was sacrificed in another. Thus, though at Memphis they adored the ox, at Mendes the goat, and at Thebes the ram; yet, in one place or other, each of these animals was used in sacrifice: but bulls and clean calves were offered up in all places. The reason of this can only be that at Memphis the ox was, in hieroglyphic learning, the symbol of some deity; at Mendes the goat; and at Thebes the ram; but the bull and calf no where: For what else can be said for the original of so

fantastical a diversity in *representative* deities within a kingdom of one national religion?—But farther: the same animal was feasted in one place, with divine honours; in another it was pursued with the direst execrations. Thus, at Arsinoë, the crocodile was adored; because having no tongue it was made in hieroglyphic writing the symbol of the divinity; elsewhere it was had in horror, as being made in the same writing the symbol of Typhon;[7] that is, it was used as a *sacred character* in the history both of their *natural* and *civil* Theology.

5. Brute-worship was, at *first,* altogether objective to their hero-gods; of whom animals were but the representatives. This is seen from the rank they hold on ancient monuments; from the unvaried worship of some few of them as the *Apis,* which still continued to be adored as the representative of Osiris:—and from the express testimony of Herodotus; who says, that, when the Egyptians addressed the sacred Animal, their devotions were paid to that God to whom the beast belonged.

6. But to make the matter still plainer, it may be observed, that the most early brute-worship in Egypt was not an adoration of the living animal, but only of its picture or image. This truth Herodotus seems to hint at in Euterpe, where he says, the Egyptians erected the first altars, images, and temples to the gods, and carved the FIGURES OF ANIMALS on stones.

(II, Book iv, Sect. iv)

These considerations are sufficient to shew that *hieroglyphics* were indeed the original of *brute-worship;* And how easy it was for the Egyptians to fall into it from the use of this kind of writing, appears from hence. In these hieroglyphics was recorded the history of their greater, and tutelary deities, their kings and lawgivers; represented by animals and other creatures. The symbol of each God was well known and familiar to his worshippers, by means of the popular paintings and engravings on their temples and other sacred monuments; so that the symbol presenting the idea of the God, and that idea exciting sentiments of religion, it was natural for them, in their addresses to any particular deity, to turn towards his representative, mark or symbol. This will be easily granted if we reflect, that when the Egyptian priests began to speculate, and grow mysterious, they feigned a *divine original* for hieroglyphic characters, in order to render them still more august and venerable. This would, of course, bring on a *relative* devotion to these symbolic figures; which, when it came to be paid to the living animal, would soon terminate in an *ultimate* worship.

But the occasional propensity to this superstition was, without question, forwarded and encouraged by the Priesthood; for it greatly supported the worship of hero-deities, by making their theology more intricate; and by keeping out of sight, what could not but weaken religious veneration in remote posterity, the naked truth, that they were only DEAD MEN DEIFIED. And these advantages they afterwards improved with notable address; by making those Symbols as well relative to new conceived imaginary qualities and influences of their first *natural gods,* the host of heaven, as to what they properly respected, in hieroglyphic writing, their later heroes and tutelary deities; Which trick, invented to keep the Egyptians in their superstition, spread so impenetrable an obscurity over paganism, as hindered the most sagacious Philosophers and knowing Antiquaries of Greece from ever get-

ting a right view of the rise and progress of their own idolatry.

(II, Book iv, Sect. iv)

I proceed then to a particular examination of this famous proof of the identity, as it is collected and digested by the learned Master of the Charter-house.[8]

The first observation I shall make upon it is, that, by the same way of arguing, one might incorporate almost any two HEROES, one meets with, in early and remote history. For as our great English poet well observes,

"Heroes are much the same, the point's agreed,
From Macedonia's madman to the Swede;
The whole strange purpose of their lives, to find,
Or make an enemy of all mankind."

To shew the reader how easily this feat may be performed, I will take any two of our Monarchs, that come first into my thoughts,—KING ARTHUR, for instance, and WILLIAM THE CONQUEROR. And now let him only imagine, when arts and empire have learnt to travel further West, and have left Great Britain in the present condition of Egypt, some future Chronologer of America, labouring to prove these Heroes one and the same, only under two different names, by such kind of Arguments as this:

1. ARTHUR and WILLIAM were both great warriors.
2. Both were of spurious or uncertain birth.
3. Both were in the management of public affairs in their early youth.
4. Both came from France to recover Britain from the Saxons.
5. Both proved victorious in their expedition.

6. Both got the crown of Britain by election, and not by descent.

7. Both had other dominions, besides Britain, to which they succeeded by right hereditary.

8. Both were frequently on military expeditions into France.

9. Both warred there with various success.

10. Both had half-brothers, by the mother, who, being made very powerful, and proving guilty of manifold extortions and acts of injustice, were punished by them, in an exemplary manner.

11. Both had rebellious sons or nephews, whom they met in the field, fought with in person, and subdued.

12. Both reigned upwards of fifty years.

13. And both died in War.

When our Chronologer had been thus successful with his argument from similar circumstances, (as in the case of Osiris and Sesostris), it is odds but he would go on; and to settle a chronology which made for some other hypothesis he had in view, he would next attempt to prove, from *similitude of names,* as before from *similitude of actions,* that WILLIAM THE CONQUEROR and WILLIAM THE THIRD, another Conqueror, were but one and the same, (as in the case of Sesostris and Sesac).

Here the number of similar circumstances, in the lives of Arthur and William, are, evidently, more characteristic of ONE, than those in the history of Osiris and Sesostris. Yet we know that Arthur and William were really two different men of two very distant ages. This will shew the critics the true value of this kind of evidence; and should reasonably dispose them to much caution in building upon it.

(II, Book iv, Sect. v)

NOTES

The modernizing of Warburton's text is that of the 4th edition of 1755–1788. Warburton's footnotes—often vast tangential essays in themselves—have been omitted except where useful for specific citations.—Ed.

1. Horap. lib. i, cap. 65.
2. Horap. lib ii, cap. 16.
3. In support here, Warburton cites Sanchoniathon according to Eusebius, *Praepar. Evang.* lib i, cap. 10.—Ed.
4. Such as the several Gentile nations of Palestine and India.
5. Deut. iv, 14–21.
6. Warburton cites Fourmont's *Réflexions critiques sur les histoire des anciens peuples,* tom. i, p. 227.—Ed.
7. The subsequent doctrine of the *Metempsychosis* soon made this the foundation of a fable, that the soul of *Typhon* had passed into a crocodile—that *Typhon* had assumed that figure, etc. See Aelian's "Hist. of Animals," lib. x, cap. 21.
8. Isaac Newton.—Ed.

NOËL ANTOINE PLUCHE

[1688–1761]

THE ABBÉ PLUCHE added a new twist to Christian Euhemerism and rationalist myth theory and thereby prefigured, though quite by accident, some of the later ideas of R. P. Knight, Friedrich Creuzer, and others about myth originating in symbolic communication. Pluche had been a professor of humanities and then of rhetoric in his native Rouen before taking holy orders for purposes of preferment. As a teacher and a literary man, he became widely known as a popularizer of ideas then in vogue. His *Spectacle de la Nature,* published in 1732, was widely reprinted and translated, as was his *Histoire du ciel,* first published in 1739.

The latter work, a defense of the Mosaic account of history and religion, takes up two main issues; it tries first to show the origin of idolatry and secondly to refute the work of Gassendi, Descartes, Newton, and other modern thinkers. Pluche clearly thought he was defending the faith from the most dangerous of old enemies—paganism—and at the same time was disposing of the most dangerous modern threat, that posed by recent science.

Pluche is a reductionist in spirit; his preface flatly claims that fables, oracles, deities, and other fabulous creatures without exception all stem simply from the abuse of the language of astronomy, an argument that would be put with more sense and less dogmatism by Dupuis and later by F. Max Müller. Pluche himself

was clearly undisturbed by complexity and unruffled by doubt; he has, in Mark Twain's phrase, the confidence of a Christian with four aces; and his theory, which is preposterous, narrow, almost entirely composed of sheer fantasy, and very likely derived from Warburton, may be summarized as follows.

Idolatry is the worship of false gods in antiquity and may be traced to Egypt. But the Egyptians were themselves descendents of Noah and were therefore presumably monotheists originally. The problem then, is to find where the Egyptians went wrong, how they lost or forgot the true faith, and how they came to worship the silly and unreal dog-headed and bird-headed idols. Pluche argued that the descendants of Noah made up a zodiac of twelve signs, each sign a symbolic representation of some simple astral event that occurred at an important point in the agricultural year. Thus all the signs taken together were a sort of agricultural calendar. This calendar of signs was then brought to Egypt by the same descendants of Noah, and though the signs no longer fit the yearly cycle accurately, they were still retained. In time, the original meanings of the signs were no longer remembered. At that point, venal priests and crafty wise men encouraged the mob to worship the signs themselves, which had now become hieroglyphic figures, while monotheism was preserved only in secret religious societies or mystery cults.

The mechanism by which all this and

much more was explained by Pluche is a fairly simple one, and can be seen in his discussion of the dog-star. In some astral event, such as the first appearance each season of a particularly bright star, men find a convenient signal that, for example, the Nile is about to commence its annual flood. The rising of the star is thus a warning, and by analogy with a watch-dog, the star is called the dog-star. For those who know little about stars and cannot recognize them, someone then puts up a sign of a dog to warn people the flood is about to begin. Soon the posting of the dog sign and the flood are associated as cause and effect. Eventually, in their ignorance and with the encouragement of the venal wise men, people begin to worship the sign of the dog and after a while can be brought to worship dogs themselves.

Pluche's work is filled with such fantasies, which are like parodies, before-the-fact, of romantic attempts to explain myth by sympathetic and imaginative reconstructions of the mythopoeic era. But however empty Pluche's scholarship, his work does in fact touch in a suggestive but brief fashion on the relations between

myth and what Pluche dimly saw to be the related matters of language, allegory, and symbol. Thus he argues, in effect, that both myth and written language originate in efforts to communicate symbolically the significance of some natural event, that mythology evolved from early written language, that painting may have arisen from these early symbols, and that allegory as a mode of thought and expression follows quite simply from the idea of written hieroglyphic or symbolical language.

R.R.

REFERENCES   Our text is from Abbé Pluche, *The History of the Heavens, Considered according to the Notions of the Poets and Philosophers, Compared with the Doctrines of Moses,* translator J. B. de Freval (London: J. Osborn, 1741), 2d ed., 2 vols. This is based on Pluche, *Histoire du ciel considéré selon les idées des poètes, des philosophes, et de Moïse,* 2 vols. (Paris, 1739). In addition to Weiss's article on Pluche in the *Biographie Universelle* (Paris, 1843) see Frank Manuel, *The Eighteenth Century Confronts the Gods* (Cambridge: Harvard University Press, 1959).

Pluche

FROM *The History of the Heavens*

It is commonly said, that Astronomy borrowed the names of men, women, animals, and other terrestrial objects, given to the signs of the Zodiack, the planets, and the other bodies that revolve in the heavens, from Paganism. The learned have

searched, and imagined they had found in antiquity, the times, places, persons, and most of the circumstances to which these names ought to refer. They have collected the several strokes of resemblance, which happened to meet between the metamorphoses of poets, and some certain events of history, both sacred and profane. They have almost all of them imagined they had brought us to the true beginnings of idolatry, by observing the several persons in history, whom flattery had deified during their lives, or whom gratitude had placed among the stars after their death. The labour of these learned men is, no doubt, very useful, and their observations often very well grounded, since 'tis certain, that in time several names of men, and many particulars in history, have been thrown into the fables and the denominations of the celestial bodies: But we are not yet informed, what was the first step that led our forefathers to idolatry, and by what gradation human reason was so far perverted as to worship dead men, after the sun, the moon, and the stars had been assigned them for their dwelling places.

The first original of this evil, the true source of idolatry, and of all superstition, is, the abuse of the language of astronomy, and of the figures of the ancient writing; which abuse was occasioned by a blind desire and an immoderate thirst after earthly riches.

Idolatry did not supply the names made use of by astronomy: but astronomy invented the names, the characters and the figures, which ignorance and lust converted into powers deserving our respect and reverence. In a word, the heaven of poets, or the primitive ground of the whole heathen mythology, is in its origin nothing more than a harmless and innocent way of writing, but stupidly mistaken, and grossly understood in the sense it offered to the eye, instead of being taken in that it was intended to offer to the mind.

(from Book I,
The Poetical Heaven, pp. 1–2)

The twelve symbolical names which signified the twelve portions both of the year and the heaven, were a prodigious help towards regulating the beginnings of sowing, mowing and harvestime, of general huntings, and other works of mankind. As they offer'd to the mind twelve objects, the figures of which are mighty obvious; in order to render the use of them more convenient, they made rough draughts of them, by delineating them on slate or stones. It was indeed but a lineary and unwrought kind of carving; but as the sketching out of a portrait is the beginning of it, these coarse delineations of the twelve celestial signs very likely gave birth to painting. But the reader will easily conceive, that images like these publickly posted up, to notify a certain kind of work determined, or two or three of these representations put together, in order to signify a certain number of months, presented to the mind something very different from what they offered to the eyes. The sight of the lion intimated the sultry heats of the summer. A maid, with a pair of scales in her hand, characteriz'd the harvest and the equinox; the end of the summer and the beginning of autumn. The sight of a balance and of a scorpion mark'd out the duration of the two months that follow the autumnal equinox. We then sensibly draw near the origin of writing, since these figures, as our characters still do, busied the mind with things quite different from what the eyes saw.   (from Book I, Chap. 1, p. 15)

It was found very convenient, to expose in publick a small figure or a single letter, as sight to inform a vast multitude of people of the exact time when certain general works were to be begun in common, and when some certain feasts were to be celebrated. The use of these figures appeared so convenient, that they by degrees extended it to more things than the order of the calendar. Several symbols fit to inform the people of certain truths, or to remind men of them by a certain analogy or relation of resemblance between the figure and the thing they had a mind to have understood, were devised. For instance, one of the most ancient symbols, since it is become universal, is the fire which was perpetually kept in the place where assemblies of the people were held. Nothing was fitter to give them a lively idea of the power, the beauty, the purity, and the eternity of the being they came thither to worship. This magnificent symbol was in use throughout the East. The Persians looked upon it as the most perfect emblem of divinity. . . . The same usage was found again in Peru, and in some other parts of America. Moses preserved the use of the perpetual fire in the holy place among the ceremonies, the choice and particular account of which he fixed and prescribed to the Israelites. And the same expressive and noble symbol, and so little capable of leading the people into errors, even now subsists in all our temples.

This method of saying or shewing one thing to intimate several others, is what introduced among the eastern nations the taste of allegories. They preserved for a long while the method of teaching every thing under symbols, fit by a mysterious outside to stir up curiosity, which was afterwards recompensed by the satisfaction of having discovered the truths which these symbols concealed. Pythagoras, who had travelled among the eastern nations, thence brought that method back to Italy. Our Saviour himself very often made use of it to keep truth hidden from all indifferent minds, and to excite those who tenderly loved that truth, to intreat him to clear it to them.

(from Book I, Chap. 1, pp. 18–19)

The son of Cham, whom the holy scripture calls Mizraim, and whom prophane histories call Menes, is the first king who by wise laws governed and ordered the colony which Cham had established in Egypt. Thot, who was, they say, the minister or the counsellor of Menes, and afterwards his successor, or some Egyptian of note not very distant from the time of the Flood, among other important services which he did to all Egypt, devised and ingraved on stone a multitude of new symbols relating to the peculiar wants of the country, and fit to let all the people into the knowledge of the common regulations: Which caused Thot to be looked upon as the inventor of the symbolical writing, though the method he used to make himself understood, was but an extension or an imitation of the figures of the zodiack, and perhaps of some others invented even before the dispersion. Very possibly Thot or Taaut may be but an imaginary person who never existed. This word, which as well as that of Anubis, seems to signify a dog, was the name given to the dog-star, for reasons which we shall very soon unfold. This symbolical dog giving the Egyptians the most important of advices, and serving to regulate the order of feasts, was afterwards looked upon as the name of the inventor of the Egyptian polity. But let the existence of Thot be what it will; the inventor of the Egyptian characters did certainly live very soon after the dispersion; and this remark is for the present sufficient. Whoever then he may have been, what concerns us here is to understand the meaning of his writing, at least as to the characters that were of more frequent use. Let us be transported into Egypt; Let us place ourselves in the times next to the confusion of languages: and if we are desirous to understand what they intended to intimate to the Egyptians in the figures perpetually exposed before their eyes, let us be first informed of the principal objects of their belief; let us be previously acquainted with their principal customs, and their most pressing wants. . . .

Religion is evidently more ancient than the Egyptians. The founders of that colony neither invented the zodiack or the first symbols. But it is to the peculiar need the Egyptians stood in of astronomy, that we are indebted for the progress and the regular form which painting and writing afterwards assumed.

Cham, and those of his children who came to inhabit the banks of the Nile and the whole lower Egypt, first there tried to cultivate the earth, according to the order of the year, and in the manner used in other countries. The earth being extremely sandy and dry, they thought it but little fit to yield corn; they sowed barley and vegetables in the spring, and with joy saw their fields quickly covered all over with verdure. The ears of their corn springing up on all parts foreboded the most plentiful harvest. But almost every year and from the month of April or May, there came from Ethiopia a violent and pestilential wind, which laid waste their gardens, flatted and sometimes wholly rooted up their barley. If they tried to repair their losses by a second ploughing and sowing, their hopes were again revived, by the almost infallible arrival of a northerly wind, which allayed the heats. All then seemed prosperous. They depended upon a richer crop than that they had lost. But they no sooner were ready to cut it down in the driest season of the year, and without the least appearance of a rain, but their river swelled to their great amazement: it flowed on a sudden over its banks, and took from them those provisions which they thought themselves already sure of. The waters continuing to rise to the

heighth of twelve, fourteen, or even sixteen cubits, covered all their plains, carried away their cattle, and even the inhabitants themselves. . . . Experience taught them how to distinguish the signs that were the forerunners of the inundation, in order to take proper measures when they should be obliged to fly, and especially to sow afterwards so critically, that they might still have time enough to gather their crop, before the coming of the waters and violent winds.

They observed from one year to another, that the overflowing was always preceded by an Etesian wind, which blowing from north to south, about the time of the passage of the sun under the stars of the crab, drove the vapours towards the south, and gathered them in the middle of the country whence the Nile came; which there caused plentiful rains, swelled the water of the river, and afterwards brought on an inundation all over Egypt, without having had the least rain there. They did not perhaps conceive that chain of effects in the manner just represented: but, without holding a needless argument on the causes and the production of the effect, they observed that the blowing of the north wind was always followed by the inundation, and that the overflowing was more or less considerable according to the strength and duration of this wind, which were not the same from one year to another. This wind, which was become the infallible sign of the rising of the waters, soon became a rule to the inhabitants. But they wanted a certain method of exactly knowing the moment when they should have all their provisions ready and their terrasses well raised, in order to repair thither with their herds and flocks. The moon afforded them no manner of assistance, as to ruling their conduct in that respect. They then had recourse to the stars, whose motion is uniform from year to year.

The flowing of the river beyond its banks happened some days sooner or later, when the sun was under the stars of the Lion. In the morning the first stars of Cancer being thirty degrees and more remote from the sun placed under Leo, begin to disingage themselves from its rays. But being very small, they are scarcely perceived. Wherefore they were little fit to serve the people for a rule. Near these stars, though pretty far from the band of the zodiack, and a few weeks after their rising, they see in the morning one of the most brilliant, if not the brightest and biggest star of the whole heaven, ascending the horizon. It appeared a little before the rising of the sun, which had rendered it almost invisible for a month or two before. The Egyptians then pitched upon the rising of this magnificent star at the approach of the day, as the infallible sign of the sun's passing under the stars of Leo, and of the beginning of the inundation. That star became the publick mark, on which every one was to keep a watchful eye, to prepare his store of provisions, and not to miss the instant of retiring to the higher grounds. As it was seen but a very little time above the horizon, towards the dawn-ing of the Aurora, which becoming every instant clearer, soon made it disappear; that star seemed to shew itself to the Egyptians, merely to warn them of the overflowing, which followed its rising not much after. It then did, with regard to every family what a faithful dog does, who warns the whole house of the approach of thieves. They then gave that star two names having a very natural relation to the helps they borrowed therefrom. It warned them of the danger; wherefore they called it the *dog,* or the *barker,* the monitor, in Egyptian *Anubis,* in Phenician *Hannobeach.* Which, by the by, shews the analogy that was between these two languages, notwithstanding the diversity of pronunciation, which made them appear quite different. Even now we call it the Dog-star, which is still but the same name. The danger which it warned the Egyptians of, was the sudden overflowing of the Nile. For this reason the people was always mindful of the time when that star disingaged itself from the rays of the sun, and in the morning ascended the horizon. The infallible connexion which was between the rising of the star and the rising of the river beyond its banks, determined the people to call it more commonly the Nile-star, or barely the Nile.

(from Book I, Chap. 1, pp. 19–27)

WILLIAM STUKELEY

[1687–1765]

A NOW obscure line of interest in the British Druids offers a convenient microcosm of the development of the interest in myth during the eighteenth century. William Blake's *Prophetic Books* are one such culmination. As traced by A. L. Owen in *The Famous Druids,* this interest began with antiquarian and patriotic interests and with the essentially casual artistic interest of poets such as Drayton and Milton. To this was added a powerful religious interest in the work of Henry Rowlands, Stukeley, and others: Druids and Druidism were "connected" in the Shuckfordian manner with biblical history, and it was suggested that Druidism was close to, or even derived from, an early patriarchal religion. A concern with Druids became common; John Toland wrote about them, attacking them for their priestcraft and making them the pretext for an anticlerical polemic. Banier mentions the Druids frequently; Fréret worked on etymological problems connected with Druidism; and with the rising interest in all religious and mythic subjects, the Druids—who, aside from the Arthurian material, were England's only hope for a real mythic heritage—came in for a great deal of careful attention both in England and in France. Patriotism may have suggested that Britain explore and publicize its own fabulous past; the nascent study of archaeology led to renewed interest in Stonehenge and other early monuments—often thought to be Druid remains during the eighteenth century; while Christianity led the patriotic antiquary to make England a seat or even the seat of primitive, pre-Mosaic Christianity.

William Stukeley, a pioneer of modern archaeology and a well-known writer on Druids in his own time, was a somewhat more colorful figure than most students of myth. Stukeley studied law and then medicine; he traveled about England observing and studying ancient remains; he became a cleric, dabbled in many fields, wrote a pedigree of Queen Anne from Noah, was a friend and correspondent of Newton and of Warburton, and was described by the latter as an honest and a learned man who was a mixture of "simplicity, drollery, absurdity, ingenuity, superstition, and antiquarianism." As an undergraduate he is said to have stolen dogs and dissected them. Later he laid out a garden with a Druid temple and an old apple tree, covered with mistletoe, in the center. Stukeley appears to have been genially crazed on the subject of Druids, sometimes signing himself "Chyndonax, Archdruid." In 1740 he brought out a handsome, beautifully engraved volume on Stonehenge, and three years later, one on Avebury. Designed as the final parts of a seven volume work (the first five books of which were never written), their argument may be conveniently gathered from the prefaces.

According to Owen, Stukeley had originally thought that Stonehenge was a "huge ideogram," a great stone hieroglyph of Druid doctrine about "unformed matter which has an innate appetite or capacity to receive forms," and Stukeley thought Druidism to have been Egyptian in origin. Why he thought this and why he later changed his mind are not known (Stukeley's interest in Stonehenge and Newton's in Solomon's Temple are intriguingly similar), but Stuckley's new theory about Stonehenge made it only a part of a much grander conception.

According to this theory, the earliest religion was that of the patriarchs before the Mosaic dispensation. This primitive religion, Stukeley argued (and in this part of his scheme he was not alone), was in fact Christianity, and the Mosaic dispensation, when it came, was only a period of darkness, a "veil intervening" between early natural Christianity and the later religion brought by Christ. Stukeley contends that descendants of the patriarchs came to Britain, where they were called Druids, and where they carried on the practice of their early and pure Christianity in temples such as Stonehenge, uncorrupted by the Mosaic dispensation. (To a Christian historian, Stukeley would seem merely to have found a way to discredit the Old Testament and thus to remove many problems posed by its non-Christian contents.) The Druidical or patriarchal doctrines were transmitted from generation to generation, eventually ending up as the doctrine of the modern Church of England. Thus for Stukeley the Druids were the means by which early Christianity was preserved from corruption and was kept alive and pure in England itself.

As Stukeley saw the Druids, they were venerable, learned, and pious; they were to be admired, studied, even emulated; they were the link connecting modern England with earliest times; they were England's guarantee of spiritual primacy. In Stukeley's interest in Druidism, many lines converge and many new attitudes can be seen evolving and emerging. For one thing, Stukeley's work is the bridge between old-fashioned antiquarian scholarship and the modern mythopoesis—the creative use of old materials—of such poets as Blake. In another way, Stukeley's antiquarianism deepened until it began to evolve into systematic archaeology, which was to provide the eighteenth and early nineteenth centuries with a substantial new body of historical material. His patriotic quest for English origins and British greatness is related to the new pre-romantic interest in primitive times and ways, while the Christian Euhemerist chronologer in Stukeley went far beyond most Euhemerism, since he took his subjects, the Druids, seriously and found much to admire in them, where the average Euhemerist normally pooh-poohed his subjects.

Scholarship on the Druids was to evolve through several further stages—the extreme and arcane theories of Rowland Jones and Edward Davies are examples—but in one sense the next real step was Blake's. Stukeley had prepared the ground: he had himself almost remythologized the Druids; but Blake actually accomplished it, and it is no accident that Blake—as well as Wordsworth, Emerson, and others—owed a large debt to the imaginative and idiosyncratic William Stukeley.

R.R.

REFERENCES Our text is from William Stukeley, *Stonehenge, a Temple restor'd to the British Druids* (London, 1740), and has been modernized in some matters of punctuation and capitalization. See also Stukeley's *Abury, a temple of the British Druids* (London, 1743). Recent commentary includes Stuart Piggott, *William Stukeley, An eighteenth-century antiquary* (Oxford: Clarendon Press, 1950), and A. L. Owen, *The Famous Druids* (London: Oxford University Press, 1962). Owen gives a useful bibliography of works on Druidism. See also G. F. Black, *Druids and Druidism: a list of references* (New York, 1920) and H. B. Walters, *The English Antiquarians of the Sixteenth, Seventeenth, and Eighteenth Centuries* (London, 1934).

S T U K E L E Y

FROM *Stonehenge, A Temple restor'd to the British Druids*

A FEW years ago I spent some time every summer in viewing, measuring, and considering the works of the ancient Druids in our Island; I mean those remarkable circles of Stones which we find all over the kingdom, many of which I have seen, but of many more I have had accounts. Their greatness and number astonish'd me, nor need I be afraid to say, their beauty and design, as well as antiquity, drew my particular attention. I could not help carrying my inquiries about them as far as I was able. My studies this way have produc'd a vast quantity of drawings and writing, which consider'd as an entire work, may thus be entitled,

Patriarchal Christianity:
or
A Chronological History
of the
Origin and Progress of true Religion,
and of Idolatry.

The parts of which the whole is composed are these:

I. *Canon Mosaicae Chronologiae,* or the year of Moses settled, by which he reckons time in the history of the old world; the time of the year fix'd when creation was begun. This is done in a new manner, and becomes an intire system of chronology from creation to the Exodus, and is exemplified by many particular Calendars of the most remarkable transactions; which are proofs of the truth of the Canon. There are interspersed a great many astronomical and historical illustrations of the sacred pages, particularly Sanchoniathon's genealogies, and Manethon's Egyptian Dynasties, are applied in a new Method to the history and chronology of the Scriptures.

II. Melchisedec, or a delineation of the first and patriarchal religion, from the best light we can gather in the sacred history: and from the most ancient heathen customs, which were remains of that religion. In this Treatise it is shewn, that the first religion was no other than Christianity, the Mosaic dispensation, as a veil, intervening; that all mankind from the creation had a knowledge of the plurality of persons in the Deity.

III. Of the mysteries of the ancients, one of the first deviations from true religion, to idolatry; this is chiefly pursu'd in an explication of the famous table of Isis, or Bembin-table, publish'd by Pignorius, Kircher, etc. wherein that knowledge which the ancients had concerning the true nature of the Deity, is further explain'd.*

IV. A discourse on the hieroglyphic

* The "table of Isis" is a large bronze covered with writing, once owned by Cardinal Bembo, and written about by Lorenzo Pignoria, *Mensa Isiaca* . . . (Amsterdam, 1669) and by Athanasius Kircher, *Oedipus Ægyptiacus* (Rome, 1652–54) and others.—Ed.

learning of the ancients, and of the origin of the alphabet of letters. Very many hieroglyphic monuments of the Egyptians are explain'd, more especially those that relate to their true notions of the persons in the Deity. The time and rise of the alphabet of letters is deduc'd from a new foundation. The present square Hebrew characters are shewn to be the primitive idea of letters, from whence all others are deriv'd. Whence the idea of every letter was taken? an explication of all the old Hebrew coins with Samaritan characters.

V. The patriarchal history, particularly of Abraham, is largely pursu'd; and the deduction of the Phoenician colony into the Island of Britain, about or soon after his time; whence the origin of the Druids, of their Religion and writing; they brought the patriarchal Religion along with them, and some knowledge of symbols or hieroglyphics, like those of the ancient Egyptians; they had the notion and expectation of the Messiah, and of the time of the year when he was to be born, of his office and death.

VI. Of the Temples of the Druids in Britain, their religious rites, orders, sacrifices, groves, tombs, their cursus's, places of sports and exercises, etc. particularly an ample and accurate description of that stupendous temple of theirs at Abury in North Wiltshire, the most august work at this day upon the globe of the earth; with many prints of ground-plots, views and admeasurements of all its parts; of their manner of sepulture; an account of my digging into many of their barrows and tumuli, with drawings of them, etc.

VII. Of the celebrated Stonehenge, another Temple of theirs, with prints of that work; an account of the barrows I dug up, and what was discover'd in them; of the knowledge the Druids had of the magnetical compass, and conjectures of

the particular times when these works were made, long before Caesar arriv'd in Britain.

I propose to publish these two first, and proceed to the speculative parts afterwards; reserving them, God willing, to the maturer time of my life.

My intent is (besides preserving the memory of these extraordinary monuments, so much to the honour of our country, now in great danger of ruin) to promote, as much as I am able, the knowledge and practice of ancient and true Religion; to revive in the minds of the learned the spirit of Christianity, nearly as old as the Creation, which is now languishing among us; to restore the first and great Idea of the Deity, who has carry'd on the same regular and golden chain of Religion from the beginning to this day; to warm our hearts into that true sense of Religion, which keeps the medium between ignorant superstition and learned free-thinking, between slovenly fanaticism and popish pageantry, between enthusiasm and the rational worship of God, which is no where upon earth done, in my judgment, better than in the Church of England. And seeing a spirit of Scepticism has of late become so fashionable and audacious as to strike at the fundamental of all revelation, I have endeavoured to trace it back to the fountain of Divinity, whence it flows; and show that Religion is one system as old as the world, and that is the Christian Religion; that God did not leave the rational part of his creation, like the colony of an ant-hill, with no other guide than instinct, but proportion'd his discoveries to the age of the world, to the learning, wisdom, and experience of it; as a wise parent does now to his children. I shall shew likewise, that our predecessors, the Druids of Britain, tho' left in the extremest west to the improvement of their own thoughts, yet advanc'd their inquiries, under all disadvantages, to such heights, as should make our moderns asham'd, to wink in the sun-shine of learning and religion. And we may with reason conclude, there was somewhat very extraordinary in those principles, which prompted them to such a noble spirit as produced these works, still visable with us, which for grandeur, simplicity and antiquity, exceed any of the European wonders.

That the doctrines and works of the Druids have hitherto been so little consider'd (since authors only transcribe from one to another, the few remaining scraps to be found in classic writers) was an incentive to me likewise in the following attempt, and at the same time it pleads for me, and bespeaks the reader's favour. I want likewise the great advantages to be had from a knowledge of the remaining Celtic languages, books, manuscripts, and history, the Cornish, Welsh, Irish, Highland, etc. the chief repository now of their doctrines and customs. . . .

And tho' there has been of late a large volume publish'd on the subject of Stonehenge, yet we may well say there has nothing been wrote upon the subject. Nor have I any other notion of this performance, than that it is as a first attempt to say something upon those famous philosophers and priests the Druids, who are never spoken of in antiquity but with a note of admiration; and are always rank'd with the Magi of the Persians, the gymnosophists of the Indians, the prophets and hierophants of the Egyptians, and those sort of patriarchal priests, whose orders commenc'd before idolatry began; from whom the Pythagoreans, Platonists, and Greek philosophers learn'd the best things they knew. To clear away rubbish, and lay a foundation only, in this difficult and obscure work, is doing somewhat. The

method of writing which I have chose is a diffusive one, not pretending to a formal and stiff scholastic proof of every thing I say, which would be odious and irksome to the reader, as well as myself. The knowledge I have acquired in these matters, was from examining and studying their works; the proofs are deriv'd from distant and different topicks, and it would be very inconvenient to marshal them syllogistically in a work of this nature; the proof results from the intire work; in all matters of so great antiquity it must be found out by the reader; and to one that has proper sagacity and judgment, conviction will steal upon him insensibly, if I am not mistaken; and he will own the evidence in general, is as strong as the nature of the subject will bear, or requires.

It was very disagreeable to me that I was forc'd to combat against a book publish'd in the name of the celebrated Inigo Jones, for whose memory I have the greatest regard.* I wonder the publisher of that work did not think of a very easy method to convince himself that he was in an error. If Stonehenge is a Roman work, it was certainly built by the Roman scale; had he reduc'd his own measures to that standard, he would have seen the absurdity of his opinion; for we cannot think that a temple, or elegant building, as he would have it, should not shew its founders by the scale on which it is form'd; they are all fractions in the Roman scale, undoubted evidence that the Romans had no hand in it. For there is no meaning, no design in the choice of the measures, neither in general nor particular; a thing unworthy of a great architect; or a great design. But it appears very evident

* Probably *The Most Notable Antiquity of Great Britain, vulgarly called Stone-Heng . . . Restored by I. J.,* ed. J. Webb (London, 1655). —Ed.

to me, that Inigo Jones had little or no part in that work, especially as it is moulded at present; and I think I have reason to be of the opinion that he never drew the designs therein publish'd, because I should be unwilling to say he knowingly falsified them. I have very much shortened what I had to say against that book, because I have no love for wrangling, and barely mention'd what was necessary, that the reader may have a true notion of this noble antiquity.

(from Preface)

ANDREW TOOKE [1673–1732]
JOSEPH SPENCE [1699–1768]

EIGHTEENTH-CENTURY interest in myth was not confined to a small group of thinkers, writers, and theologians; on the contrary, there was a great outpouring of popular mythologizing, aimed at various audiences and important in spreading ideas about mythology. Large numbers of inexpensive handbooks of mythology were printed; and some, like those of Pomey, Tooke, King, and Chompré, became well-known. There were also the more elegant, more expensive, and more sophisticated art books of Montfaucon, Spence, or Hancarville. Another level of popular mythology concerned itself with alchemy, demonology, and other esoteric subjects. (See our introduction to Pernety.) Finally the Encyclopaedias and Universal Dictionaries of the period, from Chambers's in 1728, through Diderot's, Chaufepié's, and the *Encyclopédie Méthodique,* to the early editions of the *Encyclopaedia Britannica* (first edition, 1771), represent perhaps the highest general level of popularly available knowledge about mythology in the eighteenth century. Aside from these popularizing volumes, there is also a steady stream of learned antiquarian studies.

Of the handbooks of mythology in common use during the eighteenth century, a most popular one was the *Pantheum Mythicum* of the Jesuit Pomey, and the translation, by Andrew Tooke, of this work as *Tooke's Pantheon.* Pomey's work first appeared in 1659, and by 1717 it had gone through seven editions in Latin and was still being reprinted later in the century. Tooke's English version, first published in 1698, had gone through thirty-six editions by 1831 and was at that time still being imitated, adapted, and reprinted, while a French translation of Pomey, Thenard's *Méthode pour apprendre l'histoire des anciennes divinités du paganisme,* appeared in 1715. A similar volume, William King's *History of the Heathen Gods and Heroes,* came out in 1710, reached a fifth edition in 1731, and was still being printed in 1761. Chompré's *Dictionnaire abregé de la fable,* also similar to Tooke's work, came out in 1727, went through eleven editions by 1774, was translated into Spanish in 1783 and into Portuguese as late as 1858, while the French original was re-edited by Millin in 1801 and was again re-edited in 1865. In addition to these handbooks, there were less widely used ones—for example, by Banier in 1715, by B. Hederich in 1724, by Bell in 1790, by Holwell in 1793, by Lionnois in 1795, and by Sheldon in 1810.

These handbooks were all essentially alike, and are fairly represented by *Tooke's Pantheon.* The attitude toward myth is serenely Euhemerist, with an occasional nod toward allegorical interpretation. What Pomey wrote and Tooke translated and countless others borrowed was an account of idolatry—that is, mythology—as explained by four causes: the folly and vainglory of early men, the flattery of subjects toward their princes, an immoderate love of immortality, and a wish to perpetuate the memories of good men to later ages. Pomey also has a naive anecdote showing how all false gods begin with Ninus, king of the Assyrians. These handbooks, often designed for school use, for "young readers," or as simple reference books, usually have a Christian tone and usually make an initial deprecation of myth as "heathen idolatry." As Tooke's "Jupiter," excerpted below, shows, any given article leans more toward simple allegory than toward Banier's learned Euhemerist explication.

There are, in addition, the erudite collections and compendiums by such famous antiquarians as Muratori (1709), Spanheim (1671), and J. D. Michaelis (1753, 1770). But these more specialized studies, like the popular handbooks, seem finally uninterested either in origins or in explanations. They exist to gather and provide information (usually genteel information; each new redaction of Tooke produced a chaster version than the last) about the Greek and Roman deities, including variants on the main legends, iconographic details, various names, common ideas about significance—all with a sometimes surprising wealth of detail. The handbooks' essential incuriousness about the nature and origin of myth may well be due to the fact that they were generally intended only to supply essential information about the stock mythological figures with which eighteenth-century and early nineteenth-century poetry swarms. That the Christian Euhemerist handbooks lasted as long as they did is proof of the function they performed, though it can be argued that while Chompré and Tooke lasted well into the nineteenth century, they are not typical of nineteenth-century handbooks, the tone of which is set by John Lempriere's *Classical Dictionary* in 1788, by Charles Anthon's *Classical Dictionary* in 1841, and by Thomas Bulfinch's *Age of Fable* in 1855.

Vastly different are the art books, which include Montfaucon's *L'Antiquité Expliquée,* published in 1719, and translated into English in 1721; Banier's *Les Metamorphoses d'Ovid* (1732), with illustrations by Bernard Picart; the latter's own *Cérémonies et Coutumes Religieuses de tous les peuples du monde* of 1723 (translated into English in 1737); Spence's *Polymetis,* first published in 1747, and reprinted three times before being abridged in 1764, the abridgement itself reaching a sixth edition in 1802; Winckelmann's *Geschichte der Kunst des Altertums* (1764); Comte de Caylus's *Recueil d'Antiquité* (1752–67); and Hancarville's *Recherches sur l'origine, l'esprit, et le progrès des arts de la Grèce* of 1785. These, and other books like them, are expensive folios, ornate, elegant, and lavishly illustrated with fine copper-plate engravings; and while most of them are not quite pornographic, they share a certain beady-eyed attentiveness to the female form, while the sexuality, even the sexiness of certain major figures, mostly female, rarely escapes appreciative and by no means cursory notice. In general, the serious interest of these books is in ancient art and literature, not in origins or on religious attitudes or problems. A sophisticated comparative approach is common; there is little or no interest in Euhemerizing, and often enough there is a clear anti-Christian note. Interpretation, when offered at all, is allegorical, but most interest is centered in the figures of the ancient gods themselves.

Perhaps the most influential of these art books was Joseph Spence's *Polymetis.* Spence, a friend of Pope and the author of a useful collection of literary anecdotes, succeeded Thomas Warton as Professor of Poetry at Oxford, and was later Regius Professor of Modern History. His learning was recommended in sober terms by Samuel Johnson (who had himself once projected a "History of the Heathen Mythology—with an explication of the fables both allegorical and historical, with references to the poets"), and *Polymetis* was praised by Gibbon and read by the young Keats.

Spence's idea was to use the representations of Roman deities in statues, gems, vases, and so on to illuminate the gods in Roman poetry and vice versa. The decision to ignore Greece and to confine himself to Roman work exclusively is eloquent testimony to the enduring Augustanism in England at the time. *Polymetis* is cast in dialogue form, as were a great many of the handbooks, and it is well-if not brilliantly written. The gods are domesticated within one of those extensive and elaborate English gardens for which Spence, and of course Pope, had such enthusiasm. A tone of cheerful hedonism is maintained by Polymetis's refusal to include any of the underworld deities. The general air of an elaborate private museum goes perfectly with Spence's urbane contempt for dog-headed and hawk-headed deities as tasteless and not worth inclusion. (Montfaucon's book opens with a similar remark.)

In the excerpt from the dialogue dealing with Jupiter can be seen Spence's almost incredibly simple idea about the origins of the divinities on whom he lavishes so much descriptive care. They are nothing but figures attached to the various names given by ignorance to a single deity. The brief selection concerning Venus fairly shows Spence's sensuous side, as well as his ability to compare literature and sculpture to very good purpose in his often successful search for the real vitality of any given figure. So too, his Naiads, if less real than Keats's are more alive than Akenside's, perhaps because Spence's restless searching for the life, energy, or vital center of his gods and goddesses endows his descriptions of them with something approaching credible warmth and life. Transmuted by a great poet like Keats, these divinities come to full life, compelling rather than requesting our belief. But it was such men as Spence who during the eighteenth century kept alive the attractive aspects of myth and bequeathed them to the romantic writers of the nineteenth century.

R.R.

REFERENCES Our texts are from Tooke's *Pantheon of the Heathen Gods, and Illustrious Heroes* (Baltimore: E. J. Coale, 1825) adapted from the thirty-third London edition; and from Joseph Spence, *Polymetis: or, An Enquiry concerning the Agreement between the Works of the Antient Artists* (London: R. and J. Dodsley, 1755) 2d ed. Other handbooks will be found listed in the bibliography at the end of this volume.

See also our introductions to Pernety, to Ephraim Chambers, to Fréret, and to Victorian popular mythology. Arnaldo Momigliano, *Studies in Historiography* (London, 1966), especially Chapter 1 on "Ancient History and the Antiquarian" and bibliography. L. Hautecoeur, *Rome et la Renaissance de l'Antiquité à la fin du XVIII siecle* (1912); Bernard H. Stern, *The Rise of Romantic Hellenism in English Literature, 1732–1780* (Menasha, Wisconsin, 1940); C. Justi, *Winckelmann und seine Zeitgenossen* (1866; 3d ed., 1923).

TOOKE

FROM *Tooke's Pantheon*

The Fabulous Histories
of the Heathen Gods

The Approach To the Pantheon . . .
The Origin of Idolatry

THE FABULOUS *Pantheon,* is, as its name imports, the *Temple of all the Gods,* which the superstitious folly of men have feigned through a gross ignorance of the true and only God.

The causes which have chiefly conduced to the establishment and continuance of idolatry are thus enumerated:

1. *The first cause of idolatry was the extreme folly, and vain glory of men,* who have denied to Him, who is the inexhausted fountain of all good, the honours which they have attributed to muddy streams: "Digging," as the prophet Jeremiah complains, "to themselves broken and dirty cisterns, and neglecting and forsaking the most pure fountain of living waters." It ordinarily happened after this manner: if any one excelled in stature of body, if he were endued with greatness of mind, or noted for clearness of wit, he first gained to himself the admiration of the ignorant vulgar; this admiration was by degrees turned into a profound respect, till at length they paid him greater honour than men ought to receive, and ranked the man among the number of gods; while the more

prudent were either carried away by the torrent of the vulgar opinion, or were unable or afraid to resist it.

2. *The sordid flattery of subjects toward their princes, was a second cause of Idolatry.* To gratify their vanity, to flatter their pride, and to soothe them in their self-conceit, they erected altars, and set the images of their princes on them; to which they offered incense, in like manner as to the gods; and not unfrequently, while they were living.

3. *A third cause of Idolatry, was an immoderate love of immortality in many;* who studied to attain it, by leaving effigies of themselves behind them; imagining that their names would still be preserved from the power of death and time, so long as they lived in brass, or in statues of marble, after their funerals.

4. *A desire of perpetuating the memories of excellent and useful men to future ages, was the fourth cause of Idolatry.* For to make the memory of such men eternal, and their names immortal, they made them gods, or rather called them so.

The contriver and assertor of false gods was Ninus, the first king of the Assyrians, who, to render the name of his father Belus, or Nimrod, immortal, worshipped him with divine honours after his death, which is thus accounted for:

After Ninus had conquered many nations far and near, and built the city called after his name, Nineveh; in a public assembly of the Babylonians he extolled his father Belus, the founder of the empire and city of Babylon, beyond all measure, representing him not only worthy of perpetual honour among all posterity, but also of an immortality among the gods above. He then exhibited a statue of him, curiously and neatly made, to which he commanded them to pay the same reverence that they would have given to Belus while alive; he also appointed it to be a common sanctuary to the miserable, and ordained, "that if at any time an offender should fly to this statue, it should not be lawful to force him away to punishment." This privilege easily procured so great a veneration to the dead prince, that he was thought more than a man, and, therefore, was created a god, and called Jupiter, or, as others write, Saturn of Babylon; where a most magnificent temple was erected to him by his son.

After this beginning of Idolatry, several nations formed to themselves gods; receiving into that number not only mortal and dead men, but brutes also; and even the most mean and pitiful inanimate things. For it is evident from the authority of innumerable writers, that the Africans worshipped the heavens as a god; the Persians adored fire, water, and the winds; the Lybians, the sun and moon; the Thebans, sheep and weasels; the Babylonians of Memphis, a whale; the inhabitants of Mendes, a goat; the Thessalanians, storks; the Syrophoenicians, doves; the Egyptians, dogs, cats, crocodiles and hawks; nay, leeks, onions, and garlic.

(from Introduction, Chap. 1)

We will begin with Jupiter, the father and king of gods and men, whom you see sitting in a throne of ivory and gold, under a rich canopy, with a beard, holding thunder in his right hand, which he brandishes against the giants at his feet, whom he formerly conquered. His sceptre, they say, is made of cypress, which is a symbol of the eternity of his empire, because that wood is free from corruption. On his sceptre sits an eagle, either because he was brought up by it, or because an eagle resting upon his head, portended his reign, or because in his wars with the giants an eagle brought him his thunder; and thence received the title of *Jupiter's armour bearer*. . . .   (from Pt. I, Chap. 1)

SPENCE

FROM *Polymetis*

POLYMETIS, who is as well known for his taste in the polite arts, as for his superiour talents in affairs of state, took two or three of his friends with him the last summer to his villa near the town; to breathe fresh air, and relax themselves after the business of a long session. It was customary with the old Greeks and Romans, to talk over points of philosophy at their tables. Polymetis kept up this good old custom at his house; and the part of the entertainment that was generally the most agreeable to his friends, consisted in the discourses he gave them on learning, or on the polite arts; of which he was extreamly fond. They came thither always with some expectation of it; and seldom left his table without being pleased, and perhaps improved, by their treat.

. . . You see, says Polymetis, I have followed the taste in fashion (which, as it happens, is certainly the best taste too) of making my gardens rather wild than regular. . . . The statues I got formerly from Italy, and which used to croud up all my house, are placed in them: and what I a little value myself upon, is the order in which I have placed them. Indeed, says Mysagetes, in coming through your hall, I was surpriz'd to see it deserted by all the heathen gods; that used to seem to be met there, as in council. But what is this order, I beseech you, that you value yourself so much upon? That, replied Polymetis, may lead me into a larger account than you may care for. No, interposed Mysagetes, as we shall go and see them I suppose this afternoon, I beg you would let us into your disposition of them beforehand; that we may be sufficiently prepared to admire it as we ought.

The deities of the Romans (says Polymetis) were so numerous, that they might well complain of wanting a Nomenclatour to help them to remember all their names. Their vulgar religion, as indeed that of the heathens in general, was a sort of Manicheism. Whatever was able to do good or to do harm to man, was immediately looked on as a superiour power; which, in their language, was the same as a deity.

It was hence that they had such a multitude of gods, that their temples were better peopled with statues, than their cities with men. It is a perfect mob of deities, if you look upon them all together: but they are reducible enough to order; and fall into fewer classes, than one would at first imagine. I have reduced them to six; and considering their vast number, it was no little trouble to bring them into that compass.

You see that Rotunda, with a Colonnade running round it, on the brow of the hill? Within that, are the great celestial deities; as the milder ones relating to the human mind and civil life, (Fidelity, Clemency; Peace, Concord; Plenty, Health; all the Mental or Moral Deities, of the better sort;) are placed in the Colonnade about it; one in each opening between the pillars. That temple, lower down the hill to the right, contains the beings which preside over the element of fire: which, according to the antients, had its place next to the supream mansion of the gods. You may call this, if you please, the temple of the Sun and Stars. There I have lodged all my antiques that relate to the Sun, to the Planets, to the Constellations; and to the Times and Seasons, as measured by the former. That Octogon, opposite to it on the left, is the temple of the Winds, and of the imaginary beings of the air. Those two temples on either hand below them contain, one the deities of the Waters, and the other the deities of the Earth: and if I had a temple for the Infernal beings, with the Vices of men round it, in the same manner as their Virtues are placed round the celestial one, I question whether you could name any one imaginary being in all the theology of the antients, that might not properly enough be placed in one or other of these six repositories.

What a pity it is, says Mysagetes smiling, that you should not get a Hell to adorn your garden with, and make the work compleat? Why seriously, replied Polymetis, I have thought even of that. One might have contrived a deep wood, toward the bottom of the hill, which should have led you through a narrow walk (growing every step darker and darker, as more thickened with yew and cypress) down to a vast, rough, horrid cave: in which such a gloomy light let in from above, as falls about the middle of the grotto of Pausilipo, might have half shewn you and half concealed the dismal deities and inhabitants of the lower world. . . . My collection, you know, consists wholly of antiques: and there are so few antient statues that any way relate to the subterraneous world, that I should have been at some loss for the most proper furniture for such a repository; had I been ever so fond of introducing it. . . . I think I have done right in contenting myself here with the temples of the heavens, and the four elementary ones, which you see under it: in which are all the figures I have of the imaginary beings that belong to either of them; disposed each according to his rank and character. . . .

You, Philander, know that my principal view in making this collection was to compare the descriptions and expressions in the Roman poets that any way relate to the imaginary beings, with the works that remain to us of the old artists; and to please myself with the mutual lights they might give each to the other. I have often thought when in Italy, and at Rome in particular, that they enjoy there the convenience of a sort of contemporary comments on Virgil and Horace, in the nobler remains of the antient statuaries and painters. When you look on the old pictures or sculptures, you look on the works of men who thought much in the same train with the old poets. There was generally the greatest union in their designs: and where they are engaged on the same subjects, they must be the best explainers of one another. As we lie so far north from this last great seat of empire, we are placed out of the reach of consulting these finer remains of antiquity so much, and so frequently, as one could wish. The only way of supplying this defect to any degree among us, is by copies, prints, and drawings: and as I have long had this thought, my collection is at length grown very numerous; and indeed almost as full as I could desire it, as to the point which has all along been my particular aim.

I have always admired your collection, says Philander; but might not one who has no such collection, make a shift with father Montfaucon? * That father's work, replied Polymetis, is largely stockt with figures; and perhaps too largely, to be of service in the design we are talking of. We are much obliged to him for his industry: but his choice is rather too loose and unconfined. He has taken in all the different figures he could meet with; of whatever age, or country. You have, even in the better part of his collection, Tuscan gods mixt with Roman; old Gallick figures, with those of Syria: and the monsters of Egypt, with the deities of Athens. This must bring in a great deal of confusion, and strangely multiply the appearance and attributes of almost every deity. As you see them there, the descriptions of them in the Roman poets do not agree with the artists; nor the works of the artists with the poets. As my view was a more particular one, I found myself obliged to confine my collection to the deities as received in Italy; and even in such parts of Italy only, where they

---

* The reference is to Dom Bernard de Montfaucon, *L'Antiquité expliquée et representée en figures* (Paris, 1719).—Ed.

were uniformly received. This cuts off any figures that were not of the growth, or at least made free of Rome. . . . Hence many of the Grecian deities, together with the modes of dressing them, were in a manner naturalized in Rome; and after that, may be looked upon as Roman deities. But there are some that never were so received there; and such I have endeavoured to exclude too, out of my collection.

(from Book I, Dialogue 1)

The sitting figure in the midst of this circle of deities, says Polymetis, you will easily know to be Jupiter. The distinguishing character of his person is Majesty; and everything about him carries dignity and authority with it. His look is meant to strike sometimes with terror; and sometimes with gratitude; but always with respect. It is a great pity that we have no better figures of Jupiter: among all I have seen, I have never seen one which could by any means be placed in the first class of the antient statues that remain to us. . . .

You might however easily know that this is Jupiter, by the dignity of his look; by the fullness of his hair about his face; by that venerable beard; by that mark of command in his left hand, and the fulmen in his right: but I question whether you can so easily know, what Jupiter in particular this is meant to represent. As to that, replied Philander, I am so far from being able to say what Jupiter, that I do not perfectly know what you mean. I know indeed that Cicero mentions that there were several Jupiters; but I never heard how one should distinguish them from one another. The diversity I am speaking of, says Polymetis, does not relate to those confused notions of the antient mythologists; but only to downright matter of fact. I shall explain what I mean more at large; because it is a point that is likely to occur extremely often, in what I may have to say to you.

The old Romans, as well as the rest of the heathen world, were very expert at making distinctions by names; where, according to their own notions, there was no manner of difference in the things. The thinking part of them believed that there was but one great Being, that made, and preserved, and actuated all things: which is just as much as to say that they believed there was but one God, in our sense of the word. Their best authors say this expressly, in books which they published in their lifetime; and some of them go so far as even to give the reasons why they talked vulgarly of so many gods. When they considered this one great Being as influencing the affairs of the world in different manners, they gave him as many different names; and hence came all their variety of nominal gods. When he thundered or lightened, they called him, Jupiter; when he calmed the seas, Neptune; when he guided their councils, it was Minerva; and when he gave them strength in battle, it was Mars. This was their first great distinction without a difference. They seem at first to have only made use of different names; such as Jupiter, Neptune, Minerva, and the like; they afterwards carried it farther, by using different representations of this Jupiter, Neptune, and Minerva: and at last came to consider them, vulgarly at least, as so many different persons. In time, as several distinct acts and characters were attributed even to each of these nominal deities, and as the figures of each were multiplied and varied in different places, they came by degrees to consider each of them too in different views, and this was their second great distinction without a difference. The Jupiter, for instance, when showering down blessings, was called the Kind Jupiter; and when punishing, the Terrible Jupiter. There was one Jupiter for Europe, and another for Africa: and in Europe itself, there was one great Jupiter who was the particular friend of the Athenians, and another who was the particular protector of the Romans. Nay, there was scarce a town, or hamlet perhaps, in Italy, that had not a Jupiter of its own. . . .

We had, not many centuries ago, much the same absurdities in our own country; and at any time may see them practised, the first moment we please to step out on the continent. A little before the Reformation, when our devotions were almost wholly engrossed by the virgin Mary, she had statues in every town, village, church, and chapel; and had different names and representations, according to the place that she was in, or the character she bore. There was then probably with us, as there is in Italy at present, one virgin of the mountains, and another of the valleys; one for those who travel by land to pray to, and another for such as travel by sea. Any body at that time, had they been asked the question, would have said, upon second thoughts, that there was but one virgin Mary: yet they looked upon one figure of her as more venerable than another; and there were many devout people then that gave vast presents to the virgin of Winchester, for example; who would have grudged perhaps to make the most insignificant offering to the virgin of Walsingham. They thought her more present in one place than the other; or had had sev-

eral obligations to her figure at Winchester, and none at all to that at Walsingham. . . .

In his right hand, you see, he grasps his fulmen; his thunder, as we are used to translate that word, improperly enough; for we should rather call it, his lightning. This fulmen, in the hand of Jupiter, partook something of the nature of an hieroglyphic, of old; and had different meanings, according to the different manners in which it was represented.

There were three ways of representing it most usual among the old artists. The first is a bundle of flames, as wreathed close together, and formed much in the shape of what we call the thunder-stone at present. The second is the same figure, with two transverse darts of lightning; and sometimes with wings added on each side of it, to denote its swiftness. Such was the device which all the soldiers of the thundering legion (as it is called) bore on their shields; as you see it frequently represented both on the Antonine, and Trajan pillar, at Rome; and in several other remains of antiquity: which, by the way, may serve very well to explain some lines in Valerius Flaccus, that would not be near so intelligible without their assistance. The third is an handful of flames, all let loose in their utmost fury. These three different representations of the fulmen answer very well to the three different sorts of lightning, which the Roman philosophers and divines sometimes speak of.

(from Book II, Dialogue 6)

MARK AKENSIDE

[1721–1770]

MARK AKENSIDE, the poet and doctor whose *The Pleasures of Imagination* appeared in 1743 when its author was twenty-two, also wrote a "Hymn to the Naiads" which Douglas Bush has called the "most notable mythological poem of the century."

"Hymn to the Naiads," a poem in imitation of Callimachus, takes up a mythological subject but avoids all the current Euhemerist doctrine. Not interested in religious controversy, nor in chronology, astronomy, symbolism, etymology, or allegory, Akenside approaches the Greek myths through the Greek writers themselves—through Orphism to a large extent—and he allows himself something of a free hand in rearranging certain elements of myth in his effort to "employ these ancient divinities as it is probable they were first employed." In other words, in the "Hymn to the Naiads," Akenside was deliberately trying to recapture or recreate the sort of story that the age of fable itself might have produced. Whatever its faults and feeblenesses, the poem is a deliberate step toward the poetic recreation of myth.

The lines printed below are the most vivid in the poem; the scene they describe is a Dionysian outburst, full of wine and tumult. This energetic sortie is then stilled as the poet moves on to claim that, for him, the highest poetic imagination is not associated with this Dionysian revelry, but with the gentle, Apollonian Naiads, representatives of a calmer and more re-strained spirit. Akenside acknowledges the fitness of the Dionysian spirit for some kinds of poetry, for heady or brutal or erotic subjects. Yet, for all Akenside's unusual understanding of and tolerance for the Dionysian, it was to be some time yet before this Dionysian element would be freely acknowledged or widely sought out as the primal source of poetic power. Akenside, in describing it as vividly as he does, provides, however, a glimpse of the future direction of the poetic revival of interest in myth.

In his learned notes, some of which are given below, Akenside shows a clear preference for Greek mythic thought over modern myth commentary and theory. He also reveals his tendency to Platonize, and his fondness for such things as the semi-Platonic Orphic Hymns. Orphism, an early mystery cult that later impressed Pindar and Plato, taught the transmigration of souls and emphasized moral qualities in this life, concerning itself with problems of individual guilt, with an afterlife, and so on. Orphism provides one way of reconciling paganism, Platonism, and Christianity; or at least it furnishes an attitude that can be used for such reconciliation.

One can also see, in these notes, Akenside's willingness to allow himself to make creative emendations, to fashion his own version of a myth. This attitude represents an important change in the artist's view of myth, and it seems to have come about, for Akenside at least, because he regards myth as a way of transmitting truth, not lies. Myth for Akenside is not idolatry, not corrupt stories, not even allegorical parables or historical details. Myth conveys great moral and poetic truths about the nature of things. Since myth is then an important purveyor of truth, the truth-possessing poet will have to change certain details of the old myths, as his perception of the truth changes from that of the old poets and myth-makers. But it is the very fact that myth is looked on as something of great actual value that allows the poet a free hand in reworking the old mythic expressions of truth. The "mythological passion," of which Akenside speaks, proceeds from the poet and shapes or reshapes the myths.

The final note to the poem, the explanation of the phrase "Cyrenaic shell," is the most revealing about Akenside's own purposes and hopes in the "Hymn to the Naiads." In understanding myths as "personifying natural causes" (Jupiter, for example, represents for Akenside "the vital vegetable, plastic nature"), the poet tries, not to reduce or explain away, but to re-create the early sense of divinity in nature. Not interested in derogation or allegory, Akenside goes beyond the then conventional poetic uses of myth as gen-

teel ornament, and often succeeds in generating a little of the awe, mystery, and vitality one associates with later romantic poetic attempts to re-create the world of myth in all its belief-compelling beauty. Akenside in his own limited way is, however, something more than just a fore-runner, for as his comments suggest, he looked upon both myth and poetry as means of reconciling or mediating between the physical realm and the moral or spiritual realm. Myth connects the actual world with the world of imagination; in Akenside's phrase, myths represent "the mutual agreement or opposition of the corporeal and moral powers of the world." This perception, at once Orphic, Platonic, romantic, and modern, reveals one of the central convictions later poets were to take almost for granted about the power and purpose of myth.

R.R.

REFERENCES Our text is from *The Poetical Works of Mark Akenside* (Edinburgh: James Nichol, 1857). See also Douglas Bush, *Mythology and the Romantic Tradition in English Poetry* (Cambridge: Harvard University Press, 1937).

A K E N S I D E

FROM *Hymn to the Naiads*

    . . . Ye, Naiads, Ye
With ravish'd ears the melody attend
Worthy of sacred silence. But the slaves
Of Bacchus with tempestuous clamours
    strive

To drown the heavenly strains, of highest
    Jove
Irreverent, and by mad presumption fired
Their own discordant raptures to advance
With hostile emulation. Down they rush

From Nysa's vine-empurpled cliff, the
    dames
Of Thrace, the Satyrs, and the unruly
    Fauns,
With old Silenus, reeling through the crowd
Which gambols round him, in convulsions
    wild
Tossing their limbs, and brandishing in air
The ivy-mantled thyrsus, or the torch
Through black smoke flaming, to the
    Phrygian pipe's
Shrill voice, and to the clashing cymbals,
    mix'd
With shrieks and frantic uproar. May the
    gods
From every unpolluted ear avert
Their orgies! If within the seats of men,
Within the walls, the gates, where Pallas
    holds
The guardian key, if haply there be found
Who loves to mingle with the revel-band
And hearken to their accents, who aspires
From such instructors to inform his breast
With verse, let him, fit votarist, implore
Their inspiration. He perchance the gifts
Of young Lyaeus, and the dread exploits,
May sing in aptest numbers; he the fate
Of sober Pentheus, he the Paphian rites,
And naked Mars with Cytherea chain'd,
And strong Alcides in the spinster's robes,
May celebrate, applauded. But with you,
O Naiads, far from that unhallow'd rout,
Must dwell the man whoe'er to praisèd
    themes
Invokes the immortal Muse.

                          (ll., 283–317)

               'Love . . .
       Elder than Chaos' l. 25

Hesiod in his Theogony gives a different
account, and makes Chaos the eldest of
beings, though he assigns to Love neither
father nor superior; which circumstance is
particularly mentioned by Phaedrus, in
Plato's Banquet, as being observable not
only in Hesiod, but in all the other writers
both of verse and prose; and on the same
occasion he cites a line from Parmenides,
in which Love is expressly styled the eldest
of all the gods. Yet Aristophanes in 'The
Birds,' affirms, that 'Chaos, and Night, and
Erebus, and Tartarus were first; and that
Love was produced from an egg, which
the sable-winged Night deposited in the
immense bosom of Erebus.' But it must be
observed, that the Love designed by this
comic poet was always distinguished from
the other, from that original and self existent being the TO ON or AGATHON of Plato,
and meant only the DEMIURGOS or second
person of the old Grecian trinity; to whom
is inscribed a hymn among those which
pass under the name of Orpheus, where he
is called Protogonos, or the first-begotten,
is said to have been born of an egg, and
is represented as the principle or origin of
all these external appearances of nature. In
the fragments of Orpheus, collected by
Henry Stephens, he is named Phanes, the
discoverer or discloser, who unfolded the
ideas of the supreme intelligence, and exposed them to the perception of inferior
beings in this visible frame of the world;
as Macrobius, and Proclus, and Athena-
goras, all agree to interpret the several passages of Orpheus which they have preserved.

    But the Love designed in our text is the
one self-existent and infinite mind; whom
if the generality of ancient mythologists
have not introduced or truly described in
accounting for the production of the world
and its appearances, yet, to a modern poet,
it can be no objection that he hath ventured to differ from them in this particular,
though in other respects he professes to
imitate their manner and conform to their
opinions; for, in these great points of natural theology, they differ no less remarkably

among themselves, and are perpetually confounding the philosophical relations of things with the traditionary circumstances of mythic history; upon which very account Callimachus, in his hymn to Jupiter, declareth his dissent from them concerning even an article of the national creed, adding, that the ancient bards were by no means to be depended on. And yet in the exordium of the old Argonautic poem, ascribed to Orpheus, it is said, that 'Love, whom mortals in later times call Phanes, was the father of the eternally begotten Night;' who is generally represented by these mythological poets as being herself the parent of all things; and who, in the 'Indigitamenta,' or Orphic Hymns, is said to be the same with Cypris, or Love itself. Moreover in the body of this Argonautic poem, where the personated Orpheus introduceth himself singing to his lyre in reply to Chiron, he celebrateth 'the obscure memory of Chaos, and the natures which it contained within itself in a state of perpetual vicissitude; how the heaven had its boundary determined, the generation of the earth, the depth of the ocean, and also the sapient Love, the most ancient, the self-sufficient, with all the beings which he produced when he separated one thing from another.' Which noble passage is more directly to Aristotle's purpose in the first book of his metaphysics than any of those which he has there quoted, to show that the ancient poets and mythologists agreed with Empedocles, Anaxagoras, and the other more sober philosophers, in that natural anticipation and common notion of mankind concerning the necessity of mind and reason to account for the connection, motion and good order of the world. For though neither this poem, nor the hymns which pass under the same name, are, it should seem, the work of the real Orpheus, yet beyond all question they are very an-

cient. The hymns, more particularly, are allowed to be older than the invasion of Greece by Xerxes, and were probably a set of public and solemn forms of devotion, as appears by a passage in one of them which Demonsthenes hath almost literally cited in his first oration against Aristogiton, as the saying of Orpheus, the founder of their most holy mysteries. On this account they are of higher authority than any other mythological work now extant, the Theogony of Hesiod himself not excepted. . . .

(Note A)

'Amalthea.' l. 83

The mother of the first Bacchus, whose birth and education was written, as Diodorus Siculus informs us, in the old Pelasgic character, by Thymoetes, grandson of Laomedon, and contemporary with Orpheus. Thymoetes had traveled over Libya to the country which borders on the western ocean; there he saw the island of Nysa, and learned from the inhabitants, that 'Ammon, king of Libya, was married in former ages to Rhea, sister of Saturn and the Titans: that he afterwards fell in love with a beautiful virgin whose name was Amalthea; had a son by her, and gave her possession of a neighboring tract of land, wonderfully fertile; which in shape nearly resembling the horn of an ox was thence called the Hesperian horn, and afterwards the horn of Amalthea: that fearing the jealousy of Rhea, he concealed the young Bacchus in the island of Nysa;' the beauty of which Diodorus describes with great dignity and pomp of style. This fable is one of the noblest in all the ancient mythology, and seems to have made a particular impression on the imagination of Milton; the only modern poet (unless perhaps it be necessary to except Spenser) who, in these mysterious traditions of the poetic story, had a heart to feel, and words to express, the simple and solitary genius of antiquity. To raise the idea of his Paradise, he prefers it even to—

> . . . That Nysean Isle
> Girt by the river Triton, where old Cham
> (Whom Gentiles Ammon call, and Libyan
>   Jove)
> Hid Amalthea and her florid son,
> Young Bacchus, from his stepdame Rhea's
>   eye.
>
> (Note S)

'Cyrenaic shell.' l. 327

Cyrene was the native country of Callimachus, whose hymns are the most remarkable example of that mythological passion which is assumed in the preceding poem, and have always afforded particular pleasure to the author of it, by reason of the mysterious solemnity with which they affect the mind. On this account he was induced to attempt somewhat in the same manner; solely by way of exercise: the manner itself being now almost entirely abandoned in poetry. As the mere genealogy, or the personal adventures of heathen gods, could have been but little interesting to a modern reader, it was therefore thought proper to select some convenient part of the history of nature, and to employ these ancient divinities as it is probable they were first employed; to wit, in personifying natural causes, and in representing the mutual agreement or opposition of the corporeal and moral powers of the world: which hath been accounted the very highest office of poetry.

(Note MM)

ROBERT LOWTH

[1710–1788]

ROBERT LOWTH was best known as
a literary scholar and classical translator
when elected to the usual ten-year term
as Professor of Poetry at Oxford in 1741.
Although the position obliged its holder
minimally, Lowth spent his term carrying
forward a remarkably original study,
brought together finally as *Lectures on
the Sacred Poetry of the Hebrews* (the
title of its English translation in 1787
from the original Latin, *De sacra Poesi
Hebraeorum praelectiones,* 1753). This
volume shows Lowth to be one of the
most original literary critics of the eighteenth century, a primary guide for the
coming German and English poets and
mythologists who call for and look back
to a poetry that is bardic and prophetic,
impassioned and sublime, and "mythic."
Lowth's work sought to demonstrate that
the "primitive" and the most sublime
poetry necessarily go together; and though
the "primitive" example that Lowth used
(and apparently did not wish to go beyond) was the Old Testament, his lessons
could immediately be expanded to myth
in general.

Lowth's originality appears first in his
taking up a subject almost entirely neglected by literary criticism before him:
the Old Testament as poetry like any
other poetry, whose aesthetic principles
and qualities may be analyzed and explained critically. Lowth suggests that the
Bible has never received critical attention,
in part because of piety and in part because poetic principles derived from secu-

lar literature in general (and classical literature specifically) hardly allowed one
to speak of an Old Testament poetry at
all. Lowth boldly proceeded to ignore
literary tradition: he assumed that Hebrew poetry had its own form, a form
largely determined by the uniquely divine
subject matter and source of the Bible.
The style and versification of Hebrew
poetry are governed completely by the
Hebrews' overriding desire to worship, to
express God's truths to man. Biblical
"meter" has nothing to do with the usual
prosodic rules. Hebrew verse moves instead by parallelisms, by balances and
counterbalances of units rhythmically
playing off each other, building to height-
ened religious feeling by antiphonal state-
ment-and-response. By showing how parallelism (and other devices) informs biblical poetry as prosody does secular verse,
Lowth aesthetically defended and dignified the Old Testament. In doing this,
Lowth helped prepare similar aesthetic
defending and dignifying of literary works
still considered outside the critical pale of
respectability, such as national or folk
epics and legends, or mythic poetry in
general.

Lowth's literary analysis of how Hebrew poetry used parallelism, metaphor,
allegory, or personification thus struck
forcefully at the neoclassic view that the
Old Testament was only a "naive" composition when compared to classical literature. But his analysis also helped explain what had often been a dissatisfac-

tion (or, for the orthodox, an embarrass-ment) for neoclassic and early eighteenth-century critics: the contrast between how elevated biblical style should be (as a divinely inspired work), and how simple and earthy its images and language in fact were. The Old Testament was, in short, at once too plain and too uninhibit-edly passionate. Lowth's defense of Old Testament poetry is crucially put in terms of the "sublime." And again, what Lowth says about biblical poetic sublimity is easily and inevitably applicable to all mythic poetry.

Though his main examples were of course classical, Longinus had quoted an example of the sublime from Genesis. Be-fore Lowth, the sublime had become of great interest, most influentially perhaps from Boileau's translation and interpreta-tion of Longinus in 1674, and carried in England through such critics as John Dennis. Dennis's *The Grounds of Criti-cism in Poetry* (1704) argued that "re-ligion is the basis and foundation of the greater poetry"; and Dennis gave Old Testament prophets, *Job,* the *Song of Songs* (and *Paradise Lost*) as examples. One side of Dennis's effort was to redeem "enthusiasm" from the bad name given it by rationalists and deists: Dennis (and the influential Shaftesbury) distinguishes between false and true enthusiasm, be-tween mere fanaticism and true exalta-tion. With Lowth, the Bible as such be-comes the prime example of all poetic sublimity; and the idea of the sublime, as Lowth inherited it from such critics as Dennis, approved "plain" style and dic-tion, the better to make the moment of sublimity more striking and marvellous. For Lowth, nothing is more obvious in the Bible than its "utmost brevity and simplicity" of style: there, a thought is often first stated baldly, then repeated and varied. This very simplicity is a sign of unusual fervor; what the ancient Hebrew felt, he said plainly and passionately. All poetic artificiality and "literary" effect

was scorned. In brief, the Hebrew sought God, and found sublime poetry on the way. The Hebrew did not wish to display, exposit, or only adorn God's grandeur; he felt so deeply that any image could serve. And Lowth devotes much analysis to how Hebrew imagery praised God by drawing from homely things, common objects, from parts of the body, or everyday events. These show God is everywhere, greater than any merely created thing. Old Testament language epitomizes the sublime style, for it will "strike and over-power the mind, excite the passion, and express ideas at once with perspicuity and elevation." Such descriptions of the He-brews as a nation of worshipper-poets are clearly sympathetic to later views of folk-created poetry and myth. What Lowth says about a sublimely passionate style and plain style helps in new and sympa-thetic reappraisal of "unrefined" national and folk literature, and has obvious echoes in later romantics, such as Blake or Wordsworth, who would seek eternal truth and great poetry in London's streets or in bare hills, in natural, unspoiled, and spontaneous images and feelings.

As an historian and a philologian, Lowth was admired by later historians and theorists of myth. His analysis of the unique linguistic forms and aesthetic qualities of Hebrew poetry offered a new avenue back into Hebrew thought and customs, and Lowth's admirers here in-cluded Gibbon, Sir William Jones, and the foremost eighteenth-century biblical antiquarian, J. D. Michaelis (who anno-tated the first German edition of Lowth's work in 1758). Beyond such new philo-logic-critical approaches, Lowth also ar-gued that the history of the past needed to be studied in a living, inward, and ex-periential way: thus, Lowth urges that we can understand the ancient Hebrews only if we try to think, write, and feel as they did—indeed, we must *become* them, in-sofar as possible. Lowth's disciple here is Herder, who went on to "creatively" experience Genesis, Homer, and all myth. Both sides of Lowth's approach, the philologic and the experiential, are influential in forming the mythic theories of the Göttingen philologian-critic, C. G. Heyne, and the school of "higher" biblical criticism running from Heyne through D. F. Strauss's *Life of Jesus.*

Perhaps the heart of Lowth's biblical analysis is his assumption that poetry and sublime feeling are essentially religious in origin and in effect. Religion properly seeks to express itself poetically; and conversely, the greatest poetry will have an effect essentially religious in kind. Lowth's restriction of his arguments to the Old Testament, in an orthodox Christian spirit, would hinder no later romantic poet or mythologist from applying Lowth's lesson more daringly and widely. Mythologists such as Herder and Heyne, in the Lowthian spirit and with praise for his pioneering work, would argue that religion issues into poetry quite naturally, and vice versa—and they thereby broadened the concept of myth, poetry, and religion in a new, wide, fruitful, and not a little confusing, way.

B.F.

REFERENCES   *Lectures on the Sacred Poetry of the Hebrews,* translated from the Latin by G. Gregory, with additional notes by J. D. Michaelis and S. Henley (London, 1787), 2 vols. Our text is from the one-volume London, 1847 edition of this work.

For commentary, see: Murray Roston, *Prophet and Poet: The Bible and the Growth of Romanticism* (Evanston: Northwestern University Press, 1965), for a full account of Lowth in the eighteenth-century literary setting; Christian Hartlich and Walter Sachs, *Der Ursprung des Mythosbegriffes in der Modernen Bibelwissenschaft* (Tubingen: J. C. B. Mohr, 1952), which places Lowth directly in the line of mythic thought running from Heyne through David Friedrich Strauss. The relevant work of John Dennis can be found in his *The Ground of Criticism in Poetry* (1704), in *The Critical Works of John Dennis* (Baltimore: The Johns Hopkins Press, 1939), pp. 336–381; see also his remarks on Greek myth and religion, pp. 238–251.

For a defense of the literary merit of the Bible before Lowth, see Anthony Blackwall, *The Sacred Classics Defended and Illustrated . . . towards proving the Purity, Propriety, and True Eloquence of the Writers of the New Testament* (London, 1727), which argues—far more vaguely than Lowth—that New Testament has all sublime excellencies of style and is superior to Greek or Roman classics.

LOWTH

FROM *Lectures on the Sacred Poetry of the Hebrews*

THESE observations are remarkably exemplified in the Hebrew poetry, than which the human mind can conceive nothing more elevated, more beautiful, or more elegant; in which the almost ineffable sublimity of the subject is fully equalled by the energy of the language and the dignity of the style. And it is worthy observation, that as some of these writings exceed in antiquity the fabulous ages of Greece, in sublimity they are superior to the most finished productions of that polished people. Thus, if the actual origin of poetry be inquired after, it must of necessity be referred to religion; and since it appears to be an art derived from nature alone, peculiar to no age or nation, and only at an advanced period of society conformed to rule and method, it must be wholly attributed to the more violent affections of the heart, the nature of which is to express themselves in an animated and lofty tone, with a vehemence of expression far remote from vulgar use. It is also no less observable, that these affections break and interrupt the enunciation of their impetuosity; they burst forth in sentences pointed, earnest, rapid, and tremulous; in some degree the style as well as the modulation is adapted to the emotions and habits of the mind. This is particularly the case in admiration and delight; and what passions are so likely to be excited by religious contemplations as these? What ideas could so powerfully affect a new-created mind (undepraved by habit or opinion) as the goodness, the wisdom, and the greatness of the Almighty? Is it not probable, that the first effort of rude and unpolished verse would display itself in the praise of the Creator, and flow almost involuntarily from the enraptured mind? Thus far, at least, is certain, that poetry has been nurtured in those sacred places where she seems to have been first called into existence; and that her original occupation was in the temple and at the altar.   (from Lecture I)

It would not be easy, indeed, to assign a reason, why the writings of Homer, of Pindar, and of Horace, should engross our attention and monopolise our praise, while those of Moses, of David, and Isaiah, pass totally unregarded. Shall we suppose that the subject is not adapted to a seminary in which sacred literature has ever maintained a precedence? Shall we say, that it is foreign to this assembly of promising youth, of whom the greater part have consecrated the best portion of their time and labour to the same department of learning? Or must we conclude, that the writings of those men who have accomplished only as much as human genius and ability could accomplish, should be reduced to method and theory; but that those which boast a much higher origin, and are justly attributed to the inspiration of the Holy Spirit, may be considered as indeed illustrious by their native force and beauty, but not as conformable to the principles of science, nor to be circumscribed by any rules of art? It is indeed most true, that sacred poetry, if we contemplate its origin alone, is far superior to both *nature* and *art;* but if we would rightly estimate its excellences, that is, if we wish to understand its power in exciting the human affections, we must have recourse to both. . . .

. . . Here we may contemplate poetry in its very beginning—not so much the offspring of human genius, as an emanation from heaven; not gradually increasing by small accessions, but from its birth possessing a certain maturity both of beauty and strength; not administering to trifling passions, and offering its delicious incense at the shrine of vanity, but the priestess of divine truth, the internunciate between earth and heaven. For this was the first and peculiar office of poetry—on the one hand to commend to the Almighty the prayers and thanksgivings of his creatures, and to celebrate his praises; and on the other to display to mankind the mysteries of the divine will, and the predictions of future events—the best and noblest of all employments. It is to this observation, indeed, that I would particularly point your attention; for it is plain from the general tenour of the sacred volume, that the indications of future events have been, almost without exception, revealed in numbers and in verse; and that the same spirit was accustomed to impart, by its own energy, at once the presentiment of things, and to clothe it in all the magnificence, in all the elegance of poetry, that the sublimity of the style might consist with sentiments so infinitely surpassing all human conception. When considered, therefore, in this point of view, what is there of all which the most devoted admirers of poetry have ever written or fabricated in its commendation, that does not fall greatly short of the truth itself? What of all the insinuations which its bitterest adversaries have objected against it, which is not refuted by simply contemplating the nature and design of the Hebrew poetry? Let those who affect to despise the Muses cease to attempt, for the vices of a few who may abuse the best of things, to bring in disrepute a most laudable talent. Let them cease to speak of that art as light or trifling in itself, to accuse it as profane or impious; that art which has been conceded to man by the favour of his Creator, and for the most sacred purposes; that art consecrated by the authority of God himself; and by his example in his most august ministrations.

Whether the Greeks originally derived their poetry from the fountains of nature, or received it through a different channel from a remoter source, appears a question of little importance, and not easy to be determined. Thus far, however, is evident, that an opinion was prevalent in Greece concerning the nature and origin of poetry, which appears most groundless and absurd if we contemplate only the poetry of Greece, though truly and justly applicable to that of the Hebrews. They considered poetry as something sacred and celestial, not produced by human art or genius, but altogether a Divine gift. Among them, therefore, poets were accounted sacred, the ambassadors of Heaven, men favoured with an immediate intercourse and familiarity with the gods. The mysteries and ceremonies of their religion, and the worship of their deities, were all performed in verse; and the most ancient of their compositions, their oracles, always consisted of numbers. This circumstance, I must add, rendered them not only more sublime, but more deserving of credit in the eyes of the common people; for they conceived it equally the effect of divine inspiration to foresee events, and to express them in extemporaneous verse. Thus, they seemed to have retained some traces of an opinion impressed upon the minds of men in the very earliest ages concerning the true and ancient poetry, even after they had lost the reality itself, and when religion and poetry had, by the licentiousness of fiction, reciprocally corrupted each other.

Since, therefore, in the sacred writings the only specimens of the primeval and genuine poetry are to be found, and since these are not less venerable for their antiquity than for their divine original, I conceived it my duty in the first place to investigate the nature of these writings, as far as might be consistent with the design of this institution. In other words, it is not my intention to expound to the student of theology the oracles of Divine truth, but to recommend to the notice of the youth who is addicted to politer sciences, and studious of the elegancies of composition, some of the first and choicest specimens of poetic taste.   (from Lecture II)

It became the peculiar province of poetry to depict the great, the beautiful, the becoming, the virtuous; to embellish and recommend the precepts of religion and virtue; to transmit to posterity excellent

and sublime actions and sayings; to celebrate the works of the Deity, his beneficence, his wisdom; to record the memorials of the past, and the predictions of
the future. In each of these departments
poetry was of singular utility, since, before
any characters expressive of sound were
invented, at least before they were commonly received and applied to general
use, it seems to have afforded the only
means of preserving the rude science of
the early times, and in this respect, to
have rendered the want of letters more
tolerable: it seems also to have acted the
part of a public herald, by whose voice
each memorable transaction of antiquity
was proclaimed and transmitted through
different ages and nations.

Such appears by the testimony of authors
to have been the undoubted origin of poetry
among heathen nations. It is evident that
Greece, for several successive ages, was
possessed of no records but the poetic.
. . . In the same manner, on the same
account, the Persians, the Arabs, and many
of the most ancient of the eastern nations,
preserved in verse their history and politics,
as well as the principles of religion and
morals: thus all science, human and divine,
was deposited in the treasury of the Muses,
and thither it was necessary on every occasion to resort. The only mode of instruction, indeed, adapted to human nature in
an uncivilised state, when the knowledge of
letters was very little if at all diffused, must
be that which is calculated to captivate the
ear and the passions, which assists the
memory, which is not to be delivered into
the hand, but infused into the mind and
heart.

That the case was the same among the
Hebrews—that poetry was both anciently
and generally known and practiced by
them, appears highly probable, as well
from the analogy of things, as from some

vestiges of poetic language extant in the
writings of Moses.   (from Lecture IV)

On this account difficulties must occur
in the perusal of almost every work of
literature, and particularly in poetry, where
everything is depicted and illustrated with
the greatest variety and abundance of imagery: they must be still more numerous in
such of the poets as are foreign and ancient; in the Orientals above all foreigners,
they being the farthest removed from our
customs and manners; and of all the Orientals, more especially in the Hebrews,
theirs being confessedly the most ancient
compositions extant. To all who apply
themselves to the study of their poetry, for
the reasons which I have enumerated, difficulties and inconveniences must necessarily occur. Not only the antiquity of
these writings forms a principal obstruction
in many respects; but the manner of living,
of speaking, of thinking, which prevailed
in those times, will be found altogether
different from our customs and habits.
There is, therefore, great danger, lest, viewing them from an improper situation, and
rashly estimating all things by our own
standard, we form an erroneous judgment.

Of this kind of mistake we are to be always aware, and these inconveniences are
to be counteracted by all possible diligence: nor is it enough to be acquainted
with the language of this people, their manners, discipline, rites, and ceremonies; we
must even investigate their inmost sentiments, the manner and connexion of their
thoughts; in one word, we must see all
things with their eyes, estimate all things
by their opinions; we must endeavour as
much as possible to read Hebrew as the
Hebrews would have read it. We must act
as the astronomers with regard to that
branch of their science which is called comparative, who, in order to form a more per-

fect idea of the general system and its different parts, conceive themselves as passing through and surveying the whole universe, migrating from one planet to another, and becoming for a short time inhabitants of each. Thus they clearly contemplate, and accurately estimate, what each possesses peculiar to itself, with respect to situation, celerity, satellites, and its relation to the rest: thus they distinguish what and how different an appearance of the universe is exhibited, according to the different situations from which it is contemplated. In like manner, he who would perceive and feel the peculiar and interior elegances of the Hebrew poetry, must imagine himself exactly situated as the persons for whom it was written, or even as the writers themselves: he must not attend to the ideas which, on a cursory reading, certain words would obtrude upon his mind; he is to feel them as a Hebrew hearing or delivering the same words, at the same time, and in the same country. As far as he is able to pursue this plan, so far he will comprehend their force and excellence.

(from Lecture V)

The greatness, the power, the justice, the immensity of God—the infinite wisdom of his works and of his dispensations—are the subjects in which the Hebrew poetry is always conversant, and always excels. If we only consider, with a common degree of candour, how greatly inferior the poetry of all other nations appears whenever it presumes to treat of these subjects, and how unequal to the dignity of the matter the highest conceptions of the human genius are found to be, we shall, I think, not only acknowledge the sublimity, but the divinity of that of the Hebrews.

(from Lecture XVI)

VOLTAIRE

[1694–1778]

No DISCUSSSION of the eighteenth century can avoid Voltaire, and least of all a discussion of myth in that period. This is not because Voltaire himself is very open to myth as such. Quite the opposite: like Bayle half a century before him, from whom Voltaire borrows many scandalous versions of pagan and biblical themes, Voltaire firmly and caustically rejects myth as patent superstition and historical distortion. But Voltaire everywhere touches on myth, for it is a problem rooted deeply in at least three of his central concerns: as a "universal" historian, Voltaire must consider man's earliest beginnings; as a "philosopher" of history, he must explain why those beginnings were as they were; and as a deist committed to natural religion and monotheism, he must battle myth along with other examples of *l'infâme,* past and present. But if Voltaire's work as an historian thus opened the way to making myth more important, his deist commitment denied such a conclusion.

In his *Essay on the Manners and Mind of Nations, and on the Principal Facts of History from Charlemagne to Louis XIII* (1769), Voltaire set out to complete the work of the last great "universal" historian, Bossuet. Bossuet's *Discourse on Universal History* (1681) saw history as preparing for and culminating in Israel and Christianity: it began with Adam and moved to the Flood, the Covenant with Abraham, to Moses, Troy's capture, the founding of the Temple, and finally on to

the birth of Christ and to Christianity's alliance with Rome. Voltaire brings this history down to the present; but he makes clear also that he rejects Bossuet's Christian-universal history in favor of a new secular "philosophy" of history, where Providence is replaced by progress. Voltaire thus rewrites the past so that the Bible and Greece play only minor roles. He therefore pushes historic time far back beyond Genesis to geologic time, arguing that an immense amount of time is needed for man to develop societies, arts, and sciences. Nor will Voltaire "forget three-fourths of the earth." His history begins not with the provincial Israelites, but in the Far East, the "nursery of the arts, to which the Western world owes everything it now enjoys." Voltaire begins with China, then moves slowly westward to India, Persia, Arabia, and finally to Christ and Rome.

But Voltaire's view of myth can hardly be said to undergo the enlargement of perspective implied by his secularizing and universalizing of history. For one thing, his pungent sketch of mankind's religious pluralism and primitivism conflicts with his desire to demonstrate that the earliest religions were deistically monotheistic. For example, Voltaire's argument that mankind needed an immense amount of time in which to develop might have led him to the reasonable conclusion that polytheism or primitive thought was a necessary step to a higher stage. But Voltaire is violently derogatory of such polytheistic myth, and treats polytheism as a degradation of natural religion.

Nevertheless, however much Voltaire speaks for the conquering Enlightenment, he also makes clear how deist thought could slide easily and sympathetically into romantic views affirming myth. Partly from his anti-Christian purposes, partly as a deist, he portrays and esteems the Chinese or Hindus as similar to enlightened European *philosophes,* tolerant, worldly-wise, and teaching a natural benevolence, sublimity, and religion. Voltaire claims the East as earlier than, as models and sources for, and as morally superior to Israel and Christianity (and Greece). This view of the East as a place of benign climate and unspoiled spiritual benevolence—and often as better than the restrictive, dogmatic, Old Testament Christianity, or than barbarous Greece—is a thesis much repeated by romantics, especially from Herder on (in whose thought a near-deist natural religion remained importantly alive). But many romantics also face, as Voltaire did not, the difficulty of reconciling a rational monotheistic natural religion with an irrational naturalness.

Considering that he lived after Vico's daring return to "irrational" mythic origins, and during Humes' corrosion of self-confident rationalism, Voltaire's kind of rationalism and deism can seem (not unfairly) somewhat old-fashioned. He looks back to Bayle, rather than forward to Kant or the romantics. Yet this may account in part for Voltaire's lasting importance in the history of modern mythic thought. He does not innovate any view of myth; he rather gives official stability and popular sanction to the writing of history free from Christian authority and sources. He legitimizes secularism, so to speak: he reworks openly and brilliantly the anti-orthodox arguments that earlier were well-established. He is even more daringly antireligious—but also necessarily more prudent. He is perhaps most delightfully prudent and boldly mocking in his tales, many of which parody or burlesque pious religious histories, explanations, or attitudes: *Candide,* of course, or *Mahomet, Micromegas, Zadig,* or the stories in the *Philosophical Dictionary.* Later mythologists could increasingly assume his freedom of inquiry and of expression, without having to fight the battle over again.

B.F.

REFERENCES   Our text is from *The Works of Voltaire,* with notes by T. Smollett, revised and modernized translations by William F. Fleming, 42 vols. (London and New York: G. R. DuMont, 1901), vol. XIII, pp. 63–73. For commentary, see: J. H. Brumfitt, *Voltaire, Historian* (London: Oxford University Press, 1958); H. Mason, *Pierre Bayle and Voltaire* (London: Oxford University Press, 1963); Richard A. Brooks, *Voltaire and Leibniz* (Genève: Libraire Droz, 1964); Frank Manuel, *The Eighteenth Century Confronts the Gods* (Cambridge: Harvard University Press, 1959); *La Philosophie de l'Histoire,* ed. J. H. Brumfitt (Genève: University of Toronto Press, 1969), pp. 13–78 (in *Les Oeuvres complètes de Voltaire,* vol. 59); Rene Pomeau, *La Religion de Voltaire* (Paris: Nizet, 1956); J. S. Spink, *French Free-Thought from Gassendi to Voltaire* (London: University of London, Athlone Press, 1960). For Voltaire's great interest in and limited knowledge of the East, see Raymond Schwab, *La Renaissance orientale* (Paris: Payot, 1950), esp. pp. 164–168, and W. Engemann, *Voltaire and China* (Leipzig, 1933).

FROM *Philosophical Dictionary*

FROM *On Religion*

LAST NIGHT I was meditating; I was absorbed in the contemplation of nature, admiring the immensity, the courses, the relations of those infinite globes, which are above the admiration of the vulgar.

I admired still more the intelligence that presides over this vast machinery. I said to myself: A man must be blind not to be impressed by this spectacle; he must be stupid not to recognize its author; he must be mad not to adore him. What tribute of adoration ought I to render him? Should not this tribute be the same throughout the extent of space, since the same Supreme Power reigns equally in all that extent?

Does not a thinking being, inhabiting a star of the Milky Way, owe him the same homage as the thinking being on this little globe where we are? Light is the same to the dog-star as to us; morality, too, must be the same.

If a feeling and thinking being in the dog-star is born of a tender father and mother, who have labored for his welfare, he owes them as much love and duty as we here owe to our parents. If any one in the Milky Way sees another lame and indigent, and does not relieve him, though able to do it, he is guilty in the sight of every globe.

The heart has everywhere the same duties; on the steps of the throne of God, if he has a throne, and at the bottom of the great abyss, if there be an abyss.

I was wrapt in these reflections, when one of those genii who fill the spaces between worlds, came down to me. I recognized the same aerial creature that had formerly appeared to me, to inform me that the judgments of God are different from ours, and how much a good action is preferable to controversy.

He transported me into a desert covered all over with bones piled one upon another; and between these heaps of dead there were avenues of evergreen trees, and at the end of each avenue a tall man of august aspect gazing with compassion on these sad remains.

"Alas! my archangel," said I, "whither have you brought me?" "To desolation," answered he. "And who are those fine old patriarchs whom I see motionless and melancholy at the end of those green avenues, and who seem to weep over this immense multitude of dead?" "Poor human creature! thou shalt know," replied the genius; "but, first thou must weep."

He began with the first heap. "These," said he, "are the twenty-three thousand Jews who danced before a calf, together with the twenty-four thousand who were slain while ravishing Midianitish women; the number of the slaughtered for similar offences or mistakes amounts to nearly three hundred thousand."

"At the following avenues are the bones of Christians, butchered by one another on account of metaphysical disputes. They are divided into several piles of four centuries each; it was necessary to separate them; for had they been all together, they would have reached the sky."

"What!" exclaimed I, "have brethren thus treated their brethren; and have I the misfortune to be one of this brotherhood?"

"Here," said the spirit, "are the twelve millions of Americans slain in their own country for not having been baptized." "Ah! my God! why were not these frightful skeletons left to whiten in the hemisphere where the bodies were born, and where they were murdered in so many various ways? Why are all these abominable monuments of barbarity and fanaticism assembled here?" "For thy instruction."

"Since thou art willing to instruct me," said I to the genius, "tell me if there be any other people than the Christians and the Jews, whom zeal and religion, unhappily turned into fanaticism, have prompted to so many horrible cruelties?" "Yes," said he; "the Mahometans have been stained by the same inhuman acts, but rarely; and when their victims have cried out '*amman!*' (mercy!) and have offered them tribute, they have pardoned them. As for other nations, not one of them, since the beginning of the world, has ever made a purely religious war. Now, follow me!" I followed.

A little beyond these heaps of dead we found other heaps; these were bags of gold and silver; and each pile had its label: "Substance of the heretics massacred in the eighteenth century, in the seventeenth, in the sixteenth," and so on. "Gold and silver of the slaughtered Americans," etc.;

all these piles were surmounted by crosses, mitres, crosiers, and tiaras, enriched with jewels.

"What! my genius, was it then to possess these riches that these carcasses were accumulated?" "Yes, my son."

I shed tears; and when by my grief I had merited to be taken to the end of the green avenues, he conducted me thither.

"Contemplate," said he, "the heroes of humanity who have been the benefactors of the earth, and who united to banish from the world, as far as they were able, violence and rapine. Question them."

I went up to the first of this band; on his head was a crown, and in his hand a small censer. I humbly asked him his name. "I," said he, "am Numa Pompilius; I succeeded a robber, and had robbers to govern; I taught them virtue and the worship of God; after me they repeatedly forgot both. I forbade any image to be placed in the temples, because the divinity who animates nature cannot be represented. During my reign the Romans had neither wars nor seditions; and my religion did nothing but good. Every neighboring people came to honor my funeral, which has happened to me alone . . ."

I made my obeisance and passed on to the second. This was a fine old man, of about a hundred, clad in a white robe; his middle finger was placed on his lip, and with the other hand he was scattering beans behind him. In him I recognized Pythagoras. He assured me that he had never had a golden thigh, and that he had never been a cock, but that he had governed the Crotonians with as much justice as Numa had governed the Romans about the same time, which justice was the most necessary and the rarest thing in the world. I learned that the Pythagoreans examined their consciences twice a day. What good people!

and how far are we behind them! Yet we, who for thirteen hundred years have been nothing but assassins, assert that these wise men were proud.

To please Pythagoras I said not a word to him, but went on to Zoroaster, who was engaged in concentrating the celestial fire in the focus of a concave mirror, in the centre of a vestibule with a hundred gates, each one leading to wisdom. On the principal of these gates I read these words, which are the abstract of all morality, and cut short all the disputes of the casuists: "When thou art in doubt whether an action is good or bad, abstain from it."

"Certainly," said I to my genius, "the barbarians who immolated all the victims whose bones I have seen had not read these fine words."

Then we saw Zaleucus, Thales, Anaximander, and all the other sages who had sought truth and practised virtue.

When we came to Socrates I quickly recognized him by his broken nose. "Well," said I, "you then are among the confidants of the Most High! All the inhabitants of Europe, excepting the Turks and the Crim Tartars, who know nothing, pronounce your name with reverence. So much is that great name venerated, so much is it loved, that it has been sought to discover those of your persecutors. Melitus and Anytus are known because of you, as Ravaillac is known because of Henry IV; but of Anytus I know only the name. I know not precisely who that villian was by whom you were calumniated, and who succeeded in procuring your condemnation to the hemlock."

"I have never thought of that man since my adventure," answered Socrates; "but now that you put me in mind of him, I pity him much. He was a wicked priest, who secretly carried on a trade in leather,

a traffic reputed shameful amongst us. He sent his two children to my school; the other disciples reproached them with their father's being a currier, and they were obliged to quit. The incensed father was unceasing in his endeavors until he had stirred up against me all the priests and all the sophists. They persuaded the council of the five hundred that I was an impious man, who did not believe that the moon, Mercury, and Mars were deities. I thought indeed, as I do now, that there is but one God, the master of all nature. The judges gave me up to the republic's poisoner, and he shortened my life a few days. I died with tranquility at the age of seventy years, and since then I have led a happy life with all these great men whom you see, and of whom I am the least. . . ."

I beheld a man of mild and simple mien, who appeared to me to be about thirty-five years old. He was looking with compassion upon the distant heaps of whitened skeletons through which I had been led to the abode of the sages. I was astonished to find his feet swelled and bloody, his hands in the same state, his side pierced, and his ribs laid bare by flogging. "Good God!" said I. "Is it possible that one of the just and wise should be in this state? . . . Was it also by priests and judges that you were so cruelly assassinated?"

With great affability he answered—"Yes."

"And who were those monsters?"

"They were hypocrites."

"Ah! you have said all! by that one word I understand that they would condemn you to the worst of punishments. You then had proved to them, like Socrates, that the moon was not a goddess, and that Mercury was not a god?"

"No; those planets were quite out of the question. My countrymen did not even know what a planet was; they were all arrant ignoramuses. Their superstitions were quite different from those of the Greeks."

"Then you wished to teach them a new religion?"

"Not at all; I simply said to them 'Love God with all your hearts, and your neighbor as yourselves; for that is all.' . . ."

I was on the point of begging of him to have the goodness just to tell me who he was; but my guide warned me to refrain. He told me that I was not formed for comprehending these sublime mysteries. I conjured him to tell me only in what true religion consisted.

"Have I not told you already? Love God and your neighbor as yourself."

"What! Can you love God and yet eat meat on a Friday?"

"I always ate what was given me; for I was too poor to give a dinner to any one."

"Might we love God and be just, and still be prudent enough not to intrust all the adventures of one's life to a person one does not know?"

"Such was always my custom."

"Might not I, while doing good, be excused from making a pilgrimage to St. James of Compostello?"

"I never was in that country."

"Should I confine myself in a place of retirement with blockheads?"

"For my part, I always made little journeys from town to town."

"Must I take part with the Greek or with the Latin Church?"

"When I was in the world, I never made any difference between the Jew and the Samaritan."

"Well, if it be so, I take you for my only master."

Then he gave me a nod, which filled me with consolation. The vision disappeared, and I was left with a good conscience.

DAVID HUME

[1711–1776]

THROUGH the eighteenth century, mythology served rationalist purposes as a rich source of parallels and counterclaims embarrassing to revealed religion; in Hume, for the first time in any significant way, myth becomes an embarrassment for free thought and atheism, and for rationality as well. But this is not because Hume found new intellectual power in myth. On the contrary, Hume maintains an enlightenment contempt for myth. Myth has no intellectual value or strength; it is only that reason now shows itself unexpectedly weak and limited. In effect, Hume leaves the status of myth and religion unchanged, but changes the status of reason profoundly; but one effect of this is also to change how myth and religion are to be understood.

The result of Hume's relentless empirical introspection is of course one of the best-known chapters in modern philosophy. His stringent empiricism dissolves the self and all certain knowledge of outside substances into a flow of discrete phenomena whose real causes or unifying principles escape us. For Hume, finally, there seems little, if any, justification for what rationality, especially in the seventeenth and eighteenth centuries, declared to be its triumphs—its laws of causation, or the universality and necessity of its laws governing nature and human nature, or its confidence in possessing *a priori* knowledge. For, "if we reason *a priori,* anything may appear able to produce anything"; to suppose that the mind has anything more present to it than perceptions "has no foundation in reasoning." If reason cannot establish its own laws with certainty, then reason can hardly claim to explain or judge religion. From an orthodox religious viewpoint, this outcome could seem scandalous, for it cut religion off from rational support; but from a deist or atheist viewpoint, the outcome could seem as scandalous, for it freed revealed religion and barbaric myth from rational authority and final judgment.

The brunt of Hume's skepticism is borne by natural religion, by atheism, or by any rationalism that confidently judged myth as "irrational" because its own position seemed securely "rational," or that found the thoughts of primitive men possessed of reason and monotheism because the clear laws of "human nature" and "nature" demanded such a conclusion. A typical example is Samuel Clarke's *Discourse on Natural Religion* (1706): "This Method of deducing the Will of God, from his Attributes, is of all others the best and clearest, and certainest and most universal, that the Light of Nature affords." For Hume, however, natural religion can defend its knowledge as little as can revealed religion. Thus, he begins where enlightened thought begins, but ends quite apart. *The Natural History of Religion* begins by showing myth as polytheistic absurdity, as idolatry born from fear and ignorance, never advancing beyond such anthropomorphic superstition. Hume goes on to identify this "popular religion" of paganism with all religions, including Christianity—but also including theism: "Examine the religious principles which have in fact prevailed in the world. You will scarcely be persuaded that they are anything but sick men's dreams." A polemic deist such as Toland, a skeptic such as Bayle, or a tough atheist such as Holbach might have pronounced this withering judgment on all religions. But Hume differs from earlier derogators of religion—and is akin to later "critical" thinkers such as Hamann and Kant—in permitting reason no comfortable or privileged immunity. Thus, the *Natural History* denies that mankind's first religion was monotheistic, because Hume denies that religion self-evidently shares in reason, as deists maintained. More important is Hume's conclusion on the rational side, where "doubt, uncertainty, suspence of judgment appear the only result of our most accurate scrutiny concerning this subject." The wise man, says Hume, willingly lets religious opinions fight each other, while he escapes to the regions of philosophy, which—though they are calm —are also "obscure."

Hume explores myth most directly in *The Natural History of Religion* (1757). This "history" seems remarkably unconcerned with real historical evidence, contenting itself narrowly with classical citations on one side and with reading history cavalierly on the other (that is, he says some nations have been discovered that lack religious sentiment—but which nations, or by who discovered, is left unmentioned; or, "about 1700 years ago all mankind were polytheists"). But *The Natural History of Religion* is not in fact a history of religion but a natural history of the human mind, a philosophical anatomy of psychological principles leading to religious belief. (And in such an approach, Hume's book shows genuine kinship with Trenchard's earlier *Natural History of Superstition*.) If one asks not where religion springs from in human

thought, but what truth religion may lay claim to, that subject is taken up in the *Dialogues concerning Natural Religion*.

The Natural History of Religion thus approaches myth from a double perspective: it studies myth and religious origins by looking to their psychological origins; but it also discovers something crucial about the mind by seeing what in it could give rise to such quite unreasonable notions. Mythology and psychology reflect each other. We may expect then to find myth springing from human passions alone, or perhaps better, from the natural frailty of the mind. One leading principle of human nature is its susceptibility to fear, especially of future events. Once afraid, man becomes panic-stricken as his thoughts race ahead, multiplying every conceivable kind of horror. Another human quality acts to alleviate this distress (though without, of course, coming to understand it any better). The savage mind finds some relief from nameless fears by giving them form, by personifying them, by making the unknown much like men, though somewhat superior in power and wisdom. Myth may now be said to arise in its familiar aspect: the various divinities are categorized according to their sphere of influence, leading to allegory. And since the gods are not much different or higher than mortals, it seems simple enough to elevate any local hero to divinity. Hume agrees with other Euhemerists that most pagan divinities were originally men. Because the "vulgar multitude" find it impossible to grasp the idea of an "invisible spiritual intelligence" in itself, but need the props of sensible, visible representation, poets, painters, sculptors, and priests now flourish, and declare sun, moon, and monkeys to be divinities; or, (in a more refined age) make statues, images, and pictures of their gods. Meanwhile, fabulous history and mythological tradition add to the confusion. Finally, another human failing must be considered—the human propensity for adulation, by means of which theism arises from polytheism. Having chosen a god or gods, men then outvie each other in fulsome flattery, "swelling up the titles of his divinity" till they arrive at last at infinity itself. By chance, then, men arrive at a false notion of the divine that happens to coincide with the true view reason possesses; by no means to their credit, superstitious men now speak of the divine as a perfect being, the creator of the world.

Though preserving a more or less Euhemerist account of religious origins, Hume advances a somewhat different and more original view of the origin of myth. It is impossible, he says, for monotheism to have been the original religion of mankind, because the human mind would not have been ready for such a higher view. The "natural progress" of human thought is to rise "gradually, from inferior to superior." Hume discusses this evolutionary view of human thought almost entirely in terms of the inner workings of the mind. Only by casual suggestion does he imply that all this takes place in historical time; and though Hume thus moves to the edge of a distinctly historicist and later view of myth, he remains aside from it. Nor does Hume enter into what later would be called an organic view of mind or culture, though here too he may imply it in part.

"The ancient mythologists" embraced the idea of "generation," rather than that of "creation or formation"; but this poorly explains the origins of the universe, if at all, since it supposes "gods and men to have sprung equally from the unknown powers of nature." But here the problem is complicated. For though Hume seems to reject any such explanation as myth gives, and seems to affirm that the only true cause of the universe must be external creation, the issue in Hume is uncertain. Our interest here is not and cannot be in pursuing Hume's largest view; his thought is unusually

complex and not a little elusive. But this very complexity of Hume's thought needs to be noted, for it raises a side of his thought little noted in regard to myth, but of unusual interest. On the matter of generation and myth, for example, where the issue seems settled in the *Natural History,* the issue seems to be opened again in the *Dialogues concerning Natural Religion,* especially in Part VII. For here, Philo, the skeptic, argues at least hypothetically for the plausibility of the generative myths of the ancient mythologists. Since ". . . we have no *data* to establish any system of cosmogony," and need some hypothesis, ". . . does not a plant or an animal, which springs from vegetation or generation, bear a stronger resemblance to the world" than analogies to artificial machines? For some Hume scholars, Philo represents Hume himself; whether Philo here is supporting or merely provoking an argument is an open question. But throughout the *Dialogues* especially, where the emphasis is not on offensive polytheism and religious folly, there are often passages in which a view of myth is implied quite different from Hume's more obvious enlightenment derogations. These passages occur when Hume is arguing against dogmatism of a rational or religious kind, when he is trying to show that knowledge is limited to experience. Hume never connects these arguments with myth, nor would he wish to; but the possibility is there. It sometimes seems that Hume's unenlightened savage, moving through his fearful, strange world, is an early (and unsatisfactory) version of Hume's enlightened skeptic, moving through his strange, less fearful world. The savage cannot find right order; nor can the skeptic. The savage offends, perhaps not so much in seeing the world as discrete parts, each with a finally unknowable cause and power, but in erecting all these into a pretentious "construct" —a fault deists and atheists fall into as well. "When you go one step beyond the mundane system, you only excite an inquisitive humour, which it is impossible ever to satisfy. . . ."

Hume's influence needs no rehearsing. De Brosses plagiarized much of the *Natural History* in his *Culte des dieux fétiches.* Herder was strongly influenced by the *Natural History,* and Hamann and Kant by the *Dialogues;* C. G. Heyne's earliest mythic theories drew heavily on Hume's view that primitive man could think and express himself only in images and by personification. His influence in Germany on mythic thought is probably greater than in England. But in both Germany and England, Hume's attack on rationalism and natural religion helped contribute to the remarkable freedom and urgency with which post-Kantian and romantic mythologists turned to myth. Ernst Cassirer's judgment must be agreed with: the *Natural History* remained an isolated event in the Enlightenment because the century still believed in the power of reason too much to follow Hume in renouncing it. In myth, as in philosophy, Hume's full effect is posthumous.

B.F.

REFERENCES   Our text is from *The Natural History of Religion,* in *The Philosophical Works* (Boston, 1854), vol. IV. For Hume's corrosive analysis of miracles, see his *An Enquiry concerning Human Understanding,* section X parts I and II. For commentary, see Leslie Stephen, *History of English Thought in the Eighteenth Century* (New York: Harcourt, Brace and World, 1962), vol. I, chap. VI; F. Manuel, *The Eighteenth Century Confronts the Gods* (Cambridge: Harvard University Press, 1959), chap. IV, pt. 3. James Collins, *The Emergence of the Philosophy of Religion* (New Haven: Yale University Press, 1967), with a chapter on the *Natural History.* John Cairns, *Unbelief in the Eighteenth Century as contrasted with its earlier and later history* (Edinburgh, 1881).

HUME

FROM *The Natural History of Religion*

IT APPEARS to me, that, if we consider the improvement of human society, from rude beginnings to a state of greater perfection, polytheism or idolatry was, and necessarily must have been, the first and most ancient religion of mankind. This opinion I shall endeavour to confirm by the following arguments. . . .

As far as writing or history reaches, mankind, in ancient times, appear universally to have been polytheists. Shall we assert, that, in more ancient times, before the knowledge of letters, or the discovery of any art or science, men entertained the principles of pure theism? That is, while they were ignorant and barbarous, they discovered truth: But fell into error, as soon as they acquired learning and politeness.

But in this assertion you not only contradict all appearance of probability, but also our present experience concerning the principles and opinions of barbarous nations. The savage tribes of AMERICA, AFRICA, and ASIA are all idolaters. Not a single exception to this rule. Insomuch, that, were a traveller to transport himself into any unknown region; if he found inhabitants cultivated with arts and science, though even upon that supposition there are odds against their being theists, yet could he not safely, till farther inquiry, pronounce any thing on that head: But if he found them ignorant and barbarous, he might beforehand declare them idolaters; and there scarcely is a possibility of his being mistaken.

It seems certain, that, according to the natural progress of human thought, the ignorant multitude must first entertain some grovelling and familiar notion of superior powers, before they stretch their conception to that perfect Being, who bestowed order on the whole frame of nature. We may as reasonably imagine, that men inhabited palaces before huts and cottages, or studied geometry before agriculture; as assert that the Deity appeared to them in pure spirit, omniscient, omnipotent and omnipresent, before he was apprehended to be a powerful, though limited being, with human passions and appetites, limbs and organs. The mind rises gradually, from inferior to superior: By abstracting from what is imperfect, it forms an idea of perfection: And slowly distinguishing the nobler parts of its own frame from the grosser, it learns to transfer only the former, much elevated and refined, to its divinity. Nothing could disturb this natural progress of thought, but some obvious and invincible argument, which might immediately lead the mind into the pure principles of theism, and make it overleap, at one bound, the vast interval which is interposed between the human and the divine nature. But though

I allow, that the order and frame of the universe, when accurately examined, affords such an argument; yet I can never think, that this consideration could have an influence on mankind, when they formed their first rude notions of religion.

(Chap. I)

We may conclude, therefore, that, in all nations, which have embraced polytheism, the first ideas of religion arose not from a contemplation of the works of nature, but from a concern with regard to the events of life, and from the incessant hopes and fears, which actuate the human mind. Accordingly, we find, that all idolaters, having separated the provinces of their deities, have recourse to that invisible agent, to whose authority they are immediately subjected, and whose province it is to superintend that course of actions, in which they are, at any time, engaged. . . .

It must necessarily, indeed, be allowed, that, in order to carry men's intention beyond the present course of things, or lead them into any inference concerning invisible intelligent power, they must be actuated by some passion, which prompts their thoughts and reflection; some motive, which urges their first enquiry. But what passion shall we here have recourse to, for explaining an effect of such mighty consequences? Not speculative curiosity, surely, or the pure love of truth. That motive is too refined for such gross apprehensions; and would lead men into enquiries concerning the frame of nature, a subject too large and comprehensive for their narrow capacities. No passions, therefore, can be supposed to work upon such barbarians, but the ordinary affections of human life; the anxious concern for happiness, the dread of future misery, the terror of death, the thirst of revenge, the

appetite for food and other necessaries.
(Chap. 2)

No wonder, then, that mankind, being placed in such an absolute ignorance of causes, and being at the same time so anxious concerning their future fortune, should immediately acknowledge a dependence on invisible powers, possessed of sentiment and intelligence. The *unknown causes* which continually employ their thought, appearing always in the same aspect, are all apprehended to be of the same kind or species. Nor is it long before we ascribe to them thought and reason and passion, and sometimes even the limbs and figures of men, in order to bring them nearer to a resemblance with ourselves.
(Chap. 3)

Whoever learns by argument, the existence of invisible intelligent power, must reason from the admirable contrivance of natural objects, and must suppose the world to be the workmanship of that divine being, the original cause of all things. But the vulgar polytheist, so far from admitting that idea, deifies every part of the universe, and conceives all the conspicuous productions of nature, to be themselves so many real divinities. The sun, moon, and stars, are all gods according to his system: Fountains are inhabited by nymphs, and trees by hamadryads: Even monkeys, dogs, cats, and other animals often become sacred in his eyes, and strike him with a religious veneration. And thus, however strong men's propensity to believe invisible, intelligent power in nature, their propensity is equally strong to rest their attention on sensible, visible objects; and in order to reconcile these opposite inclinations, they are led to unite the invisible power with some visible object. . . .

The deities of the vulgar are so little superior to human creatures, that, where men are affected with strong sentiments of veneration or gratitude for any hero or public benefactor, nothing can be more natural than to convert him into a god, and fill the heavens, after this manner, with continual recruits from among mankind. Most of the divinities of the ancient world are supposed to have once been men, and to have been beholden for their *apotheosis* to the admiration and affection of the people. The real history of their adventures, corrupted by tradition, and elevated by the marvellous, became a plentiful source of fable; especially in passing through the hands of poets, allegorists, and priests, who successively improved upon the wonder and astonishment of the ignorant multitude. . . .

These then are the general principles of polytheism, founded in human nature, and little or nothing dependent on caprice and accident. As the *causes,* which bestow happiness or misery, are, in general, very little known and very uncertain, our anxious concern endeavours to attain a determinate idea of them; and finds no better expedient than to represent them as intelligent voluntary agents, like ourselves; only somewhat superior in power and wisdom. The limited influence of these agents, and their great proximity to human weakness, introduce the various distribution and division of their authority; and thereby give rise to allegory. The same principles naturally deify mortals, superior in power, courage, or understanding, and produce hero-worship; together with fabulous history and mythological tradition, in all its wild and unaccountable forms. And as an invisible spiritual intelligence is an object too refined for vulgar apprehension, men naturally affix it to some sensible representation; such as either the more conspicuous parts of nature, or the statues, images, and pictures, which a more refined age forms of its divinities. (Chap. 5)

The doctrine of one supreme deity, the author of nature, is very ancient, has spread itself over great and populous nations, and among them has been embraced by all ranks and conditions of men: But whoever thinks that it has owed its success to the prevalent force of those invincible reasons, on which it is undoubtedly founded, would show himself little acquainted with the ignorance and stupidity of the people, and their incurable prejudices in favour of their particular superstitions. . . .

We may conclude, therefore, upon the whole, that, since the vulgar, in nations, which have embraced the doctrine of theism, still build it upon irrational and superstitious principles, they are never led into that opinion by any process of argument, but by a certain train of thinking, more suitable to their genius and capacity. . . .

In proportion as men's fears or distresses become more urgent, they still invent new strains of adulation; and even he who outdoes his predecessor in swelling up the titles of his divinity, is sure to be outdone by his successor in newer and more pompous epithets of praise. Thus they proceed; till at last they arrive at infinity itself, beyond which there is no farther progress: And it is well, if, in striving to get farther, and to represent a magnificent simplicity, they run not into inexplicable mystery, and destroy the intelligent nature of their deity, on which alone any rational worship or adoration can be founded. While they confine themselves to the notion of a perfect being, the creator of the world, they coincide, by chance, with the principles of reason and true philosophy; though they are

guided to that notion, not by reason, of which they are in a great measure incapable, but by the adulation and fears of the most vulgar superstition. (Chap. 6)

Since, therefore, the mind of man appears of so loose and unsteady a texture, that, even at present, when so many persons find an interest in continually employing on it the chisel and the hammer, yet are they not able to engrave theological tenets with any lasting impression; how much more must this have been the case in ancient times, when the retainers to the holy function were so much fewer in comparison? No wonder, that the appearances were then very inconsistent, and that men, on some occasions, might seem determined infidels, and enemies to the established religion, without being so in reality; or at least, without knowing their own minds in that particular.

Another cause, which rendered the ancient religion much looser than the modern, is, that the former were *traditional* and the latter are *scriptural,* and the tradition in the former was complex, contradictory, and, on many occasions doubtful; so that it could not possibly be reduced to any standard and canon, or afford any determinate articles of faith. . . .

The pagan religion, therefore, seemed to vanish like a cloud, whenever one approached to it, and examined it piecemeal. It could never be ascertained by any fixed dogmas and principles. And though this did not convert the generality of mankind from so absurd a faith; for when will the people be reasonable? yet it made them falter and hesitate more in maintaining their principles, and was even apt to produce, in certain dispositions of mind, some practices and opinions, which had the appearance of determined infidelity. . . .

Upon the whole, the greatest and most

observable differences between a *traditional, mythological* religion, and a *systematical, scholastic* one are two: The former is often more reasonable, as consisting only of a multitude of stories, which, however groundless, imply no express absurdity and demonstrative contradiction; and sits also so easy and light on men's minds, that, though it may be as universally received, it happily makes no such deep impression on the affections and understanding.   (Chap. 12)

The primary religion of mankind arises chiefly from an anxious fear of future events; and what ideas will naturally be entertained of invisible, unknown powers, while men lie under dismal apprehensions of any kind, may easily be conceived. Every image of vengeance, severity, cruelty, and malice must occur, and must augment the ghastliness and horror, which oppresses the amazed religionist. A panic having once seized the mind, the active fancy still farther multiplies the objects of terror; while that profound darkness, or, what is worse, that glimmering light, with which we are environed, represents the spectres of divinity under the most dreadful appearances imaginable. And no idea of perverse wickedness can be framed, which those terrified devotees do not readily, without scruple, apply to their deity. . . .

Here therefore is a kind of contradiction between the different principles of human nature, which enter into religion. Our natural terrors present the notion of a devilish and malicious deity: Our propensity to adulation leads us to acknowledge an excellent and divine. And the influence of these opposite principles are various, according to the different situation of the human understanding.   (Chap. 13)

What a noble privilege is it of human reason to attain the knowledge of the supreme Being; and, from the visible works of nature, be enabled to infer so sublime a principle as its supreme Creator? But turn the reverse of the medal. Survey most nations and most ages. Examine the religious principles, which have, in fact, prevailed in the world. You will scarcely be persuaded, that they are any thing but sick men's dreams: Or perhaps will regard them more as the playsome whimsies of monkeys in human shape, than the serious, positive, dogmatical asseverations of a being, who dignifies himself with the name of rational. . . .

Ignorance is the mother of Devotion: A maxim that is proverbial, and confirmed by general experience. Look out for a people, entirely destitute of religion: If you find them at all, be assured, that they are but a few degrees removed from brutes. . . .

The whole is a riddle, an aenigma, an inexplicable mystery. Doubt, uncertainty, suspence of judgment appear the only result of our most accurate scrutiny, concerning this subject. But such is the frailty of human reason, and such the irresistible contagion of opinion, that even this deliberate doubt could scarcely be upheld; did we not enlarge our view, and opposing one species of superstition to another, set them a quarrelling; while we ourselves, during their fury and contention, happily make our escape into the calm, though obscure, regions of philosophy.   (Chap. 15)

PART TWO

The Later Eighteenth Century

T HE YEARS FROM 1750 TO 1800 WITNESSED A GRADUAL TRANSITION;
classical premises of taste gave way to romantic ones, and a major part,
perhaps even a major cause, of this so-called romantic revolution was the
romantic revaluation of myth. One can see the rational and skeptical deprecation of myth losing its persuasiveness during the second half of the eighteenth
century and giving way to emotional and imaginative belief in and enthusiasm
for myth and the mythic. Where the Enlightenment cooly examined myth in
order to discredit it, romantics assented to and celebrated myth, and at times,
tried to create it.

While much enlightenment thought persists in the late eighteenth century,
and while some aspects of romantic thought are already well worked out, other
tendencies in the period had an effect on ideas about myth. Recent excavations
and expeditions in the ancient world, notably Herculaneum, Pompeii, Balbec,
and Palmyra, were turning up new artifacts, providing more knowledge about
ancient religions and myths, and lending strength to a new interest in concrete, detailed evidence. The revival of interest in Greek and Roman art,
literature, and history—one thinks of Winckelmann, Lessing, Goethe, Gibbon
—which leads also to Romantic Hellenism, had the effect of making myths and
gods seem a natural and necessary part of the study of the inspiring classical
past. And if one admired the culture of the Greeks and the Romans, one
might reasonably look with sympathy upon their religion. The rediscovery

and the very effective dissemination of knowledge about India, and of Indic literature and mythology, with its claims to being older than Greek and Hebrew literature and religion, stirred remarkable interest in and had a far-reaching effect on the study of myth, as did the discovery of the Nordic mythology contained in the *Eddas*. These two major additions to the subject led to a wholesale interest in and exploration of national mythologies and folk literatures. The revival of interest in national origins and characteristics, national religions and myths, and national literatures all worked to create an arena of increasing significance for the study of myth.

As these new interests developed and expanded, myth was seen to be important to all these new areas; and myth thus, naturally, seemed ever more important as a subject. In Charles De Brosses's *Du Culte des Dieux Fétiches*, African fetishism provided the key. De Brosses thought that Greek myth also could probably be traced back to early religious needs manifested as animism or fetishism. The Baron d'Holbach curiously chose to half defend myth in order to damn Christianity by contrast. While he might have attacked both, he did not; and one result was his affirming that there might have been, long ago, a simple, valid, nature-based worship, lightly and nobly mythologized. His famous *Système de la Nature* itself drifts in this direction. The Christians found their own religion sapped by both these works; a typical response, that of the Abbé Bergier, calls myth "the natural history of the Universe," discredits myth in its literal or overt forms, supplies a high and reverent allegorical center, and thus allows Christian truth and pagan fable to coexist. Edward Gibbon was interested in myth study as a young man, though he later emerged as a fully skeptical historian whose treatments of myth are, to say the least, cool. Robert Wood's *Essay on the Original Genius of Homer* sees natural events, such as sunsets, mirrored in myth, and he insisted that Greek myth had Greek origins, not Egyptian or Hebrew origins.

This slight shift in perspective was to have a great effect on German ideas of myth; Wood, together with Lowth and Blackwell, provided the groundwork for treating myth as a national, rather than a universal, phenomenon. Mallet's presentation of Nordic mythology, and James Macpherson's Ossianic poems provided Europe, for the first time, with an indigenous mythology, an attractive alternative to Greek and Roman myth. Heyne, in Germany, began to link myth with philology; the result was to be a new kind of historical approach to myth culminating in the work of Karl Otfried Müller. Herder, on the other hand, is perhaps the principal source of the opposing or romantic view of myth. Myth for Herder is a mode of knowing, a function of the imagination; and the subject of myth, as it was shaped by Herder, is at the center of the romantic effort to rethink religion, history, literature, nationhood, and culture.

By comparison with Herder, whose importance to romantic thought in general is in some ways equal to Rousseau's, the antiquarian researches of Jacob Bryant appear old-fashioned and unimportant, though Bryant's influence on William Blake makes him of some interest. Richard Payne Knight, another English antiquary, wrote a daring treatise that reduced religion and mythology to sexual symbolism; and to move out for a moment to the fringes of myth study—to paraphrase what James Joyce said of Shakespeare: myth has been a happy hunting ground for many minds that have lost their balance—Dom Antoine Pernety, in France, interpreted myth as an elaborate code invented to transmit the truth about alchemy, while in England an obscure dispute between Hugh Farmer and John Fell shows that mythology and demonology were still connected in some minds. In the work of Sir William Jones, the jurist and Sanskrit scholar, the impact of India on European ideas of myth and religion can be seen from the viewpoint of a scholar torn between scholarship and Christianity, while the work of Charles Dupuis shows how a secular system connecting all myth in one grand solar monomyth is now possible. With Goethe and Blake, two poets of the first rank take up myth, in quite different ways of course, and make myth central to their work. From this time on, literature and myth are seldom far apart.

R.R.

CHARLES DE BROSSES

[1709–1777]

CHARLES DE BROSSES was a magistrate, scholar, and *philosophe,* who by combining the detailed "field observation" of such early travelers as Bosman, Des Marchais, Atkins, and Lafitau with theories about primitive mentality and the psychology of religion which he derived from Fontenelle, Bayle, and especially Hume, prefigured what the next hundred years regarded as the anthropological approach to myth. De Brosses's bold concern was with fetishism, which he defined as an early form of worship in which "the cult objects are animals or inanimate beings that have been deified," or more generally as the idea of spirits, similar in general to what E. B. Tylor later called animism. De Brosses went on to claim that fetishism was a universal stage of human religion, an idea which later helped Auguste Comte formulate his idea that the earliest of the three states of man, the theological state, could be further subdivided into the fetishist, the polytheist, and the monotheist stages.

De Brosses presided over the Dijon Parlement and was later a member of the *Académie des Inscriptions et Belles-Lettres;* he wrote an early book on Herculaneum (1750), followed by his celebrated *Du culte des dieux fétiches* (1760). His popular reputation was based on a volume of Italian travel letters that was reprinted all through the nineteenth century, but he also wrote a *Traité de la formation mécanique des langues . . .* and produced a pioneer edition of Sallust,

as well as a book on Southern voyages of exploration. He got into a quarrel with Voltaire which cost him dearly in reputation. Voltaire called de Brosses "the little fetish" and denied him membership in *L'Académie Française.* Despite the fact that Diderot gave space to serpent fetishism in the *Encyclopédie* and also despite the appearance of much of *Du culte des dieux fétiches* in the atheistic *Encyclopédie Methodique,* it is true, as Frank Manuel notes, that de Brosses has never received much attention as a thinker, even though many anthropologists mention him with brief respect.

De Brosses's approach may be gathered from the closing sentence of *Du culte des dieux fétiches, or Parallèle de l'ancienne religion de l'Égypte avec la religion actuelle de Nigritie.* "It is not in his possibilities, it is in man himself that we must study man. It is not a question of imagining what he might have done or ought to have done, but of looking at what he does." With this cool, unemotional rationalism goes an interest in rite and ritual which is unusual among eighteenth-century thinkers, and it is this interest in concrete detail and in specific sources that gives *Du culte des dieux fétiches* a solidity and an interest that match its theoretical innovations.

Part one, drawing heavily from earlier travel narratives, is given to building a detailed picture of modern West African religion, which de Brosses calls fetishism (the word was orginally a fifteenth-century Portuguese term for charm or amulet). Much of the first section is spent describing the cult of the striped serpent in Juidah, which de Brosses uses as his major example of fetishism. The principal point here is to insist that the native actually worships the fetish object itself, be it serpent, plant, pebble, or stick. De Brosses will not countenance the idea that the savage is worshipping a higher power through the fetish object, or that the fetish is an image of a higher power. In de Brosses, the poor stupid savage actually worships the miserable fetish itself.

In good eighteenth-century fashion, section two undertakes to show the "conformities" between modern savage religion and ancient Egyptian and even Hebrew religion. Quoting heavily from Diodorus, Plutarch, and Cicero, de Brosses argues that the apparent zoolatry of the Egyptians, the degrading spectacle of men worshipping dog-headed and hawk-headed creatures, which Christians and Deists alike had striven to explain away, was indeed zoolatry, a form of fetishism, a savage and trivial mode of belief. De Brosses sought no higher wisdom, no secret monotheism, no cabalist or mysterious truths behind the veil. The Egyptians were originally savage, and therefore evolved a savage religion.

In arguing that the Egyptians actually worshipped animals and reptiles, to say nothing of inanimate objects, de Brosses was denouncing the allegorical mode of myth interpretation. As he saw it, allegorism was just a way to give primitive religious practices a high-minded quality they did not possess. Allegorism could be used to inject secret monotheism into mere animal worship, and such allegorism could not be trusted.

Section three is an attempt to demonstrate the means, the mechanism of ideas (*mécanique d'idées*), the actual psychology by which fetishism was to be explained. This section owes its inspiration to Hume and much of it is even a trans-

lation of Hume's *Natural History of Religion*. De Brosses presents the idea that from the despicable, ignorant, fear-ridden and hope-crazed primitive mind came the craven impulse to worship something. So the primitive worshipped the first thing he came upon and thus acquired a fetish. De Brosses then argues that due to the uniformity of human nature, religious development is the same in all places and in all times. Fetishism is found in modern Africa; it is also found in ancient Egypt. From this, de Brosses concluded that fetishism was the first great universal stage (after the Flood) of religion. If one drops the parentheses the idea remains the same.

De Brosses's approach is, as already noted, anti-allegorical. He is also quite clear in his opposition to the Christian diffusionists, who argued that from a benign and primitive monotheism men declined into savage polytheism or worse. De Brosses does, however, accept the Euhemerist interpretation of myth that, in the work of Toland, Banier, or Fourmont, argues that myth arises from worship of the dead. Implicit in de Brosses's work is the idea that a polytheistic religion centered on the worship of deified men is the second great stage of religious development, and Comte was later to make this second stage explicit.

De Brosses's concept of a fetishist stage in the universal development of religion was picked up by Comte and the word came quickly to represent a whole social state. G. H. Lewes could, in 1853, thus summarize the Comtian position;

The idea of *invariable laws* must at that time [the first age] have appeared eminently chimerical; indeed, had it arisen it would have been immediately repulsed as radically opposed to the consecrated method, which attached the explanation of every phenomenon to the *arbitrary will* of the corresponding *fétiche*. Considered in its relation to the Fine Arts, the general action of Fetishism upon the human intellect is certainly not nearly so oppressive as it is in a scientific point of view. It is indeed, evident that a philosophy which animated directly the whole of nature must have tended to favour the spontaneous impulse of the imagination, at that time necessarily having a mental preponderance. Thus, the earliest attempts in all the fine arts, not excepting poetry, are to be traced to the age of Fetishism.

Finally, fetishism was diminished and restricted as a concept by E. B. Tylor, and "animism" took the place of fetishism as a broad generic term for primitive religion and as a basis for myth interpretation. Tylor points out that de Brosses

introduced the word Fétichism as a general descriptive term, and since then it has obtained a great currency by Comte's use of it to denote a general theory of primitive religion, in which external objects are regarded as animated by a life analogous to man's. It seems to me, however, more convenient to use the word Animism for the doctrine of spirits in general, and to confine the word Fetishism to that subordinate department which it properly belongs to, namely, the doctrine of spirits embodied in, or attached to, or conveying influence through, certain material objects. Fetishism will be taken as including the worship of 'stocks and stones' and thence it passes by an imperceptible gradation into Idolatry.

In describing fetishism as a universal stage of religion, de Brosses was broaching a new and an important idea, yet it is worth recalling that his attitude toward his material is still that of the enlightenment rationalist. For de Brosses, or for those who follow his anthropological lead, there is nothing to be admired in primitive man or in his religion. Indeed, with de Brosses one begins to see a full-blown positivistic approach to myth, splitting away from the still-evolving romantic reaffirmation of primitive man, primitive religion, and myth.

R.R.

REFERENCES   The text is our translation from Charles de Brosses, *Du culte des dieux fétiches* . . . (Paris [?], 1760). For discussions, see J. M. Robertson, *Christianity and Mythology,* 2d ed. (London, 1910); Frank Manuel, *The Eighteenth Century Confronts the Gods* (Cambridge: Harvard University Press, 1959); A. Lang, *Custom and Myth* (London: Longmans, 1884), p. 378; Henri Mamet, *Le président de Brosses, sa vie et ses ouvrages* (Paris, 1874); G. H. Lewes, *Comte's Philosophy of the Sciences* (London: G. Bell and Sons, 1887) esp. pt. II, sec. vi; and E. B. Tylor, *Primitive Culture* (New York: Brentano's, 1924), 1st ed. 1871, esp. vol. 2, pp. 143–145.

DE BROSSES

FROM *On the Worship of Fetish Gods*

THE CONFUSING jumble of ancient mythology has only been, for the moderns, an indecipherable chaos or a purely arbitrary enigma, as long as we were willing to make use of the figurative approach of the late Platonic philosophers who imputed to ignorant and savage nations a knowledge of the most hidden causes in nature, or who found in the heap of trivial practices of a crowd of stupid and coarse men the

intellectual ideas of the most abstract metaphysics. We have scarcely succeeded better when by analogies, most of which are
far-fetched and poorly supported, we have
tried to recover in the mythological deeds
of antiquity the detailed but disfigured history of all that happened among the Hebrew people—a nation unknown to practically all the others, and which made a
major point of not communicating its doctrine to foreigners. But these two methods
had a marked utility for those who first
used them. The pagans sought to save the
honor of their belief from the just criticism of the Christians, and the Christians,
proselytes and persecuted, had a direct interest in tracing back to them all that was
foreign to themselves and turning into
proofs against their adversaries the ancient
traditions which the pagans still agreed
with. Moreover, allegory is a universal instrument which lends itself to everything.
Once a system of merely figurative meanings is adopted, one easily sees whatever
one wishes, as in clouds; the matter is
never troublesome, one needs no more
than wit and imagination; it is a wide field,
fertile in explanations no matter what one
needs. Also the use of images [*figurism*]
has seemed so useful that its eternal contradiction with logic and common sense
has not yet even today, in this century of
reason, lost it the ancient credit it has enjoyed for so many centuries.

Some wiser scholars, learned in the history of the first peoples whose colonies discovered the west, and versed in the knowledge of Oriental languages, after having
stripped mythology of the ill-matched lit-
ter which the Greeks loaded on it, have
finally found the true key to it in the actual
history of all these early peoples, their
opinions and their sovereigns; in the false
translations of a number of simple expressions whose meaning was no longer under-

stood by those who continued to make use
of them; in homonyms which made so
many different beings or persons from a
single object designated by different epithets. They saw that mythology was nothing but *history,* or *the recital of the deeds
of the dead,* as even its name indicates (the
Greek *mythos* being derived from the
Egyptian word *muth,* i.e. *mors,* a term
which is also found in the Canaanite language). . . . The scholarly explanations
that have been given us leave almost nothing to be desired, either in the detail of
the application of fables to actual happen-
ings in the life of celebrated persons of
profane antiquity, or in the interpretation
of terms which, reducing the story to very
simple facts for the layman, dispel the supernatural aura with which people had
liked to deck it out. But these keys, which
reveal the meaning of historical fables so
well, do not always suffice to make sense
of the singularity of dogmatic opinions and
the practical rites of the early peoples.
These two points of pagan theology depend either on the cult of the stars, known
under the name of Sabeism, or on the cult,
perhaps not less ancient, of certain terrestrial and material objects called *fetishes*
by the African negroes among whom this
cult exists, and which for this reason I
shall call *fetishism.* I ask to be allowed to
use this expression habitually, and though
in its proper sense it refers in particular to
the beliefs of the African negroes, I serve
notice in advance that I shall make equal
use of the word in speaking of any other
nation whatsoever, where the cult objects
are animals or inanimate beings that have
been deified, even in speaking sometimes
of certain peoples for whom objects of this
sort are less gods, properly speaking, than
things endowed with a divine virtue; oracles, amulets, and preservational talismans.
For it is certain that all these manners of

thinking have at bottom one source, and that it is nothing but the accessory of a common religion, spread far over the earth, which must be examined apart, as constituting a particular class among the diverse pagan religions, all quite different among themselves. Here is (it seems to me, and I intend to prove it) one of the great elements that we must use in the study of mythology, and which our most able mythologues either are not aware of, or have not known how to use, for having considered that which is in itself the most pitiable thing in the world from too beautiful an angle. It is established that among the most ancient nations of the world, those which were completely savage and coarse forged through an excess of superstitious stupidity these strange terrestrial divinities, while other less senseless peoples worshipped the sun and the stars. These two sorts of religion, abundant sources of Oriental and Greek mythology, and more ancient than idolatry properly so called, seem to demand various clarifications which the examinations of the lives of deified men cannot supply. Here the divinities are of a different kind, especially those of fetishist peoples, whose belief, so old and held for so long despite its excessive absurdity, I plan to detail. No one has yet given a plausible reason for that old usage which the Egyptians are so often reproached for, of worshipping animals and plants of all kinds. . . .

We need not go looking far away for that which is close, when we know by thousands of similar examples that there is no superstition so absurd or so ridiculous that ignorance joined to fear has not engendered it; when we see with what ease the coarsest cult establishes itself in stupid minds diseased with that passion, and roots itself through custom among the savage peoples who live their lives in a perpetual

childhood. But they are not as easily uprooted: the old customs, particularly when they have taken on a sacred tincture, live on long after one is aware of the mistake. For that matter it is not only the Egyptians that could be reproached in this manner. We shall soon see that the other nations of the Orient were no more exempt, in their early ages, from an infantile cult that we shall find spread in a general manner over all the earth and upheld particularly in Africa. It owes its birth to the time when peoples were pure savages, plunged in ignorance and barbarism. With the exception of the chosen race, there is no nation that has not been in that state, if one considers them only from the moment when one sees the memory of Divine Revelation entirely extinguished among them. I take them only from that point, and it is in that sense that everything I shall say in the following must be understood. The human race has first received from God Himself immediate instructions conforming to the intelligence with which His goodness had endowed mankind. It is so astonishing to see them later fallen into a state of brute stupidity that one can scarcely avoid considering it a just and supernatural punishment for the forgetfulness which they had made themselves guilty of toward the kind hand that had created them. A part of mankind has remained until this day in that unformed state: their customs, their ideas, their reasoning, their practices are those of children. The rest, after having passed through this state, have sooner or later come out of it by means of example, education, and exercise of their faculties. To know what once was practiced among the latter, one has only to look at what is actually happening among the former, and in general there is no better method of piercing the veils of little-known points in antiquity than to observe whether something very similar is not happening still somewhere right before our eyes. . . . Let us then first examine what in this respect is the practice of barbarian peoples where the cult in question still remains in all its strength. Nothing resembles more the absurd superstitions of ancient Egypt toward so many ridiculous divinities or would be more appropriate for demonstrating whence came this foolish usage. This discussion into which I propose to enter divides this little treatise naturally into three parts. After having shown the present-day fetishism of modern nations, I shall compare this with that of the ancient peoples, and since that parallel will lead us naturally to judge that the same actions have the same principle, we shall demonstrate quite clearly that all these peoples had the same way of thinking about the matter, for they had the same manner of behaving, which is a logical consequence of that premise.

(from Introduction, pp. 5–17)

On the Actual Fetishism of the Negroes and Other Savage Nations

The Negroes on the west coast of Africa, and even those of the interior of countries up to Nubia, a region on the border of Egypt, have as objects of worship certain gods which the Europeans call *fetishes,* a term made up by our Senegalese merchants from the Portugese word *fetisso,* that is, a *fairy object, enchanted, divine,* or *giving oracles;* from the Latin root *fatum, fanum, fari.* These divine fetishes are nothing but the first material object that the nation or the individual was pleased to select and have consecrated in a ceremony by the priests: a tree, a mountain, the sea, a piece of wood, the tail of a lion, a pebble, a shell, some salt, a fish, a plant, a flower,

an animal of a certain species, such as a cow, a goat, an elephant, a sheep; in short, anything like this you can imagine. These are gods, sacred objects and also talismans to the Negroes, who give them regular and respectful worship, address their oaths to them, offer them sacrifice, carry them in processions if it is possible to carry them, or bear them on their persons with great signs of veneration and consult them on all important occasions. They consider them generally as tutelaries of men and as powerful guardians against all kinds of accidents. They swear by them; and this is the only oath which these deceitful peoples do not dare to break. The Negroes, like most savages, have no knowledge of the worship of deified men. Among them the sun or the fetishes are the real gods, although some of them who have some faint concept of a superior being do not consider these equal to him, and some others who have a trace of Mohammedanism see them only as secondary spirits and talismans. Each country has a national fetish, aside from which each individual has one of his own for himself and his household, or even a great many, according to how susceptible he is to fear or devotion. This devotion on their part is so great that frequently they multiply their fetishes, taking the first creature they encounter, a dog, a cat, or the vilest animals. And if none appears, they in their fit of superstition choose a rock, a piece of wood, even the first object that strikes their fancy. At first the new fetish is showered with presents, together with solemn promises to honor it as a cherished patron if it lives up to the opinion that one has suddenly decided to have of its powers. Those who have an animal as a fetish will never eat its flesh: it would be an unpardonable crime to kill it, and foreigners who would commit such a sacrilege would soon be victims of the anger of the natives.

There are men among them who out of respect and fear abstain from ever seeing their fetish. Our merchants report that a king living next to the coast could not accept their invitation to come and trade with them on their ships, because the sea was his fetish, and the belief was widespread in that region that whoever set eyes on his god would die on the spot; a belief that was not limited entirely to them alone, and traces of which can be found among certain ancient nations of the Orient. "In almost all of Nigritia," says Loyer,*

there are, beside the individual fetishes, certain which are shared by the whole realm, usually some great mountain or some remarkable tree. If anyone were impious enough to cut them down or disfigure them, he would certainly be punished by death. Each village is also under the protection of its own fetish, which is decorated at public expense and invoked for the common good. The guardian of the home has an altar of reeds in the public areas, raised on four pillars and covered with palm leaves. Individuals have a place set aside for their fetishes in their wall or by their door, which they decorate according to the impulses of their own devotion and paint once a week in different colors. One finds quantities of these altars in the forest and the bush: they are loaded with all kinds of fetishes with earthenware plates and pots full of maize, rice, and fruit. If the Negroes need rain, they place empty vessels in front of the altar; if they are at war, they place swords and spears there to ask for victory; if they need meat or fish, they put bones or halters [*arrêtes*] there; to get palm wine, they leave at the foot of the altar a small knife used to make the cuts in the trees; with these marks of respect and reliance they feel they are certain to obtain what they ask for; but if they are put to shame, they attribute this to some just resentment on the part of their fetish, and they bend all their powers to finding the means of appeasing it.

It is already clear how much all these facts resemble what we are told about the

*Voyage to Issinia.

ancient religion of Egypt; I would like to mention in passing a specific point that I do not expect to return to, and that by itself would require a separate treatise; namely, the parallel that one could draw between the account of *Loyer* and the figures engraved on the obelisks where we see heads of dogs and sparrow hawks, suns, serpents, birds, et cetera, to which kneeling men are presenting little tables full of vases and fruits and so on. This would perhaps not be the worst key one could select to explain the Egyptian hieroglyphics.

(from Section One, pp. 18–24)

Examination of the causes to which Fetishism is attributable

So many similar facts, or facts of the same type, establish with the utmost clarity that what is today the religion of the African Negroes and other barbarians, was formerly that of ancient peoples, and that in all centuries, as well as all over the earth, one can perceive the dominance of this worship directly rendered, without images, to animal and vegetable productions. A crowd of proofs suffices to have established this fact. One is not obliged to give a rational explanation for a thing when there is none in it; and it would be, I think, useless enough to look for anything in it, other than the fear and folly of which the human mind is susceptible, and the facility that the mind has in such things giving birth to all sorts of superstition. Fetishism is one of those things that are so absurd that one can say that they do not even leave an opening for the reasoning that wishes to combat them. That is all the more reason why it would be difficult to allege plausible causes for such a senseless doctrine. But the impossibility of excusing it to reasonable eyes does not diminish the certainty of the fact at all, and it would assuredly be pushing historical Pyrrhonism beyond all bounds to wish to deny the reality of this simple and direct worship in Egypt and among the Negroes. Peoples have been able to agree with one another on these absurdities, or to communicate them to one another. The proximity of Africa and Egypt lends strength to this last point, whether the blacks received them from the Egyptians, or whether the latter got them from the former, for we know that Egypt borrowed from Ethiopia some of its oldest usages. But on the other hand, when one sees, in centuries and in climates so far apart, men who have nothing in common with each other, except their ignorance and barbarity, having similar practices, it is yet more natural to conclude that man is so made that left in his natural brutal and savage state, not yet formed by any reflective ideas or by any imitation, he is the same as regards primitive manners and customs in Egypt as in the Antilles, in Persia as among the Greeks; everywhere there is the same mechanism of ideas from which comes that of actions [*d'ou s'ensuit celle des actions*]. And if one is surprised on this particular point, which seems in effect very strange, if one is astounded to see Fetishism spread among all the rude peoples of the universe, in all times, in all places, then to explain this phenomenon, one need only recall the characteristic cause already cited; it is the constant uniformity of savage man—his heart perpetually open to fear, his soul which is ceaselessly and avidly hopeful—which opens the way for the derangement of his ideas, bringing him to a thousand senseless actions, when his uncultured and irrational mind is incapable of perceiving the small links that are found between certain causes and the effects that come from them. And since no one is surprised to see children fail to raise

their minds higher than their dolls, believe them alive, and act accordingly with them, why should one be astonished to see peoples who constantly pass their lives in a continual childhood, and who are never more than four years old, reason without any accuracy and act as they reason? Minds of this quality are the most common, even in enlightened centuries and among civilized nations. Also these sorts of unreasonable usages do not diminish in the same proportion as reason gains, especially when they are consecrated by inveterate habit and by a pious credulity. Their antiquity maintains them among one part of the nation while, perhaps, the other part ridicules them; they become mixed with other dominant cults and with new dogmas latterly received, as it happened in Egypt. In a word, it was with Fetishism as it was with magic, concerning which Pliny remarked that it was naturally adopted by nations who had never separated one from the other. . . . For the rest, I do not see why one should be so greatly surprised that certain people have divinized animals, while one is much less surprised that they have divinized men. This surprise, this difference in judging that we find here, seems to me a result of the self love which works secretly in us. For despite the high preeminence of man's nature over that of the animals, there is at bottom the same distance between either of them and the divine nature; that is to say, there is an equal impossibility of achieving it. A man can no more than a lion become a Divinity; it is a manner of thinking as unreasonable in the nation which maintains the one as in a nation which maintains the other. However, one finds no difficulty in saying that very civilized, very learned, very ingenious nations, such as the Greeks, the Romans, and even the Egyptians, have deified and adored mortal men at the same time that one maintains that it would be distorting the proper idea one ought to have of Egyptian wisdom, which merits so much regard, to say that these people have purely and simply deified and adored animals. But to my mind, all these varieties of idolatry are equally unreasonable, and what I find most strange is that the nations that are so proud and so worthy in so many ways should be imagined to have the power of conferring divinity or of raising mortal men to the rank of gods.

(from Section Three, pp. 182–188)

PAUL HENRI THIERY, BARON D'HOLBACH

[1723–1789]

THE BARON D'HOLBACH was the celebrated and wealthy host to a circle of *philosophes* that included Helvetius, D'Alembert, Diderot, Grimm, and Hume, as well as such men as Rousseau, Garrick, Sterne, and Akenside; he wrote for the *Encyclopédie* and was also the author of a large number of antireligious and anti-Christian works, issued under the names of Fréret, Mirabaud, Boulanger, and many others. His general reputation is that of a ranting and dogmatic atheist, a dedicated and passionate enemy of religion, which he thought of only as priestcraft and superstition, and which he called derisively the "sacred contagion." Yet it has also been pointed out that while Holbach's thought is indeed materialistic, it is also optimistic. Along with the strident atheism goes a firm belief in education, laws, civilization, and progress, and Vyverberg points out that "the combination of outright atheism and of a neo-Christian ethics was one of the most striking features of Holbach's thought." Further, Holbach makes a distinction between mythology and theology on interesting, almost romantic grounds, and in so doing demonstrates—Holbach himself being a sort of test case—how myth, taken now in a positive fashion, can move into the vacuum created by the demolition of traditionary religion.

Holbach's best-known and most influential book, the *Système de la Nature* (published in 1770 as though by Jean-Baptiste de Mirabaud, then secretary of *l'Académie française*), is an open attack on religion in the form of an essay on materialism. Holbach argues that there is nothing in the universe except matter and motion. Both are without origin, having always existed, and both are utterly subject to necessity. This necessity is universal, *not* wholly comprehensible, and it consists of the "infallible and constant tie of causes to their effects." Nonmaterial things, such as God and the soul, Holbach simply calls chimeras. Holbach was attacked by such thinkers as Voltaire, by such public men as Frederick of Prussia, and by such contemporaneous mythologues as Bergier, for his materialism, for his inconsistencies, and even for his literary style.

In the idiom of England, Holbach might have been called a secular enthusiast. The chapter on "Mythology and Theology" in the *Système de la Nature* exhibits Holbach's fierce anti-Christian quality and his open hatred of gods, theologies, and priests; it also shows an essential lack of curiosity about the origins of religion or myth, but a heavy and continuous interest in their social function. He argues initially that certain elements of nature are the first deities. The argument is close to that of de Brosses: man can, according to Holbach, make a particular god out of a particular physical object. Next however, a leisured class arises that is impressed by natural events and eager—from a sort of prehistoric *noblesse oblige*—to civilize, regulate, and enlighten the people. This impulse to civilize, to bring language, laws, and agriculture to men, is close to the missionary spirit, and in order to imprint their lessons on the minds of their new subjects, these wise civilizing strong men personify nature via poetry to make figures or images that will appeal to the popular imagination. These great men (Bacchus, Orpheus, Triptolemus, Moses, and others) "adored active nature"; indeed they worshipped the great whole, the universe, the natural order of things, and they called this universal nature Pan. (Holbach prints part of an Orphic hymn to Pan, which he apparently got out of Blackwell's *Letters concerning Mythology,* along with Blackwell's gloss on the passage.) The point here is that for Holbach mythology is "the daughter of natural philosophy, embellished by poetry, and only destined to describe nature and its parts," and as long as the wise ancients worshipped universal nature, Holbach has no objection. What he dislikes is the idea of a second religion, fit only for the people and worshipping, say, Jupiter as a person, rather than as "ethereal matter which penetrates, gives activity and vivifies all the bodies of which nature is the assemblage." The stories that form mythology were passed from generation to generation until people forgot that it was nature that lay beneath what was by then a confused heap of allegories. Next, according to Holbach, the dangerous and wicked step from mythology to theology was taken.

Metaphysicians and priests began to make a distinction between Nature and the energy in nature. Having artificially separated the two, "by degrees they made an incomprehensible being of this energy, which as before they personified; this they called the mover of nature, or God." Holbach protests that in abstracting the spirit of nature from the natural world, one is falsifying experience and creating unreal beings. The spirit of nature is

nature; God is a meaningless abstraction stemming from a philosophical error, entirely an effect of fear and ignorance. Theology, then, deals with a god or gods thought to be apart from nature, and Holbach pours scorn on the idea. "It was in the lap of ignorance, in the season of alarm and calamity, that mankind ever formed his first notions of the Divinity." What is true of Christianity is also true of pagan ideas of divinity. "It is impossible," Holbach writes, "to peruse the ancient and modern theological works without feeling disgusted at the contemptible invention of those gods which have been made objects of terror or love to mankind. To begin with the inhabitants of India and Egypt, of Greece and Rome, what littleness and foolery in their worship—what rascality and infamy in their priests," and so on.

Mythology, by contrast, is the activity that takes place before man abstracted God from Nature; it involves using convenient symbols for parts of nature while worship is directed to nature itself. This entire idea is, indeed, a protest on behalf of the concrete and the experiential, against abstraction, theologizing, and system-spinning. At the same time, however, Holbach is always the enlightened rationalist with his own true system worked out, with the result that the romantic and the rational approaches lie together uneasily.

At last, despite assurances that he himself will not personify nature, and that by "nature" he only means matter and motion, Holbach does in fact begin to personify nature, at least rhetorically, and before the end of the *Système de la Nature,* Nature is being described, addressed, and even made to speak in terms that can only be called religious. Holbach speaks of reconducting "bewildered mortals to the altar of nature"; and he argues that the worship of nature is "the only worship suitable to intelligent beings." Holbach has a high tolerance for pantheism, maintaining that "it is not out of nature we ought to seek Divinity," and in his summary Holbach even gives nature a voice:

"O thou." cries this nature to man, "who, following the impulse I have given you, during your whole existence, incessantly tend toward happiness, do not strive to resist my sovereign law. . . ."

Sometimes Nature sounds wrathful:

"For do not deceive thyself, it is I who punish, more surely than the Gods, all the crimes of the earth; the wicked may escape the laws of men, but they never escape mine."

And finally, however much it goes against the received ideas about Holbach, Nature and natural determinism, as the supreme forces in life, become for Holbach virtual divinities, or divinities *manquées,* or figures in a rhetorical pantheism, or examples of myth rising to the dignity of religion:

O Nature, sovereign of all beings! and ye her adorable daughters, Virtue, Reason, and Truth! remain for ever our only Divinities; it is to you that belong the praises of the human race; to you appertains the homage of the earth.

Holbach is still an enlightenment thinker, with roots in Fontenelle and Bayle and with affinities among the deists and the Encyclopedists. With Holbach the rational demolition of traditional theologies is complete and overt, yet the very premise of rationalism—the premise of intelligibility, the assumption that the universe can be explained by cause and effect—means that when one has eliminated God or gods as causes, one must have some cause by way of replacement. In Holbach's thought this new cause, once conveniently mythologized by the ancients as Pan, was virtually remythologized as Universal Nature.

R.R.

REFERENCES   Our text is from Paul Henri Thiery, Baron d'Holbach, *The System of Nature,* H. D. Robinson, trans. (New York: G. W. and A. J. Matsell, 1835). This was first published as *Système de la nature ou des loix du monde physique et du monde moral,* par M. Mirabaud. . . . (London [Amsterdam], 1770). Holbach published extensively under the names of others; see our introduction to Fréret.

A useful study is Henry Vyverberg, *Historical Pessimism in the French Enlightenment* (Cambridge: Harvard University Press, 1958). For Holbach's influence on Marx and Feuerbach, see Bruno Bauer's *Das Entdeckte Christentum* (Zurich, 1843). Recent useful works include Frank Manuel, *The Eighteenth Century Confronts the Gods* (Cambridge: Harvard University Press, 1959), and Basil Willey, *The Eighteenth Century Background* (London: Chatto and Windus, 1940).

HOLBACH

FROM *The System of Nature*

"Of Mythology and Theology"

THE ELEMENTS of nature were, as we have shown, the first divinities of man; he has generally commenced with adoring material beings; each individual, as we have already said, and as may be still seen in savage nations, made to himself a particular God of some physical object, which he supposed to be the cause of those events in which he was himself interested; he never wandered to seek out of visible nature the source either of what happened to himself, or of those phenomena to which he was a witness. As he every where saw only material effects, he attributed them to causes of the same genus; incapable in his infancy of those profound reveries, of those subtle speculations, which are the result of leisure, he did not imagine any cause distinguished from the objects that met his sight, nor of any essence totally different from every thing he beheld.

The observation of nature was the first study of those who had leisure to meditate: they could not avoid being struck with the phenomena of the visible world. The rising and setting of the sun, the periodical return of the seasons, the variations of the atmosphere, the fertility and sterility of the earth, the advantages of irrigation, the damages caused by floods, the useful effects of fire, the terrible consequences of conflagra-tion, were proper and suitable objects to occupy their thoughts. It was natural for them to believe that those beings they saw move of themselves, acted by their own peculiar energies; according as their influence over the inhabitants of the earth was either favourable or otherwise, they concluded them to have either the power to injure them, or the disposition to confer benefits. Those who first acquired the knowledge of gaining the ascendency over men, then savage, wandering, unpolished, or dispersed in woods, with but little attachment to the soil . . . were always more practised observers—individuals more instructed in the ways of nature, than the people. . . . The savage is a being who lives in a perpetual state of infancy, who never reaches maturity unless some one comes to draw him out of his misery. . . .

History points out to us the most famous legislators as men, who, enriched with useful knowledge they had gleaned in the bosom of polished nations, carried to savages without industry and needing assistance, those arts, of which, until then, these rude people were ignorant: such were the Bacchus's, the Orpheus's, the Triptolemus's, the Moses's, the Numas, the Zalmolxis's; in short, all those who first gave to nations their Gods—their worship—the rudiments of agriculture, of science, of theology, of jurisprudence, of mysteries, &c. It will perhaps be inquired, if those nations which at the present day we see assembled, were all originally dispersed? We reply, that this dispersion may have been produced at various times by those terrible revolutions, of which it has before been remarked our globe has more than once been the theatre. . . . Those who were able to escape from the ruin of the world . . . were not able to hand down the history of their frightful adventures, except by obscure traditions; much less to transmit to us the opinions, the systems, the arts, the sciences, anterior to these revolutions of our sphere. . . .

However it may be with these conjectures, whether the human race may always have existed upon the earth, or whether it may have been a recent production of nature, it is extremely easy to recur to the origin of many existing nations: we shall find them always in the savage state; that is to say, composed of wandering hordes; these were collected together, at the voice of some missionary or legislator, from whom they received benefits, who gave them Gods, opinions, and laws. These personages, of whom the people, newly congregated, readily acknowledged the superiority, fixed the national Gods, leaving to each individual those which he had formed to himself, according to his own peculiar ideas, or else substituting others brought from those regions from whence they themselves had emigrated.

The better to imprint their lessons on the minds of their new subjects, these men became the guides, the priests, the sovereigns, the masters, of these infant societies; they spoke to the imagination of their auditors.—Poetry, by its images, its fictions, its numbers, its rhyme, its harmony, conspired to please their fancy, and to render permanent the impressions it made: thus, the entire of nature, as well as all its parts, was personified; as its voice, trees, stones, rocks, earth, air, fire, water, took intelligence, held conversation with man, and with themselves; the elements were deified.—The sky, which, according to the then philosophy, was an arched concave, spreading over the earth, which was supposed to be a level plain, was itself made a God; Time, under the name of Saturn, was pictured as the son of heaven; the igneous matter, the ethereal electric fluid, that invisible fire which vivifies nature, that penetrates all beings, that fertilizes the earth, which is the great principle of motion, the source of heat, was deified under the name of Jupiter: his combination with every being in nature was expressed by his metamorphoses —by the frequent adulteries imputed to him. He was armed with thunder, to indicate he produced meteors, to typify the electric fluid that is called lightning. He married the winds, which were designated under the name Juno, therefore called the Goddess of the Winds; their nuptials were celebrated with great solemnity. Thus, following the same fictions, the sun, that beneficent star which has such a marked influence over the earth, became an Osiris, a Belus, a Mithras, an Adonis, an Apollo. Nature, rendered sorrowful by his periodical absence, was an Isis, an Astarte, a Venus, a Cybele.

In short, every thing was personified: the sea was under the empire of Neptune; fire was adored by the Egyptians under the name of Serapis; by the Persians, under that of Ormus or Oromaze; and by the Romans, under that of Vesta and Vulcan.

Such was the origin of mythology: it may be said to be the daughter of natural philosophy, embellished by poetry, and only destined to describe nature and its parts. If antiquity is consulted, it will be perceived without much trouble, that those famous sages, those legislators, those priests, those conquerors, who were the instructers of infant nations, themselves adored active nature, or the great whole considered relatively to its different operations or qualities; that this was what caused the ignorant savages whom they had gathered together to adore. It was the great whole they deified; it was its various parts which they made their inferior gods; it was from the necessity of her laws they made fate. Allegory masked its mode of action: it was at length parts of this great whole that idolatry represented by statues and symbols.

To complete the proofs of what has been said; to show distinctly that it was the great whole, the universe, the nature of things, which was the real object of the worship of Pagan antiquity, we shall here give the hymn of Orpheus addressed to the God Pan:—

"O Pan! I invoke thee, O powerful God! O universal nature! the heavens, the sea, the earth, who nourish all, and the eternal fire, because these are thy members, O all powerful Pan," &c. Nothing can be more suitable to confirm these ideas, than the ingenious explanation which is given of the fable of Pan, as well as of the figure under which he is represented. It is said, "Pan, according to the signification of his name, is the emblem by which the ancients have designated the great assemblage of things: he represents the universe; and, in the mind of the wisest philosophers of antiquity, he passed for the greatest and most ancient of the Gods. The features under which he is delineated form the portrait of nature, and of the savage state in which she was found in the beginning. The spotted skin of the leopard, which serves him for a mantle, represented the heavens filled with

stars and constellations. His person was compounded of parts, some of which were suitable to a reasonable animal, that is to say, to man; and others to the animal destitute of reason, such as the goat. It is thus," says he, "that the universe is composed of an intelligence that governs the whole, and of the prolific, fruitful elements of fire, water, earth, air. Pan, loved to drink and to follow the nymphs; this announces the occasion nature has for humidity in all her productions, and that this God, like nature, is strongly inclined to propagation. According to the Egyptians, and the most ancient Grecian philosophers, Pan had neither father nor mother; he came out of Demogorgon at the same moment with the Destinies, his fatal sisters; a fine method of expressing that the universe was the work of an unknown power, and that it was formed after the invariable relations, the eternal laws of necessity; but his most significant symbol, that most suitable to express the harmony of the universe, is his mysterious pipe, composed of seven unequal tubes, but calculated to produce the nicest and most perfect concord. The orbs which compose the seven planets of our solar system, are of different diameters; being bodies of unequal mass, they describe their revolutions round the sun in various periods; nevertheless it is from the order of their motion that results the harmony of the spheres." &c.

Here then is the great macrocosm, the mighty whole, the assemblage of things, adored and deified by the philosophers of antiquity, whilst the uninformed stopped at the emblem under which this nature was depicted, at the symbols under which its various parts, its numerous functions were personified; his narrow mind, his barbarous ignorance, never permitted him to mount higher; they alone were deemed worthy of being initiated into the mysteries, who knew the realities masked under these emblems.

Indeed, the first institutors of nations, and their immediate successors in authority, only spoke to the people by fables, allegories, enigmas, of which they reserved to themselves the right of giving an explanation. This mysterious tone they considered necessary, whether it were to mask their own ignorance, or whether it were to preserve their power over the uninformed, who for the most part only respect that which is above their comprehension. Their explications were always dictated either by interest, by a delirious imagination, or by imposture; thus from age to age, they did no more than render nature and its parts, which they had originally depicted, more unknown, until they completely lost sight of the primitive ideas; these were replaced by a multitude of fictitious personages, under whose features this nature had primarily been represented to them. The people adored these personages, without penetrating into the true sense of the emblematical fables recounted to them. These ideal beings, with material figures, in whom they believed there resided a mysterious virtue, a divine power, were the objects of their worship, of their fears, of their hopes. The wonderful, the incredible actions ascribed to these fancied divinities, were an inexhaustible fund of admiration, which gave perpetual play to the fancy; which delighted not only the people of those days, but even the children of latter ages. Thus were transmitted from age to age those marvellous accounts, which, although necessary to the existence of the ministers of the Gods, did nothing more than confirm the blindness of the ignorant: these never supposed that it was nature, its various operations, the passions of man and

his divers faculties, that lay buried under a heap of allegories; they had no eyes but for these emblematical persons, under which nature was masked: they attributed to their influence the good, to their displeasure the evil, which they experienced: they entered into every kind of folly, into the most delirious acts of madness, to render them propitious to their views; thus, for want of being acquainted with the reality of things, their worship frequently degenerated into the most cruel extravagance, into the most ridiculous folly.

Thus it is obvious, that every thing proves nature and its various parts to have every where been the first divinities of man. Natural philosophers studied them either superficially or profoundly, explained some of their properties; detailed some of their modes of action. Poets painted them to the imagination of mortals, imbodied them, and furnished them with reasoning faculties. The statuary executed the ideas of the poets. The priests decorated these Gods with a thousand marvellous qualities—with the most terrible passions—with the most inconceivable attributes. The people adored them; prostrated themselves before these Gods, who were neither susceptible of love or hatred, goodness, or malice; and they became persecuting, malevolent, cruel, unjust, in order to render themselves acceptable to powers generally described to them under the most odious features.

By dint of reasoning upon nature thus decorated, or rather disfigured, subsequent speculators no longer recollected the source from whence their predecessors had drawn their Gods, and the fantastic ornaments with which they had embellished them. Natural philosophers and poets were transformed by leisure into metaphysicians and theologians; tired with contemplating what they could have understood, they believed they had made an important discovery by subtly distinguishing nature from herself —from her own peculiar energies—from her faculty of action. By degrees they made an incomprehensible being of this energy, which as before they personified: this they called the mover of nature, or God. This abstract, metaphysical being, or rather, word, became the subject of their continual contemplation; they looked upon it not only as a real being, but also as the most important of beings; and by thus dreaming, nature quite disappeared; she was despoiled of her rights; she was considered as nothing more than an unwieldy mass, destitute of power, devoid of energy, and as a heap of ignoble matter purely passive, who, incapable of acting by herself, was not competent to any of the operations they beheld, without the direct, the immediate agency of the moving power they had associated with her. Thus man ever preferred an unknown power, to that of which he was enabled to have some knowledge if he had only deigned to consult his experience; but he presently ceases to respect that which he understands, and to estimate those objects which are familiar to him: he figures to himself something marvellous in every thing he does not comprehend; his mind, above all, labours to seize upon that which appears to escape his consideration; and, in default of experience, he no longer consults any thing but his imagination, which feeds him with chimeras. In consequence, those speculators who have subtly distinguished nature from her own powers, have successively laboured to clothe the powers thus separated with a thousand incomprehensible qualities: as they did not see this being, which is only a mode, they made it a spirit —an intelligence—an incorporeal being; that is to say, of a substance totally different from every thing of which we have a knowledge. They never perceived that all their inventions, that all the words which they had imagined, only served to mask their real ignorance; and that all their pretended science was limited to saying, in what manner nature acted, by a thousand subterfuges which they themselves found it impossible to comprehend. Man always deceives himself for want of studying nature; he leads himself astray, every time he is disposed to go out of it; he is always quickly necessitated to return or to substitute words which he does not himself understand for things which he would much better comprehend if he was willing to look at them without prejudice.

(from Chap. XIX)

EDWARD GIBBON

[1737–1794]

GIBBON's eminence as an historian might not by itself justify his inclusion in a history of mythic thought. On the contrary: his well-known impatience with Christianity or religion itself often suggests he is merely perpetuating the long-familiar skeptical attitudes toward myth of *philosophes* like Bayle or Voltaire. But Gibbon is worth examination because his views on myth are much more complex, or even ambiguous, than usually noted. As a boyish scholar, the later historian of the notorious chapters fifteen and sixteen of the *Decline and Fall* was an enthusiastic student of orthodox Christian chronologers and mythologists; in his literary debut with the early *Essai sur l'étude de la littérature,* Gibbon gave an eclectic and often imaginatively vivid account of the origin and growth of myth; and even in the *Decline and Fall,* he expresses admiration for certain sides of myth, while massively and ironically demolishing mythic and religious pretensions. Gibbon is, in brief, a representative witness of some large and often conflicting sides of mythic thought in his century.

As a boy, Gibbon read Ussher and Prideaux, and having become involved in chronological disputation, "presumed to weigh the systems of Scaliger and Petavius, or Marsham and Newton." At about the age of fifteen, he wrote a never published treatise on *The Age of Sesostris,* in which the approach was that of a chronologer. Following Marsham

and in defiance of Newton, Gibbon set out to show that Sesostris had been a contemporary of Solomon in the tenth century B.C. By his own later account, his proofs were elaborate and relied heavily on the technique of "connecting" Greek, Jewish, and Egyptian antiquities, a practice he later disclaimed, adding that it was "not the only instance in which the belief and knowledge of the child are superseded by the more rational ignorance of the man."

At the age of twenty-two, Gibbon wrote his *Essai,* a rambling work on the value of the study of ancient literature, in which he takes up myth in its relation to literature. His first mention of myth suggests it hardly interests him; the historian of the decline of Rome has only this to say of its founding: "The flight of a band of refugees; their squabbles with a few villagers, and the settling of a paltry town, these were the boasted labors, the great exploits of the pious Aeneas." Gibbon also compares the Greek deities, unfavorably and without irony, to the Christian deity, but repeats such ideas as Blackwell's about the civilizing mission of poets like Orpheus, Homer, and Virgil, and the need to view Greek literature from a Greek perspective. In a later section of the *Essai,* reprinted below, Gibbon takes up the subject of myth again, this time considering it as a primitive religion—as he calls it, "the pleasant and absurd system of paganism." Here Gibbon is interested in origins, and his argument, drawn from Banier and Fréret on one hand and Hume on the other, weaves together personification, allegorizing, and Euhemerism with psychological ideas. Gibbon argues that man first divinized natural forces and then created, as a first stage, nature gods. When man became more civilized, he needed other deities, so he deified moral qualities, or as Gibbon calls it, interior reality. But these latter divinities were too abstruse to be popular, and were linked therefore to the older nature gods—that is, allegory took over and "imagined a thousand fantastical relations," and gave us what we call mythology.

In the *Essai,* Gibbon shows himself a youthful assimilator of the great rationalist accountings of myth. The *Decline and Fall,* obviously, remains faithful to this elegant and ironic viewpoint. Nothing could surpass his disdainful comment, "I am ignorant, and I am careless, of the blind mythology of the Barbarians." Having set out to explain the "religious system of the German," he wonders "if the wild opinions of savages can deserve that name"; all of pagan mythology is "unsupported by any solid proofs," and wise ancients surely believed little of it. In his chapter on Julian the Apostate, Gibbon skillfully uses the absurdities and superstitions of polytheism to impugn anything similar in Christianity. In all this, however, Gibbon does not go substantially beyond a Bayle or a Voltaire.

But in another way, Gibbon gives support to the affirmation of myth emerging among the English preromantics. In chapter six of his history, for example, Gibbon mentions the recent publication of Macpherson's Ossianic fragments. The scrupulous historian admits the "doubtful mist" hanging over the authenticity of these poems. But he then goes on to draw a decidedly partisan contrast between Roman degeneracy and the "warm virtue of nature" of the untutored Caledonians. In clear reflection of Mallet's

thesis, Gibbon evokes the "generous clemency of Fingal," the bravery, tenderness, and "elegant genius" of Ossian. It is a brief but admiring portrait of the dawning age of Northern European "chivalry," which had begun to fascinate others drawn to the "Nordic" renaissance. To this may be added the half-admiring, half-disdainful portrait of German mythology in chapter nine and remarks on the *Edda* later in the same chapter. In contrast, pagan mythology is generally treated as only decorated superstition, as in chapter fifteen and chapter twenty-three. With Mallet and Blair, Gibbon imputes to the Ossianic or Caledonian mythology none of the savagery to be found in the *Eddas.*

But Gibbon's *Decline and Fall* may be seen as a grand conclusion of one strand of eighteenth-century concern with myth. For with no sympathy or even tolerance for religion or religious myth, historians could write well of the decline of peoples and nations, but less well of the problems of the origins and rise of these peoples. That would require—as the "romantic" historians coming shortly after Gibbon make clear—a quite different temper. But in his praise of Ossian and his ceaseless elegant paeans to the emerging spirit of Northern freedom and progress, Gibbon allies himself cautiously with at least part of the future.

B.F.

REFERENCES   Our text is from *An essay on the study of literature: written originally in French* (London, 1764), which is Gibbon's translation of his own work in French of 1761. See Gibbon's *Autobiography* (New York: Meridian, 1969), chap. 2 for Gibbon's youthful theological studies. For commentary, see: A. Momigliano, *Studies of Historiography* (London: Weidenfeld and Nicolson, 1966), "Gibbon's Contribution to Historical Method," pp. 40–55; G. Giarrizzo, *E. Gibbon e la cultura europea del Settecento* (Napoli, 1954).

GIBBON

FROM *An Essay on the Study of Literature*

LXV. LET US go still further, and endeavour to trace a connected series, not of facts, but of notions; to sound the human heart, and to lay hold of that chain of errours, which, from a sentiment so just, simple and universal as that *there is a power above us,* conducted by degrees to the conception of deities, which a man would blush to resemble.

Sentiment is only a conscious appeal to ourselves. Our ideas relate to objects without us; and by their number and diversity, enfeeble the sentiment. It is therefore among uncultivated savages, whose ideas are confined to their wants, and whose wants are simply those of nature, that the force of sentiment should be more keen and lively, altho' at the same time confused and indistinct. Savage man must be every moment in agitations he can neither explain nor suppress. . . . The despicable opinion he justly entertains of himself (for vanity is the creature of society) makes him perceive the existence of some superior power. It is this power whose attributes he is ignorant of, that he invokes, and of whom he asks assistance, without knowing what pretensions he may have to hope it will be granted. This sentiment, indistinct as it was, naturally produced the good deities of the primitive Greeks, and the divinities of most of the savage nations; none of whom, however, knew how to ascertain their number, attributes, or worship.

LXVI. This sentiment, in time, is modified into a notion. Savage man pays homage to every thing about him; as every thing seems to him more excellent than himself. The majestic oak, that shelters him with its spreading boughs, had afforded a shade to his ancestors, down from the first of his race. It lifted its head into the clouds, while the towering eagle lost itself in its branches. What was the duration, the size, the strength, of an human creature, compared to such a tree? Gratitude next united itself to admiration. . . . In effect, without these lights, that enable us to see how much reason alone is superior to all those necessary parts of an intelligent system, every one of them is superior to man. But wanting such lights, savage man attributes life and power to them all; and prostrates himself before imaginary beings which he hath thus created.

LXVII. The ideas of uncivilized man are singular because they are simple. To remark the different qualities of objects, to observe those which are common to many, and from that resemblance to form an abstract idea, representative of the genus of objects, without being the image of any one in particular: this is the operation of the understanding, which acts and reflects within itself; and which, overstocked with ideas, thus endeavours to relieve itself by the forms of method. In a primitive state, the soul, passive and ignorant of its faculties, is capable only of receiving external impressions: these impressions represent only single objects, and in such a manner as they seem to exist in themselves. The savage therefore sees himself surrounded with deities: every field, every forest swarms with them.

LXVIII.   Experience unfolds his ideas, for individuals as well as societies owe every thing to experience. A variety of objects becoming familiar to his perceptions, he begins to discover their common nature, and this nature becomes a new divinity superior to all particular deities. But every thing that exists has its existence determined by time or place, which distinguish its identity. . . . The God of rivers lays an indisputed claim to his local rights on the Tiber and Clitumnus; but the South wind that blew yesterday, and that we feel to-day, are both the same blustering tyrant, that stirs up the mountainous waves of the Adriatic.

LXIX.   The more the mind exercises its thoughts, the more it combines its ideas. Two species are different in some respects, and alike in others: they are destined to the same use, they are part of the same element. The stream of a fountain becomes a river, the river loses itself in the sea . . . while the earth itself contains every thing that subsists by the principle of vegetation. In proportion as mankind become enlightened, their idolatry would refine. They would become better able to perceive how the universe is governed by general laws; and would approach nearer the unity of a sole, efficient cause. The Greeks could never generalize their ideas beyond the elements of water, earth and air; which, under the names of Jupiter, Neptune, and

Pluto, comprehended and governed all things. But the Ægyptians, whose genius was better adapted to abstract speculations, arrived at length to their Osiris or principal Divinity, an intelligent principle, which operated constantly on the material principle, couched under the name and personage of Isis, his wife and sister. Those who believe in the eternity of matter, can hardly go farther than this. (The worship of the sun hath prevailed in all nations. I shall give what appear to me the reasons of it. It is perhaps the only object in the world that is at once sole and perceptible. Perceptible to all the nations upon earth, in the most brilliant and beneficent manner, it is no wonder it should attract their homage. Sole and indivisible, those who reasoned on the subject, and were not too difficult, discovered in it all the distinguishing marks of divinity.)

LXX.   Jupiter, Neptune, and gristly Pluto were brothers; the branches of whose posterity spread themselves infinitely wide, and comprehended the whole system of nature. Such was the mythology of the ancients. To the ignorant, the idea of generation was more natural than that of creation. It was more easy for them to acquire; and supposed less power exerted in the operation. This generation, however, led them to establish an hierarchy, which these beings, though free yet limited, could not possibly do without. . . .

LXXI.   This system, ill-constructed as it was, accounted for all the physical effects of nature. But the moral world, man, his destiny, and actions were without divinities. The earth, or the air, had been ill-adapted deities. The want of new Gods, therefore, forged a new chain of errours, which, joined to the former, encircled the regions of theological romance. I suspect the latter system must take its rise very late; man never thinking of entering into himself, till he had exhausted external objects.

LXXII. There are two hypotheses which always have been, and ever will, subsist. In the one, man is supposed to have received from his Creator Reason and Will; that he is left to himself to put them to use, and regulate his actions accordingly. In the other, he is supposed incapable of acting otherwise than agreeable to the pre-established laws of the Deity, of whom he is only the instrument: that his sentiment deceives him, and when he imagines he follows his own inclination, he in fact only pursues that of his master. The latter notion might be suggested to the minds of a people, little removed from a primitive state. Little instructed in the movements of so complicated a machine, they saw with admiration the great virtues, the atrocious crimes, the useful inventions of a few singular men, and thought they surpassed the powers of humanity. Hence they conceived, on every side, active deities, inspiring virtue and vice into weak mortals, incapable of resisting their impulsive influence. It was not prudence that inspired Pandarus with the design of breaking the truce, and of aiming a dart at the breast of Menelaus. It was the Goddess Minerva excited him to that attempt. The unhappy Phedra was not criminal. No. It was Venus, who, irritated by the flights of Hippolitus, lighted up an incestuous flame in the heart of that Princess, which plunged her into guilt, infamy, and death. Thus a Deity was supposed to undertake the charge of every event in life, of every passion of the soul, and every order to society.

LXXIII. These deities of the moral world, however, these passions and faculties so generalized and personated, had only a metaphysical existence, too occult for the generality of mankind. It became necessary, therefore, to incorporate them with the physical deities; in doing which, allegory has imagined a thousand fantastical relations; for the mind always requires at least the appearance of truth. It was natural enough for the God of the sea to be also that of the sailors. The figurative expression of the eye, that sees every thing at one view; of those rays, which dart thro' the immensity of the air, might easily be applied to the sun, and make an able prophet and a skilful archer, of that luminary. But wherefore must the planet Venus be the mother and goddess of love? Why must she take her rise out of the foam of the ocean? But we must leave these enigmas to such as may be able to interpret them. No sooner were these moral deities assigned their several departments, than, it is natural to conceive, they engrossed the homage of mankind. They had to do immediately with the heart and the passions, whereas the physical divinities, to whom no moral attributes had been given, fell insensibly into contempt and oblivion. Thus, it is only in the earliest ages of antiquity that I descry the smoke on the altars of Saturn.

LXXIV. From this period the Gods became particularly interested in human affairs. Nothing passed of which they were not the authors. But were they the authors of injustice? We are startled at this conclusion: an heathen, however, did not hesitate to admit, and in fact could not doubt it. His Gods often suggested very vicious designs. To suggest them, it was necessary they should concur, and even take pleasure in them. They had not the resource of a small quantity of evil admissible into the best of possible worlds. The evil, they were accessary to, was not only permitted, but authorized; besides, these several divinities, confined to their respective departments, were quite indifferent as to the general good; with which they had nothing to do. Every one acted agreeable to his own character, and inspired only the passions he was supposed to feel. The God of War was fierce, blood-thirsty and brutal; the Goddess of Wisdom, prudent and reserved: the Queen of Love, an amiable, voluptuous goddess, all charm and caprice: subtlety and low cunning distinguished the God of Trade; and the cries of the unhappy were supposed to please the ear of the inexorable tyrant o'er the dead, the gloomy Monarch of the infernal shades.

LXXVI.   A refined homage was little suitable to such a kind of deities. The multitude required sensible objects; the image of something to decorate their temples, and fix their ideas. The choice, to be sure, must be fixed on the most amiable. But which is that? The human form will doubtless be preferred by men. Should a bull have answered the question, he would probably have determined in favour of some other. Sculpture now began to improve itself in the service of devotion, and the temples were filled with statues of old men and young, women and children, expressive of the different attributes ascribed to their deities.

LXXVII.   Beauty   is   perhaps   only founded on use; the human figure being beautiful only because it is so well adapted to the functions to which it is destined. The figure of the divinity, the same, should be certainly expressive of its properties, and even of its defects. Hence came that absurd generation of deities, who composed only a celestial family, similar to those among mankind: hence their feasts of nectar and ambrosia, and the nourishment they were supposed to receive from the sacrifices. Hence also their quiet slumbers, and their afflicting pains. The Gods, thus become only a race of superior men, used often to make visits on earth, inhabit their temples, take pleasure in the amusements of mankind, join in the chace, mix in the dance, and sometimes grow susceptible of the charms of a mortal beauty, and give birth to a race of heroes.

ROBERT WOOD

[1717?–1771]

ROBERT WOOD's *Essay on the Original Genius of Homer* (1767) is at first glance only a simple and unprepossessing essay on Homer. But the book had profound implications and exerted a remarkable influence on subsequent classical studies and myth studies both in England and in Germany. For Wood's essay quietly makes four points that singly or together influenced and foreshadowed much of the new historical (anti-allegorical) approach to Greek thought and religion worked out by Herder, F. A. Wolf, K. O. Müller, and others.

Wood was a traveler, and in association with members of the newly formed English *Society of Dilettanti*—an organization that did important pioneer work in the archaeological study of classical antiquity—he published two splendidly illustrated folios on *The Ruins of Palmyra* and *The Ruins of Balbec*. He then set out "to read the *Iliad* and the *Odyssey* in the countries where Achilles fought, where Ulysses travelled, and where Homer sung," as he says in the foreword to his *A Comparative View of the Antient and Present state of the Troade. To which is prefixed an Essay on the Original Genius of Homer*, first published in 1767.

Wood began by assuming—as Schliemann was to assume later—that the tale of Troy was based on fact. He argued, accordingly, that the *Iliad* was in fact based on real, discoverable historical events. The implications of this simple assumption were startling. For if the old heroic stories reflected actual events, it might mean that myth too was grounded in historical or natural reality, and not in the inventions of priests or poets.

Wood's second point was that the geography and topography of the *Iliad* were still to be seen in Asia Minor. This was another attempt to authenticate a story long thought to be merely imaginary, and Wood's careful attention to the *locale* of the *Iliad* had at least two kinds of effects on later scholars and poets. Byron could write: "We *do* care about the authenticity of the tale of Troy. I have stood upon that plain *daily,* for more than a month in 1810. . . . I venerated the grand original as the truth of history." Wood's topographical concern also pointed to archaeology as an important tool for reinvestigating the classical past.

In the third place, Wood argued that the mythology of the *Iliad* was not derived from Egypt (as Blackwell and innumerable others had argued), but was indigenous, was characteristically Greek, and was a natural outgrowth of the Greek admiration for nature.

When the sun goes down behind the cloud-capped mountains of Macedonia and Thessaly, there is a picturesque wildness in the appearance, under certain points of view, which naturally calls to mind the old fable of the rebel giants bidding defiance to Jupiter, and scaling the heavens, as the fanciful suggestion of this rugged perspective.

This approach to the problem of the origins of myth was to lend strength to the ideas of Herder that each nation has its own characteristics, that each nation will produce its own indigenous mythology—a mythology not descended or degenerated from some other higher source. Wood's argument also allows Greek myth to be regarded seriously, and as something essentially religious; it does not reduce myth to a mere program of allegorized wisdom, cynically veiled from the ignorant.

The fourth aspect of Wood's influence was his discussion as to whether or not writing was known to Homer. According to Jebb and others, this point was of great importance to F. A. Wolf in his later and famous formulation of the "Homeric question." In this respect, as in those listed above, Robert Wood's unpretentious essay proved itself of more real use and interest than many a learned volume of recondite mythic lore, and while Wood wrote no definitive work on myth, his efforts were catalytic for much of what was best in the new historical approach to myth.

R.R.

REFERENCES   Our text is from Robert Wood, *An Essay on the Original Genius and Writings of Homer* . . . (London, 1775), first published as *A Comparative View of the Antient and Present State of the Troade. To which is prefixed an Essay on the Original Genius of Homer* (London, 1767). For commentary on Wood and Romantic Hellenism, see Bernard H. Stern, *The Rise of Romantic Hellenism in English Literature 1732–1786* (Menasha, Wisconsin, 1940); Terence Spencer, *Fair Greece Sad Relic* (London: Weidenfeld and Nicolson, 1954); Lionel Cust and Sidney Colvin, *History of the Society of Dilettanti,* 1914 (2d ed.); Donald M. Foerster, *Homer in English criticism: the historical approach in the eighteenth century* (New Haven: Yale University Press, 1947); M. L. Clarke, *Greek Studies in England, 1700–1830* (Cambridge: Cambridge University Press, 1945); J. E. Sandys, *A History of Classical Scholarship* (Cambridge: Cambridge University Press, 1908) vol. 3. For Wood's influence in Germany, see R. C. Jebb, *Homer: an Introduction to the Iliad and the Odyssey* (London, 1887), p. 107; J. L. Myres, *Homer and his critics,* ed. D. Gray (London: Routledge and Kegan Paul, 1958).

R O B E R T   W O O D

FROM *An Essay on the Original Genius and Writings of Homer*

"Homer's Religion and Mythology"

WE CANNOT well take into consideration Homer's Religion and Mythology, without some notice of his Allegory, which has opened so large a field for ancient and modern speculation. It would be needless to enter into the extravagant fancies and laboured conjectures, by which the sense of the plainest passages in the Iliad and Odyssey has been sacrificed to this allegorizing humour. Nothing can be more contrary to our idea of the character of his writings, and to that unbiassed attention to the simple forms of Nature, which we admire as his distinguishing excellence. I do not indeed think that those, who read him with true relish, and not from affectation, run any risk of falling into such refinement. However, as great pains have been taken to trace the mysterious knowledge, which the Poet is supposed to conceal under this dark allegorical veil, up to his Egyptian education; and as a late ingenious Writer [Blackwell] has attempted to shew the extensive effects of the Poet's travelling from a country, where Nature governed, to one of settled rules and a digested Polity, it may be worth while to take the best view we can of the state of learning in Greece and Egypt in Homer's time, in order to see, what foundation there is for this opinion.

Referring the reader, for the state of Homer's learning, to a particular section on that head, I shall now lay before him my reasons for thinking, that the high compliments, which have been so long paid to the knowledge and wisdom of the antient Egyptians, have not been so well founded as is generally imagined; and I shall draw those reasons from the only sources, which can furnish evidence of this matter; *viz.* first, the monuments which they have left of their taste and genius; secondly, the accounts, which other nations have given of them in these respects.

It would be difficult to form a judgment of their literary merit, without a specimen of their performance in that way: and I do not find that antiquity has transmitted to us even their pretensions to excellence in composition. I must observe, that, though Egypt produced the papyrus, its use to letters was a Greek discovery. Their hieroglyphics, indeed, have been long admired as the repository of much wisdom and knowledge; though there seems great reason to think, that they were the production of an infant state of society, not yet acquainted with alphabetical writing. And they have been preserved by means of circumstances, which were peculiar to Egypt. For this country had the driest atmosphere, and the most durable materials. Hence these memorials have been preserved, while monuments of the same early stage of knowledge have perished in other countries.

Architecture, sculpture, and painting, seem to owe little to Egypt. If the temple of Theseus stands to this day at Athens an undoubted proof of the great perfection of Greek arts, as early as the battle of Marathon: in a climate so favourable to buildings as that of Egypt, where there are still considerable remains to be seen of pyramids of such perishable materials as unburnt bricks, some fragments surely would have been preserved to justify their pretentions. But though we are apt to trace every thing back to Egypt, I believe, in those arts the Greeks are entirely original, and took their ideas from nature alone. . . .

When the Greeks first applied to the study of Nature, and travelled to Egypt (supposed to have been then the school of science) for instructions, we might reasonably expect some favourable accounts of them. But, besides, that what we are told of these early travellers is obscure, and suspicious, all we can collect from them does not raise our ideas of Egyptian knowledge. If Pythagoras sacrificed a hecatomb upon finding out the 47th proposition of the first book of Euclid, and Thales an ox on having discovered how to inscribe a rectangled triangle in a circle, after they had studied mathematics in Egypt, the parent of geometry, what opinion does it give us of the knowledge of their masters in that science? . . .

But let us proceed to a third period of their history, from which we might expect to draw something to form a judgment of their arts and sciences. When the Greeks conquered Phoenicia, Chaldaea, and Egypt, their taste, and of course their curiosity, was at the highest. Whatever accounts that elegant and learned people may have given of the school, from whence they are supposed to have received the rudiments of all their knowledge; I can find very little said of the learning or arts of Egypt, except what they brought there themselves. Homer was studied with more critical attention in Egypt than in any other country, but it was by Greeks. . . .

For these reasons I am of opinion, that Egypt, though civilized, when Greece was in a state of barbarity, never got beyond mediocrity, either in the arts of peace or war. Nor shall we find this out of the order of things, if we consider the different nature of those countries. The singualr advantage of Egypt, was, a climate so temperate, that little cloathing was necessary; and a soil so fertile, that it yielded food with very little labour. And its situation in the tract of the East India trade will account for its riches. But these circumstances, to which it owes antiquity, population, and wealth, are not favourable to genius. Great efforts and happy exertions, either of mind or body, are not to be expected in a country where Nature has so well provided against hunger and cold; and where a universal sameness of soil, and a constant serenity of sky, afford nothing to awake the fancy or rouse the passions. Compare this with the landscape of Greece, the varieties of her soil, and the vicissitude of her seasons; and we shall not think it extraordinary, that the arts of life should begin in one of those countries, and be carried to perfection in the other.

Having said thus much of the supposed nurse of that mysterious learning, which the Poet is said to have brought from Egypt, and wrapped up in allegory; let us bring the reader back to his true character as a Painter, and see if we cannot find marks of imitation even in his Religion and Mythology. I believe that a comparative view of the divine truths of his Theology, and the ingenious fictions of his Mythology, will shew, that, as far as he was at liberty, he drew both systems from an accurate and comprehensive observation of Nature, under the direction of a fine imagination, and a sound understanding.

As to his Religion, it would be idle, indeed unfair, to introduce a few general observations, which I shall offer on this head, by commonplace exclamations, against the gross extravagances of the heathen creed. For though we must acknowledge, that the general conduct of Homer's gods would even disgrace humanity; yet, when we consider the pure and sublime notions of the Divine Nature, which so frequently occur in his writings, it is but justice to such exalted sentiments of the Supreme Being, to pronounce them incompatible with the belief of those ridiculous absurdities, which distinguish the opinions of the multitude from those of the Poet.

He believed the unity, supremacy, omnipotence, and omniscience of the Divine Nature, Creator, and Disposer of all things: his power, wisdom, justice, mercy, and truth, are inculcated in various parts of the Iliad and Odyssey: the immortality of the soul, a future state, rewards and punishments, and most of the principles of sound divinity, are to be found in his writings.

This looks much less like the religion of mystery, than of common sense; and those sublime but evident truths want not the illustrations of deep learning. They are obvious to the plain understanding of every thinking man, who looking abroad and consulting his own breast, as Homer did, compares what he sees with what he feels, and from the whole draws fair conclusions.

Even his Mythology, considered with a view to his original character, will discover, if I be not mistaken, some original strokes of the Painter and of his country. It seems to constitute a very distinguishing difference between true and false religion; that while the evidence of the first is universal, of every country, and coextensive with creation, the origin of the latter may be often traced to the local prejudices of a particular soil and climate. Star worship was the native idolatry of a serene sky and desert plains, where the beauties of the heavens are as striking as the rest of the external face of Nature is dreary and lifeless. In vain should we look for Naiades, Dryades, Oriades, &c. among the divinities of a country, without springs, rivers, trees, or mountains, and almost without vegetation. These were the natural acquisitions of superstition in her more northern progress.

What share Homer had in dressing up and modelling the fables of the heathen gods, can, at this time, be little more than matter of mere conjecture; it would however be unreasonable to think, that they were of his own creation. I should rather suppose, that the liberties of poetical embellishment, which he may have taken with the popular creed of his time, were strongly engrafted upon vulgar traditional superstitions, which had already laid strong hold of the passions and prejudices of his countrymen; an advantage, which so perfect a judge of human nature would be very cautious of forfeiting. For when the religion of poetry and that of the people were the same, any attempt of sudden innovation in such an establishment would have been a hazardous experiment, which

neither a good Citizen nor a good Poet would care to undertake. I shall therefore venture to conclude, that the part of the Poet's fiction, which dishonours his Deities with the weakness and passions of human nature, was founded in popular legends and vulgar opinion, for which every good poet, from Homer to Shakespeare, has thought proper to have great complaisance. Take from that original genius of our own country the popular belief in his ghosts and hobgoblins, his light fairies and his dapper elves, with other fanciful personages of the Gothic mythology; and you sap the true foundation of some of the most beautiful fictions, that ever Poet's imagination produced. That Homer carried this too far, and studying to please neglected to instruct, may be very true; for though Plato's severity on this head has been criticised, we must find it extremely becoming his zeal for the inseparable interests of religion and virtue, if we consider that he had weighty reasons, which do not reach Shakespeare's mythology, to be alarmed at examples of vice and immorality in the very persons, who were at that time the acknowledged objects of public religious worship.

Though the persons, and perhaps some part of the action, of his fable, might have been originally taken from Egypt and the East: yet we know that his figures, I may say portraits, were his own; and the scenery of his Mythology is Grecian. And (what strengthens our conjectures with regard to his country) of the various perspectives, into which we may attempt to reduce this Greek mythological scenery, the Ionian point of view will appear predominant.

I fear, I may appear prejudiced to my subject, if I look for Nature in this imaginary province, and expect a regard for truth even in the Poet's fable. Yet I cannot help thinking, that, where his persons are most ideal, his scene is not less real;

and that when his subject carries him beyond life, and his divine agents, or (in the language of criticism) his machinery is introduced, the action is carried on with greater powers, no doubt, and upon a larger scale; but with the same attention to a just proportion, and generally in the same subordination to the invariable laws of time and place. This is a management, which, though it cannot entirely command assent, softens extravagance, and leads the reader so insensibly to fancy reality in fiction, by rendering both conformable to the same general rules of possibility and consistence, that it is not easy to say, where the Historian ends, or the Poet begins.

And yet I despair of giving satisfaction on this head, within the compass, which I have prescribed to myself: for though the important and frequent use of the machinery, in contributing so largely to a spirited sucession of interesting variety, and especially in relieving the eye from too much of the Scamandrian plain, must be obvious to every attentive reader; yet the easy transition, by which this is effected, can only be discovered by a nicer examination of those classical regions, which gave birth, or at least gave system and maturity, to his fable. If we form to ourselves a just idea of the respective situation, distance, and perspective, of Olympus, Ida, the Grecian camp, &c. we shall find Homer's celestial geography (if I may so call it) so happily connected with his Map of Troy, that the scene is shifted from one to the other naturally, and with a certain mixture of circumstantial truths, which operates unobserved, and throws at least an air of possibility into the wildest excursions of fancy. I shall explain myself by example.

Jupiter, seated on Mount Gargara, the summit of Ida, not suspecting, that any of the gods would violate the neutrality he had so strictly enjoined, turns his eyes from the slaughter upon the Scamandrian plain to the peaceful scenes of Thrace and Mysia. But Neptune, anxious for the distressed Greeks, had placed himself on the top of Samothrace, which commands a prospect of Ida, Troy, and the fleet. Having from hence observed Jupiter turn his back upon the scene of action, he resolves to seize that opportunity of annoying the Trojans. With this view he goes home to Aegos for his armour, and proceeds thence to the field of battle, putting up his chariot and horses between Imbros and Tenedos. At the same time Juno, not less interested in the Grecian cause, discovers from Olympus, what is passing at the ships. And watching the motions of Jupiter and Neptune, she forms her plan accordingly for rendering the operations of the latter effectual, by keeping Jupiter's attention diverted another way. Having with this view procured the cestus or girdle of Venus, she proceeds, first to Lemnos, to solicit the aid of the god of Sleep, and thence to Jupiter on Gargara.

I doubt much, whether any reader has ever suspected, that this fanciful piece of machinery is so geographical, that we cannot enter into the boldness and true spirit of the Poet's conceptions upon this occasion, without a map. But if he examines it in that light, he will be pleased to find, that a view of the land and water, here described, under a certain perspective, clears up the action, and converts, what may otherwise appear crowded and confused, into distinct and pleasing variety. He will then see, that the mere change of Jupiter's position, while it introduces a most beautiful contrast between scenes of innocence and tranquillity, and those of devastation and bloodshed, is essential to the episode of Neptune and Juno. He will attend those

Divinities with new pleasure, through every step of their progress. The mighty strides of the first, and the enchanting description of his voyage, long admired as one of the happiest efforts of a truly poetical imagination, will improve upon a survey of the original scenery, when its correspondence with the fable is discovered. Juno's stages are still more distinctly marked: she goes from Olympus by Pieria and Aemathia, to Athos; from Athos, by sea, to Lemnos, where, having engaged the god of Sleep in her interests, she continues her course to Imbros; and from Imbros to Lectum, the most considerable promontory of Ida; here leaving the sea, she proceeds to Gargara, the summit of that mountain.

When I attempted to follow the steps of these poetical journies, in my eye, from Mount Ida, and other elevated situations of the Aeolian and Ionian side of the Aegean Sea; I could take in so many of them as to form a tolerable picture of the whole. But I could not make this experiment with the same success from any station in European Greece. This induces me to suppose the composition to be Asiatic, and that the original idea of Neptune and Juno's journey was most probably conceived in the neighbourhood of Troy.

I must own, that in this sort of inquiry we are apt to indulge our fancy; and it is not without some apprehensions of falling into this error, that, by way of farther explanation, I risk the following conjecture. When I was in these classical countries, I could not help tracing one of the most ancient pieces of heathen Mythology up to its source, I mean the war of the Titans with the gods. For though the scene of this story lies in old Greece, yet some of its embellishments look very like the production of an Ionian imagination. I have already taken notice of the beauties of a western evening prospect from this coast.

When the sun goes down behind the cloud-capped mountains of Macedonia and Thessaly, there is a picturesque wildness in the appearance, under certain points of view, which naturally calls to mind the old fable of the rebel giants bidding defiance to Jupiter, and scaling the heavens, as the fanciful suggestion of this rugged perspective. And we find this striking face of Nature adapted to so bold a fiction with a fitness and propriety, which its extravagance would forbid us to expect; for it was by no means a matter of indifference, which mountains were to be employed, or in what order they were to be piled, to effect this daring escalade. If we compare Homer and Virgil's account of this matter with the present state of the country, we shall find a variation in their descriptions, which, while it sufficiently distinguishes the Roman copy from the Greek original, will best explain my meaning.

There was an old tradition in Greece, which is preserved there to this day, that Ossa and Olympus were originally different parts of the same mountain, of which the first formed the summit, and the latter the base, till they were separated by an earthquake. It is not improbable that their size and shape, as they appear under an eastern point of view, should have given rise to this tradition, and perhaps suggested to the inventor of the fable, or, if you please, to the Poet, who first adapted it to this Grecian scenery, the order of piling them one upon another. But Virgil, who never saw, or never attended to, this prospect, has deviated both from Homer, and Nature, in placing those mountains so as to form an inverted pyramid.

It must however be acknowledged, that Virgil seldom errs by departing from Homer: if his machinery will not bear so scrupulous a review as that of the Greek Poet, it is in general less his fault than his misfortune; nor is the manifest inferiority of the Aeneid, in this respect, to be laid to his charge. A great part of the scene of action, though it has since acquired no small share of classical fame, was not at that time sufficiently consecrated to the purposes of poetry, by the birth, habitation, intrigues, and achievements of gods and heroes. Nor is the geographical disposition of Latium so favourable to fabulous adventure as that of Greece, where a most pleasing mixture of land and water is wonderfully calculated for a quick succession of scenery, affording more distinct variety than could well be imagined within the same compass. It was here alone that the dull creed of Egypt could be extended, and modelled into that fanciful system of Mythology, which Homer has so effectually entailed upon his poetical posterity, that few of his legitimate sons have ventured to shake off that incumbrance; and perhaps not one, who has not failed in the attempt. In accommodating this most poetical religion and picturesque country to the plan of the Iliad and Odyssey, he had only to choose and shift the rich materials of this engaging fable and romantic scenery; susceptible, under his management, even to a dramatic propriety, of the most natural, and yet most diversified combinations and transitions, that fancy could suggest. While Virgil, not daring to lose sight of his great model, not only brings his gods from Greece, but his shepherds from Arcadia, and his swans from Cayster: if Diana dances, it must be on the banks of the Eurotas.

Paul Henri Mallet [1730–1807]

James Macpherson [1736–1796]

Hugh Blair [1718–1800]

DURING the second half of the eighteenth century, the growing interest in myth was being fed by a surprising amount of new material. De Brosses and Knight are examples of the new knowledge made available by anthropology and archaeology; and later in the century, Eastern mythologies, most notably from India, were to have profound effect. But by far the most influential of the new materials for myth were those published and popularized by Paul Henri Mallet, James Macpherson, Hugh Blair, and others, in what has been called the Nordic Renaissance. Neither Mallet nor Macpherson set out to create new approaches to myth or to broach new theories about it, but they did make available to the English, the French, the Germans, and the Scandinavians a whole new subject matter—the stories of Odin, Thor, or Valhalla—that could be set against Greek mythology. Mallet made available this whole new system of Nordic mythology, and Macpherson learned, perhaps from Lowth and Blackwell, how to rework old material into new myth.

Mallet and Macpherson have both been recognized as important in the history of preromanticism; but they were also crucial—indeed pivotal in some sense—in changing artists' attitudes toward mythological material. Their influence helps myth to come to mean more than

mainly Greek and Roman fables, and more than the ornament or the "machinery" for literature. They also help to separate myth still further from religion and to remove it as well from the polemical context provided in the first half of the century by orthodox Christianity. Myth was again rediscovered, this time chiefly by English and German poets as part of their own local and national history. Myth thus becomes historically and culturally important; Nordic gods, such as Thor, and Ossianic heroes, such as Fingal, seemed for the moment closer and more interesting to Europeans than were the old puzzling and foreign deities of the Mediterranean world. In Macpherson's Ossian, myth becomes something the poet both inherits and creates.

The new idea that myth is alive—that it exists and influences the present, is organically connected with poetry, and is inseparably linked with national culture and literature—can be traced from Mallet's Norse myths through Ossian, Vathek, Blake's *Prophetic Books,* and all the major English romantic poets (to follow only one of several possible lines). The new interest in myth underlies and indeed impels a new drive to write national epics, and the whole romantic movement comes more and more to be marked by the pulsing vitality and the urgent, indeed devotional, passion that had formerly been associated more with religion than with literature.

Paul Henri Mallet, a Swiss by birth and education, was appointed Professor of *Belles-Lettres* at Copenhagen in 1752, and brought out, at the age of 22 in 1755, an *Introduction à l'histoire du Dannemarc où l'on traite de la religion, des loix des moeurs et des usages des anciens Danois.* In the next year appeared the second part of this work, the *Monumens de la mythologie et de la poésie des Celtes, et particulièrement des anciens Scandinaves,* the book directly responsible for introducing the Nordic mythology contained in the *Eddas to* European notice.

Mallet's work, later expanded, re-edited, and translated widely, laid out the whole world of Odin, Thor, Loki, Valhalla, Niflheim, and the Valkyries; it gave a complete account of the origins of things and the desolate and terrifying end, and accompanied it with a running explanation of where this Norse myth came from and what it signified.

As Paul Van Tieghem points out, Mallet thought of his work as the key to the history, not only of Denmark, but of Europe, since the invasions of the northernmost peoples had determined the form of modern Europe. To know modern Europe, then, one needed to study, not the Greeks and Romans, but the Northmen, who were the source of European liberty and much else besides. Mallet also distinguished between the early Nordic religion and the late, claiming that the early religion was a pure, dignified and humane religion, not unlike ideal Christianity or deism. But this early religion had been debased and corrupted and had eventually become lost under a new wave of bloody and barbaric myth, the myths of the *Eddas.* The early religion, Mallet claimed, had been more moral and more consoling than Greek religion; it had taught respect for women, had given the profession of arms high

regard, had exalted honor, and had encouraged the lively Celtic sense of the marvelous. The later religion, as evidenced by the gloomy, warlike barbarities of Odin and the wolf Fenrir, for example, was a badly corrupted religion that had created a vicious mythology that in turn could produce only more barbarism.

Mallet, then, does not present his myths for the reader's admiration or imitation; he holds no brief for primitive nobility, and has no nostalgia for more glorious, more simple, and more heroic days. Opposed to Rousseau and to what Ossian would come to represent, Mallet believed that primitive man is unfortunate, ignorant, poor, and cruel. Yet paradoxically, he held that this dismal savagery had been preceded by a better state. Still, for all his disapproval of Nordic myth, Mallet took great care to present the stories themselves completely and colorfully; it was to prove easy for Mallet's readers to pick up the myths and to disregard Mallet's own glum estimate of their potential.

Mallet's work was translated into Danish in 1756, into German in 1765, into English in 1770 (under the title *Northern Antiquities* by Thomas Percy) and was re-edited in 1809 and again in 1847. In Germany it was picked up by Lessing, Hamann, Herder (who interpreted the Nordic myths as popular, peoples' poetry), and Goethe, to name only the best-known. In England, Gibbon cited Mallet in the *Decline and Fall,* Gray made use of Mallet's material, and Percy's *Five Pieces of Runic Poetry* took three of its five texts from Mallet. In France, Voltaire read Mallet, and a good deal of the new Nordic material got into the later volumes of the *Encyclopédie.* Mallet's influence was thus immediate, widespread, and central. He was of interest to historians, theologians, and philosophers, as well as to mythographers and poets. And when it is recalled that the later eighteenth century commonly considered the Celtic,

Gallic, Germanic, and Scandinavian peoples to be the same (the word Celt commonly covered all the rest), and that *Beowulf,* the *Chanson de Roland,* the *Nibelungenlied* and the *Kalevala* were then not yet known, it is less surprising that Germans, French, English, and Scandinavians alike looked eagerly to Mallet's new material. Blackwell had shown how it was possible to read and value a poem in its historical, geographical, and cultural context; now Europe had its own indigenous material and need no longer look to Rome or Greece. The raw material of Nordic myth was to provide whole new national literatures, closely linked to the soil and to the peoples of Northern Europe. Finally, Mallet prepared the ground for Macpherson's Ossian; the "Homer of the North" came as though to fulfill the expectation aroused by Mallet.

In 1760, James Macpherson published *Fragments of Antient Poetry collected in the Highlands of Scotland and translated from the Gaelic or Erse Language.* John Home and Hugh Blair, the latter a professor of rhetoric at the University of Edinburgh, encouraged Macpherson, and Macpherson, after a tour of the Highlands to collect more material, quickly brought out in 1762 a complete Gaelic epic, translated by himself into pearl-pale prose, called *Fingal; an Ancient Epic Poem in Six Books; Together with Several other poems, composed by Ossian the son of Fingal.* This was quickly followed by another complete epic called *Temora,* this time in eight books, published in 1763. Macpherson claimed to have worked from manuscripts and from oral tradition; he was challenged to produce the manuscripts and failed to do so, but was defended by Blair and others at such length and with such cleverness that the controversy raged on unsettled even after Macpherson's death. Despite the challenge to its authenticity, Macpherson's work was quickly and widely acclaimed by such men as Hume, Gray, Walpole, Boswell, Shenstone, Percy, Turgot, Diderot, Grimm, Lessing, Herder, Hamann, and Goethe, and while a few of these men changed their minds later, Ossian nevertheless flowed like a tide over Europe.

The Macpherson poems are largely fabrications, and to a modern ear they seem filled with languid imagery and willowy rhetoric. The endless (and derivative) prose drone of the bard, Ossian, tells stories about one Fingal, supposedly a third-century Celtic leader, about his land, Morven, and about his heroes and his bards and their numerous melancholy adventures. The poems were praised by Blair (whose *Critical Dissertation on the Poems of Ossian,* defending the poems, was of incalculable benefit in spreading the vogue) as noteworthy above all else for their tenderness and sublimity. The general tone of the poems may be adequately gathered from the excerpt from "Carthon" below.

These poems came as a revelation in their own time, and it would be hard to overestimate their impact. The English, the Germans, and the French all regarded Ossian as a primitive national bard for all of Europe, and each nation claimed Ossian for itself (Klopstock thought Ossian to have been German "because he was of Caledonian origin"). Ossian was widely compared to Shakespeare, and was often thought to have been nobler, better, and gentler than Homer; and Blair's comparison between Homer and Ossian shows how seriously the age felt obliged to take the latter. The Primitive, the Classical, and the Noble met in the Ossianic world; Ossian was even found comparable to the Bible, to Homer, and to Iroquois songs. Northern Europe was seen to be as good as, or even better than, the south, and Northern mythology was to be preferred to Greek and Roman. It was also argued that although Ossian lived after Homer, Ossian had written about a more primitive and a more noble state of society than had Homer. It should also be remarked that Mallet had postulated an earlier stage of Nordic myth, and Macpherson in fact supplied it (though apparently without having read Mallet).

Moreover, Ossian was widely thought to represent that early pure religion, that ideal noninstitutionalized and genteel deism for which so many early eighteenth-century writers had longed. Indeed, Ossian provides the only concrete example or illustration of the early simple and natural religion posited by the deists. Based as it was on the idea of a primitive, noble, rural state of nature, Ossian was also perfectly suited to Jean-Jacques Rousseau's ideas, and, as Van Tieghem points out, Ossian and Rousseau reinforced each other all through the period. The poems were proof of the idea that primitive man was refined, generous, sensitive, and happy without institutions or religions (Blair indeed argues that the reason there is no religion in Ossian is that Fingal comes after Druidism but before Christianity); and Rousseau provided the theory of benevolent, unspoiled primitive human nature, which could explain the characters and actions of Fingal, Ossian, Oscar, Carthon, Clessamor, and the other heroes of Morven.

The influence of the Ossianic poems was sudden and vast. There were endless editions, translations, reprints, and imitations; and if no major English poet was a real disciple of Ossian, still Blake, Coleridge, and Southey were heavily influenced by Ossian, as were Saint-Simon, Chateaubriand, and André Chénier in France, and Haller, Klopstock, Burger, and Schiller in Germany, in addition to those like Goethe who had taken up Ossian in the early days. Macpherson's Ossian thus had a large formative influence on the romantic imagination and hence on the modern imagination. The heavy emphases on love, on melancholy, on

fame, on the gentle and the genteel, and on sentiment found in Ossian were transmitted to the nineteenth century, as was the gloomy and misty Northern landscape. From Mallet to Ossian to William Morris and perhaps even to J. R. R. Tolkien, one can trace the Nordic and the Ossianic influence. After Mallet and Macpherson, the European artist who wished to use old myth had, for the first time, a concrete and indigenous alternative to the ancient Mediterranean mythologies.

R.R.

REFERENCES Our texts are from P. H. Mallet, *Northern Antiquities*, tr. Thomas Percy (London: Bohn, 1844), Hugh Blair, *A Critical Dissertation on the Poems of Ossian, Son of Fingal* (London, 1763), and James Macpherson, *The Works of Ossian* (London, 1765) 3d ed., vol. I. Mallet's work originally appeared as *Monumens de la mythologie et de la poésie des Celtes, et particulièrement des anciens Scandinaves* (Copenhagen, 1756); this was the second volume of Mallet's *Introduction à l'histoire de Dannemarc . . .*

A highly useful study is P. Van Tieghem, *Le Préromantisme* (Paris, 1924), especially "La mythologie et la poésie Scandinaves," and "Ossian et l'ossianisme." See also: P. Van Tieghem, *Ossian en France* (Paris, 1917); J. F. Herder, *Ossian und die Lieder alter Völker*, in *Blätter von deutscher Art und Kunst* (Hamburg, 1773); A. Gillies, *Herder und Ossian* (Berlin, 1933); R. Tombo, *Ossian in Germany* (New York, 1901); H. A. Beers, *A History of English Romanticism in the Eighteenth Century* (New York, 1899); A. Nutt, *Ossian and the Ossianic Literature* (London, 1899); Edward Snyder, *The Celtic Revival in English Literature 1760–1800* (Cambridge, Massachusetts, 1923); and F. I. Carpenter, "The Vogue of Ossian in America: a Study in Taste," *American Literature*, vol. 11 (1931).

For Blair, see R. W. Chapman, "Blair on Ossian," *Review of English Studies*, VII (1931), and O. L. Jiriczek, "Zur Bibliographie und Textegeschichte von Hugh Blair's *Critical dissertation on the Poems of Ossian*," *Englische Studien*, 1935, 181–189.

MALLET

FROM *Northern Antiquities*

*Of the Religion which Prevailed in the North, and Particularly
in Scandinavia, after the Primitive Worship had been Altered*

THE MOST striking alteration in the doctrines of the primitive religion, was in the number of the gods who were to be worshipped. A capital point in the ancient dogmas, was the pre-eminence . . . of one only all-powerful and perfect being over all the other intelligences with which universal nature was peopled. But men becoming in all appearance weary of this simplicity of religion, associated to the supreme God many of those genii or subaltern divinities who had been always subordinate to him. . . . The deep conviction we have every moment of our own weakness, prevents us from conceiving how it is possible for one single being to move and support all parts of the universe. This is, especially, inconceivable to an ignorant people who have never suspected that there is any connection between the several parts of nature, and that a general mechanism can produce so many different phenomena. Accordingly, all barbarous nations have ever substituted, instead of the simple and uniform laws of nature, which were unknown to them, the operation of spirits, genii and divinities of all kinds, and have given them as assistants to the Supreme Being in the moral and physical government of the world. If they have paid to any of them greater honours than

to others, it has usually been to those whose dominion extended over such things as were most dear to them, or appeared most worthy of admiration. This was what happened in Scandinavia. In process of time that Supreme Being, the idea of whom takes in all existence, was restrained to one particular province, and passed among the generality of the inhabitants for the God of War. No object, in their opinion, could be more worthy his attention, nor more proper to show forth his power. Hence those pictures which are left us of him in the Icelandic mythology, where he is always meant under the name of Odin. He is there called "The terrible and severe God; the father of slaughter; he who giveth victory, and reviveth courage in the conflict; who nameth those that are to be slain." The warriors who went to battle made a vow to send him a certain number of souls, which they consecrated to him; these souls were Odin's right, he received them in Valhalla, his ordinary place of residence, where he rewarded all such as died sword in hand. . . .

This terrible deity, who took such pleasure in shedding the blood of men, was at the same time, according to the Icelandic mythology, their father and creator. So easily do gross and prejudiced minds reconcile the most glaring contradictions. . . . Many ancient people, the Germans for example, attributed in like manner to the supreme God a superintendence over war. They drew their gods by their own character, who loved nothing so much themselves as to display their strength and power in battle, and to signalize their vengeance upon their enemies by slaughter and desolation. There remains to this day some traces of the worship paid to Odin in the name given by almost all the people of the north to the fourth day of the week, which was formerly consecrated to him. It is called by a name which signifies Odin's day.

The principal goddess among the ancient Scandinavians was Frigga, the wife of Odin. It was the opinion of many ancient nations, as well as of the first inhabitants of Greece, that the supreme Being or celestial God had united with the earth to produce the inferior divinities, man, and all other creatures. Upon this was founded that veneration they had for the earth, which they considered as a goddess, and the honours which were paid her. They called her Mother Earth, and Mother of the Gods. The Phenicians adored both these two principles under the name of Tautes and Astarte. They were called by some nations Jupiter and Apia; by the Thracians, Cotis and Bendis; by the inhabitants of Greece and Italy, Saturn and Ops. All antiquity is full of traces of this worship, which was formerly universal. . . . Tacitus attributes the same worship to the Germans, particularly to the inhabitants of the north of Germany. He says, "They adore the goddess Herthus, (meaning the earth,") and gives a circumstantial description of the ceremonies which were observed in honour of her in an island, which he does not name, but which could not have been far from Denmark. We cannot doubt but this same goddess was the Frigga of

the Scandinavians. Another celebrated goddess was Freyja, the Goddess of Love. It was she that was addressed in order to obtain happy marriages and easy childbirths. She dispensed pleasures, enjoyments, and delights of all kinds. . . .

The second principal god of the ancient Scandinavians was named Thor, and was no less known than Odin among the Teutonic nations. In the system of the primitive religion, the God Thor was probably only one of those genii or subaltern divinities sprung from the union of Odin, or the supreme being, and the earth. The Edda calls him expressly the most valiant of the sons of Odin. He was considered as the defender and avenger of the gods. He always carried a mallet, which, as often as he discharged it, returned back to his hand of itself; he grasped it with gauntlets of iron, and was further possessed of a girdle which had the virtue to renew his strength as often as was needful. It was with these formidable arms that he overthrew to the ground the monsters and giants, when the gods sent him to oppose their enemies.

The deities whom we have mentioned were the principal objects of the worship and veneration of all the Scandinavians; but they were not all agreed among themselves about the preference which was due to each of them in particular. The Danes seem to have paid the highest honours to Odin; the inhabitants of Norway and Iceland appear to have been under the immediate protection of Thor; and the Swedes had chosen for their tutelar deity Freyja, or rather Frey, her brother, who, according to the Edda, presided over the seasons of the year, and bestowed peace, fertility, and riches. . . . The prose Edda reckons up twelve gods and as many goddesses, to whom divine honours were due, and who, though they had all a certain power, were nevertheless obliged to obey Odin, the most ancient of the gods, and the great principle of all things. Such was Njörd, the Neptune of the northern nations, who reigned over the sea and winds. The extent of his empire rendered him very respectable; and we find in the north, to this day, traces of the veneration which was there paid him. The Edda exhorts men to worship him with great devotion.

Baldur was another son of Odin, wise, eloquent, and endowed with such great majesty that his very glances were bright and shining. Tyr, who must be distinguished from Thor, was also a warrior deity, and the protector of champions and brave men. Bragi presided over eloquence and poetry. His wife, named Iduna, had the care of certain apples, which the gods tasted when they found themselves grown old, and which had the power of instantly restoring them to youth. Heimdall was their porter. The gods had made a bridge between heaven and earth; this bridge is the rainbow. Heimdall was employed to watch at one of the extremities of this bridge, for fear the giants should make use of it to get into heaven. . . . I suppress here the names of the other gods, who made up the number of twelve; but I ought to bestow a word upon Loki, whom the ancient Scandinavians seem to have regarded as their evil principle, and whom, notwithstanding, they ranked among the gods. The Edda calls him "the calumniator of the gods, the grand contriver of deceit and frauds, the reproach of gods and men. He is beautiful in his figure, but his mind is evil, and his inclinations inconstant. Nobody renders him divine honours. He surpasses all mortals in the arts of perfidy and craft." He has had many children, besides three monsters, who owe their birth to him; the wolf Fenrir, the Midgard serpent, and Hela or Death. All three are enemies to the gods, who after various struggles have chained this wolf till the last day, when he shall break loose and rush against them. The serpent has been cast into the sea, where he shall remain till he is conquered by the God Thor. And Hela or Death has been banished into the lower regions, where she has the government of nine worlds, into which she distributes those who are sent to her. We find here and there in the Edda several other strokes concerning Loki, his stratagems against the gods, their resentment, and the vengeance they took of him, when he was seized and shut up in a cavern formed of three keen-edged stones, where he rages with such violence that he causes all the earthquakes that happen. He will remain their captive, adds the same mythology, till the end of the ages; but then he shall be slain by Heimdall, the door-keeper of the gods.

We have seen above that the Icelandic mythology reckons up twelve goddesses. . . . Besides these twelve goddesses there are numerous virgins in Valhalla, or the paradise of the heroes. Their business is to wait upon them, and they are called Valkyrior. Odin also employs them to choose in battles those who are to perish, and to make the victory incline to whatever side he pleases. The court of the gods is ordinarily kept under a great ash tree, and there they distribute justice. This ash is the greatest of all trees; its branches cover the surface of the earth, its top reaches to the highest heaven, it is supported by three vast roots, one of which extends to the ninth world. An eagle, whose piercing eye discovers all things, perches upon its branches. A squirrel is continually running up and down it to bring news; while a parcel of serpents, fastened to the trunk, endeavour to destroy him. From under one of the roots runs a fountain wherein

Wisdom lies concealed. From a neighbour-ing spring (the fountain of past things) three virgins are continually drawing a precious water, with which they water the ash tree: this water keeps up the beauty of its foliage, and after having refreshed its leaves, falls back again to the earth, where it forms the dew of which the bees make their honey. These three virgins always keep under the ash; and it is they who dispense the days and ages of men. Every man hath a destiny appropriated to him-self, who determines the duration and events of his life. But the three destinies of more especial note are Urd (the past), Verdandi (the present), and Skuld (the future).

Such were the principal deities, formerly worshipped in the north of Europe; or rather these were the ideas which the poets gave of them to the credulous people. It is easy to discover their handywork in these fictions, sometimes ingenious, but more frequently puerile, with which they thought to set off the simplicity of the ancient re-ligion; and we ought not to believe that such of them as were men of sense and discernment ever considered them in any other light. But after having shown the names and attributes of their principal deities, let us proceed to set forth, after the Edda and the poem named Völuspá, the other doctrines of their religion.

We have seen that among the qualities of which they supposed Odin or the Su-preme God to be possessed, that of the creator of heaven and earth is expressly attributed to him. What the Icelandic my-thology has preserved to us on this head merits so much the more attention, as it discovers to us the sentiments that pre-vailed at a very early period on this im-portant point, and at the same time ex-presses them frequently with a greatness and sublimity equal to the finest strokes of classical antiquity on the same subject. The Völuspá begins by a description of Chaos. "In the day-spring of the ages," says the prophetess, "there was neither sea, nor shore, nor refreshing breezes. There was neither earth below, nor heaven above, to be distinguished. The whole was only one vast abyss, without herb, and without seeds. The sun had then no palace: the stars knew not their dwelling-places, and the moon was ignorant of her power." After we are told that "there was a lumi-nous, burning, flaming world toward the south; and another, nebulous and dark, toward the north. From the latter world flowed out incessantly into the abyss that lay between the two, torrents of venom, which in proportion as they removed far away from their source, congealed in their falling into the abyss, and so filled it with scum and ice. Thus was the abyss by little and little filled quite full; but there re-mained within it a light and immoveable air, and thence exhaled icy vapours. Then a warm breath coming from the south, melted those vapours, and formed of them living drops, whence was born the giant Ymir. It is reported that whilst he slept an extraordinary sweat under his arm-pits produced a male and female, whence is sprung the race of the giants; a race evil and corrupt, as well as Ymir their author. Another race was brought forth, which formed alliances with that of the giant Ymir: this was called the family of Bor, so named from the second of that family, who was the father of Odin. The sons of Bor slew the giant Ymir, and the blood ran from his wounds in such abundance, that it caused a general inundation, wherein perished all the giants, except only one, who saving himself in a bark, escaped with all his family. Then a new world was formed. The sons of Bor, or the gods, dragged the body of the giant in the abyss, and of it made the earth: the sea and rivers were composed of his blood; the earth of his flesh; the great mountains of his bones; the rocks of his teeth and of splinters of his bones broken. They made of his skull the vault of heaven, which is supported by four dwarfs named North, South, East, and West. They fixed there tapers to enlighten it, and assigned to other fires certain spaces which they were to run through, some of them in heaven, others under the heaven: the days were distinguished, and the years were numbered. They made the earth round, and surrounded it with the deep ocean, upon the outward banks of which they placed the giants. One day, as the sons of Bor, or the gods, were taking a walk, they found two pieces of wood floating upon the water; these they took, and out of them made a man and a woman. The eldest of the gods gave them life and souls; the second motion and knowledge; the third the gift of speech, hearing and sight, to which he added beauty and raiment. From this man and this woman, named Ask and Embla, is descended the race of men who are permitted to inhabit the earth."

It is easy to trace out in this narration vestiges of an ancient and general tradition, of which every sect of paganism has altered, adorned or suppressed many circumstances, according to their own fancy, and which is now only to be found entire in the books of Moses. Let the strokes we have here produced be compared with the beginning of Hesiod's Theogony, with the mythology of some Asiatic nations, and with the book of Genesis, and we shall instantly be convinced that the conformity which is found between many circumstances of their recitals, cannot be the mere work of chance. Thus in the Edda the description of the Chaos; that vivifying breath which produces the giant Ymir;

that sleep during which a male and female spring from his sides; that race of the sons of the gods; that deluge which only one man escapes, with his family, by means of a bark; that renewal of the world which succeeds; that first man and first woman created by the gods, and who receive from them life and motion: all this seems to be only remains of a more ancient and more general belief, which was carried into the north, and altered there more slowly than in other countries. One may discover also in the very nature of these alterations the same spirit of allegory, the same desire of accounting for all the phenomena of nature by fictions, which has suggested to other nations the greatest part of the fables with which their theology is infected. To conclude, the style itself, in which the expressions, one while sublime, one while extravagant and gigantic, are thrown together without art, the littlenesses that accompany the most magnificent descriptions, the disorder of the narrative, the uniform turn of the phrases, confirms to all who read this work an idea of a very remote antiquity, and a mode of thinking and writing peculiar to a simple and gross people, who were unacquainted with any rules of composition, and whose vigorous imagination, despising or not knowing any rules of art, displays itself in all the liberty and energy of nature. . . .

The other precepts of this religion probably extended no farther than to be brave and intrepid in war, to serve the gods, and to appease them by sacrifices, not to be unjust, to show hospitality to strangers, to keep their words inviolably, and to be faithful to the marriage bed. . . . It is now time to discuss another of its doctrines, that of the state of man after death, and the final destiny of the world he now inhabits.

"There will come a time," says the Edda,

"a barbarous age, an age of the sword, when iniquity shall infest the earth, when brothers shall stain themselves with brothers' blood, when sons shall be the murderers of their fathers, and fathers of their sons, when incest and adultery shall be common, when no man shall spare his friend. Immediately shall succeed a desolating winter; the snow shall fall from the four corners of the world, the winds shall blow with fury, the whole earth shall be hard bound in ice. Three such winters shall pass away without being softened by one summer. Then shall succeed astonishing prodigies; then shall the monsters break their chains and escape; the great serpent shall roll himself in the ocean, and with his motions the earth shall be overflowed; the earth shall be shaken, the trees shall be torn up by the roots, the rocks shall be dashed against each other. The wolf Fenrir, broke loose from his chains, shall open his enormous mouth which reaches from heaven to earth; the fire shall flash out from his eyes and nostrils; he shall devour the sun; and the great serpent who follows him shall vomit forth upon the waters, and into the air, great torrents of venom. In this confusion the stars shall fly from their places, the heaven shall cleave asunder, and the army of Surtur shall break in. But Heimdall, the doorkeeper of the gods, rises up, he sounds his clanging trumpet; the gods awake and assemble; the great ash-tree shakes its branches; heaven and earth are full of horror and affright. The gods fly to arms; the heroes place themselves in battle array. Odin appears armed in his golden casque and his resplendent cuirass; his vast scimitar is in his hands. He attacks the wolf Fenrir; he is devoured by him, and Fenrir perishes at the same instant. Thor is suffocated in the floods of venom which the serpent breathes forth as he expires. Loki

and Heimdall mutually kill each other. The fire consumes everything, and the flame reaches up to heaven. But presently after a new earth springs forth from the bosom of the waves, adorned with green meadows; the fields there bring forth without culture, calamities are unknown, a palace is there raised more shining than the sun, all covered with gold. This is the place that the just will inhabit, and enjoy delights for evermore. Then the powerful, the valiant, he who governs all things, comes forth from his lofty abodes, to render divine justice. He pronounces decrees. He establishes the sacred destinies which shall endure for ever. There is an abode remote from the sun, the gates of which face the north; poison rains there through a thousand openings: this place is all composed of the carcasses of serpents: there run certain torrents, in which are plunged perjurers and assassins."

Notwithstanding the obscurities which are found in these descriptions, we see that it was a doctrine rendered sacred by the religion of the ancient Scandinavians, that the soul was immortal, and that there was a future state reserved for men, either happy or miserable, according to their behaviour here below. All the Teutonic nations held the same opinions, and it was upon these they founded the obligation of serving the gods, and of being valiant in battle: but although the Greek and Latin historians who have spoke of this people, agree in attributing these notions of them, yet none of them have given any particular account of the nature of these doctrines; and one ought to regard in this respect the Icelandic mythology as a precious monument, without which we can know but very imperfectly this important part of the religion of our fathers. I must here sacrifice to brevity many reflections, which the picture I have here copied from thence naturally presents to the mind. Many in particular would arise on the surprising conformity that there is between several of the foregoing strokes, and those employed in the gospel to describe the same thing. A conformity so remarkable that one should be tempted to attribute it to the indiscreet zeal of the Christian writer who compiled this mythology, if the Edda alone had transmitted to us this prophecy concerning the last ages of the world, and if we did not find it with the same circumstances in the Völuspá, a poem of greater antiquity, and in which nothing can be discovered that has an air of interpolation, or forgery.

One remark, however, ought not to be omitted, which is, that this mythology expressly distinguishes two different abodes for the happy, and as many for the culpable; which is what several authors who have written of the ancient religion of Europe have not sufficiently attended to. The first of these abodes was the palace of Odin named Valhalla, where that god received all such as died in a violent manner, from the beginning to the end of the world, that is, to the time of that universal desolation of nature which was to be followed by a new creation, and what they called Ragnarök, or the twilight of the gods. The second, which after the renovation of all things was to be their eternal abode, was named Gimli, that is, the palace covered with gold, the description of which we have seen above, where the just were to enjoy delights for ever. It was the same as to the place of punishments; they distinguished two of those, of which the first, named Niflheim, was only to continue to the renovation of the world, and the second that succeeded it was to endure for ever. This last was named Náströnd, the shore of the dead; and we have seen in the description of the end of the world, what idea was entertained of it by the ancient Scandinavians. With regard to the two first places, the Valhalla and Niflheim, they are not only distinguished from the others in being only to endure till the conflagration of the world, but also in respect to rewards and punishments. Those only whose blood had been shed in battle, might aspire to the pleasures which Odin prepared for them in Valhalla. The pleasures which they expected after death show us plainly enough what they relished during life. "The heroes," says the Edda, "who are received into the palace of Odin, have every day the pleasure of arming themselves, of passing in review, of ranging themselves in order of battle, and of cutting one another in pieces; but as soon as the hour of repast approaches, they return on horseback all safe and sound back to the hall of Odin, and fall to eating and drinking. Though the number of them cannot be counted, the flesh of the boar Saehrimnir is sufficient for them all. . . . A crowd of virgins wait upon the heroes at table, and fill their cups as fast as they empty them." Such was that happy state, the bare hope of which rendered all the inhabitants of the north of Europe intrepid, and which made them not only to defy, but even seek with ardour the most cruel deaths. Accordingly King Ragnar Lodbrok, when he was going to die, far from uttering groans, or forming complaints expressed his joy by these verses. "We are cut to pieces with swords; but this fills me with joy, when I think of the feast that is preparing for me in Odin's palace. Quickly, quickly seated in the splendid habitation of the gods, we shall drink beer out of curved horns. A brave man fears not to die. I shall utter no timorous words as I enter the Hall of Odin."   (from Chap. V)

MACPHERSON

FROM *Carthon*

[The death of Carthon and Ossian's apostrophe to the Sun]

JOY ROSE in Carthon's face; he lifted his heavy eyes.—He gave his sword to Fingal, to lie within his hall, that the memory of Balclutha's king might remain on Morven.—The battle ceased along the field, for the bard had sung the song of peace. The chiefs gathered round the falling Carthon; and heard his words, with sighs. Silent they leaned on their spears, while Balclutha's hero spoke. His hair sighed in the wind, and his words were feeble.

"King of Morven," Carthon said, "I fall in the midst of my course. A foreign tomb receives, in youth, the last of Reuthámir's race. Darkness dwells in Balclutha; and the shadows of grief in Crathmo. But raise my remembrance on the banks of Lora, where my fathers dwelt. Perhaps the husband of Moina will mourn over his fallen Carthon."

His words reached the heart of Clessámmor: he fell, in silence, on his son. The host stood darkened around: no voice is on the plains of Lora. Night came, and the moon, from the east, looked on the mournful field; but still they stood, like a silent grove that lifts its head on Gormal, when the loud winds are laid, and dark autumn is on the plain.

Three days they mourned above Carthon; on the fourth his father died. In the narrow plain of the rock they lie; and a dim ghost defends their tomb. There lovely Moina is often seen; when the sun-beam darts on the rock, and all around is dark. There she is seen, Malvina; but not like the daughters of the hill. Her robes are from the stranger's land, and she is still alone.

Fingal was sad for Carthon; he desired his bards to mark the day when shadowy autumn returned. And often did they mark the day, and sing the hero's praise. Who comes so dark from ocean's roar, like autumn's shadowy cloud? Death is trembling in his hand! his eyes are flames of fire!—Who roars along dark Lora's heath? Who but Carthon, king of swords! The people fall! see! how he strides, like the sullen ghost of Morven! But there he lies, a goodly oak which sudden blasts overturned! When shalt thou rise, Balclutha's joy! lovely car-borne Carthon? —Who comes so dark from ocean's roar, like autumn's shadowy cloud?

Such were the words of the bards in the day of their mourning; I have accompanied their voice; and added to their song. My soul has been mournful for Carthon: he fell in the days of his valour; and thou, O Clessámmor! where is thy dwelling in the air? Has the youth forgot his wound? And flies he on the clouds with thee?—I feel the sun, O Malvina! leave me to my rest. Perhaps they may come to my dreams: I think I hear a feeble voice.—The beam of heaven delights to shine on the grave of Carthon: I feel it warm around.

O thou that rollest above, round as the shield of my fathers! Whence are thy beams, O sun! thy everlasting light? Thou comest forth in thy awful beauty; and the stars hide themselves in the sky; the moon, cold and pale, sinks in the western wave; but thou thyself movest alone. Who can be a companion of thy course? The oaks of the mountains fall; the mountains themselves decay with years; the ocean shrinks and grows again; the moon herself is lost in heaven: but thou art for ever the same, rejoicing in the brightness of thy course.

When the world is dark with tempests, when thunder rolls and lightning flies, thou lookest in thy beauty, from the clouds, and laughest at the storm. But to Ossian, thou lookest in vain, for he beholds thy beams no more: whether thy yellow hair flows on the eastern clouds, or thou tremblest at the gates of the west. But thou art, perhaps, like me, for a season; and thy years will have an end. Thou shalt sleep in thy clouds, careless of the voice of the morning. Exult then, O sun, in the strength of thy youth! age is dark and unlovely; it is like the glimmering light of the moon, when it shines through broken clouds, and the mist is on the hills: the blast of the north is on the plain, the traveller shrinks in the midst of his journey.

BLAIR

FROM *A Critical Dissertation on The Poems of Ossian, The Son of Fingal*

AMONG the monuments remaining of the ancient state of nations, few are more valuable than their poems or songs. History, when it treats of remote or dark ages, is seldom very instructive. The beginnings of society, in every country, are involved in fabulous confusion; and though they were not, they would furnish few events worth recording. But, in every period of society, human manners are a curious spectacle; and the most natural pictures of ancient manners are exhibited in the ancient poems of nations. These present to us what is much more valuable than the history of such transactions as a rude age can afford—the history of human imagination and passion. They make us acquainted with the notions and feelings of our fellow creatures in the most artless ages; discovering what objects they admired, and what pleasures they pursued, before those refinements of society had taken place, which enlarge, indeed, and diversify the transactions, but disguise the manners of mankind.

Besides this merit which ancient poems have with philosophical observers of human nature, they have another with persons of taste. They promise some of the highest beauties of poetical writing. Irregular and unpolished we may expect the production of uncultivated ages to be; but abounding, at the same time, with that enthusiasm, that vehemence and fire, which are the soul of poetry: for many circumstances of those times which we call barbarous, are favorable to the poetical spirit. That state, in which human nature shoots wild and free, though unfit for other improvements, certainly encourages the high exertions of fancy and passion.

In the infancy of societies, men live scattered and dispersed in the midst of solitary rural scenes, where the beauties of nature are their chief entertainment. They meet with many objects, to them new and strange; their wonder and surprise are frequently excited; and by the sudden changes of fortune occurring in their unsettled state of life, their passions are raised to the utmost; their passions have nothing to restrain them, their imagination has nothing to check it. They display themselves to one another without disguise, and converse and act in the uncovered simplicity of nature. As their feelings are strong, so their language, of itself, assumes a poetical turn. Prone to exaggerate, they describe every thing in the strongest colors; which of course renders their speech picturesque and figurative. Figurative language owes its rise chiefly to two causes; to the want of proper names for objects, and to the influence of imagination and passion over the form of expression. Both these causes concur in the infancy of society. Figures are commonly considered as artificial modes of speech, devised by orators and poets, after the world had advanced to a refined state. The contrary of this is the truth. Men never have used so many figures of style, as in those rude ages, when, besides the power of a warm imagination to suggest lively images, the want of proper and precise terms for the ideas they would express, obliged them to have recourse to circumlocution, metaphor, comparison, and all those substituted forms of expression, which give a poetical air to language. An American chief, at this day, harangues at the head of his tribe in a more bold and metaphorical style than a modern European would adventure to use in an epic poem. . . .

(from pp. 1–2)

As Homer is, of all the great poets, the one whose manner, and whose times, come the nearest to Ossian's, we are naturally led to run a parallel in some instances between the Greek and Celtic bard. For though Homer lived more than a thousand years before Ossian, it is not from the age of the world, but from the state of society, that we are to judge of resembling times. The Greek has, in several points, a manifest superiority. He introduces a greater variety of incidents; he possesses a larger compass of ideas; has more diversity in his characters; and a much deeper knowledge of human nature. It was not to be expected, that in any of these particulars Ossian could equal Homer. For Homer lived in a country where society was much farther advanced; he had beheld many more objects; cities built and flourishing; laws instituted; order, discipline, and arts, begun. His field of observation was much larger and more splendid: his knowledge, of course, more extensive; his mind also, it shall be granted, more penetrating. But if Ossian's ideas and objects be less diversified than those of Homer, they are all, however, of the kind fittest for poetry: the bravery and generosity of heroes, the tenderness of lovers, the attachments of friends, parents, and children. In a rude age and country, though the events that happen be few, the undissipated mind broods over them more; they strike the imagination, and fire the passions in a higher degree; and, of consequence, become happier materials to a poetical genius, than the same events when scattered through the wide circle of more varied action and cultivated life.

. . . Both poets are eminently sublime; but a difference may be remarked in the species of their sublimity. Homer's sublimity is accompanied with more impetuosity and fire; Ossian's with more of a solemn and awful grandeur. Homer hurries you along; Ossian elevates, and fixes you in astonishment. Homer is more sublime in actions and battles; Ossian in description and sentiment. In the pathetic, Homer, when he chooses to exert it, has great power; but Ossian exerts that power much oftener, and has the character of tenderness far more deeply imprinted on his works. No poet knew better how to seize and melt the heart. With regard to dignity of sentiment, the pre-eminence must clearly be given to Ossian. This is indeed a surprising circumstance, that in point of humanity, magnanimity, virtuous feelings of every kind, our rude Celtic bard should be distinguished to such a degree, that not only the heroes of Homer, but even those of the polite and refined Virgil, are left far behind by those of Ossian. . . .

(from pp. 22–23)

. . . For it is perfectly absurd to imagine, as some critics have done, that Homer's mythology was invented by him "in consequence of profound reflection on the benefits it would yield to poetry." Homer was no such refining genius. He found the traditionary stories, on which he built his Iliad, mingled with popular legends concerning the intervention of the gods; and he adopted these because they amused the fancy. Ossian, in like manner, found the tales of his country full of ghosts and spirits; it is likely he believed them himself; and he introduced them, because they gave his poems that solemn and marvellous cast, which suited his genius. This was the only machinery he could employ with propriety; because it was the only intervention of supernatural beings which agreed with the common belief of the country. . . .

As Ossian's mythology is peculiar to himself, and makes a considerable figure in his other poems, as well as in Fingal, it may be proper to make some observations on it, independent of its subserviency to epic composition. It turns for the most part on the appearances of departed spirits. These, consonantly to the notions of every rude age, are represented not as purely immaterial, but as thin airy forms, which can be visible or invisible at pleasure; their voice is feeble, their arm is weak; but they are endowed with knowledge more than human. In a separate state, they retain the same dispositions which animated them in this life. They ride on the wind; they bend their airy bows; and pursue deer formed of clouds. The ghosts of departed bards continue to sing. The ghosts of departed heroes frequent the fields of their former fame. "They rest together in their caves, and talk of mortal men. Their songs are of other worlds. They come sometimes to the ear of rest, and raise their feeble voice." All this presents to us much the same set of ideas concerning spirits, as we find in the eleventh book of the Odyssey, where Ulysses visits the regions of the dead; and in the twenty-third book of the Iliad, the ghost of Patroclus, after appearing to Achilles, vanishes precisely like one of Ossian's, emitting a shrill, feeble cry, and melting away like smoke. . . .

(from pp. 33–34)

It is a great advantage of Ossian's mythology, that it is not local and temporary, like that of most other ancient poets; which of course is apt to seem ridiculous, after the superstitions have passed away on which it is founded. Ossian's mythology is, to speak so, the mythology of human nature; for it is founded on what has been the popular belief, in all ages and countries, and under all forms of religion, concerning the appearances of departed spirits. Homer's machinery is always lively and amusing; but far from being always supported with proper dignity. The indecent squabbles among his gods surely do no honour to epic poetry. Whereas Ossian's machinery has dignity upon all occasions. It is indeed a dignity of the dark and awful kind; but this is proper; because coincident with the strain and spirit of the poetry. A light and gay mythology, like Homer's, would have been perfectly unsuitable to the subjects on which Ossian's genius was employed.   (from p. 38)

CHRISTIAN GOTTLOB HEYNE

[1729–1812]

CHRISTIAN GOTTLOB HEYNE was the most important classical scholar in Germany in the second half of the eighteenth century; but in a way not true of most classicists in his time and before, he was also one of the revolutionary forces leading to new views of myth. For with Heyne, two changes occur, both crucial to mythic thought through to our time. First, Heyne joins mythic speculation to philologic rigor, as the earlier eighteenth century had not been able to do; and next, he helps institute a powerful historical-philologic approach to myth, important in itself and as part of the rising tide of philology finally so triumphant in the nineteenth century. To grasp Heyne's innovation, the earlier conflict between speculative mythology and philologic antiquarianism needs to be recalled briefly. From Fontenelle through Voltaire—and on through Herder—*philosophe* or deist mythologists were generally disdainful of the narrowness or dullness of the *erudit* historians, not without reason: Voltaire mocked a Calmet's or a Hardion's banal orthodox conclusions about religious origins, even as he exploited their rich collections of historical detail; Fréret's combination of philologic expertise and speculative breadth was notoriously unique among members of the *Académie des Inscriptions et Belles-Lettres;* the greatest English classicist, Bentley, or such French savants as Montfaucon or LeClerc, showed little if any interest in the deeper problems revealed by the study of myth.

In his influential essay, "How the Ancients Depicted Death" (1769), Lessing succinctly expressed the difference between "antiquarian" and "archaeologist": the antiquarian "has inherited the *fragments,* the archaeologist the *spirit* of antiquity . . . before the former can say *it was so,* the latter already knows whether it *could be so.*" The breach between grand *a priori* mythic theorizing and carefully documented philology was occasionally bridged, with immediately interesting results by such men as Lessing, Fréret, Thomas Blackwell, or Winckelmann.

Wide change here showed itself first in Germany. There, as elsewhere, by the early eighteenth century the teaching of classical languages had generally become lifeless. In Germany especially, Greek was ignored or derogated, partly because of the larger neoclassic preference for Roman "refinement" over Greek "barbarism," partly from Pietist attacks on the heathen pagans. But by about 1795, as J. L. Myres notes in his *Homer and His Critics,* there was, in contrast, a positive German vogue for studying Homer in the original. One major source of such change is Göttingen, where from 1734 J. M. Gesner began to revive Greek studies and a new humanistic spirit. Gesner's successor at Göttingen from 1763 was Heyne. In that same year, Winckelmann's *History of Greek Art* appeared, initiating the German (and modern) renaissance in the study of Greek plastic art by uniting bold theorizing and solid erudition. Heyne does as much for Greek mythic study through philology. But he also advances "archaeology" in Lessing's sense: in 1767, Heyne gave what may have been the first academic course offered on archaeology.

Heyne was born in 1729, the same year as Lessing, twenty years before Goethe; but Heyne's real career begins in 1763 and extends influentially to his death in 1812. He is at once an original theorist of myth and the "founder" of an important mythic school, an ally of Herder, and for almost half a century his country's most influential classical teacher, scholar, and writer. For forty-two years he edited the leading classical journal, the *Commentationes Societatis Regiae scientarum Gottingensis,* in which most of his work appeared. His vast influence doubtless derived in part from his astonishing industry: an early biographer, Heeren, records that besides his many books, Heyne wrote more than 7500 reviews in his career. Measured by his students, Heyne was plainly a great teacher: these students include Friedrich and August Schlegel, Creuzer, and Wilhelm von Humboldt; the prominent mythic historians, M. G. Hermann, Buttmann, K. F. Heinrich, Dornedden, J. J. Wagner, and Kanne; such pioneering philologians as Zoega; and he partly taught and profoundly influenced the two most important German Homeric scholars, J. H. Voss, the great translator of Homer, and F. A. Wolf—though these were both too irascibly independent to acknowledge themselves anyone's student. Besides these classicists, Heyne had as pupils and disciples the new biblical critics, J. G. Eichhorn and Gabler, whose daring methods descend from Heyne and pass onward through G. L. Bauer and De Wette to D. F. Strauss.

With this nineteenth-century German school of radical biblical "demythologizing" in mind, modern scholars have begun to treat Heyne's mythic thought as independently original, rather than in the usual way as only a sidelight to Herder. The most thorough study of Heyne's influence, by C. Hartlich and W. Sachs, rightly begins by showing how strongly Heyne was impressed in one way by Lowth's philologic analysis of Hebrew poetry, and by Hume in another. Lowth sought to demonstrate how the uniquely sublime Old Testament *style* must refer back to the Bible's unique *content;* that is, revealed inspiration. Heyne approaches Greek myth similarly. He assumes that mythic content existed as such, and was only afterwards shaped into the "mythic poems" (such as Homer's) that have come down to us. In separating myth from a later, refined poetic treatment of myth, Heyne moves away from most *philosophes,* but also (though not consistently) from such a claim as Herder's that folk-poetry afforded more direct access to earliest myth. With Heyne now, the real access to early myth is by rigorous philologic analysis of the poetry that stands between us and the original mythic content. "Mythic" poetry itself offers a possibility for such philologic analysis, for such poetry goes through a series of developing phases—as seen in the varying complexity of devices such as similes or tropes or allegories. Through these, one can work from the later stages of poetry back to the earliest, and thence back to the mythic raw material.

Heyne also drew on Hume's genetic view of myth as expressing the "childhood of mankind": Hume saw myth springing from fear and rational weakness—primitive man could think only simply, concretely, rudely; conceptual and abstract thought comes later. Heyne's explanation of what myth originally meant has a rationalist edge: "raw" myth expressed either plain historical events or crude philosophic gropings. Such primitive philosophizing is what Heyne, in a famous term, called *philosophemes:* they include cosmogonies or savage moralities or efforts to explain causes. But primitive minds, unable to generalize abstractly, could explain causes only as a kind of "begetting."

The immediate implications of Heyne's approach are several. Myth is to be distinguished from poetry: poets did not invent, but only inherited and reshaped mythic material. Moreover, poetic intention is different from, or even in conflict with, mythic intention—thus, Heyne dismisses all allegoric interpretation of myth as later poetic intrusions. But since myth has been perpetuated and elaborated mainly by poetic transmission, much "myth" is the result of misunderstandings. Such "disease of language" can be corrected only by philologic cure. The force of Heyne's approach lies here: that not creative intuition so much as philologic rigor may be the best way to reach the original mythic intentions. (It should be noted, however, that Heyne seems to have preached this need for philologic rigor more powerfully than he practiced it: as Sandys notes, Heyne's own editions and commentaries show rather more interest in the historical and aesthetic dimensions of a classical work than in exact textual criticism.) But Heyne's mythic theorizing often goes further abroad: as myth springs from primal fear and inadequate rationality, so mythic cults seem to institutionalize these psychological reactions. He also argues at times that fetishism is the oldest religion, from which—as among the Pelasgians—there arise the somewhat more symbolic forms of nature worship, of divinized rivers or beasts or mountains, with star worship as an even higher step.

Heyne's ideas, for all their Humean stringency, nonetheless could ally themselves with some of Herder's leading themes. One link here is their common emphasis on historic growth—Heyne is one of the first to praise Blackwell and Robert Wood's historizing interpretation of Homer, and Heyne's own genetic phi-lology properly anticipates F. A. Wolf's philologic disintegration of "Homer" into Greek oral traditions. Another link to Herder is in Heyne's allegiance to the Lowthian principle that real penetration of poetic structure demands sympathetic entry into the inner living spirit of the past. Heyne's Humean insights and philologic methods could also be applied to the Bible—a step first taken by Eichhorn in his *Urgeschichte* (1779), a work edited and elaborated on by Eichhorn's own pupil, Gabler. Like Greek myth and poetry, the Bible is now seen as content and form developing in history, amenable thus to genetic linguistic analysis. Such an approach leads naturally to seeking the original mythic content embedded in scriptural language. In many ways, Eichhorn and Gabler approach the Old and New Testament as if the ancient Israelites, like pagan primitives, were driven to "religion" through fear and inarticulate reason: "Jehovah" may be a Hebrew "god." What is new here, again, is not the tendency to debunk Holy Writ, but the weapons used to do it: the Bible is tested, not by *bon sens* or the "light of reason" or universal nature, but by philologic dissection. The later development of this Heynean approach, in an important way, issues into the "Higher Criticism" of the Bible; and this is perhaps best taken up as part of the immediate history of that great early nineteenth-century scandal, David Friedrich Strauss's *Life of Jesus* (1835).

B.F.

REFERENCES The texts are our translations from *Quaestio de causis fabularum seu mythorum veterum physicis* (1764), published in Heyne's *Opuscula Academica* (Göttingen, 1785), and from *Sermonis Mythici seu Symbolici Interpretatio ad Causas et Rationes Ductasque inde Regulas Revocata (Comm. Soc. Reg. Gott.,* 1807). Most of Heyne's voluminous writings on myth appeared in the *Opuscula Academica* (Göttingen, 1785–1812) or in the *Commentationes Societatis Regiae scientiarum Gottingensis.* Most of his writing is in Latin, and to our knowledge is almost entirely untranslated. No standard edition of his works exists.

For a listing of some important essays here, see Otto Gruppe, *Geschichte der klassischen Mythologie und Religionsgeschichte* (Leipzig, 1921), pp. 112–13 for bibliography (Gruppe classifies Heyne's writings as on cults, art-mythology, and the emergence of mythology). A useful bibliographic notice is given in Christian Hartlich and Walter Sachs, *Der Ursprung des Mythosbegriffes in der Modernen Bibelwissenschaft* (Tübingen, 1952), pp. 11–12. For Heyne's thought and influence, see Gruppe, *op. cit.,* pp. 107–120 for a very useful summary. See Hartlich and Sachs, *op. cit.,* chap. 2 and *passim* for a crucial study placing Heyne in the mainstream of mythologic study leading from Lowth to D. F. Strauss and the "Higher Criticism," and for helpful sections on Eichhorn, Gabler, Herder, J. J. Hess, G. L. Bauer, de Wette, and Strauss. Heyne is discussed in F. Leo, "Heyne," in *Festschrift zur Feier des 150j. Best. d. Konigl. Gesellsch. zu Göttingen* (1901), pp. 155–234.

For briefer discussions, see K. O. Müller, *Introduction to the Scientific Study of Mythology* (1825), "Appendix" which discusses

Heyne's theories. Jan De Vries, *Forschungsgeschichte der Mythologie* (München: Verlag Karl Alber, 1961), pp. 142–149 for discussion and selection of text (which gives a loose German translation of sections in part covering texts given in our volume). A summary of some of Heyne's ideas are found in his "Vorrede" to the work of his disciple, M. G. Hermann, *Handbuch der Mythologie, 2 Bde. (1787–90).* P. B. Stadler, *Wilhelm von Humboldts Bild der Antike* (Zürich and Stuttgart, 1959) discusses Heyne's influence. J. H. Voss, *Mythologische Briefe,* 2 Bde. (Königsberg, 1794) polemicizes against Heyne's mythologic approach. Heyne's place in philologic history is sketched in H. A. Erhard, *Das Wiederaufblühn der klassischen Studien in Deutschland* (Halle, 1864); in C. Bursian, *Geschichte der klassischen Philologie bis zum Gegenwart* (Munich and Leipzig, 1883); in J. E. Sandys, *A History of Classical Scholarship* (New York: Hafner, 1964), Vol. 3.

For biography, see A. H. Heeren, *Christian Gottlob Heyne. Biographisch dargstellt* (Göttingen, 1813), and a review of this book by Thomas Carlyle, "Life of Heyne," in his *Critical and Miscellaneous Essays* (New York, 1865), pp. 115–127. R. Benz, *Wandel des Bildes der Antike in Deutschland* (Munich, 1948).

HEYNE

FROM *Inquiry into the Causes of Fables or the Physics of Ancient Myths*

IT MAY be asked why stories and judgments about the earliest origins of people and historical events arose first of all from myth, and why from myth too there came early inquiries into nature and philosophizing about morality. It can be answered that our understanding here depends importantly on seeing how physical or natural causes shaped myth and its various transformations. Such physical or natural causes derive partly from human nature, partly from the capacities men have to form their conceptions through language, and partly from the world of external nature which most powerfully shapes these conceptions. . . . One kind of natural cause is seated in human nature: in its childhood, mankind had not yet become skilled in using its own mental powers or in reasoning or observing subtly. The mind of early man became confused when it perceived many rather than a few things. Certainly, a deeper impression is made when one vivid sense-impression stamps itself on the mind; when there is less to perceive in the external world the mind responds more intensely to what it does perceive; and however often recalled by memory or other mental activity, this one vivid sense-impression will still be perceived intensely. And these intense impressions don a new garment, multiply and expand themselves, and also become greater and more wondrous by borrowing from each other. It is through language, through speech, that what is seen or heard changes itself into pure wonder. But such experiences cannot be very precisely remembered or very exactly described, for neither language and words nor reason is as yet strongly enough developed. So it is that the origin of all mythology is ignorance concerning what causes appearances.

Language and words had as much influence in forming those myths by which man tried to explain and express his sense-impressions. But since language and words were themselves weak, they could hardly furnish expressions adequate to the concepts newly awakening in the mind. The soul set forth then to discover new means, that is, new sounds and new words, with which these sense-impressions could be expressed. . . . But the poverty of speech

could reproduce only a small part of what was perceived. Man needed gestures, expressive voice, movements of limbs and eyes—in short, the expressiveness of the entire body. Yet just this made a great impact on the mind: what could be perceived could be grasped by the mind, not only through the eye but through the ear. Whoever makes a judgment about the eloquence of early man must avoid all the usual conventional ideas here—instead, one should compare what has been heard about the races living in North America. Such early kinds of speech lack suitable words, and tend to express the concrete through the abstract; thoughts are transposed into events; what was awakened in the mind by reflection becomes reproduced once more as a deed. In this way, the most ancient life provided not only men but living and inanimate nature as material for myths of ever new and wondrous kinds. Out of these elements, led by the development of and guided by ever more selective speech, arose allegories, tropes, and especially metaphor. . . .

. . . Since we moderns do not have other and more satisfactory words, we speak of "religion," "God," "divinities," of "divine nature." Precisely because of this we must abandon any hasty conceptualizing, if we wish to understand the concepts and judgments of primitive men. A mind that is capable of grasping only simple things through the senses cannot rise to metaphysical conceptions. But this must mean too, that each of our judgments must remain vague and unclear when we set out to learn in a strict way what early man thought about God and divine nature. . . .   (pp. 190–196)

FROM *An Interpretation of the Language of Myths or Symbols Traced to Their Reasons and Causes and Thence to Forms and Rules*

I SEE indeed that some time has passed since Hellenic mythology has been set free from the perverse interpretations of those who would trace all Greek antiquity back to the Hebrews, Egyptians, and the Phoenicians, whither it had been led by means of the accessions of the barbarians and the corruptions of the Phrygians and cut off from Hellenic antiquity. That our own studies should now progress is desirable and admirable in itself. While formerly that study might proceed only with difficulty beyond the ruins of Egypt, now it extends from where the mythology of the Indians is more abundantly narrated. Monuments of the wisdom of the Zoroastrians have been brought to light. And though there are many disputes regarding the religions of the Near East, I see the talents of learned men applied toward the Indians and the philosophemes of the Persian people, and religion moving toward a single explanation and consensus, and so to speak establishing some sort of oneness [*henoticum*] of all philosophy and religion, or at least of all the primitive ones. If you maintain that perceptions are implanted by nature within primitive man, I would accept this entirely. But if by this same argument you go even further and falsely attribute the metaphysical subtlety of our era to that early one; or if you seek to derive from divine admonition and heavenly precept divinely disclosed in the infancy of the same human race, those things which would be known only by a later people in the cities and established kingdoms; and finally if you reduce the documents of diverse men, of diverse peoples, and of lands of diverse climate, with all their inclination, ways of life, mores, and usages, to the same meaning and further recall this to some fixed doctrines or formulas of doctrines: then, you will surely have an easy and happy advance of effort, such as I would not want even to predict or to pray for.

The myths of single peoples, I am convinced, have manifested themselves each in a separate way not at all only with respect to the myths of other peoples; they each demand to be collected and to be interpreted and understood in terms of the popular tradition and only in the sense in which each has been accepted and handed down. In this way are the myths of the Indians to be displayed, since they are in no way responsive to interpretation from other directions. As so similarly should the myths of the Egyptians be compared and examined with respect to their historical and religious monuments to the sun; but at the same time certainly with respect to the recorded interpretations preserved in another time of ancient and more recent peoples. So too should be studied the myths of the Phoenicians, Assyrians, Babylonians, Medes, Persians, Phrygians, Thracians, and Hellenes—that is, according to the thinking of the times and of the authors and from the viewpoint of the faith, truth, authority, and judgment of those who handed these things down, and further, in the same manner and according to the same cautions advanced by the critics.

Thus, finally, with the myths of diverse peoples and times observed systematically and according to their own diverse natures, it would be possible to compare them safely, and to see in what and to what extent these myths do agree among themselves: what properly is unique, what common to all, in what sense and in what acceptation; and to see by how much these myths differ from later usage and our own notions. For even if upon first glance they appear most similar, they still remain alien to our way of thinking.

In such a way, then, are religions mixed and coalesced from many others which were so mutually inharmonious; or in other ways twisted out of their proper shape; and too, if their origins, ages, and circumstances were more closely looked into, so obscure, ambiguous, and much more, that you should scarcely dare to pronounce anything emphatically—only in such confusing ways will religions offer themselves willingly. All such things will greatly slow the process of interpretation down, if you try to gain an understanding of the orgies and mysteries, of the Orphic and Bacchic rites, of the Mother of the Gods, of Venus, of Adonis, and of the other religions and myths of that kind. In the meantime, through such explorations as these, the facts will appear: what is ancient, what is domestic as opposed to what is received from foreign rites adopted through outside opinion or through invention. The unique advantage, however, of each kind of investigation will lie in its initial conception, that is, whether it happens that you are able through this learned study to comprehend and substantially encompass a general idea of myth; or, through comparison

with other more ascertainable and acknowledged facts, you are able to understand the nature and form, the type, as I call it, the essential character of myth. For by this is myth recognized, even if you are able neither to see it all distinctly or to set it all straight, nor to assert anything very confidently, yet still getting an insight through probable inference into the true sense of myth in general.

Rarely is it possible to proceed further with really deficient arguments. You are able to follow up to the point where you must turn your mind toward distinguishing times and ages, toward separating in particular those ages in which poets and philosophers have translated or altered myths by fitting their imaginations merely to their own opinions, by embellishing, or by setting out to stitch different ages together. In this respect, almost everything is to be relegated to vulgar superstition or to priestly commentaries, such as frequently occur in Pausanias or further in Plutarch. For the diverse commentaries are largely confused and interwoven. And unless you have diligently looked into these and set them in their proper contexts, your researches will have no effect in explaining a single thing. Much less will you succeed if you confuse the opinion of earlier men, which is usually saturated with the flavor of myth, with true ancient myths—especially if you accept such opinions as they were idiosyncratically expressed in the very ages during which the usages of symbolic speech could only have originated from the customs of the vulgar.

If you carry through in this and separate what is true from false, certain from uncertain, what is probable from mere soothsayings, you will have so discriminated that you will be enabled then to make a great advance toward understanding the history of the human race, the complex ways of philosophy and the opinions of philosophers of diverse ages, their superstitions and their daydreams, and finally advance toward the investigation of the origins of these things. In this way will those learned men be deservedly honored for their study of history and philosophy, who will bring into the light, liberated from involuted mythographers, the opinions and the religions of Plotinus and his school of philosophy, and who will with learning declare their characters, origins, and ingenious subtlety. Thus, truly, in our great knowledge of things advanced through the most polished age and men, and in our new increments of knowledge thence obtained, I have faith where indeed previously I hoped but with some doubts. I have faith now even if I place in the balance the chance that through these difficult cogitations, untying the rough and knotty style of that language, it would come about that we are brought back to primitive simplicity and speaking.

And if at length we perceive the variety of conjecturing to be utterly and impenetrably infinite, and the varying ways of expression contained in recorded opinion to be extraordinarily abundant and diverse; and if we find the boundaries of knowledge, moreover, to be most narrow; then, there will be no dawn unless you take into account the effects and properties of a newly known nature, and unless you deal with new usages and grow accustomed to being profoundly enlarged. These things, which will be understood from the learned and just interpretation of myths, I will communicate at length with sufficient clarity. Certainly, I myself will try to advance the understanding of the *concept of myth* and of the *diversity of myths,* and then, the nature of *mythical*

interpretation and its several natures and causes.   (pp. 285–289)

Thus, thought early man, the stars and movements of the stars were set up through intelligent beings and those who participated in divine nature. In this way the various orders and ranks of the gods were set up differently among different people; here, too, come spirits, demons, and heroes; also, the ideas of things understood by the mind were experienced in terms of spirits; and the orders and ranks of spirits and angels and all the rest who were generated out of such ideas.

(p. 292)

I. Hence follow all the precepts for the interpretation of mythic narrations—or the words, and sentences, and expressions of mythical usage. First, 1): we know that in very ancient mythic or symbolic ways of speaking, the senses and thoughts were communally uttered (in our own popular usages of speech nothing is accepted except what is grammatically or literally useful or understandable); what these words, sentences, and formulas meant then is to be seen with respect to their rising from the senses and desires of ancient man and from the customs of speaking in those ages. Otherwise, our interpretation would deviate from the mythic reasons for speaking and narrating as they did—by which kind of deviation it happens that in innumerable commentaries and among many learned frauds, the interpretations of antiquity is only entangled. . . .   (p. 300)

Now moreover in regard to those things that have been preserved from rude antiquity, not by the authors or their contemporaries themselves, but transmitted and fixed by those coming later who shifted and altered much according to their own notions; here, too, the soul of speech is recalled to very ancient habits; so that will have been the use of language through many ages:

II. We should thus try to see 1) whether the saying and stories of myth are from an earlier or later age; 2) whether they show primitive or more sophisticated kinds of invention; 3) whether they are of domestic or foreign origin; and further, 4) which was the more ancient, the first native habitat of myth; and what were the motives for the later ornamental and even arbitrary additions deriving from poetic ingenuity, or why did the errors of mythographic commentary and interpolation of inept mythographers ever begin? Further, severe judgment is to be turned upon the faith and authority of the writers, whence we derive our own myths as well. First it is a matter of the antiquity of the myth. Then it is to be seen, with the utmost diligence, if Diodorus, Plutarch, and the other famous writers are the appropriate writers to follow, at least to the extent we can make an estimate. Last, 5) the types of the ancient mythical sayings can be only two, the one historical, the other physical and ethical (which have come to be called *philosophemes*); it is then to be seen whether it is any fact or event that is being narrated or whether it is a judgment of reason and supposition or phantom that is turned into narration.   (p. 301)

JOHANN GOTTFRIED HERDER

[1744–1803]

HERDER holds a unique and commanding place in the history of early modern myth study: his work is the culmination of the earlier eighteenth-century period and becomes in turn perhaps the most enduring influence on nineteenth-century approaches to myth, whether romantic or historical. More comprehensively than any earlier mythologist, he makes myth indispensable to rethinking the meaning of religion, history, literature, nationhood, and culture. Indeed, except for Vico, Herder is the first major thinker to put the problem of myth at the center of a bold effort to found a new science of humanity. But where Vico remained scarcely known, too original for his age, Herder's thought had immediate, profound impact on his own generation and after. For Herder's originality, far from isolating him, reveals him instead the representative mythic thinker of his period. His innovations issue from the several mainstreams of eighteenth-century ideas. He makes distinct and cohesive what had been half formulated or only partially implied by English preromantics about poetry and genius; by German Pietists, such as Hamann, about the wisdom of primitive language; by Shaftesburian or Rousseauian exaltations of natural benevolence and harmony; and by the importance assigned by Montesquieu and others to environment, organic historical growth, and national spirit. But crucially, Herder also carries forward—to unexpected, radical conclusions—the enlightenment confidence that myth is best understood in terms of its origins; and he extends such inner critiques of rationalism as that found in Hume's radical empiricism. Herder's work is the first to reshape these possibilities into a theory forceful enough to provide a decisive challenge to the dominant *philosophe* mythologizing.

At the same time, Herder himself inaugurates a new mythologic mainstream. His is the first important expression of the romantic affirmation of myth as creative primal wisdom and sublime spiritual power, of myth as vitally true for the present as for the past, not only in "high" religion or art but in its "savage," folk forms. As his impact on Goethe alone shows, Herder inspires the first great modern poetic revitalizing of myth. Also with Herder, the allegorical mode of interpreting myth gives way to new and still current symbolic interpretations. Through such German romantic descendents of Herder as the Schlegels or Schelling, Herder's thought influences English romantic interest in myth, and, through Quinet or Michelet, French romantic interest in myth.

Herder is also the most important catalyst in interpreting myth as an organic historical process. Just as importantly, he stimulates new and deeper study of national, social, and cultural history, of folk songs, ballads, traditional lore, and language. He is the prime source as well of new literary and mythic enthusiasm for

India, leading in one way to the romanticizing of India as the cradle of mankind and the great source of all religion, and in another to a scientific comparative philology. In the largest sense, finally, Herder is the first really influential thinker to emancipate myth from rationalist or Christian context and strictures, opening it to world horizons, the dimension of historical time and cultural relativism, and deepening its meaning as a profound mode of truth.

Nonetheless, while his influence is strikingly clear, Herder's own position is difficult to fix or even to circumscribe distinctly. One reason is that so many of his ideas have been restated more systematically, with more evidence and refinement, by so many diverse minds: Herder is always in danger of vanishing among those he influenced. It is however also true that Herder is always more the practicing critic or inspiring innovator than the systematic theorist or scholar. His fragmentary, excited, and exciting insights reveal how transitional a figure he is, poised and mediating between the Enlightenment and romanticism, and also between "new" German thought and older French and English mythic positions. Herder helps instigate and always reflects the phenomenal rise to prominence—or even dominance—of German mythologizing from the latter eighteenth century.

Johann Gottfried Herder (he was ennobled late in life) was born in 1744 in East Prussia. From 1762 to 1764, he studied at Königsberg, a student of Kant (in the pre-Critical period), but also a disciple of the remarkable Kierkegaard-like religious thinker, Hamann. That Kant remained devoted to rationalism while Hamann even then was Germany's most profound opponent of the *philosophes* reveals one basic, unresolved and fruitful tension in Herders' own thought. Moreover, Herder matures in a Germany striving to attain its own maturity as a nation, philosophically and artistically: in Herder's youth, Winckelmann and Lessing promote a German criticism and artistic identity independent from and opposed to French and other neoclassicism; Heyne revivifies German classical philology at Göttingen; Moser, among others, had already called for serious attention to German history. Herder's acquaintance with Goethe from 1770 on is a familiar part of the *Sturm-und-Drang* literary movement; and Herder is a main channel through which English preromantic criticism, the literary historizing of Blackwell and Wood, and the cult of Shakespeare and Ossian pass into German culture. All this he absorbs and puts to new uses in his own thinking about myth.

Herder's mythologizing begins around 1764 with his earliest writings. He is then still assimilating Humean and Heynean ideas about myth originating in fear and intellectual poverty. But he already shows strong allegiance to Hamann's celebrating of language as the creative mother-tongue of the human race. From the start, he champions the need to see myth in its national setting, and takes up the problem of how modernity can find its own myths. He opposes the tyrannical dominance of Greek myth, and praises the *Eddas* or Chinese or Indic myth as equally worthy of study. He soon displays reservations about the Bible as revealed truth or as the oldest document. By the time of his *Travel Diary* and *Critical Forests* of 1769, Herder reaches an independent position.

No single work of Herder's encompasses his whole mature thought about myth: each of his works takes up the same main motifs, but in endlessly rich variation. A summary description best approaches him, perhaps, through such major motifs: among these, the most important are the organic and indivisible unity of all human experience, the autonomy of cultures, the relation of myth to particular nations or to a *Volk,* the role of Providence in history, and the need for a radically historical perspective.

First, Herder affirms the integrity and dignity of any single myth because he so strongly defends the uniqueness of the historical "particular." As perhaps no one before him, he sees history as a radical empiricist: scanning mankind, he sees nothing but discrete cultures, single peoples, different epochal viewpoints, and varied languages, poetries, and religions; he refuses to reduce these to some seemingly more elementary or higher, or universal and homogeneous source or principle. In part, this reflects Herder's own quick ability to enter the inner spirit of different peoples or ages with a remarkable selflessness and imaginative sympathy. In the *Travel Diary,* by evoking the wondrous state of mind of an ancient Greek mariner, he dramatically shows why the sea might indeed have seemed so pregnant with menacing or kindly gods —and he argues that Greek myth is best read while in that mood on shipboard. The miraculous coming of dawn is rhapsodically evoked as a clue to Genesis. Skillfully, lavishly, often ecstatically, he describes what it must be like to think, talk, or feel as did an ancient Egyptian or Iroquois or a German peasant-poet. His *Volkslieder* (1778), for example, includes not only German but also Italian, French, Spanish, Estonian, Lithuanian, Lettish, Eskimo, Old Norse, Greek, Danish, medieval Latin, and Inca folk poems.

Against all antiquarianism or abstract rationalism, he insists that myth can be understood only if livingly assented to in the spirit of those who created and believed such myths. Myth thus is never simply false, but only relatively so; that is, false to those who have other myths, other world-views. But more daringly, Herder moves beyond such imaginative empathy with other ways of life—he seems to have coined the German word

Einfühlung—to seek the total spirit of history from which these endlessly varied forms arise. He becomes a new kind of philosopher of history, and a new kind of mythologist. In short, all myth not only seems alive and true to its believers, but indeed *is* true. Herder's arguments here lead on one side to his affirmation of the *Volk,* on another to poetry as a mode of truth and power.

All poetry and myth, all "theology," is necessarily national and epochal. His conception of the nation or *Volk* intends nothing political or biological: the *Volk* is simply the natural unity in which man must exist and become more or less developed, an organism through which inchoate natural energy moves to some human wholeness and formed perfection. Herder sees each historical nation or moment as if it developed "by nature," in a necessary way. That such natural growth can seem "good" shows his deep conviction that some preestablished harmony exists between man and his world. Herder's commentators have pointed out how often he sounds like an optimistic supporter of natural religion—but with this difference: he always dissolves the religion of nature into the flow and variety of history. Like Burke, Herder moves instinctively to the biological analogy. Every individual and every nation strives toward fulfillment, slowly, partially successfully—but always as modified by its own origins and living traditions, and by external factors such as climate, neighbors, and chance.

What guarantees that the "natural" (or as accurately, the primitive) generally aims at the healthy and the true is a great guiding and unifying principle that Herder—like Vico earlier—assigns to Providence. Underlying this panorama of historic differentiation is divine wisdom that guides indirectly, through secondary causes. "Philosopher in a northern valley, with the infant's scales of your century in your hand, do you know better than Providence?" History itself reveals no undeniably fixed clear purposes or goals, no inevitable perfectability, no one absolutely binding revelation as Christianity claims, nor—as Winckelmann taught—some single culture such as the Greek as the surpassing ideal. Greek myth and art remain noble human achievements, but are "only" Greek. No one myth subsumes all the others; but taken together, all myth shows man's "divine" creativity. It follows that creative poetry best leads us to truth and spiritual energy.

"Poetry is originally theology and the noblest, greatest poetry will always remain theology in essence." What mediates between man and nature is language. In his *Origin of Langauge* (1772), Herder denies two formidable earlier views: that language is either divinely and perfectly bestowed on man; or, is merely humanly contrived. On the contrary: through language, man imitates not nature but divine creativity itself. In Herder's paraphrase of Shaftesbury, the primitive poet is nothing other than a "second creator." Language contains the seeds of divinity *in potentia;* myth is the necessary result of this. When primitive man "projects" himself into his surroundings, he does not therefore falsify nature, but rather discovers what is true there. He rightly feels himself in everything, because everything is contained in himself. Myth and poetry are thus creative: personifying nature, man "impresses" his own "form" on what was hitherto void —Herder deliberately draws here on Hebrew vocabulary. Herder prefers the earliest expression to the later, that is, the oral over the written. When he says, "The wilder a people, the livelier its songs," he seeks no return to naive innocence or noble savagery, but to what is still vital and energetic. As long as the *Volk* remains growing, mythopoesis goes on continually, as all folksongs show. But myth

is always the result of communal poetizing: Herder endorses no hope for individual mythmaking.

If such primal poetizing reveals human-divine truth, any later division of man's totality into really separate spheres must be rejected. Herder denies the analysis of human powers into the conflicting faculties of thought, feeling, imagination, and action—and denies as well the divisive categories of poetry, philosophy, or religion. He blurs or dissolves the distinction between irrational and rational, between "primitive" and "enlightened" man. Shakespeare, Mahomet, but also Newton and Buffon and Eskimos and Indians, are all "poets." By insisting on the indivisible unity of man—"myth" is the evidence from the past and "folk-poetry" is present evidence—Herder fosters and anticipates the romantic enthusiasm for the symbol. If truth is always immanent, the allegoric interpretation of myth finds itself frustrated, for the meaning of myth cannot now be referred outside of myth itself. Since mythic truth is also "total" and unified, myth cannot be dismissed as mere poetic fancy or ignorance. Similarly, the communally spontaneous origin of myth denies allegory's self-conscious manipulation of levels of meaning.

Two results of Herder's approach to myth emerge immediately. First, the meaning of myth becomes enormously difficult to clarify by any rational or external standard; the tendency rather may be to declare myth an autonomous "symbolic" mode of knowing, and indeed, perhaps the deepest ground of knowing and expressing humanity—the romantics pursue this implication. Connected with this, modern poetry may find myth indispensable: any interest in making poetry genuinely "philosophic" or in giving it "prophetic" or religious scope will gravitate toward myth. But Herder's insistence that what is true for our culture must come from our own cultural roots, presents a challenge to the modern poet and critic. No return to classical myth or art is possible. The modern must find his own authentic myths, or at least assimilate the past in a way wholly true to the present.

B.F.

REFERENCES   Our texts are from the following: 1—"Excerpt from a correspondence . . ." and "On contemporary uses . . ." are our translations from the standard edition of Herder, *Sämmtliche Werke,* ed. B. Suphan, 33 vols. (Berlin, 1877–1913); 2—*Reflections on the Philosophy of the History of Mankind,* tr. T. Churchill (London, 1800) for selections from Book VIII, Chap. 2 and Book XIII, Chap. 2, and from *Ideas for a Philosophy of the History of Mankind,* in *J. G. Herder on Social and Political Culture,* translated, edited, and with an introduction by F. M. Barnard (Cambridge: Cambridge University Press, 1969) for last selection from Book XIII; 3—*Journal of My Voyage in the Year 1769 (Travel Diary)* in F. M. Barnard, *Ibid.,* pp. 71–72; 4—*The Spirit of Hebrew Poetry,* tr. J. Marsh, 2 vols. (Burlington, 1833).

For commentary, see: A. Gillies, *Herder* (Oxford: Basil Blackwell, 1945); Robert T. Clark, Jr., *Herder: His Life and Thought* (Berkeley: University of California Press, 1955); Fritz Strich, *Die Mythologie in der deutschen Literatur von Klopstock bis Wagner,* 2 vols. (Halle, 1910), esp. 1, 26–68, 115–185; A. Leslie Willson, *A Mythical Image: The Ideal of India in German Romanticism* (Durham: Duke University Press, 1964), for Herder's role in promoting Indic myth; Isaiah Berlin, "Herder and the Enlightenment," in Earl R. Wasserman, ed., *Aspects of the Eighteenth Century* (Baltimore: The Johns Hopkins Press, 1965), pp. 47–104; A. Gillies, *Herder und Ossian* (Berlin, 1933); Robert S. Mayo, *Herder and the Beginnings of Comparative Literature* (Chapel Hill: University of North Carolina Press, 1969); Henri Tronchon, *La fortune intellectuelle de Herder en France* (Paris: Rieder, 1920); Paul Kluckhohn, *Die Idee des Volkes im Schrifttum der deutschen Bewegung von Möser und Herder bis Grimm* (Berlin: Juncker-Dunnhaupt, 1934); Gustav Brandt, *Herder und Görres 1798–1807* (Berlin, 1939). Erich Aron, *Die deutsche Erweckung des Griechentums durch Winckelmann und Herder* (Heidelberg, 1929).

HERDER

FROM *"Excerpt from a Correspondence on Ossian and the Songs of Ancient Peoples"* (*1773*)

YOUR OBJECTIONS are strange. You yield to me on the matter of ancient Gothic songs, as you like to call them, rhymed poems, romances, sonnets, and such artful or even artificial stanzas, but not when it comes to the ancient unaffected songs of savage, uncivilized peoples. Savage, uncivilized peoples? I can hardly subscribe to your point of view. So you think that Ossian and his noble and great Fingal belong merely to a savage, uncivilized people? Even if he had idealized everything he wrote about, would someone who could idealize like that, or someone who found his nightly dreams, his daily example, his relaxation and greatest pleasure in such images, such stories—would he be savage and uncivilized? We find ourselves in the strangest places when trying to rescue our favorite opinions!

Know then, that the more savage, that is, the more alive and freedom-loving a people is (for that is the simple meaning of the word), the more savage, that is, alive, free, sensuous, lyrically active, its songs must be, if it has songs. The more distant a people is from artful cultivated thinking, language, and letters, the less will its songs be written for paper— dead literary verse. The lyrical, the living and therefore rhythmical elements of song, the living presentness of the imagery, the continuity and force of the contents and invention, the symmetry of words, syllables, even letters, the melody and the hundreds of other things that belong to and disappear with the living word, the songs of a language and a nation—on this and this alone depends the natures, the purpose, the whole miraculous power of these songs, their charm, the driving force that makes them the timeless song of the heritage and joy of our people. These arrows of a savage Apollo, pierce hearts and carry souls and thoughts with them. The longer a song is to last, the stronger and more sensuous the rousers of the soul must be, in order to defy the powers of time and changing circumstances of centuries—what do you say to that?

. . . You laugh at my enthusiasm for savages as Voltaire laughed at Rousseau for wanting to walk on all fours. Don't think because of that that I despise our customary civilized preferences in any way. The human race is fated to a progression of scenes, cultures, and customs; woe to the man who is dissatisfied with the scene he is supposed to appear in, act his part,

and spend his life! But woe also to the philosopher of mankind and customs who considers his own scene the only one, and insists on dismissing the earliest scenes as the worst! Since they all belong in the whole of the continuous drama, each one demonstrates a new and remarkable side of mankind—and take care that I don't haunt you with some psychology from Ossian's poetry next time! The idea of it at least lies deep and vivid in my heart, and you might see many peculiar things.

You believe that we Germans should also have many more such poems as I indicated when speaking of Scottish romance—I not only believe it, but I know it. In more than one province I am acquainted with folksongs, regional songs, peasant songs that certainly would lack nothing when it comes to liveliness and rhythm, naivete and strength of language. But who is collecting them? or who cares about them? the songs of the people, from streets and alleys and fishmarkets, in the traditional roundelays of the country folk? songs that are often unscanned and poorly rhymed, who would collect them? who would print them for our critics who are so good at syllable-counting and scanning?

. . . All unpolished peoples sing and act; they sing about what they do and thus sing histories. Their songs are the archives of their people, the treasury of their science and religion, their theogony and cosmogony, the deeds of their fathers and the events of their history, an echo of their hearts, a picture of their domestic life in joy and in sorrow, by bridal bed and graveside. Nature has given them a comfort against many of the miseries that oppress them and a substitute for many of the so-called blessings we enjoy: that is, love of freedom, leisure, ecstasy and song.

Here everyone portrays himself and appears as he is. The warrior nation sings of brave deeds; the tender sings of love. A clever people makes up riddles; a people with imagination makes allegories, similes, living tableaux. The people with warm passions knows only passion, as the people under terrible conditions creates terrifying gods for itself. A small collection of such songs from the mouth of each nation, about the noblest conditions and deeds of their lives, in their own language but at the same time properly understood and explained, accompanied with music: how much it would enliven the chapter that the student of man reads most eagerly in every travelogue, "the nature and customs of the people! their science and letters, their games and dances, their music and mythology!" All of these would give us better concepts of the nation than we get through the gossip of a traveler or an "Our Father" copied down in their language! As a natural history describes plants and animals, so the peoples depict themselves here. We would gain an intuitive understanding of everything; and from the similarities or differences in language, contents, and tone among these songs, particularly of ideas of cosmology and the history of their forefathers, a great deal could be concluded with certainty about the ancestry, propagation, and intermingling of peoples.

FROM *"On Contemporary Uses of Mythology"* (1767)

I NOW wish to indulge in a few practical considerations of how we can use mythology for the cultivation of our inventive powers, in order to approach the ancients in spirit rather than through imitation.

What was mythology to the ancients? Partly history, partly allegory, partly religion, partly mere poetic scaffolding! How did they arrive at it, how did they beautify it, use it, change it? And in all this, can we learn something from them?

What kind of Greek imagination is responsible for the elevation of strong yeomen soldiers into Herculi, heroes, demigods; for dressing them in all the wealth of poetic value; for incarnating so creatively in poetic bodies, and inspiring with poetic soul the journey of the Argonauts, the siege of Troy, the scaling of heaven, and all those legends that have their origins in history? What is Scamander, and Olympus, and all the sacred places and stories that were the original material of their mythology? I study them in travelogues, I remove their poetical ornamentation in the ancient legends, and what are they?—heavens! All this I have in my own country, in my own history; all around me lies the material for this poetic structure. Only one thing is missing: poetic inspiration. We are forced to admire you, you ancients, and to lower our eyes before you: you lift trivia from the dust to a splendid height; we let all of creation mourn deserted and barren around us, to plunder you instead, and employ our spoils miserably. . . .

Though the Greek Pindar only praises the heroes of his own city-state, how well he knows how to use every interesting circumstance of the city from the day of its founding. He demonstrates its characteristics, its advantages over others, the ancestors of the families of its heroes; when the venerable age and worth of a person permits, he surrounds this or that forefather and progenitor with the rays of Olympus, forges the genealogical chain up to the throne of a god, or calls a place sacred precisely because gods have acted there: thus his ode becomes full of mythology. But why? in order to show off his scholarship or artistry? in order to have written a mythological ode?—Not at all! his mythology is the history of his fatherland, the history of his city-state, the family tree and ancestral pride of his heroes, the origin of each event he celebrates. And what, in consequence, is his verse? A sacred, national, timeless, and patronymic hymn, worthy to be preserved in golden letters in the temple of the god and the archives of the city he celebrates; the heirloom of a race, and more than a gallery of heroes, as the noble pride of Pindar himself was well aware.

Do we in our own age have such poets, who are and shall be all those things to the event, person, or age of which they sing? . . .

In short, let us study the mythology of the ancients as poetical heuristics, to become inventors ourselves. A collection of the god- and hero-myths edited from this point of view—a few of the greatest ancient writers analyzed in this manner— that, or nothing in the world, must produce poetical genius. But what a great man must he be who is to convey to us this *Steps to Parnassus,* this *Horn of Plenty,* this *Matter of the Poets' Inventions,* this *Gold Mine of Mythology* (or some such high-sounding title . . .).

But this inventive ability requires two qualities that are rarely found together and frequently counteract each other: the capacity to reduce and imagine philosophic analysis as against poetic synthesis. Thus,

here there are many obstacles to creating a whole new mythology for ourselves. It is certainly easier to know that we will find a mythology in the world of images of the ancients; that lifts us above imitation and distinguishes rather the poet. . . .

Can we illuminate a new event with a fiction from the old mythology? . . . That favorite fable by Lessing, *Zeus and the Horse,* where the camel is created before our eyes, the one that puts a tough skin on the donkey to comfort it, the one that explains to us straight from the council of the gods why the sheep is defenseless, where the goat got his beard and so on; these are small anecdotes of a poet who is simultaneously a witness and a messenger of the gods, and an explainer of Nature. . . . In short, I believe the most poetical use of fables, and the source of the most beautiful and captivating images, is to explain a fact, a discovery, or an event in a poetically probable and poetically beautiful manner.

This brings us to another usage: that of adding a new feature so skillfully to the old mythology from the modern age and its customs that the new becomes venerable and the old rejuvenated.

To this relates a third liberty, that of giving the ancient fables a certain intellectual sense, without their pleasing us the less. Since our higher level of culture has gained intellectually what it has lost in sensuous awareness, we seek to inspire the fables with a new spirit, so that gods and heroes no longer act as strong, savage men of their times, but let us perceive a meaning that suits our taste. Bacon considered mythology a political picture gallery because his eye habitually saw things in a political light; others envisioned mythology as a chemical and alchemical laboratory; still others look at it historically; others study the natural science of the ancients in it. The philosophical poet may inspire it with a new poetic sense that captivates them all.

To conclude, the happy artistry that our Ramler displays in all his poetry is to relate a new event to an old one, so that the new, dressed in the old, takes on worthy wealth, status, and charm from it. His masterly use of mythology is witness to this, though I still have a slight suspicion that his odes would be even better without the mythology. A poetic personality like him, who sees the hollow backs of mountainsides in temples and palaces, and the stones of Deucalion coming alive in the statues of artists—such a poet could, according to my earlier dream, be the first to make for himself a political mythology, as some modern poets have begun to make a theological one. But as long as no one dares to undertake this, the earliest and surest way is to use the mythology of the ancients, which is an already erected scaffolding for poetry, and which with an easy and unfettered imitation still certainly permits us much poetic spirit and achievement.   (Sect. 7)

FROM *Reflections on the Philosophy of the History of Mankind*

THIS, I conceive, is the key of the mystery. Were all notions as clear to us, as those we acquire by the sight; had we no other ideas, than those which we derive from visual objects, or can compare with them; the source of errour and deception would be stopped, or at least soon discoverable. But at present most national fictions spring from verbal communications, and are instilled into the ear. The ignorant child listens with curiosity to the tales, which flow into his mind like his mother's milk, like choice wine of his father, and form its nutriment. They seem to him to explain what he has seen: to the youth they account for the way of life of his tribe, and stamp the renown of his ancestors: the man they introduce to the employment suited to his nation and climate, and thus they become inseparable from his whole life. The Greenlander and Tungoose see in reality all their lives only what they heard of in their infancy, and thus they believe it to be evidently true. Hence the timid practices of so many nations, even far remote from each other, in eclipses of the Sun or Moon: hence their trembling belief in spirits of the air, sea, and other elements. Wherever there is motion in nature; wherever any cause seems to exist and produce change, without the eye being able to discover the laws, by which the change is effected; the ear hears words, which explain to it the mystery of what is seen, by something unseen. The ear is in general the most timorous, the most apprehensive, of all the senses: it perceives quickly but obscurely: it cannot retain and compare things, so as to render them clear, for its objects hasten to the gulf of oblivion. Appointed to awaken the mind, it can seldom acquire clear and satisfactory information, without the aid of the other sense, particularly the eye.

3.   Thus it appears *among what people the imagination is most highly strained;* among those namely, who love solitude,

and inhabit the wild regions of nature, deserts, rocks, the stormy shores of the sea, the feet of volcanoes, or other moving and astonishing scenes. From the remotest times the deserts of Arabia have fostered sublime conceptions, and they who have cherished them have been for the most part solitary, romantic men. In solitude Mohammed began his Koran: his heated imagination rapt him to Heaven, and showed him all the angels, saints, and worlds: his mind was never more inflamed, than when it depicted the thunders of the day of resurrection, the last judgment, and other immense objects. To what extent has the superstition of the Shamans spread itself! From Greenland and the three Laplands, over the whole benighted coast of the Frozen Ocean, far into Tartary, and almost throughout the whole of America. Magicians every where appear, and fearful images of nature every where form the world in which they dwell. Thus more than three fourths of the Globe receive this faith: for even in Europe most nations of Finnish or Slavian origin are still addicted to the sorceries of the worship of Nature, and the superstition of the Negroes is nothing but Shamanism moulded to their genius and climate. In the polished countries of Asia, indeed, this is suppressed by positive, factitious religion, and political institutions: yet it is discernible, wherever it can peep out, in solitude, and among the populace; till on some of the islands in the South Sea it again rules with powerful sway. Thus the worship of Nature has gone round the Globe, and its reveries have seized on those local objects of power and alarm, on which human wants confine. In ancient times it was the worship of almost all the nations upon Earth.

4. *That the way of life and genius of each nation have powerfully cooperated in*

this, scarcely requires to be mentioned. The shepherd beholds nature with different eyes from those of the fisherman or hunter: and again, in every region these occupations differ as much as the character of the people, by whom they are exercised. I was astonished, for instance, to observe in the mythology of the Kamtschadales, dwelling so far to the north, a lasciviousness, that might have been more naturally expected from a southern nation: but their climate and genetic character afford us some explanation of this anomaly. Their cold land is not without burning mountains and hot springs: benumbing cold and melting heat there contend against each other; and their dissolute manners, as well as their gross mythological tales, are the natural offspring of the two. The same may be said of the fables of the passionate, talkative Negro, which have neither beginning nor end: the same of the fixed concise mythology of the North American: the same of the flowery reveries of the Hindoo, which breathe, like himself, the voluptuous ease of Paradise. The gods of the last bathe in seas of milk and honey: his goddesses repose on cooling lakes, in the cups of fragrant flowers. In short, the mythology of every people is an expression of the particular mode, in which they viewed nature; particularly whether from their climate and genius they found good or evil to prevail, and how perhaps they endeavoured to account for the one by means of the other. Thus even in the wildest lines, and worst-conceived features, it is a philosophical attempt of the human mind. which dreams ere it awakes, and willingly retains its infant state.

(from Book VIII, Chap. 2)

The mythology of the Greeks flowed from the fables of various countries: and these consisted either of the popular faith; the traditionary accounts, that the different generations preserved of their ancestors; or the first attempts of reflecting minds, to explain the wonders of the Earth, and give a consistency to society. However spurious and new-modified our hymns of the ancient Orpheus may be; still they are imitations of that lively devotion and reverence of Nature, to which all nations in the first stage of civilization are prone. The rude hunter addresses his dreaded bear; the Negro, his sacred fetish; the Parsee mobed, his spirits of nature and the elements; nearly after the Orphic manner: but how is the Orphic hymn to Nature refined and ennobled, merely by the Grecian words and images! And how much more pleasing and easy did the Greek mythology become, as in time it rejected even from its hymns the fetters of mere epithet, and recited instead, as in the songs of Homer, fables of the deities! In the cosmogonies, too, the harsh primitive legends were in time amalgamated together, and human heroes and patriarchs were sung, and placed by the side of the gods. Happily the ancient relaters of theogonies introduced into the genealogies of their gods and heroes such striking, beautiful allegories, frequently with a single word of their elegant language, that when subsequent philosophers thought fit merely to unfold their signification, and connect with it their more refined ideas, a new delicate tissue was formed. Thus the epic poets in time laid aside their frequently repeated fables of the generation of the gods, the storming of Heaven, the actions of Hercules, and the like, and sang more human themes for the use of man.

(from Book XIII, Chap. 2)

Finally, *religion* is the most exalted mark of man's humanity. No one needs to be startled by my referring to religion in this manner and mentioning it in this context. The human understanding is the most exquisite gift of man, the business of which is to trace the connection between cause and effect, and to divine it where it is not apparent. The human understanding does this in every action, occupation and art, for even where it follows an accepted practice, some understanding must originally have settled the connection between cause and effect, and thus have established it. To be sure, we cannot discern the inner cause of natural phenomena. There is little or nothing that we know about how things operate even within ourselves. In a sense, therefore all the phenomena around us are but a dream, a conjecture, a name, though we regard it as reality if and when we observe the same effects linked with the same occasioning circumstances, often and constantly enough. This is how philosophy proceeds, and the first and last philosophy has always been religion. Even the most primitive peoples have practised it, for there is not a single people upon earth that has been found entirely without some form of religion, just as there is no human society without the capacity for reasoning, without language, without connubial relations, or some traditional morals and customs. Where men could see no visible author of events, they supposed an invisible one; yet in spite of the darkness they continued to search into the causes of things. It is true that they focused more on the external manifestations of phenomena than on their intrinsic nature, and were more impressed by the terrifying and transitory aspects of things than by their more lasting and beneficial elements. Similarly they rarely succeeded in subsuming a multiplicity of causes under one basic cause. Nonetheless, man's first endeavours along these lines were religious in character. To maintain that religion originated in *fear,* that fear invented the gods of most people, is to say very little indeed, and to explain even less. Fear, as such, invents nothing. It merely rouses the mind to seek an understanding of given phenomena, to venture into the unknown by conjecture, by true and false hunches. As soon as man, therefore, learned to apply his mind at the slightest prompting, that is to say, as soon as he looked upon the world differently from an animal, he was bound to believe in more powerful invisible beings that helped or injured him. These he sought to make his friends or to keep as his friends, and thus religion was born. True or false, right or wrong, it served man as guide and comforter in a life full of perplexity, danger, and sizeable areas of darkness . . .

It is not difficult to see why in all religions of the world either God has been invested with human, or man with divine, properties; for we know of no form that is superior to our own. Whatever was to move man and make him more human had to be capable of being thought and felt in human terms. Thus nations that thought and felt in essentially aesthetic terms exalted the human form to divine beauty; whilst others, more inclined to abstract thought, represented the perfections of the Invisible by means of symbols. Even in those instances where God is said to have revealed Himself to man, His words and actions were interpreted in *human* terms and in accordance with the prevailing temper of the times.

(from Book XIII)

FROM *Travel Diary*

THE SEA-FARING folk still remain particularly attached to superstition and the marvellous. Since they have to attend to wind and weather, to small signs and portents, since their fate depends on phenomena of the upper atmosphere, they have good reason to heed such signs, to look on them with a kind of reverent wonder and to develop as it were a science of portents. And since these things are supremely important, since life and death depend on them, what man will not pray in the tempest of a dark and fearful night, in a violent storm, in places where pale death beckons? Where human help ceases, man always assumes the reality of divine aid, if only for his own comfort—especially the ignorant man, who out of every ten phenomena of nature sees only one as

natural, and who is terrified by the fortuitous, the sudden, the amazing, the inescapable. Oh, he will believe and pray, even if he is coarse and dissolute otherwise. He will have pious formulas in his mouth where things of the sea are concerned, and will not ask, 'How did Jonah get inside the whale?' For nothing is impossible to almighty God, even if the man thinks himself otherwise quite capable of making a religion for himself and sets no store by the Bible. The whole language of shipboard life, the reveille, the calling of the hours, is therefore framed in pious stock phrases and is as solemn as a chant from the bowels of the ship itself.—In all this lie data which explain the earliest ages of mythology. When man in his ignorance of nature listened to signs, nay, had to listen to them, it is scarcely surprising that for sailors coming to Greece, unfamiliar with the waters, the flight of a bird was a solemn matter—as indeed it still is in the vast expanse of air and on the desolate sea. Likewise the lightning of Jupiter gave cause for anguish and fright—as lightning still does at sea. Zeus thundered through the sky and forged bolts to strike sinful groves and waters. With what awe did men then worship the silent silver moon, which stands so huge and solitary and so powerfully affects the air, the seas and the seasons. With what avidity did men then look to certain help-bringing stars, to Castor and Pollux, Venus, etc., as seamen still do on a foggy night. Even I, who from youth on had seen and known all these things in an entirely different perspective, have found that the flight of a bird and the lightning on the sea and the silent moon in the evening made impressions on me that were quite different from those they had made on land—so what must have been their effect on a seafarer who, ignorant of the sea—perhaps as an exile from his homeland, as a youth guilty of some crime—was seeking a strange land? How readily he would kneel before thunder and lightning and eagles! How natural for him to see Jupiter's seat in the sphere of the upper air! And how comforting for him to feel he could influence these things by his prayers! How natural for him to paint the sun sinking into the sea with the colours of chariot-driving Phoebus and to deck Aurora in all her beauty! A thousand new and more natural explanations of mythology, a thousand more profound appreciations of its most ancient poets, come to mind when one reads Orpheus, Homer, Pindar—and especially the first—on shipboard. Sailors brought the Greeks their earliest religion; all Greece was a colony on the sea coast. Hence she could not have a mythology like that of the Egyptians and Arabs beyond their sandy deserts, but developed a religion of foreign lands, of the sea and of sacred groves. Therefore her mythology must be read at sea. What would I have given to have been able to read Orpheus and the *Odyssey* on board! When I do read them again, I will throw myself back into their times. How far the Greek imagination went in matters relating to the sea is illustrated by their stories of dolphins. There is nothing beautiful or friendly to men in the appearance of these creatures; but their gambols around the ship, their swift pace in calm weather, their leaping and diving, gave occasion for legends about them. To say, 'a dolphin abducted him' was as much as to say, 'Aurora stole him away': two circumstances occur together and one must therefore be the result of the other. So the transformed ships in Vergil, the nymphs, sirens, tritons, etc. are both easily explicable in terms of the sea, and also perfectly credible, especially if one imagines the terror of night, and fog, and so on . . .

(from Book IV)

FROM *The Spirit of Hebrew Poetry*

[EUTHYPHRON:] All Northern languages imitate the sounds of natural objects, but roughly, and as it were only by the mechanism of the outward organs. Like the objects they imitate, they abound with creaking, and rustling, and whizzing, and crashing sounds, which wise poets may employ sparingly with effect, but which the injudicious will abuse. The cause of this is obviously to be found in the climate, and the organs, in and by which the languages were originally formed. The further South, the more refined will be the imitation of nature. Homer's most sounding lines do not creak and hiss, they are sonorous. The words have passed through a refining process, been modified by feeling, and moulded as it were, in the vicinity of the heart. Thus they do not present uncouth forms of mere sound and noise, but forms on which feeling has placed its gentler impress. In this union of feeling from within, and form from without, in the roots of their verbs, the Oriental languages, I meant to say, are the best models.

A[LCIPHRON:] Is it possible you are speaking of those barbarous and uncouth gutturals? And do you venture to compare them with the silvery tones of the Greek?

E. I make no comparison. Every language suffers by being thus compared with another.

(from Vol. I, Dialogue I, pp. 33–34)

The first rays of the dawn were not yet visible, when the two friends found themselves together at an appointed spot, a delightful eminence, that furnished a wide and beautiful prospect. They saw before them all the objects of nature lying yet formless and undistinguished, for the night had wrapt them up in its veil of obscurity. But soon the night breeze sprang up, and the morning appeared in its loveliness. Its going forth was as if the Almighty had cast a reviving look upon the earth and renovated its existence; while his glory accompanied it, and consecrated the heavens as his magnificent and peaceful temple. The higher it rose, the more

elevated and serene appeared the golden firmament, that gradually purified itself from the subsiding waters, clouds and vapours, till it stood displayed, as an upper ocean, an expanse of sapphire interwoven with gold. In the same manner also the earth seemed to rise up before them. Its dark masses became distinguished, and at length it stood forth like a bride adorned with herbage and flowers, and waiting for the blessing of Jehovah. The soul of man elevates and purifies itself like the morning sky; it wakes and rouses itself from slumber, like the virgin earth; but at no moment is the delightful view attended with such sacred awe, as at the first existence of light, the breaking forth of the dawn, when, as the Hebrews say, the hind of the morning is struggling with the shades of night, and, with its head and knees bended together, waits for the moment of release. It is, as it were a birth of the day; and every being shudders with a pleasing dread, as if conscious of the presence of Jehovah. The most ancient nations made a distinction between the light of the dawn and that of the sun; considering it an uncreated being, a brightness that gleamed from the throne of Jehovah, but was returned again, so soon as the sun awoke to shine upon the earth. It is the viceregent of the Deity, behind which Jehovah himself is concealed.

E. Observe, my friend, the peculiarity and splendour of the view which at this moment opens before us. It was from this that knowledge first dawned upon the human mind, and this perhaps was the cradle of the first poetry and religion of the earth.

A. You agree then with the author of "The Earliest Monuments" [Herder], but remember his views have been controverted.

E. So far as our purpose is concerned, nothing has been or can be objected to them, so long as the morning dawn remains what it is. Have we not at this moment beheld and admired all the changing scenes in this vast work of creation? From the dark moving pictures of night to the magnificent uprising of the sun, with whom all beings in air and water, in the ocean and upon the earth seem to awake into being, the whole has passed before us. Is it objected, that the moon and stars do not come forth simultaneously with the sun? Perhaps too you may add with equal force on the other hand, that all the phenomena of the morning belong to every day, while those of creation are to be divided into the labours of six. But why waste our time with such discussions? Not only the first brief history of the creation, but all the Hebrew songs in praise of it, nay the very names of those glorious phenomena, that we just now saw before and around us, were for the most part formed, as it were, in the immediate view of those very scenes; and it was this view that prompted the most ancient poetry of nature on the subject of the creation.

A. When, and by whom, was such poetry formed?

E. I know not, for my understanding cannot carry back its researches to the cradle of human improvement. It is sufficient, that the poetical roots of the language, the hymns, that celebrate the creation, and fortunately the first sketch of a picture, after or in conjunction with which both seem to have been formed, are still extant. What if we, in our present interview, inquire into the earliest ideas, derived from the contemplation of nature, and from the connexion and progress of its changing and varied scenes, which are exhibited in this childlike and beautiful poetry of nature? We can hardly spend our morning hours in a more suitable manner.

A. With all my heart; and I am convinced, that to the great being who pervades and surrounds us, nothing is more acceptable than the thankful offering of our inquiring thoughts. The morning of the day will remind us of the morning of intellectual illumination, and give to our souls the vigour of youth, and the freshness of the dawn. In general I have remarked, that the poetry of every people is characterized by the influence of the climate, in which it is formed. A depressing, cold, cloudy atmosphere, gives rise to images and feelings of the same character; where the sky is serene, open, and expanded, the soul also expands itself, and soars without restraint.

E. I could say much against such a theory, but let it pass. Those features of poetry, and those images, to which I wish now to direct your attention, are those which spring from the earliest and most childlike intuitions and feelings of the human mind, and are occasioned by the more obvious appearances and events of the external world. These are every where the same. In all climates, and under every sky, night is night, and morning is morning. The heavens and the earth are every where spread above and beneath us; and the spirit of God, which fills them, which gives to man his elevation and, at the view of the glories around him, kindles up the native poetry of the heart and the understanding, extends to all its creative energies.

A. Begin, then, if you please, with the primitive notion of the human mind.

E. With what else could I begin, than with the name of Him, who in this ancient poetry animates and binds every thing together; whom it denominated the *strong* and the *mighty;* whose power was every where witnessed; whose unseen presence was felt with a shuddering of reverential fear; whom men honoured; whose name gave a sanction to the solemnities of an oath; whom they called by way of eminence the Great Spirit, and whom all the wild and untaught nations of the earth still seek after, and feel and adore. Even among the most savage tribes, how elevated does poetry and sentiment become through the all-pervading feeling of this infinite invisible Spirit! To them the remarkable phenomena, and the active powers of nature, appear as the index of his immediate presence and agency, and they fall down and worship him. Not from slavish fear and senseless stupidity, but with the lively feeling, that in these manifestations of his power, he is nearer to them, they offer up, in honour of the great Spirit, their dearest possessions with childlike forms, and awe-struck adoration. This feeling pervades the history of all ancient people, their languages, their hymns, their names of God and their religious rites, of which, from the ruins of the ancient world, a multitude of monuments and proofs will occur to your observation.

A. They do so, but the philosophers have explained this feeling of awe in a far different manner. Fear and ignorance, say they, have produced imaginary gods. Slavish terror and brutal stupidity have paid them homage, as powerful but malignant beings, in short as invisible and evil demons. In all languages religion employs terms of fear and dread, and in the Hebrew they adduce as proof a catalogue of the most ancient names of God.

E. The hypothesis, like most others that are brought forward, is not a new one, and I fear is as false as it is old, for nothing is more easily misinterpreted by frigid, and at the same time superficial thinkers, than unsophisticated human feeling. So far as I am acquainted with antiquity, I think I discover continually increasing

evidence, that this feeling of reverential homage is, in its simple and primitive character, neither the servile homage of a slave, nor the stupidity of a brute. The circumstance, that all nations worship gods of some kind, distinguishes them from the brutes; and almost universally the feeling has prevailed, that our existence is a blessing, not a curse; that the Supreme Being is good, and that the service, which we ought to yield to him, must not be an offering of fear and terror, presented as to an evil demon.

A. But are you not acquainted with many observances that spring from terror, and have you never read the books of an author [Boulanger], who derives all religions from the desolation of the world by the flood, and fearful forebodings of renewed destruction?

E. Do not disturb his ashes—He was a superintendent of bridges and dikes, and so must ex-officio believe in a Neptunian philosophy. His books are so bad, his learning so full of uncertainty, and his imagination so confused, that they altogether very much resemble the waters of the deluge. But we will go upon safe ground, and admit, that the religion of many ancient nations had indeed a mixture of terror; especially of nations who dwelt in inhospitable regions, among rocks and volcanoes, on the shores of a tempestuous sea, or in caves and mountain cliffs, or whose minds were impressed by some great devastation, or other terrible events. But these are plainly exceptions, for the whole earth is not a perpetual deluge, nor a burning Vesuvius. The religion of nations in milder regions we find mild, and even among those most impressed with ideas of the terrific, the existence of a powerful good spirit is never wholly given up, and still almost always predominates in its influence.

Finally, all these appendages, the off-spring of fear, superstition, and priestcraft, belong in fact to later times. The ideas of the most ancient religions, are grand and noble. The human race seems to have been originally furnished with a fine treasure of knowledge, unbiassed and uncorrupted; but their degeneracy, their wanderings and misfortunes, have alloyed it with baser metal.

(from Vol. I, Dialogue II, pp. 47–52)

Poetry is a Divine language, yet not in the sense that we understand by it what the Divine Being in himself feels and utters; whatever was given to the most godlike men, even through a higher influence, to feel and experience in themselves, was still human. If we knew more of the psychological and historical circumstances, connected with these higher influences, and with the intercourse of the Elohim with the first children of creation, we might perhaps give also a more definite conclusion respecting the origin of their language and mode of representation. But, since the most ancient history of the human mind has denied us this, we must argue from the effect to the cause, from the outward working to the inward form of feeling, and thus we treat of the origin of poetry only as human.

The spirit of poetry, therefore, was first exhibited in a dictionary of significant names, and expressions full of imagery and of feeling, and I know of no poetry in the world, in which this origin is exhibited in greater purity than in this. The first specimen, which presents itself in it, is a series of pictures exhibiting a view of the universe, and arranged in accordance with the dictates of human feeling.

Light is the first uttered word of the creator, and the instrument of Divine efficiency in the sensitive human soul. . . . In giving names to all, and ordering all from the impulse of his own inward feeling, and with reference to himself, he becomes an imitator of the Divinity, a second Creator, a true *poetes,* a creative poet. Following this origin of the poetick art, instead of placing its essence in an imitation of nature, as has generally been done, we might still more boldly place it in an imitation of that Divine agency, which creates, and gives form and determinateness to the objects of its creation. Only the creative thoughts of God, however, are truly objective, have actuality in their outward expression, and stand forth existent and living in the products of creative power. Man can only give names to these creations, arrange and link them together; beyond this, his thoughts remain but lifeless forms, his words and the impulses of his feelings are not in themselves living products. Yet, the clearer the intuition, with which we contemplate and systematize the objects of creation, the more unsophisticated and full the impulse of feeling, which impels us to impress every thing with the purest character and fullest measure of humanity—that which marks the analogy of our being to that of God—the more beautiful, the more perfect, and, let us not doubt, the more powerful will be our poetick art. In this feeling of natural beauty and sublimity the child often has the advantage of the man of gray hairs, and nations of the greatest simplicity have in their natural imagery and expressions of natural feeling, the most elevated and touching poetry.

(from Vol. II, 1, pp. 6–8)

JACOB BRYANT

[1715-1804]

JACOB BRYANT was one of the most renowned English mythologists of the end of the eighteenth century—though perusal of his work may make the reason for his renown at first puzzling. He was born in 1715, and died at a ripe age in 1804. His career was spent as an antiquarian, librarian, and mythologist, mostly under the patronage of the Marlboroughs (who were his quite lavish financial supporters). His writings focussed on antiquities and religious history: he wrote on Josephus as a witness of Jesus, on the language of the Gypsies, on there never having been a Troy, on the plagues of Egypt. Bryant also edited and helped get Robert Wood's landmark essay on Homer expanded and republished in 1775. Bryant's reputation is however entirely tied to his *A New System, or, an Analysis of Ancient Mythology* of 1774. This went into a second edition in 1775–76 (in three volumes) and a third edition in 1807 (in six volumes). John Wesley thought enough of the work to publish his own abridgment of it, while John Richardson (with Sir William Jones's help) saw fit to publish an attack. William Blake was an apprentice to the engraver of the *New System*, James Basire, and Blake himself seems to have designed one or more of the plates in the book. Moreover, Blake later incorporated much of Bryant into his own poetry and mythic system. Indeed, it is doubtless Blake's name that has kept Bryant from vanishing.

To come on Bryant's mythic work of 1774 is to feel oneself not in 1774 but in 1674. For Bryant's real kin among the mythologists are those late seventeenth-century polymaths like Bochart, Kircher, John Spencer, or Marsham. Like these, Bryant held the Bible to be the single text and history needed to explain all pagan myth. Bryant also thought etymologizing and scholastic collation of texts relating to rite and dogma an adequate method. The textually myopic methods and pious assumptions of Bochart and others were of course a chief target of the entire enlightenment revolution in myth, but Bryant writes as if the force of Fontenelle's or Fréret's or Brosses's arguments and evidence had not decisively impugned the older approach to myth. The result is a late-blooming version of a dead era in mythic thought.

The *New System* proposes itself a vast plan and vast scope. Bryant's subtitle shows his ambitions: he will try to divest tradition of all fable, reduce the truth to its original purity, and also give a history of the Babylonians, Chaldeans, Egyptians, Canaanites, Helladians, Ionians, Leleges, Dorians, Pelasgi, Scythae, Indo-Scythae, Ethiopians, Phenicians. He intends to give a true account of the "first ages," from the Flood to the dispersion of all peoples. By correctly analyzing this history (as he claims none had done before him), Bryant proposes to deduce the true source and therefore the true meaning of pagan myth. Admittedly, it was a staple thesis of Christian mythology to see pagan myths and religious practices as only a degraded plagiarism of the true Mosaic account. In this familiar and narrow orthodox Christian framework, Bryant adds what is essentially a small correction. He too begins with the Flood as the epochal event, after which the ensuing world dispersion led men to misremember the revealed origins and earlier sacred history. Bryant concentrates now on the descendents of Ham, especially the Cuthites, who he sees as constituting the single although vastly dispersed "gentile" family. The Cuthites—or Amonians (from Ham)—are declared the real, chief founders of gentile-pagan cities, the institutors of pagan gods, heroes, and demons. All pagans thus hold to one religion: Ham or Amon is identified with the Sun; Amon is worshipped as the Patriarch, the head of their line; the Sun is worshipped as the visible ancestor of life. In fact, Bryant's "new" thesis amounts to this insistence that pagan religion was simply sun worship, in turn only a degenerate form of the pure Israelite worship of the one God.

With sun worship as his leading key, Bryant proceeds to muster proof. He dismisses all pagan myth as having no autonomous source or integral history. His method is overwhelmingly simple: he seeks to show by word-roots that all the sacred traditions of the heathens—the names of their gods, cities, sacred places, even their sacred plants or minerals—are but mistaken memorials of the Flood and before. Gentile religion thus results from "disease of language," and corrective etymology is the right approach. Further, since all pagan language and rites descend from the "original" Amonian language (developed after the Flood), these rites and dogmas will necessarily show a strong family relationship—in this way (though no such Amonian language was known before or found since his book) Bryant undertakes a "comparative" mythology. Bryant sets down the "radicals," or basic

elements, of this Amonian language, from which all the sacred pagan words have been constructed. These radicals include, for example, Ham or Cham (which give rise to such place-names as Cham Ar, Cham Ur, Choman, Comara, etc); Chus, Nimrod, Theuth or Thoth (from which comes the main Greek word for god, *theos*), Ab, El, On-Eon, Ait, Ad, Ees-Is, San-Son-Zan (or Sun), and so on. His method is self-proving: from Feronia, the name of a goddess, Bryant can deduce Fer-On, in accord with his key idea that all such sacred titles derive from sun or fire worship; having got this far, he can then proceed to explore ancient writers, such as Strabo or Pliny, for scholarly confirmation.

Bryant is as rigidly Euhemerist in explaining myth as Isaac Newton or Samuel Shuckford, who forty years before Bryant were already thought to be too narrowly reductive. In accounting for Bryant, perhaps one ought to remember that though he published his mythic system in 1774, fifteen years after Hume, Bryant was educated before 1735. Perhaps, too, if Bryant's system had been published—like so many others it resembled—around 1740, it would have been buried or briefly remembered by the orthodox. Coming so late, however, Bryant's book reaped new opportunities. First, even if his out-of-date mythology might be wholly unimportant for serious mythic scholarship, it could find a response among certain poets and speculative religious minds sympathetic to his orthodox viewpoint—or, at least, among those profoundly dissatisfied with the triumph of skeptical rationalism and deism. The greatest of these minds with respect to Bryant is of course William Blake. For Blake, Bryant's cavalier disregard of the new rationalist mythology could seem not outmoded but rather a defense of the true and ancient faith against the corrosive disbelief perpetrated by that Blakean trio of Satanic arch-rationalists, "Bacon, Newton, and Locke" (for Blake,

Newton was only a scientist). Not only Blake, but also John Wesley and that later eccentric orthodox Christian mythologist, G. S. Faber, admired Bryant for some of these same reasons.

Even though Bryant did not affirm ancient myth as spiritual truth, his rigid reduction of all pagan myth to one "gentile" idolatry did present myth as universally coherent. Blake made this clear when he said: "The antiquities of every Nation under Heaven, is no less sacred than that of the Jews. They are the same thing as Jacob Bryant . . . proved." As Blake also showed, with all ancient religion and history able to be related to one primal source, the way may be open to writing a new poetic system indeed.

B.F.

REFERENCES   Our text is from *A New System, or, an Analysis of Ancient Mythology* (London, 1774). For commentary, see: E. B. Hungerford, *Shores of Darkness* (New York: World, 1963); Albert J. Kuhn, "English Deism and the Development of Romantic Mythological Syncretism," PMLA, LXXI, no. 5, pp. 1094–1116; Ruthven Todd, *Tracks in the Snow* (New York, 1947).

Northrop Frye, *Fearful Symmetry* (Boston: Beacon Press, 1962; orig. 1947), pp. 173–175, suggests that Blake in fact did not read Bryant very carefully. Mary S. Hall, "*Tiriel*: Blake's Visionary Form Pedantic," BNYPL, LXXIII (1969) and Nancy Bogen, "A New Look at Blake's *Tiriel*," *ibid.*, both discuss Blake's borrowing of the figure of Tiriel from Bryant. A. L. Owen, *The Famous Druids* (Oxford: Clarendon Press, 1962) for Bryant in this context. Edgar Allan Poe's *Eureka* mentions Bryant and uses him extensively.

BRYANT

FROM *A New System,*
or,
An Analysis of Ancient Mythology

IT IS MY purpose in the ensuing work to give an account of the first ages; and of the great events, which happened in the infancy of the world. In consequence of this I shall lay before the Reader, what the Gentile writers have said upon this subject, collaterally with the accounts given by Moses, as long as I find him engaged in the general history of mankind. By these means I shall be able to bring surprising proofs of those great occurrences, which the sacred penman has recorded. And when his history becomes more limited, and is confined to a peculiar people, and a private dispensation; I shall proceed to shew, what was subsequent to his account after the migration of families, and the dispersion from the plains of Shinar. When mankind were multiplied upon the earth, each great family had by divine appointment a particular place of destination, to which they retired. In this manner the first nations were constituted, and kingdoms founded. But great changes were soon effected; and colonies went abroad without any regard to their original place of allotment. New establishments were soon made; from whence ensued a mixture of people and languages. These are events of the highest consequence: of which we can receive no intelligence, but through the hands of the Gentile writers.

It has been observed by many of the learned, that some particular family betook themselves very early to different parts of the world; in all which they introduced their rites and religion, together with the customs of their country. They represent them as very knowing and enterprizing: and with good reason. They were the first, who ventured upon the seas, and undertook long voyages. They shewed their superiority and address in the numberless expeditions, which they made, and the difficulties, which they surmounted. Many have thought that they were colonies from Egypt, or from Phenicia; having a regard only to the settlements, which they made in the west. But I shall shew hereafter, that colonies of the same people are to be found in the most extream parts of the east: where we may observe the same rites and ceremonies, and the same traditional histories, as are to be met with in their other settlements. The country called Phenicia could not have sufficed for the effecting all, that is attributed to these mighty adventurers. It is necessary for me to acquaint the Reader, that the wonderful people, to whom I allude, were the descendents of Chus; and called Cuthites, and Cuseans. They stood their ground at the general migration of families: but were at last scattered over the face of the earth. They were the first apostates from the truth; yet great in worldly wisdom. They introduced, wherever they came, many useful arts; and were looked up to, as a superior order of beings: hence they were styled Heroes, Daemons, Heliadae, Mac-

arians. They were joined in their expeditions by other nations; especially by the collateral branches of their family, the Mizraim, Caphtorim, and the sons of Canaan. These were all of the line of Ham, who was held by his posterity in the highest veneration. They called him Amon: and having in process of time raised him to a divinity, they worshiped him as the Sun: and from this worship they were styled Amonians. This is an appellation, which will continually occur in the course of this work: and I am authorized in the use of it from Plutarch; from whom we may infer, that it was not uncommon among the sons of Ham. He specifies particularly in respect to the Egyptians, that, when any two of that nation met, they used it as a term of honour in their salutations, and called one another Amonians. This therefore will be the title, by which I shall choose to distinguish the people; of whom I treat, when I speak of them collectively: for under this denomination are included all of this family; whether they were Egyptians, or Syrians, or of Phenicia, or of Canaan. They were a people, who carefully preserved memorials of their ancestors; and of those great events, which had preceded their dispersion. These were described in hieroglyphics upon pillars and obelisks: and when they arrived at the knowledge of letters, the same accounts were religiously maintained both in their sacred archives, and popular records. . . .

I should be glad to give the Reader a still further insight into the system, which I am about to pursue. But such is the scope of my inquiries, and the purport of my determinations, as may possibly create in him some prejudice to my design: all which would be obviated, were he to be carried step by step to the general view, and be made partially acquainted, according as the scene opened. What I have to exhibit, is in great measure new: and I shall be obliged to run counter to many received opinions, which length of time, and general assent, have in a manner rendered sacred. What is truly alarming, I shall be found to differ not only from some few historians, as is the case in common controversy; but in some degree from all: and this in respect to many of the most essential points, upon which historical precision has been thought to depend. My meaning is, that I must set aside many supposed facts, which have never been controverted: and dispute many events, which have not only been admitted as true; but have been looked up to as certain eras, from whence other events were to be determined. All our knowledge of Gentile history must either come through the hands of the Grecians; or of the Romans, who copied from them. I shall therefore give a full account of the Helladian Greeks, as of the Iönim, or Ionians, of Asia: also of the Dorians, Leleges, and Pelasgi. What may appear very presumptuous, I shall deduce from their own histories many truths, with which they were totally unacquainted; and give to them an original, which they certainly did not know. They have bequeathed to us noble materials, of which it is time to make a serious use. It was their misfortune not to know the value of the data, which they transmitted, nor the purport of their own intelligence.

It will be one part of my labour to treat of the Phenicians, whose history has been much mistaken: also of the Scythians, whose original has been hitherto a secret. From such an elucidation many good consequences will, I hope, ensue: as the Phenicians, and Scythians have hitherto afforded the usual place of retreat for ignorance to shelter itself. It will therefore

be my endeavour to specify and distinguish the various peoples under these denominations; of whom writers have so generally, and indiscriminately spoken. I shall say a great deal about the Aethiopians, as their history has never been compleatly given: also of the Indi, and Indo-Scythae, who seem to have been little regarded. There will be an account exhibited of the Cimmerian, Hyperborean, and Amazonian nations, as well as of the people of Colchis: in which the religion, rites, and original, of those nations will be pointed out. I know of no writer, who has written at large of the Cyclopians. Yet their history is of great antiquity, and abounds with matter of consequence. I shall therefore treat of them very fully, and at the same time of the great works which they performed: and subjoin an account of the Lestrygons, Lamii, Sirens, as there is a close correspondence between them.

As it will be my business to abridge history of every thing superfluous, and foreign; I shall be obliged to set aside many ancient lawgivers, and princes, who were supposed to have formed republics, and to have founded kingdoms. I cannot acquiesce in the stale legends of Deucalion of Thessaly, of Inachus of Argos, and Aegialeus of Sicyon: nor in the long line of princes, who are derived from them. The supposed heroes of the first ages in every country are equally fabulous. No such conquests were ever atchieved, as are ascribed to Osiris, Dionysus, and Sesostris. The histories of Hercules, and Perseus, are equally void of truth. I am convinced, and hope I shall satisfactorily prove, that Cadmus never brought letters to Greece: and that no such person existed as the Grecians have described. What I have said about Sesostris and Osiris, will be repeated about Ninus, and Semiramis, two personages, as ideal as the former. There never were such expeditions undertaken, nor conquests made, as are attributed to these princes: nor were any such empires constituted, as are supposed to have been established by them. I make a little account of the histories of Saturn, Janus, Pelops, Atlas, Dardanus, Minos of Crete, and Zoroaster of Bactria. Yet something mysterious, and of moment, is concealed under these various characters: and the investigation of this latent truth will be the principal part of my inquiry. In respect to Greece, I can afford credence to very few events, which were antecedent to the Olympiads. I cannot give the least assent to the story of Phryxus, and the golden fleece. It seems to me plain beyond doubt, that there were no such persons as the Grecian Argonauts: and that the expedition of Jason to Colchis was a fable. . . .

In the execution of the whole there will be brought many surprising proofs in confirmation of the Mosaic account: and it will be found from repeated evidence, that every thing, which the divine historian has transmitted, is most assuredly true. And though the nations, who preserved memorials of the Deluge, have not perhaps stated accurately the time of that event; yet it will be found the grand epoch, to which they referred; the highest point, to which they could ascend. This was esteemed the renewal of the world; the new birth of mankind; and the ultimate of Gentile history. Some traces may perhaps be discernible in their rites and mysteries of the antediluvian system: but those very few, and hardly perceptible. It has been thought, that the Chaldaic, and Egyptian accounts exceed not only the times of the Deluge, but the era of the world: and Scaliger has accordingly carried the chronology of the latter beyond the term of his

artificial period. But upon enquiry we shall find the chronology of this people very different from the representations, which have been given. This will be shewn by a plain and precise account, exhibited by the Egyptians themselves: yet overlooked and contradicted by the persons, through whose hands we receive it. Something of the same nature will be attempted in respect to Berosus; as well as to Abydenus, Polyhistor, and Apollodorus, who borrowed from him. Their histories contained matter of great moment: and will afford some wonderful discoveries. From their evidence, and from that which has preceded, we shall find, that the Deluge was the grand epocha of every ancient kingdom. It is to be observed, that when colonies made any where a settlement, they ingrafted their antecedent history upon the subsequent events of the place. And as in those days they could carry up the genealogy of their princes to the very source of all; it will be found, under whatever title he may come, that the first king in every country was Noah. For as he was mentioned first in the genealogy of their princes, he was in aftertimes looked upon as a real monarch; and represented as a great traveller, a mighty conqueror, and sovereign of the whole earth. This circumstance will appear even in the annals of the Egyptians: and though their chronology has been supposed to have reached beyond that of any nation, yet it coincides very happily with the accounts given by Moses.

In the prosecution of my system I shall not amuse the Reader with doubtful and solitary extracts; but collect all, that can be obtained upon the subject, and shew the universal scope of writers. I shall endeavour particularly to compare sacred history with profane, and prove the general assent of mankind to the wonderful events recorded. My purpose is not to lay science in ruins; but instead of desolating to build up, and to rectify what time has impaired: to divest mythology of every foreign and unmeaning ornament; and to display the truth in its native simplicity: to shew, that all the rites and mysteries of the Gentiles were only so many memorials of their principal ancestors; and of the great occurrences, to which they had been witnesses. Among these memorials the chief were the ruin of mankind by a flood; and the renewal of the world in one family. They had symbolical representations, by which these occurrences were commemorated: and the ancient hymns in their temples were to the same purpose. They all related to the history of the first age; and to the same events, which are recorded by Moses.   (from Preface)

The materials, of which I propose to make use in the following enquiries, are comparatively few, and will be contained within a small compass. They are such, as are to be found in the composition of most names, which occur in ancient mythology; whether they relate to Deities then reverenced; or to the places where their worship was introduced. But they appear no where so plainly, as in the names of those places, which were situated in Babylonia and Egypt. From these parts they were, in process of time, transferred to countries far remote; beyond the Ganges eastward, and to the utmost bounds of the Mediterranean west; wherever the sons of Ham under their various denominations either settled or traded. For I have mentioned, that this people were great adventurers; and began an extensive commerce in very early times. They got footing in many parts; where they founded cities,

which were famous in their day. They likewise erected towers and temples: and upon headlands and promontories they raised pillars for sea-marks to direct them in their perilous expeditions. All these were denominated from circumstances, that had some reference to the religion, which this people professed; and to the ancestors, whence they sprang. The Deity, which they originally worshiped, was the Sun. But they soon conferred his titles upon some of their ancestors: whence arose a mixed worship. They particularly deified the great Patriarch, who was the head of their line; and worshiped him as the fountain of light: making the Sun only an emblem of his influence and power. They called him Bal, and Baal: and there were others of their ancestry joined with him, whom they styled the Baalim. Chus was one of these: and this idolatry began among his sons. In respect then to the names, which this people, in process of time, conferred either upon the Deities they worshiped, or upon the cities which they founded; we shall find them to be generally made up of some original terms for a basis, such as Ham, Cham, and Chus: or else of the titles, with which those personages were in aftertimes honoured. These were Thoth, Men or Menes, Ab, El, Aur, Ait, Ees or Ish, On, Bel, Cohen, Keren, Ad, Adon, Ob, Oph, Apha, Uch, Melech, Anac, Sar, Sama, Samaïm. We must likewise take notice of those common names, by which places are distinguished, such as Kir, Caer, Kiriath, Carta, Air, Col, Cala, Beth, Ai, Ain, Caph, and Cephas. Lastly are to be inserted the particles Al and Pi; which were in use among the Egyptians.

Of these terms I shall first treat; which I look upon as so many elements, whence most names in ancient mythology have been compounded; and into which they may be easily resolved: and the history, with which they are attended, will, at all times, plainly point out, and warrant the etymology.

HAM or CHAM

The first of the terms here specified is Ham; at different times, and in different places, expressed Cham, Chom, Chamus. Many places were from him denominated Cham Ar, Cham Ur, Chomana, Comara, Camarina. Ham, by the Egyptians, was compounded Am-On. . . . Ham, as a Deity, was esteemed the Sun: and his priests were stiled Chamin, Chaminim, and Chamerim. His name is often found compounded with other terms, as in Cham El, Cham Ees, Cam Ait: and was in this manner conferred both on persons and places. From names, which seemed to have any correspondence with the Zeus of Greece, Amoun or Ammon was the most peculiar, and adequate.

(from pp. 1–3, "Radicals")

RICHARD PAYNE KNIGHT

[1750–1824]

RICHARD PAYNE KNIGHT, a wealthy collector of ancient bronzes and gems, an arbiter of taste who publicly opposed England's acquisition of what he called "Elgin's Phidian freaks," wrote and in 1786 published *A Discourse on the Worship of Priapus*. In this work, he proposed the still unrefuted theory that all mythology and theology, including that of Christianity, is ultimately derived from primitive fertility cults in which the male and female genitalia are the symbols through which men worshipped the procreative power. Knight's bold thesis further claimed that most of the symbolism in ancient art was derived from or related to sex and the genitalia, and he used innumerable artifacts, especially coins, gems, and medals, as well as more conventional and more familiar written texts, to argue his case. The *Discourse* caused great offense, partly because of the obvious relish with which Knight approached his subject; it was withdrawn, only to surface again in 1818, in very sober dress and without the wittily obscene illustrations of the earlier work, as *The Symbolical Language of Ancient Art and Mythology,* in which Knight's leading idea is masked behind a duller style and a great deal of pedantic mythographizing.

All through the eighteenth century, the prominence of sex in Greek myth had been discussed, with indignation by the Christians, with irony by men such as Bayle and Gibbon, and with speculative sobriety by Hume, who had tried to explain the promiscuity of so much early mythology by claiming that a savage mind could more easily understand the idea of generation or procreation, which is readily communicable via sexual objects and scenes, than abstract ideas, such as that of creation out of nothing. One also finds eighteenth-century attitudes toward sex and myth ranging from decorous ribaldry to smirking lasciviousness in unusual as well as in expected places: in Banier, in Spence, in Diderot, in Sylvain Maréchal, and in Hancarville, the last being one of Knight's important and acknowledged sources. De La Croze and Jablonski helped publicize sexual aspects of early Indic and Egyptian culture, while the discovery of innumerable artifacts of obvious sexual significance from Herculaneum and Pompeii gave added impetus to collectors, antiquaries, and travelers (such as Wood), and added importance to the growing collections of antique objects, the implications of which were nearly impossible to ignore. Indeed, so impressive were the artifacts themselves—the statuettes, gems, medals, coins, cups, paintings, and so on—that Knight made them his basic source, using written records only for corroboration. Faced with this mass of new, concrete, and undeniable evidence of sex worship, which seemed to support certain parts of the written records that were often overlooked, made fun of, or misinterpreted, it was only a matter of time before someone decided to consider seriously the idea that sexuality had once been an important part of religion. This bold approach is part of the novelty of Knight's argument.

In standard enlightenment language Knight postulates a universal human nature that is always essentially the same, though it can be temporarily altered or repressed. Knight deplores warring sects, remarking innocently that men usually worship the same thing under different forms. Then, drawing upon medals and coins and upon some passages from Plutarch's *Isis and Osiris,* Knight smoothly explains that the phallus is "a very natural symbol of a very natural and philosophical system of religion." He interprets Orphicism and the Eleusinian mysteries as concerned with phallus worship and he provides a very simple and clear argument. Since the phallus "represented the generative or creative attribute," men worshipped the creator by paying homage to His creative principle, the most convenient symbol of which is the erect "organ of generation."

Knight dismisses the idea that ancient symbol or myth arose from verbal ambiguities, arguing briefly that since words are symbols of ideas, the ideas must exist before the words. He next parodies abstract theology and its scholastic discussions of Being, and offers instead his own stout notion that when men of common sense wish to worship Being, they simply set up a phallus and worship that instead of resorting to abstractions. He goes on to remark that the evidence of the medals and gems suggests that the female genitalia generally represent the generative power of Nature, while the male genitalia usually represent the generative power of a force beyond Nature, of God. From this point, Knight ranges off into a demonstration that most ancient and indeed most modern symbols can be reduced to or derived from either the male or the female genitalia. He includes the bull, the egg, the sun, the moon, the serpent, the shell, the scepter and innumerable others.

(Knight is also a scandalmonger. He enjoys telling tales of goats and girls, drawing parallels between Christianity and pagan obscenities, and then quoting orthodox bishops like Warburton for support; or he makes sly comparisons between, say, Christ and a statue of a cock [penis] mounted on a cock's [rooster's] head mounted on a man's shoulders and inscribed "The Saviour of the World.") Much of the remainder of the essay is commentary upon various Greek sexual symbols and upon the clearly sexual objects and statues from such places as the caves of Elephanta in India. From direct sexual symbols, Knight passes to indirect symbols, claiming at one point that the Cross adored by the Christians is nothing more than a late and stylized version of the male genitalia. At length, according to Knight, the symbols degenerated into poetic myth, and the poetic myths were in turn abstracted and allegorized by philosophers. Knight's essay ends by implying that Christianity itself is to be traced back to Bacchic and eventually to Priapic origins.

Thirty-two years later, Knight published *The Symbolical Language of Ancient Art and Mythology,* which was also issued serially in the *Classical Journal.* The book was reissued in 1836 (and again, with sweeping changes, in 1876). The central thesis is the same, but Knight gives greater weight now to the literary texts, admits a vague and general nature worship as the primitive religion, and fortifies his argument with a good deal more study and with appropriate arguments from writers on myth from Fontenelle to Jacob Bryant. He also puts more emphasis on the idea of symbols as a sort of primitive language (which develops later into written language) than on what was being symbolized; that is, he puts more emphasis on the nature of symbolic communication than on the sexual nature of the material. Knight has not abandoned his central idea, but he has altered his approach and shifted his emphases, and he has written in a greyer, duller prose, presumably more acceptable than his earlier flamboyant excursions into Priapism.

Knight's earlier essay remains the more interesting, though it is a difficult piece to assess. One is not quite sure whether it is to be considered as a scholarly work, as a critical essay, or as a piece of mildly arch eroticism. Perhaps the ambiguous tone of *A Discourse on the Worship of Priapus* is due to the various and divergent interests of the author and to his failure to draw lines between his enlightened scorn for religion and priestcraft, his scholarly discoveries and announcements, and his marked and genuine enthusiasm for the earlier and more primitive religions that in a natural and healthy way recognized and rejoiced in the necessary connection between Eros and religion.

Knight, like de Brosses, used new and nonliterary discoveries to formulate a new theory of myth; but unlike de Brosses,

Knight's work is related to romanticism —Knight's growing interest in symbolic communication shows this clearly—and at last one must admit that however unlikely or unstable the tone of the piece, Knight is one of the first to clearly recognize and call attention to the importance of Eros in religious and mythic ideas, and to the importance of fertility and sexuality in the mythic rituals and in mythic art.

R.R.

REFERENCES   Our text is from Richard Payne Knight, *A Discourse on the Worship of Priapus and its connection with the mystic theology of the Ancients,* in *Sexual Symbolism* (New York, 1957), intro. by Ashley Montagu. See also Knight's *The Symbolical Language of Ancient Art and Mythology* (London, 1818). See also Otto Gruppe, *Geschichte der klassischen Mythologie und Religionsgeschichte* (Leipzig, 1921).

KNIGHT

FROM *A Discourse on the Worship of Priapus and Its Connection with the Mystic Theology of the Ancients*

MEN, considered collectively, are at all times the same animals, employing the same organs, and endowed with the same faculties: their passions, prejudices and conceptions, will of course be formed upon the same internal principles, although directed to various ends, and modified in various ways, by the variety of external circumstances operating upon them. Educa-

tion and science may correct, restrain, and extend; but neither can annihilate or create: they may turn and embellish the currents; but can neither stop nor enlarge the springs, which, continuing to flow with a perpetual and equal tide, return to their ancient channels, when the causes that perverted them are withdrawn.

The first principles of the human mind

will be more directly brought into action, in proportion to the earnestness and affection with which it contemplates its object; and passion and prejudice will acquire dominion over it, in proportion as its first principles are more directly brought into action. On all common subjects this dominion of passion and prejudice is restrained by the evidence of sense and perception; but, when the mind is led to the contemplation of things beyond its comprehension, all such restraints vanish: reason has then nothing to oppose to the phantoms of imagination, which acquire terrors from their obscurity, and dictate uncontrolled because unknown. Such is the case in all religious subjects, which, being beyond the reach of sense or reason, are always embraced or rejected with violence and heat. Men think they know, because they are sure they feel; and are firmly convinced, because strongly agitated. Hence proceed the haste and violence with which devout persons of all religions condemn the rites and doctrines of others, and the furious zeal and bigotry with which they maintain their own; while perhaps, if both were equally well understood, both would be found to have the same meaning, and only to differ in the modes of conveying it.

Of all the profane rites which belonged to the ancient polytheism, none were more furiously inveighed against by the zealous propagators of the Christian faith, than the obscene ceremonies performed in the worship of Priapus; which appeared not only contrary to the gravity and sanctity of religion, but subversive of the first principles of decency and good order in society. Even the form itself, under which the god was represented, appeared to them a mockery of all piety and devotion, and more fit to be placed in a brothel than a temple. But the forms and ceremonials of a religion are not always to be understood in their direct and obvious sense; but are to be considered as symbolical representations of some hidden meaning, which may be extremely wise and just, though the symbols themselves, to those who know not their true signification, may appear in the highest degree absurd and extravagant. It has often happened, that avarice and superstition have continued these symbolical representations for ages after their original meaning has been lost and forgotten; when they must of course appear nonsensical and ridiculous, if not impious and extravagant.

Such is the case with the rite now under consideration, than which nothing can be more monstrous and indecent, if considered in its plain and obvious meaning, or as a part of the Christian worship, but which will be found to be a very natural symbol of a very natural and philosophical system of religion, if considered according to its original use and intention.

What this was, I shall endeavour in the following sheets to explain as concisely and clearly as possible. Those who wish to know how generally the symbol, and the religion which it represented, once prevailed, will consult the great and elaborate work of Mr. D'Hancarville, who, with infinite learning and ingenuity, has traced its progress over the whole earth. My endeavour will be merely to show, from what original principles in the human mind it was first adopted, and how it was connected with the ancient theology: matters of very curious inquiry, which will serve, better perhaps than any others, to illustrate that truth, which ought to be present in every man's mind when he judges of the actions of others, *that in morals, as well as in physics, there is no effect without an adequate cause.* If in doing this, I frequently find it necessary to differ in opinion with the learned author above-mentioned, it will be always with the utmost deference and respect; as it is to him that we are indebted for the only reasonable method of explaining the emblematical works of the ancient artists.

Whatever the Greeks and Egyptians meant by the symbol in question, it was certainly nothing ludicrous or licentious: of which we need no other proof, than its having been carried in solemn procession at the celebration of those mysteries in which the first principles of their religion, the knowledge of the God of Nature, the First, the Supreme, the Intellectual[1] were preserved free from the vulgar superstitions, and communicated, under the strictest oaths of secrecy, to the initiated; who were obliged to purify themselves, prior to their initiation, by abstaining from venery, and all impure food. We may therefore be assured, that no impure meaning could be conveyed by this symbol, but that it represented some fundamental principle of their faith. What this was, it is difficult to obtain any direct information, on account of the secrecy under which this part of their religion was guarded. Plutarch tells us, that the Egyptians represented Osiris with the organ of generation erect, to show his generative and prolific power: he also tells us, that Osiris was the same deity as the Bacchus of the Greek mythology; who was also the same as the first-begotten Love (*Eros protogonos*) of Orpheus and Hesiod.[2] This deity is celebrated by the ancient poets as the creator of all things, the father of gods and men;[3] and it appears, by the passage above referred to, that the organ of generation was the symbol of his great characteristic attribute. This is perfectly consistent with the general practice of the Greek artists, who (as will be made appear hereafter) uniformly represented the at-tributes of the deity by the corresponding properties observed in the objects of sight. They thus personified the epithets and titles applied to him in the hymns and litanies, and conveyed their ideas of him by forms, only intelligible to the initiated, instead of sounds, which were intelligible to all. The organ of generation represented the generative or creative attribute, and in the language of painting and sculpture, signified the same as the epithet (*paggenetos*) in the Orphic litanies.

This interpretation will perhaps surprise those who have not been accustomed to divest their minds of the prejudices of education and fashion; but I doubt not, but it will appear just and reasonable to those who consider manners and customs as relative to the natural causes which produce them, rather than to the artificial opinions and prejudices of any particular age or country. There is naturally no impurity or licentiousness in the moderate and regular gratification of any natural appetite; the turpitude consisting wholly in the excess or perversion. Neither are organs of one species of enjoyment naturally to be considered as subjects of shame and concealment more than those of another; every refinement of modern manners on this head being derived from acquired habit, not from nature: habit, indeed, long established; for it seems to have been as general in Homer's days as at present; but which certainly did not exist when the mystic symbols of the ancient worship were first adopted. As these symbols were intended to express abstract ideas by objects of sight, the contrivers of them naturally selected those objects whose characteristic properties seemed to have the greatest analogy with the Divine attributes which they wished to represent. In an age, therefore, when no prejudices of artificial decency existed, what more just and natural image could they find, by which to express their idea of the beneficent power of the great Creator, than that organ which endowed them with the power of procreation, and made them partakers, not only of the felicity of the Deity, but of his great characteristic attribute, that of multiplying his own image, communicating his blessings, and extending them to generations yet unborn?

In the ancient theology of Greece, preserved in the Orphic fragments this deity, the *Eros protogonos,* or first-begotten Love, is said to have been produced together with Æther, by Time, or Eternity (*Kronos*), and Necessity (*Ananke*) operating upon inert matter (*Chaos*). He is described as eternally begetting (*aeignetes*); the Father of Night, called in later times, the lucid or splendid (*phanes*), because he first appeared in splendour; of a double nature (*diphnes*), as possessing the general power of creation and generation, both active and passive, both male and female.[4] Light is his necessary and primary attribute, co-eternal with himself, and with him brought forth from inert matter by necessity. Hence the purity and sanctity always attributed to light by the Greeks.[5] He is called the Father of Night, because by attracting the light to himself, and becoming the fountain which distributed it to the world, he produced night, which is called eternally-begotten, because it had eternally existed, although mixed and lost in the general mass. He is said to pervade the world with the motion of his wings, bringing pure light; and thence to be called the splendid, the ruling Priapus, and self-illumined (*antanges*).[6] It is to be observed that the word *Priepos,* afterwards the name of a subordinate deity, is here used as a title relating to one of his attributes; the reasons for which I shall endeavour to explain hereafter. Wings are figuratively

attributed to him as being the emblems of swiftness and incubation; by the first of which he pervaded matter, and by the second fructified the egg of Chaos. The egg was carried in procession at the celebration of the mysteries, because, as Plutarch says, it was the material of generation (*ule tes geneseos*)[7] containing the seeds and germs of life and motion without being actually possessed of either. For this reason, it was a very proper symbol of Chaos, containing the seeds and materials of all things, which, however, were barren and useless, until the Creator, fructified them by the incubation of his vital spirit, and released them from the restraints of inert matter, by the efforts of his divine strength. The incubation of the vital spirit is represented on the colonial medals of Tyre, by a serpent wreathed around an egg; for the serpent, having the power of casting his skin, and apparently renewing his youth, became the symbol of life and vigour, and as such is always made an attendant on the mythological deities presiding over health. It is also observed, that animals of the serpent kind retain life more pertinaciously than any others except the Polypus, which is sometimes represented upon the Greek medals, probably in its stead. . . .

The Creator, delivering the fructified seeds of things from the restraints of inert matter by his divine strength, is represented on innumerable Greek medals by the Urus, or wild Bull, in the act of butting against the Egg of Chaos, and breaking it with his horns. It is true, that the egg is not represented with the bull on any of those which I have seen; but Mr. D'Hancarville[8] has brought examples from other countries, where the same system prevailed, which, as well as the general analogy of the Greek theology, prove that the egg must have been understood, and that the attitude of the bull could have no other meaning. I shall also have occasion hereafter to show by other examples, that it was no uncommon practice, in these mystic monuments, to make a part of a group represent the whole. It was from this horned symbol of the power of the deity that horns were placed in the portraits of kings to show that their power derived from Heaven, and acknowledged no earthly superior. The moderns have indeed changed the meaning of this symbol, and given it a sense of which, perhaps, it would be difficult to find the origin, though I have often wondered that it has never exercized the sagacity of those learned gentlemen who make British antiquities the subject of their laborious inquiries. At present it certainly does not bear any character of dignity or power; nor does it ever imply that those to whom it is attributed have been particularly favored by the generative or creative powers. But this is a subject much too important to be discussed in a digression. . . .

To the head of the bull was sometimes joined the organ of generation which represented not only the strength of the creator, but the peculiar direction of it to the most beneficial purpose, the propagation of sensitive beings. . . .

Sometimes this generative attribute is represented by the symbol of the goat, supposed to be the most salacious of animals, and therefore adopted upon the same principles as the bull and the serpent. The choral odes, sung in honour of the generator Bacchus, were hence called *tragodiai* or songs of the goat; a title which is now applied to the dramatic dialogues anciently inserted into these odes, to break their uniformity. On a medal struck in honour of Augustus, the goat terminates in the tail of a fish, to show the generative power incorporated with water.

Under his feet is the globe of the earth, supposed to be fertilized by this union; and upon his back, the cornucopia, representing the result of this fertility.

Mr. D'Hancarville attributes the origin of all these symbols to the ambiguity of words; the same term being employed in the primitive language to signify God and a Bull, the Universe and a Goat, Life and a Serpent. But words are only the types and symbols of ideas, and therefore must be posterior to them, in the same manner as ideas are to their objects. . . .

(from pp. 25–44)

NOTES

Knight's notes are given in most cases, except when referring to plates in text.—Ed.

1. Plutarch, *de Isis et Osiris.*
2. *Ibid.*
3. Orph. *Argon.* 422.
4. Orph. Argon ver 12. This poem of the Argonautic Expedition is not of the ancient Orpheus, but written in his name by some poet posterior to Homer; as appears by the allusion of Orpheus's descent into hell; a fable invented after the Homeric times. It is, however, of very great antiquity, as both the style and the manner sufficiently prove; and, I think, cannot be later than the age of Pisistratus, to which it has been generally attributed. The passage here referred to is cited from another poem, which at the time this was written, passed for a genuine work of the Thracian bard: whether justly or not matters little, for its being thought so at that time proves it to be of the remotest antiquity. The other Orphic poems cited in this discourse are the Hymns, or Litanies, which are attributed by the early Christian and later Platonic writers to Onomacritus, a poet of the age of Pisistratus; but which are probably of various authors. . . . They contain however nothing which proves them to be later than the Trojan times; and if Onomacritus, or any later author, had anything to do with them, it seems to have been only in new-versifying them, and changing the dialect. . . . Had he forged them, and attempted to impose them upon the world, as the genuine compositions of an ancient bard, there can be no doubt but that he would have stuffed them with antiquated words and obsolete phrases; which is by no means the case, the language being pure and worthy the age of Pisistratus. These poems are not properly hymns, for the hymns of the Greeks contained the nativities and actions of the gods, like those of Homer and Callimachus; but these are compositions of a different kind, and are properly invocations or prayers used in the Orphic mysteries, and seem nearly of the

same class as the Psalms of the Hebrews. The reason why they are so seldom mentioned by any of the early writers, and so perpetually referred to by the later, is that they belonged to the mystic worship, where everything was kept concealed under the strictest oaths of secrecy. But after the rise of Christianity, this sacred silence was broken by the Greek converts, who revealed everything which they thought would depreciate the old religion or recommend the new; whilst the heathen priests revealed whatever they thought would have contrary tendency; and endeavored to show, by publishing the real mystic creed of their religion, that the principles of it were not so absurd as its outward structure seemed to infer; but that when stripped of poetical allegory and vulgar fable, their theology was pure, reasonable, and sublime. . . . Perhaps there is no surer rule for judging than to compare the epithets and allegories with the symbols and monograms on the Greek medals, and to make their agreement the test of authenticity. The medals were the public acts and records of the State, made under the direction of the magistrates, who were generally initiated into the mysteries. We may therefore be assured that whatever theological and mythological allusions are found upon them were part of the ancient religion of Greece. It is from these that many of the Orphic Hymns and Fragments are proved to contain the pure theology of mystic faith of the ancients, which is called Orphic by Pausanias (lib. i., c. 39) and which is so unlike the vulgar religion, or poetical mythology, that one can scarcely imagine at first sight that it belonged to the same people; but which will nevertheless appear, upon accurate investigation, to be the source from whence it flowed, and the cause of all its extravagance. . . .

5. See Sophocles, Oedipus Tyr., vers, 1436.
6. Orph. Hymn. 5.
7. Symph. I. 2.
8. Recherches sur les Arts, lib 1.

ANTOINE PERNETY

[1716–1801]

THE ALCHEMICAL theory of myth put forward by Dom Antoine Pernety illustrates one of the furthest reaches of the allegorical mode of myth interpretation in the eighteenth century. In Pernety's work, the thinness of argument, the uninformed confidence, and the esoteric excesses are indications that simple allegorism is no longer broadly useful as an approach to myth. While the mainstream of myth study lies through the mainstream of romanticism, certain obscure and dimly related eddies and backwaters make a series of interesting but hard to follow connections between myth and occultism. We could follow myth into Astrology, Demonology, Rosicrucianism, Freemasonry, and Cabalism; into Swedenborg, Boehme, and the *Illuminati,* as well as into Alchemy. All these movements and currents, like their modern counterparts—the interest, for example, in Mme Blavatsky, in the Tarot, and in the *I Ching*—are often indications of a curious hunger to institutionalize primal forces, to find suitable symbols for a dark, nonrational vision of life, and to combine these symbols into some sort of system.

Antoine Pernety, an obscure French *érudit* (once flatteringly but typically mistaken by Frederick of Prussia for his cousin Jacques Pernetti, another obscure French *érudit*) was a translator of Swedenborg, the founder of a group of *Illuminati* in Avignon, and an apologist for alchemy. His two books on the latter, *Les Fables égyptiennes et grecques dévoilées*

. . . (1758, 2d ed. 1787) and the *Dictionnaire mytho-hermétique* . . . (1787), undertake to show that myth is nothing more than an elaborate language deliberately worked out by early Egyptian alchemists as a way of concealing their ideas from the common people. Pernety argues that once the early chemists had discovered how to make gold and how to stay young forever (the philosophers' stone and the elixir of life), it was necessary to hide this knowledge lest every peasant, and worse, every woman, should gain the knowledge, become rich, and live forever. Pernety himself, in divulging the secrets, tried to maintain the veil. His two books need to be taken together; each refers to the other at crucial points, and one sometimes finds oneself referred back and forth as one pursues a point. An example of Pernety's approach is the claim that the fable which says that Hercules was the son of Jupiter and Alcmena is a secret formula for deriving mercury, since Hercules equals Mercury, Jupiter equals tin, and Alcmena equals dry earthly matter. At the same time that Pernety claimed that the Greek fables were arcane chemical formulae, he also claimed that alchemy, in its broad outlines and general aims, was an eminently Christian science. And indeed in the late eighteenth century, the alchemy that the young Goethe enthusiastically studied approached the making of gold as increasingly less important than the seeking of high philosophical, mystical, or religious truth via secret teachings and symbols. In some aspects alchemy was becoming a material approach to transcendental ideas and states.

At any rate, as Weiss records in his notice of Pernety in the *Biographie Universelle,* Pernety died in 1801 firmly convinced that he had found the way to prolong his life for several centuries. As his work is reminiscent of theories of hidden Egyptian wisdom from Kircher onward, the idea that fables are allegories is the other cornerstone of Pernety's work. For other correspondences between myth and alchemy, one can go back to Olympiodorus, whose *Meteorologica* connects lead with the planet Saturn, copper with Venus, electrum with Jupiter, and so on, or one can look forward to Goethe, to Melville, whose *Pierre* contains traces of a dark fusion of alchemical and mythic ideas, to Jung, and to Mircea Eliade, whose *The Forge and the Crucible* reinterprets alchemy as an expression of man's desire to participate in the processes of nature as nature perfects itself.

And if it can be maintained that myth is intricately bound up with the need to reconcile natural and supernatural, fact and wish, object and desire, man and deity, then alchemy and indeed many of the occult sciences have strong connections with myth since these sciences themselves mediate between the actual world and the world of imagination, and like myth, they provide symbologies.

R.R.

REFERENCES The texts are our translations from Antoine Pernety, *Les Fables égyptiennes et grecques dévoilées, et réduites au même principe avec une explication des Hiéroglyphes, et de la guerre de Troye* (Paris, 1758), and *Dictionnaire mytho-hermétique, dans lequel on trouve les allégories fabuleuses des poètes, les métaphores, les énigmes et les termes barbares des Philosophes Hermétiques expliqués* (Paris, 1787). See also Mircea Eliade, *The Forge and the Crucible* (New York, 1962), and R. D. Gray, *Goethe the Alchemist* (Cambridge: Cambridge University Press, 1952).

PERNETY

FROM *Egyptian and Greek Fables Unveiled*

IT IS THEN beyond doubt that the Chemical Art of Hermes was known among the Egyptians. It is hardly less sure that at least some of the Greeks who traveled in Egypt learned the art there, and having hidden it under hieroglyphs, they taught it afterwards under the veil of fables. . . . (from p. 36)

FROM *Mythic-Hermetic Dictionary*

NO SCIENCE ever had so much need of a Dictionary as Hermetic Philosophy.

Those into whose hands fall books on this subject can scarcely sustain a half hour's reading of them; the outlandish names one finds there seem void of sense, and the equivocal terms which are placed by design in nearly every phrase present no settled meaning. The authors themselves warn that one should not understand them literally, that they have given a thousand names to the same thing, that their works are nothing but a tissue of enigmas, metaphors, and allegories, themselves presented under the veil of ambiguous terms, and that it is necessary to distrust the places that seem easy to understand on first reading. They make a mystery of everything and seem only to have written in order to be not understood. They protest however that they write only to teach and to teach a science that they call the key to all the others. The love of God, of neighbor, of truth puts the pen in their hand. Recognition of so signal a favor as that of having received from the Creator intelligence of so lofty a mystery does not permit them to remain silent. But they have received it, they add, in the shadows of mystery; it would be a crime worthy of anathema to raise the veil that hides it from the eyes of the vulgar. Can't they dispense with mysterious writing? If one exposed to broad daylight this science in its simplicity, women, even children, would want to put it to the test. The most stupid peasant would leave his plough to labor like Jason in the field of Mars. He would cultivate philosophical ground, in which the work would be only an amusement for him, whose abundant harvest would procure him immense riches, with a very long life and unfailing health to enjoy them.

So one must keep this science in obscurity, must speak of it only by hieroglyphs, by fictions, in imitation of the ancient priests of Egypt, the Brahmins of India, the first philosophers of Greece and of all countries, as soon as one senses the necessity of not overturning all the order and harmony established in civil society. . . .   (from Preface, pp. v–vii)

Jupiter

[Pernety begins with a brief and quite conventional account of Jupiter and of his amours, follows this with a suggestion of a great mystery for the solution of which he refers the reader to his other work, then, after printing the heading *Jupiter* again, gives the following.]

THE CHEMISTS give this name to the metal we commonly call tin, but the alchemists often understand something else, as in the explication they give for the fable of Amphytrion and of Alcmena, where Jupiter is taken for that celestial heat and that innate fire which is the primal source, and as the efficient cause of metals; this is why they say that Mercury, which is their first and principal agent in the great work, is represented under the guise of Hercules, born of Alcmena and Jupiter, because Alcmena is taken as the symbol of the dry earthly matter which is like the matrix of metallic humidity upon which Jupiter acts.   (p. 230)

JOHANN WOLFGANG VON GOETHE

[1749–1832]

KARL PHILIPP MORITZ

[1756–1793]

IF ONE characteristic of modern literature is a persistent interest in myth—running from Blake or Hölderlin to Melville and Wagner through Nietzsche, Joyce, Yeats, Mann, and Eliot—Goethe's use of myth precedes all these others. His poetic revitalizing of myth begins about 1770, twenty years before Blake, and almost half a century before Keats or Nerval. Goethe is unique in other ways. Not only is the use of myth in his early verse at once daring and masterful, his creative vitality with myth never dissipates or ossifies: he is even more inventive, flexible, and wide-ranging in the last twenty years before his death at eighty-two in 1832. Goethe is successful in any and every genre: lyric, epic, narrative, fiction, drama—all contribute to what T. S. Eliot has called his amplitude, abundance, and universality, and in all these Goethe puts myth to new use. But compared to the writers mentioned above, the young Goethe works in isolation, with no vital mythopoetic tradition or great examples to sustain his bold efforts; he singlehandedly creates the poetry that Herder only theorized about. In contrast, the only comparably early and daringly innovative poet of myth, Blake, descends from and continues the English tradition of "prophetic" poetry vigorously launched by Milton. Yet, where Blake was wholly ignored by the dominant line of English romantic mythic poetry, Goethe was at first uniquely famous and influential, then swiftly elevated to the largely ineffectual status of a monument.

Before he was fifty, he was acclaimed by younger German romantics as having first triumphantly demonstrated what modern poetry might do with myth. But as Nietzsche said, Goethe is an "event without consequence" in German cultural history—or put differently, as far as myth is concerned, Goethe saw himself as an event with romantic consequences he neither enjoyed nor desired. In Germany, those "romantic" or "modern" consequences became the fountainhead of modern literary mythologizing—in no small part by absorbing Goethe's poetic and critical innovations and insights, then transforming and carrying these forward to quite different ends. One result has been that Goethe's mythic originality has been admired officially and neglected in fact. Only in our century, for example, has the virtuosity, scope, and bold irreverence toward tradition of Part Two of *Faust* been recognized as anticipating and rivalling a pioneering "modern" work like Joyce's *Ulysses*.

Goethe was born in 1749, and reached

maturity in the late blossoming of German literature, nationalism, and enthusiasm for Greece over Roman-French "classicism." But though the older Goethe eulogized Winckelmann's idealizing of Greek formal perfection and harmony, Goethe's earliest interest in myth—from 1770—is quite otherwise excited by Herder's rhapsodic teachings about myth as primal, creatively striving, and dynamic. By 1771, the youthful Goethe rejects the whole decorative Hellenism prevailing in Germany and elsewhere; and even before Herder—not to mention Nietzsche's *Birth of Tragedy*—he exalts and explains Greek tragic power as an outgrowth of religious music, dance, and ecstasy. In 1772, he wrote "Wandrers Sturmlied," a lyric that can lay first claim to marking the modern literary revolution in myth. In this lyric—and in other lyrics and odes in the next few years, such as "Prometheus," "Ganymed," "An Schwager Kronos," "Meine Göttin"—Greek myth is not alluded to or simply "imitated," but rather re-created in its inner spirit: Goethe seeks directly to rewaken the wondrous, terrible, and beautiful vitality of living myths. In doing so, he recovers for his poetry what would later be called the Dionysian side of Greece: myth becomes the source and realm of wild energy, heroic greatness, or Titanism; the gods become power realized, not morality personified.

Goethe's enormous poetic achievement in myth cannot be summarized here, or even adequately listed. His fascination with Greek myth and art is lifelong, but moves restlessly, always to new viewpoints. Thus, after his Italian journey from 1784 to 1786, and the resulting personal renaissance, his early lyrics of mythic power transmute themselves into the classic chasteness and tragic tranquillity of *Iphigenie auf Tauris* (1787); his *Nausicaa* and *Achilleis* are brilliant, fragmentary efforts to write epic and tragedy in a modern vein but with a pagan spirit; his *Helena* (1800) is the

basis for the remarkable classical episode of *Faust*, II. Through Greek myth and art, he moves from a Werther-like despair and *Stürmer* frenzy to that surpassing sanity, wholeness, and objectivity, that Goethean wisdom summed up in his most subtly "naive" word, Nature. One side of this maturing wisdom—especially during his alliance with Schiller in the 1790s—issues into a polemic against the excess and decadence he saw in much of romanticism's Christian mysticism, aesthetic medievalizing, or subjectivity. Classical now means health; romantic means illness. After about 1805, Goethe's classical severity diminishes somewhat—due more perhaps to his undeluded sense that Greekness is irrecoverable than to any sympathy with more radical modern ideals. Yet it was always true that even as he battled—and alienated—his romantic admirers, he contributed most greatly to romantic literary mythic achievements: his youthful *Werther* had indeed praised Ossian over Homer; his drama *Götz* joined Shakespearean freedom and irregular splendor to a medieval German subject; his *Reynard the Fox* (1794) makes high epic of a folk theme. With Herder, he promotes romantic enthusiasm for folk songs and the East, poetizing Indian, Chinese, and Moslem themes—and particularly medieval Persian material in the *West-East Divan* (1814–19), an incredible series of several hundred philosophic love lyrics written when he was over sixty-five.

But *Faust* remains his major poetic effort with myth, literally a lifework: first taken up in 1769, published as *Fragment* in 1790, as Part I in 1808, with Part II completed only weeks before his death. First, *Faust* is at once a *summa* of romantic and modern mythic themes and styles, pagan and Christian, Mediterranean and Nordic, romantic and classic; but it is also as much a critique of the whole coming literary mythic enthusiasm. Stated most summarily, one difference between Goethe's *Faust* and the subsequent romantic use of myth is this: *Faust* achieves and seeks a balance between these contrasting and often contradictory mythic elements that later writers either deliberately destroy or lose. The point may be clarified a bit by looking forward: poets like Wordsworth or Whitman or Melville often seek a mythic "condition" for their thought and gain it largely by dismissing traditional myths in any original, integral form; Novalis or Hölderlin or Wagner do retain older myths, but subordinate them decisively to Christian and modern purposes; a poet like Keats, seeming to deal directly with Greek myths, profoundly transforms these into original symbols; in Joyce's *Ulysses,* the "mythic" dissolves into ironic or shadowy background. On the contrary, *Faust* keeps the various Nordic, pagan, and Christian myths in their original identity and integrity of meaning—this is not to say he does not re-create them; he does; otherwise he could not make them come alive again. But rather than coalescing mythic diversity into any monomyth or to some "higher" position, Goethe conciliates the disparities. One example from *Faust* is that in the midst of the Christian creation, the pagan afterworld exists in seemingly complete autonomy; or, alongside God the Creator, the mythic-pagan "Mothers" (a Goethean elaboration from Plutarch) are genuine life-giving forces.

To put the differences here as provocatively as possible, Goethe may be said to stand against what has become a too familiar side of literary mythologizing since romanticism—what Goethe protested against as the modern "unmitigated striving for absolutism in this thoroughly conditional world." He rejects using myth as a religious or mystic avenue to any unconditional or ultimate ground by which to transcend or ignore what concrete, living nature allots to man. One aspect of this is that where later my-

thopoesis often aspires to being prophetic or tragic, Goethe always strives to mediate and reconcile. He is thus not simply using myth for aesthetic purposes, no matter how refined; nor finally promoting "superior" modern viewpoints in a "classical" style or temper. Unlike a Christianizing Blake or Wagner or Eliot, or a radically atheist-nihilist and "creative" Nietzsche, Goethe seats myth in the great, normal, benevolent, abiding order of nature itself.

Goethe also contributes importantly to the emerging view of myth as symbolic expression. Basic to this development is Goethe's insistence that nature is best understood as Gestalt or organic form in which the ideal manifests itself in sensuous, perfected form. In his critical and scientific works, Goethe expresses this in terms of *Ur*-forms—the *Ur*-plant, the *Ur*-landscape, the *Ur*-phenomenon: all these and many others point to the immanence in all things of a natural harmonious striving toward fulfillment. The *Ur*-forms never exist abstractly, and are never absent from any living thing: borrowing Aristotle's word, Goethe also calls them "entelechies." Goethe goes so far as to claim Homer's poems as natural *Ur*-forms, not an imitation of nature, but nature itself finding expression. Greek sculpture is similarly "nature." Thus, "Statues of gods in themselves have no meaning outside themselves, but are really what they represent." A statue of Jupiter thus expresses the "idea" of majestic power, but not allegorically: the statue is, rather, the form majestic power would itself take could it become plastic. Art deals then in objective, not subjective, truths. Goethe rejects synthesizing all such various forms into one unity: as nature is variously perfect and self-sufficiently developed, so is every work of art and myth. All this transfers easily and inevitably to thinking of representations as "symbols," distinct from allegory. The symbol is a mode of truth not to be reduced or referred outside itself to some more "true" reality or meaning as in allegory. Symbols are "general ideas given form by art."

Goethe's ideas about symbolism developed extensively during the 1780s, partly in collaboration with Karl Philipp Moritz, the novelist and art critic. In 1787, with Goethe's help, Moritz began a treatise on myth, published in 1792 as *Götterlehre,* which develops Goethean ideas on myth as symbol and Gestalt. Nature reveals itself through art in the form of the "gods." Myth depicts not moral truth, but the truth of nature as a totality of striving creativities. Zeus conquers the older gods because Zeus is more "formed," his power more ordered—and, thus, more beautiful. Moritz frees myth from Christian constraint—his mythology is indeed anti-Christian, an attempt to return wholly to the realm of Greek myths as a world of powers ceaselessly in conflict and self-perfection. Like Goethe, Moritz divorces myth from history but not from nature; and like Goethe also, Moritz makes the aesthetic symbol almost wholly autonomous while remaining essentially natural.

B.F.

REFERENCES Our texts are from the following sources: Goethe, "Prometheus," translated by Theodore Martin, from *The Permanent Goethe,* edited by Thomas Mann (New York: Dial Press, 1948), p. 4; Karl Philipp Moritz, *Götterlehre oder mythologische Dichtungen der Alten* (Vienna/Prague, 1801; 2d ed.), our translation. Another English translation of *Götterlehre* is: *Mythological Fictions of the Greeks and Romans,* tr. from 5th German ed., by C.F.W.J. (New York, 1830). The wealth of Goethe's writing and its ready availability have prompted us to give one example only and that from his earliest poetry of myth.

Among the voluminous commentaries on Goethe, some useful works are: Humphrey Trevelyan, *Goethe and the Greeks* (Cambridge: Cambridge University Press, 1941); Oskar Walzel, *Das Prometheussymbol von Shaftesbury zu Goethe* (Munich, 1932); Momme Mommsen, *Studien zum West-Ostlichen Divan* (Berlin: Akademie Verlag, 1962); Wilhelm Emrich, *Die Symbolik von Faust II* (Berlin, 1943); H. Jantz, *Goethe's Faust as a Renaissance Man* (Princeton: Princeton University Press, 1951).

For commentary on Moritz, see: Rudolf Fahrner, *K. Ph. Moritz' Götterlehre, ein Dokument des Goetheschen Klassizismus* (Marburg, 1932); H. Trevelyan, *op. cit.,* p. 145 and *passim;* H. Hatfield, *Aesthetic Paganism in German Literature* (Cambridge: Harvard University Press, 1964), pp. 102–103.

GOETHE

"Prometheus"

CURTAIN thy heavens, thou Jove, with clouds and mist,

And, like a boy that mows down thistle-tops,

Unloose thy spleen on oaks and mountain-
     peaks;
Yet canst thou not deprive me of my earth,
Nor of my hut, the which thou didst not
     build,
Nor of my hearth, whose cheerful little
     flame
Thou enviest me!

I know of nought within the universe
More slight, more pitiful than you, ye
     gods!
Who nurse your majesty with scant
     supplies
Of offerings wrung from fear, and
     mutter'd prayers,
And needs must starve, were't not that
     babes and beggars
Are hope-besotted fools!

When I was yet a child, and knew not
     whence
my being came, nor what before it lay,
Up to the sun I bent my wilder'd eye,
As though an ear were there
To listen to my plaint,
A heart, like mine,
To pity the oppress'd.

Who gave me succour
Against the Titans' over-mastering force?
Who rescued me from death—from
     slavery?

Thou!—thou, my soul, burning with
     hallow'd fire,
Hast not thyself alone accomplished all?
Yet didst thou, in thy young simplicity,
Glow with misguided thankfulness to him,
That slumbers on unheeding there above!

I reverence thee?
Wherefore? Hast thou ever
Lighten'd the sorrows of the heavy-laden?
Hast ever stretched thy hand, to still the
     tears
Of the perplexed in spirit?
Was it not
Almighty Time, and ever-during Fate—
My lords and thine—that shaped and
     moulded me
Into the MAN I am?

Belike it was thy dream,
That I should hate life—fly to wastes and
     wilds,
Because the buds of visionary thought
Did not all ripen into goodly flowers?

Here do I sit, and frame
Men after mine own image—
A race that may be like unto myself,
To suffer, weep; enjoy, and have delights,
And take no heed of thee.
As I do!

MORITZ

FROM *Treatise on the Gods,*
or Mythologic Poem of the Ancients

MYTHOLOGIC poems must be considered as a language of imagination: as

such, they make a world for themselves,
so to speak, and are lifted out of the inter-

connectedness of actual things. Imagination rules in its own realm according to what is pleasing, and nowhere thrusts beyond this. The essence of imagination is to form and shape; it creates a broad realm of play in which it carefully avoids all abstract and metaphysical concepts which might disturb its forms. Most of all it shuns the concept of metaphysical infinity and the unconditioned, since in these the charming creations of imagination would immediately vanish as in a desolate waste. It flees the concept of a being which has no beginning; in imagination, all is origin, procreation and birth, as in the most ancient stories of the gods. None of the higher essences or beings which imagination represents is eternal; none derive from unbounded power. Imagination also avoids the concept of omnipresence, which would inhibit life and movement in the world of the gods.

As often as possible, imagination seeks to tie its forms to time and place; it rests and hovers happily on actuality; but since any actuality that is too close or distinct would harm its dawning light, imagination thus nestles itself gladly in the shadowy world of primal history, where time and place themselves are often wavering and indistinct and therefore have more free room to play: Jupiter, the father of gods and men, was nursed in Crete on goat's milk and raised by wood nymphs.

Now since at the same time a clue to the most ancient lost histories lies hidden in the mythological poems—and since these are not empty dreamshow or simple play of wit expanding into air, but remain important and serious through their inner interweaving with the most ancient events —it is all the more worthwhile to keep these mythologic poems from being dissolved into mere allegory.

To wish to transform the ancient his-tories of the gods into mere allegories, through all kinds of interpretations, is as foolish an undertaking as if one sought through strained interpretations to transform these poems into simply true stories. . . .

Not to distort these lovely poems, it is first of all necessary (disregarding all preconceptions) to take them as they are; and, as often as possible, to consider them from the viewpoint of the whole, so as gradually to comprehend the most remote influences and relations among what have come down to us mostly as fragments.

So when it is said, for example, that Jupiter signifies the upper air, what is meant is nothing less than the concept Jupiter, in which must be included everything that imagination once placed within that concept; by this imaginative inclusiveness, this concept retains a kind of completeness in and for itself, and does not need to explain itself by first looking outside itself.

In the realm of imagination, the concept Jupiter first of all signified itself, just as Caesar signified Caesar in the succession of actual historical events. So who, when glancing at the image of Jupiter from Phidias' master-hand, would first of all think of the higher air as what Jupiter might signify, except he who has denied all feeling for nobility and beauty, and who has become capable of viewing the highest work of art as a hieroglyph or dead letter whose whole worth lies in expressing something beyond itself.

A true work of art, a lovely poem, is something complete and finished in itself, existing for its own sake; its worth lies within itself, and in the well-ordered relation of its parts. . . .

So all the less should one ask about the high poetic beauty of Homer . . . what does the Iliad mean? what does the Odyssey mean?

All that a beautiful poem means lies within itself; in its great or small circumference it mirrors the relations of things, of life, and the fate of men . . . but all this is subordinated in poetic beauty, and is not the main intention of poetry. Poetry thus teaches better because its purpose is not to teach, because its teaching submits itself to beauty, and triumphs through grace and charm.

In mythologic poems, the teaching is certainly subordinated in this way, and must not be sought therein, however outrageous the entire tissue of these poems may appear to us.

In these poems of higher essences or beings, then, man is something so inferior that little regard is taken of him or his moral needs. Often he is a sport of higher powers which reign over all, elevating and casting him down according to whim, and punishing not so much man's injuries to man as rather much more each sign of man's encroachment on the prerogatives of the gods.

Least of all are these higher powers moral essences or beings. The primary principle in them is power, to which all else is secondary. The ever-enduring youthful force which they possess expresses itself in them in their entire luxuriant fullness.

Thus, each of these beings born from imagination in some way represents Nature complete with all its luxurious, wanton growths and its whole brimming over-flow, and is represented as such, raised beyond all concept of morality. . . .

Imagination, however, flees all generalizing concepts, and seeks to make its forms as individualized as possible; so imagination transfers the concept of these higher and prevailing powers over to beings now represented as actual, and to these are attributed the birth, names, genealogy, and form of men.

As often as possible, imagination allows the beings it creates to play in the realm of the actual. The gods enjoy themselves with the daughters of men, and make them mothers of heroes who ride to immortality through great deeds.

It is here, then, where the realm of imagination and actuality border each other most closely; and whence it comes about, too, that the language of imagination or mythologic poetry should be seen simply as it is, and above all protected from all hasty historical explanations. Thus these mixtures of truth and poetry in the most ancient histories fasten our mental horizon to the twilight horizon, so to speak, as far back as we can peer. To have a new dawn here, it is necessary that the mythic poems, as old folk legends, be separated as far as possible in order to find once more the thread to their gradual interweavings and transformations. In this light, the task of a general mythology is to place the oldest folk legends coming down to us beside each other, for which we can at present—restricted as we are here to the mythology of the Greeks and Romans—only offer a hand from afar.

(from pp. 1–7)

SIR WILLIAM JONES

[1746–1794]

THE RELIGION, literature, and mythology of Ancient India first came into wide European notice in the second half of the eighteenth century. It was then that Europeans first learned Sanskrit, and first brought back authentic Indic texts. The Oriental or Indic Renaissance that resulted from this massive influx of non-western material had an enormous effect on the study of language, history, and religion, and on nineteenth-century literature in Germany, France, England, and America, as Raymond Schwab's *La Renaissance orientale* makes admirably clear.

The first great name in Indic studies is that of Anquetil-Duperron (1731–1805). Having seen a manuscript of the Parsee *Vendidad,* which had been given to Oxford in 1718 by a merchant and which no one in Europe could read, Anquetil-Duperron made it his life's ambition to learn the Oriental languages and to discover and publish old and unknown texts. He believed, as many did not, that authentic versions of the earliest true Vedas would one day be found; and despite the numerous false Shastras that found their way to Europe via Abraham Roger, Marco dalla Tomba, Holwell, and others, and despite the pessimism of Sonnerat, Wilkins, and Colebrook as to the existence of authentic Indic texts, Anquetil's faith was eventually vindicated by nineteenth-century scholarship. He himself went to India in 1755, and while he never learned Sanskrit, he did eventually obtain copies and translations of the *Zend-Avesta,* which he published in 1771 after his return to France. Schwab dates the Oriental Renaissance from this publication: "The *Zend-Avesta* of 1771 marks the first coming of an Asiatic text totally independant both of the biblical tradition and of the classical tradition. The history of languages, and history through language both begin here."

The mastery of Sanskrit and the first publication of authentic Sanskrit texts belong to the English in India. Warren Hastings encouraged the study of native law, language, and literature, and it was under his encouraging auspices that the great work of Jones and Wilkins began. In 1784 the Asiatic Society of Bengal was founded at Calcutta. The next year saw the publication of the Wilkins translation of the *Bhagavad Gita,* the first direct and complete translation of a great Sanskrit text. In 1787 came Wilkins's translation of the *Hitopadesa,* and in 1789 came Jones's celebrated translation of the *Sacontala* of Calidasa. This last work caused a literary sensation in Europe and was a major factor in the rapid spread of Indic studies and interest to Germany and France.

Sir William Jones is the most important figure in this spectacular growth and spread of interest in Indic literature, language, religion, and myth. A pioneer Orientalist, he knew thirteen languages well and twenty-eight moderately well; he undertook to codify Hindu Law, he learned Sanskrit, founded and presided over the Asiatic Society, and wrote numerous essays for its journal, the widely reprinted and translated *Asiatick Researches.*

Jones translated a Persian *Life of Nadir Shah* in 1770, wrote a treatise on Oriental poetry in the same year, and a *Poeseos Asiaticae commentatorium libri sex* (modelled on Lowth's work on Hebrew poetry) in 1774, all before setting out for India. Besides the *Sacontala,* Jones edited Calidasa's *Ritusamhara,* and wrote on Indian plants, medicines, chronology, history, customs, language, geography, religion, and mythology. Jones was celebrated in his own time as an Orientalist, as a jurist, and as a linguist; his work lasted long after his death in 1794, and was used by such writers as Tennyson and Melville.

Perhaps his most influential piece was the essay "On the Gods of Greece, Italy, and India," delivered before the Asiatic Society in 1785 and printed in 1799. This piece begins with Jones's observation that there are numerous similarities between Indian, Greek, Italian, Egyptian, Chinese, Persian, and Gothic systems of mythology. To explain such similarities, Jones lists four main causes of myths: historical, astronomical, poetical, and metaphysical. (H. Bruce Franklin has argued that this section of Jones's essay provides the long-sought key to Melville's *Mardi.*) Jones believes, though he is at pains to be open to other argument, that the Vedas were written after the Flood and that Genesis is therefore the older or truer book. But the effect of this essay, and of much subsequent writing on Hindu myth—such as that of Priestley—was to place the Jewish and Christian Scriptures yet more firmly within historical time and within a comparative context in which they might still be considered true, but less and less as the only truth.

The bulk of Jones's essay is a detailed description of the deities in the Hindu pantheon, with an elaborate comparison of each deity with his or her Roman or Greek counterpart. Jones finds similarities between Ganesa and Janus, between Menu and Saturn (and Noah), between Jupiter and Indra, between Jupiter and the triple divinity of Vishnu, Siva, and Brahma, between Cali and Proserpina, and so on. Indeed, the general effect of the essay owes less to its theories about the gods, and more to its careful, detailed, and imaginative presentation of the Indic myths, often told at a length that precludes easy anthologizing. As with Mallet's Nordic mythology, the stories and figures outshone the theories and ideas with which they were connected. In addition, Jones dwells on sun worship and emphasizes the Indic concept of a single deity who is at the same time a creator, a preserver, and a destroyer, a triune arrangement that could seem as sensible as the Christian trinity. And though Jones seems unclear or uncommitted on the then momentous question of origins, it should be noted that in an essay "On the Antiquity of the Indian Zodiack" he argued that both the Greeks and the Hindus (and everyone else) got their zodiac from Chaldea, that is, from Babylonia, which Jones argues was the source of Egyptian, Greek, Italian, Hindu, and Scandinavian versions. Elsewhere, Jones reworked Indian chronology to make it roughly consistent with the Mosaic account, while in "On the mystical poetry of the Persians and Hindus," he argues for Indian, rather than Egyptian, origins.

Jones's great contribution, however, was his observation, in 1786, that

The Sanskrit language, whatever may be its antiquity, is of wonderful structure: more perfect than the Greek, more copious than the Latin, and more exquisitely refined than either, yet bearing to both of them a stronger affinity, both in the roots of verbs and in the forms of grammar, than could have been produced by accident: so strong that no philologer could examine all the three without believing them to have sprung from some common source which, perhaps, no longer exists. There is a similar reason, though not quite so forcible, for supposing that both the Gothic and the Celtic, though blended with a different idiom, had the same origin with the Sanskrit.

This brilliant perception has been claimed as the starting point of modern comparative philology and of the so-called Aryan thesis.

Indic studies were carried forward into the nineteenth century by Colebrook, Brian Hodgson, and H. H. Wilson in England, but the center of speculative interest and creative energy in Indic studies shifted during the 1790s to Germany (see our introduction to "German Romantic Mythology and India") and to France where Anquetil-Duperron and Sylvestre de Sacy gave it new impetus. In general it may be claimed that the new Indic material made Europe aware of what seemed to be a higher antiquity than that of the familiar biblical and classical periods. Thus the new Indic material presented a serious challenge to Christianity as well as to the study of history and language, and myth. Indeed the modern study of language begins with Anquetil-Duperron and Jones. Indic studies also lent new impetus to the search for a single source for civilization. It was also the first important non-western culture to have a major influence on the intellectual and artistic development of Europe and America.

Finally, it should be noted that the remarkable enthusiasm for Indic culture was obscured, during the middle of the nineteenth century or a little after, by the more dramatic discoveries in Egypt and the spectacular deciphering of the hieroglyphics, although the ancient Egyptian civilization thereby revealed does not antedate Indian civilization or outweigh it in intrinsic interest. Indic studies also suffered from a chauvinist anti-Indian missionary movement in England in the early nineteenth century.

R.R.

REFERENCES Our text is from Sir William Jones, "On the Gods of Greece, Italy, and India," published in *Asiatick Researches* (1799). See also *The Works of Sir William Jones,* ed. Anna Maria Jones, with a life by J. Shore, Baron Teignmouth (London, 1799) 6 vols., and *The Letters of Sir William Jones,* ed. G. Cannon (Oxford, 1969) 2 vols., which has a good bibliography of works on Jones.

The best general treatment of the impact of India on the West is Raymond Schwab, *La Renaissance orientale* (Paris, 1950) with excellent bibliographies. See also A. L. Willson, *A Mythical Image: The Ideal of India in German Romanticism* (Durham: Duke University Press, 1965); Guy R. Welbon, *The Buddhist Nirvāna and its Western Interpreters* (Chicago: University of Chicago Press, 1968); Thomas A. Sebeok, ed., *Portraits of Linguists: A Biographical Source Book for the History of Western Linguistics 1746–1963* (Bloomington: Indiana University Press, 1966); and Holger Pedersen, *Linguistic Science in the Nineteenth Century,* tr. J. W. Spargo (Cambridge: Harvard University Press, 1931).

JONES

FROM *"On the Gods of Greece, Italy, and India"*

WE CANNOT justly conclude, by arguments preceding the proof of facts, that one idolatrous people must have borrowed their deities, rites, and tenets from another; since Gods of all shapes and dimensions may be framed by the boundless powers of imagination, or by the frauds and follies of men, in countries never connected; but, when features of resemblance, too strong to have been accidental, are observable in different systems of polytheism, without fancy or prejudice to colour them and improve the likeness, we can scarce help believing, that some connection has immemorially subsisted between the several nations, who have adopted them: it is my design in this essay, to point out such a resemblance between the popular worship of the old *Greeks* and *Italians* and that of the *Hindus;* nor can there be room to doubt of a great similarity between their strange religions and that of *Egypt, China, Persia, Phrygia, Phoenice, Syria;* to which, perhaps, we may safely add some of the southern kingdoms and even islands of *America;* while the *Gothick* system, which prevailed in the northern regions of *Europe,* was not merely similar to those of *Greece* and *Italy,* but almost the same in another dress with an embroidery of images apparently *Asiatick.* From all this, if it be satisfactorily proved, we may infer a general union or affinity between the most distinguished inhabitants of the primitive world, at the time when they deviated, as they did too early deviate, from the rational adoration of the only true GOD.

There seem to have been four principal sources of all mythology. I. Historical, or natural, truth has been perverted into fable by ignorance, imagination, flattery, or stupidity; as a king of *Crete,* whose tomb had been discovered in that island, was conceived to have been the God of *Olympus,* and MINOS, a legislator of that country, to have been his son, and to hold a supreme appellate jurisdiction over departed souls; hence too probably flowed the tale of CADMUS, as BOCHART learnedly traces it; hence beacons or volcanos became one-eyed giants and monsters vomiting flames; and two rocks, from their appearance to mariners in certain positions, were supposed to crush all vessels attempting to pass between them; of which idle fictions many other instances might be collected from the *Odyssey* and the various *Argonautick* poems. The less we say of *Julian* stars, deifications of princes or warriours, altars raised, with those of APOLLO, to the basest of men, and divine titles bestowed on such wretches as CAJUS OCTAVIANUS, the less we shall expose the infamy of grave senators and fine poets, or the brutal folly of the low multitude:

but we may be assured, that the mad apotheosis of truly great men, or of little men falsely called great, has been the origin of gross idolatrous errors in every part of the pagan world. II. The next source of them appears to have been a wild admiration of the heavenly bodies, and, after a time, the systems and calculations of Astronomers: hence came a considerable portion of *Egyptian* and *Grecian* fable; the *Sabian* worship in *Arabia;* the *Persian* types and emblems of *Mihr* or the sun, and the far extended adoration of the elements and the powers of nature; and hence perhaps, all the artificial chronology of the *Chinese* and *Indians,* with the invention of demigods and heroes to fill the vacant niches in their extravagant and imaginary periods. III. Numberless divinities have been created solely by the magick of poetry; whose essential business it is, to personify the most abstract notions, and to place a nymph or a genius in every grove and almost in every flower; hence *Hygieia* and *Jaso,* health and remedy, are the poetical daughters of AESCULAPIUS, who was either a distinguished physician, or medical skill personified; and hence *Chloris,* or verdure, is married to the *Zephyr.* IV. The metaphors and allegories of moralists and metaphysicians have been also very fertile in Deities; of which a thousand examples might be adduced from PLATO, CICERO, and the inventive commentators on HOMER in their pedigrees of the Gods, and their fabulous lessons of morality: the richest and noblest stream from this abundant fountain is the charming philosophical tale of PSYCHE, or the *Progress of the Soul*; than which, to my taste, a more beautiful, sublime, and well supported allegory was never produced by the wisdom and ingenuity of man. Hence also the *Indian* MÁYÁ, or, as the world is explained by some *Hindu* scholars, "the first inclina-

tion of the Godhead to diversify himself (such is their phrase) by creating worlds" is feigned to be the mother of universal nature, and of all the inferiour Gods; as a *Cashmirian* informed me, when I asked him, why CÁMA, or *Love,* was represented as her son; but the word MÁYÁ, or *delusion,* has a more subtile and recondite sense in the *Vedanta* philosophy, where it signifies the system of *perceptions,* whether of secondary or of primary qualities, which the Deity was believed by EPICHARMUS, PLATO, and many truly pious men, to raise by his omnipresent spirit in the minds of his creatures, but which had not, in their opinion, any existence independent of mind.

In drawing a parallel between the Gods of the *Indian* and *European* heathens, from whatever source they were derived, I shall remember, that nothing is less favourable to enquiries after truth than a systematical spirit, and shall call to mind the saying of a *Hindu* writer, "that whoever obstinately adheres to any set of opinions, may bring himself to believe that the freshest sandal wood is a flame of fire": this will effectually prevent me from insisting, that such a God of *India* was *the* JUPITER of *Greece*; such, *the* APOLLO; such, *the* MERCURY: in fact, since all the causes of polytheism contributed largely to the assemblage of *Grecian* divinities (though BACON reduces them all to refined allegories, and NEWTON to a poetical disguise of true history), we find many JOVES, many APOLLOS, many MERCURIES, with distinct attributes and capacities; nor shall I presume to suggest more, than that, in one capacity or another, there exists a striking similitude between the chief objects of worship in ancient *Greece* or *Italy* and in the very interesting country, which we now inhabit.

The comparison, which I proceed to lay

before you, must needs be very superficial, partly from my short residence in *Hindustan,* partly from my want of complete leisure for literary amusements, but principally because I have no *European* book, to refresh my memory of old fables, except the conceited, though not unlearned, work of POMEY, entitled the *Pantheon,* and that so miserably translated, that it can hardly be read with patience. A thousand more strokes of resemblance might, I am sure, be collected by any, who should with that view peruse HESIOD, HYGINUS, CORNUTUS, and the other mythologists; or, which would be a shorter and a pleasanter way, should be satisfied with the very elegant *Syntagmata* of LILIUS GIRALDUS.

Disquisitions concerning the manners and conduct of our species in early times, or indeed at any time, are always curious at least and amusing; but they are highly interesting to such, as can say of themselves with CHREMES in the play, "We are men, and take an interest in all that relates to mankind." They may even be a solid importance in an age, when some intelligent and virtuous persons are inclined to doubt the authenticity of the accounts, delivered by MOSES, concerning the primitive world; since no modes or sources of reasoning can be unimportant, which have a tendency to remove such doubts. Either the first eleven chapters of *Genesis,* all due allowances being made for a figurative Eastern style, are true, or the whole fabrick of our national religion is false; a conclusion, which none of us, I trust, would wish to be drawn. I, who cannot help believing the divinity of the MESSIAH, from the undisputed antiquity and manifest completion of many prophesies, especially those of ISAIAH, in the only person recorded by history, to whom they are applicable, am obliged of course to believe the sanctity of the venerable books,

to which that sacred person refers as genuine; but it is not the truth of our national religion, as such, that I have at heart: it is truth itself; and, if any cool unbiassed reasoner will clearly convince me, that MOSES drew his narrative through *Egyptian* conduits from the primeval fountains of *Indian* literature, I shall esteem him as a friend for having weeded my mind from a capital error, and promise to stand among the foremost in assisting to circulate the truth, which he has ascertained. After such a declaration, I cannot but persuade myself, that no candid man will be displeased, if, in the course of my work, I make as free with any arguments, that he may have advanced, as I should really desire him to do with any of mine, that he may be disposed to controvert. Having no system of my own to maintain, I shall not pursue a very regular method, but shall take all the Gods, of whom I discourse, as they happen to present themselves; beginning, however, like the *Romans* and the *Hindus,* with JANU or GANESA. . . .

(pp. 319–326)

We come now to SATURN, the oldest of the pagan Gods, of whose office and actions much is recorded. The jargon of his being the son of Earth and of Heaven, who was the son of the Sky and the Day, is purely a confession of ignorance, who were his parents or who his predecessors; and there appears more sense in the tradition said to be mentioned by the inquisitive and well informed PLATO, "that both SATURN or *time,* and his consort CYBELE, or the *Earth,* together with their attendant, were the children of *Ocean* and THETIS, or, in less poetical language, sprang from the waters of the great deep." CERES, the goddess of harvests, was, it seems, their daughter; and VIRGIL describes "the mother and nurse of all as crowned with turrets, in a car drawn by lions, and exulting in her hundred grandsons, all divine, all inhabiting splendid celestial mansions." As the God of time, or rather as *time* itself personified, SATURN was usually painted by the heathens holding a scythe in one hand, and in the other, a snake with its tail in its mouth, the symbol of perpetual cycles and revolutions of ages: he was often represented in the act of devouring years, in the form of children, and sometimes, encircled by the seasons appearing like boys and girls. By the *Latins* he was named SATURNUS; and the most ingenious etymology of that word is given by FESTUS the grammarian; who traces it, by a learned analogy to many similar names, *à Satu*, from planting, because, when he reigned in *Italy*, he introduced and improved agriculture: but his distinguishing character, which explains, indeed, all his other titles and functions, was expressed allegorically by the stern of a ship or galley on the reverse of his ancient coins; for which OVID assigns a very unsatisfactory reason, "because the divine stranger arrived in a ship on the *Italian* coast;" as if he could have been expected on horseback or hovering through the air.

The account, quoted by POMEY from ALEXANDER POLYHISTOR, casts a clearer light, if it really came from a genuine antiquity, on the whole tale of SATURN; "That he predicted an extraordinary fall of rain, and ordered the construction of a vessel, in which it was necessary to secure men, beasts, birds, and reptiles from a general inundation."

Now it seems not easy to take a cool review of all these testimonies concerning the birth, kindred, offspring, character, occupations, and entire life of SATURN, without assenting to the opinion of BOCHART, or admitting it at least to be highly probable, that the fable was raised on the true

history of NOAH; from whose flood a new period of *time* was computed, and a new series of ages may be said to have sprung; who rose fresh, and, as it were, newly born from the waves; whose wife was in fact the universal mother, and, that the earth might soon be repeopled, was early blessed with numerous and flourishing descendants: if we produce, therefore, an *Indian* king of divine birth, eminent for his piety and beneficence, whose story seems evidently to be that of NOAH disguised by *Asiatick* fiction, we may safely offer a conjecture, that he was also the same personage with SATURN. This was MENU, or SATYAVRATA, whose pratronymick name was VAIVASWATA, or child of the SUN; and whom the *Indians* believed to have reigned over the whole world in the earliest age of their chronology, but to have resided in the country of *Dravira*, on the coast of the Eastern *Indian* Peninsula: the following narrative of the principal event in his life I have literally translated from the *Bhagavat*; and it is the subject of the first *Purana*, entitled that of the *Matsya*, or *Fish*. . . .   (pp. 329–332)

Be all this as it may, I am persuaded, that a connexion subsisted between the old idolatrous nations of *Egypt, India, Greece,* and *Italy,* long before they migrated to their several settlements, and consequently before the birth of MOSES; but the proof of this proposition will in no degree affect the truth and sanctity of the *Mosaick* History, which, if confirmation were necessary, it would rather tend to confirm. The *Divine Legate,* educated by the daughter of a king, and in all respects highly accomplished, could not but know the mythological system of *Egypt*; but he must have condemned the superstitions of that people, and despised the speculative absurdities of their priests; though some of their traditions concerning the creation and the flood were grounded on truth. Who was better acquainted with the mythology of *Athens* than SOCRATES? Who more accurately versed in the Rabbinical doctrines than PAUL? Who possessed clearer ideas of all ancient astronomical systems than NEWTON, or of scholastick metaphysicks than LOCKE? In whom could the *Romish* Church have had a more formidable opponent than in CHILLINGWORTH, whose deep knowledge of its tenets rendered him so competent to dispute them? In a word, who more exactly knew the abominable rites and shocking idolatry of *Canaan* than MOSES himself? Yet the learning of those great men only incited them to seek other sources of truth, piety, and virtue, than those in which they had long been immersed. There is no shadow then of a foundation for an opinion, that MOSES borrowed the first nine or ten chapters of *Genesis* from the literature of *Egypt:* still less can the adamantine pillars of our *Christian* faith be moved by the result of any debates on the comparative antiquity of the *Hindus* and *Egyptians,* or of any inquiries into the *Indian* Theology. Very respectable natives have assured me, that one or two missionaries have been absurd enough, in their zeal for the conversion of the *Gentiles,* to urge, "that the *Hindus* were even now almost *Christians,* because their BRAHMA, VISHNU, and MAHESA, were no other than the *Christian* Trinity;" a sentence, in which we can only doubt, whether folly, ignorance, or impiety predominates. The three *powers, Creative, Preservative,* and *Destructive,* which the *Hindus* express by the triliteral word *Om,* were grossly ascribed by the first idolaters to the *heat, light,* and *flame* of their mistaken divinity, the Sun; and their wiser successors in the East, who perceived that the Sun was only a created thing, applied those powers to its creator; but the *Indian* Triad, and that of PLATO, which he calls the Supreme Good, the Reason, and the Soul, are infinitely removed from the holiness and sublimity of the doctrine, which pious *Christians* have deduced from texts in the Gospel, though other *Christians,* as pious, openly profess their dissent from them. Each sect must be justified by its own faith and good intentions: this only I mean to inculcate, that the tenet of our church cannot without profaneness be compared with that of the *Hindus,* which has only an apparent resemblance to it, but a very different meaning. One singular fact, however, must not be suffered to pass unnoticed. That the name of CRISHNA, and the general outline of his story, were long anterior to the birth of our Saviour, and probably to the time of HOMER, we know very certainly; yet the celebrated poem, entitled *Bhagavat,* which contains a prolix account of his life, is filled with narratives of a most extraordinary kind, but strangely variegated and intermixed with poetical decorations: the incarnate deity of the *Sanscrit* romance was cradled, as it informs us, among *Herdsmen,* but it adds, that he was educated among them, and passed his youth in playing with a party of milkmaids; a tyrant, at the time of his birth, ordered all new-born males to be slain, yet this wonderful babe was preserved by biting the breast, instead of sucking the poisoned nipple, of a nurse commissioned to kill him; he performed amazing, but ridiculous, miracles in his infancy, and, at the age of seven years, held up a mountain on the tip of his little finger: he saved multitudes partly by his arms and partly by his miraculous powers; he raised the dead by descending for that purpose to the lowest regions; he was the meekest and best-tempered of beings, washed the feet of the *Brahmans,* and preached very nobly, indeed, and sublimely, but always in their favour; he was pure and chaste in reality, but exhibited an appearance of excessive libertinism, and had wives or mistresses too numerous to be counted; lastly, he was benevolent and tender, yet fomented and conducted a terrible war. This motley story must induce an opinion that the spurious Gospels, which abounded in the first age of *Christianity,* had been brought to *India,* and the wildest parts of them repeated to the *Hindus,* who ingrafted them on the old fable of CESAVA, the APOLLO of *Greece.*

As to the general extension of our pure faith in *Hindustan,* there are at present many sad obstacles to it. The *Muselmans* are already a sort of heterodox *Christians:* they are *Christians,* if LOCKE reasons justly, because they firmly believe the immaculate conception, divine character, and miracles of the MESSIAH; but they are heterodox, in denying vehemently his character of Son, and his equality, as God, with the Father, of whose unity and attributes they entertain and express the most awful ideas; while they consider our doctrine as perfect blasphemy, and insist, that our copies of the Scriptures have been corrupted both by *Jews* and *Christians.* It will be inexpressibly difficult to undeceive them, and scarce possible to diminish their veneration from MOHAMMED and ALI, who were both very extraordinary men, and the second, a man of unexceptionable morals: the *Koran* shines, indeed, with a borrowed light, since most of its beauties are taken from our Scriptures; but it has great beauties, and the *Muselmans* will not be convinced that they were borrowed. The *Hindus* on the other hand would readily admit the truth of the Gospel; but they contend, that it is perfectly consistent with their *Sastras*: the deity, they say, has appeared innumerable times, in many parts of this world and of all worlds, for the salvation of his creatures; and though we adore him in one appearance, and they in others, yet we adore, they say, the same God, to whom our several worships, though different in form, are equally acceptable, if they be sincere in substance. We may assure ourselves, that neither *Muselmans* nor *Hindus* will ever be converted by any mission from the Church of *Rome,* or from any other church; and the only human mode, perhaps, of causing so great a revolution will be to translate into *Sanscrit* and *Persian* such chapters of the Prophets, particularly of ISAIAH, as are indisputably Evangelical, together with one of the Gospels, and a plain prefatory discourse containing full evidence of the very distant ages, in which the predictions themselves, and the history of the divine person predicted, were severally made publick; and then quietly to disperse the work among the well-educated natives; with whom if in due time it failed of producing very salutary fruit by its natural influence, we could only lament more than ever the strength of prejudice, and the weakness of unassisted reason.

CHARLES DUPUIS

[1742–1809]

CHARLES FRANÇOIS DUPUIS, a scholar and politician who flourished before and during the French Revolution, and who dedicated his great work *Origine de tous les cultes ou la Religion universelle* to the Assembly in 1795, was in many ways the last important mythographer of the Enlightenment. In assigning to myth an astronomical and zodiacal basis, his work is akin to that of Newton or Pluche; in his generally antireligious outlook and in his conclusion that myths are allegorical veils, he not only takes an old Christian argument and turns it against Christianity, but he resembles the Encyclopedists and the Holbachians in his rejection of everything except visible nature as a starting point for myth. In his use of the fear-theory and the priestcraft theory, he follows lines that go back at least to Bayle, Fontenelle, and the deists. Dupuis is, in fact, an eclectic culmination of the mythical theories of the rationalists; the result is a species of comparative skepticism in which one finds gathered up and nearly harmonized all the important ideas that had been used to undermine, disparage, and degrade myth during the previous hundred years.

Dupuis studied theology at first, then became professor of Rhetoric at the college of Lisieux at the age of twenty-four; he also studied law, mathematics, and astronomy, becoming a lawyer in 1770. In the late 1770s he began to formulate his theory of the origin of myth, religion, and civilization, and he published what were to become parts of his great work in the *Journal des Savants* in June, October, and December of 1778, and in February of 1781 (these were also published in book form in 1781 as *Mémoire sur l'origine des constellations et sur l'explication de la fable par le moyen de l'astronomie*). Dupuis took a chair of Humanities in the College of France, became a member of the *Académie des Inscriptions,* and then became a moderate member of the National Convention upon the outbreak of the French Revolution. In the middle of a distinguished and active political career, Dupuis brought out his *Origine des tous les cultes* in 1795, in two different formats. The work raised a storm of controversy, was twice epitomized, once by Destutt de Tracy and once by Dupuis himself, was reissued in 1835, was refuted by Becchetti, by Joseph Priestley, and by J. S. Bailly, played a part in Napoleon's expedition to Upper Egypt, and long enjoyed a certain prestige in liberal circles in France, England, and America. Dupuis's own *precis* went through four editions early in the century, and was being reprinted as late as 1897: a flurry of pamphlets and books about Dupuis's theory of solar myths was seen in England in the 1870s, after F. Max Müller had again made the subject popular.

Dupuis, who knew Mallet's Nordic myths and something of Indic myth, nevertheless traced much of Western civilization, religion, and myth to the development of the zodiac. He argued the zodiac must have arisen in North Africa, in upper Egypt and Ethiopia, about fifteen thousand years ago, since the constellations and their signs were matched best at that time and place. The zodiac, Dupuis thought, was an astronomical and agricultural calendar, the first and most important schematization of the astral, solar, and lunar events that interested early man, and the general source of most early stories, personifications, and myths. Early man, according to Dupuis, worshipped nature and the forces of nature: he did not worship some abstract or nonexistent force behind or above nature. The idea could have come to Dupuis from Holbach, or from the deists via Holbach, for they all give much the same emphasis to the adequacy and grandeur of physical nature, nature being thought of as not only the green world, but the entire visible universe.

Dupuis goes on to argue that all nations have worshipped nature, especially the sun, the moon, and the stars. He explains how all the mystic numbers refer to natural events (seven is the number of the planets and of the days of the week, twelve is the number of signs in the zodiac and the number of months, and so on). He points out the prevalence of equinoctial and solstitial festivals and goes on to list, in numbing detail, the nature worship of the Greeks, the Persians, the Indians, the Arabs, the Japanese, the Chinese, as well as that of Siam, Thule, the Molluccas, the Philippines, Formosa, Madagascar, and a great many other places. Indeed Dupuis relies heavily for his effect on his ability to document even the simplist rite by citing dozens of examples culled from the increasingly voluminous travel literature, and the *Origine de tous les cultes* was to be a major mine of mythic detail for the nineteenth century. Faber used Dupuis, as did Freemasons, theosophists, and others.

Having shown that all nations worship nature, Dupuis now emphasizes certain

major points. All people, he claims, were impressed by the generative power of nature, by the principle of fecundity, and they saw in nature both active and passive sexuality. Heaven and earth were seen as male and female respectively; hence, (and this is all apparently independent of Knight) Bacchic and Priapic worship, Indian Lingam worship, fertility cults, and so on. Similarly, Dupuis claims that all early men saw in nature the twin and opposed principles of light and dark, or good and evil, which eventually were personified as a good deity versus an evil one.

In addition to the active and passive generative principles and the principles of light and dark, and more important than them, is the sun, universally recognized by early man as the most impressive, most awesome force of nature. The first passage printed below is one of Dupuis's attempts to dramatize for the reader the advent of solar worship and solar myth. The coming dawn and day are described from the imagined point of view of early man, and we are asked to understand and even to be present at the psychological moment of mythmaking. The section from Dupuis's own epitome of *Origine* that summarizes the argument that Hercules is the sun and his labors are allegories of his celestial passage, is the second selection here, and is an excellent example of Dupuis's ability to read astronomical events into any and all myths. Indeed Dupuis comes close to being the first monomythographer in his effort to relate almost all myth to the passage of the sun across the sky.

Other sections of the book identify Isis as the moon, Bacchus as the sun in his generative aspect, and Jason and Christ as two more sun-gods. All stories, poems, and scriptures are approached as allegories put up by silly poets or wicked priests as veils to cover elemental nature worship. Christianity is shown to be just another version of sun worship and, as the third selection below shows, Dupuis attacks Christianity with special malice. Indeed, as the work proceeds, Dupuis's anger rises, first against Christianity, then against all creeds, cults, churches, priests, and scriptures. Rant and scorn are at times elevated into Isaiah-like denunciations, at times debased into mere name-calling; but the dominant idea is that man has been tragically and needlesly betrayed by religion.

This is the foundation of all worship and every religion, which is putting man in relation with the gods, and Earth with the Heavens, in other words, that all organized worship, which is practised by the priests, has for its basis an ideal order of invisible beings, whose business is, to grant a chimerical succor through the intercession of sharpers.

Dupuis attacks all ideas of immortality and metempsychosis, and he equates all mysteries with plain fraudulence. The great praise of the French Revolution is that it has at long last delivered mankind from the grip of the priests and from their mumbo jumbo: Reason and Nature have replaced Faith and Superstition. Like Holbach before him, Dupuis finally conceded that if we want to worship something, we had best worship nature pure and simple.

The many editions and versions of Dupuis's major work attest to its influence. Destutt de Tracy and Dulaure spread Dupuis's ideas, Volney composed his *Ruines* after a conversation with Dupuis, John Adams and many others read him in America. His own wide reading and his inexhaustible references underpinned and lent credence to his pervasive disbelief; he is at last not only anti-clerical and anti-Christian, but anti-religious, anti-primitive, anti-immortality,

and of course, anti-myth. His great effort is to subdue myth to the enlightenment program; his great weakness is the vehemence that ends by remythologizing the just unveiled nature behind all myth. But perhaps this was inevitable, for one of the most interesting things about Dupuis's work on myth is his continual and deliberate effort to relate it to the present. The purpose of Dupuis's work is not the mere antiquarian illumination of the past, but the liberation of the present. And if all the old myths are swept away, revealing great nature itself, it will be that very nature, experienced in all the intensity of romanticism and revolution, that provides a starting point for new myths.

R.R.

REFERENCES   Our text is from Charles Dupuis, *The Origin of all religious worship* (New Orleans, 1872). This is a translation of Dupuis's own 1798 epitome of the longer *Origine de tous les cultes ou la Religion universelle* (Paris, 1794) which was issued in two formats, 3 volumes in quarto, and an Atlas, and 12 volumes in octavo. Dupuis's epitome appeared in 1798 in one volume.

See also deTracy, *Analyse raisonée de l'Origine de Tous les Cultes* (Paris, 1804), J. A. Dulaure, *Des Cultes qui ont précédé et amené l'îdolatrie et l'adoration des figures humaines* (Paris, 1805), and the same writer's *Des divinités génératrices, ou Du culte du phallus chez les anciens et les modernes* (Paris, 1805). Dupuis has been discussed by J. M. Robertson in *A History of Freethought* (London: Watts and Co., 1936) and by Frank Manuel in *The Eighteenth Century Confronts the Gods* (Cambridge: Harvard University Press, 1959), and in his *The New World of Henri Saint-Simon* (Cambridge: Harvard University Press, 1962).

Dupuis

from *The Origin of All Religious Worship*

Of the Great Divisions of Nature into
Active and Passive Causes and into
the Principles of Light and Darkness

IN THE midst of the shades of an
intensely dark night, when Heaven is
charged with thick and heavy clouds, when
all the bodies have disappeared before our
eyes, when we seem to live alone with ourselves and with the black shades surrounding us, what is then the measure of our
existence? How little does it differ from
complete nonentity, especially when not
surrounded in memory and thought with
the image of the objects, which broad daylight has shown us? All is dead for us and
in some respect, we ourselves are dead to
Nature. Who can give us life again and
draw our soul from that mortal lethargy,
which chains its activity to the shades of
chaos? A single ray of light can restore us
to ourselves and to entire Nature, which
seems as if it had withdrawn from us. Here
is the principle of our veritable existence,
without which our life would be only a
sensation of continued weariness. It is the
want of light in its creative energy, which
has been felt by all men, who have not
seen anything more dreadful, than its absence. Here is then the first Divinity, the
fiery splendour of which, spouting out
from the midst of Chaos, caused man and
the whole Universe to spring into exist-

ence according to the principles of the
theology of Orpheus and Moses. This is
that God *Bel* of the Chaldeans, the Oromaze of the Persians, whom they invoke
as the source of all the blessings of Nature,
whilst the origin of all the evil is placed
in darkness and in Ahriman its Chief.
They hold therefore Light in great veneration and stand in dread of Darkness.
Light is the life of the Universe, the friend
of man and his most agreeable companion; with it he never feels lonesome; he
looks for it as soon as missed, unless in
order to rest his tired limbs, he should
desire to withdraw from the spectacle of
the World and seek repose in sleep.

But how much is he annoyed, when he
awakes before daylight and is forced to
await its reappearance. How glad is he, as
soon as he has a glimpse of its first rays,
and when Aurora, whitening the horizon,
restores again to his sight all those pictures, which had disappeared in the shades
of night. He sees again those children of
the Earth, stretching out their gigantic
forms high into the air, those lofty mountains, crowning with their ridges his horizon, and forming the circular barrier,
which terminate the course of the Stars.
The earth slopes down towards their feet
and spreads out in vast plains, intersected
by rivers, and covered with meadows,
woodland and crops, the aspect of which

was hidden from his view a little while ago by that gloomy veil, which Aurora with beneficent hand is now tearing away. All Nature appears again entirely at the command of the Divinity which sheds the light, but the God of Day is hiding himself yet from the sight of man, in order that his eye might imperceptibly be accustomed to support the brilliant splendour of the rays of the God, whom Aurora comes to usher into the temple of the Universe, of which he is the father and the soul. The gate, by which he has to make his entrance, is already shaded with a thousand colors, and vermillion roses seem to be sown under his footsteps; the gold, mixing its splendour with the azure, forms the triumphal arch, under which the conqueror of night and darkness shall pass. Before him has disappeared the troop of Stars, and left him free passage through the fields of Olympus, of which he alone shall hold the scepter. Entire Nature awaits him; the birds celebrate his approach with their warbling, and the sound of their concerts reecho in the plains of the air, over which his chariot shall move, and which is already agitated by the sweet breath of his coursers; the tops of the trees are gently rocked by the fresh breeze, which rises in the East; the animals, which are not afraid of the proximity of man and which live under his roof, awaken with him and receive from Day and Aurora the signal, that they can seek again their food in the meadows and fields, the grass, plants, and flowers of which are wet with a gentle dew.

At last this beneficent God makes his appearance, surrounded with all his glory. His empire shall extend over the whole Earth, and His rays shall light up His altars. His majestic disk spreads in large waves the light and the heat, of which he is the great center. By degrees, as he ad-

vances in his career, Shadow his eternal rival, like Typhon and Ahriman, clinging to coarse matter and bodies which produce it, flies before him, always in the opposite direction decreasing by degrees as he rises and awaiting his retreat, in order to reunite with the gloomy night, in which the Earth is plunged again at the moment, when she sees no more the God, the father of Day and Nature. With a Giant's stride he has overcome the interval, which separates the East from the West, and he descends below the horizon as majestic as when he ascended. The trace of his step is still lit up by the light, which he leaves on the clouds, shaded with a thousand colors, and in the air, which he whitens and where the rays, which he sheds in the atmosphere some hours after his retreat, are broken manifoldly and in various ways, in order to accustom us to his absence and to spare us the terror of a sudden night. But finally the latter arrives imperceptibly, and already is her black pall spread over the Earth, which grieves for the loss of a beneficent father. . . .

(from Chap. IV, pp. 79–82)

An Explanation of the Heracleid or of the Sacred Poem on the Twelve Months and on the Sun, Worshipped under the Name of Hercules

As soon as man had attributed a soul to the World, with life and intelligence to each of its parts, when he had placed Angels, Genii, Gods in every Element, in each Star and especially in that beneficent luminary, which vivifies entire Nature, engenders the seasons and dispenses to the Earth that active heat, which brings forth all the blessings from its bosom and sets aside the evils, which the principle of darkness pours into matter, there remained only one step more to make, in order to put into action in sacred poems all the intelligences or spirits scattered over the Universe, giving them character and habits analogous to their nature, and creating as many personages, each of which played his part in those poetical fictions and religious songs, as if they had played them upon the brilliant stage of the World. Thence originated the poems on the Sun, which was described under the name of Hercules, Bacchus, Osiris, Theseus, Jason, &c., such as the Heracleid, the Dionysiacs, the Theseid, the Argonautics, poems, of which some have reached us complete, others only in part.

There is not one of the heroes of these various poems, who had not reference to the Sun, nor is there one of these songs, which was not a part of the songs on Nature, on the cycles, on the seasons and on the Luminary, which engenders them. Such is the nature of the poem on the twelve months, known by the name of songs on the twelve labors of Hercules or of the solstitial Sun.

Whatever may have been the opinions about Hercules, he was surely not a petty Grecian Prince, renowned for his romantic adventures, invested with all the charms of poetry, and sung from age to age by men, who had succeeded the heroic ages. It is the mighty luminary, which animates and fructifies the Universe, the Divinity of which has been honored everywhere by the erection of temples and altars, and consecrated in religious songs by all nations. From Meroë in Ethiopia, and Thebes in upper Egypt, to the British isles and to the snows of Scythia; from ancient Taprobane and Palibothra in the Indies to Cadiz and the shores of the Atlantic Ocean; from the forests of Germany, to the burning sands of Lybia, wherever the blessings of the Sun were experienced, there the worship of Hercules is found established; there are

sung the glorious deeds of this invincible God, who showed himself to man only, in order to deliver him from his evils, to purge the Earth of monsters and chiefly of tyrants, who may be classed amongst the greatest scourges, of which our weakness has to stand in fear. Many centuries before the epoch, which is assigned to the son of Alcmena or to the supposed hero of Tirynthia, as the time, when they made him live, Egypt and Phoenicia, which surely did not borrow their Gods from Greece, had erected temples to the Sun, under the name of Hercules, and had carried its worship to the island of Thasus and to Cadiz, where they had also consecrated a temple to the Year and to the Month, which divided it into twelve parts, or in other words, to the twelve labors, or twelve victories, which conducted Hercules to immortality.

It is under the name of Hercules Astrochyton, or of the God clad in a mantle of Stars, that the poet Nonnus designates this Sun-God, worshipped by the Tyrians. The titles of the King of Fire, of Lord of the World and of the Planets—of nourisher of mankind, of the God, whose glowing orb, revolves eternally around the Earth, and who while followed in his track by the Year, the daughter of Time and mother of the twelve Months, draws along in regular succession the seasons, which renew and reproduce themselves—are so many traits of the Sun, that we should recognize them, even if the poet had not given to his Hercules the name of Helios or the Sun. "It is," says he, "the same God, which is worshipped by many nations under different names: as Belus, on the shores of the Euphrates, as Ammon in Lybia, as Apis at Memphis, as Saturn in Arabia, as Jupiter in Assyria, as Serapis in Egypt, as Helios at Babylon, as Apollo at Delphi, as Aesculapius throughout

Greece, &c." Martianus Capella, in his magnificent hymn on the Sun, also the poet Ausonius and Macrobius confirm this multiplicity of names, which were given by different nations to this luminary. . . .

It is evident, that if Hercules is the Sun, as we have shown by the above cited authorities, that the fable of the twelve labors is a solar fable, which can have reference only to the twelve months and to the twelve signs, of which the Sun travels over one in each month. This inference shall become a demonstration by the comparison, which we shall make of each of the labors with each one of the months, or with the signs and constellations, which mark the division of time in the Heavens, during each of the months of the annual revolution.

Amongst the different epochs, at which formerly the year began, that of the summer solstice was one of the most remarkable. It was on the return of the Sun to this point, that the Greeks fixed the celebration of their Olympic feasts, the establishment of which was attributed to Hercules: this was the origin of the most ancient era of the Greeks. We shall there-

fore fix the departure of the Sun Hercules there, in its annual route. . . .

But before we shall compare month for month the series of the twelve labours with that of the Stars, which determine and mark the annual route of the Sun, it is well to observe, that the Ancients, in order to regulate their sacred and rural Calendars, employed not only the signs of the Zodiac, but more frequently also remarkable Stars, placed outside of the Zodiac, and the various constellations, which by their rising and setting indicated the place of the Sun in each sign. The proof of this will be found in the *Fastes of Ovid*, in Columella, and chiefly in the Ancient Calendars, which we have published as a sequel to our larger work. It is in conformity, with this known fact, that we shall draw the picture of the subjects of the twelve songs, compared with the constellations, which presided over the twelve months, in order to convince the reader, that the poem of the twelve labors is only a sacred calendar, embellished with all the charms, of which allegory and poetry made use of in these remote ages, in order to give soul and life to their fictions.

CALENDAR

First Month

Passage of the Sun under the sign of the celestial Lion, called the Lion of Nemea, fixed by the setting in the morning of the *Ingeniculus* or the constellation of the celestial Hercules.

Second Month

The Sun enters the sign of the Virgin, marked by the total setting of the celestial

POEM

Title Of The First Canto Or Of The First Labor

Victory of Hercules over the Nemean Lion.

Second Labor

Hercules slays the Lernean Hydra, the heads of which grew together again, whilst

Hydra, called the Lernean Hydra, the head of which rises again in the morning with the Cancer.

he is cramped in his labor by a crawfish or Cancer.

Third Month

Passage of the Sun at the commencement of autumn to the sign of the Balance, fixed by the rising of the celestial Centaur, the same, whose hospitality Hercules enjoyed. This constellation is represented in the Heavens, with a leather bottle, filled with wine, and a Thyrsus adorned with vine leaves and grapes, image of the season's product. Then rises in the evening the celestial Bear, called by others the Boar and the animal of Erymanthia.

Third Labor

A Centaur gives hospitality to Hercules; his fight with the Centaurs for a cask of wine; victory of Hercules over them; he slays a terrible wild Boar, which devastated the fields of Erymanthia.

Fourth Month

The Sun enters the sign of the Scorpion, fixed by the setting of Cassiope, a constellation, which was formerly represented by a Hind.

Fourth Labor

Triumph of Hercules over a Hind with golden horns and feet of brass, which Hercules took on the Sea shore, where it was reposing.

Fifth Month

The Sun enters the sign of the Sagittarius, consecrated to the Goddess Diana, whose temple was at Stymphalia, in which the Stymphalian Birds were to be seen. This passage is fixed by the rising of three birds, the Vulture, the Swan, and the Eagle, pierced by the arrow of Hercules.

Fifth Labor

Hercules gives chase near Stymphalia to the Birds of the Stymphalian lake, which are represented in number three in the medals of Perinthus.

Sixth Month

Passage of the Sun to the sign of the Goat or the Capricorn, the son of Neptune according to some, and grandson to the Sun, according to others. This passage is marked by the setting of the River of the Aquarius, which flows under the stable of the Capricorn, and the source of which is in the hands of Aristeus, son of the river Peneus.

Sixth Labor

Hercules cleans the Stables of Augias, the son of the Sun, or according to others the son of Neptune. He makes the river Peneus run through it.

Seventh Month

The Sun enters the sign of Waterman or Aquarius, and at the place in the Heavens, where the full Moon was found every year, which served to denote the epoch for the celebration of the Olympic games. This passage was marked by the Vulture, placed in the Heavens alongside the constellation called Prometheus, at the same time that the celestial Bull of Pasiphae and Marathon culminated in the meridian, at the setting of the Horse Arion or Pegasus.

Seventh Labor

Hercules arrives at Elis. He was mounted on the horse Arion; he drags along with him the Bull of Creta, beloved by Pasiphae, which afterwards ravaged the plains of Marathon. He institutes the celebration of the Olympic Games, where he is the first to enter the lists; he kills the Vulture of Prometheus.

Eighth Month

Passage of the Sun to the sign of the Fishes, fixed by the rising in the morning of the celestial Horse, the head of which is bearing on Aristeus, or on the Aquarius the son of Cyrene.

Eighth Labor

Hercules makes the conquest of the Horses of Diomedes, the son of Cyrene.

Ninth Month

The Sun enters the sign of the Ram, consecrated to Mars, and which is also called the Ram of the Golden Fleece. This passage is marked by the rising of the ship Argo, by the setting of Andromeda or of the celestial Woman and of her Girdle; by that of the Whale; by the rising of Medusa, by the setting of the Queen Cassiope.

Ninth Labor

Hercules embarks on board the ship Argo, in order to make the conquest of the Ram of the Golden Fleece; he fights with martial women, daughters of Mars, from whom he takes a magnificent girdle and liberates a Maiden exposed to a Whale or a Sea-monster, like the one to which Andromeda, the daughter of Cassiope was exposed.

Tenth Month

The Sun leaves the Ram of Phrixus and enters the sign of the Bull. This transit is marked by the setting of Orion, who was in love with the Atlantides, or with the Pleiades; by that of Bootes, the Driver of the Oxen of Icarus; by that of the River Eridanus; by the rising of the Atlantides and by that of the Goat, the wife of Faunus.

Tenth Labor

Hercules after his voyage with the Argonauts in order to conquer the Ram, returns to Hesperia, to make the conquest of the Oxen of Geryon; he also kills a tyranical Prince, who persecuted the Atlantides, and arrives in Italy at the house of Faunus at the rising of the Pleiades.

Eleventh Month

The sun enters the sign of the Twins, which transit is indicated by the setting of the Dog Procyon; by the cosmical rising of the great Dog, followed by the stretching out of the Hydra and by the rising in the evening of the celestial Swan.

Eleventh Labor

Hercules conquers a terrible Dog, the tail of which was a Serpent, and the head of which was bristling with serpents; he defeats also Cygnus, or the Prince Swan, at the time in which the Dog-star scorches the Earth with its fire.

Twelfth Month

The Sun enters the sign of the Cancer, which corresponds with the last month, indicated by the setting of the Stream of the Waterman, and of the Centaur, by the rising of the Shepherd and his Sheep, at the time when the constellation of Hercules Ingeniculus is descending towards the occidental regions, called Hesperia, followed by the Polar Dragon, the guardian of the Apples growing in the garden of the Hesperides; which Dragon he puts under his feet, as marked in the sphere, and which falls near him towards the setting.

Twelfth Labor

Hercules travels in Hesperia, in order to gather Golden Apples, guarded by a Dragon, which, in our spheres, is near the pole, according to others, in order to carry off sheep with a Golden Fleece. He is preparing to make a sacrifice and puts on a robe dyed in the blood of a Centaur, whom he had slain at the passage of a river. By this robe he is consumed with fire; he dies and ends thus his mortal career, in order to resume his youth in Heaven and to enjoy there immortality.

This is the comparative picture of the cantos of the poem of the twelve labors and of the celestial aspects during the twelve months of the annual revolution, achieved by the Sun under the name of the indefatigable Hercules. The reader may judge of the relation, which may exist between the poem and the calendar, and to observe up to what point they may agree. . . .

Even if the Ancients had not told us, that Hercules was the Sun; even if the universality of its worship did not show plainly, that a petty Grecian Prince could never have had such an astonishing good luck in the religious World, and that such a high destiny did not belong to a mortal, but alone to that God, whose blessings are felt over the whole Universe, it would be sufficient to understand thoroughly all the

relations of this double picture, in order to come with the greatest verisimilitude to the conclusion, that the hero of the poem is the God, who measures the time, who conducts the year, who regulates the seasons and the months, and who distributes the light, heat and life throughout Nature. When the adventures of a man or a prince are there looked for, it becomes a monstrous story, which never agrees with any chronology at all: but when we discover in it the God, who fecundates the Universe, then it becomes at once a grand and ingenious poem. All is motion, all is life there. The solstitial Sun is there represented with all the attributes of power, which it has acquired at that epoch, and which contains in him the depository of the universal power of the World; he is clothed with the skin of the Lion and armed with the club. Boldly he strides onward in the career, which he is by Nature's eternal law obliged to travel. . . .

There is still another inference to be drawn from this comparative picture, which has demonstrated, that Hercules was not a mortal, who was raised to the rank of the Gods on account of his courage and of the benefits, which he had conferred on mankind, nor that the events of his pretended life were historical facts, but that they were simply astronomical realities. That conclusion is, that the testimony of many centuries and of many nations in favor of the existence, as mortals, of the heroes of the different religions, whose memory is consecrated by worship, and by poems and legends, is not always a sure guarantee of their historical reality. The example of Hercules puts this inference in its full evidence. The Greeks very generally believed in the existence of Hercules as a Prince, who was born, and had lived and died amongst them, after having travelled all over the Universe. . . .

Temples, statues, altars, feasts, solemn games, hymns, sacred traditions, scattered over different countries, reminded the Greeks of the sublime deeds of the hero . . . and also of the blessings, which he had bestowed on the Universe in general, and on the Greeks in particular; yet, notwithstanding all this, we have just seen, that the great Hercules . . . is the great God of all nations; that strong and fecundating Sun, which engenders the Seasons and measures time in the annual circle of the zodiac, divided into twelve sections, which designate and to which are united the various animals, representing the constellations, the only monsters, which the hero of the poem had fought.

What matter for reflection ought it be for those, who are drawing a great argument from the evidence of one or several nations, and of several centuries, in order to establish a historical fact, chiefly in matter of religion, where the very first duty is to believe without examination. The philosophy of a single individual in this case is better than the opinion of many thousands of men, and of many centuries of credulity. Those reflections will find their application in the solar fable, invented on the chief of the twelve apostles, or in other words on the hero of the legend of the Christians, and eighteen centuries of imposture and ignorance will not destroy the striking likeness, which this fable has with the other sacred romances, which have been made on the Sun, called by Plato the only son of God. The universal benefactor of the World—when he quitted the skin of the solstitial Lion, in order to take that of the equinoctial Lamb of Spring—shall not escape our researches under this new disguise, and the Lion of the tribe of Judah shall still be the Sun. . . .   (pp. 86–98)

An Explanation of the Fable, in which the Sun is the Object of Worship under the Name of Christ

When we shall have shown,—that the pretended history of a God, born of a Virgin at the winter solstice, who resuscitates at Easter or at the equinox of spring, after having descended into hell; of a God, who has twelve apostles in his train, whose leader has all the attributes of Janus; of a God-conqueror of the Prince of Darkness, who restores to mankind the dominion of Light, and who redeems the evils of Nature—is merely a solar fable, like all those, which we have analysed, it will be quite as indifferent, or of as little consequence to examine, whether there ever existed a man by the name of Christ, as it would be to enquire, whether some Prince was called

Hercules, provided it will be conclusively demonstrated, that the being, consecrated by worship under the name of Christ, is the Sun, and that the marvelousness of the legend or of the same poem, has that luminary for its object, because it would seem then to be proved, that the Christians are mere worshippers of the Sun, and that their priests have the same religion as those of Peru, whom they have caused to be put to death.   (from Chap. IX)

WILLIAM BLAKE

[1757–1827]

OF ALL the English poets who devoted themselves to myth, Blake has probably received the most attention and been most exhaustively explored. In his own time and for some decades after his death, he was of course largely neglected by the main line of English literary development. Even as his reputation began to grow toward the end of the nineteenth century, he was still considered a remarkably isolated figure, a solitary prophet whose mythic and poetic concerns seemed appropriate more to our times than to his. But since the criticism of Damon, Percival, Frye, and others, it has become increasingly clear that Blake can be seriously understood only by grasping his own intellectual, religious, and mythic tradition and roots. It has become clear, too, that however labyrinthine his symbolism or bewildering his mythology, these difficulties are not mainly due to his eccentric erudition or private system. Blake is no longer considered to be "outside" of some single main tradition of English poetry. He is rather at the center of one of those main traditions—one that has been increasingly obscured and neglected from Blake's time on.

Even a summary list of Blake's sources or kinships is formidable. These must include at least the heterodox teachings of Christianity; teachings assimilated also from hermetic, gnostic, Cabalist, alchemical, Orphic, and Neoplatonic mysteries; from minds like Paracelsus, Boehme, and Swedenborg; and from the mythology of British druidism, still excitedly pursued by many in Blake's time, such as Davies or Evans or Williams, and reaching back to Stukeley and Milton. Once the outlines of this learning come into sight, Blake is seen to be no less original as poet and mythologer, but only less isolated. To all this must be added his large knowledge and interests in contemporary scholarship and myth study. He is much influenced by the revival of classicism as he found it, for example, in Winckelmann (translated by Blake's friend, Fuseli) and in friends such as Flaxman; he is absorbed in the Platonic and Neoplatonic translations by Thomas Taylor (who gave the first complete English translation of Plato in Blake's time); he is versed in such mythic works as Mallet's *Northern Antiquities,* in Percy and ballads, and in the preromantic experiments with mythic themes or moods in poetry by Gray or Macpherson; and Blake exploited at least the details of a Dupuis or Bryant. Naturally, Blake's sources explain only part of his achievement; without that background, however, he can only be misread. An adequate view of Blake demands that he be seen as a consummation of older, as well as a pioneer of new, mythic and mythopoetic concerns. It is crucial, too, to see that Blake's effort is centrally akin to the whole poetic-critical fascination with myth, appearing during his time in England but also in Germany and elsewhere.

But consideration of Blake as a mythologizing poet might fairly begin with how original and bold his work seems at first sight. Coming shortly after the genteel preromantic "mythic" criticism of a Hurd or Blair, or the conventionalist mythic theories of a Jones or Bryant, or the mildly mythic poetry of a Gray, Blake seems astonishingly new in his use of myth.

Of the major European poets, only Goethe precedes Blake's new mythopoetic efforts. Blake's first characteristic work appears between 1788 and about 1796, with the *Songs of Innocence* and *Songs of Experience, The Marriage of Heaven and Hell,* and his first ambitious attempts at mythopoesis—such works as *The Book of Thel, The First Book of Urizen,* or *America*—what Blake called "Prophecies" or "Visions." Probably in 1796 he began a much more elaborate mythic poem, *The Four Zoas*: that is, the four eternals, or eternal aspects of the divine and human involved in the creation or fall of man and eternity, from which "nature," "history," and traditional religion emerged. This poem remained unfinished, but provided the torso and model for his greatest mythic poems, *Milton* (perhaps between 1804–1810) and *Jerusalem* (perhaps 1804–1820). The scale and complexity with which Blake developed his mythology simply baffles any summary description. He created an entire new set of spiritual types and symbols, such as Los, Orc, Urizen, Luvah, Tharmas, and others; a new hierarchy of beings, Eternals, Spectres, Emanations, and so on; and new spiritual realms such as Ulro or Golgonooza. Taken together, his poems set forth a new cosmogony, and a new interpretation of man's creation, fall, and redemption. But "new" in Blake always means in part a new emphasis on or selection from such older "sources" as mentioned.

If Blake stands alone in his time in a real way, this is not mainly because his aims were uniquely visionary or mythopoetic. That is as true of Hölderlin or Wordsworth. Blake, however, tries something not really attempted by any other English or even European poet of his time or before. He single-mindedly and successfully sets out to create nothing less than a complete mythic *system*—rivalling Scripture itself in scope and grandeur. As "Los," Blake's mythic figure of the poet, proclaims in *Jerusalem,* "I must create a System, or be enslav'd by another Man's." Certainly other contemporaries, such as Novalis, sketched such systems; but beside Blake's grandly elaborated visions, Novalis's "system" seems only small and bare. Coleridge may have had Blake's relentless systematizing of symbols in mind when he said that Blake's poetry bespoke a "despotism of symbols." Where most romantic poets, English and German, mythicized mainly in the lyric mode with occasional ventures into larger forms, Blake at his greatest is almost entirely a poet of mythic epics, each of which forms part of a greater whole.

Like other mythologists, particularly the German romantics, Blake explicitly views myth more as a prophetic or religious agency than as an aesthetic mode. Indeed, Blake's systematic poetizing does what the early Friedrich Schlegel's universal mythopoesis only promised. But here again, Blake remains apart. However universal or cosmic his mythologizing, he nonetheless—as several critics have maintained—always needs to be seen as an English poet. Certainly, Blake goes further than any contemporary in seating myth in the present moment and everyday reality. He weaves myth into and out of explicit political and social events and issues of the day, even out of the very London streets. If Wordsworth found a way to do something similar in *The Prelude,* Blake goes beyond this to integrate all such material into a genuinely cosmic system. English, biblical, Nordic, and Indian myth and history are blended into one symbolic whole. "Albion," for example, is thus the Adam Kadmon of the Cabalists, the druid "Wicker Man" of religious sacrifice, but also recognizably and specifically the war-tormented England of the Napoleonic Wars. No poet in his time goes so far in extending the meaning or province of myth: Felpham can gain mythic parity with Egypt, since Blake does not reserve mythic privilege to special times or places. Nor, for all his attractiveness to later modern mythic interests, does Blake finally or mainly find his new mythology in decisively modern spiritual or personal experiences or insights, like Schlegel and Wordsworth.

Blake remains firmly within the Christian tradition—again with a difference. It was of course a staple of romantic myth, especially German, to affirm Christianity anew by returning to "true" primal mythic origins in turn identified as in some way most deeply Christian. Blake seeks to do the same, but through unfamiliar means. He claims to find support for a mythic revision of Christian tradition from within the Christian tradition on its heresiarchal side. Blake's image of Christ can seem closer to the gnostic rebelling against the tyrant-God, or Neoplatonic emanation, than to Old Testament creating *ex nihilo*. (Kathleen Raine goes so far as to say Blake created the first Christian polytheism—which might provoke an interesting comparison to Hölderlin.)

From such a heterodox Christian view, Blake could agree with other mythologists that there was a golden age or true revelation from which all myths and religions derive. The Bible, though indispensable, is only a dimmed memorial of that time, and needs correcting, as do all other myths, histories, and faiths. Guided by the primal oneness of the divine, such a correction is possible. So is a kind of comparative mythology, which equates or analogizes similar elements in all myths. Thus, Blake can treat as one continuing tradition the Old Testament, King

Arthur and English history, and Eddaic mythology; thus, he moves easily through all "occult" writings—the Smaragdine Tablet of Hermes, Jehovah's tablets, even Newton's laws; thus, Greek myth derives from and supplements Scripture. Thus, too, Blake melds Christ the Redeemer with Orphism and the Platonic Demiurge, the rebel or Christ with Prometheus or Balder.

Moreover, Blake can describe his own poetic visions as continuing the one enduring, although obscured, truth. In his "Descriptive Catalogue," for example, he says his two pictures of Pitt and Nelson are

compositions of a mythological cast, similar to those Apotheoses of Persian, Hindoo, and Egyptian Antiquity, which are still preserved on rude monuments, being copies from some stupendous originals now lost. . . .

"Vision" or "Prophecy" is Blake's most triumphant word, signalling his confidence at having penetrated to those "stupendous originals." To have done that meant for Blake to have penetrated the falsities of pagan myth to reach the truer origins of Christianity. But to have so urgently felt the need to recover those origins at all, to have discarded the orthodox traditions of Christianity as a reliable guide to those beginnings, and to have relied instead on heterodox wisdom and poetic inspiration —in retrospect, that could show Blake clearly allied with the romantic mythic movement of his time. But in point of priority, in singularity of insight and approach, he remains apart from the other romantics: as individual, unclassifiable, and ambitious as his only early peer, Goethe.

B.F.

REFERENCES　Our texts are from *The Poetry and Prose of William Blake,* ed. David V. Erdman, commentary by Harold Bloom (New York: Doubleday, 1965). Some useful commentaries are: D. J. Sloss and J. P. R. Wallis,

The Prophetic Writings of William Blake, 2 vols. (Oxford: Clarendon Press, 1926; reprinted 1957, 1964); D. Saurat, *Blake and Modern Thought* (New York, 1929); M. O. Percival, *William Blake's Circle of Destiny* (New York, 1938); Northrop Frye, *Fearful Symmetry* (Princeton: Princeton University Press, 1947); E. B. Hungerford, *Shores of Darkness* (New York: World, 1963), Part One; Peter F. Fisher, *The Valley of Vision* (Toronto: University of Toronto Press, 1961); Kathleen Raine, *Blake and Tradition,* 2 vols. (Princeton: Princeton University Press, 1969); Desiree Hirst, *Hidden Riches: Traditional Symbolism from the Renaissance to Blake* (New York: Barnes and Noble, 1964); Ruthven Todd, *Tracks in the Snow* (London: The Grey Walls Press, 1946), pp. 29–60, "William Blake and the Eighteenth-Century Mythologists."

BLAKE

FROM *Jerusalem*

JERUSALEM the Emanation of the Giant Albion! Can it be? Is it a Truth that the Learned have explored? Was Britain the Primitive Seat of the Patriarchal Religion? If it is true: my title-page is also True, that Jerusalem was & is the Emanation of the Giant Albion. It is True, and cannot be controverted. Ye are united O ye Inhabitants of Earth in One Religion. The Religion of Jesus: the most Ancient, the Eternal: & the Everlasting Gospel— The Wicked will turn it to Wickedness, the Righteous to Righteousness. Amen! Huzza! Selah!

"All things Begin & End in Albions Ancient Druid Rocky Shore."

Your Ancestors derived their origin from Abraham, Heber, Shem, and Noah, who were Druids: as the Druid Temples (which are the Patriarchal Pillars & Oak Groves) over the whole Earth witness to this day.

You have a tradition, that Man anciently containd in his mighty limbs all things in Heaven & Earth: this you received from the Druids. "But now the Starry Heavens are fled from the mighty limbs of Albion."

Albion was the Parent of the Druids; & in his Chaotic State of Sleep[,] Satan & Adam & the whole World was Created by the Elohim.

The fields from Islington to Marybone,
To Primrose Hill and Saint Johns Wood:
    Were builded over with pillars of gold,
And there Jerusalems pillars stood.

Her Little-ones ran on the fields
The Lamb of God among them seen
    And fair Jerusalem his Bride:
Among the little meadows green.

Pancrass & Kentish-town repose
Among her golden pillars high:
    Among her golden arches which
Shine upon the starry sky.

The Jews-harp-house & the Green Man;
The Ponds where Boys to bathe delight:
    The fields of Cows by Willans farm:
Shine in Jerusalems pleasant sight.

She walks upon our meadows green:
The Lamb of God walks by her side:

And every English Child is seen,
Children of Jesus & his Bride,

  Forgiving trespasses and sins
Lest Babylon with cruel Og,
  With Moral & Self-righteous Law
Should Crucify in Satans Synagogue!

  What are those golden Builders doing
Near mournful ever-weeping Paddington
  Standing above that mighty Ruin
Where Satan the first victory won.

Where Albion slept beneath the Fatal Tree
And the Druids golden Knife,
  Rioted in human gore,
In Offerings of Human Life

  They groan'd aloud on London Stone
They groan'd aloud on Tyburns Brook
  Albion gave his deadly groan,
And all the Atlantic Mountains shook

· · · · · ·

(from Chap. 2, "To the Jews")

FROM *"A Descriptive Catalogue"*

THE TWO Pictures of Nelson and Pitt are compositions of a mythological cast, similar to those Apotheoses of Persian, Hindoo, and Egyptian Antiquity, which are still preserved on rude monuments, being copies from some stupendous originals now lost or perhaps buried till some happier age. The Artist having been taken in vision into the ancient republics, monarchies, and patriarchates of Asia, has seen those wonderful originals called in the Sacred Scriptures the Cherubim, which were sculptured and painted on walls of Temples, Towers, Cities, Palaces, and erected in the highly cultivated states of Egypt, Moab, Edom, Aram, among the Rivers of Paradise, being originals from which the Greeks and Hetrurians copied Hercules, Farnese, Venus of Medicis, Apollo Belvidere, and all the grand works of ancient art. They were executed in a very superior style to those justly admired copies, being with their accompaniments terrific and grand in the highest degree. The Artist has endeavoured to emulate the grandeur of those seen in his vision, and to apply it to modern Heroes, on a smaller scale.

No man can believe that either Homer's Mythology, or Ovid's, were the production of Greece, or of Latium; neither will any one believe, that the Greek statues, as they are called, were the invention of Greek Artists; perhaps the Torso is the only original work remaining; all the rest are evidently copies, though fine ones, from greater works of the Asiatic Patriarchs. The Greek Muses are daughters of Mnemosyne, or Memory, and not of Inspiration or Imagination, therefore not authors of such sublime conceptions. Those wonderful originals seen in my visions, were some of them one hundred feet in height; some were painted as pictures, and some carved as basso relievos, and some as groupes of statues, all containing mythological and recondite meaning, where more is meant than meets the eye. The Artist wishes it was now the fashion to make such monuments, and then he should not doubt of having a national commission to execute these two Pictures on a scale that is suitable to the grandeur of the nation, who is the parent of his heroes, in high finished fresco, where the colours would be as pure and as permanent as precious stones though the figures were one hundred feet in height.   (from Number II)

The characters of Chaucer's Pilgrims are the characters which compose all ages and nations: as one age falls, another rises, different to mortal sight, but to immortals only the same; for we see the same characters repeated again and again, in animals, vegetables, minerals, and in men; nothing new occurs in identical existence; Accident ever varies, Substance can never suffer change nor decay.

Of Chaucer's characters, as described in his Canterbury Tales, some of the names or titles are altered by time, but the characters themselves for ever remain unaltered, and consequently they are the physiognomies or lineaments of universal human life, beyond which Nature never steps. . . .

The Plowman is simplicity itself, with wisdom and strength for its stamina. Chaucer has divided the ancient character of Hercules between his Miller and his Plowman. Benevolence is the plowman's great characteristic, he is thin with excessive labour, and not with old age, as some have supposed.

"He would thresh and thereto dike and
    delve
For Christe's sake, for every poore
    wight,
Withouten hire, if it lay in his might."

Visions of these eternal principles or characters of human life appear to poets, in all ages; the Grecian gods were the ancient Cherubim of Phoenicia; but the Greeks, and since them the Moderns, have neglected to subdue the gods of Priam. These Gods are visions of the eternal attributes, or divine names, which, when erected into gods, become destructive to humanity. They ought to be the servants, and not the masters of man, or of society. They ought to be made to sacrifice to Man, and not man compelled to sacrifice to them; for when separated from man or humanity, who is Jesus the Saviour, the vine of eternity, they are thieves and rebels, they are destroyers.

The Plowman of Chaucer is Hercules in his supreme eternal state, divested of his spectrous shadow; which is the Miller, a terrible fellow, such as exists in all times and places, for the trial of men, to astonish every neighbourhood, with brutal strength and courage, to get rich and powerful to curb the pride of Man.

(from Number III)

The three general classes of men who are represented by the most Beautiful, the most Strong, and the most Ugly, could not be represented by any historical facts but those of our own country, the Ancient Britons; without violating costume. The Britons (say historians) were naked civilized men, learned, studious, abstruse in thought and contemplation; naked, simple, plain, in their acts and manners; wiser than after-ages. They were overwhelmed by brutal arms all but a small remnant; Strength, Beauty, and Ugliness escaped the wreck, and remain for ever unsubdued, age after age.

The British Antiquities are now in the Artist's hands; all his visionary contemplations, relating to his own country and its ancient glory, when it was as it again shall be, the source of learning and inspiration. Arthur was a name for the constellation Arcturus, or Bootes, the Keeper of the North Pole. And all the fables of Arthur and his round table; of the warlike naked Britons; of Merlin; of Arthur's conquest of the whole world; of his death, or sleep, and promise to return again; of the Druid monuments, or temples; of the pavement of Watling-street; of London stone; of the caverns in Cornwall, Wales, Derbyshire, and Scotland; of the Giants of Ireland and Britain; of the elemental beings, called by us by the general name of Fairies; and of these three who escaped, namely, Beauty, Strength, and Ugliness. Mr. B. has in his hands poems of the highest antiquity. Adam was a Druid, and Noah; also Abraham was called to succeed the Druidical age, which began to turn allegoric and mental signification into corporeal command, whereby human sacrifice would have depopulated the earth. All these things are written in Eden. The artist is an inhabitant of that happy country; and if every thing goes on as it has begun, the world of vegetation and generation may expect to be opened again to Heaven, through Eden, as it was in the beginning.

The Strong man represents the human sublime. The Beautiful man represents the human pathetic, which was in the wars of Eden divided into male and female. The Ugly man represents the human reason. They were originally one man, who was fourfold; he was self-divided, and his real humanity slain on the stems of generation, and the form of the fourth was like the Son of God. How he became divided is a subject of great sublimity and pathos. The Artist has written it under inspiration, and will, if God please, publish it; it is voluminous, and contains the ancient history of Britain, and the world of Satan and of Adam.

In the mean time he has painted this Picture, which supposes that in the reign of that British Prince, who lived in the fifth century, there were remains of those naked Heroes, in the Welch Mountains; they are there now, Gray saw them in the person of his bard on Snowdon; there they dwell in naked simplicity; happy is he who can see and converse with them above the shadows of generation and death. The giant Albion, was Patriarch of the Atlantic; he is the Atlas of the Greeks, one of those the Greeks called Titans. The stories of Arthur are the acts of Albion, applied to

a Prince of the fifth century, who conquered Europe, and held the Empire of the world in the dark age, which the Romans never again recovered. In this Picture, believing with Milton, the ancient British History, Mr. B. has done, as all the ancients did, and as all the moderns, who are worthy of fame, given the historical fact in its poetical vigour; so as it always happens, and not in that dull way that some Historians pretend, who being weakly organized themselves, cannot see either miracle or prodigy; all is to them a dull round of probabilities and possibilities; but the history of all times and places is nothing else but improbabilities and impossibilities; what we should say was impossible if we did not see it always before our eyes.

The antiquities of every Nation under Heaven, is no less sacred than that of the Jews. They are the same thing as Jacob Bryant, and all antiquaries have proved. How other antiquities came to be neglected and disbelieved, while those of the Jews are collected and arranged, is an enquiry, worthy of both the Antiquarian and the Divine. All had originally one language, and one religion, this was the religion of Jesus, the everlasting Gospel. Antiquity preaches the Gospel of Jesus. The reasoning historian, turner and twister of causes and consequences, such as Hume, Gibbon and Voltaire; cannot with all their artifice, turn or twist one fact or disarrange self evident action and reality. Reasons and opinions concerning acts, are not history. Acts themselves alone are history, and these are neither the exclusive property of Hume, Gibbon nor Voltaire, Echard, Rapin, Plutarch, nor Herodotus. Tell me the Acts, O historian, and leave me to reason upon them as I please; away with your reasoning and your rubbish.

(from Number V)

FROM *"A Vision of the Last Judgment"*

THE LAST JUDGMENT is not Fable or Allegory but Vision Fable or Allegory are a totally distinct & inferior kind of Poetry. Vision or Imagination is a Representation of what Eternally Exists. Really & Unchangeably. Fable or Allegory is Formd by the daughters of Memory. Imagination is Surrounded by the daughters of Inspiration who in the aggregate are calld Jerusalem. . . . The Hebrew Bible & the Gospel of Jesus are not Allegory but Eternal Vision or Imagination of All that Exists. . . .

Let it. here be Noted that the Greek Fables originated in Spiritual Mystery & Real Vision and Real Visions Which are lost & clouded in Fable & Alegory . . . ⟨while⟩ the Hebrew Bible & the Greek Gospel are Genuine Preservd by the Saviour's Mercy The Nature of my Work is Visionary or Imaginative it is an Endeavour to Restore ⟨what the Ancients calld⟩ the Golden Age*   (pp. 544–545)

* Blake's text is here reproduced as in the Erdman edition.—Ed.

PART THREE

The Nineteenth Century to 1860

THERE ARE SEVERAL WAYS TO DESCRIBE THE ENORMOUS IMPACT the study of myth had on the first half of the nineteenth century; indeed, both mythology itself (that is to say, bodies of myth) and mythography (the study of myth) have a three-fold character during this time. Myth is in one sense simply a body of knowledge consisting of collections of myths, of detailed knowledge of myths, and of investigation into the narrative, linguistic, and historical particulars of these myths. In another sense, myth is assumed to be a creative process, a mode of the imagination usually directed toward art or literature. And in a third sense, myth is seen, by the romantics especially, to have a religious quality; myth becomes a way of redeeming modern man and restoring him to his early simplicity—his original and primeval union with God and nature.

As a body of knowledge, myth increased during the early nineteenth century by the expanded knowledge of Indian, Egyptian, and Polynesian mythology and by the expansion of philology, while the study of myth became increasingly sophisticated and increasingly central to the study of history, language, and culture. As a mode of the imagination, mythopoesis became for the nineteenth-century writer a common activity, or at least a frequent goal. From Goethe and Friedrich Schlegel to Thoreau and Whitman, writers called for and got new myths for modern man and heroic literature for the modern adventure. Myth is a major concern of romantic literature, as

Rene Wellek and M. H. Abrams have insisted; it has even been described as one of the distinguishing characteristics of romantic writing. Allied to myth as literature as well as to myth as religion, the new interest in symbolism and symbolic communication developed strongly in this period.

The religious quality of romantic mythic concern—and one is using "religious" here in a broad sense—finds expression in the gradual movement away from a rationally apprehended universal culture to a localized national culture, in a growing renewal of faith in natural and spontaneous ways of life, in the new optimism about humanity and its democratic experiments in France and America, and in the remarkable connections that persist, especially in Germany, among philosophy, religion, and myth. Perhaps this third or religious quality of myth may be best appreciated if we say that myth was a major vehicle by which Christianity was secularized into romanticism, and that in a wholly secular way, myth was a major bridge between Augustan or enlightenment classicism and romantic classicism.

During the first half of the nineteenth century, then, many fields of learning, many artistic aims, and much philosophical and religious thought converged on the subject of myth. German romanticism, a movement of short duration and great intensity and complexity, lies behind many nineteenth-century developments in myth and has therefore been treated below as an entity, emphasizing the interdependence of German romantic art and thought, the way these men took myth for granted, and the new seriousness with which the subject was treated. The short essay on the German romantics also stresses the many and strong connections between myth and the new organic views about man, nature, and history proposed by German philosophical thought.

Friedrich Schlegel's work shows the impact of mythic thought on literary criticism; the argument is that an understanding of the real nature of myth (as a synthesizing force) will lead the critic to a new and higher position from which he can make more comprehensive syntheses. This interest in myth also led Schlegel to call for a new kind of art that would embrace, subsume, and synthesize everything. The primal unity that can still be glimpsed in myth is the means by which a new unity can be forged. Another way to put this is to call, as Schlegel did, for writers to create new myths. It was, however, through August Schlegel, the most moderate of the German romantics, that the new organic view of myth spread most influentially beyond Germany to Europe, England, and America. August Schlegel's well-known lectures on dramatic literature emphasized the element of myth in Greek tragedy; and he also argued that the modern poet may either work in the spirit of myth, creating new stories, or use the old myths, whether or not he believes in them, for poetic purposes.

The writings of Hölderlin and Novalis show how these new and extreme

versions of myth can be used in poetry. Hölderlin, indeed, is an example
of how far one could go in regarding ancient Greek myth as still-vital religion
—an example of the great poet whose work is inconceivable apart from myth;
and his emphasis on the dark, tragic aspects of myth give him a profundity
not always associated with mythological poetry. For Novalis, poetry is also
closely tied to myth. Both these poets are closely involved with other German
writers and thinkers, and both are strongly marked by the idealist and the
organicist aspects of the new German philosophy during this period.

In the work of Majer, and in Friedrich Schlegel's Indic work, the impact
on Germany of Indian myth and religious thought becomes evident. India
was widely taken to be the cradle of man and the original fountain of religion
or myth; and German romanticism saw itself, to a rather large extent, as a
renaissance of Eastern thought and religion, though Schlegel later turned
against the nihilism he came increasingly to see in Indic thought.

Joseph Görres also points to India as the ancient source of myth; but
Görres's difficult style, his indifference to fact, and his mystical streak (coupled
with a patriotic urge that began to warp Herder's emphasis on the *Volk* into
something less noble) led Görres to invoke an Indic and mythic oneness for
the modern German spirit. Görres's utterance is near-orphic: "man is the great
creative word spoken by the earth." Görres influenced Friedrich Creuzer,
whose great work, the *Symbolik,* also had for its historical thesis the by now
routine idea about Indic origins. The *Symbolik,* however, is the first modern
work to deal exclusively and specifically with symbolism and myth, to make
a clear distinction between them, and to argue, in a very modern way, that
myths are a species of symbolic communication.

Wilhelm and Jacob Grimm show how the study of folklore springs from
the romantic concern with myth. Arguing that myth was a residue of an
earlier nobler state of man, Jacob Grimm refused to posit a single earlier
state of man and instead posited many coequal early states of man. Thus the
German earlier age was equivalent to the Greek earlier age and the mythology
of Germany was just as good as (and for a good German, better than) that
of Greece. But all that remained of German myth was buried in folklore and
fairy tales, to which Grimm then turned. Grimm's method could of course
be turned on any national body of folk material, and the work of Thomas
Keightley shows how the Grimms' idea were applied in England.

George Faber, an obscure English divine, is included for the rather startling
manner in which he anticipates modern archetype criticism. His work also
shows that one important root of such criticism lies in the Christian tradition
of typological criticism. Leigh Hunt shows the essential sanity and balance that
mark most of the English romantic concern with myth. Although his work,
and that of Wordsworth, Keats, Shelley, Coleridge, and Byron, lacks most

of the qualities usually found in German romantic writing, myth was nevertheless important to the English poets in many ways, ranging from the
ornamental to the religious.

The impressive work of Karl Otfried Müller, the great German classicist,
is marked by a broad and scholarly concern with humane learning, and by a
desire to comprehend Greek culture in its entirety. Müller takes myth, with
philology, not only as a crucial tool for scholarly investigation but also as
the single most important key to the Greek mind. In its avoidance of special
pleading and its far-reaching illumination of Greek culture, Müller's work
is one of the high points of nineteenth-century myth study. In France,
Jules Michelet and Edgar Quinet show how narrower German ideas can be
made to fit French history, how myth lends power to patriotism, and how
myth can be invoked as a charter for present action, even for revolution.
The French romantics show a predictable interest in myth generally, and
one may particularly note that in Nerval and in Baudelaire one can see
the symbolist movement in literature developing from the romantic use of
mythology and symbolism.

Schelling applied systematic philosophy to myth, raised the philosophy
of mythology to equal standing with other branches of philosophy, and
indeed argued for the central metaphysical importance of myth. At one time
he believed that myth shows "the pre-established harmony between the
the ideal and real worlds," and later he came to think that myth belongs
to the blind, dark, and unconscious aspect of man's nature as it gropes
upward toward expression and self-awareness. As Karl Otfried Müller is
the high point of myth studied historically, so Schelling is the high point of
myth as philosophy in the nineteenth century.

D. F. Strauss's notorious *Das Leben Jesu* uses the new mythic method
to undercut and deny the historical reality of Christ, and Strauss's very
influential work shows where the serious study of myth had been pushing
Christian scholarship for nearly a hundred and fifty years. Quinet's refutation of
Strauss in *Voices of the Church against Strauss* (not included here) makes
the same point, but in a different cause and with a different spirit. In Arthur
de Gobineau's work on *The Inequality of the Human Races,* German mythic
thought is twisted into potentially vicious racist theory; while in Richard
Wagner, Germany had an artist who drew from mythic thought the idea for
a new, grand, comprehensive art that would exalt, ennoble, and unite the
German people. It would be hard to find an artist whose work was more
fully shaped in form, content, and spirit by myth and mythic thought.

In the widely used handbooks of Thomas Bulfinch and others, one can
begin to see a process at work simplifying, refining, and bowdlerizing myth
for popular consumption. This purifying of myth is given vast impetus

and even vaster prestige by the work of F. Max Müller, who tried, with enormous philological learning, to reduce all myths to mere locutions for simple solar events, such as dawn.

But before myth became so genteel, it had one final triumph in the masterwork of the American romantics. In Emerson, Thoreau, Whitman, Poe, Melville, and even perhaps in Hawthorne, myth fed and inspired a series of attempts to create a new series of myths for the common man and a heroic literature for the heroic age of democracy. In *Representative Men,* in *Walden,* in *Moby Dick,* and in *Leaves of Grass,* the nineteenth century saw the last major triumph of mythic thought and art before the achievements of the twentieth century. At about the same time, the writings of Feuerbach and especially of Marx laid the still-impressive groundwork for the widespread modern view of myth as a vehicle for the ideology of any given cultural unit or group.

If the romantic reappraisal of myth included an affirmation of the Dionysian, the violent, the sexual, and the darkly fatalistic elements of myth, it therefore included within its approval the whole irrational side of myth: that side of myth that often lies buried, that may be connected with the unconscious and the instinctual, and that seeks expression in dark symbolism or in awesome conceptions of Necessity, Fate, or Destiny. But the Victorian revaluation of myth largely ignored or rejected this entire side of myth, and in filtering myth through a mesh of decorous and sunny gentility, robbed the subject of much of its seriousness, much of its dignity, much of its capacity to nourish tragedy, and many of its deep connections with what Melville called the "underformings of the mind." Indeed, the later nineteenth-century assessment of myth—which this volume does not pretend to treat—may be described as a revival of rationalism, a second Enlightenment that confined its serious interest in myth to anthropology and gave myth back to the not very highly esteemed "savage mind." So Andrew Lang set out to explain what to him were the "extremely gross and irrational" stories of the ancient Greeks, and he provided, in his *Myth, Ritual, and Religion* (1888), a special appendix praising Fontenelle's approach to the problem as the right one.

If the late nineteenth-century scholarly study of myth, dominated by historians, anthropologists, and sociologists as it was, appears as a second Enlightenment, perhaps the twentieth-century revival of sympathetic interest in myth (one thinks of Nietzsche, Jane Harrison, Cornford, Gilbert Murray, Freud, and of T. S. Eliot, Mann, and Yeats) may indeed be called a second romantic revival and reaffirmation of the power and truth of myth.

R.R.

German Romanticism and Myth

ONE REMARKABLE aspect of the German romantic movement as it first rises to prominence and achievement around 1797 is how its greatest figures—such as Friedrich and August Schlegel, Hölderlin, Novalis, Schelling—seem from the start to *assume* myth as naturally central to their own deepest preoccupations and hopes. As Gibbon had earlier described his education steeped in orthodox religious disputations about biblical chronology and dynasties, so these younger romantics are steeped from their earliest education in the new intellectual and creative excitement about myth that is reflected in the work of Winckelmann, Heyne, Herder, and Goethe. In Schiller's derisive verse written against the excessive romantic Hellenic cult already swelling by the middle 1790s—

Hardly has the cold fever of Gallomania left us
Then there breaks out a burning fever, Greekomania

—"Greekomania" might rightly be translated "mythomania." All the romantics move in a pervasive atmosphere where philology, philosophy, history, biblical criticism, art criticism, and the greatest modern German poetry ceaselessly nourish an interest in myth, either directly or indirectly: if not in Herder's praise of mythic wisdom and Volk-myths and in his historicizing analysis of religion, then in Lessing's different but no less emphatic historicizing of religious development or in his widely read *Essay on the History of Fable*, in which he defines fable as "an example of practical morality"; or if not in Heyne's philologic-historic analysis of myth, then in F. A. Wolf's revolutionary interpretation of Homer as oral poetry of the folk; if not in Goethe, then in Schiller's famous poem, "The Gods of Greece," which unfavorably compares Christianity and modernity with an utterly lost but higher Greek religion, or in his essays on why ancient mythic "naivete" is incompatible with the highest, truest modern idealist aspirations. In a similar way, what is announced in Kant's philosophy, or in the idealist philosophies deriving from him, can lead easily to more interest in myth: Kant's emphasis on art as a kind of mediating solution to the problems of human duality, as carried forward differently by Schiller and by Schelling, approached myth as the ultimate paradigm of the imaginative mode for reconciling dualities.

The most intense and original romantic interest in myth occurs between about 1795 and 1810; that is, between the first tentative but prescient suggestions of the young Schlegels and Schelling and the massively erudite and ambitiously systematic mythologies of Görres and Creuzer. In this period, certain historical factors reinforce the romantic interest in myth, but also lead it to a profound break with the older German mythic thought from Winckelmann through Goethe. Among these are the compactness of German cultural life, centering in and radiating from one smallish city or university circle to another, a mutually responsive web of intellectual activity; the vitality of a newly rising national culture, whose sense of its own newness and possibilities is another force making for intimate contact between established and emerging thinkers; the intensifying of German nationalism under such inner pressure, but also under pressure from the French revolutionary wars and Napoleonic invasions; the unusual closeness and sympathetic alliance between German philosophers and poets, famously exemplified in the youthful friendship of Hölderlin, Hegel, and Schelling—these and other historical factors could quicken, enrich, and spread interest in a subject such as myth, which seemed to cut across all these problematic areas, giving promise of a greater literature, a spiritual support to patriotism, and even a radically unifying solution to the dilemmas appearing in knowledge and faith.

In great part, of course, many of these elements had served to stimulate the mythic innovations of the older German generation. What is partly new here are the problems the romantics begin to feel as peculiarly their own—a growing sense of the loss of tradition and belief, of deepening division within the self and between the self and the world, and of political and national pressures. What is also remarkably new, however, is the assumption by so many of the greatest early romantics that myth is doubtlessly involved in any effort to solve these perennial problems, not only philosophic, religious, and aesthetic, but political and personal.

One cause for this German romantic confidence in myth has been broached above and may be briefly pursued. It may be claimed that for the romantics, the idea of myth as a high mode of truth is now not so much a fascinating possibility as something like a settled presupposition. This was by no means the case for such earlier mythic explorers as Herder or Goethe, for example. For while myth was indeed a central theme and resource for both of these men, it is also true that the mythic enterprise of both is a personal venture: Herder or Goethe neither exist as part of any distinct school of mythic thought nor really descend from one— except in the sense that behind their full-

bodied views of myth lies a suggestive but disorganized body of "preromantic" possibilities. With the romantics, however, the very idea of myth as worthy of the most serious philosophic or poetic attention no longer seems to need fighting out again. It is perhaps plausible to speak of the German romantics as forming a real "school" of myth—indeed, perhaps the first real such school since the orthodox Christian mythology began to collapse near the end of the seventeenth century. For however interested some enlightenment figures were in myth, or however broad an area of agreement among some of them, *philosophes* and deists generally seem to have ended with myth, rather than beginning with it. But the romantics (though sometimes ending elsewhere) in contrast seem to begin with myth, almost as a matter of course. Thus, for example, the Schlegels both studied with Heyne and moved very early to write criticism in which myth is inextricably mixed with all their thoughts on almost any other subject, literary, political, religious, historical. Thus, too, Schelling's school dissertation in 1792 is on the mythic problems posed by Genesis 3—a subject already raised by Eichhorn and Gabler, Heyne's pupils and admirers of Herder; and Schelling's first published essay, in 1793, is significantly titled "On Myths, Historical Fables and Philosophemes of the Most Ancient World." Or, Hölderlin's Master's essay in 1790, titled "History of the Fine Arts Among the Greeks," is redolent more of mythic speculation than of art history.

It might be expected that these younger romantics would make far more ambitious claims for myth than did their elders. Goethe's sardonic complaint that the romantics inevitably tended to Catholicism pointed up such a real difference between the older and newer generation: how deeply committed the romantics were to Christianity (if not Catholicism simply), and by contrast how ambiguously or indifferently Christian were Goethe, or Herder, Lessing, and Winckelmann. Romantic myth quickly becomes a deliberate religious program and vehicle—a way back or forward to a deep, progressively expanding and unifying spirituality modelled on (or as often, fulfilling) Christianity. In contrast, Herder and Goethe, however daringly they affirmed myth as a mode of truth, never exalted myth as promising such a transcending unity. Herder emphasized that each *Volk* was and should be autonomous and different, that each such *Volk* is needed to give full expression to what *Humanität* might mean; Goethe stressed individuation, both in human and in natural development. Taken together, the romantics in their early phase stress the opposite: that the true goal of human and natural striving is to seek and find the undetermined, the primally undivided and the formless, the infinite and boundless, the oneness behind all seeming separateness. And they usually describe myth so as to support this view.

Romantic myth may in part be described fairly as a revival in secular or idealist form of an older Christian hope. Instead of being an aspect of organic historical or natural growth, myth now becomes more a mode of redeeming a humanity separated from a lost primal unity. The romantics do not conceive any return to that primal unity as a real possibility. But myth may provide a key to reconciling the intensely felt dualities of necessity and freedom, finitude and infinity, sensuousness and divinity. Their emphasis moves then to what myth portends, rather than what it was or is. The final goal of myth is often described as striving to make wholly conscious, universalized, and free what in the original myths was only unconscious, instinctual, blindly necessary, or partial. Myth will be most truly fulfilled when all contradictions are resolved and all potentialities realized and synthesized. Novalis could assert that "progressive, ever augmenting evolutions

are the stuff of history. What does not now attain fulfillment will attain it. . . ." Friedrich Schlegel spoke of a "universal, progressive poetry" that would redeem the world. Neither of these remarks— with echoes in Schelling and Hölderlin and others—intends any theory of progress in the rationalist style of a Condorcet or Comte, but a vision of a "return" in fullness of what had been in the beginning. Novalis's mythic story "Klingsohr's Fairy Tale" shows that the "iron age" is redeemed when the daughter of Mind and Imagination, called Fable, at the end sings a triumphant song announcing total, transcending harmony.

The romantics offer two broad avenues by which myth may serve thus to redeem what had been shadowed forth in primal myth. On the one hand, in F. Schlegel's manifestoes or in Novalis's or Hölderlin's poetry, there arises a hope of achieving a radically self-conscious creation of myth out of modern ideals and materials. On the other hand, they pursue the hope of finding some mythic origin wholly consonant with romantic Christian-idealist aspirations. A most striking expression of this is in the romantic exaltation of India, now seen not only as one great example of mythic wisdom among many others, but often as the single true source of all mythic wisdom. Here, for the first time, India begins to replace Greece or Egypt —or Israel itself—as the primary mythic-religious image.

B.F.

REFERENCES Works dealing with German romanticism in terms of literature, philosophy, religion, history, or mythology tend for obvious reasons to cross-refer or overlap; works cited here are selected from those most directly concerned with myth.

Fritz Strich, *Die Mythologie in der deutschen Literatur von Klopstock bis Wagner*, 2 vols. (Halle, 1910) is an indispensable, exhaustive survey but with minimal bibliography; Strich's *Deutsche Klassik und Romantik*

(Bern: Francke Verlag, 1962, 5th edition) surveys similar ground thematically. Henry Hatfield, *Winckelmann and His German Critics* (New York, 1943). Carl Justi, *Winckelmann und seine Zeitgenossen,* ed. W. Rehm (Cologne, 1956, 5th edition). Wolfgang Schadewaldt, *Winckelmann und Homer* (Leipzig, 1941). Rudolf Suhnel, *Die Götter Griechenlands in der deutschen Klassik* (Wurzburg, 1935). Walther Rehm, *Götterstille und Göttertrauer* (Berlin: Francke Verlag, 1951). Walther Rehm, *Griechentum und Goethezeit* (Bern, 1952). Karl Borinski, *Die Antike in Poetik und Kunsttheorie* (Leipzig, 1914–1922).

Humphrey Trevelyan, *Goethe and the Greeks* (Cambridge: Cambridge University Press, 1941). Oscar Walzel, *Deutsche Romantik* (Leipzig: B. G. Teubner, 1923). Rene

Wellek, *History of Modern Criticism. II: The Romantic Age* (New Haven: Yale University Press, 1955). W. Erbt, *Gottesdienst und Göttersage der Germanen* (1941); René Gerard, *L'Orient et la Pensée romantique allemande* (Paris: Didier, 1963); G. Dumézil, *Mythes et Dieux des Germanes* (Paris, 1939). Erich Aron, *Die deutsche Erweckung des Griechentums durch Winckelmann und Herder* (Heidelberg, 1920). E. M. Butler, *The Tyranny of Greece over Germany* (Cambridge: Cambridge University Press, 1935). Raymond Schwab, *La Renaissance Orientale* (Paris: Payot, 1950). A. Leslie Willson, *A Mythical Image: The Ideal of India in German Romanticism* (Durham: Duke University Press, 1964). Herbert Anton, "Romantische Deutung griechischer Mythologie," in *Die Deutsche Romantik,* hrsg. H. Steffen (Göttingen, 1967).

FRIEDRICH SCHLEGEL

[1772–1829]

FRIEDRICH SCHLEGEL's name is most familiarly linked with his important role in pioneering and codifying the new German romantic movement as it comes to fruition by 1800. His new use of the old word "romantisch" provides the title for the new movement, and his periodical *Athenäum* (begun in 1798 with his older brother, August) is generally recognized as first and most influentially outlining the crucial lines of the romantic program. Novalis—who himself was often exalted by Schlegel and others as the kind of romantic poet par excellence—paid Schlegel a remarkable compliment in 1800: "If anyone was born to be the apostle for our time, it is you . . . the St. Paul of the new religion . . . with this religion begins a new world history. You understand the secrets of the age." The extravagant language aside, literary history has come to see Schlegel, like Coleridge, as one of the most seminal and original nineteenth-century critics. But as Novalis's emphasis on "new religion" makes clear, it is literary criticism with a difference. Schlegel's literary criticism reveals him also as an innovator in shaping several important modern approaches to myth, especially regarding myth's centrality for literature. With Schlegel's work, indeed, it becomes unmistakably clear for the first time that literary criticism as a whole is being revolutionized by the new importance of myth. The result is not only a series of new critical approaches and insights, but a radical revaluation of the meaning and possibility of literary criticism itself.

Friedrich Schlegel began in law, but soon moved to the study of classics, now more than ever a center of German intellectual and creative excitement. With his brother August, Schlegel studied at Göttingen in 1790 under the great classicist, Heyne. As might be expected in an age dominated by men such as Heyne, Herder, Winckelmann, Goethe, and Schiller, Schlegel's classical studies broadened inevitably into art, myth, and history. His early notebooks, essays, and projected works are dazzlingly wide-ranging, and always emphasize how any particular work or epoch must be understood in its historical, philosophic, and religious totality.

He begins by paying allegiance to Winckelmann, but soon moves away from the Winckelmannian image of classical calm and simplicity, and from classicism itself. He stresses more the wildly sensuous Dionysian side of Greece. And this connects intimately with his quickening interest in the possibility of a dynamic art of the future. After 1796, Schlegel becomes the most prominent spokesman for an art that only modernity can understand and achieve—what he calls the modern, the "romantic," or in his earlier term, the "interesting." One influence here obviously is Schiller, who taught how a "sentimental" modernity has lost a classically "naive" easiness with nature, and how modern thought must go beyond the "finite" classic view to fulfill the higher modern ideals of striving for the infinite. Schlegel's famous statement of this modern hope is in the *Athenäum,* Fragment 116, where he calls for a "progressive, universal poetry." Such a poetry or art, deliberately breaking the limits set in the past, will blend philosophy with poetry, will blend all genres, will reconcile all dualities, and will realize all possibilities.

One distinctly new feature here is Schlegel's buoyant optimism that such a truly modern-romantic art might accomplish all he hoped. What feeds such optimism is in large part Schlegel's absorption in and assumptions about myth. For myth points back to what poetry seemed to be in the primal beginnings of the human race, a unity of thought, art, and belief such as Schlegel hoped to realize in the future. This vision of a paradisal original oneness is assimilated both to a Herderian view of organic historical growth and, as importantly, to a Christian vision of the ultimate spiritualization of all things. What Schlegel intends here is doubtless too wide for the word *literature,* and too unorthodox for the word *religion* as both were traditionally used before him. But *myth* fits his new meaning ideally. Myth seems to join literature and religion inseparably; myth illuminates for modernity the missing link between art and faith, for myth shows both the origin and the goal implicit in both art and religion.

The outcome of such ideas becomes manifest from 1798 in his "literary" criticism, in his *Athenäum* essay fragments, in his 1800 "Discourse on Poetry," and in his writings at least to about 1805. His criticism—looked at here only with myth in mind—does two things at once, both revolutionary: on the one side, it proposes various radical new critical insights and artistic programs; on the other, it begins to claim a radically new role for literary criticism itself. He gives the first modern manifesto clearly calling for a self-conscious effort by individual poets to create wholly new myths in wholly modern terms—stated succinctly in his 1800

"Discourse on Mythology"; this broke with the earlier view held by Herder or Goethe and others that true myth could not be created by individual figures. Schlegel is one of the first to promote a systematic break with the older German "classical" Greece, stressing instead the Dionysian, uncontrollably ecstatic side of Greek culture—and he seeks also to transfer this to modern cultural goals. He is one of the first to exalt Indian myth and religion as particularly akin to romantic aims, and is the first German in the modern period to undertake direct, scholarly study of Sanskrit, as early as 1802—and his 1808 *On the Wisdom and Language of the Indians* stands as probably the first adequate philologic-philosophic study of Hinduism. Finally, with his brother August, he literally reshapes the modern critical view of Western literature in terms of historical perspectives, providing perhaps the main source for later, pervasive interpretations of literature as either "modern" or "ancient" in spirit—Friedrich Schlegel's most widely-known contribution here is his *The History of Ancient and Modern Literature* (1812).

Even such a baldly summary sketch of some of Schlegel's critical themes may nonetheless suggest how his enthusiasm for myth changes the very concept of what literary criticism might and should be. As myth originally transcended—by including in itself—philosophy and poetry and history, so the critic who understands this truth about myth reaches a higher synthesizing position than he could by studying either philosophy or poetry or history (or religion) alone. Thus, the Schlegelian critic is now not merely a critic, standing outside poetry and explicating its qualities: the critic himself now practices a kind of "transcendental poetry." Criticism is a creative act, a deeper, higher, living entry into creativity than artistic or intellectual creativity itself can know. As Schlegel put it, "poetry can only be criticized by poetry." Such a view has obvious affinities to its English offspring in the criticism of Coleridge, though Schlegel goes aggressively beyond Coleridge's steady attention to the poetic object. But like Coleridge, Schlegel would be misunderstood as mainly a literary critic who had philosophic or other interests. Schlegel is not a literary critic also interested in myth; criticism as he conceives it aims at nothing less than becoming a new *summa* of all human knowledge, arts, and action. While Doctor Johnson or Goethe were prodigiously learned men, Schlegel's *deliberate* cultivating of all realms of human knowledge as properly part of the critical province is something new. Moreover, where Johnson or Goethe remain moderate in their critical insights or goals, guided perhaps by a sense of the necessary imperfections or partiality of human wisdom, and doubtful of any single mode that claims to unite in itself all wisdom, Schlegel goes beyond because he can appeal to what seems just such a single all-uniting mode —i. e., myth.

No brief account of Schlegel could ignore or in any way cover his influence on his time and later; and only the most exhaustive account could untangle the excited cross-influences playing between himself, his brother, Novalis, Schelling, Jean Paul, Hölderlin, or others of his generation. He impressed—and often irritated—everyone, from Schiller and Goethe to Madame de Staël, Hegel, Heine, and Carlyle. His influence was overshadowed finally by that of his brother, perhaps because of August's more moderate positions. But Schlegel's own many-sided career contributed to this as well: he seems to be an early case of the writer who is considered "brilliant but unsound" —but also "lazy" (so few works brought to conclusion) or "immoral" (primarily because of his daring novel, *Lucinde*) or finally, a Catholic convert and political reactionary.

The substance or force of these charges against him has disappeared. But with myth in mind, it would be misleading to dismiss the importance in his thought of Catholicism, or Christianity in general, for it is always in his thought as a model and agent of universal spirituality. The final turn in Schlegel's view of myth, indeed, shows the triumph of his Christian commitment over his early enthusiasm for myth. In part, his deep study of Indic religion directly in Sanskrit, rather than through the enhancing medium of romanticism, helped to effect this—but a fuller account of his interest in India must be delayed here. The start of Schlegel's break with myth shows clearly by his 1804–1806 lectures where he argues against Schelling's defense of pantheism. His 1808 study of Indic religion carries this rejection of pantheism—and thus of myth—further. As he became more devoutly Catholic and socially conservative, the older Schlegel's views on mythic limitations hardened. In his 1828 *Philosophy of Life*—published the year before his death—he speaks harshly of mythology as "olden heathenism" that is generally a "materialism assuming poetic form and expression," at last a "heathenish deification of nature." He still affirms, as earlier, that man lives through symbols: "Terrestrial nature, in all its organic productions and warring elements of life, is throughout symbolical"; man is "surrounded by a symbolical world of sensuous emblems"—but the signification of these spiritual symbols for him is now truly explained not by myth but by Catholic Christianity.

B.F.

REFERENCES Our texts are from *Dialogue on Poetry and Literary Aphorisms,* translated, introduced, and annotated by Ernst Behler and Roman Struc (University Park: Pennsylvania State University Press, 1968). Most of Schlegel's work remains untranslated.

Schlegel's works on Indic myth are excluded here; see References to "German Romantic Mythology and India."

Useful standard editions include: *Friedrich Schlegel: Seine prosaische Jugendschriften,* ed. Jakob Minor (Vienna, 1882); *Kritische Friedrich Schlegel Ausgabe,* ed. E. Behler with J. J. Anstett and H. Eichner (Paderborn-Darmstadt-Zürich, 1958), projected in 22 volumes; *Athenäeum,* 3 vols. (Berlin, 1798–1800, reprinted Stuttgart, 1960); *The Philosophy of Life, and Philosophy of Language,* translated by A. J. W. Morrison (London: Bohn, 1847).

Useful commentaries include: F. Strich, *Die Mythologie in der deutschen Literatur von Klopstock bis Wagner,* 2 vols. (Halle, 1910), II; F. Strich, *Deutsche Klassik und Romantik* (Bern: Francke Verlag, 1962, 5th edition); Oskar Walzel, *German Romanticism,* translated by A. E. Lussky (New York: Putnam's Sons, 1932), pp. 34–48, 85–91, 224–244; H. Hatfield, *Aesthetic Paganism in German Literature* (Cambridge: Harvard University Press, 1964), Chap. 10; R. Wellek, *A History of Modern Criticism, II: The Romantic Age* (New Haven: Yale University Press, 1955). Klaus Briegleb, *Aesthetische Sittlichkeit; Versuch über Friedrich Schlegels Systementwurf zur Begründung der Dichtungskritik* (Tübingen: M. Niemeyer, 1962). N. A. Busch, "The Chief Metamorphoses of Friedrich Schlegel's Concept of Mythology," University of Washington Ph.D. dissertation, unpublished, 1965. A. Béguin, *L'Âme romantique et le rêve* (Paris: Librairie Corti, 1963).

F. SCHLEGEL

"Talk on Mythology"

CONSIDERING your serious reverence for art, I wish to challenge you, my friends, to ask yourselves this question: should the force of inspiration also in poetry continue to split up and, when it has exhausted itself by struggling against the hostile element, end up in lonely silence? Are the most sacred things always to remain nameless and formless, and be left in darkness to chance? Is love indeed invincible, and is there an art worthy of the name if it does not have the power to bind the spirit of love with its magic word, to make the spirit of love follow and obey it, and to inspire its beautiful creations in accordance with its necessary freedom?

You above all others must know what I mean. You yourselves have written poetry, and while doing so you must often have felt the absence of a firm basis for your activity, a matrix, a sky, a living atmosphere.

The modern poet must create all these things from within himself, and many have done it splendidly; up to now, however, each poet separately and each work from its very beginning, like a new creation out of nothing.

I will go right to the point. Our poetry, I maintain, lacks a focal point, such as mythology was for the ancients; and one could summarize all the essentials in which modern poetry is inferior to the ancient in these words: We have no mythology. But, I add, we are close to obtaining one or, rather, it is time that we earnestly work together to create one.

For it will come to us by an entirely

opposite way from that of previous ages, which was everywhere the first flower of youthful imagination, directly joining and imitating what was most immediate and vital in the sensuous world. The new mythology, in contrast, must be forged from the deepest depths of the spirit; it must be the most artful of all works of art, for it must encompass all the others; a new bed and vessel for the ancient, eternal fountainhead of poetry, and even the infinite poem concealing the seeds of all other poems.

You may well smile at this mystical poem and the disorder that might originate from the abundance of poetic creations. But the highest beauty, indeed the highest order is yet only that of chaos, namely of such a one that waits only for the touch of love to unfold as a harmonious world, of such a chaos as the ancient mythology and poetry were. For mythology and poetry are one and inseparable. All poems of antiquity join one to the other, till from ever increasing masses and members the whole is formed. Everything interpenetrates everything else, and everywhere there is one and the same spirit, only expressed differently. And thus it is truly no empty image to say: Ancient poetry is a single, indivisible, and perfect poem. Why should what has once been not come alive again? In a different way, to be sure. And why not in a more beautiful, a greater way?

I plead with you only not to give in to disbelief in the possibility of a new mythology. Doubts from all sides and in all directions would be welcome, so that the investigation may become that much more free and rich. And now lend my conjectures an attentive ear. More than conjectures, considering the situation of the matter, I cannot hope to offer. But I hope that these conjectures through you yourselves will become truths. For if you want to employ them in such a way, they are to a certain extent suggestions for experiments.

If a new mythology can emerge only from the innermost depths of the spirit and develop only from itself, then we find a very significant hint and a noteworthy confirmation of what we are searching for in that great phenomenon of our age, in idealism. Idealism originated in just this way, from nothing as it were, and now it has constituted itself in the spiritual sphere as a firm point from which the creative energy of man can safely expand, developing in all directions, without losing itself or the possibility of return. All disciplines and all arts will be seized by the great revolution. You can see it already at work in physics where idealism erupted of its own before it was touched by the magic wand of philosophy. And this wonderful, great fact can at the same time be a hint for you of the secret correspondence and inner unity of the age. Idealism—from a practical view nothing other than the spirit of that revolution—and its great maxims which we are to practice and propagate from our own energy and freedom; this idealism, considered theoretically, as great as it manifests itself at this point, is yet only a part, a branch, a mode of expression of the phenomenon of all phenomena: that mankind struggles with all its power to find its own center. It must, as things are, either perish or be rejuvenated. What is more probable, and what does one not hope for from such an age of rejuvenation? Remote antiquity will become alive again, and the remotest future of culture will announce itself in auguries. Yet this is not what matters to me at this point, for I do not want to pass over anything but to lead you step by step to the certainty of the most sacred mysteries. Just as it is the nature of spirit to determine itself and in perennial alternation to expand and return to itself, and as every thought is nothing but the result of such an activity; so is the same process generally discernible in every form of idealism, which itself is but a recognition of this very law. The new life, intensified by this recognition, manifests its secret energy in the most splendid manner through the infinite abundance of new ideas, general comprehensibility, and lively efficacy. Naturally this phenomenon assumes a different form in each individual; this is why success must often fall short of expectation. But our expectations cannot be disappointed in what the necessary laws allow us to expect for the development as a whole. Idealism in any form must transcend itself in one way or another, in order to be able to return to itself and remain what it is. Therefore, there must and will arise from the matrix of idealism a new and equally infinite realism, and idealism will not only by analogy of its genesis be an example of the new mythology, but it will indirectly become its very source. Traces of a similar tendency you can now observe almost everywhere, especially in physics where nothing is more needed than a mythological view of nature.

I, too, have long borne in me the ideal of such a realism, and if it has not yet found expression, it was merely because I am still searching for an organ for communicating it. And yet I know that I can find it only in poetry, for in the form of philosophy and especially of systematic philosophy realism can never again appear. But even considering a general tradition, it is to be expected that this new realism, since it must be of idealistic origin and must hover as it were over an idealistic ground, will emerge as poetry which indeed is to be based on the harmony of the ideal and real.

Spinoza, it seems to me, has an identical fate as the good old Saturn of the fable. The new gods pulled down the sublime one

from the lofty throne of knowledge. He faded back into the solemn obscurity of the imagination; there he lives and now dwells with the other Titans in dignified exile. Keep him here! Let his memories of the old mastery melt away in the song of the Muses into a soft longing. Let him put away the militant attire of systematic philosophy and share the dwelling in the temple of new poetry with Homer and Dante, joining the household gods and friends of every god-inspired poet.

Indeed, I barely comprehend how one can be a poet without admiring Spinoza, loving him, and becoming entirely his. In the invention of details your own imagination is rich enough; to stimulate it, to excite it to activity, and to provide it with nourishment there is nothing better than the creations of other artists. In Spinoza, however, you will find the beginning and end of all imagination, the general basis on which all individual creation rests; and especially the separation of the original, the eternal aspect of imagination from the individual and the typical must be very welcome to you. Seize the opportunity and observe. You are granted a profound view into the innermost workshop of poetry. Spinoza's feeling is of the same kind as his imagination. It is not a sensitivity to this or that nor a passion that smolders and dies again, but a clear fragrance that hovers invisibly visible over the whole; everywhere eternal longing finds an accord from the depths of the simple work which in calm greatness breathes the spirit of original love.

And is not this soft reflection of the godhead in man the actual soul, the kindling spark of all poetry? Mere representation of man, passions, and actions does not truly amount to anything, as little as using artificial forms does, even if you shuffle and turn over the old stuff together millions of times. That is only the visible, the external body, for when the soul has been extinguished what is left is only the lifeless corpse of poetry. When that spark of inspiration breaks out in works, however, a new phenomenon stands before us, alive and in the beautiful glory of light and love.

And what else is any wonderful mythology but hieroglyphic expression of surrounding nature in this transfigured form of imagination and love?

Mythology has one great advantage. What usually escapes our consciousness can here be perceived and held fast through the senses and spirit like the soul in the body surrounding it, through which it shines into our eyes and speaks to our ear.

This is the crucial point: that in regard to the sublime we do not entirely depend on our emotions. To be sure, he whose emotions have run dry, in him they will nowhere spring forth; this is a well-known truth which I am not in the least inclined to oppose. But we should take part everywhere in what is already formed. We should develop, kindle, and nourish the sublime through contact with the same in kind, the similar, or if of equal stature the hostile; in a word, give it form. If the sublime, however, is incapable of being intentionally created, then let us give up any claims to a free art of ideas, for it would be an empty name.

Mythology is such a work of art created by nature. In its texture the sublime is really formed; everything is relation and metamorphosis, conformed and transformed, and this conformation and transformation is its peculiar process, its inner life and method, if I may say so.

Here I find a great similarity with the marvelous wit of romantic poetry which does not manifest itself in individual conceptions but in the structure of the whole, and which was so often pointed out by our friend for the works of Cervantes and Shakespeare. Indeed, this artfully ordered confusion, this charming symmetry of contradictions, this wonderfully perennial alternation of enthusiasm and irony which lives even in the smallest parts of the whole, seem to me to be an indirect mythology themselves. The organization is the same, and certainly the arabesque is the oldest and most original form of human imagination. Neither this wit nor a mythology can exist without something original and inimitable which is absolutely irreducible, and in which after all the transformations its original character and creative energy are still dimly visible, where the naive profundity permits the semblance of the absurd and of madness, of simplicity and foolishness, to shimmer through. For this is the beginning of all poetry, to cancel the progression and laws of rationally thinking reason, and to transplant us once again into the beautiful confusion of imagination, into the original chaos of human nature, for which I know as yet no more beautiful symbol than the motley throng of the ancient gods.

Why won't you arise and revive those splendid forms of great antiquity? Try for once to see the old mythology, steeped in Spinoza and in those views which present-day physics must excite in every thinking person, and everything will appear to you in new splendor and vitality.

But to accelerate the genesis of the new mythology, the other mythologies must also be reawakened according to the measure of their profundity, their beauty, and their form. If only the treasures of the Orient were as accessible to us as those of Antiquity. What new source of poetry could then flow from India if a few German artists with their catholicity and profundity of mind, with the genius for translation which is their own, had the opportunity which a nation growing ever more dull and brutal barely knows how to use. In the Orient we must look for the most sublime form of the Romantic, and only when we can draw from the source, perhaps will the semblance of southern passion which we find so charming in Spanish poetry appear to us occidental and sparse.

In general, one must be able to press toward the goal by more than one way. Let each pursue his own in joyful confidence, in the most individual manner; for nowhere has the right of individuality more validity—provided individuality is what this word defines: indivisible unity and an inner and vital coherence—than here where the sublime is at issue. From this standpoint I would not hesitate to say that the true value, indeed the virtue of man is his originality.

And if I place so much emphasis on Spinoza, it is indeed not from any subjective preference (I have expressly omitted the objects of such a preference) or to establish him as master of a new autocracy, but because I could demonstrate by this example in a most striking and illuminating way my ideas about the value and dignity of mysticism and its relation to poetry. Because of his objectivity in this respect, I chose him as a representative of all the others. This is the way I reason. Just as the *Theory of Knowledge,** in the view of those who have not noticed the infinitude

* Published by Fichte in 1794.

and eternal abundance of idealism, remains a perfect form, a general system for all knowledge, so, too, is Spinoza in a similar way the general basis and support for every individual kind of mysticism. And this, in my opinion, even those who have no special understanding of either mysticism or of Spinoza will readily acknowledge.

I cannot conclude without urging once more the study of physics, from whose dynamic paradoxes the most sacred revelations of nature are now bursting forth in all directions.

And thus let us, by light and life, hesitate no longer, but accelerate, each according to his own mind, that great development to which we were called. Be worthy of the greatness of the age and the fog will vanish from your eyes; and there will be light before you. All thinking is a divining, but man is only now beginning to realize his divining power. What immense expansion will this power experience, and especially now! It seems to me that he who could understand the age—that is, those great principles of general rejuvenation and of eternal revolution—would be able to succeed in grasping the poles of mankind, to recognize and to know the activity of the first men as well as the nature of the Golden Age which is to come. Then the empty chatter would stop and man would become conscious of what he is: he would understand the earth and the sun.

This is what I mean by the new mythology.

FROM *The Athenaeum*

Aphorism No. 116
ROMANTIC poetry is a progressive universal poetry. Its mission is not merely to reunite all separate genres of poetry and to put poetry in touch with philosophy and rhetorics. It will, and should, now mingle and now amalgamate poetry and prose, genius and criticism, the poetry of art and the poetry of nature, render poetry living and social, and life and society poetic,

poetize wit, fill and saturate the forms of art with solid cultural material of every kind, and inspire them with vibrations of humor. It embraces everything poetic, from the greatest system of art which, in turn, includes many systems, down to the sigh, the kiss, which the musing child breathes forth in artless song. It can lose itself in what it represents to such a degree that one might think its one and only goal were the characterization of poetic individuals of every type; and yet no form has thus far arisen appropriate to expressing the author's mind so perfectly, so that artists who just wanted to write a novel have by coincidence described themselves. Romantic poetry alone can, like the epic, become a mirror of the entire surrounding world, a picture of its age. And yet, it too can soar, free from all real and ideal interests, on the wings of poetic reflection, midway between the work and the artist. It can even exponentiate this reflection and multiply it as in an endless series of mirrors. It is capable of the highest and the most universal education; not only by creating from within, but also from without, since it organizes in similar fashion all parts of what is destined to become a whole; thus, a view is opened to an endlessly developing classicism. Among the arts Romantic poetry is what wit is to philosophy, and what society, association, friendship, and love are in life. Other types of poetry are completed and can now be entirely analyzed. The Romantic type of poetry is still becoming; indeed, its peculiar essence is that it is always becoming and that it can never be completed. It cannot be exhausted by any theory, and only a divinatory criticism might dare to characterize its ideal. It alone is infinite, as it alone is free; and as its first law it recognizes that the arbitrariness of the poet endures no law above him. The Romantic genre of poetry is the only one which is more than a genre, and which is, as it were, poetry itself: for in a certain sense all poetry is or should be Romantic.

Aphorism No. 125

Perhaps a completely new epoch of sciences and arts would arise, if symphilosophy and sympoetry became so universal and intimate that it would no longer be unusual if several characters who complement each other would produce common works. Sometimes one can scarcely resist the idea that two minds might actually belong together like separate halves, and that only in union could they be what they might be. . . .

Aphorism No. 238

There is a poetry whose One and All is the relationship of the ideal and the real: it should thus be called transcendental poetry according to the analogy of the technical language of philosophy. It begins in the form of satire with the absolute disparity of ideality and reality, it hovers in their midst in the form of the elegy, and it ends in the form of the idyll with the absolute identity of both. But we should not care for a transcendental philosophy unless it were critical, unless it portrayed the producer along with the product, unless it embraced in its system of transcendental thoughts a characterization of transcendental thinking: in the same way, that poetry which is not infrequently encountered in modern poets should combine those transcendental materials and preliminary exercises for a poetic theory of the creative power with the artistic reflection and beautiful self-mirroring, which is present in Pindar, the lyric fragments of the Greeks, the ancient elegy: and among the moderns, in Goethe: thus this poetry should portray itself with each of its portrayals; everywhere and at the same time, it should be poetry and the poetry of poetry.

FRIEDRICH W. J. SCHELLING

[1775–1854]

SCHELLING'S career as a mythologist is exceptionally long and productive. His two earliest writings, at age eighteen in 1793, were on myth; and he was still elaborating his most ambitious effort on the same subject, *Einleitung in die Philosophie der Mythologie,* when he died, almost eighty years old, in 1854. Despite this long and impressive span of work, Schelling's contribution to mythic thought is unusually difficult to assess. On the one hand, he has been seen as surpassing even Vico in giving myth its first ambitious metaphysical and systematic modern philosophic exposition. Ernst Cassirer has indeed defended Schelling's claim to be the first philosopher to have set up a "philosophy of mythology" as an equal alongside all other philosophic disciplines. On the other hand, Schelling has often been regarded as finally unoriginal and even quite narrow, obscurantist, or semi-mystical. Leaving aside the formidable inner complexities of his thought, there are important external reasons for such divergent judgments on Schelling as a mythologist. One of these is that through his long career, he remained devoted to the deep aesthetic or religious importance that the early romantics assigned to myth; another is that through the various "phases" of his philosophizing, Schelling always claimed that the only true "science" of myth lay in an idealist metaphysical approach. Schelling's own ambiguous reputation reflects the decline both of romantic attitudes toward mythology and of the

kind of philosophic idealism that he and other romantics found so attractive.

During Schelling's early precocious career, from 1792 to about 1797, he was a disciple of Fichte's early transcendental revision of Kant; at the same time, a proponent of Heyne's view that myth embodied rude "philosophemes" and history. From 1797 to 1804, he broke with Fichte to develop his own absolute idealism, and also moved close to the emerging new romanticism. In this period, he stressed nature as an organic spiritualized realm, human consciousness as a higher stage beyond nature, and described both as resulting from God's creative self-unfolding. The supreme document and tool for understanding this creative movement of Spirit is found in art; and myth is seen as a primal expression of art on one side, and as its ultimate culmination on the other. From 1804, Schelling's thought entered a new phase: the meaning of religion and God move to the center of his thinking, and myth, rather than art, is the indispensable key here. His work to the end of his life sought to refine and synthesize these ideas.

But Schelling's greatest influence came very early in his career, with the result that he has often seemed to be merely the idealist philosopher of romantic myth. And Schelling's kind of absolute idealism could also seem mainly an "episode," a transition between Fichte and Hegel. As is well-known, as Hegel's star rose, Schelling's place as the foremost transcendental philosopher faded rapidly. The same is true of the high value Schelling found in myth—in Hegel's system, so dominant thereafter, myth occupies a much less important place than it did in Schelling's system. From about 1809, Schelling's philosophic isolation was manifest: between then and his death, he published only two small works, confining himself to lecturing and to private writing. After Hegel's death, Schelling went to Berlin in 1841 to teach his philosophy of religion. In these lectures, Schelling propounded his later mythic thought and his "positive" philosophy, that anticipates, in part, existentialism; his audience included Bakunin, Engels, Burckhardt, and Kierkegaard, but the response was finally disappointing. Nevertheless, these last lectures of Schelling's may be counted as the last important bid by the older romantic-idealist mythology to regain its failing fortunes. As early as 1810, the romantic reinterpretation of myth had already lost its most gifted and enthusiastic supporters, through death or apostasy; the romantic view is championed most strongly now by the mystic or Neoplatonizing systems of Görres or Creuzer. Thus, Schelling's later and most ambitious theorizing on myth, clearly emerging and deepening in the decade or so after Creuzer, was done as the newer historical and philological disciplines began to displace romantic and idealist prestige. Schelling's culminating synthesis in the *Philosophy of Mythology* reached print only two years before the mythic work standing at its intellectual antipodes, F. Max Müller's *Comparative Mythology*.

But Schelling is misleadingly narrowed to romanticism or to a transitional place in philosophic idealism. He remains apart from both sides: he was more rigorously systematic in his thinking about myth than any other major romantic was or wished to be; and conversely, he was probably more committed to myth's central metaphysical importance than any other important modern philosopher. Whatever its final merits, Schelling's ambition to erect a total metaphysical system of myth is bold and original. Here—beyond parallels with Friedrich Schlegel or Schelling's debt to Fichte, Boehme, Spinoza, or Baader—it is perhaps Vico who best brings Schelling's ambition into proper focus. No question of influence is involved here, only kinship of aims. Both Schelling and Vico claim that myth is a decisive key to the purposes of Divine Providence (as Vico put it), or Absolute Spirit or God (as Schelling put it). Both agree, moreover, that such discoveries can be ordered into a grand system. What Vico called the "ideal eternal history" of what "had, has and will have to be" is the subject of his "new science," to be as strictly developed as geometry. Schelling's effort and approach are the same, though cast now in Kantian, rather than Cartesian, terms. Vico's mythologizing yielded a "rational civil theology," an ideal history primarily of human civilization under Providence. Schelling, however, goes much further. His philosophy of myth intends to explain not only the theologic reasons of human civilization, but the divine causes for the rise of nature and human consciousness as well, and even more, of the reasons within Providence itself—the inward necessity and freedom inherent in God's own wish to manifest Himself.

What might then be called Schelling's metaphysics of myth falls roughly into two main phases. Between 1797 and about 1803, along with the Schlegels, Novalis, and Hölderlin, he is deeply influenced by Fichte's effort to find objective grounds once again for metaphysical truth, which Kant had made most problematic when he placed the thing-in-itself beyond certain human knowledge or proof. Fichte was uninterested in myth; but his approach was fruitful. Fichte argued that an objectively true world can be directly known because human consciousness can be said to "make" its own objective world. The inner subjective and outer objective realities build up as consciousness plays dialectically back and forth between awareness of itself as against what it finds is not itself. This anticipates "idealism," and romanticism as well—for as a result of its own dynamic, successful striving to realize itself against what is not itself, the ego "creates" its world.

Schelling's first independent position begins here, and goes beyond. In several works on philosophy of "Nature," between 1797–1799, and especially in his *System of Transcendental Idealism* (1800), he expands Fichte's creatively striving, self-transcending human subject into a creatively striving, self-transcending Absolute Mind or Spirit. Spirit now comes to know itself by objectifying itself, by moving progressively into what is not itself. The history of all creation, from brute matter to highest human self-consciousness, is simply the history of the Odyssey of Spirit. In part, at least, Schelling's system is much like the biblical-Christian view of God as a creating, self-incarnating Spirit. What Schelling adds, importantly, is an insistence that Spirit must move through distinct, progressive stages—not through the stages of mere empirical history, but through enduring "moments"; or put otherwise, through what Schelling calls "potencies," ascending levels of spiritual possibility. Spirit progresses through three such unfolding moments or potencies, each higher than the one before: first, Spirit moves into the objectively real, or "Nature"; then into subjectivity, or human consciousness as it grasps the ideal; but then into the still higher recognition of the identity between the ideal and real. This entire process may rightly be called the "poetry" of Spirit, for the whole process shows Spirit literally "making" itself real. Nature as such is therefore still the "primitive, un-

conscious poetry of the Spirit"; man is nature become conscious of itself.

Myth gives the first sign that man has truly glimpsed the "preestablished harmony between the ideal and real worlds" that pervades all seeming contraries and antitheses. This deepest truth, conveyed by all early historical myth, is found in myth's typical act of reconciling the finite with the infinite, the shaping of divine power into form. Myth also first shows the deepest meaning of all art. For art is precisely just such an act of reconciliation between the ideal and real, a free playing with given necessity, a vision of the whole in the part, a unity out of multeity (in the language of Schelling's sometime plagiarizer and disciple, Coleridge). The *Philosophie der Kunst* (1803) extends these ideas. The mythic gods are explained as finite expressions of the infinite, as imaginative symbolic forms of the Spirit. As in Goethe and Moritz (whom Schelling admired), the mythic gods refer to no higher truth outside themselves, but are autonomously real. In Greek myth, says Schelling, every possibility that mind can conceive is given perfection of form: Jupiter thus expresses (or *is*) the identity between ideal and real, Vulcan the forming principle at work in the material world. But unlike Goethe or Moritz, Schelling makes these perfect aesthetic and symbolic forms of myth only a first "moment." Their limitation can be seen in their stress on distinct form. Christianity goes beyond this by recognizing Spirit as an Idea, and as one Idea. The "Trinity," for example, breaks all possibility of mere form. Again, Schelling's system of three unfolding potencies appears: the pagan myth of nature and Christian Idea are both essential but not sufficient; both need to be reconciled on a higher level—that is, in a new mythology. In the same way, Schelling argues in his *Bruno* (1802) that the higher truth of Spirit is found neither in poetic mythology nor in esoteric philosophic mysteries; to take one or the other alone is to lose the higher identity underlying and needing both. The Odyssey of Spirit must complete itself, returning in consciousness to the harmony of the beginning: this will be the task of the new mythology. How this will come about, Schelling is unsure. Against Friedrich Schlegel's early optimism, Schelling denies that an individual poet can create myth, which must be the poetic work of a whole people.

From 1804, with his *Philosophie und Religion,* and more fully by 1815, Schelling's mythic thought takes a serious redirection. Though still seeking a rigorous conceptual system, he begins to revise his earlier way of interpreting divine creativity. To say that Absolute Spirit must and will manifest itself in three unfolding upward stages in one way seems to deny freedom to God or to man, who would now be only "made." In his new view, Schelling sees the divine creation as radically free creativity, which finally defies explanation. Looking back to Jacob Boehme (but also forward to Kierkegaard), Schelling sees the world as a "Fall": "From the Absolute to the real there is no continuous transition. The origin of the sensate world can be thought of only as an utter breaking-away from the Absolute by means of a leap." Creation thus occurs when any being posits its own freedom apart from divine unity. "History is an epic poem issuing from the divine Spirit . . . the departure of humanity from its Center to the furthest limits . . . and its return to the Center. The first part is like the Iliad, the other like the Odyssey." Schelling's emphasis now is on the dark loss that a creative Fall shows. To become finite or particular is to become separate and capable of evil; to "return" to the center is now no longer cosmically and impersonally assured (as his earlier system implied), but is achieved only through free struggle. With this view of man as radically free in relation to God, Schelling begins to stress man as an "existential," contingent being —his "positive" philosophy takes its start in immediate, even blind restlessness and striving.

The outcome of these views for Schelling's mythology becomes increasingly visible from 1815 to his death. In the *Ages of the World* (1815), the influence of Boehme is marked. Spirit's creativity, and life itself, result from struggle. In Boehme and now clearly in Schelling, God is described as having a higher and a darker aspect, love and anger; out of this inner struggle in the divine, all creation results; and all being can reach a higher state through struggle against what is not itself. "There is no life without simultaneous death. In the very act whereby existential being is posited, one such existent being must die that another may live." In his *Über die Gottheiten von Samothrace* (1815), using Creuzer's discussion of the Mysteries of Samothrace, Schelling tied his theosophic views directly to myth. Creuzer had explained these mysteries, involving the Kabiri and Ceres, as an esoteric theory of emanation. But Schelling sees it as a movement upward from dark, blind depths to higher, free divinity. Ceres thus rightly represents essential, metaphysical hunger and desire (much like Boehme's primal and empty ground of being). The mysteries depict, through rising steps, the ascent to the free Demiurge.

The *Philosophy of Mythology* is elaborated by Schelling at least from 1825 to his death. The essence of myth is now clearly assigned to what is "hungry and desirous," "blind, unfree and spiritual." This is not to dismiss myth, but the opposite: myth becomes crucial to Schelling's system. For myth is the realm of the necessary, the unconscious, man at his furthest remove from the "center." But because myth nonetheless always expresses an intuition of ultimate spiritual harmony, myth is thus at the same time the condition for man's free striving to regain the "center." This intuition of the divine One is unconsciously lived, rather than consciously understood; and mythic man therefore lives the life and death of his gods as real.

For Schelling's system, the relation between mythology and revelation is all-important. At the beginning of all human history, there is monotheism, but not true revelation; and this monotheism is only a "relative" kind: that is, it contains potentials that can be fulfilled only in the course of time. Man in the first moment then lives an undifferentiated life; polytheism is a break from, a release from, and an elevation above, such undifferentiated life: the manyness of the gods mirrors man's increasing sense of his own differentiation and thus of his freedom. Man moves on through ascending levels of consciousness, aimed toward reunion with God. This divinely intended and supported level of ascension can be seen within myth itself—Schelling describes polytheism as being "successive": one god succeeds and prepares another, each in turn being higher than the last: for example, Uranus, Cronos, and Zeus. Myth thus "repeats" the cosmic process, but in its own terms. But only with Revelation itself does a full expression of human freedom come, through God's free willing. Christian Revelation makes actual what myth only intuited and represented. Judaism signals the end of myth, but even here only the Father is present; the Son must still appear as man to actualize the truth.

The *Philosophy of Mythology* contains Schelling's most richly detailed and cogent criticism of other mythic theories. He rejects any effort to interpret myth by explaining it away: he insists thus that Revelation continues (not refutes) myth, and he rejects all allegorizing, all nature-divinizing, all Euhemerism, and all ideas of myth as mere "disease of language." He resists the view that there is a single

historical origin for all myth, and thus rejects the exclusive mythic enthusiasm for India. He insists that myth can unfold and evolve only in history, among living, believing men; but myth cannot be reduced to this. He affirms the symbol as the mode of truth. From this viewpoint, he criticizes Creuzer as having separated sense and sign, making myth merely the outward garb of pure truth. Myth is a real "moment" of the Spirit; the gods are indeed what they represent, and mean more than their believers can know, too. Schelling sought in these ways to restore myth to itself. The ambitiousness of his effort contrasts with his lack of real influence; but it may be that very ambitiousness which is a main cause for his neglect.

B.F.

REFERENCES   Our texts are from *Selections from System of Transcendental Idealism,* translated by A. Hofstadter, in *Philosophies of Art and Beauty,* edited by A. Hofstadter and R. Kuhns (New York: Random House, 1964); and *Einleitung in die Philosophie der Mythologie,* Erstes Buch, 6. Vorlesung and 9. Vorlesung, in *Schellings Werke,* Bd. VI, hrsg. Manfred Schröter (Munich: Beck u. Oldenbourg, 1928), our translation. Specific reference to Schelling's other writings on mythology may be omitted here; his entire corpus needs to be considered: see *Schellings Werke* for complete edition.

Some useful translations are: Vladimir Jankélevitch, *Introduction à la Philosophie de la Mythologie,* 2 vols. (Paris: Aubier, 1945), which renders *Einleitung in die Philosophie der Mythologie,* the first half of *Philosophie der Mythologie;* F. de W. Bolman, *The Ages of the World,* translated with introduction and notes (New York: Columbia University Press, 1942); James Gutmann, *Schelling: Of Human Freedom* (Chicago: The University of Chicago, 1936). For bibliography, *Friedrich Wilhelm Joseph von Schelling. Eine Bibliographie,* G. Schneebergen (Bern, 1954).

For commentary, see: Adolf Allwohn, *Der Mythos bei Schelling* (Charlottenburg: Pan-

Verlag Heise, 1927); Gerbrand Dekker, *Die Rückwendung zum Mythos; Schellings Letze Wandlung* (Munich/Berlin: Oldenbourg, 1930), for the complex manuscript history of *Philosophie der Mythologie;* Christel M. Schröder, *Das Verhältnis von Heidentum und Christentum in Schellings Philosophie der Mythologie und Offenbarung* (Munich, 1936); Vladimir Jankélevitch, *L'Odyssée de la conscience dans la dernière philosophie de Schelling* (Paris: Alcan, 1933); Fritz Strich, *Die Mythologie in der deutschen Literatur von Klopstock bis Wagner,* 2 vols. (Halle, 1910) and *Deutsche Klassik und Romantik* (Munich, 1962, 5th edition); Ernest Cassirer, *The Philosophy of Symbolic Forms, Volume Two: Mythical Thought,* translated by R. Manheim (New Haven: Yale University Press, 1955), especially pp. 1–26; Frederick Copleston, *A History of Philosophy* (New York: Doubleday, 1965), Vol. VII, Part I, Chaps. 5–7. H. Zeltner, *Schelling* (Stuttgart: Fromanns Verlag, 1954), esp. pp. 217–233. K-H. Volkmann-Schluck, *Mythos und Logos. Interpretation zu Schellings Philosophie der Mythologie* (Berlin: de Gruyter, 1969).

Schelling

FROM *System of Transcendental Idealism*

1. . . . PHILOSOPHY starts out from an infinite dichotomy of opposed activities; but all aesthetic production rests on the same dichotomy, which latter is completely resolved by each artistic representation. What then is the marvelous faculty by which, according to the assertions of philosophers, an infinite opposition annuls itself in productive intuition? We have until now been unable to make this mechanism fully comprehensible because it is only the faculty of art that can fully disclose it. This productive faculty under consideration is the same as that by which art also attains to the impossible, namely, to resolve an infinite contradiction in a finite product. It is the poetic faculty which, in the first potency, is original intuition, and conversely it is only productive intuition repeating itself in the highest potency that we call the poetic faculty. It is one and the same thing that is active in both, the sole capacity by which we are able to think and comprehend even what is contradictory—the imagination. Hence also it is products of one and the same activity that appear to us beyond consciousness as real and on the hither side of consciousness as ideal or as a world of art. But precisely this fact, that under otherwise entirely identical conditions of origin, the genesis of one lies beyond consciousness and that of the other on this side of consciousness, constitutes the eternal and ineradicable difference between the two.

For while the real world proceeds wholly from the same original opposition as that from which the world of art must proceed (bearing in mind that the art world must also be thought of as a single great whole, and presents in all of its individual productions only the one infinite), nevertheless the opposition beyond consciousness is infinite only to the extent that an infinite is presented by the objective world as a *whole* and never by the individual object, whereas for art the opposition is infinite in regard to *each individual object,* and every single product of art presents infinity. For if aesthetic production proceeds from freedom, and if the opposition of conscious and unconscious activity is absolute precisely for freedom, then there exists really only a single absolute work of art, which can to be sure exist in entirely different exemplars but which yet is only one, even though it should not yet exist in its most original form. To this view it cannot be objected that it would be inconsistent with the great freedom with which the predicate "work of art" is used. That which does not present an infinite immediately or at least in reflection is not a work of art. Shall we, e.g., also call poems works of art that by their nature present merely what is individual and subjective? Then we shall also have to apply the name to every epigram that records a merely momentary feeling or current impression. Yet the great masters who worked in these literary types sought to achieve objectivity only through the *whole* of their writings, and used them only as means whereby to represent a whole infinite life and to reflect it by a many-faced mirror.

2. If aesthetic intuition is only intellectual intuition become objective, then it is evident that art is the sole true and eternal organon as well as document of philosophy, which sets forth in ever fresh forms what philosophy cannot represent outwardly, namely, the unconscious in action and production and its original identity with the conscious. For this very reason art occupies the highest place for the philosopher, since it opens to him, as it were, the holy of holies where in eternal

and primal union, as in a single flame, there burns what is sundered in nature and history and what must eternally flee from itself in life and action as in thought. The view of nature which the philosopher composes artificially is, for art, original and natural. What we call nature is a poem that lies hidden in a mysterious and marvelous book. Yet if the riddle could reveal itself, we would recognize in it the Odyssey of the spirit which, in a strange delusion, seeking itself flees itself; for the land of fantasy toward which we aspire gleams through the world of sense only as through a half-transparent mist, only as a meaning does through words. When a great painting comes into being it is as though the invisible curtain that separates the real from the ideal world is raised; it is merely the opening through which the characters and places of the world of fantasy, which shimmers only imperfectly through the real world, fully come upon the stage. Nature is nothing more to the artist than it is to the philosopher; it is merely the ideal world appearing under unchanging limitations, or it is merely the imperfect reflection of a world that exists not outside but within him.

What is the derivation of this affinity of philosophy and art, despite their opposition? This question is already sufficiently answered by the foregoing.

We conclude therefore with the following observation. A system is completed when it has returned to its starting point. But this is precisely the case with our system. For it is just that original ground of all harmony of the subjective and the objective which could be presented in its original identity only by intellectual intuition, that was fully brought forth from the subjective and became altogether objective by means of the work of art, in such a way that we have conducted our object, the ego itself, gradually to the point at which we ourselves stood when we began to philosophize.

But now, if it is art alone that can succeed in making objective with universal validity what the philosopher can only represent subjectively, then it is to be expected (to draw this further inference) that as philosophy, and with it all the sciences that were brought to perfection by it, was born from and nurtured by poetry in the childhood of science, so now after their completion they will return as just so many individual streams to the universal ocean of poetry from which they started out. On the whole it is not difficult to say what will be the intermediate stage in the return of science to poetry, since one such intermediate stage existed in mythology before this seemingly irresolvable breach occurred. But how a new mythology (which cannot be the invention of an individual poet but only of a new generation that represents things as if it were a single poet) can itself arise, is a problem for whose solution we must look to the future destiny of the world and the further course of history alone.

FROM *Introduction to the Philosophy of Mythology*

AFTER THE preceding discussion . . . it seems no longer doubtful that we must abide by the explanation according to which polytheism was preceded by monotheism—not monotheism in any general way but historically so, and indeed monotheism from the age when the peoples first separated. The only question still in doubt is whether polytheism preceded the separation of the peoples or not, and this question, we believe, has already been settled . . . the birth of peoples is entirely due to polytheism. This is the basis of our further inquiry here. . . .

When mankind divided itself into different peoples, in place of the earlier consciousness of unity there came to be different gods; similarly, we can conceive that earlier unity of mankind only in terms of a positive underlying cause, which could hardly have been so decisively maintained except through the consciousness of a God universal and common to all mankind.

But nothing decisive is found here regarding whether this God, universal and common to all men, was necessarily God in the sense of monotheism and indeed in the sense of the One God of revealed monotheism, or whether this God is generally simply unmythologic, with all mythology excluded from him. . . .

But this question cannot be answered without going more deeply than usual into the nature of polytheism . . . we must draw attention to a difference in polytheism itself . . . there is a great difference between a polytheism which includes a greater or smaller number of lesser gods subordinated to one enduring highest and ruling God; and a polytheism which includes many gods, each of which at any given time is the highest and ruling God, and which can thus only succeed each other as ruling Gods. Let us imagine Greek history as having shown not the three races of gods but only one, perhaps that of Zeus; there would then have been only coexisting and simultaneous gods, all of which found their common unifying point in Zeus—there would have been only a *simultaneous* polytheism. But in fact there are three systems of the gods, and in each only one god is highest: Uranus in the first, Cronos in the second, Zeus in the third. These three gods cannot be simultaneous but rather mutually exclude each other, and follow one another in time. So long as Uranus rules, Cronos cannot, and when Zeus rules, Cronos must disappear. This kind of polytheism may be called *successive*. . . .

. . . It is this second kind of polytheism which clearly demands explanation, it is successive polytheism which is the riddle. . . .

If we judge the problem correctly, we see it is the successive character of mythology in which the actual historical and thus the actual true aspect of myth resides; and by considering this successive character, we thus find ourselves on the historical ground of the actual course of mythical events.

That this succession of gods really expresses the actual history of the rise of mythological gods may be seen when one compares the mythologies of different peoples. One sees that in the mythologies of more recent peoples, the teachings about the gods are given only as if related to the past, while in more ancient peoples these are held to be real and in the present. . . . In the chief god, say of the exclusively ruling God of the Phoenicians, the Greeks recognize with complete certainty the Cronos of their own history of the gods, and name him as such. It is quite easy to show how different and wholly unrelated are the Greek and Phoenician gods; but all these differences can be explained by noting that in Phoenician mythology Cronos still rules alone, while in the Greek Cronos is already a god of the past, replaced by another. How could the Greeks recognize

their god in the Phoenician mythology unless Cronos was really an actual god for them, not simply imagined and fictitious?

How many incredible explanations would have been avoided, if instead of speaking of polytheism in a general way, it was seen completely and always as historical! . . . It goes against what is natural for anyone to believe in anything that has only been in the past—rather, it is true anything can only become past, but this begins from my sense of the present, for what I feel as past I must first of all have felt as once present. What has no reality for us can seem only a mere phase, a moment; but the earlier gods . . . must have ruled man's consciousness and entered living into it, or else when it disappeared . . . it would not have been remembered. . . .

Indeed, mythology has no reality outside consciousness. But though mythology develops only in the determinations of consciousness, thus in representations [*Vorstellungen*], that development, that succession of representations cannot be once more simply something to be represented—it must have been held to be real, to have really affected consciousness. These representations did not create mythology, but it is mythology which created them, for mythology is finally only the totality of its teachings on the gods as they actually followed one another, and mythology is the product of this succession. . . .

Mythology is not simply teachings about the gods successively represented. A struggle between successive gods, as spoken of in the theogonies, would never have been found in mythologic representations unless these had already really existed in the consciousness of peoples. . . . The succeeding gods have one after the other actually dominated and affected man's consciousness. Mythology, as a history of the gods, thus as mythology properly speaking, is surely begotten in life; but it demands to be lived and experienced.

. . . From what has been said to now, it may be said that . . . an absolute monotheism, a one God besides whom there can be no other, is not necessary to explain mankind's primal unity or later divisions. . . . We must decide between the two possibilities of an absolute or relative monotheism, and ask whether a relative monotheism does not explain original unity and its fragmentation better than positing an absolute monotheism in the beginning. . . .

. . . How do different peoples come to be? . . . most feel explanations here only superfluous: no special causes need be found here; people create themselves, spontaneously. If from our present viewpoint, . . . we must admit that the spiritual differences which become apparent in the divergence of peoples and of divergent teachings about the gods have always existed in man since his origin, though only potentially and without effect; and these have become expressed and actualized only in the course of ever-evolving generations. . . . If a certain point of development is reached, the differences become actual. . . . The birth of peoples is not something that occurs in simply regular order, from preexisting conditions; but is rather something by which a previous existing order of things is broken through and an entirely new one put in its place. The passage from a homogeneous existence to a higher and more developed one . . . happens no more spontaneously than the passage from inorganic to organic nature, to which it might be compared. . . . The principle that kept man in a state of unity cannot then be an absolute principle, but it must be such that it can be followed by

another, by which it is agitated, changed, even at last conquered.

But as soon as this second principle begins to exercise its effect on mankind, all the possible conditions . . . appear, in some immediate, in others still distant. . . . It is quite possible that the gods of the Greek theogony . . . (Uranus, Cronos, Zeus), were only different successive forms of one or of the first god, and that the succeeding god, though necessarily passing into this form, was entirely outside and foreign, and his own name is still not yet known. If the first forms of the gods are given, those succeeding are given as well, though only as still distant possibilities. To the different forms of the gods correspond divergent, materially different teachings about the gods that exist already potentially, in accord with the second principle. . . . To the different teachings about the gods correspond the different peoples, and thus these are at first in a potential condition . . . since they move into actuality not all at once but only in measured succession. It is through the successive aspect of polytheism that the peoples make their entry and appearance in history not all at once, but one after the other. Until its moment is come . . . each people remains in a potential state, part of a mankind as yet undifferentiated though destined to be. . . . But since the crisis . . . extends universally over all mankind, so a people meant for a later time and a later decision move through all the moments, not indeed as an actual people but as part of mankind as yet still not come to the point of decision. Only in this way is it possible that the moments distributed among the different peoples can become united in the consciousness of the last of these as a completed mythology.

. . . Polytheism was inflicted on mankind in order to destroy not that which was truly One, but that which was distortedly One, a merely relative monotheism. Despite appearances to the contrary . . . polytheism was nevertheless the true passage to the better condition, to the freeing of mankind from a power making man content, but a power oppressive to his freedom, all development and the highest knowledge.

. . . One could respond to our explanations: what you have claimed is incontestable, if there had been no revelation. In the simple natural progress of mankind, a one-sided monotheism could be the first kind. But revelation—what has this to do with that? . . . Now admittedly, man lost Paradise through his own fault, i. e., fell from his original position of having simply essential relations with God. But one cannot consider this without also thinking how man changed, and even how God Himself changed, i. e., without thinking that there was an alteration in religious consciousness . . . such an alteration corresponds to what might be called relative monotheism. God said, in effect: Behold, man is become as one of us; thus—how can one interpret the words otherwise?— he is no longer the entire divinity, but as one of us, as are the Elohim.*

(from Lecture VI)

If, from the viewpoint at which we have thus far arrived, we look back at the purely exterior premises by which earlier hypotheses thought to explain mythology (and revelation was such a hypothesis), we see that a great step forward toward a philosophic inquiry into mythology is to derive myth from primitive mankind's

* Schelling refers earlier in this Sixth Lecture to Elohim as the "angels" whose name *Elohim* can be translated "gods," but without therefore meaning anything involving true polytheism. See *The Ages of the World*, pp. 161–162.—Ed.

inward, spiritual capacity. And more, to admit that it was not poets, cosmogonic philosophers, or followers of a historically prior religious doctrine who have been the creators of mythology, but rather human consciousness which ought to be deemed the true seat and generating principle of mythologic notions and representations.

. . . The last result we arrived at was that mythology in general arises as a consequence of a process, especially of a theogonic character, in which human consciousness finds itself engaged by its own nature . . . it is this process which henceforth will be the single object of the science developed here.

. . . We saw that the mythologic notions and representations created by myth have for men . . . a subjective necessity, a subjective truth. That does not prevent seeing, as is clear, that considered objectively, mythologic notions may be false and arbitrary. . . . All earlier explanations were based on presuppositions which did not go beyond the limits of historical time; now we have established an explanation which ascends to a process transcending history; and here we find some unexpected predecessors. It is a very ancient opinion to see in paganism . . . a consequence of original sin. . . . But in whatever form, this view merits consideration for the sake of the insight that mythology does not seem to be explainable except by a real separation of men from their original condition. Such a view agrees with our own interpretation; but on the other hand, our views diverge, since this older view finds it necessary to appeal to nature and to explain polytheism as an idolatrizing of nature. By seeing man lapsing into the idolatry of nature in this way, the theological approach differs from other well-known analogous interpretations. But with such an explanation based on nature idolatry, the theologic approach turns back again into the categories of explanations already proposed. Led by original sin into the sphere of attraction of nature, and sinking into it ever more deeply, men confuse the creature with Creation, which now ceases to be one and becomes plural. . . . In mystical terms, this can be expressed more precisely: We must by all means start not from a primal knowledge, however splendid, but rather from the *existence* of man within the divine unity. Man was created at the center of this Godhead, and it is essential for him to remain in that center, since that alone is his true place. As long as man remains in the center, he sees things not from an exterior, spiritless, and divided view, but as they exist in God progressively interpenetrating each other, ascending through man as its chief agent, and through him to God. As soon as man moves from the center and falls, the periphery confuses him, divine unity becomes chaotic, and then man himself is no longer divinely above things, but sunken to the same level. But even though fallen, man may still wish to claim his central position and the intuitions connected with it. Then, man's struggles and gropings to cling fast to this disordered and fragmented but still primally divine moment will produce a mediating world—and this world we may call the world of the gods, that higher existence men have dreamt about ever since they knew themselves fallen from that higher world. This world of the gods is produced in an involuntary manner as a consequence of the necessity imposed on man through his primal condition . . . and man, now come to self-consciousness, gives himself over to this external godly world, happy to be released from an immediate condition that he can no longer affirm, and he does this the better to put in its place a mediating condition which leaves him free. . . .

The mythologic process, whose underlying causes are the theogonic potencies as such, is not simply religious in general, but rather has an objectively religious meaning; for it is these God-positing potencies which are at work in the mythologic process. But we have still not reached the last formulation here, since much has been said of a monotheism that became fragmented and splintered into polytheism. . . . According to this, mythology could only be man's earliest consciousness, but now deformed, broken and corrupted. Such monotheism, decomposed into polytheism, is thought of as above all an historical event occurring at some specific epoch in this history of the human race. . . . But we have had to give up the idea of such a monotheism. And we have accepted in its place an essential, i. e., a potential monotheism of the primal consciousness. It is this which has been destroyed in the theogonic process, and one might now say: these same potencies, in their cooperation and unity, create a God-positing consciousness; but these same potencies when divided become the underlying causes of the process through which the gods arise, and thus produces mythology.

. . . Mythology is essentially a successive polytheism, which can arise only through an actual successive sequence of potencies, in which each power supposes and makes necessary what follows and is completed by what preceded, so that true unity is established again at last. . . .

. . . "But," one may ask, "is polytheism then not a false religion, and are there no false religions finally?" Our view is that mythology is not false in itself, but true, because of the premises on which it rests . . . and as for whether there is no false religion, it has already been explained that each Moment of mythology is false not in itself but when abstracted from its relations with all other such Moments. It must be stressed that the mythologies of different peoples really ought to be considered as so many Moments, as Moments of the same process involving all mankind. Each polytheistic religion of a people becoming fixed and stagnant is, as such, a false religion, since it is already an unchanging isolated Moment. But we do not really observe mythology in terms of these encapsulated Moments; we see mythology as a totality, in its unbroken unity through all the Moments of a perpetual activity and movement. . . .

. . . But polytheism, considered in the totality of its successive moments, is the way to truth, and is thus truth itself. Indeed, the conclusion might be as follows: the true religion will be the last mythology which reunites all previous Moments.

. . . The following scheme can be given of a rapid glance at different conceptions of mythology as they appear when seen from the viewpoint of objective truth.

A

There is no truth as such in mythology: it is

1—to be understood in a purely poetic sense; if it contains truth, it does so only by accident;

2—or, it is composed of representations (and ideas) lacking meaning, born of ig-

norance, elaborated later by poetic art and belonging to a poetic realm (J. H. Voss).

B

There is truth in mythology, but not in mythology as such. Mythology is

1—only the garb, the external covering of

a—an historical truth (Euhemerus)

b—a physical truth (Heyne);

2—or, mythology is a misunderstanding, a distortion of

a—a pure scientific truth (thus essentially irreligious) (G. Hermann)

b—of a religious truth (W. Jones; Creuzer).

C

There is truth in mythology as such.

. . . the third conception truly comprises the synthesis of the other two; the first being mythology in the literal sense, but refusing to it all doctrinal meaning, the second insisting on the contrary on doctrinal meaning in myth or even affirming that truth is involved there, but a truth now masked and deformed. While the third affirms that mythology rightly understood directly reveals its truth. This last viewpoint is, as must be clear, possible only through the interpretation advanced here, for we are obliged to admit in mythology an origin in what is necessary, and we are thus as obliged to recognize in mythology a necessary content, i. e., truth.

(from Lecture IX)

FRIEDRICH HÖLDERLIN

[1770–1843]

HÖLDERLIN's poetic career was as brief, as intensely and greatly mature, and as quickly stopped as Keats's. His greatest work was done in about six years, from 1797 to 1803, when he entered a madness and poetic silence almost unbroken thereafter to his death at seventy-three, in 1843. He was born in 1770 and trained for the ministry at Tübingen from 1788 to 1793, with Hegel and Schelling among his fellow-students and friends. Hölderlin's seminary theses show the same enthusiasm for mythic-religious subjects prominent in the youthful works of other budding romantics. In 1790, he wrote a school essay, "Parallel between Solomon's Proverbs and Hesiod's Works and Days," that was partly a stylistic comparison, partly also a rendering of the by then familiar German view of myth as a "first energy of the soul" among primitive peoples. In the same year, he wrote another sketchy school essay, "History of the Fine Arts among the Greeks," one of whose points is to emphasize how (unlike the Egyptian-Oriental practice) the Greeks embodied their gods in sensuous beauty, and how Greek myth rose from this same natural joyousness. His early verse is Schilleresque in tone, style, and in theme. By 1797, he reached poetic maturity, published the first version of his Greek romance, *Hyperion,* and started his much-revised long poem about Empedocles; up to 1803, his writing was prolific, brilliantly sustained, and developing.

But his poetic triumphs cannot be separated from a ceaseless spiritual crisis that Hölderlin never solved, but rather always deepened for himself. His mature poems express a most intense and original search for religious belief and certainty. Part of Hölderlin's originality lies in his hope to satisfy his religious longing within the realm of Greek myth and the gods, or in some realm where Greek myth livingly joins Christian or Germanic or Indic divinities. In daring to believe that the Greek gods are still somehow alive and accessible, Hölderlin went far beyond his predecessors and contemporaries in hoping to revitalize "ancient" myth. For him, Greek myth is not mainly an historical or even aesthetic expression, and certainly not allegory or a debased or crude version of revealed Christian truth, but the real possibility of a compelling, genuine religion. Certainly Hölderlin's celebrations of the gods were always deeply qualified and stimulated by his continuing commitment to Christian ideals and to idealist assumptions. But how far he departed from the former can be seen in his incessant but futile struggle to boldly reconcile Christ with the classical pantheon of gods. How far he departed from idealist philosophy may be seen by comparing his vivid dithyrambic evocations of divine mythic presences with an earlier sketch of 1795, his *The Oldest System Programme of German Idealism* (preserved in Hegel's handwriting and paraphrased by Schelling in 1795–1796), which explicitly calls for a new mythology, a "mythology of reason," where reason is defined as an "aesthetic act" directed toward a vaguely Platonic idea of beauty. His richest characteristic poetry is however much more an effort to surrender fully to a living religious experience, but never naively or programatically: Hölderlin's greatest poems are mythopoetic in two senses—a worshipping of the archaic divinities from within their own sphere, combined with a self-conscious awareness that the archaic divine is now "silent" and thus can be resurrected again only by a new kind of poetic creation.

Neglected while alive, Hölderlin's rank among the greatest German poets is by now unassailable. Still his work in general or use of myth in particular cannot be adequately explained by conventional romantic allegiances. He exploits the romantic longing for a golden age and infinite harmony, and is deeply influenced as well by the romantic conviction that this is best embodied in Indic religion. But rather than remaining another poet of romantic myth, he has increasingly come to be that poet in whose art romantic myth, more than being a special viewpoint, becomes the adequate basis of a large poetic achievement. Hölderlin is the first important German poet whose work cannot be discussed on any side except in terms of myth. More accurately, perhaps, he is the first—and finally, maybe the only—major modern poet about whom this is a suitable assertion. This points again, of course, to Hölderlin's uniquely single-minded effort to write mythic poetry as a religious act. This is one crucial reason why Hölderlin's is one of the most difficult mythopoetic achievements in the modern period.

He seeks to grasp the mythic in its own terms. But though this means becoming a pagan once more, the implications of this are not easily grasped: Hölderlin seems early to have endorsed pantheism, and later, in some form, polytheism, and

yet frequently seems also to subsume all this into a kind of monotheism. But he holds none of these positions in any conventional sense. Thus, Hölderlin can write about gods that he alone has named, such as "Father Aether" or "Germania." The difficulties in ascertaining what myth or what the "gods" actually signify here is increased considerably when Hölderlin speaks of Christ as brother of Hercules, or of the "Father" in the same way as he speaks of Bacchus. If the gods were mainly allegoric or aesthetic abstractions for Hölderlin, shadow-spirits to be reconciled with a higher view, there would be no difficulty; but his gods seem always actual, real, livingly present and autonomous. If his "gods" are indeed really divine, then reconciliation between them and Christ should be possible: the divine, after all, must be one. But most other mythologists achieved cosmic harmony by choosing either the gods or God. In part, too, Hölderlin is difficult because he takes literally what romantic mythologists from Herder on taught but never practiced so intensely: that myth must be livingly experienced to be understood, and that regaining such mythic depth and life may help redeem modern man. Hölderlin carries this program out, or tries to. But instead of the large optimism about myth, shown by many romantics, Hölderlin shows that radical modern mythopoesis can lead to tragic conclusions, to high and wondrous but also unexpectedly perilous and baffling dilemmas as well.

This reappearance of tragic myth is apparent early in his short poetic career. His Greek novel, *Hyperion,* shows a familiar romantic Hellenism. Hyperion is a young Greek of the eighteenth century who hopes to help free his country from Turkish rule, and the novel consists of letters between Hyperion and some German friends, mainly discussing Greece and the world, ancient and modern. The hope for freedom fails because of modern Greek venality, but Germany turns out to be just as decadent. Still, ancient beauty and nature, Greek art and the gods remain pure, alive, "waiting." Such waiting for divine appearance is one of Hölderlin's great themes, a hope held sometimes with soaring Christian confidence, sometimes darkly pagan. That the divine might be gained by passive surrender was a romantic and ultimately Christian theme. But Hölderlin's pious celebration of "waiting" stands in frequent contrast to the often aggressive romantic thrust toward grasping the divine or the mythic, such as in Novalis's "magic idealism," or in Friedrich Schlegel's omnivorous "universal, progressive" poetry. In the same way, Hölderlin's poems often yield a despair rarely if ever encountered among earlier mythic poets—an unbearable sense of expectation, wedded always to an awareness of how inscrutable the divine is. The gods are near, and yet most difficult to grasp, give men highest joy, yet are the "alien ones"; even Christ is now silent. Too boldly, Empedocles dares to name the gods and to explain the mysteries, and he comes to know the impiety of *hubris*—an agonizing knowledge for any pious mythopoetic poet to bear, as Hölderlin makes clear. The poet remains torn, unable to know with certainty whether the gods are benevolent or cruel, attentive to men or indifferent. Despair comes too because the gods—and Christ —may not have vanished, but may have only withdrawn because of man's own indifference, corruption, and "forgetfulness." In a poem perhaps parodying Herder in its title, "The Voice of the People," Hölderlin shows not the rise to creative fulfillment of the *Volk,* but its ruin. Against Herder's primitive *Volk*-as-poet, Hölderlin stresses the need now for a sophisticated poet who comes (and can only come) "late." Such a poet can at least announce the divine "return" and perhaps prepare for it by teaching his nation a right piety. But the true return of the gods does not mean reinstituting the

Olympian religion, but that the Golden Age itself comes again. Hölderlin here introduces a most un-Greek element and hope into his view of the gods; at the same time, he introduces a most un-Christian element into his love of Christ, by demanding a reconciliation between Christ and Hercules. In his poem "The Only One," Apollo, Zeus, and Hercules, but also Christ and the Christian Father, are brought together on the same hopeful level. Such a transcending vision, however, could also yield a transcendent despair: for when this vision of primal harmony fails to be achieved, myth fails too, in its claim to universality.

There is another difficulty in Hölderlin that brings forward another side of his originality: he approaches myth most powerfully through the lyric poem. Goethe preceded Hölderlin here, but Goethe also went on to work with myth in epic, narrative, and dramatic form; Hölderlin remained the lyricist. From antiquity to modernity, poetry has mostly treated myth through epic or narration, as much as through the lyric—Homer and Virgil, obviously, and modern examples include *Faust,* Blake's *Prophetic Books,* Keats's narrative mythic poems, *Thus Spake Zarathustra,* the *Waste Land,* Yeats's *Vision, Moby Dick, Ulysses,* and Mann's *Joseph.* Hölderlin's "tradition" includes Pindar before him, and Rilke after. The lyric clearly frustrates mythic system-building or coherent articulation through action and character. To explain then what the poet means by his rapt mythic songs is difficult; but in Hölderlin, this obscurity clearly points to what he seemed able to sense intuitively about mythic meaning. His odes and hymns are a worshipping, but also an illumined delineation of the sense of being (or wanting to be) invaded and possessed by the mystery of divine power. His lyrics do not recosmologize the divine, as Blake tried to do. Not the least side of Hölderlin's achievement is his refusal or honest reluctance to make myth more rational, more aesthetic, or more systematic—despite his Christian hopes—than it may have been.

B.F.

REFERENCES Our texts are from Friedrich Hölderlin, *Poems and Fragments,* translated by Michael Hamburger (Ann Arbor: University of Michigan Press, 1967). *Sämtliche Werke,* ed. F. Beissner, 6 vols. (Stuttgart: Kohlhammer, 1943–1961) is the standard edition. Among much commentary, see the following: Wilhelm Böhm, *Hölderlin,* 2 vols. (Halle-Saale, 1928–1930); Karl Viëtor, *Die Lyrik Hölderlins* (Frankfurt am Main, 1921); Romano Guardini, *Hölderlin* (Munich, 1955); E. L. Stahl, *Hölderlin's Symbolism* (Oxford, 1945; Paul Böckmann, *Hölderlin und seine Götter* (Munich, 1935); Lothar Kempter, *Hölderlin und die Mythologie* (Horgen-Munich und Leipsig, 1929); Marshall Montgomery, *Friedrich Hölderlin and the German Neo-Hellenic Movement* (Oxford, 1923); A. Leslie Willson, *A Mythic Image: The ideal of India in German Romanticism* (Durham: Duke University Press, 1964); Henry Hatfield, *Aesthetic Paganism in German Literature* (Cambridge: Harvard University Press, 1964).

HÖLDERLIN

"In My Boyhood Days . . ."

IN MY boyhood days
   Often a god would save me
      From the shouts and the rod of men;
         Safe and good then I played
           With the orchard flowers
              And the breezes of heaven
               Played with me.

And as you make glad
The hearts of the plants
When toward you they stretch
Their delicate arms,

So you made glad my heart,
Father Helios, and like Endymion
I was your darling,
Holy Luna.

O all you loyal,
Kindly gods!

Would that you knew how
My soul loved you then.

True, at that time I did not
Evoke you by name yet, and you
Never named me, as men use names,
As though they knew one another.

Yet I knew you better
Than ever I have known men,
I understood the silence of Aether,
But human words I've never understood.

I was reared by the euphony
Of the rustling copse
And learned to love
Amid the flowers.

I grew up in the arms of the gods.

"The Only One"

WHAT is it that
To the ancient, the happy shores
Binds me, so that I love them
Still more than my own homeland?
For as though in heavenly
Capitivity cowering, in flaming air
I am where the stones tell Apollo walked

In the guise of a king
And Zeus condescended
To innocent youths, and sons in a holy
fashion
Begot, and daughters,
The exalted, amid mankind.

(ll. 1–12, second version)

"Germania"

NOT THEM, the blessed, who once
appeared,
Those images of gods in the ancient land,
Them, it is true, I may not now invoke,
but if,
You waters of my homeland, now with you
The love of my heart laments, what else
does it want, in
Its hallowed sadness? For full of
expectation lies
The country, and as though it had been
lowered
In sultry dog-days, on us a heaven today,
You yearning rivers, casts prophetic shade.
With promises it is fraught, and to me
Seems threatening too, yet I will stay with
it,
And backward now my soul shall not
escape
To you, the vanished, whom I love too
much.
To look upon your beautiful brows, as
though
They were unchanged, I am afraid, for
deadly
And scarcely permitted it is to awaken the
dead.

Gods who are fled! And you also,
present still,
But once more real, you had your time,
your ages!
No, nothing here I'll deny and ask no
favours.
For when it's over, and Day's light gone
out,
The priest is the first to be struck, but
lovingly
The temple and the image and the cult
Follow him down into darkness, and none
of them now may shine.
Only as from a funeral pyre henceforth
A golden smoke, the legend of it, drifts
And glimers on around our doubting
heads
And no one knows what's happening to
him. He feels
The shadowy shapes of those who once
were here,
The ancients, newly visiting the earth.
For those who are to come now jostle us,
Nor longer will that holy host of beings
Divinely human linger in azure Heaven.

(ll. 1–32)

NOVALIS

[1772–1801]

IF THERE IS a single poet *par excellence* of German romantic myth, it is Novalis. His poems and mythic romances are creative embodiments of the oracular ambitions and excited theories that he, the Schlegels, and others poured out in notebooks, aphorisms, and bold manifestoes: the program of a total poetry, a "poetry of poetry," of a new mythology to be based on idealism and dynamic nature; of Schiller-derived formulas about the modern ideal aiming at the infinite and freedom, and of a new poetry that will raise past and present to the highest power; of the romantic-Christian vision of a spiritually unified medievalism projected fervently to the future; of the dream of India as the paradisal homeland and fathomless mythic well of all poetry and religion; of the poet as magical seer and creative priest of nature. Novalis's best work cannot be confined to these formulas, but neither are these mere formulas. Some of the most intense and extreme ideas of German romanticism were formed and developed by Novalis himself; his short life and necessarily brief poetic career were both lived out entirely within the period of the rise of early German romanticism.

"Novalis" was born Friedrich von Hardenberg in 1772, to a noble, ancient, and pietist family. He trained for law, attended Schiller's lectures at Jena in 1790–91, and became intimate with the Schlegels, Tieck, and Schleiermacher. His life reaped some of the mysterious poetic quality his writing strove for, if unhappily so. At twenty-two, he fell in love with a precocious, gifted twelve-year-old girl, Sophie von Kuhn, and became engaged to her in 1794. In 1797, following a long illness, Sophie died; the tragedy became the direct inspiration for his best poem, *Hymns to the Night* (1799–1800). But by 1801, Novalis himself was dead of tuberculosis. In the few years before his death, besides the *Hymns,* he finished a series of *Spiritual Songs* (1799–1802), some of which became popular church hymns, and *Christianity or Europe* (1799), an essay on the medieval unifying of Europe through Christianity, the decay of modern Europe through rationalist godlessness, and the need for reunification through a higher Christian revival. He also wrote a mass of brilliant aphorisms, many of which were printed in the Schlegels' *Athenäum,* and two unfinished mythic romances: *The Novices of Sais* (1798), a rhapsodic-didactic portrayal of nature as offering symbolic knowledge, using the cult of Isis in the temple at Sais in ancient Egypt; and his most ambitious work, *Heinrich von Ofterdingen,* a *Bildungsroman* modelled after Goethe's *Wilhelm Meister* but set now in medieval Germany, which describes the initiation of the hero, not into the "world" at large, but into the higher mysteries of life that were thought to reside in the realm of the mythic. The initiation is symbolized by Heinrich's quest for the magical "blue flower."

Heinrich von Ofterdingen has, at its center, certain teachings about the true meaning of poetry, which Heinrich learns from the master-poet Klingsohr. Klingsohr imparts this wisdom appropriately through a symbolic myth (Part I, Chapter 9), in which all human and cosmic antitheses become prophetically reconciled. This myth begins with an "iron age" now fallen on the cosmos, symbolic of the loss of original paradise. As in Blake, the characters here are spiritual powers blending old and new mythology: some from Greek myth, like the Sphinx, the Fates, Eros, and Perseus; some from Arabic or Indic myth, like Ginnistan (Hindostan is one root here); Freya comes from Northern myth; some are invented, like Fable, the Father, the Scribe, Sophia, and Arcturus. The cosmos here is threefold: it is a spiritual geography, consisting of an upper world, perhaps heaven, now frozen; the middle realm, earth, ruled by the Father (or Mind); and the underworld, inhabited by the forces of necessity and blind nature, the Fates and Sphinx. The action involves reuniting into oneness all the scattered fragments of primal harmony, and is accomplished primarily through the indefilable purity of the child, Fable. The start of the tale suggests the desired end: "Once Fable gains her ancient right once more/ The world shall rewaken fire in Freya's womb." Freya epitomizes total harmony now paralyzed. Freya's mother, Sophia or Wisdom, has left the upper world to live in the middle, earthly realm. In that middle realm are born the instruments of redemption: Fable, the daughter of Mind and Imagination, and Eros, the son of Mind and Heart. Eros unsuccessfully quests for Freya, but becomes impotently enthralled by sensuousness. Now reason —in its "petrified form"—tyrannically seizes rule of the earth; but Fable escapes, to begin the awakening of the creative but sleeping cosmic powers. First, the power of nature itself is destroyed: the sun is stripped of its glory and becomes a dead stone. Following this, Fable goes to the underworld and destroys both the Fates and the Sphinx. Master of power now, Fable next rewakens the sleeping ancient giant of earth by using lightning. "The earth is awakened again . . . the ancient times are returning." The tale ends with Eros married to Freya. Fable is awarded the spindle of fate to "spin forever an unbreakable golden thread." An apotheosis of cosmic joy and unity ensues forever:

Established is the empire of eternity,
In love and peace all enmity is ended,
The long, long dream of sad pain is ended,
Sophia now is forever Priestess in our
     hearts.

Novalis's view of myth looks radically toward the future, toward actualizing all human and historic possibilities. Myth of the earliest or historical past thus becomes the raw material for a new and necessary mythopoesis. Underlying such a prophetic flowering of all potentiality is, of course, Novalis's ardent Christian hope. But as Klingsohr's mythic prophecy shows, the Christian strain in Novalis's own myth-making remains somewhat ambivalent. What Christ traditionally did as the redeemer, Fable now does, and Christ is nowhere mentioned as such. Perhaps Blake offers some illuminating affinities with Klingsohr's myth. Sophia, like Blake's Jerusalem, is fallen into self-dividedness; Blake's Christ (the true artist), like Novalis's Fable, descends into the world now ruled by false gods ("petrified reason" in Novalis, stony Urizen in Blake). And Novalis, like Blake, absorbed something of his view of Sophia from Jacob Boehme's near-Gnostic teaching about fallen Wisdom. But where Blake can often seem to hold to Christ without Christianity, so Novalis as often can seem to hold to Christian hopes without Christ. Like Blake, too, Novalis's redemption is to be immanently attained by human imaginative power flowering out into cosmic oneness; the need for external redemption vanishes. But unlike Blake, Novalis's conception of imaginative power is heavily stamped by philosophic idealism, particularly by Fichte's view of the ego "creating" its own world by an act of will.

This joining of Christian eschatology and extreme metaphysical subjectivism often makes an unstable mixture in Novalis's mythopoetic practice. Sometimes his myth-creating poet seems primarily the human vehicle and prophet of a still recognizably Christian apotheosis; sometimes, however, his poet makes myths as an autonomous creator who can transform and synthesize all reality at will through his own ecstatic "magic." Herder and others had already taught that myth exemplified the human ability to transform physical nature into a higher spiritual truth. Novalis pushes the creative power of mythic poetry to much more extreme lengths: poetry now will subsume myth, and will bring to free, self-conscious fulfillment all that myth implied. "The world becomes dream, dream becomes the world." What seems to guide Novalis's thought is the image of the absolute poem, a *Totalwissenschaft,* in which all reality becomes poetry. Indeed, he suggested to Friedrich Schlegel in 1797 that all books should aim at being the Bible. For Novalis, the ideal book takes the form of the *Märchen,* the fairy tale: "The fairy tale is entirely the canon of poetry—everything poetic must be like fairy tales." Nothing merely childish or naive is intended here. The *Märchen* is the final, self-contained, self-referring expression of all in one, and its ideal condition is like music or dream, "without coherence, an ensemble of marvels and events . . . nature itself." All apparent obstacles to complete unity will be broken through; Novalis's account of the quest for the "blue flower" symbolizes this. *Hymns to the Night* similarly celebrate death, not as the end but as the beginning. In that poem, a "singer" born in Greece goes out to worship the newborn Christ, and passes thence to "Hindostan." The birth of the new world pervades the whole of time and space. The *Hymns* end with death issuing mankind into eternal dream: "Dream bursts our bonds and sinks us free/ To our father's arms eternally."

In Novalis, myth does more than give an historical opportunity for poetry to arise: poetry is alone the meaning of myth, "Poetry is what is truly and absolutely real . . . the more poetic, the more true." But it is also true, therefore, that any true poesis must be mythopoesis.

B.F.

REFERENCES Our text is from *Novalis, Hymns to the Night and Other Selected Writings,* translated with introduction by Charles E. Passage (New York: Bobbs-Merrill, 1960). *Schriften,* 4 vols., ed. J. Minor (Jena: E. Diederich, 1923) is a standard edition. Useful translations include: *Henry of Ofterdingen,* translated by J. Owen (Cambridge, Massachusetts, 1842; 2d ed., 1853); *The Novices of Sais,* translated by Ralph Manheim, with introduction by Stephen Spender (New York: Curt Valentin, 1949).

For commentary see: Thomas Carlyle, *Novalis,* 1829; Jutta Hecker, *Das Symbol der Blauen Blume im Zusammenhang mit der Blauensymbolik der Romantik* (Jena, 1931); Frederick Hiebel, *Novalis* (Chapel Hill: University of North Carolina Press, 1954); Theodor Haering, *Novalis als Philosoph* (Stuttgart, 1954); Bruce Haywood, *Novalis: The Veil of Imagery* (Cambridge: Harvard University Press, 1959); Michael Hamburger, *Reason and Energy* (New York: Grove Press, 1957), Chap. II; A. Leslie Willson, *A Mythical Image: The ideal of India in German Romanticism* (Durham: Duke University Press, 1964), pp. 147–170, for best guide to Novalis's interest in Eastern myth; James Trainer, "The Märchen," in *The Romantic Period in Germany,* ed. S. Prawer (New York:

Schocken, 1970); R. Benz, *Märchendichtung der Romantik* (Jena, 1926, 2d ed.). M. Lüthi, *Märchen* (Stuttgart: Metzlersche Verlag, 1962).

NOVALIS

FROM "Klingsohr's Fairy Tale"

IN *Henry of Ofterdingen*

I

THE LONG night had just come on. The ancient hero struck upon his shield so that it resounded far and wide in the empty streets of the city. Thrice he repeated the sign. Thereupon the high colored windows of the palace began to brighten from within and their figures stirred. They stirred with greater animation the stronger the reddish light became, which began to illuminate the streets. Gradually also the mighty columns and walls themselves were seen to grow bright; finally they stood in the purest milky-blue shimmer, exuded the softest hues. The entire region was visible now, and the reflection of the figures, the tumult of lances, swords, shields, and helmets, which from all sides bowed down before crowns that appeared now here, now there, and which finally, like them, disappeared, yielding place before a smooth green wreath around which a broad circle was closed— all this was reflected in the frozen sea that surrounded the mountain upon which the city stood, and even the distant girdle of mountains that enclosed the sea was clothed to its depths in a mild glow. Nothing could be clearly distinguished. Yet a wondrous din was to be heard, as from a far-off gigantic smithy. The city, on the other hand, appeared bright and clear. Its smooth transparent walls reflected the beautiful rays, and the excellent symmetry, the noble style of all edifices, and their fine ordering were revealed. Before all the windows stood delicate clay vessels full of the most diverse ice-flowers and snow-flowers, which glittered most charmingly.

Most splendid of all stood out the garden in the great square before the palace, which consisted of metal trees and crystal plants and which was sown with jewel-blossoms and fruits. The diversity and exquisiteness of the forms and the vividness of the lights and colors afforded the most magnificent spectacle, the splendor of which was completed by a lofty fountain frozen to ice in the midst of the garden. The hero was slowly walking past the gate of the palace. From within a voice cried his name. He pushed against the gate, which opened with a gentle ringing tone, and stepped into the hall. Before his eyes he held his shield.

"Have you discovered nothing yet?" said the beautiful daughter of Arcturus in a voice of lamentation.

She was lying against silken cushions upon a throne artfully constructed from a single large sulphur-crystal, and several maidens were assiduously rubbing her tender limbs, which seemed to be commingled of milk and crimson. Under the hands of the maidens lovely light emanated from her, wondrously illuminating the palace. A fragrant breeze wafted through the hall. The hero was silent.

"Allow me to touch your shield," she said softly.

He approached the throne and trod upon the rare carpet. She took his hand, pressed it with tenderness to her heavenly bosom, and touched his shield. His armor rang, and a permeating strength animated his body. His eyes flashed and his heart beat audibly against his armor. The beautiful Freya seemed more cheerful, and the light that streamed from her flared more fiery.

"The King is coming!" cried a magnificent bird that sat in the recess of the throne.

The waiting-women drew a sky-blue coverlet over the Princess, covering her even above the bosom. The hero lowered his shield and looked up toward the dome, to which two broad staircases wound their way on either side of the room. A faint music preceded the King, who presently appeared in the dome with a numerous retinue and descended.

The beautiful bird unfolded its gleaming pinions, softly stirred them, and, as though with a thousand voices, sang toward the approaching King:

The handsome stranger will not long delay.
Warmth nears, eternity begins its reign.
The Queen will wake from long dreams
    where she lay

When in love's ardor melt both land and
    main.
Cold night will quit the places of his stay
Once Fable wins her ancient right again.
In Freya's womb the world shall kindle
    fire.
And each desire discover its desire.

The King embraced his daughter with tenderness. The spirits of the constellations ranged themselves about the throne, and the hero took his place in the procession. An untold throng of stars in ornamental groups filled the hall. The waiting-women brought in a table and a casket wherein lay a quantity of leaves of paper bearing holy and profound symbols composed solely of star-formations. Reverently the King kissed these leaves, carefully shuffled them, and handed several of them to his daughter. The rest he retained for himself. The Princess drew them forth one by one and laid them on the table. Then the King closely consulted his own and selected with much reflection before adding one to the rest. At times he seemed to be constrained to select this leaf or that. But often his joy could be seen when with a lucky leaf he could lay down a fine harmony of signs and symbols. As the game began, signs of the most avid absorption could be observed among all the onlookers, and the strangest expressions and gestures, as if each held in his hands an invisible instrument with which he was eagerly operating. Simultaneously a soft but deeply moving music was to be heard in the air, which seemed to arise from the stars that were wondrously interweaving in the hall, and from the other strange movements. The stars kept moving about, now slowly, now swiftly, in constantly altering patterns, and, at the pace of the music, kept taking up most dextrously the formations on the leaves of paper. Ceaselessly the music varied, like the symbols upon the table, and wondrous and intricate as the transitions not infrequently were, one simple theme seemed nevertheless to connect them all. With incredible lightness the stars flew toward the symbols. They were beautifully disposed now in one great concentration and then again in separate clusters; now the long array disintegrated like a beam of light in countless sparks, and now in ever augmenting smaller circles and patterns there was again realized one great astounding configuration. During this time the colored forms in the windows remained stationary. The bird kept constantly stirring the cloak of its precious feathers in the most varied ways. Up until now the ancient hero had also been busily carrying on his invisible operation, when suddenly the King, full of joy, exclaimed:

"All shall go well. Cast your sword, Iron, into the world, so they may learn where Peace rests."

The hero wrested his sword from his hip, held it with the point toward heaven, then seized it and threw it from the opened window across the city, across the sea of ice. Like a comet it flew through the air and seemed to burst asunder against the girdle of mountains, for it fell as sheer sparks.

V

Expectation was fulfilled and surpassed. All perceived what they had lacked, and the room had become a place of waiting for the blessed. Sophia said: "The great mystery has been revealed to all, yet remains eternally unfathomable. Out of sufferings the new world is born, and in tears are the ashes dissolved into the drink of eternal life. In each one dwells the heavenly Mother in order to bear each child eternally. Do you feel the sweet birth in the throbbing of your breasts?"

What remained in the vessel she poured down into the altar. The earth quaked in its depths. Sophia said: "Eros, hasten with your sister to your beloved. You shall all see me again soon."

Fable and Eros departed quickly with their retinue.

A mighty springtime was spread across the earth. Everything was rising and stirring. The earth floated closer under the veil. The moon and clouds with joyous turmoil were moving northward. The King's citadel shed a magnificent radiance across the sea, and upon the parapet stood the King in full splendor with his retainers. Everywhere they glimpsed dust whorls in which known forms seemed to be taking shape. They encountered numerous bands of youths and maidens streaming toward the citadel and welcoming them with exultation. On many a hill sat a happy pair just awakened, in long foregone embrace, taking the new world for a dream and unable to cease assuring themselves of the lovely truth.

Flowers and trees were growing and putting forth green with all their might. Everything seemed infused with soul. Everything was talking and singing. Fable greeted old acquaintances everywhere. Beasts approached the awakened humans with friendly greetings. Plants entertained them with fruits and fragrances and adorned them most fairly. No stone lay any longer on any human heart, and all burdens had collapsed of themselves to form a solid floor. They came to the sea. A barque of polished steel lay tied up at the shore. They stepped in and loosened the cable. The bow directed itself toward north, and the boat, as though in flight, clove the amorous waves. Whispering reeds halted its impetus, and it touched lightly to shore. They hurried up the broad stairs. Love marveled at the royal city and its treasures. In the courtyard leaped the fountain which had come to life, the grove was astir with the sweetest tones, and a wondrous life seemed to well and surge in its hot stems and leaves, in its glittering flowers and fruits. The ancient hero received them at the gates of the palace.

"Venerable ancient," said Fable, "Eros needs your sword. Gold had given him a chain, one end of which reaches down into the sea and the other end of which is wound about his heart. Take hold of it with me and lead us into the hall where the Princess rests."

Eros took the sword from the hand of the ancient, set the pommel against his heart, and inclined the tip forwards. The double doors of the hall flew open, and Eros with ecstasy approached the slumbering Freya. Suddenly there fell a mighty thunderbolt. A bright spark leaped from the Princess to the sword; the sword and the chain flashed. The hero held little Fable who had almost collapsed. Eros' helmet-crest rose in undulations. "Cast away the sword," cried Fable, "and awaken your beloved." Eros dropped the sword, flew to the Princess, and ardently kissed her sweet lips. She opened her great dark eyes and recognized her beloved. A long kiss sealed the eternal bond.

Down from the dome came the King with Sophia by the hand. The constellations and the spirits of Nature followed in resplendent ranks. An indescribably bright daylight filled the hall, the palace, the city, and the sky. A countless throng poured into the broad royal hall, and with silent reverence saw the lovers kneel before the King and Queen, who solemnly consecrated them. The King took his diadem from his head and placed it upon Eros' golden locks. The ancient hero removed his armor from him, and the King cast his mantle about him. Then he placed the lily in his left hand, and Sophia clasped a precious bracelet round the entwined hands of the lovers, while simultaneously placing her own crown upon Freya's brown hair.

"Hail to our ancient rulers!" cried the people. "They have always dwelt among us and we did not recognize them! Hail to us! They shall rule over us forever! Bless us also!"

Sophia said to the new Queen: "Cast the bracelet of your union into the air so that the people and the world shall remain bounden to you."

The bracelet melted in the air, and presently rings of light were to be seen around every head and a glittering circlet formed over the city and the sea and over the earth, which was celebrating an eternal festival of springtime. Perseus entered carrying a spindle and a small basket. He brought the basket to the new King. "Here," said he, "are the remains of your enemies." Within there lay a stone plate with black and white squares, and beside it a number of figures in alabaster and black marble. "It is a chessboard," said Sophia. "All war is charmed onto this board and into these figures. It is a memorial of the old troubled time." Perseus turned to Fable and gave her the spindle. "In your hands this spindle shall delight us forever, and out of yourself you will spin us a golden thread unbreakable." The Phoenix flew with a melodious sound to her feet and spread its wings before her; whereon she mounted, and it hovered with her above the throne without alighting. She sang a celestial song and began to spin, while the thread seemed to unwind out of her breast. The people were seized with new rapture and the eyes of all hung upon the lovely child. A new exultation arose at the door. The old Moon entered with his strange court, and behind him the people bore in Ginnistan and her bridegroom as in a triumph.

They were wreathed with garlands of flowers. The royal family received them with the most cordial tenderness, and the new regal pair proclaimed them their regents on earth.

"Grant me," said the Moon, "the realm of the Fates, whose strange buildings have just risen out of the earth in the courtyard of the palace. There I will delight you with spectacles with which little Fable will assist me."

The King accorded the request, little Fable nodded agreement, and the people looked forward with pleasure to the oddly entertaining pastime. The Hesperides expressed their best wishes upon the accession to the throne and their request for protection in their gardens. The King bade them welcome, and in this fashion followed countless joyous embassies. Mean-

while the throne had imperceptibly become transformed and had turned into a magnificent nuptial couch over the canopy of which hovered the Phoenix with little Fable. Three Caryatides of dark porphyry bore up the rear of it, and in front it rested upon a sphinx of basalt. The King embraced his blushing beloved, and following the King's example, the people embraced one another. Nothing was to be heard but sweet names and the whispering of kisses. At last Sophia said: "The Mother is among us, her presence will make us happy eternally. Follow us to our dwelling. In the temple there we shall dwell forever and guard the mystery of the world."

Fable went on busily spinning and with a loud voice sang:

Established is the empire of eternity,
In love and peace concluded is all enmity,
The long-drawn dream of dreary suffer-
    ing departs,
Sophia is forever Priestess in our hearts.

AUGUST WILHELM SCHLEGEL

[1767–1845]

BEYOND his early, important part in helping found German romanticism, August Wilhelm Schlegel shared with his younger brother Friedrich a wide but central range of interests: in literature, the arts, and myth; in a cult of Hellenism, of medievalism and Christianity, Indianism and modernism; in classical and also Sanskrit philology (though August began studying Sanskrit later than did his brother, he went on to occupy the first German university chair for Indian subjects in 1818 at Bonn). But in a way never quite true of Friedrich, August Schlegel early gained and held a most influential critical place in European romanticism in general. Indeed, through the popularizing work of Madame de Staël, *On Germany* (1813), some of August Schlegel's critical attitudes came almost to epitomize the essence of the whole surprisingly rich renaissance of recent German culture as it became newly known to a larger European audience. Schlegel's critical gifts and temper in many ways ideally fitted him for such a role. For of all the greater German romantics, Schlegel was perhaps the most moderate in tone and judgment, much more the equable consolidator of romantic innovations than, for example, the fertilely brilliant but restless Friedrich. Or put otherwise, August was more the calmly detached practicing literary critic than the boldly speculative theorist, a superb sympathetic interpreter of a prodigious spread of subjects.

As much is true of August Schlegel's views on myth. Like Friedrich, he early commits himself to myth as a higher and most ancient mode of truth and poetry, indispensable to any understanding of human history or achievement. But rather than stressing myth as a revolutionary literary or philosophic program, Schlegel mediates between what is praiseworthy in myth and its art as against romantic-Christian ideals and art; and if the modern "poetry of longing" is finally higher, Schlegel urges always a ground of middle sympathy for both. One far-reaching result of his balanced, catholic criticism is that the new idea of myth moves from Germany into general European sight, with its more radical side already somewhat mitigated, and thus, more assimilable. Schlegel affirms how myth is the primal organic form from which poetic organicism arises, but his real achievement is in giving perhaps the first great critical demonstration of how literature unifies multiplicity—and his critical analyses are closely detailed, spacious, and flexible (if not finally as subtle) as those of his admirer and "plagiarizer," Coleridge.

Schlegel's two major and best-known works are his *On Literature and the Fine Arts* of 1801–1804, and his *On Dramatic Art and Literature* of 1809–1811. In the first series of lectures, mythology is treated at length in the chapter on the theory, criticism, and history of poetry. The ideas here are a blend of familiar

German mythic thought from Herder, Schiller, Schelling, and Friedrich Schlegel. Following a main line of German romanticism, myth is a higher wisdom implicit in primal language, a first true worldview; myth also reveals how man moves from sensuous confinement into the higher spirituality of awareness of freedom. Myth teaches that an ultimately ideal meaning dwells in nature. And each time the Greeks personified natural powers as gods, they gave symbolic expression to their intuition of the ideal abiding amid all chance and change. Poetry is a refined "new recognition" of this true content of myth; Homer or the tragic poets, for example, show the mythic tension between man caught in necessity and yet aspiring to freedom, which is one meaning of the Promethean or Titanic struggles against tyrannic fate or gods. Even though civilized progress must mean an ensuing loss of naive belief in myth, still the crucial truths will remain embedded in mythic poetry—and Schlegel suggests that these truths remain latent in all poetry, for all higher poetry, he says, is "an artistic production of mythic conditions, a free and waking dream." Christianity more fully and freely actualizes these mythic intuitions by teaching that the god becomes man willingly, in love and sacrifice: Christ transcends Prometheus. Triumphing over paganism, Christianity is, however, importantly still an expansion of mythic insight: the Reformation shows this partly by its battle against mythic remnants in Christianity; but on the other hand, works such as *Faust* express how Christian-romantic ideals are deeply akin to a mythic sense of the deep, secret, even "magic" powers of nature.

In the later Vienna lectures on drama, myth is important in two general ways: historically, as the Greeks knew and believed it; and aesthetically, as a paradigm of how poetry fuses diversity and unity. Taken historically, Greek myth must re-main "exotic plants," foreign to modern minds. But still, only a sympathetic acceptance of what myth meant to the Greeks can help us rightly understand their tragic art. For Greek tragedy is necessarily rooted in mythic themes and rituals, since Greek myth held in itself all national and religious traditions. What Greek tragedy did was to find it possible to give dramatic "distance" to these piously and stringently held traditions. Tragedy, however freely it transformed myth, saw itself still a solemnly religious art, and remained faithful to the spirit if not the letter of older myths. Moreover, the spirit of myth helps art attain true artistic autonomy. Since myth is finally a symbolic manifesting of divine freedom, an art using this raw material is led to comprehend its own independently imaginative status. Tragedy is not allegory, therefore, but like myth, is created by the imagination for purposes of its own, the transfiguring of reality.

One result of this is that Schlegel argues against either slavish devotion to the merely external rules of ancient drama or against mechanical usage of ancient mythic themes. Impelled to regain the simplicity, grandeur, and wondrousness that ancient myth offered the Greek poet, the modern poet finds himself in great difficulty: ancient myth is not his own, and tends to enter modern poetry more decoratively than organically. Schlegel does not urge that the problem be solved by turning (as Friedrich Schlegel and others urged) to self-conscious individual modern mythopoesis; that hope is dubious, if only because no individual seems able to create the myths from which older poetry grew. August Schlegel's solutions seem to go in two directions. The modern poet should concentrate on the inward spirit of myth, rather than its letter—and here, Schlegel daringly suggests that Shakespearean-romantic drama in some ways fulfills mythic intent even better than did ancient tragedy: for such "romantic" art "blends into one harmonious whole" all contraries, nature and art, prose and poetry, spirituality and sensuality. But the modern poet may also turn directly to using ancient mythic themes. As Hatfield emphasizes, Schlegel's solution is characteristically a compromise, with enormous influence and resonance in modern times: that is, myth may be used by modern poets, even though not necessarily believed in. Goethe had said he was a polytheist for poetic purposes; but Goethe still remained committed to a broad, even severe classicism. With August Schlegel, myth begins to detach itself from either pagan belief or deeply held classicism, and moves far toward becoming an explicitly aesthetic device useful for evoking the effect of spiritual and historical depth.

B.F.

REFERENCES   Our texts are from: *Die Kunstlehre,* hrsg. Edgar Lohner (Stuttgart: Kohlhammer, 1963), which is part one of Schlegel's *Vorlesungen über schöne Literatur und Kunst* (Berlin lectures, 1801) as first published in critical edition, 1884 (our translation); *A Course of Lectures on Dramatic Art and Literature,* translated by John Black, 2 vols. (London, 1815), which renders *Über dramatische Kunst und Literatur,* Schlegel's Vienna lectures of 1808, published 1809–11. See also *Oeuvres de M. A. G. de Schlegel, écrites en français* (Leipzig: E. Bocking, 1846), tome I, pp. 317–329, "De la Mythologie Grecque."

For commentary, see: René Wellek, *A History of Modern Criticism, II: The Romantic Age* (New Haven: Yale University Press, 1955); A. Leslie Willson, *A Mythical Image: The ideal of India in German Romanticism* (Durham: Duke University Press, 1964), pp. 199–220 for August Schlegel as Indologist; Fritz Strich, *Die Mythologie in der deutschen Literatur von Klopstock bis Wagner,* 2 vols. (Halle, 1910), II.

AUGUST SCHLEGEL

FROM *Lectures on Literature and Fine Art*

WE CAN at the same time interpret ourselves and the mythic creation of the world through the images of dreams, for dreams never allow any doubt to enter about the reality of their transitory images, however unrelated or even contradictory these images are to each other. Moritz has made excellent use of this regarding ancient mythology by showing that even the lack of method and system in myth is not disturbing, that a seeming chaos can coexist with an inner harmony and poetic consistency. . . . Poetry is an artistic production of those mythic conditions, a free and waking dream.

Wherever human nature develops in accord with necessity and without being intruded on by mere arbitrariness, it cannot fall into error. Mythology is an essential and involuntary creation of imagination in the progress of human civilization: truth must reside in it fundamentally. The fabulous is thus not simply to be taken as the truth, but rather is in a certain sense true. One can say that in the spirit of genuine poetry all truth lies concealed . . . each poetic reanimation of myth is a recognition of the truth dwelling there.

Man remains for himself always the center of all things, a center from which he ventures out and to which he returns. He can represent himself in his mythology either as a sensuous being who is part of nature, or as a being striving to make himself independent and transcendent of nature. The former will yield an earthly and natural religion; the latter, a holy and spiritual religion. In the first case, man is before all a sensual being, and thus this kind of religion will be the first to come to prominence and arise as the natural religion everywhere. The other kind of religion will be spread only through the influence of special men of surpassing wisdom, and will thereby gain the character of a revealed religion. The double principle in mankind—the real and the ideal—will express itself in both, though taking one or the other direction. In one direction the aspiration toward the infinite works through the corporeal, through giddiness and anxiety; in the other direction, the need is to show that the merely sensual and immediate are spiritual. . . .

We are familiar with a great mass of realistic mythologies, from differing ages and nations, raw and cultivated, poor and rich. The most interesting and universal, however, the one too that moved most completely into poetry and art and became immortalized through them, is the Greek. Of opposed kinds, we know only the Christian religion in its real essence. It appears different from related spiritualities in the East, from which of course Christianity descends to us. . . .

We move on to view Greek mythology, in which three different subjects can be distinguished: the physical, the mystic, and the idealistic. . . .

As we have already remarked in connection with the primal origin of language, it is improbable for childlike men to set before themselves any kind of active quality other than that which they feel in themselves. Each cause of change thus becomes for these men an acting, willing, passionate being; all the powers of nature are humanized. Among the flux of appearances that bring them forth, these beings are permanent, but nevertheless untransformable, unexplorable, incomparable, and incommensurable with men themselves, that is, gods. Thus the heavens and earth are peopled with various forms of gods. The elements will be personified in different ways and with their own characteristics. So Zeus signifies the upper air in Greek myth, Juno the lower air. . . .

(from pp. 282–286)

Mythology is frequently declared by Greeks themselves as the common root of poetry, history, and philosophy. The relation to poetry has been sufficiently clarified here previously. Myth furnishes a much more refined matter than simple nature: it is nature in poetic costume. It is certainly already poetry, but it can through a consciously free usage be reduced once more to . . . simple elements. We also find these materials significantly designated in the different kinds of Greek poetry. . . . The epic is most of all simple passive transmitting of tradition. Lyric poetry shows its greater freedom in its choice of allusions, it touches the myths only fleetingly, links up the very remote, and so forth. The tragic poets, finally, deal most freely with the myths, and model them entirely according to their own purposes.

(from p. 293)

Up to now we have quickly surveyed in an approximate way the ruling representations of the Greeks. Everything derived from nature. The gods themselves were part and power thereof, only more powerful than mankind, but otherwise divided from them by no unbridgeable gap. So long as mankind viewed and felt themselves as simply beings of nature, they dissimulated and conspired against these gods as against other natural things that must be won over or be suffered from. They were children of chance. . . . So soon, however, as a higher possibility awoke in man, namely freedom, the consciousness of a more primal and absolute self-determination, he could no longer remain in such an attitude to the world as before. Even the limitlessness of nature, which is well expressed in the always expanding polytheism and the chaotic form of the whole mythology, did not satisfy him. He noted the lack of an absolute there, and since he found it in no particular, he was forced to transfer it outside and beyond nature, completely as an object of the absolute, thus as absolute

necessity. But the existence of such an absolute necessity especially meant the collapse of the world of the gods, since the gods too belonged to the realm of nature. On the other side, however, this [idea of necessity] was the view that myth had of how the world was ruled on the whole. That is the dark fearful idea which one first finds hinted at in Homer, though first developed further by the tragic poets, so completely indeed that its entire art turns round its axis. . . . Within the bounds of nature, man was at one with himself, and we find the experience of a harmonious existence nowhere so perfectly expressed as in the Greek world; but on the farther side of nature begins the conflict, and man buys the feeling of his own divinity only at a price. Fate was not itself moral, but only the criterion of morality. . . thus the highest triumph of pagan religion is really the possibility of striving against the gods, and all great noble races of antiquity can imagine man in the image of Prometheus. . . .   (from p. 297)

FROM *Lectures on Dramatic Art and Literature*

THE GREEK tragedy, in its pure and unaltered state, will always for our theatres remain an exotic plant, which we can hardly hope to cultivate with any success, even in the hot-house of learned art and criticism. The Grecian mythology, which constitutes the materials of ancient tragedy, is as foreign to the minds and imaginations of most of the spectators, as its form and mode of representation. . . .

I have called mythology the chief materials of tragedy. We know, indeed, of

two historical tragedies, by Grecian authors: the *Capture of Miletus,* of Phrynichus, and the *Persians,* of Aeschylus. . . . The sentence passed by the Athenians on Phrynichus, whom they subjected to a pecuniary fine because, in the representation of contemporary calamities which with due caution they might have avoided, he had agitated them in too violent a manner, however hard and arbitrary it may appear in a judicial point of view, displays however a correct feeling with respect to the subject and the limits of art. The mind suffering under the near reality of the subject cannot possess the necessary repose and self-possession which are necessary for the reception of pure tragical impressions. The heroic fables, on the other hand, appear always at a certain distance, and in the light of the wonderful. The wonderful possesses the advantage of being believed, and in some degree disbelieved, at the same time: believed in so far as it is founded on the connexion with other opinions; disbelieved while we never take such an immediate interest in it as we do in what wears the hue of the every day life of our own age. The Grecian mythology was a web of national and local traditions, held in equal honour as a part of religion and as an introduction to history; every where preserved in full life among the people by customs and monuments, and by the numberless works of epic and mythical poets. The tragedians had only therefore to engraft one species of poetry on another: they were always allowed the use of certain established fables, invaluable for their dignity, and grandeur, and remoteness from all accessory ideals of a petty description. Every thing, down to the very errors and weaknesses of that departed race of heroes who claimed their descent from the gods, was consecrated in the eyes of the people. Those heroes were painted as beings endowed with more than human strength; but, so far from possessing unerring virtue and wisdom, they were also represented as under the dominion of furious and unbridled passions. It was a wild age of effervescence: the cultivation of social order had not as yet rendered the soil of morality arable, and it yielded at the same time the most beneficent and poisonous productions, with the fresh and luxuriant fulness of a creative nature. Here the monstrous and ferocious were not a necessary indication of that degradation and corruption with which they are necessarily associated under the development of law and order, and which fill us with sentiments of horror and aversion. The criminals of the fabulous ages are not, if we may be allowed the expression, amenable to the tribunals of men, but consigned over to a higher jurisdiction. . . .

A few mythological fables only seem originally marked out for tragedy: such, for example, as the long-continued alternation of aggressions, vengeance, and maledictions, which we witness in the house of Atreus. When we examine the names of the pieces which are lost, we have great difficulty in conceiving how the mythological fables on which they are founded, as they are known to us, could afford sufficient materials for the development of an entire tragedy. It is true, the poets, in the various relations of the same story, had a great amplitude of selection; and this very variety justified them in going still farther, and making considerable alterations in the circumstances of an event, so that the inventions added to one piece sometimes contradict the accounts given by the same poet in another. We are, however, principally to ascribe the productiveness of mythology, for the tragic art, to the principle which we observe so powerful throughout the whole historical range of Grecian cultivation; namely, that the power which preponderated for the time assimilated everything to itself. As the heroic fables, in all their deviations, were easily developed into the tranquil fullness and light variety of epic poetry, they were afterwards adapted to the object which the tragedians proposed to accomplish, by earnestness, energy, and compression; and what in this change of destination appeared inapplicable to tragedy still afforded materials for a sort of half sportive, though ideal representation, in the subordinate walk of the *satirical drama*.

(from pp. 80–85)

From the very commencement, the Eumenides stands on the very highest tragical elevation: all the past is concentrated as it were in one focus. Orestes has merely been the passive instrument of fate; and free agency is transferred to the more elevated sphere of the gods. Pallas is properly the principal character. The opposition between the most sacred relations, which frequently appears beyond the power of mortal solution, is represented as a contention in the world of the gods.

And this leads me to the deep import of the whole. The ancient mythology is in general symbolical, although not allegorical; for the two are quite distinct. Allegory is the personification of an idea, a fable solely undertaken with such a view; but that is symbolical which has been created by the imagination for other purposes, or which has a reality in itself independent of the idea, but which at the same time is easily susceptible of a symbolical explanation; and even of itself suggests it.

The Titans, in general, mean the dark primary powers of nature and of mind; the later gods, what enters more within the circle of consciousness. The former are more nearly related to original chaos, the latter belong to a world already subjected to order. The Furies are the dreadful powers of conscience, in so far as it rests on obscure feelings and forebodings, and yields to no principles of reason. In vain Orestes dwells on the just motives for the deed, the voice of blood resounds in his ear. Apollo is the god of youth, of the noble ebullition of passionate discontent,

of the bold and daring action: hence this deed was commanded by him. Pallas is cool wisdom, justice, and moderation, which alone can allay the dispute.

(from pp. 104–105)

Comedy at its commencement, namely, in the hands of its Doric founder, Epicharmus, borrowed its materials chiefly from the mythical world. Even in its maturity it appears not to have renounced this choice altogether, as we may see from many of the titles of the lost pieces of Aristophanes and his contemporaries; and at a later period, in the interval between the old and the new comedy, for particular reasons, it returned again to mythology, with a peculiar degree of predilection. But as the contrast between the materials and the form is here in its proper place, and nothing can be more directly opposed to the exhibition of the ludicrous, than the most important and serious concerns of men, the peculiar subject of the old comedy was naturally therefore taken from public life and the state. It is altogether political, and the private and family life, beyond which the new never soars, was only introduced occasionally and indirectly, with a reference to the public. The chorus is therefore essential to it, as being in some sort a representation of the public: it must by no means be considered as something accidental, which we may account for in the local origin of old comedy; we may assign as a more substantial reason, that it belongs to the complete parody of the tragic form.   (from pp. 198–199)

I come now to a more important point, namely, to that of the materials not being handled in a manner suitable to their nature and quality. The Greek tragedians, with a few exceptions, always selected objects from their native mythology. The

French tragedians borrow theirs sometimes from the ancient mythology, but much more frequently from the history of almost all ages and nations, and their manner of treating mythological and historical subjects is but too often not properly mythological, and not properly historical. I shall explain myself more distinctly. The poet who selects an ancient mythological fable, that is, a fable connected by sacred tradition with the religious belief of the Greeks, should enter himself, and in like manner enable his spectators to enter, into the spirit of antiquity; he should preserve the simple manners of the heroic ages, with which such violent passions and actions could alone be consistent or credible; his persons should bear that near resemblance to the gods which from their descent, and the frequency of their immediate intercourse with them, the ancients believed them to possess; what is wonderful in the Grecian religion should not be purposely avoided or under-stated, but placed in its true character before the imaginations of the spectators, who ought to be supposed capable of entering fully into the belief of it. Instead of this however the French poets have given to their mythological heroes and heroines the refinement of the fashionable world, and the court manners of the present day. . . . The Grecian tragedians certainly allowed themselves a great latitude in changing the circumstances of the fables, but the alterations were always consistent with the general ideas of the heroic age. On the other hand they always left the characters as they received them from tradition and early fable, by means of which the cunning of Ulysses, the wisdom of Nestor, and the impetuous rage of Achilles, had almost become proverbial. Horace particularly insists on the rule. But how unlike the Achilles in Racine's *Iphigenia* to the Achilles of Homer! The gallantry ascribed to him is not merely a sin against Homer, but it renders the whole story improbable. Are human sacrifices conceivable among a people whose chiefs and heroes are so susceptible of the most tender feelings? In vain recourse is had to the power of religious motives: history teaches us that a cruel religion becomes always milder with the manners of a people.

In these new exhibitions of ancient fables, the wonderful has been studiously rejected as foreign to our belief. But when we are once brought from a world in which it belonged to the order of things into a world entirely prosaical, and consistent with historical ideas, we then find any wonderful thing, which the poet can only exhibit in an insulated state, so much the more incredible. In Homer, and in the Greek tragedians, every thing takes place in the presence of the gods, and when they are visible, or display themselves in any wonderful manner, we are in no manner astonished. On the other hand, all the labour and art of the modern poets, all the eloquence of their narratives, cannot reconcile our minds to these exhibitions.

(from pp. 360–364)

German Romantic Mythology and India

FRIEDRICH MAJER [1772–1818]

FRIEDRICH SCHLEGEL [1772–1829]

ARTHUR SCHOPENHAUER [1788–1860]

THE FIRST great literary and speculative response to the new Indic materials introduced by Sir William Jones and others occurred in Germany: Herder is its most prominent catalyst before 1800, and the younger romantics its zealots for at least a decade or so after 1800. Only after 1820 does a response of similar intensity appear in France, with the romantics. Moreover, the German image of India, and mythic theories generating out of that, have some important influence on French attitudes toward myth: for example, through Herder on Michelet, through Friedrich Schlegel on Baron Eckstein and thus on Hugo, through Creuzer and Görres on Quinet. For these reasons, then, space may be allowed for a brief glance at German interest in Indian mythology. But it should be emphasized in passing that in philology and history, France, Germany, and England each contribute equally in the early part of the century, as Raymond Schwab shows in his detailed history, *La Renaissance orientale*.

There is another reason for examining the German response to India. For early in the course of that enthusiastic response, there emerged a crisis whose outcome has had profound effect on the study of mythology, even into our own century as well: the spiritual, aesthetic, and specu-

lative approach to myth, favored by the German romantics, comes into sharp conflict—as early as 1808 or 1810—with the new philologic and historical schools and their quite different aims and methods. Much of this centers on the knowledge of Sanskrit. As the indispensable key to the whole Indo-European system of languages, and through that to the earliest religions and history, Sanskrit philology undercut or bypassed the romantic effort to unify the meaning of myth on non-linguistic artistic, religious, or philosophic grounds. Two prominent romantic devotees of Indian myth help clarify this impending collision and turning point in mythic thought: Friedrich Majer, an important Indic encyclopedist and catalyst for romanticism; and Friedrich Schlegel, the first German romantic to study Sanskrit directly, one outcome of which was his break with some main romantic views.

The rise of German romantic enthusiasm about Indian religion and myth properly begins with Herder's early works. As early as 1770, he begins to exalt the Orient (though vaguely) as the source of language; and in works over the next fourteen years he goes on to describe India as the pure homeland of the human race, a view repeated in his *Ideas* of 1784. At this point, comments Schwab, Herder knew no more about India than Voltaire. In 1791, however, Georg Forster translated into German Jones's 1789 English translation of the *Sacontala,* and Herder immediately praised it as a literary masterpiece and as the epitome of Indic spiritual sublimity and richness. Goethe too was "extravagantly impressed" with this drama, and it may have influenced his "Theater Prelude" to *Faust.* And in general, from the 1790s, German renderings of previously translated English works from Sanskrit proliferated enormously.

With the Schlegels and Novalis, Indic myth explicitly becomes an important part of the whole romantic program, the epitome of primal spiritual purity, innocence, and cosmic-human harmony. Friedrich Schlegel's shift from classicism to promoting modern, "interesting" or "romantic" poetry around 1797 coincides with his new praise of the *Sacontala.* In his poem, "The Ages of the World" (1800), Schlegel makes India the earliest and holiest manifestation of religious wisdom, and employs symbols of light, flowers, and children, derived from Indic literature; and in the *Athenäum,* Schlegel announced that "we must seek the highest romanticism in the Orient." In his 1801–1804 lectures on literature and fine art, August Schlegel treated Indian religion (in the section on the history and characteristics of romantic literature) as the likely source underlying all religions. Novalis reveals the same ardent dedication to this view in his aphorisms, and particularly in his Christian-Indic poem, *Hymns to the Night,* and his mythic fable, *Heinrich von Ofterdingen,* with its famous "blue flower." A. Leslie Willson shows how Novalis drew this consummate romantic symbol of longing and boundless beauty from Indic themes, most probably from the *Sacontala.* The "blue flower" is at once a symbol of mythic immanence, sleep and mystery, organic flowering and growth, and total reconcili-

ation of all dualities. In Hölderlin's poetry, Indic influence is reflected in the importance assigned to Dionysus, the ecstatic god come to Greece from the East; "Asia" stands for the first golden age of divine presence and natural innocence, and suggests the birth and fulfillment of Christ and Christianity out of India. Schelling also exalts India, more as a phase of the evolving of spirit than as its true essence. His *Lectures on University Study* (1803) allies the "idealistic" Indian religion with Christianity against what he calls the "realistic" Greek religion. By 1810, such mythologists as Gotthilf Schubert, F. Ast, J. A. Kanne, Görres, and Creuzer systematize and often inflate this speculative mythology. In 1813–1814, at Weimar, Schopenhauer began his first deep exploration of Indic religion under Majer's personal guidance. Goethe was another who turned to Majer for expertise on India.

Friedrich Majer. Majer's mythic views were not original, but were instead exemplary of German romantic attitudes toward India; and in this exemplary role lies much of Majer's importance. His work gives entry not only into the general level of Oriental and other mythologic erudition commanded by the nonphilologic mythologists in Germany, but also into how, in the early nineteenth century, mythology was still a seemingly integrated whole, not yet splintered into philologic, historical, and other special disciplines.

As several historians have noted, Majer is an undeservedly neglected figure. He did as much as or more than any other writer of his time to consolidate and thus make easily available the vast but diffuse flood of new mythic materials from India, and elsewhere as well. Besides Goethe and Schopenhauer, Friedrich Schlegel may have been inspired to his pioneering study of Sanskrit through Majer.

Majer was educated for the law, but was a student and lifelong admirer of

Herder. During much of his life, he moved in leading romantic circles in Jena, Weimar, and Heidelberg. He early became famous as a fervent devotee of Indic myth especially, but of all mythic lore as well. His first book concerning myth was *Zur Kulturgeschichte der Völker* (with foreword by Herder) in 1798. He lectured from 1796 on myth, and published numerous important interpretations and German retranslations of Oriental texts in leading journals. His major work, the *Allgemeines Mythologisches Lexicon,* appeared in 1803 and 1811–1813. The *Lexicon* was designed to be universal in scope, one part to cover all classical myth, the other all nonclassical myth. The title page of his 1803 nonclassical volume claims to present the myths of the Chinese, Javanese, Hebrews, Indians (especially Brahmanist and Lamaist), North-Asians, Parsees, Arabians and Moslems, Africans, Slavs, Finns, Lapps, Greenlanders, Scandinavians, Germans, primitive Americans (such as the Aztecs and Incas), and aboriginal Australians. Majer's personal circumstances prevented this first volume from proceeding in subject beyond A–I, partly because of political upheavals, and worse, because of the devastating loss later of a lifetime's collection of notes; he did however publish the volume on classical myth before this loss occurred. Undaunted, he planned still another enormous work wholly on Indic myth and religion, projected in four parts, on Brahmanism, Sivaism, Vishnuism, and Buddhism. Only one volume of this— *Brahma*—came out before his death in 1818.

In their reach of erudition, Majer's efforts were astonishing—the more so, since in his Indian specialty he knew no Sanskrit. He gleaned his information everywhere: from such early works as Thomas Hyde's on Persian religion, from later innumerable travelers and historians, from the *Asiatick Researches,* from translations

in almost any European language. His footnoted sources are an encyclopedia in themselves of the remarkable amount of mythic information available by his time. (Another indication of this, outside Majer, may be had by noting that Majer's contemporary, Christoph Meiners, in his *Allgemeine Kritische Geschichte der Religionen* [1806], prefaced his study with a bibliography of 305 separate titles covering travels, histories, and religious and mythic treatises and texts.)

As Majer's introduction to his *Allgemeines Mythologisches Lexicon* of 1803 makes clear, he was wholly committed to the romantic cult of India. By his *Brahma* of 1818, however, Majer's methods as well as goals and interpretations could seem more and more merely speculative, as would the mass of mythic speculation about India that he helped to inform. The opposition from more scientific historical and philological studies had already begun. Friedrich Schlegel is a crucial and illuminating point of transition between the old and new views.

Friedrich Schlegel. By 1800 the romantic exalting of Indic myth had reached a high intensity, and by 1810 would culminate in the works of that year published by Görres and Creuzer, which sought to demonstrate once and for all that India was the first and only origin of Greek, European, and even all myth. Also, during this decade, Friedrich Schlegel became modern Germany's first competent Sanskritist, and his 1808 *On the Language and Wisdom of India* is the first adequate scholarly study and the first mortal philologic blow at romantic Indic mythologizing. Ironically, Schlegel's study of Sanskrit was undertaken as an effort not to attack but to corroborate the romantic Indic vision. That effort grew out of his increasing dissatisfaction with a mainly aesthetic approach to myth and religion: he hoped to find in actual historical religion a way to reconcile religious, historic, and moral dualities. But just as rationalists such as Bayle or Voltaire had vastly stimulated the study of actual history while they themselves worked to prove mere historical knowledge decisively unreliable, so Schlegel began the study of Sanskrit to prove his romantic assumptions decisively right, but his work was to have unexpected and contrary results. The initial assumption—as August Schlegel optimistically suggested in 1801—that philology would become part of art, proved wrong. As Willson emphasizes, such a philological approach could only mean the inevitable collapse of the romantic dream-vision of India as the homeland and preserver of paradisal spirituality; once that vision ceased being poetically sustained and became instead accessible to the closest linguistic and historical scrutiny, the result was foreordained.

Schlegel's hopes for exploiting philologic discoveries were fed by remarkable developments in the study of language and comparative philology. Jones had suggested that Latin, Greek, and Sanskrit "may have sprung from one common source"; and comparative philologists such as Schlözer or Gyarmathi advanced the work. The knowledge of world languages was extended and systematized, with Pallas's and Adelung's vast surveys. Knowledge of Indic languages was meanwhile deepening: through the *Asiatick Researches,* through Anquetil-Duperron's Persian translation, through the establishment of regular teaching of Chinese in Naples as early as 1732, and through historical accident—Alexander Hamilton, a Sanskritist and member of the Asiatick Society of Calcutta, caught in France during the Napoleonic wars, spent his time translating Sanskrit texts and instructing in the language; Friedrich Schlegel became one of Hamilton's students in 1803.

In the early phases of his Sanskrit study, Schlegel remained buoyantly optimistic. But by the publication of his In-

dic study in 1808, he had become disillusioned, clearly in part from increasingly direct knowledge of India and Indic religion. His 1804–1806 writing, *Kritik der Philosophischen Systeme,* sees pantheism leading to fatalism, to a negative idea of God, or worse, to a "complete annihilation" of self, to "nihilism."

His 1808 book extends this indictment of the worth of Indic myth. In the first section, Schlegel gives what has often been considered the first serious program for a scientific comparative philology based on Sanskrit as the root language; at the least, his work here founded scientific philology in Germany. Schlegel also calls for a genuinely scientific comparative mythology—myth, like language, shows a common inner structure throughout. But Schlegel declares the comparative study of myth much more difficult than that of language; not only does myth encompass the tangled history of the human spirit, but not enough historical data are yet available for any decisive judgments. The oldest Indian thought is found in theories about metamorphosis and emanation; pantheism is much more recent, though more important. Schlegel differentiates between emanation and pantheism and seeks to give due credit to both: pantheism teaches that all is good, all is one; emanation naturally suggests a divinely higher oneness. But both doctrines lead finally to spiritual impotency or degradation. Indian emanation equates being with nothingness. Indian pantheism (indeed, all pantheism) cancels out all differences between good and evil, and induces an indulgent complacency that all is one and that no further individual striving is required—a provocative position with regard to much romantic endorsement of pantheism. Meanwhile, the profound influence of India on European thought and faith is not denied, but Schlegel claims that Indian teaching passed into the West always somewhat "polluted," as it was at the source. Pythagorean ideas about metamorphosis originated in India, as did Egyptian religion and myth. Indian myth is indeed higher than the Greek, but is itself finally only suitable as a kind of "educational commentary" on the higher truths manifested in Scripture. Indian myth departed from original revelation with disastrous results, where Judaism and Christianity strongly forbade and resisted the slide into superstition.

One result of Schlegel's study is to reaffirm the romantic view of a primal revelation but to restore it now to the Christian framework—and whether as cause or consequence, Schlegel converted to Catholicism in 1808.

The great achievements in comparative philology immediately following Schlegel led in a similar way to further impugning of romantic mythic assumptions or speculations. Modern scientific comparative philology is founded partly in the work of Rask on Old Norse or Icelandic, which in its extended 1818 form lays early claim to creating an adequate comparative Indic-European grammar. Sanskrit became more widely known as University chairs were established to provide regular teaching in the subject (at the Collège de France, 1814; in Bonn, 1818, with August Schlegel the first occupant—August Schlegel also began printing Sanskrit texts the same year at Bonn). Franz Bopp studied at Paris, and his *Conjugationssystem* (1816) lays the groundwork for his great philologic treatise, *Comparative Grammar of the Sanskrit, Zend, Greek . . .* (1833–1852). In 1819, Jakob Grimm published his *Deutsche Grammatik,* revised in 1822 to include his discoveries of the "sound-shift" (independently anticipated by Rask). Champollion deciphered the Rosetta stone in 1822. In 1826, Eugène Burnouf began his epoch-making studies with his work on Pali, laying the basis for an adequate approach to Buddhism; in 1833, his *Commentaire sur le Yaçna* founds modern Avestan

study; in 1844, he gives the first great study of Buddhism, with his *Introduction à l'histoire du buddhisme indien*. The outcome of these developments in philology prepares the rise and eventual dominance from about mid-century of the philologic-historic school, whose public voice is most prominently that of F. Max Müller.

Arthur Schopenhauer. From the time of his introduction to Indian materials, by Majer in 1813–1814, Schopenhauer set out to construct a synthesis of post-Kantian philosophy and Indian religion. His *The World as Will and Representation* (1818) exalted the *Upanishads*. In the new edition of his neglected work (1844), Schopenhauer saw Buddhism as closest to his own thought. His exposition of the need for "denial of will," with his linking of this to Brahman and Buddhist teachings and to the asceticism of Christianity, is an original philosophic step, and with familiarly important effect on admirers such as Wagner and Nietzsche. In the earlier and later editions, Schopenhauer seems to separate the purer Indian teachings from their more popular "mythic" versions. But his reasons for doing this are quite different than those of earlier condemners of myth. He speaks of myth often as if it were only a false or deceiving story. But by his appeal to the lofty purity of Buddhism, he seems at the same time to be bringing to the West a new kind of myth—for Buddhism is after all, as Schopenhauer admits, alien to the West. Yet, he does not describe Buddhism as only another myth. Buddhism might rather be called Schopenhauer's version of the final mythology, that which destroys all former "myth" or half-truth and self-deception: it is that myth, perhaps, that will make us free of myth once and for all, and will offer us what myth so often seemed to proffer, a direct perception of primal reality. The deepest effect of Schopenhauer's thought begins after our period, notably on Nietzsche, though clearly acknowledged by Wagner shortly after mid-century. Schopenhauer, Wagner, and Nietzsche may be seen perhaps as the last great expression of the nonphilological speculative school of Indian mythology.

B.F.

REFERENCES Our texts are from: Friedrich Majer, *Allgemeines Mythologisches Lexicon* (Weimar, 1803) our translation; Friedrich Schlegel, *On the Language and Wisdom of the Indians*, in *The Aesthetic and Miscellaneous Works of Frederick von Schlegel*, translated by E. J. Millington (London, 1849), from *Über die Sprache und Weisheit der Indier* (Heidelberg, 1808); Arthur Schopenhauer, *The World as Will and Representation*, translated by E. F. J. Payne, 2 vols. (Indian Hills, Colorado: Falcon's Wing Press, 1958).

For Majer, see: A. Leslie Willson, *A Mythical Image: The ideal of India in German Romanticism* (Durham: Duke University Press, 1964), especially pp. 93–104 and *passim;* Guy R. Welbon, *The Buddhist Nirvana and its Western Interpreters* (Chicago: University of Chicago Press, 1968), pp. 158–159; Raymond Schwab, *La Renaissance orientale* (Paris: Payot, 1950), pp. 64–65, 220–224, and *passim.*

For F. Schlegel, see: Willson, *op. cit.,* pp. 83–85, 88–93, and especially 199–220; F. Imle, *Friederich von Schlegels Entwicklung von Kant zum Katholizismus* (Padeborn, 1927); Ursula Oppenberg, *Quellenstudien zu Friedrich Schlegels Übersetzungen aus dem Sanskrit* (Marburg: Elwert, 1965). C. Enders, *Friedrich Schlegel. Die Quellen seines Wesens und Werdens* (1913); A. Emmetsleben, *Die Antike in der romantischen Theorie. Die Gebrüder Schlegel und die Antike* (1937).

For Schopenhauer, see: Welbon, *op. cit.,* pp. 155–170; R. K. Das Gupta, "Schopenhauer and Indian Thought," *East and West,* New Series, vol. XIII, No. 1 (March, 1962), pp. 32–40; Edward Conze, "Buddhist Philosophy and Its European Parallels," *Philosophy East and West, XIII* (1963–1964), pp. 9–23.

For general background, see: Willson, *op. cit.; Welbon, op. cit.; Schwab, op. cit.,* pp. 507–514 for excellent general bibliography; Henri de Lubac, *La Rencontre du bouddhisme et de l'occident* (Paris: Aubier, 1952); Ernst Windisch, *Geschichte der Sanskrit-Philologie und indische Altertumskunde,* 2 vols. (Strassburg: Trubner, 1917); Holger Pedersen, *Linguistic Science in the Nineteenth Century,* translated by J. W. Spargo (Cambridge: Harvard University Press, 1931); Fritz Strich, *Die Mythologie in der deutschen Literatur von Klopstock bis Wagner,* 2 vols. (Halle, 1910), II. Helmut Glasenapp, *Das Indienbild deutscher Denker* (Stuttgart: Koehler, 1960). H. Cordier, *Un orientaliste allemand. Jules Klaproth* (Paris, 1917). Rene Girard, *L'Orient et la pensée romantique allemand* (Paris: Didier, 1963).

For the influence of Creuzer on German romantic interest in Indic myth, see for example: Niklas Müller, *Glauben, Wissen und Kunst der alten Hindus und im Gewande der Symbolik* (Mainz, 1822). For full study and bibliography of Kanne, see: Dieter Schrey, *Mythos und Geschichte bei Johann Arnold Kanne und in der romantischen Mythologie* (Tubingen: Max Niemeyer, 1969), esp. Chap. V on Indic myth. Susanne Sommerfeld, *Indienschau und Indiendeutung romantischer Philosophie* (Zurich: Rascher, 1943).

MAJER

FROM *Universal Mythological Lexicon*

"Introduction"

IF MEANS and circumstances, with ever so slight an encouragement from the present time, are granted to me, even only to some degree, then undoubtedly the most highly desired goal of my efforts will remain the dedication of the greatest part of my life to the completion of such a work. The intimation of results infinitely important for the entire human race draws me as a guiding star to untiring exertions, so that the completion of this work, far off and yet perhaps near, can rediscover and unveil the most sacred secrets of the pre-world. Then this wonderful sign language and esoteric symbolism from the early spring of mankind will be seen to contain even more than the essence of the most important knowledge discovered and imagined in the first experience and observation of the pre-world concerning the appearance and nature of the invisible in the visible guide of nature. For we may also find in it a *revelation of the Eternal,* whose pure glory the blinded eye of mortals can hardly endure. Tradition and prophecy about this invisible in visible guise is the essence of all religion and mythology among all peoples and in all areas of the world. Strange memories tell us that once it was not invisible to us, and that we shall again find what we have lost. Then what now is life to us will in another memory seem to have been only a sleep, in which dreams of the past and a future life played around us in manifold shapes. Nowhere has the reality of this eternal truth been so beautifully and joyously expressed as in *those three kindly, related figures* of the Christian religion, whose love-inspiring image stands before this work in gentle outlines as the incarnate echo of the inner, never vanishing voice of all peoples.   (pp. vii–viii)

"Brahma"

A sacred awe seizes the soul at this representation come to us from the past of the endless, eternal, self-emanating, unfathomable Being, the Prime Mover of all things, in his being, ordering, and acting. In childlike times the modest wisdom of the East tried to express the ancient memories that mankind had of an eternal existence in this elevated poetry. These ideas of the Highest Being could not be depicted. They had no images of the Eternal One, no temples were dedicated to him in particular, for under all the names of his thousand creations he was included, represented, and even honored and worshipped. But the weakness of the great mass of men demanded a representation of the invisible Prime Mover of the universe that was scaled to their ability to understand and could be seen. So these metaphysical and speculative ideas were embodied in accordance with empirical observation and exploration of a universal visible *threefold* emanation of power from the Highest Being. By personifying this trinity of united powers, three basic deities were made, whose personalities, taken together according to their characteristics and activities, should represent the infinite God as cognizable, in the condition of his revelation and activity outside himself. This revelation and activity is shown in a creating, sustaining, and destroying power, as the universe teaches and confirms in all its parts, from the wide realm of heaven with its glittering bodies down to the smallest lichen on the naked cliffs of our earth. This power was honored in those firstborn gods; Brahma the Creator, Vishnu the all-permeating Preserver, and Shiva the Destroyer. It is also possible that the idea of the highest God was derived only after those three great powers of nature had already been worshipped for a long time, and that it was first honored in the divine trinity, or even in its three distinct figures separately. This could happen in and through the honor which the different sects of worshippers of Vishnu and Shiva tendered each of these gods exclusively as the only Highest Being. The worship of Brahma was soon pushed aside, perhaps because the creative power is less visible in the mere external appearance of nature, than are the sustaining and destroying forces. But on the other hand, the followers of Vishnu, as well as of Shiva, each honored in their god the highest God, incorporating the three great powers of nature; for they noticed that the propagation of all of nature arose from the uniting of all three powers, since even while they collided with each other in their activity and seemed to cancel each other, they promoted the preservation and rejuvenation of nature. Often preservation comes about through destruction, and new life proceeds from it. Each sect attributed the highest characteristics of nature to the god which they worshipped as the highest, and robbed the others of these powers. One should then not mind too much if in the following fragments from the sacred texts of the Indians on the nature of Godhead and the origin of the world, now Brahma, now Vishnu, or Shiva, is referred to or made to speak as the highest eternal God. Everywhere and in all figures the passages speak of the eternal, infinite, self-sustaining Being, and the poor language of man has perhaps nowhere spoken what his earthly dreams dimly perceived of the Highest Being in more beautiful truth and splendour than in those bewitching countries that in all probability were the cradle of humanity and the first workshop of God on our earth.   (pp. 238–240)

FRIEDRICH SCHLEGEL

FROM *On the Language and Wisdom of the Indians*

IT IS AN opinion very generally entertained, that the original condition of man was one of almost unreasoning stupidity, from which, impelled by necessity or other external incitements, he gradually attained, by successive efforts, to certain degrees of intelligence. Independently of the consideration that this idea is completely at variance with all known systems of philosophy, it must be acknowledged, that so far from being supported by the testimony of ancient historical records, it is, on the contrary, contradicted, and proved to have been adopted on arbitrary and insufficient grounds. Without mentioning the Mosaic records, which I shall reserve for examination in the third book of this treatise, the numerous ancient monuments existing in Asia, and the general progress of events, afford sufficient and incontrovertible evidence that, in the earliest steps of his mortal career, man was not left without God in the world. In India especially, many surprising discoveries have been made, which remarkably illustrate the progress of human intelligence in those ancient times; and the little we already know of Oriental literature has elucidated so many difficult points, that we may confidently anticipate that still more satisfactory results will attend the further prosecution of our researchers.

Having in the first book considered the Indian language in the relation it bears to the most important languages of Asia and Europe, Indian Mythology, the parent of so many other systems, appears to offer an appropriate subject for consideration in the second. We must, however, be on our guard against an error, into which the British Society in Calcutta has too often been betrayed, and not lay too much stress upon isolated and often deceptive appearance, while attempting to prove that an internal uniformity of structure exists both in the language and mythology, and that the similarity of the ground tissue in each, notwithstanding slight subordinate alterations, sufficiently indicates congeniality of origin. It is true that there is no dearth of such surprising coincidences as cannot be merely casual; but, before being received as such, they require to be more strictly investigated than even the language, the peculiarities of mythology being more variable and uncertain, and their delicate and evanescent spirit more difficult to seize and retain. Mythology presents the most complicated structure ever devised by human intellect; inexhaustibly rich, but at the same time most variable in its signification; and that being a point of the highest moment, requires to be scrupulously examined; the slightest variation of meaning is of importance, and should be considered in its simple individuality, apart from any consideration of time or place. Greek and Roman mythology, for instance, we are accustomed to treat as one and the same, unless forbidden by distinct historical records; and yet, any one whose researches have been carried back to the earliest origin of these people, will be sufficiently alive to the difference existing between them to feel that Venus and Aphrodite, Mars (Mavors) and Ares, &c. cannot justly be regarded as one and the same divinity. How widely do the Hellenic cities differ among themselves! how great is the difference between Corinth and Athens, or between Dorians in Sparta and Sicily; the symbolic representation of certain peculiar features in the history, and even the name of the divinity, may be common to many distant nations, and long preserved among them; but it is the signification, the idea conveyed by these symbols, which is the really essential point, and this everywhere assumes a different aspect. A great number of facts must be adduced, and many different sources explored, before it will be possible to adopt, with any degree of success, the only method which can in this instance be available; that is, to enter into a full analysis of the system, displaying all its peculiar features in their just proportions, whether of internal development or external admixture, noticing even each trace of gradual change or variation: the scarcity of our materials makes it impossible at present to accomplish this in the Indian Philosophy.

(from Book II, Chap. 1)

In a word, the Indian doctrine of Emanation, if treated as the offspring of natural reason, is totally inexplicable; but, considered as a perverted conception of revealed truth, becomes at once intelligible. We have, then, ample reason to conclude, from historical evidence alone, as well as upon far higher grounds, that the same glorious Being by whom man was so majestically formed and highly gifted, vouchsafed to the newly created one glance into the mysterious depth of his own existence; thus for ever raising him above the bondage of his mortal condition, placing him in communion with the invisible world, and enriching him with the lofty, yet dangerous boon—the faculty of eternal happiness or misery.

We cannot suppose that original revelation to have been communicated by the immediate teaching of the Father, in symbolic and expressive language, although even that idea were far from utterly empty and futile; still it was probably rather an impulse of the inner feeling; and where the living principle of truth exists, appropriate words and symbols immediately suggest themselves, and these will be full and expressive in proportion to the grandeur of the feeling which inspires them. But again: how could truths so divinely imparted become involved in the mists of error? I would explain it in this manner. Man, if without the gifts of revelation, would occupy a place with other animals in the general plan of creation; perhaps holding the first and highest rank, perhaps, on the contrary, the most intrinsically wild and savage of them all. Without the free operation and comprehension of divine truth, he would soon become debased into a merely blind and senseless instrument. This primitive error, which sprang from an abuse of the divine gifts, and an eclipsing and misinterpretation of holy wisdom, is clearly to be traced in all the Indian records; and in proportion as our knowledge of this, the most highly cultivated nation of antiquity, becomes more perfect and complete, the influence of error and distorted views will be more clearly and palpably evident. The Indian mythology and philosophy is the first system which was substituted for the pure light of truth: notwithstanding some lingering traces of a holier origin, wild inventions and savage errors everywhere predominate, and an impression of anguish and sorrow, naturally resulting from the first rejection of an estrangement from revealed truth.

It will readily be acknowledged that the unfathomable abyss which was supposed to intervene between the idea of infinite perfection in the creative essence and the visible imperfection of the world around, could hardly be more easily and naturally filled up than by the doctrine of Emanation: it is, indeed, not merely the root and basis of all primitive superstition, but an ever-welling spring of poetry and imagination. According to that doctrine, every thing is an emanation of divinity, each distinct existence being, as it were, but a more obscure and limited reflection of the supreme head; consequently the world, thus inspired and vivified, becomes an assemblage of Divine Beings, or Gods, —Hylozoismus, not merely Polytheism, but, if one may so speak, "all-götterie,"— an universality of Gods or Pantheism, for the Indian divinities are indeed of countless numbers. Every mythology rising from the same fertile source is remarkable from the richness of its original inventions, and is thus sufficiently distinguished from all less perfect systems, or, to speak more properly, from those which lie yet more widely distant from the stream of old legendary tradition. Still no mythological system has as yet been discovered which can be entirely separated from all dependence on nobler ideas, and more cultivated nations; on those, in short, whose creations were drawn more immediately from the true and living spring of poetry and fancy. Even the Greek philosophy, different as it is in genius and character, partakes, in common with the Indian, of this overflowing abundance of indwelling living treasures. . . .

The doctrine of Emanation is seen in the most beautiful and favourable light when considered as a system of reunion with the divine essence. The divine origin of man is continually inculcated to stimulate his efforts to return, to animate him in the struggle, and incite him to consider a reunion and re-incorporation with divinity as the one primary object of every action and exertion. To this we may attribute the holy tendency of so many Indian laws, customs, and manners, and the severe and serious simplicity of their entire life. Still the spirit of those institutions may have early vanished, leaving only dead forms and penitential exercises too quickly assailed and undermined by the growth of error and superstition.

(from Book II, Chap. 2)

The adoration of the elements, however, is not the only characteristic feature of this religion; heroes and warriors, also, became objects of worship; yet they were no longer adored merely as destroyers and conquerors, nor reverenced on account of their physical strength and vigour, but as heavenly conquerors of the giants, triumphant over the powers of darkness and the spirits of hell. . . .

Vishnoo frequently appeared upon earth, under the various forms of a king, a sage, a wonder-working warrior and hero, but always with the intention of checking the progress of crime, exterminating giants and unfriendly powers, and animating all good genii to support and protect their leader, the high-souled Indrá.

This noble idea has been greatly defaced by arbitrary fables and inventions; feigning that God, like another Proteus, assumed not only the human form, and appeared in the character of a philosopher or hero, but also took that of a turtle, a boar, a man-lion, and a fish. Still, the mere conception of so grand an idea as the incarnation of a God, is an abiding proof of the profound reflective character of the Indian mind, and of the high degree of intelligence with which that people was endowed. The same pure and beautiful idea of affording salvation to the pure in heart, and annihilating all evil and destructive powers, may be seen under every variety of form. We occasionally find in other systems of mythology, if based on high moral principles, such descriptions of heroes as almost answer to our ideas of god-like virtue; heroes, who, obedient to sublime laws, and in the performance of glorious duties, laboured only to subvert the wicked, and raise and protect the good. But in no Hercules or hero of the poet's song is the idea of deified humanity so vividly embodied as in that of the Indian Ramá, the generous conqueror, whose voluntary exile and loneliness, and sometimes fortunate, sometimes unhappy affection for Sita, has been so sweetly and deliciously sung. . . .

This system is not purely poetical, although many and indeed the most beautiful among the Persian and Indian fables were founded on the doctrine of the two principles and the worship of the free spirit of nature. The full meaning and intention of many fictions of the Greek and Latin mythology also, as well as the Northern, is first seen when they are considered as forming part of that cycle of ideas. Still, notwithstanding their inherent poetic spirit, they will generally be found susceptible of a philosophical construction and interpretation. Even in the symbolism of the Persians we discover a certain regular proportion in the symbolic figures, a form symmetrically constructed, and the first germ of which is in Dualism, in the antagonism

or alternate manifestation of the primary powers. It seems highly probable that a philosophical system of similar intent and spirit was also common among the Indians. . . .

Some foreign admixtures may be discovered in almost every branch of Indian writings, but the Puranas are unquestionably the first in which the religion and fictions of Vishnoo predominate, partly, indeed, in the same philosophical sense which they bear in later systems. We also meet in the Puranas with personages and histories borrowed from the Holy Scriptures; not merely those which, like the history of Noah, were familiar to all nations and people, but others also which appear peculiar to the sacred writings; the history of Job, for example: still we must not too hastily conclude that they were borrowed immediately from the records of the Old Testament by Indian poets and sages, for it is probable that the Hebrews and Persians, and again the Persians and Indians, may have had more ideas in common than is usually supposed.

(from Book II, Chap. 4)

Instead of bewildering myself and my readers with isolated comparisons between the Indian and different other systems of mythology, I shall rather attempt to give a general outline of the earliest Oriental modes of thought, according to the evidence supplied by authentic records. The darkness and confusion of that period can only be satisfactorily elucidated by a thoroughly comprehensive review of the entire scheme of mythology; and such a review, if properly combined at the same time with an inquiry into the historical genealogy of the language, will afford a clue to assist our progress through that ancient labyrinth, and to point out to us the way of return to holiness and light. . . .

The first germ of polytheism is contained in the doctrine of Emanation,—that is to say, of the eternal and progressive development of the Divinity, and of universal spiritual animation. The belief in astrology, and the sensual adoration of nature, called forth the abounding riches of ancient mythological fables, which were subsequently softened, beautified, and enriched by the doctrine of the two principles—the religion of light, and the pious and divinely inspired hero-worship; but as soon as pantheistic ideas were introduced, at whatever period that may have been, mythology, ere long, became regarded merely in the light of allegory, or as an esoteric veil of poetic fancy and diction. The Greek mythology is perhaps the richest in symmetrical development, but the Indian is far more comprehensive in its mystical ideality; which, indeed, appears to have been transfused from thence into every other system. It would be difficult to point out any idea or doctrine, common in either of the different intellectual systems, which was not also known among the Indians; nor any fable holding a distinguished place in merely poetical mythologies, the counterpart of which does not exist also in the Indian. . . .

Let us not, like ordinary letter-learned critics, study the form alone without the spirit, but rather contemplate the inner life of that mythology, and we shall find that all their poems are of one description, mythic and heroic. If we reject all immaterial differences of outward form, we shall see that in Homer as well as in Aeschylus, in Pindar as in Sophocles, the blending of that originally wild and gigantic power with softer and sweeter impulses, gives a peculiar fascination to their writings; though all may vary much in proportion to their different degree of deviation from, or approximation to, the primary idea, or in individual traits of loveliness or harshness.

This, and this alone, is true poetry; all to which that name has been given in later times, when art had annexed so much to the original germ, becomes so only when it breathes a kindred spirit with those old heathen fictions, or because it springs from them.   (from Book III, Chap. 1)

SCHOPENHAUER

FROM *The World as Will and Representation*

KANT's philosophy is therefore the only one with which a thorough acquaintance is positively assumed in what is to be here discussed. But if in addition to this the reader has dwelt for a while in the school of the divine Plato, he will be the better prepared to hear me, and the more susceptible to what I say. But if he has shared in the benefits of the *Vedas,* access to which, opened to us by the *Upanishads,* is in my view the greatest advantage which this still young century has to show over previous centuries, since I surmise that the influence of Sanskrit literature will penetrate no less deeply than did the revival of Greek literature in the fifteenth century; if, I say, the reader has also already received and assimilated the divine inspiration of ancient Indian wisdom, then he is best of all prepared to hear what I have to say to him. It will not speak to him, as to many others, in a strange and even hostile tongue; for, did it not sound too conceited, I might assert that each of the individual and disconnected utterances that make up the *Upanishads* could be derived as a consequence from the thought I am to impart, although conversely my thought is by no means to be found in the *Upanishads.* (Vol. I, pp. xxiii–xxiv)

The vivid knowledge of eternal justice, of the balance inseparably uniting the *malum culpae* with the *malum poenae,* demands the complete elevation above individuality and the principle of its possibility. It will therefore always remain inaccessible to the majority of men, as also will the pure and distinct knowledge of the real nature of all virtue which is akin to it, and which we are about to discuss. Hence the wise ancestors of the Indian people have directly expressed it in the *Vedas,* permitted only to the three twice-born castes, or in the esoteric teaching, namely in so far as concept and language comprehend it, and in so far as their method of presentation, always pictorial and even rhapsodical, allows it. But in the religion of the people, or in exoteric teaching, they have communicated it only mythically. We find the direct presentation in the *Vedas,* the fruit of the highest human knowledge and wisdom, the kernel of which has finally come to us in the *Upanishads* as the greatest gift to the nineteenth century. It is expressed in various ways, but especially by the fact that all beings of the world, living and lifeless, are led past in succession in

the presence of the novice, and that over each of them is pronounced the word which has become a formula, and as such has been called the *Mahavakya: Tatoumes,* or more correctly, *tat tvam asi,* which means "This art thou." For the people, however, that great truth, in so far as it was possible for them to comprehend it with their limited mental capacity, was translated into the way of knowledge following the principle of sufficient reason. From its nature, this way of knowledge is indeed quite incapable of assimilating that truth purely and in itself; indeed it is even in direct contradiction with it; yet in the form of a myth, it received a substitute for it which was sufficient as a guide to conduct. For the myth makes intelligible the ethical significance of conduct through figurative description in the method of knowledge according to the principle of sufficient reason, which is eternally foreign to this significance. This is the object of religious teachings, since these are all the mythical garments of the truth which is inaccessible to the crude human intellect. In this sense, that myth might be called in Kant's language a postulate of practical reason (*Vernunft*), but, considered as such, it has the great advantage of containing absolutely no elements but those which lie before our eyes in the realm of reality, and thus of being able to support all its concepts with perceptions. What is here meant is the myth of the transmigration of souls. This teaches that all sufferings inflicted in life by man on other beings must be expiated in a following life in this world by precisely the same sufferings. It goes to the length of teaching that a person who kills only an animal, will be born as just such an animal at some point in endless time, and will suffer the same death. It teaches that wicked conduct entails a future life in suffering and despised creatures in this world; that a person is accordingly born again in lower castes, or as a woman, or as an animal, as a pariah or Chandala, as a leper, a crocodile, and so on. All the torments threatened by the myth are supported by it with perceptions from the world of reality, through suffering creatures that do not know how they have merited the punishment of their misery; and it does not need to call in the assistance of any other hell. On the other hand, it promises as reward rebirth in better and nobler forms, as Brahmans, sages, or saints. The highest reward awaiting the noblest deeds and most complete resignation, which comes also to the woman who in seven successive lives has voluntarily died on the funeral pile of her husband, and no less to the person whose pure mouth has never uttered a single lie—such a reward can be expressed by the myth only negatively in the language of this world, namely by the promise, so often occurring, of not being reborn any more: *non adsumes iterum existentiam apparentem;* or as the Buddhists, admitting neither *Vedas* nor castes, express it: "You shall attain to Nirvana, in other words, to a state or condition in which there are not four things, namely birth, old age, disease, and death."

Never has a myth been, and never will one be, more closely associated with a philosophical truth accessible to so few, than this very ancient teaching of the noblest and oldest of peoples. Degenerate as this race may now be in many respects, this truth still prevails with it as the universal creed of the people, and it has a decided influence on life today, as it had four thousand years ago. Therefore Pythagoras and Plato grasped with admiration that *non plus ultra* of mythical expression, took it over from India or Egypt, revered it, applied it, and themselves believed it, to what extent we know not. We, on the

contrary, now send to the Brahmans English clergymen and evangelical linen-weavers, in order out of sympathy to put them right, and to point out to them that they are created out of nothing, and that they ought to be grateful and pleased about it. But it is just the same as if we fired a bullet at a cliff. In India our religions will never at any time take root; the ancient wisdom of the human race will not be supplanted by the events in Galilee. On the contrary, Indian wisdom flows back to Europe, and will produce a fundamental change in our knowledge and thought.

(Vol. I, pp. 355–357)

Therefore that great fundamental truth contained in Christianity as well as in Brahmanism and Buddhism, the need for salvation from an existence given up to suffering and death, and its attainability through the denial of the will, hence by a decided opposition to nature, is beyond all comparison the most important truth there can be. But it is at the same time entirely opposed to the natural tendency of mankind, and is difficult to grasp as regards its true grounds and motives; for, in fact, all that can be thought only generally and in the abstract is quite inaccessible to the great majority of people. Therefore, in order to bring that great truth into the sphere of practical application, a *mythical vehicle* for it was needed everywhere for this great majority, a receptacle, so to speak, without which it would be lost and dissipated. The truth had therefore everywhere to borrow the garb of fable, and, in addition, had to try always to connect itself in each case with what is historically given, and is already known and revered. That which *sensu proprio* was and remained inaccessible to the great masses of all times and countries with their low mentality, their intellectual stupidity, and their general brutality, had to be brought home to them *sensu allegorico* for practical purposes, in order to be their guiding star. Thus the above-mentioned religions are to be regarded as sacred vessels in which the great truth, recognized and expressed for thousands of years, possibly indeed since the beginning of the human race, and yet remaining in itself an esoteric doctrine as regards the great mass of mankind, is made accessible to them according to their powers, and preserved and passed on through the centuries. Yet because everything that does not consist throughout of the indestructible material of pure truth is subject to destruction, whenever this fate befalls such a vessel through contact with a het-erogeneous age, the sacred contents must be saved in some way by another vessel, and preserved for mankind. But philosophy has the task of presenting those contents, since they are identical with pure truth, pure and unalloyed, hence merely in abstract concepts, and consequently without that vehicle, for those who are capable of thinking, the number of whom is at all times extremely small. Philosophy is related to religions as a straight line is to several curves running near it; for it expresses *sensu proprio,* and consequently reaches directly, that which religions show under disguises, and reach in roundabout ways.

(Vol. II, pp. 628–629)

English Romanticism and Myth

ARCHIBALD ALISON [1757–1839]

WILLIAM WORDSWORTH [1770–1850]

SAMUEL TAYLOR COLERIDGE [1772–1834]

ROBERT SOUTHEY [1774–1843]

LEIGH HUNT [1784–1859]

THOMAS CARLYLE [1795–1881]

ONE STRIKING aspect of English poetry in the first half of the nineteenth century is the sudden appearance of so many poets so newly preoccupied with myth. Where Blake stood alone in 1790, every major romantic poet is now deeply involved—Wordsworth, Coleridge, Landor, Byron, Shelley, Keats, and Tennyson. Remarkably often, the celebrated works of the period center decisively around the theme of myth or mythopoesis—Wordsworth's *The Prelude,* Coleridge's *Rime of the Ancient Mariner,* Shelley's *Prometheus Unbound* or *Ode to the West Wind,* Keats's *Endymion* or *Hyperion* or the *Odes,* Byron's *Don Juan,* Tennyson's *The Lotos-Eaters* or *Idylls of the King.* On a less exalted level, mythic themes and furbishings become a cliché in such poets as Southey, Scott, Macaulay, Hood, Moore, and in countless others.

But though the romantic absorption in myth is obvious and impressive, the reasons for this new and enduring concern with myth are not easily described. For one thing, the English romantics show scant interest in discussing myth theoretically, or in trying to clarify very directly the tangled philosophic, theological, and historical relations between myth and poetry. There is no English equivalent of Herder's pioneering theories, of Friedrich Schlegel's explicit mythopoetic program, or of Schelling's philosophy of mythology. If the English romantics speak constantly about mythology, they mainly mean by this the traditional corpus of past myth they had always drawn on for allusion or story.

In one obvious way, the English romantics might be said to have had little need for scholarly theorizing or explicit programs about myth. For at least as far as mythopoesis was concerned, they already possessed an adequate equivalent in the whole body of familiar romantic concepts formulated around the ideas of the organic, nature, imagination, emotion, genius, or the particular. These in turn derived in part from the preromantic exploration of mythic themes such as folk and national poetry, the primitive, and the natural sublime; and these were already yielding new sources of poetry. For the English romantics, then, the issue of mythopoesis was already contained in their larger striving to redefine or reshape the meaning of poetry and the poet. As M. H. Abrams and other critics have stressed, the problem and status of poetry—so crucial to the romantics—in fact recapitulated central mythologic and mythopoetic issues. The discussion about Imagination and Fancy; the poetry and religion of nature; the reconciling activity of poetry; the new high claims for poetry as an organic and primal mode of truth and prophecy—all this and more emphasized and energized mythopoetic possibilities, in fact if not quite in name.

English romantic poetry gravitated to mythopoesis for other reasons. Traditional mythology had of course already been denied much or all of its claim to religious truth by deists, skeptics, and orthodox Christians alike. The academic myth scholarship of a Jacob Bryant or Sir William Jones, influential with romantics, reinforced this tendency by placing pagan mythology more or less firmly under Christian domain. Much eighteenth-century verse accelerated the process by making mythology primarily ornamental, learned or witty allusion, or an occasion for travesty. If the romantics generally treated mythic material with dignity and even great respect as appropriate to the most serious poetry, they also however did not undo the denial of myth as religious truth. Instead, they urged a universal religious sense to be found now in nature or in a transcending creative imagination. Leigh Hunt's essay on myth makes clear this side of English interest in myth: his eye is on the human, not the divine; the Greek gods for him are touchstones to a higher sense of humanity, rather than to a debased or wildly ecstatic sense of Deity. For Hunt, myth

is not so much a religious substitute for a decayed Christianity as a source of greater awareness of the present, though also a deepened awareness of that "other world" imagination can reveal. In the prophetic prose of Thomas Carlyle, however, the other side may be glimpsed: new myths are needed to replace antiquated Christianity; and *Sartor Resartus* and *Heroes and Hero-Worship* grandly announce and try to solve that modern need.

What English romanticism also brings to the revitalizing of mythic poetry is a rereading or a rededication to England's own literary past. Romantic mythopoesis always moves with an extraordinary sense of alliance and debt to its greatest predecessors—to Chaucer, Spenser, Shakespeare, Milton, and the Old Testament especially. As the romantics read these poets—or others like them, such as Dante or Aeschylus—they could find a poetry of vision and prophecy, sublime power and epic scope, the supernatural wedded to the natural, or what might loosely be called a poetry of myth. In the historical events of their own age, too, such as the French Revolution, the English romantics found subjects of seemingly large and perhaps almost mythic size; and their sense of living through a moment of epochal revolutionary bliss or disillusion, portentous with divine meaning, contributes greatly to the romantic striving for the grand mythic-prophetic poem.

Certainly English romanticism did not ignore traditional mythology as such. Every major poet among them directly took up Greek or Roman myth; most of them also employed some side of Nordic or Druid mythology, and Indian, Arabic, or Persian themes besides. But these traditional myths were recast profoundly by being viewed through the medium of romantic ideas about imagination or nature. The earliest greater romantics, Wordsworth or Coleridge, indeed either neglect traditional myth or (with Wordsworth) return to it only after having moved mythopoesis in a radically new direction. In this new direction, Wordsworth, Coleridge, and those after find a way to write with remarkable mythopoetic power about nonmythical subjects—the earth, winds, flowers, birds, or humble or inner human life. In 1790, the critic Archibald Alison foretold how ancient myth would be reborn in different form through the sublimity or beauty being found in Nature: "The beautiful forms of ancient mythology, with which the fancy of poets have peopled every element, are now ready to appear to their minds upon the prospect of every scene"—that readiness to find mythic significance in all scenes, prosaic or even conventionally mythological, is consummated first in Wordsworth.

Wordsworth's contribution here comes earliest, is most influential, and in many ways remains the most daring and innovative. If his special effort can be summarily stated, it is in one way to make myth out of what before him had seemed nonmythic subjects, and in another way, to assimilate traditional myths to his own complex natural religion. These go together—Wordsworth must stand as the foremost poetic destroyer of traditional mythology in English poetry; and his razing is so successful because he can powerfully reaffirm myth on quite new grounds. As Basil Willey has suggested, in Wordsworth's poetry "there must be no abstractions, no symbols, no myths, to stand between the mind and its true object." Wordsworth conceives a mythology without myths in the usual sense. In the *Excursion* (vii, 728–740), Wordsworth speaks of "old Bards" who in "idle songs" tell of "Pan and Apollo, veiled in human form"; against this, he poses a new mythmaking that "through a simple rustic garb's disguise" sees the "spirit of a hero" walking in the "unpretending valley." Through his earlier great verse, myth is similarly recast: the woods, waterfalls, rocks, crags, and clouds of the Simplon Pass can seem "blossoms upon

one tree,/ Characters of the great Apocalypse,/ The types and symbols of Eternity"; the "mighty heart lying still" in London; the "mighty Being" awake, revealing itself in the converse of sea with heaven. The *Prelude* expands these themes to genuinely epic or mythic scope; the hero becomes the poet, his divinized history that of the growth of his poetic vision of Imagination, that "awful Power," a vision rising from the prophetic wisdom to be found in living folk communities and in the poet's own memory and experience of the eternal. At the same time, Wordsworth revivifies traditional myth through this immediately experienced sense of natural divinity—for example, in "the sight of Proteus rising from the sea," in the *Ode to Lycoris, Laodamia,* or in passages in the *Excursion.*

Some of Coleridge's remarks on mythology show his independent version of ideas familiar from (and adapted from) German mythic thought: Coleridge contrasts a uniquely modern "inwardness or subjectivity" with Greek mythic "finiteness." But much more in the English spirit of kinship with Old Testament sublimity, Coleridge praises Isaiah or Paul, compared to whom he finds Homer or Virgil "disgustingly *tame,*" and even Milton "barely tolerable." Though he was superbly equipped to theorize extensively on myth and mythopoesis, Coleridge's views here are at best scattered and sketchy. Coleridge's poetic use of mythic themes and techniques is original, but, coming to it from his explicit criticism of myth, somewhat unexpected as well. His poetry does not exalt pagan myth, but neither does it fit very well or at all the image of Hebrew sublimity. In lesser poems, such as *Hymn to Sunrise,* Coleridge did treat nature, as he said, "in the manner of the Psalms." But in greater poems, such as the *Rime of the Ancient Mariner,* he creates a magically autonomous realm in which any particular can be (or must be) invested with a mythically transcendent yet mysterious significance.

Keats moves the mythological poem perhaps even closer than Coleridge to a kind of symbolic autonomy, and develops the mode more brilliantly and fully. This shows partly in Keats's way of beginning with formal mythic subjects, but ending elsewhere: while he names and portrays the gods or heroic figures of legend, they seem to move continually toward becoming new, sensuous imaginative symbols. His gods attain an aspect of amoral power and beauty closer possibly to Goethe's or Hölderlin's lyrics than to any comparable poetry in English. Not the least of Keats's originality with myth is his ability to use such symbols to evoke a felt sense of sadness or joy, moving hauntingly back and forth between ideal types and the utterly sensuous and experiential—the *Ode on a Grecian Urn* is only the most famous example of this. And Keats, like Coleridge, can use the ballad form to mix folk-like simplicity and wonder with a sophisticated magic-mythic mysteriousness, as in *La Belle Dame Sans Merci*.

Part of Shelley's achievement is to blend the new mythology of nature with traditional mythic subjects, as in the Dionysian nature imagery filling his *Prometheus Unbound*. But *Prometheus Unbound* also shows Shelley's aspiration to speak to modern political and intellectual problems by using but recasting traditional myths; his romantic Platonism may be another instance of this. Like other romantics, Shelley often makes mythopoesis one of his main themes: his description of the poet as the "unacknowledged legislator" of mankind deals with the poet as visionary mythmaker in an explicit way, while *Ode to the West Wind,* as Harold Bloom suggests, is a poem about the process of making myths. *Adonais* not only approaches Keats through myth, but strives to turn him into a mythic paradigm.

Byron's use of myth is often slack or banal, by comparison with the other romantics: no other major poet of the time so frequently drummed out vulgarly mythic-exotic topics—the *Giaour, The Bride of Abydos,* the *Corsair,* and so on. Beyond such obviously ambitious mythicizing poems as *Cain,* however, it might be argued that his *Don Juan* is something wholly new in the mythic poetry of his time—perhaps the only successful treatment of a modern mythic character through irony, wit, and most serious comic parody. Tennyson in many ways signals the exhaustion of English romantic genius for revitalizing myth in poetry, most clearly in the sentimentalities of *Sir Galahad, Lady of Shalott,* and much of the *Idylls of the King.* But in *The Lotos-Eaters* or *The Kraken* and other lyrics, Tennyson reaches a sensuous richness and magically effective symbolism reminiscent of Keats. Still, for all his musical resources, Tennyson shows how the earlier and grander romantic preoccupation with myth as a high road to truth or art has by mid-century often narrowed to decorativeness or thinned to a lovely decorousness.

B.F.

REFERENCES Our texts are from: Archibald Alison, *Essays on the Nature and Principles of Taste* (Edinburgh, 5th edition; 1st edition, 1790); *Collected Letters of Samuel Taylor Coleridge,* edited by E. L. Griggs, 2 vols. (Oxford: Clarendon Press, 1956), vol. I; William Wordsworth, *The Prelude (Text of 1805),* edited by E. De Selincourt (London: Oxford University Press, revised impression, 1969); and *The Excursion* in *The Poetical Works of Wordsworth,* edited by T. Hutchinson, new edition revised by E. De Selincourt (London: Oxford University Press, 1964); *The Poetical Works of Robert Southey,* 10 vols. (Boston, 1896), vol. IV; Leigh Hunt, "Spirit of the Ancient Mythology," in *A Day* by the Fire (London, 1870); Thomas Carlyle, Sartor Resartus, in Works, ed. H. D. Traill (London, 1896–1899).

For general commentary: Douglas Bush, Mythology and the Romantic Tradition in English Poetry (Cambridge: Harvard University Press, 1937) limits itself to Greek and Roman myth, but is excellent for guide and bibliography to major and innumerable minor figures; see also Douglas Bush, Pagan Myth and Christian Tradition in English Poetry (Philadelphia: American Philosophical Society, 1965), Chap. 2; Stephen Larrabee, English Bards and Grecian Marbles (New York: Columbia University Press, 1943); M. H. Abrams, The Mirror and the Lamp (New York: Oxford University Press, 1953), especially pp. 290–297; Helen H. Law, Bibliography of Greek Myth in English Poetry (New York: American Classical League Service, Bulletin 27; Supplement, 1941); Edward Hungerford, Shores of Darkness (New York: Columbia University Press, 1941); A. J. Kuhn, "English Deism and the Development of Romantic Mythological Syncretism," PMLA 71 (1956), 1094–1115; Alex Zwerdling, "The Mythographers and the Romantic Revival of Greek Myth," PMLA 79 (1964), 447–456.

For Wordsworth, see Basil Willey, The Seventeenth Century Background (London: Chatto & Windus, 1934), "On Wordsworth and the Locke Tradition." For Coleridge: see his "Poesy and Art" (1818) for primitive language and "music of savage tribes"; his Lecture XI (Lectures, 1818) on Asiatic and Greek mythologies, with Schellingian influence; "On the Prometheus of Aeschylus" (May 18, 1825) and "Summary of an Essay" on myth and ancient mysteries. See G. N. G. Orsini, Coleridge and German Idealism (Carbondale: Southern Illinois University Press, 1969), esp. Chaps. 8 and 9. John Armstrong, The Paradise Myth (London: Oxford University Press, 1969).

For Shelley: Harold Bloom, Shelley's Mythmaking (New Haven: Yale University Press, 1959, reprinted 1969). For Keats: Margaret Sherwood, Undercurrents of Influence in English Romantic Poetry (Cambridge: Harvard University Press, 1934), "Keats' Imaginative Approach to Myth"; Paul de Man, "Keats and Hölderlin," Comparative Literature 8 (1956–1957), 28–45; Edward S. LeComte, Endymion in England (New York: King's Crown Press, 1944). For Tennyson: M. W. Maccallum, Tennyson's Idylls of the King and Arthurian Story from the XVIth Century (Glasgow: Maclehose, 1894). W. D. Paden, Tennyson in Egypt (Lawrence: University of Kansas, 1942) for excellent background and particulars. For illuminating remarks on Robert Burns's use of myth-folklore material in "Tam O'Shanter" (written for the antiquary Grose, and appearing in the latter's Antiquities of Scotland), see David Daiches, Robert Burns (London: Macmillan, 1950, revised 1966), pp. 249–251.

For the interest in folklore shown by Southey, Scott, Allan Cunningham, and others, see Richard M. Dorson, The British Folklorists (Chicago: University of Chicago Press, 1968), pp. 91–137, and Peasant Customs and Savage Myths Selections from the British Folklorists, edited by Richard Dorson, 2 vols. (Chicago: University of Chicago Press, 1968), Chap. I. See also: George Dyer, Poetics (London, 1812), I, pp. xvii–xviii and 148–149 for poetic use of mythology. Hartley Coleridge, "On the Poetical Use of the Heathen Mythology" (1822), repr. in Essays and Marginalia, ed. D. Coleridge (London, 1851), I, pp. 18 ff. John Ogilvie, Philosophical and Critical Observations on the Nature, Characters and Various Species of Composition (London, 1774), I, pp. 332–333 on using heathen mythology. Marie E. de Meester, Oriental Influences in the English Literature of the Nineteenth Century (Heidelberg: Anglistische Forschungen, Heft 46, 1901). R. Sencourt, India in English Literature (London, 1925). Byron P. Smith, Islam in English Literature (Beirut: American Press, 1939).

ALISON

FROM *Essays on the Nature and Principles of Taste*

THERE ARE many other instances equally familiar which are sufficient to show that whatever increases this exercise or employment of imagination, increases also the emotion of beauty or sublimity.

This is very obviously the effect of all associations. There is no man who has not some interesting associations with particular scenes, or airs, or books, and who does not feel their beauty or sublimity enhanced to him by such connections. The view of the house where one was born, of the school where one was educated, and where the gay years of infancy were passed, is indifferent to no man. They recall so many images of past happiness and past affections, they are connected with so many strong or interesting emotions, and lead altogether to so long a train of feelings and recollections, that there is hardly any scene which one ever beholds with so much rapture. There are songs also that we have heard in our infancy, which, when brought to our remembrance in after years, raise emotions for which we cannot well account, and which, though perhaps very indifferent in themselves, still continue from this association, and from the variety of conceptions which they kindle in our minds, to be our favorites through life. The scenes which have been distinguished by the residence of any person whose memory we admire produce a similar effect. *Movemur enim, nescio quo pacto, locis ipsis, in quibus eorum, quos diligimus, aut admiramur adsunt vestigia.** The scenes themselves may be little beautiful, but the delight with which we recollect the traces of their lives blends itself insensibly with the emotions which the scenery excites, and the admiration which these recollections afford seems to give a kind of sanctity to the place where they dwelt, and converts everything into beauty which appears to have been connected with them. . . .

The delight which most men of education receive from the consideration of antiquity, and the beauty that they discover in every object which is connected with ancient times, is in a great measure to be ascribed to the same cause [of associative imagination]. The antiquarian in his cabinet, surrounded by the relics of former ages, seems to himself to be removed to periods that are long since past, and indulges in the imagination of living in a world which, by a very natural kind of prejudice, we are always willing to believe was both wiser and better than the present. All that is venerable or laudable in the history of those times present them-

* Cicero, *De Legibus,* II, iv: "For we are moved, I know not in what way, by those places in which traces remain of those we love or admire."—Ed.

selves to his memory. The gallantry, the heroism, the patriotism of antiquity rise again before his view, softened by the obscurity in which they are involved, and rendered more seducing to the imagination by that obscurity itself, which, while it mingles a sentiment of regret amid his pursuits, serves at the same time to stimulate his fancy to fill up, by its own creation, those long intervals of time of which history has preserved no record. The relics he contemplates seem to approach him still nearer to the ages of his regard. The dress, the furniture, the arms of the times are so many assistances to his imagination, in guiding or directing its exercise, and offering him a thousand sources of imagery, provide him with an almost inexhaustible field in which his memory and his fancy may expatiate. . . . Even the peasant, whose knowledge of former years extends but to a few generations, has yet in his village some monument of deeds or virtues of his forefathers, and cherishes with a fond veneration the memorial of those good old times, to which his imagination returns with delight and of which he loves to recount the simple tales that tradition has brought him.

And what is it that constitutes that emotion of sublime delight which every man of common sensibility feels upon the first prospect of Rome? It is not the scene of destruction which is before him. It is not the Tiber, diminished in his imagination to a paltry stream and stagnating amid the ruins of that magnificence which it once adorned. It is not the triumph of superstition over the wreck of human greatness, and its monuments erected upon the very spot where the first honors of humanity have been gained. It is ancient Rome which fills his imagination. It is the country of Caesar, and Cicero, and Virgil, which is before him. It is the

mistress of the world which he sees, and who seems to him to rise again from her tomb to give laws to the universe. All that the labors of his youth or the studies of his maturer age have acquired, with regard to the history of this great people, open at once before his imagination, and present him with a field of high and solemn imagery which can never be exhausted. Take from him these associations, conceal from him that it is Rome that he sees, and how different would be his emotion!

The effect which is thus produced by associations, in increasing the emotions of sublimity or beauty, is produced also, either in nature or in description, by what are generally termed "picturesque objects." Instances of such objects are familiar to every one's observation: an old tower in the middle of a deep wood, a bridge flung across a chasm between rocks, a cottage on a precipice, are common examples. If I am not mistaken, the effect which such objects have on every one's mind is to suggest an additional train of conceptions beside what the scene or description itself would have suggested, for it is very obvious that no objects are remarked as picturesque which do not strike the imagination by themselves. They are, in general, such circumstances as coincide but are not necessarily connected with the character of the scene or description, and which, at first affecting the mind with an emotion of surprise, produce afterwards an increased or additional train of imagery. . . .

The influence of such additional trains of imagery in increasing the emotions of sublimity or beauty might be illustrated from many other circumstances equally familiar. I am induced to mention only the following, because it is one of the most striking that I know, and because it is probable that most men of education have at least in some degree been conscious of it—the influence, I mean, of an acquaintance with poetry in our earlier years in increasing our sensibility to the beauties of Nature. . . . In most men at least, the first appearance of poetical imagination is at school, when their imaginations begin to be warmed by the descriptions of ancient poetry and when they have acquired a new sense, as it were, with which they behold the face of Nature.

How different from this period become the sentiments with which the scenery of Nature is contemplated by those who have any imagination! The beautiful forms of ancient mythology, with which the fancy of poets peopled every element, are now ready to appear to their minds upon the prospect of every scene. The descriptions of ancient authors, so long admired and so deserving of admiration, occur to them at every moment, and with them all those enthusiastic ideas of ancient genius and glory, which the study of so many years of youth so naturally leads them to form. Or, if the study of modern poetry has succeeded to that of the ancient, a thousand other beautiful associations are acquired, which, instead of destroying, serve easily to unite with the former and to afford a new source of delight. The awful

forms of Gothic superstition, the wild and romantic imagery which the turbulence of the Middle Ages, the Crusades, and the institution of chivalry have spread over every country of Europe, arise to the imagination in every scene, accompanied with all those pleasing recollections of prowess and adventure and courteous manners which distinguished those memorable times. With such images in their minds, it is not common nature that appears to surround them. It is nature embellished. . . .

Nor is it only in providing so many sources of association that the influence of an acquaintance with poetry consists. It is yet still more powerful in giving *character* to the different appearances of nature, in connecting them with various emotions and affections of our hearts, and in thus providing an almost inexhaustible source of solemn or cheerful meditation. . . .

Associations of this kind, when acquired in early life, are seldom altogether lost, and whatever inconveniences they may sometimes have with regard to the general character, or however much they may be ridiculed by those who do not experience them, they are yet productive to those who possess them of a perpetual and innocent delight.

WORDSWORTH

FROM *The Prelude*

. . . to the open fields I told
A prophecy: poetic numbers came
Spontaneously, and cloth'd in priestly robe
My spirit, thus singled out, as it might
    seem,
For holy services: great hopes were mine;
My own voice chear'd me, and, far more,
    the mind's
Internal echo of the imperfect sound;
To both I listen'd, drawing from them both
A chearful confidence in things to come.

    Whereat, being not unwilling now to
        give
A respite to this passion, I paced on
Gently, with careless steps; and came,
    erelong,
To a green shady place where down I sate
Beneath a tree, slackening my thoughts
    by choice,
And settling into gentler happiness.
'Twas Autumn, and a calm and placid
    day,
With warmth as much as needed from a
    sun
Two hours declin'd towards the west, a
    day
With silver clouds, and sunshine on the
    grass,
And, in the shelter'd grove where I was
    couch'd
A perfect stillness. On the ground I lay
Passing through many thoughts, yet mainly
    such

As to myself pertain'd. I made a choice
Of one sweet Vale whither my steps should
    turn
And saw, methought, the very house and
    fields
Present before my eyes: nor did I fail
To add, meanwhile, assurance of some
    work
Of glory, there forthwith to be begun, . . .

Time, place and manners; these I seek,
    and these
I find in plenteous store; but nowhere such
As may be singled out with steady choice;
No little Band of yet remember'd names
Whom I, in perfect confidence, might hope
To summon back from lonesome banish-
    ment
And make them inmates in the hearts of
    men
Now living, or to live in times to come.
Sometimes, mistaking vainly, as I fear,
Proud spring-tide swellings for a regular
    sea,
I settle on some British theme, some old
Romantic tale, by Milton left unsung;
More often resting at some gentle place
Within the groves of Chivalry, I pipe
Among the Shepherds, with reposing
    Knights
Sit by a Fountain-side, and hear their
    tales.
Sometimes, more sternly mov'd, I would
    relate

How vanquish'd Mithridates northward
    pass'd,
And, hidden in the cloud of years, became
That Odin, Father of a Race, by whom
Perish'd the Roman Empire . . .

Sometimes it suits me better to shape out
Some Tale from my own heart, more near
    akin
To my own passions and habitual thoughts,
Some variegated story, in the main
Lofty, with interchange to gentler things.
But deadening admonitions will succeed
And the whole beauteous Fabric seem to
    lack

Foundation, and, withal, appears
    throughout
Shadowy and unsubstantial. Then, last
    wish,
My last and favourite aspiration! then
I yearn towards some philosophic Song
Of Truth that cherishes our daily life;
With meditations passionate from deep
Recesses in man's heart, immortal verse
Thoughtfully fitted to the Orphean
    lyre . . .
                (from Book I, ll. 59–86; 169–189;
                                        200–234)

FROM *The Excursion*

                                Say why
That ancient story of Prometheus chained
To the bare rock, on frozen Caucasus;
The vulture, the inexhaustible repast
Drawn from his vitals? Say what meant
    the woes
By Tantalus entailed upon his race,
And the dark sorrows of the line of
    Thebes?
Fictions in form, but in their substance
    truths,
Tremendous truth? familiar to the men
Of long-past times, nor obsolete in ours.

Exchange the shepherd's frock of native
    grey
For robes with regal purple tinged; convert
The crook into a sceptre; give the pomp
Of circumstance; and here the tragic Muse
Shall find apt subjects for her highest art.
Amid the groves, under the shadowy hills,
The generations are prepared; the pangs,
The internal pangs, are ready; the dread
    strife
Of poor humanity's afflicted will
Struggling in vain with ruthless destiny.
                (from Book VI., ll. 539–557)

COLERIDGE

FROM *a letter to John Thelwall*

17 December 1796

. . . You say the Christian is a *mean* Religion: now the Religion, which Christ taught, is simply 1 that there is an Omnipresent Father of infinite power, wisdom, & Goodness, in whom we all of us move, & have our being & 2. That when we appear to men to die, we do not utterly perish; but after this Life shall continue to enjoy or suffer the consequences & [natur]al effects of the Habits, we have formed here, whether good or evil.—This is the Christian *Religion* & all of the Christian *Religion*. That there is *no fancy* in it, I readily grant; but that it is mean, & deficient in *mind,* and *energy,* it were impossible for me to admit, unless I admitted that there *could be* no dignity, intellect, or force in any thing but *atheism.*—But tho' it appeal not, itself, to the fancy, the truths which it teaches, admit the highest exercise of it. Are the 'innumerable multitude of angels & archangels' less splendid beings than the countless Gods & Goddesses of Rome & Greece?—And can you seriously think that Mercury from Jove equals in poetic sublimity 'the mighty Angel that came down from Heaven, whose face was as it were the Sun, and his feet as pillars of fire: Who set his right foot on the sea, and his left upon the earth. And he sent forth a loud voice;

and when he had sent it forth, seven Thunders uttered their Voices: and when the seven Thund[ers] had uttered their Voices, the mighty Angel lifted up his hand to Heaven, & sware by Him that liveth for ever & ever, that TIME was no more? ['] Is not Milton a *sublimer* poet than Homer or Virgil? Are not his Personages more sublimely cloathed? And do you not know, that there is not perhaps *one* page in Milton's Paradise Lost, in which he has not borrowed his imagery from the *Scriptures*?—I allow, and rejoice that *Christ* appealed only to the understanding & the affections; but I affirm that, after reading Isaiah, or St Paul's Epistle to the Hebrews, Homer & Virgil are disgustingly *tame* to me, & Milton himself barely tolerable. You and I are very differently organized, if you think that the following (putting serious belief out of the Question) is a mean flight of impassioned Eloquence; in which the Apostle marks the difference between the Mosaic & Christian Dispensations—'For ye are not come unto the Mount that might be touched' (i. e. a *material* and earthly place) 'and that burned with fire; nor unto Blackness, and Tempest, and the sound of a Trumpet, and the Voice of Words, which voice they who heard it intreated that it should not be spoken to them any more; but ye are come unto Mount Sion, and unto the city of the living God, to an innumerable multitude of Angels, to God the Judge of all, and to the Spirits of just Men made perfect!'— *You* may prefer to all this the Quarrels of Jupiter & Juno, the whimpering of wounded Venus, & the Jokes of the celestials on the lameness of Vulcan—be it so (The difference in our tastes it would not be difficult to account for from the different feelings which we have associated with these ideas)—I shall continue with Milton to say, that

> Sion Hill
> Delights *me* more, and Siloa's Brook that
>   flow'd
> Fast by the oracle of God!

SOUTHEY

FROM *The Curse of Kehama*

SEVERAL years ago, in the introduction of my "Letters to Mr. Charles Butler, vindicating the 'Book of the Church,' " I had occasion to state, that, while a schoolboy at Westminster, I had formed an intention of exhibiting the most remarkable forms of mythology which have at any time obtained among mankind, by making each the groundwork of a narrative poem. The performance, as might be expected, fell far short of design; and yet it proved something more than a dream of juvenile ambition.

I began with the Mahommedan religion, as being that with which I was then best acquainted myself, and of which every one, who had read the "Arabian Nights' Entertainments," possessed all the knowledge necessary for readily understanding and entering into the intent and spirit of the poem. Mr. Wilberforce thought that I had conveyed in it a very false impression of that religion, and that the moral sublimity which he admired in it was owing to this flattering misrepresentation. But "Thalaba the Destroyer" was professedly an Arabian tale. The design required that I should bring into view the best features of that system of belief and worship which had been developed under the Covenant with Ishmael, placing in the most favorable light the morality of the "Koran," and what the least corrupted of the Mahommedans retain of the patriarchal faith. It would have been altogether incongruous to have touched upon the abominations ingrafted upon it, first by the false Prophet himself, who appears to have been far more remarkable for audacious profligacy than for any intellectual endowments, and afterwards by the spirit of Oriental despotism which accompanied Mahommedanism wherever it was established.

Heathen mythologies have generally been represented by Christian poets as the work of the Devil and his angels; and the machinery derived from them was thus rendered credible, according to what was during many ages a received opinion. The plan upon which I proceeded in "Madoc" was to produce the effect of machinery, as far as was consistent with the character of the poem, by representing the most remarkable religion of the New World such as it was,—a system of atrocious priestcraft. It was not here, as in "Thalaba," the foundation of the poem, but, as usual in what are called epic poems, only incidentally connected with it.

When I took up, for my next subject, that mythology which Sir William Jones had been the first to introduce into English poetry, I soon perceived that the best mode of treating it would be to construct a story altogether mythological. In what form to compose it was then to be determined. No such question had arisen concerning any of my former poems. I should never for a moment have thought of any other measure than blank verse for "Joan of Arc" and for "Madoc," and afterwards for "Roderick." The reason why the irregular, rhymeless lyrics of Dr.

Sayers were preferred for "Thalaba" was that the freedom and variety of such verse were suited to the story. . . .

The same sense of fitness which made me choose for an Arabian tale the simplest and easiest form of verse, induced me to take a different course in an Indian poem. It appeared to me, that here neither the tone of morals nor the strain of poetry could be pitched too high; that nothing but moral sublimity could compensate for the extravagance of the fictions; and that all the skill I might possess in the art of poetry was required to counterbalance the disadvantage of a mythology with which few readers were likely to be well acquainted, and which would appear monstrous if its deformities were not kept out of sight. I endeavored, therefore, to combine the utmost richness of versification with the greatest freedom. The spirit of the poem was Indian, but there was nothing Oriental in the style. I had learnt the language of poetry from our own great masters and the great poets of antiquity.

(from Preface)

HUNT

FROM *Spirit of the Ancient Mythology*

THE GREATEST pleasure arising to a modern imagination from the ancient mythology is in a mingled sense of the old popular belief and of the philosophical refinements upon it. We take Apollo, and Mercury, and Venus, as shapes that

existed in popular credulity, as the greater fairies of the ancient world: and we regard them at the same time, as personifications of all that is beautiful and genial in the forms and tendencies of creation. But the result, coming as it does, too, through avenues of beautiful poetry, both ancient and modern, is so entirely cheerful, that we are apt to think it must have wanted gravity to more believing eyes. We fancy that the old world saw nothing in religion but lively and graceful shapes, as remote from the more obscure and awful hintings of the world unknown, as physics appear to be from the metaphysical; as the eye of a beautiful woman is from the inward speculations of a Brahmin; or a lily at noonday from the wide obscurity of night-time.

This supposition appears to be carried a great deal too far. We will not inquire, in this place, how far the *mass* of mankind, when these shapes were done away, did or did not escape from a despotic anthropomorphitism; nor how far they were driven by the vaguer fears, and the opening of a more visible eternity, into avoiding the whole subject, rather than courting it; nor how it is that the nobler practical religion which was afforded them has been unable to bring back their frightened theology from the angry and avaricious pursuits into which they fled for refuge. But, setting aside the portion of terror, of which heathenism partook in common with all faiths originating in uncultivated times, the ordinary run of pagans were perhaps more impressed with a sense of the invisible world, in consequence of the very visions presented to their imagination, than the same description of men under a more shadowy system. There is the same difference between the two things as between a populace believing in fairies and a populace not believing. The latter is in the high road to something better, if not drawn aside into new terrors on the one hand or mere worldliness on the other. But the former is led to look out of the mere worldly commonplaces about it, twenty times to the other's once. It has a sense of a supernatural state of things, however gross. It has a link with another world, from which something like gravity is sure to strike into the most cheerful heart. Every forest, to the mind's eye of a Greek was haunted by superior intelligences. Every stream had its presiding nymph; who was thanked for the draught of water. Every house had its protecting gods, which had blessed the inmate's ancestors, and which would bless him also, if he cultivated the social affections: for the same word which expressed piety towards the gods expressed love towards relations and friends. If in all this there was nothing but the worship of a more graceful humanity, there may be worships much worse as well as much better. And the divinest spirit that ever appeared on earth has told us that the extension of human sympathy embraces all that is required of us, either to do or to foresee.

Imagine the feelings with which an ancient believer must have gone by the oracular oaks of Dodona; or the calm groves of the Eumenides; or the fountain where Proserpine vanished under ground with Pluto; or the Great Temple of the mysteries at Eleusis; or the laurelled mountain Parnassus, on the side of which was the temple of Delphi, where Apollo was supposed to be present in person. Imagine Plutarch, a devout and yet a liberal believer, when he went to study theology and philosophy at Delphi: with what feelings must he not have passed along the woody paths of the hill, approaching nearer every instant to the divinity, and not sure that a glance of light through the trees was not the lustre of the god himself going by! This is mere poetry to us, and very fine it is; but to him it was poetry, and religion, and beauty, and gravity, and hushing awe, and a path as from one world to another.

With similar feelings he would cross the ocean, an element that naturally detaches the mind from earth, and which the ancients regarded as especially doing so. He had been in the Carpathian sea, the favourite haunt of Proteus, who was supposed to be gifted above every other deity with a knowledge of the causes of things. Towards evening, when the winds were rising, and the sailors had made their vows to Neptune, he would think of the old "shepherd of the seas of yore," and believe it possible that he might become visible to his eyesight, driving through the darkling waters, and turning the sacred wildness of his face towards the blessed ship.

In all this there is a deeper sense of another world than in the habit of contenting oneself with a few vague terms and embodying nothing but Mammon. There is a deeper sense of another world, precisely because there is a deeper sense of the present; of its varieties, its benignities, its mystery. It was a strong sense of this which made a living poet, who is accounted very orthodox in his religious opinions, give vent, in that fine sonnet, to his impatience at seeing the beautiful planet we live upon, with all its starry wonders about it, so little thought of, compared with what is ridiculously called *the world*. He seems to have dreaded the symptom, as an evidence of materialism, and of the planets being dry self-existing things, peopled with mere successive mortalities, and unconnected with any superintendence or consciousness in the universe about them. It is abhorrent from all we think and feel, that they should be so: and yet Love might make heavens of them, if they were.

The world is too much with us. Late and
    soon,
Getting and spending we lay waste our
    powers:
Little we see in Nature that is ours:
We have given our hearts away, a sordid
    boon!
This Sea that bares her bosom to the moon;
The Winds that will be howling at all hours,
And are upgathered now like sleeping
    flowers;
For this, for everything, we are out of
    tune;
It moves us not.—Great God! I'd rather be
A Pagan suckled in a creed outworn;
So might I, standing on this pleasant lea,
Have glimpses that would make me less
    forlorn;
Have sight of Proteus rising from the sea;
Or hear old Triton blow his wreathèd horn.

            —Wordsworth

CARLYLE

FROM *Sartor Resartus*

The Everlasting Yea

". . . WAS IT not to preach forth this same HIGHER that sages and martyrs, the Poet and the Priest, in all times, have spoken and suffered; bearing testimony, through life and through death, of the Godlike that is in Man, and how in the Godlike only has he Strength and Freedom? Which God-inspired Doctrine art thou also honoured to be taught; O Heavens! and broken with manifold merciful Afflictions, even till thou become contrite, and learn it! O, thank thy Destiny for these; thankfully bear what yet remain: thou hadst need of them; the Self in thee needed to be annihilated. By benignant fever-paroxysms is Life rooting out the deep-seated chronic Diseases, and triumphs over Death. On the roaring billows of Time, thou art not engulfed, but borne aloft into the azure of Eternity. Love not Pleasure; love God. This is the EVERLASTING YEA, wherein all contradiction is solved: wherein whoso walks and works, it is well with him."

And again: "Small is it that thou canst trample the Earth with its injuries under thy feet, as Old Greek Zeno trained thee; thou canst love the Earth while it injures thee, and even because it injures thee; for this a Greater than Zeno was needed, and he too was sent. Knowest thou that 'Worship of Sorrow'? The Temple whereof, founded some eighteen centuries ago, now lies in ruins, overgrown with jungle, the habitation of doleful creatures: nevertheless, venture forward; in a low crypt, arched out of falling fragments, thou findest the Altar still there, and its sacred Lamp perennially burning."

Without pretending to comment on which strange utterances, the Editor will only remark, that there lies beside them much of a still more questionable character; unsuited to the general apprehension; nay wherein he himself does not see his way. Nebulous disquisitions on Religion, yet not without bursts of splendour; on the "perennial continuance of Inspiration"; on Prophecy; that there are "true Priests, as well as Baal-Priests, in our own day": with more of the like sort. We select some fractions, by way of finish to this farrago.

"Cease, my much-respected Herr von Voltaire," thus apostrophises the Professor: "shut thy sweet voice; for the task appointed thee seems finished. Sufficiently hast thou demonstrated this proposition, considerable or otherwise: That the Mythus of the Christian Religion looks not in the eighteenth century as it did in the eighth. Alas, were thy six-and-thirty quartos, and the six-and-thirty thousand other quartos and folios, and flying sheets or reams, printed before and since on the same subject, all needed to convince us of so little! But what next? Wilt thou help us to embody the divine Spirit of that Religion in a new Mythus, in a new vehicle and vesture, that our Souls, otherwise too like perishing, may live? What! thou hast no faculty in that kind? Only a torch for burning, no hammer for building? Take our thanks, then, and—thyself away.

"Meanwhile what are antiquated Mythuses to me? Or is the God present, felt in my own heart, a thing which Herr von Voltaire will dispute out of me; or dispute into me? To the 'Worship of Sorrow' ascribe what origin and genesis thou pleasest, *has* not that Worship originated, and been generated; is it not *here?* Feel it in thy heart, and then say whether it is of God! This is Belief; all else is Opinion,—for which latter whoso will let him worry and be worried."

"Neither," observes he elsewhere, "shall ye tear-out one another's eyes, struggling over 'Plenary Inspiration,' and such-like: try rather to get a little even Partial Inspiration, each of you for himself. One BIBLE I know, of whose Plenary Inspiration doubt is not so much as possible; nay with my own eyes I saw the God's-Hand writing it: thereof all other Bibles are but leaves,—say, in Picture-Writing to assist the weaker faculty."

(from Book II, Chap. 9)

JOSEPH GÖRRES

[1776–1848]

JOSEPH GÖRRES had at least three different careers: as nationalist, educator, and mythologist. At first a partisan of the French revolution, he turned away after 1800 to become finally one of the foremost publicists for German nationalism —the side of his career for which he is still most generally remembered. Throughout his life he was a teacher as well, first of the sciences in the higher secondary schools, then, from 1806 to 1808, of German literature and history at the University of Heidelberg, and after more political writing and exile, Professor of History at Munich from 1826. His main work in myth began in 1806 when he joined the Heidelberg circle whose other members included Arnim, Brentano, and Creuzer. Arnim and Brentano had been collecting German folksongs since 1802, and their three-volume work, *Des Knabens Wunderhorn* (1806–1808), was a landmark collection. In 1807 Görres published *Die teutschen Volksbücher;* in 1817, a collection of *Altteutsche Volks- und Meisterlieder;* in 1813, he edited *Lohengrin;* and he translated and projected other works in the same field. In 1810, culminating an intense interest in Indian myth, he published his most ambitious work, *Mythengeschichte der asiatischen Welt.*

But it is perhaps more accurate to say that Görres had not three careers, but only one with three aspects. For his nationalist, educative, and mythic activities all reflect each other. His effort to foster older German literature is fed by and fed back into his nationalist enthusiasms. As critics have noted, to edit *Lohengrin* and to collect folksongs between 1806 and 1813 had obvious political point, since that was the time of the Napoleonic occupation. In the same way, Görres is said to be the first (in 1808) to give secondary school lectures on medieval German literature. As passing remarks in his book on Indian myth show, he explicitly urged that the deeper spirituality he thought he found in the East be utilized for a needed revival of spiritual depth in a Germany he thought debilitated by rationalist skepticism and pedantry. Though generally free of the cruder cult of Teutonism promoted by other contemporary nationalists such as "Father" Jahn or the poet Arndt, Görres also clearly shows the shift from Herder's cosmopolitan embracing of all folklore to the theory of *Volk* now enlisted in the service of immediate patriotism. (An interesting comparison with Görres here is Heinrich Julius Klaproth [1783–1835], who precociously published his *Asiatisches Magazin* at Weimar in 1802, with articles by leading Indic scholars, and thereafter pursued a remarkable career as traveler, linguist, geographer, and patriot—as Raymond Schwab notes, Klaproth rejects "Indo-European" philology in favor of "Indo-Germanic," foreshadowing similar tendencies in Gobineau and Wagner.)

Görres's *Mythic History of the Asiatic World* is hardly a history of its purported subject; it is rather his own vast, oracular, part-romantic part-mystic system fastened to what Görres claims as the higher truth, not only of Indian myth, but also of Egyptian, Chaldean, Persian, Chinese, and Greek myth, and finally of the German spirit. The historical spine in his book is that India is the cradle and source of all world religions, from which the purest religious wisdom spreads outward to the Far East, Africa, and the West, in the course of which it becomes more or less degraded. To support this theory, Görres marshals a singularly self-indulgent set of documents and interpretations. He claims to prove the *Vedas* the oldest and truest Indian (and thus, world) religious documents by evidence from the *Oupnek'hat,* which he says is a "true abridgement" of the *Vedas.* Görres used Anquetil-Duperron's translation of the *Oupnek'hat* (1801–1802), but ignored the serious problems raised about Anquetil's use not of a Sanskrit text but of a dubious Persian version. For Egyptian mythology, Görres relied decisively on the Hermes Trismegistus fragments, despite Isaac Casaubon's complete demonstration as early as 1614 of the spurious antiquity of this work: a fact Görres admitted, but oracularly dismissed as puerilely blind to the demands of a transcending intuitive truth.

Opaque as his Indic mythicizing often is, Görres's ideas become more clear when seen as part of the earlier romantic perception of India as the cradle of religion, and about myth as manifesting the oneness of all wisdoms. Görres diffusely asserts a view familiar at least from the early Schelling: that religion and myth begin when the Godhead, to comprehend and realize itself, manifests itself in matter and time. But Görres seems to go further, apparently denying matter or nature any intrinsic worth or reality. Nature is only the visible expression of God's Word, and man is the great creative Word spoken by the earth—and so, too, plants, organs, stars are but spiritually sensuous emblems. Moreover, what men call "history"—the flow of real, decisive events—is only the narrow "circle" of total Spirit they narrowly comprehend. Almost as in Blake, there is no true natural religion or history: eternal Spirit "is in constant struggle with the circle in which Nature would like to trap it." But religion "in its innermost essence has like God no history." The Godhead is always present and omnipresent. Görres seems to suggest that myth or true religion is best understood as a perpetually present incarnation. Indian mythic religion exemplifies this completely, and Görres portrays these original men as in an Eden. Mythic men did come to worship the stars, then the sun. But this meant they participated in Spirit innocently, fully, openly. However, the later religions and history of mankind occur as the emanative process goes further, as part separates further from the source and the whole. "Mere" history now begins. In migrations from India, priests carry the truth abroad; divisive languages spring up as mankind separates. But in all parts of the world there remain still inextinguished remnants of the golden age in language, doctrine, ritual, and history. Indeed, the *Mythic History* is in large part an effort to collect just such evidence from all and any sources.

Görres's system in the end seems a romantic version of the older Christian interpretation of myth as a "plagiarism" of true revelation. What Görres expounded ecstatically, his friend and disciple in mythology, Friedrich Creuzer, expressed in a more moderate, scholarly, and profound way in his famous *Symbolik,* also published in 1810. It was under Görres's influence that Creuzer published his first mythologic effort in this direction, his *Idee und Probe alter Symbolik* (1806); and Creuzer chose as his epigraph to his *Symbolik* a long quotation from Görres's *Mythengeschichte*.

B.F.

REFERENCES   The text is our translation from *Mythengeschichte der asiatischen Welt,* 2 vols. (Heidelberg, 1810). Görres's works are found in *Gesammelte Schriften,* ed. M. Görres, 6 vols. (Augsburg, 1854–1860). For commentary see the long, admiring note on Görres's mythology by J. D. Guignaut in his French translation of Creuzer's *Symbolik* under the title of *Religions de l'antiquité considerées principalement dans leurs formes symboliques et mythologiques,* 4 vols. (Paris, 1825–1851), I, 523–528; Max Koch, *Deutsche National-Litteratur* (Stuttgart, 1891), Bde. 146, I, i–clxii, which usefully discusses Görres and his relation to the Heidelberg circle; A. Leslie Willson, *A Mythical Image: The ideal of India in German Romanticism* (Durham: Duke University Press, 1964), 105–108; Fritz Strich, *Die Mythologie in der deutschen Litteratur von Klopstock bis Wagner,* 2 vols. (Halle, 1910), II, *passim*; Gustav A. Brandt, *Herder und Görres 1797–1807* (Berlin: Fr.-Wilhelms Universität, 1939); Otto Gruppe, *Geschichte der klassischen Mythologie und Religionsgeschichte* (Leipzig, 1921), 133–136; J. N. Sepp, *Görres* (Berlin, 1896).

GÖRRES

FROM Mythic History of the Asiatic World

IN THE beginning the Godhead came forth from its holy mysteries, and its manifestation was matter and the visible universe. That is the first word that it spoke, calling itself by its own name; those are the first holy books, that are written with letters of fire on the heavens; and as the worlds entered with celebration in their orbits, the first hymns resounded from their choirs to the hidden secret from which they had come forth. The second incarnation followed, in order even more to announce the splendor of the being. Among all the forms of nature, life was dominant. Then it gathered in each to a flame, as the waters of the earth gathered into streams, and the secret approached closer to the light, and only threw a light veil of elements around it, and wove the hieroglyphs of the previous incarnation into distinct pictures, so that it now could understand itself and the great ancestors and the even greater Godhead. The mysteries of nature became manifest in mankind; what had remained dark and secretive in the great work should now be resolved in history, so that every thing could arrive at a clear understanding of the whole. Thus all world history is the history of nature spelled out. The gates of the great temple of nature, the earth, have opened, and from the inner sanctum a train has emerged; led by priests and prophets, and then guided by poets, heroes, and sages, it will pass through the wide realm of the Father, giving and receiving testimony to his miraculous power and making clear and evident the dark words that God spoke into the world. But for this reason did the world come into existence, that the Godhead might be able to comprehend itself, as it comprehends itself whole and undivided in its own idea, in the same way also in its infinity, taken in all its parts.

In mankind as well the same eternal sun shines, there as well it wants to beam in a great spring, and history in its entire course and in all its phases represents the second creation of the creating Godhead, in which the Idea of life strives for higher universal self-consciousness, like that which it reached in the first creation. Before all time and beyond all space is the first image of God. Time and space and all that they contain are this Idea revealing itself and tied to it through free necessity.

No time, no people, no circumstance has ever been without the pure Idea of Godhead; had it withdrawn itself for a moment, the moment itself would have disappeared, and would never have become part of the sequence. Thus, it is not this Idea that history strives for—it cannot be the goal of strife since it gives itself quite freely to the seeker, as life gave itself to him. Godhead in its essence, and thus in all its manifestations, has no history; in the abyss of eternity there are no currents, no ebb and flood; only when the stream of endless time has broken from it, then fall and succession begin, and with that, history. This continuous presence of Godhead in time and space in all natures and through all developments is the basic axiom of the entire following historical examination. In it there is no progress and no change, but what progresses and changes is that which, having come from Being, is reflected in forms, breaks into spectrums, flows piecemeal into words, divides itself into thoughts.

The perception, then, that each particular time held of the nature of things and of God, was tied to the general relationships of reflections at that time. Early nature was narrowly restrained; the concept of Being in early nature had to condense itself into simple, limited terms; Godhead could not reveal itself wider in it than it could be comprehended with undeveloped organs. . . . As the times widen, as the organs develop, as the circle of reflections spreads, each revelation too becomes greater and more inclusive; the concept of Godhead grows as the universe and history grow, and this growth has no limits. And as religion, grounded in Being, in this omnipresent Idea, is not bound to one time, has no beginning and will have no end, and does not propagate things through some tradition from age to age, but returns eternally young in each age, thus also this outward incarnation of religion is in no way tied to a particular revelation: it is not a closed matter to be transmitted to coming generations through books, but it progresses with history. Each age has its prophets and its God-inspired men, but they speak the language of the age, and their word must not remain behind the width of the reflexion that the perception of Godhead reaches in them. Religion therefore in its innermost essence has like God no history, only in its positive outwardness it becomes history, and ultimately all history is religious history, as all life is divine life.

The first religion was practised by the first-born people of the stars. Then the sun was hierophant (high priest) and each planet according to its order. . . . Then the sacrificial dances and the ceremonial paths of the skychildren in their orbits, and silently the great mysteries were fulfilled. Other races rose from the deep; they stood at the gates of the temple and gazed in astonishment at the innumerable people that crowded in its halls.

But the childhood of the species was different from the childhood of the individual; not bound to the common chain of generations, it had broken forth from another realm; the elements themselves had been pregnant with it, its childhood had great teachers, life allowed it great wonderful memories. It must have encountered memorable things; the monuments of ancient times were as yet not withered, many witnesses of the past still lived, it could begin with a rich treasure of the observation of nature. As in the Indian myth, the universe first became as a drop of dew, then as a mustard-seed, then as a pearl, and finally as an egg, from which the heaven and earth formed, thus from this solid core of nature observation soon in continuing growth a great history must develop. But development is different in the growing life and in the closed universe. Nature, on which the beginning history rests, consumes its activity in always circular motions.

But these elements tie together in a great cycle, days accumulate to years. The form of this transfer is that line which results between any point on the periphery of the smaller circle and a greater one, that is, the radius. In greater periods human years pile up, as in the Indian mythical view, to star years, divine years; the formula for the curve becomes more complex, but always the circle remains the ground and the end of all development, and the *cycloid* the line of progress from the point and to infinity.

. . . But wherever higher intellectual activity gains the victory over the lower life, there a new element as well enters the development. The spirit is self-sufficient and striving in its innermost nature, it is free from the law of inertia which all matter is subject to, it strives to control, to be a law to itself and every thing else. It therefore is in constant struggle with the circle in which Nature would like to trap it.

There was one worship and one myth in the beginning of time, one church and also one state and one language.

The three races of which we spoke earlier took shape. The black race descended to the interior of Africa, and we will most naturally signify its order and its nature when we determine it as the drop that resulted when the two other races separated themselves from the cosmic herd of life, and the race now most closely related to night and to its dark figures also was clothed in its darkness and became the lowest stratification. Before that first separation all the elements were undivided. The old traditions of the pre-world lived among the men of the first law; all were tied together in one family, ruled by the powers of Nature that spoke by the mouth of their priests and prophets and in the middle of the ancient world that state was founded that however apparently had a different relation to the elements. With the separation, however, history began, the first mass migration as the multitudes departed to seek their homes. First the children of night had found theirs; those that the morning had claimed followed them; the mainstream however, after it had given off these branches, turned toward the west.

The first state however that included all the races still together in their original home, was a natural state and therefore a theocracy ruled by a priesthood.

Thus the state grew generally from the priesthood, as by the laws of gravity it centered around them; in simple lineaments the outlines of the government were drawn up; simple law, plain and just customs; that was the Golden Age, that great ancient realm of which the traditions of all peoples speak. Nature first brought forth simple but great forms. The perception of nature at that time was also simple but great, the reflected light from the giant youth of the race lay upon it, witnesses had much to say of the past, the tradition lived for many ages, all voices led back to the world of the elements. At the gates of this realm, under the halls of entry, the mountains, mankind knelt in supplication and asked for knowledge of the streams from the closed temple, and sought to understand the speech of thunder.

The worship was simple, without temple and images. They looked up from the earth, only in heaven was the true realm of fire, there the sun always burned, there the stars, wanderers or fixed, struck like flames through the darkness, and eternal and unconcealed fire burned there, though it only flowed thriftily on earth. Then the worship of fire became worship of the stars; the sun and the heavenly hosts, below them the worshipping elements, were the great immortal powers, the priests of heaven; the world itself was the reflection of Godhead that exists in itself, dependent on nothing; the religion thus in this sense was *pantheism*. With awe they gazed at the shining face of Godhead, and the priests comprehended its features; and they studied the abodes and the motions of the elements; and they learned wisdom from the animals; and they prayed to the choirs of holy beings that stood brilliant upon the firmaments, and saw sun and moon and planets passing through this multitude.

(from I, pp. 1–21)

FRIEDRICH CREUZER

[1771–1858]

FRIEDRICH CREUZER was for more than fifty years a professor of philology and ancient history at Heidelberg, and one of Germany's most distinguished classical scholars. With the publication of his *Symbolik und Mythologie der alten Völker, besonders der Griechen* in 1810, he also became one of the most controversial mythologists in his half of the century; and more than this, a turning point in the fortunes of romantic mythology. His book provoked a long and heated public debate about his ideas and methods, and thus also about the entire romantic approach to myth—for Creuzer's work was easily the most commanding scholarly exposition and defense of main romantic beliefs in myth as filled with esoteric religious wisdom and pure spirituality, in the key role of the symbol, and in India and the East as the source of Greek and pagan religions. Some modern historians of mythology, such as Walter Otto and Jan de Vries, have argued that the decisive disparaging of Creuzer's effort marked the beginning of a long scholarly disdain or dry cautiousness about bold speculation or enthusiastic sympathy with the living religious side of myth. But however Creuzer failed to carry his historical claims about India and Greek religion, his penetrating analysis of symbolism looks forward to some dominant positions on symbolism in our own century.

Creuzer set out to prove that Greek religion derived from India. He argued that Indian priests migrating to a spiritually impoverished Greece brought with them the high, pure monotheistic Indic religion in its originally pure symbolic forms. But to satisfy the ignorant popular Greek needs, the symbols had to be adjusted to the crude native polytheism and demand for stories or myths. Still, the priests preserved and concealed the purer teachings in the symbolism of the mystery cults, and Creuzer found such traces in Orphism, in Eleusinian and Samothracian mysteries, in Pythagoreanism, or in Neoplatonism. But the explicit subject of Creuzer's book gives little idea why his work provoked so much rebuttal and admiration. At first sight, indeed, his work seems only one more contribution to the already well-worked German romantic enthusiasm for synthesizing India and Greece, symbols and myth, mysticism and history. Among others, for example, J. J. Wagner and J. A. Kanne in 1808 or Joseph Görres in 1810 had also sought to prove India the mythic source of all religion, particularly the Greek. It was also under Görres's influence at Heidelberg that Creuzer published an early version of his symbolic theories in 1806, and became deeply interested in the cult of Dionysus and its Oriental affinities, on which he published in 1809.

Creuzer's system, however, provoked unusual attacks from all sides, from within the romantic camp as well as from unsympathetic scholars, and with good reason. For one thing, Creuzer's book seemed to codify and demonstrate, in the most formidable academic way, romantic views that had often enough indulged extravagant religious and historical theories, eccentric or merely enthusiastic scholarship. But it was with a genuine solidity of learning that Creuzer tried to seat the original monotheistic revelation in the historically specific locale and epoch of earliest Indian religion and thence to trace the higher Greek religion. Precisely such an ambitious and academic historical claim set off a long, loud, and seriously damaging rebuttal. C. A. Lobeck, in his enormous *Aglaophamus* (1829), dissolved Creuzer's interpretation of the mysteries and Neoplatonism in terms of Indic religion, in large part by deriding the mysteries themselves. K. O. Müller attacked Creuzer for favoring an external uniform Indic source over the more important, indigenous Greek historical and mythic traditions. J. H. Voss, the eminent Homer translator and an irascible mythologist himself, depicted poor Creuzer as a kind of mysticizing scoundrel and "Jesuit."

Within the romantic school or its sympathetic periphery, Creuzer's views raised almost as much controversy. The problems here arose mainly from Creuzer's effort to separate symbol distinctly from myth. The ultimate issue was how Creuzer interpreted and valued symbols as against myth. Creuzer held that as the divine mysteriously and wonderfully showed itself, the original revelation thus took the form of symbolic portent. This then is the first meaning Creuzer assigns to symbolism: those radiant signs resulting when divinity breaks its bounds and shines forth. But since these primal portents were not only full of signficance and provocative of wonder, but also necessarily only suggestive and "dark," further interpretation is demanded. This is the second meaning of symbolism: wise men, like Indian priests or Zoroaster, benev-

olently explain these dark, portentous symbols, giving exterior form to these in images or pictographs. Such symbols or pictographs preserve the wondrous primal union of spirit and matter. Image precedes speech, then, as symbols precede myth or narration. Or put most drastically, the symbolic or direct contemplation of spirit precedes and is higher than the indirect *told* or narrated stories about the gods. Symbols directly show mystic oneness, myths portray this through human action and history; symbols teach monotheism, myths polytheism.

By driving an essential distinction between symbol and myth, of course, Creuzer was clearly impugning the claims of myth to yield the real or earliest religious truth. And it is here that defenders of mythic worth and dignity joined debate with him. K. O. Müller, for example, defended myth as making more clear, rather than less, any earlier symbolic meaning; and Müller argued too that some myths are simply identical with what Creuzer called symbols. Schelling similarly attacked Creuzer's division between symbol and myth, charging that Creuzer in this way finally reduced myth to mere allegory. For Schelling, Creuzer's primal symbols really only reworked the older orthodox Christian mythology, since for Creuzer myth only "plagiarized" and distorted the true earlier content of the monotheistic revelation into polytheist falsities.

It is at this point, perhaps, that Creuzer's work can be seen as presenting enormous difficulties, so that an introduction to this thought must remain as much an inventory of puzzles and problems as of insights. Put most succinctly, Creuzer seems to have assigned to symbols what other romantics, from Herder through Schelling, had assigned to myth. For Creuzer, symbols indeed do what myth had been thought to do: the symbol keeps the infinite and finite, the spiritual and transient, in indivisible unity. The

Creuzerian symbol *is* the thing symbolized, where myth now only *represents* it; symbol contains truth, where myth now only communicates it; symbols overflow with meaning, where myth now can only discuss meaning. In a sense, Creuzer seems to "solve" the meaning of myth, but nevertheless leaves everything still as problematic, since now those old and largest problems formerly presented by myth are the problems presented by symbols. As Gottfried Hermann insisted at the time, Creuzer wavers between what the symbol means: he wants the symbol to be irreducibly live with true divine significance on the one hand, but also rationally accessible in terms of philosophic doctrine on the other. For Hermann, this was a serious inconsistency. But Creuzer himself admitted that the symbol had just such a "double nature," and this is part of the strength and subtlety of his analysis of the symbol. The human soul, he says, floats between the ideal and the sensible world, and the symbol reflects this in its way of harmonizing, though unstably, the immense disproportion between what is divine and what is human, pure being and existent finite form. This "indecision" inherent in the symbol is what gives it its profound energy, radiance, and inexhaustible significance. The wealth of analysis Creuzer brings to this view may be glimpsed in the second selection reprinted below.

It may be suggested, finally, that Creuzer's approach to myth has its deep affinities with much modern thought on the subject. It is crucial to Creuzer's approach to interpret the meaning of myth apart from its indigenous historical development, and to appeal instead to a body of enduring symbolic truths that transcend history.

B.F.

REFERENCES The text is our translation from *Symbolik und Mythologie der alten Völker, besonders der Griechen,* 4 Bde. (Leipzig/Darmstadt, 1810–1812). A second edition appeared in 1819. For complete bibliography of Creuzer's works to 1847, see F. Creuzer, *Deutsche Schriften,* Bde. I. 5th Abteilung (Leipzig, 1848), 344–357. The French translation is by J. D. Guignaut, *Religions de l'antiquité considerées principalement dans leurs formes symboliques et mythologiques,* 4 vols. (Paris, 1825–1851); Ernest Renan reviewed this translation in a long essay on Creuzer with an encyclopedic survey of modern mythic thought in *La Revue des Deux Mondes,* May 15, 1853, pp. 821–850.

For selections and references to the controversy over the *Symbolik,* see Ernst Howald, *Der Kampf um Creuzers Symbolik* (Tübingen, 1926), which gives texts by J. H. Voss, Gottfried Hermann, Lobeck, Menzel, K. O. Müller, and Ludwig Preller; for Schelling's critique of the *Symbolik,* see *Einleitung in die Philosophie der Mythologie,* in *Schellings Werke,* hrsg. M. Schröter (Munchen: Beck und Oldenbourg, 1928), Bde. VI, 4. Vorlesung and *passim;* Otto Gruppe, *Geschichte der klassischen Mythologie und Religionsgeschichte* (Leipzig, 1921), 126–133 on Creuzer's system, and pp. 133–139 for Creuzer's adherents, disciples, and disputants; F. Cumont, *Recherches sur le symbolisme funéraire des Romains* (Paris, 1942); Pinard de la Boullaye, *L'Étude comparée des Religions,* 2 vols. (Paris: Beauchesne, 1922), I, pp. 261–268 for general discussion and bibliography.

CREUZER

FROM *Symbolism and Mythology of Ancient Peoples*

OUR INTENTION in this survey is not to encompass all the religions of the Orient, nor to portray the development of symbols and myths in these religions. There is enough material in that for yet another substantial work of research. . . . We proceed from the accounts and monuments of the Greeks and Romans; and since we shall enter into the bases of the symbolism and mythology that the Egyptians and Near Eastern peoples accepted because of their close ties to the Greeks, we choose the standpoint here, therefore, of classical documents. From this standpoint, however, we perceive only the Near East in bright light, which fades into dimness as one moves beyond. The religions of these peoples who the Greeks later called barbarians reveal their essence only through the evidence of silent customs, few and fragmentary legends and unmoving statues. But this evidence even the oldest Greek that we know about would have listened to only half-attentively. His gaze had already turned westwards. From thence came the troops of warriors whose battles preoccupied him. And thus each bright world-mirror of Homeric poetry shows us a select and masterful mankind in the midst of life and action; and shows us too a world of gods only as the nobler side and image of human life. We see the battles and sorrows of the heroes together with

the help and sympathy of gods who act and feel in a most human way. But the arena in which these deeds occur is in fact the greatest dividing point between East and West, and thus all Greek poetry draws a most decisive line between the shadowy indefiniteness of Near Eastern worship and the bright and variously formed warrior of the mythical gods. In accordance with laws unknown to most of the polytheistic primitive world, Fate placed in the Greek spirit a marvellous aspiration to form images of the gods out of that Oneness called Divinity—images somewhat idealizing men, but nonetheless based on a clear inward and individual intuition, and set in decisive acts and sorrows.

With its races of gods who through heroes and heroines lost themselves in mankind, with its battles between heroes and gods, Greece is and remains the mother of myths, and Homer is the most fitting and prolific son of this mother. His spirit is hearkened to now by the Greek peoples, they make his song the law of their beliefs, their songs, and their poems: his light puts the priestliness of the Asiatic primal epic in the shadow. What the Near East had taught and practiced, partly openly, partly esoterically, was forgotten by the Greeks amid the full clarity of their Olympus. There still sounded forth the orgiastic hymns from the Phrygian and Thracian hills, but their marvellous contents were no longer understood by the Hellenes. In Greek cities, the devotions of the Syrians and Phoenicians were still practiced but their inner meaning scarcely known or guessed at. A Daedalus had wakened the old images of the Egyptians from their long sleep; entreaties and exertions, like those of the Greeks kneeling before these images, called them forth. From half-opened coverings there burst forth the winged signs of myths. The old holy house of the great goddess of Ephesus swarmed with a noisy crowd of Ionians, and stripped of her Asiatic veils and her wondrous image-bedecked garment, she fled like a gay huntress into the mountains. Instead of the old peace and Asiatic contemplativeness, now there was action, humanly felt and thought, and this became the center of religion; and legends now concerned themselves with such external, public devotions. The insatiable expansiveness of the oldest symbols of the gods was submitted to Greek measure and proportion. A lovely sensuousness and plastic form expelled the deepest content of the older meaning along with all monstrosities.

When the Greek spirit had been dominated for a century by this Homeric rule, which unified the religions of the Greeks through its very power, the old royal houses gradually disappeared or else were expelled by citizens who as lawgivers led each freeborn Greek to a great arena of public activity through the establishing of free constitutions. That self-reliance, nourished in everyone through public and primarily religious academies, set up beauty of form as a fundamental alongside fulfillment of personality and decisiveness of character. This transformation of the nature of the community had great effects on the spirit of religion. The performance of devotions became one with the claims of the state, and the organization both of the holy choral dances and of the drama was at the same time a fulfillment of the duties of citizens. So tragedy and comedy, deriving anciently from the old worship of nature, now betray such a public and external spirit. Each uses the legends of the heroes and gods to promote the renown of the city before which they are presented; and tragedy and comedy show the freedom of their form in the freedom with which they judge public persons. Thus it was in Greece that the religion of the people, assembled from their poetry and art, became plastic and political.

However, the eternal spirit of nature had an entirely different effect in the Near East. First in the Ionian cities, then in the mainland of Greece itself, this great school of experienced citizen-life bore quite other fruit. Life became more civil, cultivated, and serious. The youthful joyousness of the heroic age, forever newly excited and amused by an always thriving mythic abundance, now had to give way to more meaningful aspirations, at least among the educated people. Cultivated men, wearied by the wretched confusion into which the One and the Divine had been splintered, expressed healthy doubts, complained about the innumerable and absurd myths, and—distinguished by an honest spirit of inquiry—departed from the vulgarities of the mob. These were the masters of the old Ionian philosophy who had grasped the harm being done to religion and philosophy by the tyranny of Homeric poetry through the entrenched power of myth. They sought to bring the susceptible soul of the Greeks from the excitements of myths back to calmness, to bring the contemplation of the One and All back from the distractions of the Many. Symbols had been cast aside by the endless babble of old stories, and these masters now set symbols up again in their old dignity: the symbol that was primarily born from sculpture but which, bodied forth through words, through meaningful syllables, through the totality and compact vitality of its essence, could interpret the unity and inexpressibility of religion in a way legend could not. In the form of their teaching, Pherecydes of Syros, one of the oldest of Ionian sages, and Pythagoras, the founder of the Italian school, both look back not to the Hellenic fatherland but rather to the Orient and Egypt.

But what am I saying about the East? Was this form then a new phenomena in Greece? Was it not much older than the mythic form we call Homeric after a great poet? Thus, before the rhapsodes captivated the enchanted Greek people by their ever new songs and legends, a race of priestly singers had placed the mainland Greeks under the healthy protection of religion. The ancient Thracians, later the very image of barbarism, had once, through the natural advantages of their land, enjoyed prosperity and a cultivated state under monarchic form. These kings had by their side—and, it appears, even above them— an honored class of priests who, as in Egypt (and from there comes the most reliable history of their origin), controlled all teaching of the people through the power of music and poetry. In this education through religion, it appears that here as in Egypt there was a very complex gradation of ranks. Destiny has bequeathed us through reliable witnesses (one of whom is that reasonable investigator, Aristotle) many dogmas of this Orphic religion in symbolic and mythic form. These show a quite great affinity with Eastern teachings, and with the dogmas of the old Ionian school of Pherecydes and also Pythagoras. The newer Ionian philosophy was now joined to this older Ionian teaching, and the majority of

the principal teachings themselves agree exactly with the contents of the Orphic priestly teachings—as for example, "concerning the soul, which ruling in the universe unifies all through all"; or, "concerning the double harmony that through the All grasps the beyond"; or, "concerning the identity of life and death."

However, the worthy spirit of religion remained known only to the wise. The poetry that brought the people together round the seat of the rhapsode or into the theater kept its power over the people's feelings and was little disturbed by the most serious researches or profound philosophy. The cults of the people, made sacrosanct by legislators and constitutions, promoted and needed an abundance of legends; the people had to know the history of those before whom they bowed; and the administrators of public devotions jealously watched over the sacred status of all this. Thus the purer oral teachings passed over into the obscurities of the Samothracian, Attic, and other Mysteries, and into the thickets of esoteric philosophy.

In this way also the relation of philosophers to mythical and state religion was determined. The philosophers sometimes entered into a dangerous conflict, attacking myth and the seductive poetry allied to it; or else they risked complaints against Homer, the god of the people, and (in order to be understood by the people) announced the pains that would be suffered in the underworld by the betrayers of religion; or again, they censured, but mildly. The remark of the Egyptian priests is to be taken in this spirit: "O Solon, you Greeks remain forever children!"

The directors of the Mysteries, especially the Attic ones, agreed with the concerns of the philosophers. They knew the power that poetry exercised on the Greek soul and they sought to elevate the Greeks with poems which (though under a disguise) taught the unity of nature as found in the old religions. That the form of these poems was a product of later culture (they may in part belong to the golden age of Athens, and this is particularly true of the Orphic hymns) cannot be doubted, even though such weighty authorities as Herodotus, Plato, and Aristotle do not mention it. But that the basis of these poems is old Orphic symbols and teachings, and also that many voices of old hymns echo in them, is attested by the fragments of the old Ionian philosophy, though uncertainty still remains about this.

With Alexander's expeditions, the Orient was opened to the Greek soul—or in a wider sense, the East itself was embraced. Now, the Greeks ruled there, and from the time of this great mixing of peoples the Greeks were either born in the East themselves or else spent a great deal of their lives there. The same heaven arching over the richly imaginative Orientals arched over the Greeks, and the poetry of old Asia calmed their spirit as well. The Greeks saw the palace of Persepolis, a wondrous symbolic architecture, the fabulous beasts of the Far East, the animal-plants on the carpets of Babylon. At the same time, too, there were the impressions from external nature itself, that wild and luxurious vegetation, that overpowering animalistic experience, and finally the immense numbers and meanings in the astrology and cosmogony of the Chaldeans.

Thus was the impressionable Greek imagination now aroused and nourished in so many different ways.

Moreover, that world-colony, Alexandria in Egypt, influenced the Greek thinkers through its great stream of peoples. The climate of this land was anomalous by any standard, developing there a spirit of melancholy and seriousness. The Greeks felt

this influence too. The constant sight of those gigantic monuments of a profound priestly world now vanished must have had on those who observed them the effect of urging the reflective soul to withdraw from the external world.

But another cause here was the decline of Greek freedom—that freedom whose entire revolution of the community's nature by its ancient constitutions had constantly invited the soul to action, and then had kept the soul involved in ceaseless activity. As a replacement for this sensuous mastery found in ancient citizen-life, and as a consolation for such a sad outcome, there was the learned leisure bestowed by the grace of a cultivated prince.

Also of the greatest influence in causing this decisive split between epochs was the heaping up of literary treasures in each world-city, the accelerated exchange of ideas that resulted from this, the acquaintance with the religious teachings of the East, with the theories of the old Magi, with the metamorphoses of the gods in the Indian system, and finally the influence of monotheism from the many Hebrews living in Alexandria. And shortly before this, Plato, standing amid the high noon of all culture and education, had conquered and made his own all the light of the East and all the knowledge of Western philosophy. His view of nature and of the soul would have a long and crucial effect on the numerous schools of philosophers.

From all this, the following phenomena in religion and philosophy can now be explained. 1) The extraordinary spread of religion and philosophy among the Greek people, with all kinds of spiritually enriching influences. 2) The pragmatic use of myth. The learned thinker now sought more than ever to win profit from his knowledge and life. The youthful poetic view of the old fabulous realms was now

subordinated to a more serious and inquiring viewpoint. 3) The revival and return to mysticism and symbolism in mythology, and the enduring authority of
mysticism and symbols thereafter.

The human spirit, aroused, enlarged, and
set striving in a thousandfold way, began
to think in terms of itself, and contemplation turned within. . . .

(from Book I, Chap. VI)

Modern writers, especially since the researches of Goguet, have claimed that only
a crude historical painting underlies all
symbols, and have tried to derive the whole
of hieroglyphics from the so-called kyriologic writing. According to this approach,
at the beginning of all efforts to represent
figuratively, there is hypothesized some
kind of knotted cord (*Quipos*) of the Peruvians, or else the nails that the ancient Romans hammered into their temples for their
calendars or other observances. All this ac-
cords perfectly with the efforts of a weak
and helpless people who, either in delineating on soft material or engraving on hard
substance, sought only to portray the corporeal in a truly slavish corporeal way. But
in all this we find the still corporeal but
already simplified figures, compelled by a
thousand earlier reasons to become just
such abbreviated images. Each effort at
representing figuratively became raw material for alphabetic writing, as can be seen
in the accepted view that the 80,000 characters of Chinese writing, based on six
elements and combined in innumerable
ways, derived from some such kyriology.
But in all such efforts at representing figuratively, the path divides. Here, word-
syllables and finally alphabetic writing are
born, with the first efforts to depict sounds.
There, the invisible and incorporeal is
gradually portrayed as a corporeal image
to the eye of the soul. In letters there is

an image of sound, and in hieroglyphs a
visible image of a concept.

We will not try to show whether the
great invention of alphabetical writing can
be explained in this way. But that the essence of symbols was not discovered in
this manner must be clear immediately. The
symbol and figure differ not only in degree
but generically from kyriologic writing.
The whole of figurative representation
[*Ikonismus*] can be divided into two essential orders whose centers, however one tries
to reconcile them, remain apart. We mean
the kyriologic order and the symbolic order. To understand symbols, one cannot
merely extend a crude inquiry into kyriology; rather, one must seek the root of
all imaginative representations in terms of
the symbol.

A glance at the poems and religions of
all peoples shows us as an undeniable fact
the common ruling belief in the life of
things. The primitive world, especially, that
grasped all with naive and direct thought,
was still unacquainted with the separation
between the corporeal and spiritual so familiar to us. This primitive kind of thinking usually understood any particular thing
by thinking it alive—or rather not merely
as alive but as human. What is announced
so generally and so often in any epoch
whose representations diverge from the
way of nature, but not because of bad
education, must for that very reason have
been permitted by the natural drives and
voices of nature. And with that we recognize a necessity that men decide to place
themselves at the center of their world, and
amid all the realms of nature to mirror only
themselves. We do not wish here to reach
back to the source and primal spring of
this kind of thinking, or to seek it out via
the thread of philosophic speculation. . . .
We have rather to turn our view backward
to the realm of figurative representation it-

self, in order to make clear there the variousness and forms of the products of each natural instinct. To this end, we content ourselves with this one principle and the following few laws:

First of all, it is the simplest observation that the ruling clarity and figurativeness of writing and speech in all poetizing and thinking cannot be taken as merely willful and arbitrary, but is rather a plainly necessary kind of expression.

To this we add that these high needs place man in the center of the entire creation; all the rays of being collect in him as in a microcosm; and consequently he sees all nature in his own nature, and thus cannot see otherwise except according to the laws of his own being. What the abstract mind calls an active force is only a person to the primitive native way of seeing. Herewith the sexual and all that is connected with it is acknowledged and accepted as immediate consequences: love and hate, unity and division, corruption and birth, or death and decline, or again, life newly born from death.

Thus it follows that what we call the figurative is nothing else than the impress of a form of our thinking, a necessity that the most abstract and weighty soul cannot escape from; antiquity bore this necessity willingly. As monuments of this figurative manner there remain the religions of the most ancient world, especially the polytheistic; and also the poems before our time, especially the Theogonies and Cosmogonies whose fundamental nature rests on the active power of personification, and in whom Eros has so great a significance. That way of thinking was in Greece a widely spread article of faith to which the people clung ardently, as shown in their metaphors and in the mythic character of their speech. These same feelings and metaphorical speech perceived the inno-

cent primal world in the elements and forces of nature. Man knew nothing else than to sense nature through joy and pain and to express his feelings in speaking images. The death of a loved and admired hero was mourned by the very soil of the fatherland as much as by the people. The earth must bring forth flowers that in color and expressive character join their grief to that of men; and so that the memory of the grief-stricken be not lost, an annual ceremony is ordained, to which the mute language of each plant serves as the most fitting sign of remembrance. . . .

Now we shall consider myth in itself and in its relation to the other figurative types. First of all, its origin. But who can count the innumerable causes for the existence of myth, especially when actual heroic legends are also entangled here? Once there was a cultivated stranger who, thrown among wild tribes, spread the seeds of a foreign culture; or else a distinguished tribal chieftain who, because of his bodily or spiritual qualities, is called a son of the gods, and feasts are ordained in thanks for this blessing. In this way gratitude and admiration no longer know boundaries, and the whole that these legends encompass soon advances into the infinite. Festivals and games and annual ceremonies were decreed in order not to let these memorable occurrences fade from memory. Images, processions, tableaux, and mimes must help exalt the celebration of the time and place. First of all formulas and then invocations and songs proclaim the reason for this celebration and praise the object being celebrated. Thus it is the substance of legendary traditions which is the forerunner of history. The legendary tradition takes the place of written annals, as does a regularly recurring cycle of feasts. The physical causes are perhaps still more numerous than the historical. Now, for instance, the extraordinary character or power of an animal gives rise to a legend, or now it is the very expressive form or some qualities of a natural body that seem most unusual; and the effort to explain this is the seed of an expressive myth. But the hidden forces of nature arouse the poetic imagination even more. Their secret activity and images and their living breath penetrating all beings must then have tempted reflection all the more, since ancient man yielded himself entirely to nature's immediate influence. . . .

The content of myth divides into two main branches. Either it encompasses old events and is thus called legend; or it encompasses old beliefs and teachings. We use one word for both: tradition. The old epic songs already divided it these two ways, as in the following from the *Theogony* of Hesiod . . .

> The praiseworthy deeds of ancient
>   times
> and the gods on the blessed peak of
>   Olympus.

That each of these two elements comprises manifold other types needs no special notice. We condense what follows to what is essential. First of all, the historical branch widens itself out into different limbs: legends come from strangers, events of the ancient Asiatic ages, wonder before foreign lands and especially of Egypt, and travel-legends and reports of other travelers. Or else the people proclaim experiences of their own tribe, the colonizing of a region, the founding of a city, the deeds

of a tribal prince, or the memorable experiences from an old palace. As much is true of the other branch of myth. Here too essential constituents should be differentiated that are rather inconveniently assembled under the name of *philosophemes.* Much more suitable would be the expression *theologumeme* or more precisely still, *theomyths,* in which recognizably there lies the whole essence of the collected beliefs and knowledge of the oldest peoples in the various off-shoots of religion. We may also distinguish here between the smaller elements in each main branch. First of all, the special persuasions concerning men, nature, and God as the objects of a holy faith, which usually construe myth in a narrow sense. Then the specific ethical principle that makes up the entire content of some myths; further, the specifically physical traditions wherein old natural and especially astral evidence remains. Finally such myths that already betray a more educated way of thinking and in which speculations from the older wisdom are clarified or elaborated. . . .

We now discuss the character of myth, its developmental phases and its relation to symbol and other kinds of figurative representation. In symbol a universal concept takes on earthly garment, and steps meaningfully before the eye of the soul as an image. In myth the pregnant soul expresses its presentiments or knowledge in a living word. It is also an image but of the kind that, in a way different from symbol, goes through the ear to attain inner meaning.

(from Book I, Chap. III)

GEORGE STANLEY FABER

[1773–1854]

FABER WAS an obscure English divine, the author of some twenty-seven books, mostly on standard theological subjects, or on such topics as *The Revival of the French Emperorship Anticipated from the Necessity of Prophecy,* which had five editions in the 1850s. He was also a latter-day Christian mythologer intent upon the old business of explaining away all myths and gods as simply corrupt versions of the Bible. Faber's contributions to the study of myth include *Horae Mosaicae; or, a View of the Mosaical Records with respect to their coincidence with Profane Antiquity. . . and their connection with Christianity,* 1801; *A Dissertation on the Mysteries of the Cabiri; or the Great Gods of Phenicia, Samothrace, Egypt, Troas, Greece, Italy and Crete,* 1803, and *The Origin of Pagan Idolatry ascertained from historical testimony and circumstantial evidence,* 1816.

Faber seems to have been unaware of the growing affirmative revaluation of myth in Germany or England, the new archaeological discoveries, or the new philosophy. In his insular, complacent, and interminable (1658 pages) *Origin of Pagan Idolatry,* Faber sets out (as had Bochart in the seventeenth century and Newton or Shuckford in the eighteenth) to show how pagan idolatry or mythology is a diffused corruption of patriarchal religion. In particular, he tried to show how all "Great Father" gods are versions of Noah, how all "Great Mother" goddesses are derived from and refer back to

the Ark, and how all the triads of Divinities are shadows of the three sons of Noah. Faber's aims are thus very much out of date by 1816, and his methods are woefully behind contemporaneous thought and scholarship. Yet partly for this very reason, and partly because of the methodological excesses Faber whips himself to, his work provides a convenient, oddly lucid and wholly unexpected opportunity to see how the mode of scriptural interpretation called "typology" is essentially similar to and a possible source of the symbol and archetype criticism currently associated with the ideas of Carl Jung and Northrop Frye, to mention only two of the most distinguished of the modern proponents of archetype theory.

Typology is the branch of theology that undertakes to show the unity of the Bible by means of the principle that everything in the Old Testament can be explained by reference to the story of Christ in the New. Thus, Isaac is a "type" of the "antitype" (or "antetype" or "prototype" or "archetype" or "original") Christ. Similarly, Christ's crucifixion is the antitype or archetype of which the sacrifice of Isaac is the type. In orthodox Christian typology, one then proceeds to explicate the sacrifice of Isaac as though it were a deliberate historical foreshadowing of the sacrifice of Christ. Typology was customarily distinguished from allegory (considered as another way to demonstrate the essential harmony and unity of Scripture). Patrick Fairbairn's *The Typology of Scripture* (1845) claimed that "the typical is not properly a different or higher sense, but a different or higher application of the same sense." Typology accepts the literal level, allegory seeks a level beyond the literal. Thus the type or typical can be distinguished from the symbol because the type is always real; that is to say, it is historical, and "not a fictitious or ideal symbol." An example of allegory is Philo's claim that the five cities of the Plain are the five senses; an example of symbol is the horn that symbolizes strength in the book of Daniel; and the dove returning to Noah is an example of a type of the descent of the Holy Ghost in the form of a dove to Christ upon his baptism.

Typology is as old as the Bible itself and the early Fathers used the technique. It flourished during the Reformation, when allegory and the scholastic fourfold interpretations were abandoned in favor of literalism. Typology has the advantage, for Protestantism, of being a way of reconciling texts without going beyond the literal level. Typology declined during the eighteenth century, then underwent a revival in the nineteenth. Usually confined to the problem of unifying the Bible, typology was boldly applied by Faber to the problem of unifying pagan mythology. As Faber uses it, typology becomes more than a technique for reducing the Old Testament to a series of shadows or types of the archetypal myth of Noah and the Ark.

Faber commences with the same problem that has served so often as a starting point for myth investigation: why are there so many resemblances and similarities to be found among the world's far flung mythologies and religions? *The Origin of Pagan Idolatry* sets out to show that all the non-biblical gods, demons, and stories are versions of an early religion based on the worship of Noah that rose sometime after the confusion of

tongues and the dispersal of the nations at Babel. Faber's principal problem is that much more was known about the world's religions by 1816 than had been known a hundred years before, and Faber had to strain much harder than earlier orthodox Christian mythologers to crowd them all into his monomyth (the story of Noah). In his efforts to do so, he uses Euhemerist ideas and diffusionist ideas; he dabbles in etymology (and invents indigestible jargon like "Noëtic," "Naviform," "luniform," and "Magistratual"), and always falls back on the cry of priestcraft. All these approaches are well-worn and old-fashioned by 1816, and indeed, Faber's main ideas and devices are all derivative. He draws on Kircher, Bochart, Cudworth, Prideaux, Shuckford, Warburton, Banier, Hurd, Mallet, Moor, Maurice, Bryant, Davies, Volney, Jones, Wilford, and Voss, though most of the last half dozen are taken up only to be refuted. But it is not Faber's main ideas or his principal assumptions that make him of interest; it is rather the style of his interpretation and his application of the hermeneutic technique known as typology that make his work interesting.

Faber argues that all the pagan deities were originally deified men, that the men so deified were those of the golden age, and that there were, in effect, two golden ages, one associated with Adam and the other with Noah. The second golden age was thought to be a repetition or a reenactment of the first. Hence Noah was thought to duplicate or reembody Adam, while Noah's sons were replicas or reincarnations or types of Adam's sons; and the Ark, from which the earth was repopulated, was thought to be a latter-day version of the Earth, or the Great Mother of all life of Adam's time. (Faber does not explain why neither Eve nor Noah's wife are even to be considered here.) From the idea of a second golden age duplicating the first came mythologic or false ideas about multiple creations and destructions, and hence about a series or plurality of worlds, and about successive incarnations or metempsychosis. Cyclical ideas about history were another logical extension, and the idea of there being numerous avatars of a given deity comes, Faber argues, from the same source. After seeing Faber uncover so many patterns of repetition in history, the reader is not completely surprised to find Faber arguing next that all male deities (excluding God, of course) are the same deity, are usually symbolized by and associated with the sun, and are at last only versions of the one Great Father, which is Noah, which is Adam. Similarly, all female divinities are the same, are usually symbolized by the moon and by ships, and are only versions of the original Great Mother, which is the Ark, which meant also the Earth. So too all triadic divinities, such as those of the Hindu Trimurti, are to be considered as versions or types of the original (or archetype) of the sons of Noah, who in turn are a type of the sons of Adam. Just how it first happened that men abandoned "true" religion and came to Euhemerize Noah/Adam is explained by Faber as the doing of some wicked Priest-Kings seeking power and dominion.

Mistaking inclusiveness for comprehensiveness, Faber labors to include all the gods of Greece, Egypt, India, Persia, Britain, China, America, Scandinavia, and the South Seas in his pattern, arguing that they all fit his scheme. This is made easier since he admits that he looks for similarities, rather than differences. "I have made no distinction between the mythologies of different nations, but have considered them all together as jointly forming a single well-compacted and regular system."

The section below on the identity of the Great Goddesses shows the range and style of Faber's application of typology to myth. Faber finds that all the Great Goddesses were associated with earth and the Moon; later he claims that the crescent moon is the Ark and the earth is Mount Ararat; thus all the goddesses are types of the original Great Mother, the Ark itself.

The section "On the Origination of Romance from old mythologic Idolatry" is even more interesting in that it shows how a technique once limited to the Bible can be applied not only to other religious stories and scriptures and to other mythologies but also to works of imaginative literature. Faber considers the archetype of "the entrance of the Great Father into the ship" (Noah boarding the Ark), and traces it through classical literature and Arthurian romance. He takes up archetypes of the sacred lake, of the fairy or female divinity presiding over it, of the wonderful cavern, of the oracular tomb, and so on, and traces them in Hindu legend, in Celtic story, in Ariosto and in Shakespeare. Faber even considers saints' lives as a branch of imaginative literature and finds them conforming to the same pattern.

In showing that much or even all of imaginative literature depends on and repeats mythic archetypal patterns, Faber thinks to belittle the mythic element in literature. But he is himself susceptible to literature and his very sympathies may suggest how short a step it is from Faber's pious archetype criticism, intended to discredit myth and exalt Scripture, to modern archetype criticism, which finds its archetypes in man's mind instead of in the Bible, and works to exalt the mythic element in literature.

R.R.

REFERENCES   Our texts are from G. S. Faber, *The Origin of Pagan Idolatry ascertained from historical testimony and circumstantial evidence* (London, 1816). Noah Webster's essay on the "Origin of Mythology," printed in *Memoirs of the Connecticut Academy of Arts and Sciences,* Vol. I, pt. 1 (New Haven,

1810) draws heavily on Faber, as does much nineteenth-century writing on the symbolic wisdom of Freemasonry. See, for example, Albert Pike, *Morals and Dogma of the Ancient and Accepted Scottish Rite of Freemasonry* . . . (Charleston, A.˙. M.˙. 5680 [1923?]) 1st edition 1871, pp. 234, 581ff., 591ff.

On Typology see, for example, Patrick Fairbairn, *The Typology of Scripture* (Edinburgh, 1845). Edward B. Hungerford refers to Faber in *Shores of Darkness* (New York: Columbia University Press, 1941), as does A. L. Owen in *The Famous Druids* (Oxford: Clarendon Press, 1962) and W. D. Paden, in *Tennyson in Egypt* (Lawrence: University of Kansas Publications in Humanistic Studies, no. 27, 1942) pp. 75–88, 154–159.

FABER

FROM *The Origin of Pagan Idolatry*

ALL THE Goddesses of Paganism will be found ultimately to melt together into a single person, who is at once acknowledged to be the great mother and the earth: yet that person is also declared to have assumed the form of a ship when the mighty waters of the vast deep universally prevailed, to have peculiarly presided over navigation, to have sprung from the sea and yet to have been born from that sacred mountain whence flowed the holy rivers of Paradise, to have contained within her womb all those hero-gods who are literally said to have each sailed in an ark, to have been in some remarkable manner connected with the dove and the rainbow, or to have had a ship for her special representative.

(Vol. 1, Book I, Chap. 1, p. 21)

"Concerning the Identity
and Lunari-terrene Character
of the great Goddesses
of the Gentiles."

I now proceed to consider the character of the great goddesses of the Gentiles, which will be found to bear a close analogical reference to that of their great gods. The female divinities, however apparently multiplied according to the genius of polytheism, ultimately resolve themselves into one, who is accounted the great universal mother both of gods and men: and this single deity is pronounced to be alike the Moon in the firmament and the all-productive earth.

I. On the present point both the eastern and the western mythologists are remarkably explicit. The Hindoos inform us, that, although each god has his own proper consort; yet, as the gods coalesce first into three and afterwards into one, so the goddesses in like manner blend together, first becoming three who are the wives of their three chief divinities, and afterwards one who is the mystic consort of their self-triplicating great father. Sometimes the order of speaking of this personage is inverted: and then we are told, that Devi or the goddess (as their great mother is styled by way of eminence) multiplies herself into the three forms of Parvati, Lacshmi, and Saraswati, and afterwards assumes as many subordinate forms or characters as there are female divinities in the mythology of Hindostan. Yet each of these is severally, we are assured, both the Moon and the Earth: and each accordingly, is represented by the common symbols of the cow and the lotos. Such is always the case with the mysterious female, who still remains one, however she may be multiplied. Whether she be Devi, or Iva, or the White Goddess, or Ila, or Anna-Purna, or Sita, or Isi; she is equally Maya or the great mother: and this great mother is pronounced to be at once the Earth and the Moon.

II. As Isi, she is manifestly, according to the just remark of Sir William Jones, the Isis of the Egyptians. Nor is she proved to be the same by the mere identity of names: the whole of her character minutely agrees with that of Isis; and the Brahmens themselves acknowledge, that the mythology of Egypt is but a transcript of their own. But Isis, like Isi, is declared to be equally the Moon and the Earth and she is at the same time unanimously determined by the ancient theologists to be one with Ceres, Proserpine, Minerva, Venus, Diana, Juno, Rhea, Cybele, Jana, Atargatis, Semiramis, Vesta, Pandora, Io, Bellona, Hecate, Rhamnusia, Latona, the Phenician Astartè, the Lydian and Armenian Anaïs and the Babylonian Mylitta. These again are said to be mutually the same with each other: and if we descend to particulars, we still find them indifferently identified with the Earth and the Moon.

Isis was equally worshipped among the Gothic tribes under the appellation of *Frea:* and they sometimes bestowed upon her the title of *mother Herth,* as Tacitus

writes the word; a title, which is plainly no other than our English *Earth.*

The same great goddess was likewise venerated by the old Britons under the names of *Ceridwen, Ked, Sidee, Devi, Andrastè,* and *Esaye* or *Isi.* This deity, as both her general character and her title *Ceridwen* may serve to testify, and as Artemidorus positively asserts, is the Ceres of the classical writers. She is also, as her other names no less than her character sufficiently intimate, the Sita or Devi or Isi of Hindostan. We are told that she was astronomically the Moon: and since she is celebrated as a botanist, and as the goddess of corn, and since her mystic circle is declared to be the circle of the World, we may reasonably infer, that she was also worshipped as the Earth, agreeably to the general analogy of Paganism.

III. Such being the universal intercommunion between the Moon and the Earth the great mother being alike deemed a personification of each, both those planets bore the common name of *Olympias* or *Olympia:* by which was meant the World; for mount Olympus, as we have already seen, was no other than the Indian mount Ilapu or Meru, which is fabled to be crowned with the mundane circle of Ila or Ida. Accordingly the Moon was deemed a sort of celestial Earth, bearing a close affinity to this our nether world.

(Vol. 3, Book 5, Chap. 1, pp. 3–5)

"On the Origination of Romance
from old mythologic Idolatry"

The mythology of one age becomes the popular romance of another: and so completely have the minds of men been preoccupied with the ancient universal system of Idolatry, that almost every fictitious legend, whether ancient or modern, bears its unequivocal impress. On this singular subject it was easy to write a volume. Brevity however must be consulted. I shall therefore content myself with bringing together a few scattered notices respecting romance secular, romance ecclesiastical, and romance magical or necromantic.

I. Secular romance I do not confine solely to those chivalrous fictions, which ordinarily bear that name. I consider the substance, rather than the mere appellation: and, as with equal propriety Hercules may be styled a *knight-errant* and Amadis *a hero,* I scruple not to place together under the same division of my subject warriors of very different ages and countries; though it must be acknowledged, that, in generous courtesy at least, if not in martial prowess, the cavaliers of the middle ages far transcend their barbarous predecessors.

1. The entrance of the great father into the Ship formed a very prominent feature of old mythology: and, as his liberation from it was esteemed his birth into the new World, he was often represented as a helpless infant exposed in a wooden ark. This ark is sometimes set afloat on the sea, while at other times it is mentioned *simply* without any specification of such a circumstance: and, though the great father himself is occasionally exhibited as an infant, yet we are not unfrequently told without any disguise that he constructed a ship and embarked in it with certain companions. All these various particulars have been duly transcribed into the page of romance both ancient and modern: and the channel of communication seems to have been a well preserved, though at length mistaken, remembrance of the diluvian Mysteries. Each aspirant was imitatively deemed an infant, and in the course of his initiation was committed to the

sacred infernal boat. Hence originated the numerous tales of persons having experienced such a calamity during their childhood.

(1.) Let us first attend to legends of an exposure in an ark, either at sea or on the stream of a river. Of this it is easy to produce a considerable variety of examples.

The classical Perseus, and Telephus, and Anius, and Tennes, are all equally said, like the god Bacchus, to have been set afloat in an ark, during the period of their infancy, on the surface of the ocean, and to have all in due time come safe to shore. A precisely similar story is told respecting the British Taliesin, the Persian Darab, the Latin Romulus, the Indian Pradyumna, the Amadis of Gothic romance, and the Brahman and Perviz and Parizadè of Arabic fiction. The child Taliesin is committed to sea in a coracle: the infant Darab is set afloat on the Gihon in a small wooden ark: Romulus and his brother are exposed in the same manner on the Tiber: Pradyumna is inclosed in a chest and thrown into the sea, is swallowed by a fish, and is ultimately brought safe to land: Amadis, while a child, is shut up in a little ark, and cast into the main ocean: and the two princes and their sister are successively placed in wicker baskets, and thus committed to a stream which flowed beneath the walls of their father's palace.

(2.) Sometimes we meet with a story of a person being inclosed within an ark, unattended by the circumstance of its being set afloat on the water.

Thus Cypselus, an ancient prince of Corinth, is said to have been preserved in an ark, when his enemies sought his life: and this ark, which continued to be shewn in the days of Pausanias, was afterwards consecrated in Olympia by his posterity, who from him were denominated *Cypselidae.* Thus Jason, the captain of the Argo, was inclosed in an ark during his infancy as one dead; and in that state was bewailed by the women of his family, precisely in the same manner as the females of Egypt and Phenicia lamented the untimely fate of the ark-concealed Osiris and Adonis. Thus Ion, the son of the Babylonic Xuth and the reputed ancestor of the Ionic Greeks, is fabled to have been exposed in an ark, which was decorated with an olive-branch. Thus the primeval Athenian prince Erechthonius, whose form was compounded of a man and a serpent, was inclosed in an ark by Minerva, and committed to the care of the three daughters of Cecrops who were certainly priestesses of the triplicated great mother. . . .

(3.) Occasionally the idea of infancy is dropped; and the hero of romance, at an adult age, performs some extraordinary voyage.

Such is the exploit of Hercules, when a golden cup conveys him in quest of adventures over the surface of the mighty ocean. Such is the voyage of Theseus to encounter the Cretan Minotaur: for, in what light his ship was viewed by the Athenians, may easily be collected, from the circumstance of its being preserved with high veneration even to the time of Demetrius Phalereus, and from the positive declaration of antiquity that he was one of the mariners of the Argo. And such is the bold adventure of the British Merlin and his associated bards, who dared the perils of the ocean in a house of glass and were never heard of more. This is said to be one of the three disappearances from the isle of Britain. The tale most probably originated from the loss of some unfortunate aspirants, who were carried out to sea in their coracle while going through the process of a navicular initiation: for, in the ancient song of Taliesin which treats of the entrance of the just man

with his seven companions into the inclosure of the ship-goddess Sidi, that vessel is styled *the inclosure of glass*. As for the appellation itself, it was certainly borrowed from the glass boat or lunette which the Druids used in the celebration of their Mysteries.

To the same class we may refer the various romances of our British king Arthur.

It is not unlikely, that such a prince actually fought with the Saxons: but the mythologic history of a primeval Arthur, from whom he received his name, has become romantic fiction when engrafted upon the exploits of the literal sovereign. Hence we find king Arthur described as entering into a wonderful ship or inclosure with seven companions, during the time of a general desolation produced by a mighty flood of waters. Hence, in allusion to the triplicated White goddess, he is said to have had three wives; each of whom was denominated *Gwenhwyvar* or *the Lady on the summit of the water*. And hence he is represented, as having a sister, who is styled *the Lady of the lake*. He is placed at the head of three knights; who are said, like himself, to have been imprisoned in a very remarkable manner. The mode of this imprisonment evidently shews, that the story was borrowed from the inclosure of the aspirant within the mystic stone cell of Ceridwen which typified the womb of the ship-goddess. Three nights, we are told, was Arthur confined in the inclosure of wrath and the remission of wrath; three nights, with the lady of Pendragon; and three nights, in the person of Kud or Ceridwen under the flat stone of Echemeint. This stone was his allegorical bed or sepulchre: and, accordingly, a vast stone in the centre of a round table, which crowns a hill in the district of Gower, is still denominated *Arthur's stone*. Monuments of such a description are sometimes called his *quoit* or his *table:* but both the one and the other of these imaginary implements were equally derived from the sacred ring of Ila, which the Druids symbolized by Stonehenge styling it *the Ark of the World.* Accordingly, the redoubtable knights of the round table are sometimes fabled to man the infernal ship and to ferry the souls of the dead over the lake of Hades: and the sacred inclosure, into which Arthur enters with his seven companions when a flood destroys the rest of mankind, and which we find variously denominated his *quoit* and his *table,* is declared to be Caer-Sidi by which appellation the bards distinguished Stonehenge. His round table is the same also as his shield: and that shield we find to be a ship, in which he performs a wonderful voyage over the ocean. It was called *Prydwen,* which signifies *the lady of the World;* a title, not particularly applicable to a buckler, but strictly descriptive of that mundane Ship which was personified as a lady or a goddess.

With respect to his military exploits, he copies and rivals Osiris or Dionysus or Sesostris or Myrina. He drives the Saxons out of England. He conquers Scotland, Ireland, Denmark, and Norway. He makes the kings of Iceland, Gothland, and Swedeland, his tributaries. He subdues all France. He completely routs the emperor of Rome, by name *Lucius:* and, in the same battle, slays the Greek emperor and five paynim kings to boot. The next year he enters the capital of the world as a conqueror; and solemnly receives the imperial crown from all the cardinals. But the greatest warriors must die: and so must king Arthur. Returning to Britain, he is treacherously slain by his kinsman Mordred; just as Osiris, after all his victories, perished by the villainy of Typhon. Though mortally wounded, he

is unable to die till his magical sword Excalibar is thrown into the Severn. The charge is entrusted to duke Lukyn; who at length fulfils it, though sorely against his inclination. He casts the noble blade into the midst of the stream: when lo, ere it touches the water, a hand and arm is seen to grasp it, to flourish it thrice in the air, and then to sink with it beneath the waves. When the duke returns, Arthur is no longer visible: but he perceives a self-moved boat put off at the same instant from the land, and hears the piercing shrieks of unseen ladies. Popular superstition long believed, that the king was not really dead; but that he was conveyed by the fairy Morgana, in an enchanted ship, to a paradisiacal region within the recesses of the ocean. From this island of the blessed he will return after a certain pre-determined interval, and reign again over the world with his pristine authority.

I need not formally point out, whence this wild and beautiful fiction originated. Yet, although Arthur thus disappeared, his grave was shewn in the sacred peninsula, where the abbey of Glastonbury was founded. Some writers say, that our Henry the second examined it, and discovered a stone beneath which was a wooden coffin: but Polydore Virgil treats the whole account as an idle fiction. I believe him to be right in his scepticism: for every particular in the romance of king Arthur, no less than the insular situation of the tomb itself, leads me to believe that it was a sepulchre of a similar nature to those of Osiris or Jupiter or Bacchus or Apollo or Buddha.

Closely allied to the magical bark of Arthur, as originating from a common source, are the inchanted boats, which are so often prepared in romance to convey knights errant to some desperate adventure. The cavalier finds a small skiff on the shore of the ocean. He is immediately convinced, that some brother in arms or some distressed damsel, imprisoned in an insular castle, needs the assistance of his invincible arm. He steps into the vessel: and, in an instant, like the navigators of the infernal boat which conveys the souls of the dead from Gaul to Britain, he is wafted, by the unseen agency of some friendly magician, full three thousand leagues to the precise scene of action. . . .

2. We shall equally find in romance the sacred lake, the fairy or female divinity presiding over it, the wonderful cavern, the oracular tomb of imprisonment, the sleeping giant, and the upright figure eternally seated upon a large stone like the Memnon and other colossal statues of Egypt.

(1.) In British fiction, we have a Lady of the lake, who is said to have been the sister of king Arthur, and who is celebrated by the name of *Morgana* or *Viviana*. She is clearly the same being as the Persic Mergian Peri and as the Sicilian Fata Morgana, whose splendid illusive palaces float upon the surface of the sea. Boiardo represents her as gliding beneath the waters of an inchanted lake, while she caresses a vast serpent into which form she had metamorphosed one of her lovers: and other romance-writers describe her as the perfidious paramour of Merlin, who was wont to denominate her *the white serpent*. Her character has been taken from that of the White goddess; who presided over the sacred lake, and who as the navicular serpent was the diluvian vehicle of the great universal father.

As for Merlin, he was the son of a fair virgin by an infernal spirit: and he was at once the lover of the lady Morgana, and her instructor in the profound science of magic. Like the old Cyclopians or Telchines, he was a most skilful architect. He surrounded Caermarthen with a wall of brass: he compelled the demons to labour for him in a cavern of the island of Barry in Glamorganshire; where (as Camden remarks) you may still, by the exertion of a moderate degree of fancy, hear them at work: and, having built the stupendous circle of Stonehenge, he conveyed it in a single night, partly by sea and partly by land, from the neighbouring country of Ireland to the plain of Salisbury. He was sometimes called *Ambrosius;* and, agreeably to that appellation, such stones as those of which his temple is composed were of old denominated *Ambrosian stones;* while a town in its immediate vicinity still bears the name of *Ambrosbury*. All his magical skill however could not preserve him from the treachery of his mistress, the Lady of the lake. He became enamoured of her at the court of Uther Pendragon; where he established the famous round table, wrought many wonderful works, and uttered a number of prophecies. Previous to his death, he constructed a tomb capable of holding him and the lady: and taught her a charm, which would so close the stone that it could never be opened. The tomb is represented, as being formed out of a rock; and the entrance into it was beneath a huge inchanted slab. Into this cavern, and under this slab, she one day prevailed upon him to go; pretending, that she wished to ascertain whether it was sufficiently large. As soon as he was fairly within, she pronounced the fatal charm, and made him her rock-inclosed prisoner. Here he died: but his spirit, being likewise confined by the potent spell, continued to give oracular answers to those who consulted him.

The poetical wizard Ariosto has made a beautiful use of this palpably mythologic fiction: and it is remarkable, that he has strictly adhered in every particular to the descriptions which have come down to us of the ancient fatidical grotto. Bradamant descends into an immense cave. At the bottom of it she finds a spacious portal, which leads into an inner cavern. Here she beholds the rocky tomb of Merlin, within which he was confined by the Lady of the lake: and, conducted by the priestess Melissa, whom the poet has distinguished by the very name of an ancient priestess of the infernal great mother, she receives an answer to her inquiries from the enthralled spirit.

It is almost superfluous to point out the mode, in which this legend has been borrowed from old idolatry. Merlin, the reputed builder of Stonehenge in which he sails across the Irish channel, is a Druidical hierophant, the professed representative of him, who constructed the mundane Ark shadowed out (as the bards inform us) by that vast circular monument. His mysterious birth is a transcript of the virgin-birth of Buddha. And the stone tomb, within which he becomes a prisoner, is the mystic cell or Cromlech; within which the aspirant was said to be confined by the great mother, where he was reputed to die and to be buried, and which was deemed the oracular grave of the deceased great father. We have seen, that Arthur was similarly confined, with the self-same lady of Pendragon, in the prison of Kud beneath the flat stone of Echemeint. In both cases, no doubt, the tale of the imprisonment was derived from the Druidical rite of initiation within the stone cell of Ceridwen.

Nearly allied to Merlin and king Arthur is the valourous Sir Launcelot of the lake, whose title explains itself, and who is celebrated as one of the bravest of the knights of the round table. This personage is made the paramour of Queen Gwenhwyvar; whose name, as we have seen, denotes *the Lady on the summit of the water:* and he is described as accomplishing an adventure, the outlines of which have been palpably taken from the infernal shews of the Mysteries and from the allegorical death or slumber of the great father. In the course of his wanderings, the knight arrives before the sacred inclosure of Chapel perilous. Tying his steed to a small wicket, he undauntedly enters within the fence; and beholds right before him thirty gigantic cavaliers, who grin a horrible defiance against the daring intruder. For a moment his courage fails him: but, soon recovering himself, he rushes forward with his drawn sword; and the phantoms instantly give place. He now advances through the portal of the chapel: and, by the dim light of a single lamp, he perceives in the midst of it the recumbent figure of a dead warrior with his faulchion lying by his side. The inchanted weapon he forthwith seizes, and prepares to make the best of his way out of this scene of nocturnal horror; when he is charged in a grimly voice by the phantom knights without to relinquish the sword, as he values his life. Regardless of the menace, he again passes without opposition through the midst of his yielding antagonists, and regains his steed in safety.

(Vol. 3, Book 5, Chap. VIII, p. 314–323)

It seems doubtful, whether Shakespeare was acquainted with the ancient Orphic poems: I am rather inclined to believe, though he introduces the name of Hecate, that his magical cauldron and his three weird-sisters [in *Macbeth*] were traditionally derived from a different though kindred source; I mean the old Celtic mythology of the Druids. His witches are no mere beldames in mortal bodies; but the great infernal mother, revealing herself in three shapes and oracularly responding to those who consult her. They are the same persons, as the furies or Parcae of the Orphic poet and as the Valkyriur or fatal sisters of Gothic mythology. Hence their magical rites bear a mixed resemblance to the Orgies of Ceridwen-Erinnys and to the Colchian incantations of the Cuthic Medea. Their cauldron appears evidently to be the cauldron of the British goddess, and that cauldron again may be identified with the circular pit prepared by Jason. Each, though differently used, is used for a similar purpose: and the dance of the weird-sisters round the cauldron is perfectly analogous to the horrible dance of the three Parcae and the two infernal goddesses round the pit. Ultimately however both the cauldron and the pit are transcripts of the deep boiler employed in the celebration of the sepulchral Mysteries.

(Vol. 3, Book 4, Chap. VIII, p. 347)

JACOB GRIMM [1785–1863]
WILHELM GRIMM [1786–1859]

THE WORK of Jacob and Wilhelm Grimm is a clear and early indication of how folklore emerges from broad romantic mythic ideas and then, narrowed and redirected, finally becomes a separate discipline. Jakob's interest in medieval literature began as early as 1805, though Wilhelm's *Altdänische Heldenlieder, Balladen und Märchen* (1811) is the first important work of either. Wilhelm's later career remained centered on folk literature, folk tradition, and German myth. Jacob pursued two careers: besides his continuing interest in German mythic and folk material, he is of course one of the great pioneering philologists, especially in his *Deutsche Grammatik* (1819–1837) and *Geschichte der deutschen Sprache* (1818)—in these and other titles, "German" might be translated "Teutonic" or "Germanic." But these philologic studies began in and remained always complementary to his writings on myth.

The first joint work of the brothers—renowned ever after as the "Brothers Grimm"—is their *Kinder– und Hausmärchen* or *Fairytales* (1812–1815), the first important and still most famous collection of fairy tales. To this collection, the Grimms added a strict, copious philologic commentary. One important result was that where the inspiration for the Grimms' own collection, Arnim and Brentano's literarily retouched *Des Knabens Wunderhorn* (1806–1808), had mostly a literary impact, the *Märchen*

can be said to have founded scientific folklore study. Together, also, the brothers put out important editions such as the *Edda* (1815). In 1816–1818, their *Deutsche Sagen* appeared; in 1852, the first part of their *Deutsches Wörterbuch*. Meanwhile, Wilhelm published his *Über deutsche Runen* (1821), *Die deutsche Heldensage* (1829), and Jacob his *Deutsche Rechts-Alterthümer* (1828). In 1835, Jacob published the first edition of his most important mythic work, his *Deutsche Mythologie*; a second edition, with an important preface, appeared in 1844, and a fourth, with posthumous additions, in 1875–1878.

The early work of the Grimms began under romantic auspices. Between 1804–1807, both studied under Savigny, whose own pioneering studies of law as deriving from a whole cultural development showed strong Herderian influence. The Grimms' romantic ideas are gained most influentially through their association with the Heidelberg group, including Arnim and Brentano, Görres and Creuzer (the Grimms were early contributors to this group's journal, which promoted folk literature and history). This period of the Grimms' early development bristled with scholarly and critical disputes about Nordic and German myth and tradition. These involved recurrent quarrels about the literary worth, authenticity, and usefulness of, for example, Ossian or the *Edda*. The Grimms defended Ossian as authentic, and the *Nibelungenlied* as expressing genuine folk ideals. The Grimms indeed were, from the start, folk enthusiasts, mixing a kind of cult of old German naivete with romantic exaltation of creative poetic mythmaking. Though the Grimms approached this through scrupulous scholarship, they could still provoke August Schlegel's polemic against their folk collections as a "devotion to triviality." What lies behind this polemic in part also is the influence on the Grimms of Görres. Like Görres, they saw myth and language rising from primal oneness, from some central homeland of the human race. Myth is the residue of this lost but once universal original revelation. Thus the Grimms judged mythic folk literature—natural, ideal, national—superior to the more refined, higher and later literature Schlegel praised.

But the central interest of the Grimms lay not in the mythic origins but in its residue—the German residue. They believed the oldest German history and spiritual forces could be recovered through German legends. If Herder is a predecessor here, the Grimms narrowed Herder's cosmopolitan mythic approach down to Germanic myth. In this, they were never narrowly nationalist, but they might well be called spiritual patriots. Thus, what Jacob Grimm affirms most in his own mythology is that part of Herder's thesis stressing how each nation must find its own way to develop. Every nation, says Jacob, seems "impelled by nature to isolate itself, to keep itself unspoiled by foreign ingredients. Its language, its epos are truly happy only in the home circle . . . [the] undisturbed development of all its own energies and innermost impulses proceeds from this source." Against this is opposed what Jacob calls the "Foreign," all that is other than the *Volk*. (With Grimm, this took the form of an enlightened patriotism, as can be seen in his role during the 1848 National Assembly at Frankfurt.) Grimm shows once more the kinship

between romantic myth and nationalism; and the romantic era is, of course, the period when forgotten national literatures are fervently sought out and acclaimed as priceless treasures. (The Old Saxon *Heliand* was recovered in 1830, the Finnish *Kalevala* in 1835.)

By 1844, in the preface to the second edition of his *Teutonic Mythology,* Jacob Grimm could claim that though national lore was earlier thought to be a "barren" field of study, there was now a "glut" of such studies; and he could suggest rightly that his own work had contributed importantly to this very reversal. This preface makes clear what anchored and stimulated the Grimms' single-minded dedication to German lore. In one way, their view owes something to Görres's mystic mythicizing. Since all gods emanate from the One, comparative mythology is thus an indispensable pursuit for anyone seriously interested in myth. In fact, however, for Jacob Grimm comparative mythology is mostly useful as a means of sifting out what is not natively Germanic myth. All through the *Teutonic Mythology,* he urges exploring other European, ancient, and Eastern or Indian-derived myths; but at the same time, his preface and text fight an endless running battle against any foreign encroachment on German mythic integrity. Most of all, and understandably, Grimm argues passionately that Germanic myth is neither inferior to nor necessarily derived from Greek or Roman or even Christian sources. The view that German myth is "barbarous" is, he says, slander and ignorance; and only a "disloyal scholarship" could think it inevitable that Tannhauser must turn out to be Ulysses! And if it must be admitted that a certain "grossness" exists in German heathen myths, this would surely have disappeared in the course of time—had not Roman and Christian domination intervened, leaving the native Germanic traditions only half-fulfilled. Grimm admits the early Germanic mythology was heathen and polytheistic; but he also says that all polytheism—"innocently," if primitively—simply descends from and carries on monotheism. Moreover, Germanic myth independently achieved much of the "fullness" Greek myth had, in comparison to the "theosophic propensity" in Indian or Celtic myth.

Grimm has several answers to the question of why the authentic Germanic myths are still not very widely or deeply known. First, Germanic and Nordic myths became confused in history, and need to be separated. If Germanic myth has nothing so pure as the *Edda,* this is because Germanic lands were Christianized and Romanized earlier, and the development of their native mythic roots was cut off and buried under Roman-Christian and other encrustations. To dig out the buried Germanic divinities and religion, Grimm urges turning to written and oral memorials, particularly traditional legends, fairy tales, and superstitious beliefs, to runes and to early language and names; all these often preserve the untainted historical beginnings and earliest times. Such Germanic mythology is found for example in Yule-plays, in medical lore, and so on. And Grimm's mythic study, like his philological studies, assumes that the earliest is the more "perfect" form and expression. The body of Grimm's work is a staggering display of minute erudition, a kind of super-etymologizing and endless vertical digging-out of local, lost lore. To say the least, the theoretic or speculative side is not dominant or even prominent in Grimm. He comes as close as anyone in the nineteenth century to giving us another massively accreted *Golden Bough.* Like the *Golden Bough,* too, Grimm's work bulks large especially in the public image of mythology. Certainly Grimm, more than Herder or others, is responsible for the development by which mythologic study has become the study mainly of folklore.

B.F.

REFERENCES   Our text is from Jacob Grimm, *Teutonic Mythology,* translated from the Fourth Edition with Notes and Appendix by James Steven Stallybrass (New York: Dover, 1966, reprinted from 1883–1888 edition), Vol. III. For collection, see Jacob Grimm, *Kleinere Schriften,* 8 Bde (Berlin, 1964–1969).

For commentary, see: W. Scherer, *Jacob Grimm* (Berlin, 1885, 2d edition); Reinhold Steig, *Goethe und die Brüder Grimm* (Berlin, 1892) and *Clemens Brentano und die Brüder Grimm* (Stuttgart/Berlin, 1914); Richard M. Dorson, *The British Folklorists* (Chicago: The University of Chicago, 1968), especially pp. 61–66 and *passim;* Fritz Strich, *Die Mythologie in der deutschen Literatur von Klopstock bis Wagner,* 2 vols. (Halle, 1910), II, *passim.* Max Lüthi, *Märchen* (Stuttgart: Metzlersche Verlag, 1962), pp. 47–51 and 55 ff, with useful bibliography.

GRIMM

FROM *Teutonic Mythology*

Now THAT I am able to put my germinated sprout of German Mythology into its second leafing, I do it with a firmer confidence in the unimpeded progress of its growth. When the first shyness was once overcome, seeking and finding came more quickly together; and facts, that rebuked any effeminate doubt of the reality of scientific discoveries on a field till then considered barren, started up on every side, till now there is a glut of them. . . .

Criticism, often brilliantly successful on foreign fields, had sinned against our native antiquities, and misused most of the means it had. The immortal work of a Roman writer had shed a light of dawn on the history of Germany, which other nations may well envy us: not content with suspecting the book's genuineness (as though the united Middle Ages had been capable of such a product), its statements, sprung from honest love of truth, were cried down, and the gods it attributes to our ancestors were traced to the intrusion of Roman ideas. Instead of diligently comparing the contents of so precious a testimony with the remnants of our heathenism scattered elsewhere, people made a point of minimizing the value of these few fragments also, and declaring them forged, borrowed, absurd. Such few gods as remained unassailed, it was the fashion to make short work of, by treating them as Gallic or Slavic, just as vagrants are shunted off to the next parish—let our neighbours dispose of the rubbish as they can. The Norse Edda, whose plan, style and substance breathe the remotest antiquity, whose songs lay hold of the heart in a far different way from the extravagantly admired poems of Ossian, they traced to christian and Anglo-Saxon influence, blindly or wilfully overlooking its connexion with the relics of eld in Germany proper, and thinking to set all down to nurses and spinning-wives, whose very name seemed, to those unacquainted with the essence of folklore, to sound the lowest note of contempt.

They have had their revenge now, those norns and spindle-bearers.

One may fairly say, that to deny the reality of this mythology is as much as to impugn the high antiquity and the continuity of our language: to every nation a belief in gods was as necessary as language. No one will argue from the absence or poverty of memorials, that our forefathers at any given time did not practise their tongue, did not hand it down; yet the lack or scantiness of information is thoughtlessly alleged as a reason for despoiling our heathenism, antecedent to the conversion, of all its contents, so to speak. History teaches us to recognise in language, the farther we are able to follow it up, a higher perfection of form, which declines as culture advances; as the forms of the thirteenth century are superior to our present ones, and those of the ninth and the fifth stand higher still, it may be presumed that German populations of the first three centuries of our era, whose very names have never reached us, must have spoken a more perfect language than the Gothic itself. Now if such inferences as to what is non-extant are valid in language, if its present condition carries us far back to an older and oldest; a like proceeding must be justifiable in mythology too, and from its dry watercourses we may guess the copious spring, from its stagnant swamps the ancient river. Nations hold fast by prescription: we shall never comprehend their tradition, their superstition, unless we spread under it a bed on still heathen soil. . . .

I am met by the arrogant notion, that the life of whole centuries was pervaded by a soulless cheerless barbarism; this would at once contradict the loving kindness of God, who has made His sun give light to all times, and while endowing men with gifts of body and soul, has instilled into them the consciousness of a higher guidance: on all ages of the world, even those of worst repute, there surely fell a foison of health and wealth, which preserved in nations of a nobler strain their sense of right and law. One has only to recognise the mild and manly spirit of our higher antiquity in the purity and power of the national laws, or the talent inherited by the thirteenth century in its eloquent, inspired poems, in order justly to appreciate legend and myth, which in them had merely struck root once more.

But our inquiry ought to have the benefit of this justice both in great things and in small. Natural science bears witness, that the smallest may be an index to the greatest; and the reason is discoverable, why in our antiquities, while the main features were effaced, petty and apparently accidental ones have been preserved. I am loth to let even slight analogies escape me, such as that between Bregowine, Freáwine, and Gotes friunt. . . .

True to my original purpose, I have this time also taken the Norse mythology merely as woof, not as warp. It lies near to us, like the Norse tongue, which, having stood longer undisturbed in its integrity, gives us a deeper insight into the nature of our own, yet not so that either loses itself wholly in the other, or that we can deny to the German language excellences of its own, and to the Gothic a strength superior to both of them together. So the Norse view of the gods may in many ways clear up and complete the German, yet not serve as the sole standard for it, since here, as in the language, there appear sundry divergences of the German type from the Norse, giving the advantage now to the one and now to the other. Had I taken the rich exuberance of the North as the basis of my inquiry, it would have perilously overshadowed and choked the

distinctively German, which ought rather to be developed out of itself, and, while often agreeing with the other, yet in some things stands opposed. The case appears therefore to stand thus, that, as we push on, we shall approach the Norse boundary, and at length reach the point where the wall of separation can be pierced, and the two mythologies run together into one greater whole. If at present some new points of connexion have been established, more important diversities have revealed themselves too. To the Norse antiquarians in particular, I hope my procedure will be acceptable: as we gladly give to them in return for what we have received, they ought no less to receive than to give. Our memorials are scantier, but older; theirs are younger and purer; two things it was important here to hold fast: first, that the Norse mythology is genuine, and so must the German be; then, that the German is old, and so must the Norse be.

We have never had an Edda come down to us, nor did any one of our early writers attempt to collect the remains of the heathen faith. Such of the christians as had sucked German milk were soon weaned under Roman training from memories of home, and endeavoured not to preserve, but to efface the last impressions of detested paganism. . . .

The Fairy-tale (märchen) is with good reason distinguished from the Legend, though by turns they play into one another. Looser, less fettered than legend, the Fairy-tale lacks that local habitation, which hampers legend, but makes it the more homelike. The Fairy-tale flies, the legend walks, knocks at your door; the one can draw freely out of the fulness of poetry, the other has almost the authority of history. As the Fairy-tale stands related to legend, so does legend to history, and (we may add) so does history to real life.

In real existence all the outlines are sharp, clear and certain, which on history's canvas are gradually shaded off and toned down. The ancient mythus, however, combines to some extent the qualities of fairy-tale and legend; untrammelled in its flight, it can yet settle down in a local home. . . .

In addition to the fairy-tale and folk-tale, which to this day supply healthy nourishment to youth and the common people, and which they will not give up, whatever other pabulum you may place before them, we must take account of Rites and Customs, which, having sprung out of antiquity and continued ever since, may yield any amount of revelations concerning it. I have endeavoured to shew how ignition by friction, Easter fires, healing fountains, rain-processions, sacred animals, the conflict between summer and winter, the carrying-out of Death, and the whole heap of superstitions, especially about path-crossing and the healing of diseases, are distinctly traceable to heathen origins. Of many things, however, the explanation stands reserved for a minute inquiry devoting itself to the entire life of the people through the different seasons of the year and times of life; and no less will the whole compass of our law-antiquities shed a searching light on the old religion and manners. In festivals and games comes out the bright joyous side of the olden time; I have been anxious to point out the manifold, though never developed, germs of dramatic representation, which may be compared to the first attempts of Greek or Roman art. The Yule-play is still acted here and there in the North; its mode of performance in Gothland bears reference to Freyr. On the bear's play I intend to enlarge more fully elsewhere. Sword-dance and giant's dance, Berchta's running, Whitsun play, Easter play, the induction of summer or May, the violet-hunt and the swallow's welcome are founded on purely heathen views; even the custom of the kilt-gang, like that of watchmen's songs, can be traced up to the most antique festivities. . . .

Such investigations and similar ones capable of indefinite expansion, some of them not even dreamt of at present, may gradually become important to the internal aspect of our own Mythology: a still more urgent task is, to establish its relation to the Religions of Other Nations; nay, this is really the hinge on which mythological study in general turns. But seldom have their mutual influences or differences been so successfully explored, as to educe therefrom a safe standard for the treatment of any one mythology.

Every nation seems instigated by nature to isolate itself, to keep itself untouched by foreign ingredients. Its language, its epos feel happy in the home circle alone; only so long as it rolls between its own banks does the stream retain its colour pure. An undisturbed development of all its own energies and inmost impulses proceeds from this source, and our oldest language, poetry and legend seem to take no other course. But the river has not only to take up the brooks that convey fresh waters to it from hill and mountain, but to disembogue itself at last in the wide ocean: nations border upon nations, and peaceful intercourse or war and conquest blend their destinies in one. From their combinations will come unexpected results, whose gain deserves to be weighed against the loss entailed by the suppression of the domestic element. If the language, literature and faith of our forefathers could at no time resist at all points the pressure of the Foreign, they have one and all undergone the most disruptive revolution by the people's passing over to Christianity. . . .

These examples are well known, and are here chosen merely to make good for Mythology also a distinction between material that was common from the first and that which was borrowed and came in later. Our scholarship, disloyal to its country, inured to outlandish pomp and polish, loaded with foreign speech and science, miserably stocked with that of home, was prepared to subordinate the myths of our olden time to those of Greece and Rome, as something higher and stronger, and to overlook the independence of German poetry and legend, just as if in grammar also we were free to derive the German ist from est and *esti,* instead of putting the claims of these three forms perfectly on a par. Giving the go-by to that really wonderful and delightful consonance, whose origin would have had to be pushed far back, they struggled, however much against the grain, to hunt up any possible occasions of recent borrowing, so as to strip their country of all productive power and pith. Not content even with handing over our mythology to foreign countries, they were eager, with as little reason, to shift its contents into the sphere of history, and to disparage essentially unhistoric elements by expounding them as facts.

Why hold our tongues about the mischief and the caprices of this criticism? Mone, an honest and able explorer, whose strenuous industry I respect, will often come half-way to meet the truth, then suddenly spring aside and begin worrying her. By hook or by crook the Reinhart of our apologue must be resolved into a historical one, the Siegfried of our heroic lay into Arminius, Civilis and Siegbert by turns, Tanhäuser into Ulysses. In all that I had gathered by a careful comparison of original authorities on sorcery and witches, he of course can see neither circumspectness nor moderation, who gravely imagines that

witchcraft was once a reality, who from the minutes of a single trial in 1628 jumps at once to the Greek Dionysia, makes the devil Dionysus, and warms up again the stale explanation of hexe (witch) from Hecate. This is allowing the devil a great antiquity in comparison with those heroes; to me Reinhart and Isengrim seem to reach up far higher than the ninth century, and Siegfried even beyond Arminius, therefore a long way before the time when the term devil first came into our language. Several designations of the giants are unmistakably connected wth the names of surrounding nations; Mone's view applies them to Indians, Frisians, Persians, according as the words ent and wrise suit his purpose; let no one be startled to find that Caucasus comes from our Gouchsberg (cuckoo's hill)!

A later work . . . comes in not unseasonably here. Soldan agrees in my opinion on the atrocity and folly of the witch-persecutions, but he would dispute the connection of witches with German mythology, and derive all our magic and demonology from the Greeks and Romans again. The resemblance of the medieval notions to classical antiquity strikes him so forcibly, that he seems to think, either that Germany and all barbarian Europe till their early contact with the Romans were without any magic or belief in ghosts, or that such belief suddenly died out. The Walburgis-night, it seems, was suggested by Roman lares praestites, even the practice of bidding for fiefs by floralia and averruncalia, and the cutting of henbane by the fruges excantare: why may not our es also come from id, our auge from oculus, our zehn from decem? At that rate Wuotan might without more ado be traced back to Jupiter, Holda to Diana, the alp to the genius, all German mythology to Roman, and nothing be left us of our own but the bare soil that drank in the foreign doctrine. . . .

I do not deny for a moment, that beside this mysterious diffusion of myths there has also been borrowing from without, nay, that they could be purposely invented or imported, though it is a harder matter than one would imagine for this last sort to take root among the people. Roman literature has from early times spread itself over other European lands, and in certain cases it may be quite impossible to strike the balance between its influence and that inner growth of legend. And nowhere is extrinsic influence less a matter of doubt than where, by the collision of christian doctrine with heathenism among the converted nations, it became unavoidable to abjure the old, and in its place to adopt or adapt what the new faith introduced or tolerated.

(from Preface, 2d Edition)

KARL OTFRIED MÜLLER

[1797–1840]

IN THE WORK of Karl Otfried Müller, probably the most eminent classicist of the years from 1820 to 1840, the study of myth becomes, along with the study of language, the central and dominant tool for the scholarly study of the classical past. Myth thus achieved at last, though without much fanfare, a crucial place in historical investigation, a central place in classical studies, and an academic prestige that it had not enjoyed before. Müller, born in 1797, studied under J. G. Schneider and L. F. Heindorf (the latter a pupil of F. A. Wolf) at Breslau, and under Böckh at Berlin, and was appointed adjunct professor of Ancient Literature at Göttingen in 1819, where he taught until 1839. In that year he went to Greece to pursue his work, caught a fever at Delphi and died at Athens in 1840.

The ambition of his life was to understand Greek civilization as a whole, and the thrust of all his work was therefore integrative and synthetic. He is an example of German academicism at its broadest and most attractive. During his career, he lectured on mythology and the history of religion, on Greek antiquities, Latin literature, and comparative grammar. His voluminous writings include the three-volume *Geschichten Hellenischer Stämme und Städte,* the first volume of which was called *Orchomenos und die Minyer* and the second and third volumes *Die Dorier.* He also wrote books on the Etruscans, the Macedonians, and on the antiquities of Antioch. Among his best-known works, those translated into English are the *Introduction to a Scientific System of Mythology,* the *Handbook of Ancient Art and its remains: or a Manual of the Archaeology of the Arts,* and the *History of the Literature of Ancient Greece.* His work consolidates the great gains of his gifted predecessors, but it also makes advances in its own right and in some ways represents a high point in myth scholarship because of Müller's command of the various fields involved, his ambition to be comprehensive, and his temperate and objective tone.

Müller's work shows the influence of Herder's ideas about the essentially national character of myth. Müller argues against the idea that Greek myth came from the East, and works to show how it rose naturally, organically, and historically from Greek history, language, customs, geography, and religion. (It may be noted parenthetically that whatever the drawbacks of enlightenment and rationalist myth study, it had pressed myth toward universal significance and toward international interpretations, while Herder's influential insistence on national origins ultimately reversed this drift. Thus K. O. Müller's important work on myth takes in only Greek myths—though Müller himself was well aware of Nordic, African, and Polynesian myths—and thus helps form the notion perpetuated by Bulfinch and most other handbook writers of the late nineteenth century that myth is mainly to be thought of as Greek, or, at best, as Greek and Roman. It has been principally in the modern field of history of religions that the broad enlightenment attempt to embrace all myth has lived on.) Müller's work also shows the influence of Heyne and others in its insistence on philology as a major tool. Müller's attempt to understand ancient Greece excluded no method and no field of learning: he used archaeology to extend and to make concrete the traditional historical and literary sources; he used philology, the archaeology of words, to connect the history of language with the history of the people; and he used mythology as a collection of clues to early history, custom, migrations, and religious beliefs and practices.

Philology and mythology are Müller's favored tools because they tend to unify disparate materials, rather than to further fragment the objects of study. Philology in Müller's work is usually subordinate to mythology: hence mythology is the master key to the Greek mind. This position reflects Müller's conviction that the religious, imaginative, and artistic concerns that so naturally find an expression in myth are indeed crucial to an understanding of ancient Greece.

The *Introduction to a Scientific System of Mythology,* written in 1825 and translated into awkward English by John Leitch in 1844, is a young man's book, intent upon its method and confident of success. The account of the Perseus myth, reprinted here, is one of Müller's own examples of the application of his ideas. Usually said to have mediated between the positions of Creuzer and Lobeck, Müller may also be considered as trying to reach, by openly eclectic means, a position somewhere between pure allegorism and pure historicism. He argues that myths represent the confluence of the real and the ideal, the historical and the imagined, the remembered and the invented. Myths are formed when materials

of various kinds come together; the student is advised to seek what, in any myth, may be historical, what may relate to local religious worship or to colonization, what word may have geographical hints, and by such means to locate the myth and set the period of its origin. In a section that prefigures much modern anthropological work, Müller argues that much religious worship seems to precede myth and give rise to myth. Myth then becomes a way of explaining something one already does. In another place, Müller anticipates the ground of much modern criticism when he points out that "ancient Greece possessed only two means of representing and communicating ideas on deity—the mythus and the symbol. The mythus relates an action . . . the symbol renders it visible to the sense."

The *Introduction to a Scientific System of Myth* amply demonstrates the quality of Müller's scholarship. When he was not writing for specialists alone, he was capable of the sort of broad, lucid and informative general survey of Greek religion and myth that can be seen in the second chapter (reprinted below) of his *History of the Literature of Ancient Greece.* Müller here argues that religion generally precedes poetry in a given society, and that behind the Homeric pantheon, composed of deities fit for warriors, huntsmen, and chieftains, there was, earlier, an ancient Pelasgic religion suited to agricultural people, focussed on a single deity, probably Demeter, with a number of other figures, such as Persephone and Dionysius, who were personified powers of the natural world and were associated with its cyclical processes. Later, as Greek society moved into its heroic phase, there evolved the familiar Homeric deities, while the cults of Demeter and Dionysius, associated still with natural process and with mystical ideas—such as rebirth or resurrection—turned into the mystery religions of Eleusis, Samothrace, and elsewhere. Enlightenment mythographers had been quick to speak of the two observable Greek religions as a cynical contrivance, one religion for the wise initiates and another for the mob. Müller, with other romantic thinkers, places Greek religion and myth in history and can thus argue more plausibly that the evolution of religion keeps pace with and is connected with the evolution of society.

Müller's influence was wide, both in scholarly circles and among the general public who read his *History of the Literature of Ancient Greece,* initially commissioned and translated for publication in England. After K. O. Müller, myth studies are inescapably central to all serious study of ancient history, religion, literature, and language.

R.R.

REFERENCES Our texts are from K. O. Müller, *A History of the Literature of Ancient Greece* (London, 1840), trans. Lewis and Donaldson, and *Introduction to a Scientific System of Mythology* (London, 1844), trans. Leitch. The latter was first published in German in 1825.

Müller's place in classical scholarship has been discussed in J. E. Sandys, *A History of Classical Scholarship* (Cambridge University Press, 1958) vol. 3. Otto Gruppe, *Geschichte der klassischen Mythologie und Religionsgeschichte* (Leipzig, 1921), pp. 157–162 for Müller's mythic theories with bibliography, and pp. 163–172 for Müller's vast influence as a mythic theorist and classical scholar, and the names and bibliographies of his prominent disciples or students; Karl Hillebrand, *Unbekannte Essays* (Bern: Francke Verlag, 1955), "Otfried Müller," pp. 184–241 (originally published 1865).

For the work of one of K. O. Müller's teachers, see the essays by Karl W. F. Solger, "Über die ältesten Ansichten der Griechen von der Welt," and "Über die Religion der Griechen und einiger anderer Völker des Altertums," both in *Nachgelassenen Schriften* (Leipzig, 1826). Other useful accounts include Pinard de la Boullaye, *L'Étude comparée des religions* (Paris, 1922–1923) and G. P. Gooch, *History and Historians in the Nineteenth Century* (London: Longmans, 1913).

The following excerpts show first Müller's scrupulous historical approach to a given myth (one may compare Müller's treatment of Perseus with Bulfinch's) and secondly the broad historical ideas Müller could generalize from such study. The starting point in both excerpts is Müller's disavowal of an early Greek monotheism, and his consequent acceptance of polytheistic Greek religion.

K. O. MÜLLER

FROM *Introduction to a Scientific System of Mythology*

ANOTHER EXAMPLE may be drawn from an entirely different, and, indeed one of the darkest legendary cycles of Grecian mythology, the mythus* of Perseus and

---

* A number of nineteenth-century scholars used "mythus" and "mythi" to mean a single myth and several myths respectively.—Ed.

---

the Gorgons. I will first relate the main fact after Pherecydes,[1] from whom Apollodorus excerpts,[2] and whose chief sources were probably Hesiodic lays; (for that he drew from an ancient epic poet, is proved even by the accurate agreement with Pindar,[3] who, in *his* relation, assuredly does not follow Pherecydes.)[4] Acrisius king of Argos shuts up his daughter Danaë in a brazen tower; on account of a threat that death would come upon him from her offspring. But Zeus streams down to her from heaven in a golden shower, and begets by her Perseus. Mother and child are enclosed in a chest, and thrown into the sea. Dictys of Seriphus rescues them from the waves; but his brother, Polydectes, king of the island, wishes to take Danaë to himself. He pretends that he is going to woo Hippodamia, the daughter of Œnomaus, and calls upon his vassals, on occasion of a banquet, to fit him out for the bridal journey.[5] Now, when he demands a horse from each, Perseus, who was by this time grown up, says to him, as it would seem in anger, that he should have the Gorgon's head. Polydectes takes him at his word, and threatens, if he fail, that he will take his mother. Perseus undertakes the adventure with the help of the gods. With the shoes of Hermes, and the shield of Aides, he flies invisible over sea and land to Oceanus at the end of the world, where he finds the Gorgons; and looking only at the reflection of Medusa's petrifying countenance in his shield, succeeds in severing her head from the trunk, and places it in his pocket reversed. But Pegasus and Chrysaor spring forth from the body. On returning home, he turns Polydectes and his people to stone, and then gives the Gorgoneion to his protectress Athena, who fixes it upon her shield. An extraordinary tale of wonder, indeed, which, if told in our times, might well be thought the mere play of a grotesque fancy; but for higher antiquity that idea is inadmissible. It will scarcely answer to determine at the outset what portion of it is popular tradition, and what poetical embellishment. The whole has an equally fantastic and fictitious appearance; and

although we know that the mythus of Perseus was in its native soil at Argos, Mycenae, and Tiryns, still that does not lead us to the interpretation, unless we also learn, besides, what circumstances, relations, and institutions of the ancient Argives, gave rise to the mythus, or co-operated in its creation. If we succeed in determining these, though only in the leading points of the mythus, we can then hope to take up more and more threads, and, in the end, to unravel the whole. Now, the main point is manifestly the cutting off the Gorgon's head by Perseus. With regard to this Gorgonian head, *Gorgein Kephale,* it can be easily perceived that it was a far-famed bug-bear in ancient Greece. The *Gorgoneion* is nearly in the mythus what the *mormolukeia* are in later nursery tales. Odysseus fears to admit more shades from the infernal world to the blood-drinking, lest Persephoneia might also send forth on him the Gorgonian head of the terrific monster. The Gorgoneion, accordingly, was a creature sprung from terror of the gods, who, as experience taught, send evil as well as good. But the Gorgon is almost always introduced with reference to Athena. As early as Homer, Athena is armed with "the Gorgonian head of the terrible monster, the dreadful, the appalling, the prodigy of Aegis-shaking Zeus." [6] The very mythus which we are examining, closes with saying, that Athena places the Gorgon's head on her aegis, and through her also did Perseus accomplish the feat.[7] But this cannot well be a deliberate extension of the legend, a deduction from the rest, particularly for this reason, that the head and blood of the Gorgon figure in the popular legends of various districts, in connexion with the worship of Pallas, without even any mention being made of Perseus. The earth-born Erichthonius, according to the Attic tradition in Euripides,[8] was said to have received from Pallas two drops of the Gorgon's blood, the one having power to kill, the other to cure. It is told there that Athena herself slew the Gorgon, in the Phlegraean gigantomachy, where the reference to the general battle of the gods may not be the oldest portion of the narrative.[9] In like manner, they fancied at Tegea, where there existed from the earliest times a worship of Athena, that they had hairs of Medusa, which the goddess had given to Cepheus, the hero of the city, and which they only required to show from the wall to the beseiging army, in order to scatter it in flight.[10] Nay, the relation between Athena and the Gorgon is so close, that both are even taken for one mythic form, the goddess herself being called Gorgon by Euripides,[11] and in several other authors. Whence we may venture to conclude, that the Gorgon was imagined to be a hostile Pallas who could sometimes be united with her, as Demeter is called Erinnys, and Persephone Brimo and Daeira, and sometimes regarded as an antagonist being, detested by the goddess herself.

The Argive worship of Pallas, therefore, is the leading circumstance in the creation of the mythus. The goddess had her temple beside Zeus Larissaeus, on the summit of the citadel, which was fortified by Perseus with Cyclopean walls. She was thence called Athena *Akria* or *Akris*.[12] According to tradition, Acrisius himself lay buried in the temple of Acria,[13]—a coincidence of names too remarkable for me not to prefer the interpretation thereby suggested to any other.[14] In like manner, the fable of the taming of Pegasus by Bellerophon, according to Pindar's account, is wholly connected with the sanctuary of Pallas Hippia at Corinth.[15] There was also in Seriphus a temple to Athena, where Perseus was said to have been reared.[16] On

that island, as appears from Pausanias, he was paid divine honours, as *paredros* of the goddess, and, moreover, as the coins of the island almost invariably refer to the Corintho-Argive worship of Pallas, the opinion[17] is not improbable, that its earlier inhabitants were derived from those regions. If so, then the entire connexion of Seriphus and Argos in the mythus is explained.

However much all this may serve to strengthen the position laid down, still it does not open for us the way to the explanation of the mythus, because we know nothing yet of the character of that ancient worship of Athena. Now, we may at once assume, that the ideas of the Homeric poesy are here inapplicable, and that we must rather call to aid the ancient legends of the neighbouring Athenians, which, at all events, give the idea of a deity, through whom the produce of the fields, and the children of men receive nourishment, light, warmth, and increase, growing up and blooming under such benign influences.[18] Even yet traces of such ideas present themselves in the Argive mythus of Danaus; and it is a certain rule that we must be so much the more careful in turning all such traces to account the less they harmonize with later ideas. Danaus, the parched field of Argos, suffers through the contest between Poseidon and Athena, until the former impregnates his daughter, the fountain Amymone, and fills the lake of Lerna; but, throughout his whole life, he was protected by the goddess, and on this account, even built her at Rhodes a famous sanctuary, which was transplanted into various colonies. Nay, it seems to me clear, that the Rhodian legend of the golden rain of Zeus at the birth of Athena, is nothing else than a transference and modification of the Argive tradition that Perseus was begotten by a golden shower, the latter having been carried over from the mother-city.

Now, I think we already see the path we must enter, in the interpretation of the mythus, distinctly traced before us, especially by the main position: Perseus a daemonic being in close union with the ancient Argive Pallas, as a goddess who blessed the land with fruitfulness. His daemonic nature is proved, not only by his wonderful achievements, but also in the clearest manner by the divine worship which he received in Seriphus and Argive Tarsus. It is perhaps on account of the latter that Aeschylus places the Gorgonian fields in the east, as the Libyan worship of Pallas occasioned another nearly opposite transplantation of the mythus.

But in the interpretation itself let us not require an allegorical explanation of every individual feature of the legend, for precisely thereby would its falsity be immediately shown. Only the signification of the main features is to be pointed out; the rest was afterwards naturally formed on these, just because the whole is a *mythos*.

The dry sealed up soil in the land of Pallas, *Danae 'Akrisione*, thirsts for rain, and Zeus, the father of life, descends into its bosom in fructifying, bounteous, and therefore golden shower, in like manner as the cloud in which Zeus embraces Hera, is called in Homer, a golden one from which glittering dewdrops fall.[19] The child of this connexion is *Perseus*, an obscure name of which I have seen no satisfactory explanation; but this much, however, seems to be clear that *Persephoneia*, the daughter of Zeus by the Earth-mother, is from the same root. Perseus is the favourite of the fruit-producing Pallas, also a merely imaginary, not an externally-existing being, a *Genius Palladis*. But the god of the nether world, called the Much-receiver, *Polydectes* also *Dictes,* the Catcher, for

both brothers probably signify the same thing, wishes to take *Danae* to himself. The night of chaos and eternal horror is about to overshadow her. This danger is averted by Perseus delivering the goddess from her anti-type, the dreadful *Gorgo,* through whom the moonbeams become baleful, and the soil is turned to stone. The influence of her look is turned upon the infernal world itself, and its circuit fastened in the deep; while, at the same time, her full power is restored to the benign goddess, the kindly nurse of seeds and plants. Then spring up the clear and living fountains, of which the horse is the symbol— as, in general, so Pegasus in particular, who was born at the fountains of Oceanus, was caught beside fountains, struck out fountains with his hoofs, in his name also a horse of fountains. Polydectes' demand of horses, and then the procuring of one by Perseus, are also a remnant of the symbolical legends.

Accordingly, this mythus may be called a physical one if we only discard the idea of instruction in the powers of nature. The operations of nature are conceived by a powerful fancy, and introduced into the creed of the deity; and thence arises a daemon-story, which afterwards passed into the heroic mythus. I have designedly avoided too particular references, although even the ancients interpreted in this sense. Thus the Orphici explained the *Gorgoneion* to be the *facies in orbe lunae,* with which then Aristotle's interpretation of Pallas as the moon would very well agree;[20] but although this interpretation manifestly suits some expressions of that deity's nature, I fear, however, that it still oftener leaves us in the lurch, and proves too narrow and restricted; and I bring the principles above advanced here also into application. But the mythus is thoroughly symbolical; and as to its age, some idea may be formed from this, that even in the time of Homer and Hesiod it had become ordinary heroic fable. The symbolical character gives it a peculiar representability, and attracted elder art, which was still able to represent but little by expression and characteristic portraiture. Hence, a Gorgoneion, as a work of the Cyclopes at Argos;[21] the Gorgonea, as impressions on very old Attic, even Etruscan, coins; scenes from the combat of Perseus on the coffer of Cypselus,[22] and among the brazen reliefs of Gitiadas;[23] Perseus cutting off the Chimaera's head, and Chrysaor springing forth, in a very ancient terracotta,[24] and the rising up of Pegasus, in a relief of a very early style, found at Selinus.[25]

(from Chap. XIV)

FROM *History of the Literature of Ancient Greece*

Greek Religion

NEXT TO THE formation of language, religion is the earliest object of attention to mankind, and therefore exercises a most important influence on all the productions of the human intellect. Although poetry has arisen at a very early date among many nations, and ages which were as yet quite unskilled in the other fine arts have been distinguished for their poetical enthusiasm, yet the development of religious notions and usages is always prior, in point of time, to poetry. No nation has ever been found entirely destitute of notions of a superior race of beings exercising an influence on mankind; but tribes have existed without songs, or compositions of any kind which could be considered as poetry. Providence has evidently first given mankind that knowledge of which they are most in need; and has, from the beginning, scattered among the nations of the entire world a glimmering of that light which was, at a later period, to be manifested in brighter effulgence.

This consideration must make it evident that, although the Homeric poems belong to the first age of the *Greek poetry*, they nevertheless cannot be viewed as monuments of the first period of the development of the *Greek religion*. Indeed, it is plain that the notions concerning the gods must have undergone many changes before (partly, indeed, by means of the poets themselves) they assumed that form under which they appear in the Homeric poems. The description given by Homer of the life of the gods in the palace of Zeus on Olympus is doubtless as different from the feeling and the conception with which the ancient Pelasgian lifted up his hands and voice to the Zeus of Dodona, whose dwelling was in the oak of the forest, as the palace of a Priam or Agamemnon from the hut which one of the original settlers constructed of unhewn trunks in a solitary pasture, in the midst of his flocks and herds.

The conceptions of the gods, as manifested in the Homeric poems, are perfectly suited to the time when the most distinguished and prominent part of the people devoted their lives to the occupation of arms and to the transaction of public business in common; which time was the period in which the heroic spirit was developed. On Olympus, lying near the northern boundary of Greece, the highest mountain of this country, whose summit seems to touch the heavens, there rules an assembly or family of gods; the chief of which, Zeus, summons at his pleasure the other gods to council, as Agamemnon summons the other princes. He is acquainted with the decrees of fate, and is able to guide them; and, as being himself king among the gods, he gives the kings of the earth their power and dignity. By his side is a wife, whose station entitles her to a large share of his rank and dominion; and a daughter of a masculine complexion, a leader of battles, and a protectress of citadels, who by her wise counsels deserves the confidence which her father bestows on her; besides these a number of gods, with various degrees of kindred, who have each their proper place and allotted duty in the divine palace. On the whole, however, the attention of this divine council is chiefly turned to the fortunes of nations and cities, and especially to the adventures and enterprises of the heroes, who, being themselves for the most part sprung from the blood of the gods, form the connecting link between them and the ordinary herd of mankind.

Doubtless such a notion of the gods as we have just described was entirely satisfactory to the princes of Ithaca, or any other Greek territory, who assembled in the hall of the chief king at the common meal, and to whom some bard sang the newest song of the bold adventures of heroes. But how could this religion satisfy the mere countryman, who wished to believe that in seed-time and in harvest, in winter and in summer, the divine protection was thrown over him; who anxiously sought to offer his thanks to the gods for all kinds of rural prosperity, for the warding off of all danger from the seed and from the cattle? As the heroic

age of the Greek nation was preceded by another, in which the cultivation of the land, and the nature of the different districts, occupied the chief attention of the inhabitants (which may be called the *Pelasgian period*), so likewise there are sufficient traces and remnants of a state of the Grecian religion, in which the gods were considered as exhibiting their power chiefly in the operations of outward nature, in the changes of the seasons, and the phenomena of the year. Imagination—whose operations are most active, and whose expressions are most simple and natural in the childhood both of nations and individuals—led these early inhabitants to discover, not only in the general phenomena of vegetation, the unfolding and death of the leaf and flower, and in the moist and dry seasons of the year, but also in the peculiar physical character of certain districts, a sign of the alternately hostile or peaceful, happy or ill-omened coincidence of certain deities. There are still preserved in the Greek mythology many legends of a charming, and at the same time touching simplicity, which had their origin at this period, when the Greek religion bore the character of a worship of the powers of Nature. It sometimes also occurs that those parts of mythology which refer to the origin of civil society, to the alliances of princes, and to military expeditions, are closely interwoven with mythical narratives, which when minutely examined are found to contain nothing definite on the acts of particular heroes, but only describe physical phenomena, and other circumstances of a general character, and which have been combined with the heroic fables only through a forgetfulness of their original form; a confusion which naturally arose, when in later times the original connexion of the gods with the agencies of Nature was more and more forgotten, and those of their attributes and acts which had reference to the conduct of human life, the government of states, or moral principles, were perpetually brought into more prominent notice. It often happens that the original meaning of narratives of this kind may be deciphered when it had been completely hidden from the most learned mythologists of antiquity. But though this process of investigation is often laborious, and may, after all, lead only to uncertain results, yet it is to be remembered that the mutilation and obscuring of the ancient mythological legends by the poets of later times affords the strongest proof of their high antiquity; as the most ancient buildings are most discoloured and impaired by time.

An inquiry, of which the object should be to select and unite all the parts of the Greek mythology which have reference to natural phenomena and the changes of the seasons, although it has never been regularly undertaken, would doubtless show that the earliest religion of the Greeks was founded on the same notions as the chief part of the religions of the East, particularly of that part of the East which was nearest to Greece, Asia Minor. The Greek mind, however, even in this the earliest of its productions, appears richer and more various in its forms, and at the same time to take a loftier and a wider range, than is the case in the religion of the oriental neighbors of the Greeks, the Phrygians, Lydians, and Syrians. In the religion of these nations, the combination and contrast of two beings (Baal and Astarte), the one male, representing the productive, and the other female, representing the passive and nutritive powers of Nature, and the alternation of two states, viz., the strength and vigour, and the weakness and death of the male personification of Nature, of which the first was celebrated with vehement joy, the latter with excessive lamentation, recur in a perpetual cycle, which must in the end have wearied and stupefied the mind. The Grecian worship of Nature, on the other hand, in all the various forms which it assumed in different places, places *one* deity, as the highest of all, at the head of the entire system, the God of *heaven* and *light;* for that this is the meaning of the name *Zeus* is shown by the occurrence of the same root (*Diu*) with the same signification, even in the Sanscrit, and by the preservation of several of its derivatives which remained in common use both in Greek and Latin, all containing the notion of *heaven* and *day*. With this god of the heavens, who dwells in the pure expanse of ether, is associated, though not as a being of the same rank, the goddess of the Earth, who in different temples (which may be considered as the mother-churches of the Grecian religion) was worshipped under different names, *Hera, Demeter, Dione,* and some others of less celebrity. The marriage of Zeus with this goddess (which signified the union of heaven and earth in the fertilizing rains) was a sacred solemnity in the worship of these deities. Besides this goddess, other beings are associated on one side with the Supreme God, who are personifications of certain of his energies; powerful deities who carry the influence of light over the earth, and destroy the opposing powers of darkness and confusion: as *Athena,* born from the head of her father, in the height of the heavens; and *Apollo,* the pure and shining god of a worship belonging to other races, but who even in his original form was a god of light. On the other side are deities, allied with the earth and dwelling in her dark recesses; and as all life appears not only to spring from the earth, but to return to that whence it sprung, these deities are for the most part also connected with death: as *Hermes* who brings up the treasures of fruitfulness from the depth of the earth, and the child, now lost and now recovered by her mother Demeter, *Cora,* the goddess both of flourishing and of decaying Nature. It was natural to expect that the element of water (*Poseidon*) should also be introduced into this assemblage of the personified powers of Nature, and should be peculiarly combined with the goddess of the Earth: and that fire (*Hephaestus*) should be represented as a powerful principle derived from heaven and having dominion on the earth, and be closely allied with the goddess who sprang from the head of the god of the heavens. Other deities are less important and necessary parts of this system, as *Aphrodite,* whose worship was evidently for the most part propagated over Greece from Cyprus and Cythera by the influence of Syrophoenician tribes. As a singular being, however, in the assembly of the Greek deities, stands the changeable god of flourishing, decaying, and renovated Nature, *Dionysus,* whose alternate joys and sufferings, and marvellous adventures, show a strong resemblance to the form which religious notions assumed in Asia Minor. Introduced by the Thracians (a tribe which spread from the north of Greece into the interior of the country), and not, like the gods of Olympus, recognized by all the races of the Greeks, Dionysus always remained to a certain degree estranged from the rest of the gods, although his attributes

had evidently most affinity with those of Demeter and Cora. But in this isolated position, Dionysus exercises an important influence on the spirit of the Greek nation, and both in sculpture and poetry gives rise to a class of feelings which agree in displaying more powerful emotions of the mind, a bolder flight of the imagination, and more acute sensations of pain and pleasure, than were exhibited on occasions where this influence did not operate.

(from Chap. 2)

NOTES

1. Fragm. 2. p. 72 sqq.; 10. p. 90 sqq. Sturz.
2. II. 4, 1, 2.
3. P. xii. 11 sqq.
4. Comp. Shield, 216; Theog., 274; Homer Il., xiv. 318.
5. Comp. Welcker, Prometh., p. 381.
6. Il., v., 738.
7. Pindar, P. x. 45.
8. Ion, 1018.
9. V. 1006.
10. Paus., viii. 47. 4. Apollod., ii 7.3, where Hercules forms the connecting link.
11. Helena, 1316, and the frag. of Erechtheus.
12. Pausan., ii. 24, 4. Comp. Hesych. s. v., 'Akria.
13. Clem. Alex. Protr., p. 29, Sylb.
14. Even to that of Welcker's Prometh., p. 387.
15. Comp. Böckh, Expl., p. 218.
16. Hygin., f. 63.
17. Of Spanheim, *De Praest. Num.* i. p. 265.
18. *Minerv. Poliad.,* i.
19. Il., xiv. 351.
20. *Min. Pol.,* p. 5.
21. Paus., ii. 20.5.
22. Ib., v. 18. 1.
23. Ib., iii. 17.3.
24. Millingen, *Monum. ined.* W. 5, 2.
25. Treatise by Pisani. Compare with reference to the whole of this treatment of the fable, besides the brief notice in the Dorians, vol. i. p. 412, the profound and ingenious views of Völcker in his Mythology of the Jopetidae, p. 200 sqq.

French Romanticism and Myth

ANDRÉ CHÉNIER [1762–1794]

F. R. DE CHATEAUBRIAND [1768–1848]

HONORÉ DE BALZAC [1799–1850]

GÉRARD DE NERVAL [1808–1855]

VICTOR HUGO [1802–1885]

JULES MICHELET [1798–1874]

COMPARED TO Germany and England, the major French literary achievement involving myth comes late. Only from about 1820 does an important mythopoetic movement appear: among the poets, first with Lamartine, Vigny, Hugo, and Musset, then with Nerval, Baudelaire, and Leconte de Lisle; with Balzac among the new novelists; and with Quinet and Michelet among the historians. Perhaps only from 1840 or even 1850 does the greatest French poetry of myth appear. By then, of course, the vitality and important originality of German and English mythopoesis is virtually over. It is undeniable that the French romantic approach to myth, coming as late as it does, is crucially influenced by these already matured romanticisms, by their artistic examples, their theories, and as well by the sheer quantity of mythology and information about myth becoming available. Some of these cross-contacts are well-known: the influence of Friedrich Schlegel on Baron Eckstein and thus on Hugo, or of August Schlegel on Madame de Staël; Herder and Creuzer on Quinet; Milton and English preromanticism on Chateaubriand. But it is as true that French romantic work with myth decisively evolves from singular French conditions, and these importantly account for the relatively slow rise but also the independent direction and remarkable endurance and vitality of this mythopoetic interest.

What needs to be seen first is that, like French literature in general, the nascent French movement toward mythopoesis undergoes a serious interruption as it emerges from the end of the eighteenth century—in the twenty-year creative hiatus resulting from the Revolution and the Empire. For at least from Rousseau, there was considerable French preparation for what could nourish a mature romantic art of myth. The wealth of these native French currents can be only hinted at. There is obviously Rousseau's all-important, although diffused, contribution to a romanticism of nature and sentiment. In the later eighteenth century, and continuing, there was also much interest in occultism, in illuminism, in Freemasonry, and in visionaries such as Swedenborg. On another side, there was increasing interest in national history, poetry, and legend; by the end of the century, for example, a genuine cult of the troubadours emerged, as did editions of Provencal poetry, books about medieval lore, and a cult of the exotic, such as Saracen or Gothic. There was much attention, although generally confused, paid to India and the East, as in Anquetil-Duperron's Zend translation or as transmitted through English or later German philology.

Much of this appears blended in the greatest early French romantic writer, Chateaubriand, himself a prime catalyst for what was to come. His novel *Atala* (1801) daringly uses mythic and primitivist themes and atmosphere to illuminate a new sense of modern malaise, not least through a voluptuous prose more symbolist perhaps than descriptive. He introduces into French style something of a romantic-Miltonic mood; and in his *Genius of Christianity* (1802), he praises Christian mythic "marvellousness" and beauty over the superficiality of pagan myth. But Chateaubriand is also a mythic syncretist in a later romantic way, at once enthusiastically Christian, Ossianic, Homeric, antique, and modern. Madame de Staël's *On Germany* (1814), banking heavily on August Schlegel's theories, portrays to France the "new" romantic Germany as a land of poets and thinkers, whose inwardness and imaginative spirituality may serve to revitalize French culture and literature.

But these and other new beginnings take effect only after 1820. What intervenes crucially can be laid to the cultural counterrevolution of the Revolution and Empire: a modish, monumental and often shallow "Roman" neoclassicism is sponsored and imposed politically and patriotically; and either openly or subtly, from within or without, artistic innovation is discouraged or inhibited. However inhibiting such an atmosphere was to new mythopoetic stirrings, in another way it helped to embed classical mythology in all the minor poets of the period, and to sustain at least the great tradition of French antiquarian scholarship. This historical era, during which there is much mythic material available without any dominant artistic or intellectual force shaping it, may help account for why the new French romantics are quite eclectic about myth. It is a familiar part of French romantic history, for example, that Lamartine's *Méditations* in 1820—frequently taken as the first clearly decisive announcing of the new school—came only a year after the posthumous publication of André Chénier's poetry, which quickly became a romantic cult and inspiration. But Chénier (who died during the Reign of Terror) gained such quick fame perhaps because of his own acceptable eclecticism. His verse is most often in a neoclassic bucolic, elegiac or Theocritean mode; and his unfinished *Hermès* broaches an ambitious mythopoetic plan to represent the world under the "metaphoric emblem of a great animal" whose life, death, and metamorphoses will encompass history, uniting the old gods to Newton. In Lamartine, Vigny, or Musset, a poetry of natural sublimity and personal emotion moves easily into or from classical or medieval themes.

The syncretist tendency shows most powerfully in Hugo's remarkably versatile range of styles and themes: his youthful novel, *Han d'Islande,* draws on Mallet and Nordic myth; his early *Odes* and *Ballades* use classic and folk material; his *Les Orientales* moves to the East; his *La Légende des Siècles* attempts a full canvas of all Christian myth and much pagan, Islamic, and Indian as well. As Raymond Schwab makes clear, the French romantic period is excitedly interested in Indian myth—Hugo, Vigny, Lamartine, Balzac, or Baudelaire employ Indian themes and are only some of the most important figures involved here, for one could point as well to Nodier, Ballanche, Nerval, Michelet, or Quinet.

Such eclecticism or syncretizing is one reason why French mythopoesis of this period is not easily treated in terms of very distinct phases or currents. Another reason is that unlike the brief, intense outburst of German and English romantic mythic poetry, French poetry of myth has an unusually long vitality and continuity, almost spanning the century: after Lamartine or Hugo (himself the most enduring), new directions appear around mid-century with Nerval and Baudelaire, and even then Rimbaud, Mallarmé, Laforgue, and Valéry are still to come. If French mythopoesis is approached through individual figures, here again the long careers and unexpected inner shifts of many of these make categorization difficult. As an example, Nerval translates *Faust* (Part One) in 1828, but his masterpieces of poetic myth, such as "El Desdichado," are written almost at the end of his career in 1853; Vigny's early poems of 1826, using formal mythic topics, are quite different from his later and more personal use of myth in the 1840s and then again in the 1850s; and in Hugo's phenomenal career, the changes are themselves phenomenal.

In another way, too, some broad inner currents in French romantic mythicizing help frustrate classification, even as they provide some unifying threads. Some central tendencies seen in German or English romanticism reappear in French romantic myth. There are still, for example, the romantic views of the poet as mythmaker and seer, and the hope of myth as yielding a purer poetry, or a more primal, holy or magical language or spirituality. But much more than among the Germans or English, French mythic poetry—especially from 1830 on—reflects the new pressures of a society becoming commercialized, radically politicized, and bourgeois. Sometimes this leads to greater focus on the self, or the occult and mystic and magical, but usually to ever-bolder artistic experimentation or synthesizing of older traditions.

A minimal list of important French romantic achievement in myth would probably include the following: Vigny's *Poèmes antiques et modernes* (1826), Lamartine's *La Chute d'un ange* (1838), Hugo's *Odes et Ballades* (1823; 1826–1828), his *La Légende des Siècles* (1859–1883), his posthumous *Fin du Satan* and *Dieu* (written 1853?); Nerval's *Les Chimères* (1854); Baudelaire's *Les Fleurs du Mal* (1857); Leconte de Lisle's *Poèmes antiques* and *Poemes barbares* (1862). To this would have to be added several of Balzac's novels, *Louis Lambert, Séraphita, La Peau de Chagrin*, and numerous lyric poems, such as Musset's *Les Nuits*.

Lamartine's *La Chute* might be said to make clear, by its failures and few successes, what makes Lamartine important to French mythic poetry. His early verse brought to French verse a poetic medium wonderfully evocative of nature and natural bliss, though as often monotonously pearl-smooth in facility. *La Chute* sets up a large mythic theme: the fall of an angel through love of a woman (who is descended from Cain), and the angel's nine-fold incarnation and redemption; but what works best in the poem is what works best elsewhere in Lamartine—the eloquence or even music of natural benignity and a Christian pantheism. Lamartine may indeed exemplify how close a philosophic poetry of nature can come to mythopoesis without entering it.

Hugo's vast work and its variety neutralizes any summary comment. There is scarcely a mythic province he does not draw from: besides classic, biblical, Christian, Arabic, and Near Eastern and Eastern, he studies and uses Cabbalist and occult themes. His mythicizing poetry encompasses all styles, often mixing genres with dazzling virtuosity: if *Les Orientales* is mostly external local color and exoticism, the late *La Trompette du Jugement* is lyrically powerful and symbolically immediate; he can rhapsodize optimistically, and yet turn mythical topics to the poignant cosmic cruelties of a poem like *Horror*; he can write myth and evoke the qualities of myth in lyrics as well as in epics. *La Légende des Siècles* may seem to be all of these in one: it is a long poem with ambitious scope, conceived as recounting all human history from mythic times to the present and on to the visionary future. It explicitly uses biblical and Christian myth, but also (though less of) classical, Mohammedan, and Indian mythology. Perhaps more important is the great sweep of the poem through history, which seems to evoke a primal mythic power pressing forcefully through all time, space, civilizations: here, plants, animals, rivers, planets, as well as men and angels, speak, joining the marvellous to the real.

It is possible to describe Vigny, Musset, Nerval, or Baudelaire at first as lyric poets of myth in whom there runs a quite pronounced emphasis on cosmic and personal suffering, exacerbated nerves, or visionary anguish. If this obviously cannot describe their achievement, the emphasis can point to part of what is original in their treatment of myth. In these poets, more than in English or German romantics, the mythicizing poet begins to exploit his private experience by bringing it openly into the poem, and by using it to build up a private mythology or to rework traditional mythology in a bold new subjective way. Vigny is perhaps most puzzling here: his private pessimism seems everywhere evident, yet given distance and form by being cast into mythic themes; sometimes he uses biblical themes, as in *Moïse* or *Le Deluge,* and gains a striking mixture of warm feelings

and stylistic hardness; sometimes—as in *La Bouteille à la mer*—he writes a magic "symbolist" poem reminding one of the *Rime of the Ancient Mariner*. In *Les Chimères,* especially in "El Desdichado," and "Artemis," Nerval alludes to an astonishing array of mythic lore—alchemical, classical, Christian, folk, occult. But this alluded myth tradition is also hauntingly and mysteriously coalesced with quite private symbols—with loved women, places seen or dreamt of, his personal history: the unique effect is to make traditional myth part of his personal history, and his personal history part of traditional myth.

Even more than Nerval, Baudelaire's poetry marks an unmistakable shift from the earlier romantic to the decisively modern manner. His kinships or debt to older romantic mythopoesis remain evident, even as he radically transforms that tradition. His theory of correspondences, his bold symbolist theories and practice, his cult of art as autonomous truth, as an avenue to some kind of salvation, his deliberate blending of sensations—these have been embedded in early modern mythopoesis since Goethe or Friedrich Schlegel or Keats. But Baudelaire can use all this for new effect, for irony, more than sublime optimism or celebration, for exposing what is dark and sinister as well as for seizing naked holiness. *The Albatross* has romantic props, the divine winged poet, the bird of destiny, but the poem yields a new, nobly bitter irony; *Voyage to Cytherea* moves from its idyllic opening toward shocking images of mutilation. Baudelaire superbly meshes older mythology with his private life and visions, to form a new mythology whose roots lie more in his memory than in historical memory: in *The Swan,* there is a dizzying shift from ancient Andromache to the new Louvre to the poet's remembrance of old Paris to the sight of a real swan to mythic Greece again, and so on. Similarly new is Baudelaire's vision of

Paris as itself a cosmos and symbol, the modern city now not played off against the mythic splendor of the past (as for example in Wordsworth) but now the seat of myth itself.

Balzac is a peer and predecessor of Baudelaire in treating Paris as nothing less than a mythic cosmos, through whose commerce, people, and politics there swells and flows a positively mythic and primal energy. Balzac treats Paris as if it were a deposit of mythologies, a vast organic history whose every smallest life or nuance contributes to the whole. And Balzac often views the relation of the individual to society, or to himself, in explicit mythic terms. His Louis Lambert philosophizes in a mythic-Swedenborgian way about the correspondence of mind and matter; Balzac's *Séraphita* is both male and female, a version of the androgynous myth. Baudelaire did not hesitate to say that Balzac was not so much a realist or materialist as a "visionary."

Beyond its impact on poets and novelists, mythology is cultivated by a wide range of philosophers, historians, scientists, and scholars in general: some of the most prominent include Victor Cousin, J. J. Ampère, Silvestre de Sacy, Guigniaut, Benjamin Constant, and Émeric-David. But the full-blown impact of myth is perhaps best seen in Jules Michelet and Edgar Quinet. Their early intellectual development has deep affinities: Michelet as a young man was overwhelmed by his discovery of Vico, and first translated him into French; the young Quinet, under the strong influence of Görres and Creuzer, translated Herder's *Ideas*. Both went on to write historical works in which mythology, national legend, the spirit of the *Volk*, and the spiritual history of mankind are leading or even obsessive themes. But both also went on to a clear effort at making myths, as well as explaining and recording them. In Edmund Wilson's phrase, "Michelet tries to live his history": his *History of the Revolu-* tion has as its explicit heroes the French people, French land and cities, the whole organic evolution of French history; and Michelet's histories openly aim at creating or recreating his nation as a living mythic unity. Quinet, too, moved from analyzing myth (as in his *De l'Origine des dieux* of 1828) to direct efforts at writing and making myths. As Schwab points out, Quinet's epic poem *Ahasverus* is a signal new effort to write a French epic in the Germanic-Faustian mode, melding an enthusiasm for the Nibelungs and the *Vedas*. In other epics such as *Promethée* and *Napoléon,* each as unsuccessful in a literary sense, Quinet labored toward the same goal. (It might be noted that in Napoleon, the French had an authentic possibility around which a modern myth could be developed; and besides Quinet, Balzac, Hugo, or even Stendhal, among others, contributed to doing just this.) Like Michelet, too, Quinet's mythic enthusiasm fulfilled itself in part by becoming life itself: both became ardent patriots, and may be said finally to have ended by substituting France for Humanity as a goal and ideal.

B.F.

REFERENCES Our texts are from: André Chénier, *Oeuvres complètes de André Chénier,* publiées d'après les manuscrits par Paul Dimoff, 2 vols. (Paris: Delagrave, 1953), II; our prose rendering has been given. Chateaubriand, *The Genius of Christianity,* translated by Charles I. White (Baltimore, 1856); *The Works of Honoré de Balzac,* edited by George Saintsbury (Philadelphia: Avil, 1901), vol. II: *Seraphita*; Nerval, "El Desdichado," translated by Richmond Lattimore, in *An Anthology of French Poetry from Nerval to Valery,* edited by Angel Flores (New York: Doubleday, 1958); *La Legende des Siècles,* in *The Works of Victor Hugo* (New York: Athenaeum Society, n.d.), our prose rendering; Michelet, *Historical View of the French Revolution,* translated by C. Cocks (London: Bell, 1908).

For general comments and surveys, see:

Paul Van Tieghem, *Le Préromantisme, Études d'Histoire Littéraire Européene* (Paris: Rieder, 1924), v. I; Thor J. Beck, *Northern Antiquities in French Learning and Literature 1775–1855* (New York: Columbia, 1934); Albert Béguin, *L'Ame romantique et le rêve, essai sur le romantisme allemand et la poesie francaise* (Paris: Corti, 1939); Rene Canat, *L'Hellénisme des romantiques,* 3 vols. (Paris, 1951–1955); Henri Peyre, *Bibliographie critique de l'hellénisme en France de 1843 à 1870* (New Haven: Yale, 1932); Louis Bertrand, *La Fin du Classicisme et Le Retour à L'Antique* (Paris: Hachette, 1897); Auguste Viatte, *Les Sources occultes du Romantisme,* 2 vols. (Paris, 1928); H. Tronchon, *La Fortune intellectuelle de Herder en France* (Paris, 1920); Denis Saurat, *La Littérature et l'occultisme* (Paris, 1928); Bernard Faÿ, *La Franc-Maconnerie francaise et la revolution intellectuelle du dix-huitième siècle* (Paris, 1935). Raymond Schwab, *La Renaissance orientale* (Paris: Payot, 1950); E. Dumeril, *Le lied allemagne et ses traductions poetiques en France* (Paris, 1934); M. Braunschvig, *Notre Littérature étudiée dans les textes,* 2 vols. (Paris: Colin, 1958), II, pp. 633–635 for brief survey of French scholarly institutions relating to study of mythology.

For Chénier: F. Scarfe, *André Chénier, his Life and Work 1762–94* (Oxford: Clarendon Press, 1965). For Chateaubriand: Gilbert Chinard, *L'Exotisme dans l'Oeuvre de Chateaubriand* (Paris, 1918); Yves LeFebvre, *Le Génie du Christianisme* (Paris, 1929). For Balzac: Albert Béguin, *Balzac visionnaire* (Skira, 1946); Mircea Eliade, *La* coincidentia oppositorum *et le mystère de la totalité* (Zurich: Rhein-Verlag, 1959).

For Hugo: Denis Saurat, *La religion de Victor Hugo* (Paris, 1929); J. B. Barrere, *La Fantaisie de Victor Hugo* (Paris, 1949); Richard B. Grant, *The Perilous Quest: Image, Myth and Prophecy in the Narratives of Victor Hugo* (Durham: Duke University Press, 1968); A. Py, *Les mythes grecs dans la poésie de Victor Hugo* (Paris, 1963); P. Berret, *La philosophie de Victor Hugo en 1854–1859 et deux mythes de la Légende des Siècles* (Paris, 1910).

For Nerval: Albert Béguin, *Gérard de Nerval* (Paris, 1945, edit. aug.); Albert Dubruck, *Gérard de Nerval and the German Heritage* (The Hague: Mouton, 1965); Charles Dedeyan, *Gérard de Nerval et l'Allemagne,* 2 vols. (Paris: SEDES, 1957); Jean Richer, *Gérard de Nerval et les doctrines ésotériques* (Paris: Griffon d'or, 1947).

For Quinet: P. Gautier, *Un prophète: Edgar Quinet. Edition nouvelle de ses articles sur l'allemagne d'après les textes originaux* (Paris, 1917); Ulrich Molsen, *Philosophie und Dichtung bei Quinet* (Altona, 1913); Horst Neumann, *Das Deutschland-Erlebnis bei Edgar Quinet* (Hamburg, 1933); Herbert J. Hunt, *The Epic in Nineteenth-Century France* (Oxford: Blackwell, 1941), pp. 101–143; Henri Tronchon, *Le Jeune Edgar Quinet, ou l'Aventure d'un Enthousiaste (Allemagne-France-Angleterre)* (Paris, 1937), esp. for Quinet as popularizing Herder.

For Michelet: P. Viallaneix, *La Voie royale. Essai sur l'idée de peuple dans l'oeuvre de Michelet* (Paris: Delagrave, 1959). For Leconte de Lisle: Joseph Vianey, *Les Poèmes Barbares de Leconte de Lisle* (Paris: SFELT, 1946); Alison Fairlie, *Leconte de Lisle's Poems on the Barbarian Races* (Cambridge: at the University Press, 1947). For Barthélémy: *L'Abbeé J. J. Barthélémy et l'hellénisme en France dans la seconde moitié du 18e siècle* (Paris, 1926). For Baron d'Eckstein: P. N. Burtin, *Le Baron d'Eckstein* (Paris, 1931); Schwab, op. cit., *passim.* W. L. Schwartz, *The Imaginative Interpretation of the Far East in Modern French Literature 1800–1925* (Paris, 1927). P. Jourda, *L'Exotisme dans la littérature française depuis Chateaubriand. Le Romantisme,* 2 vols. (Paris, 1938).

Chénier

from *America*

I MUST completely invent a species of *probable* and poetic mythology with which I can replace the gracious tableaux of the ancients. . . .   (IV, i, p. 109)

from *Invention*

WHATEVER you finally become, young poet, you should work, should dare to achieve this illustrious conquest. Patterns and examples, what use are they? A great work is itself a powerful witness. Show what can be done by doing it yourself. If for you seclusion is a supreme joy, if each day the poetry of the great masters makes your blood race and your hair stand on end, if each day you feel these transports, these flames, and animated by their spirit need to create, then exert yourself.

In the quarries of Paros, the radiant block is to vulgar eyes only insensible stone. But the cunning chisel sees and traces and finds the life and the soul and all its qualities in its inmost heart. All Olympus breathes in the secret recesses of the stone. There, live Venus' beauties; there, curve the supple muscles and bulging veins; there, we find some backs unbowed by labor to relieve Atlas of his celestial burdens. To the will of the iron their vast exterior surfaces give way, grow soft and fall, and from this shapeless block the brilliant Gods spring forth. There is Apollo himself, honored among Gods. There is Alcide, conqueror of the Nemean monsters. There is the terrible death of the venerable Trojan, there the prince and defender of the wandering Hebrews. God himself lives in the thought-breeding marble. O heavens, can you not hear the creative voice of the world breaking forth from its depths?

O that among us inventive spirits would attain the heights of Virgil and Homer, knowing that they had, in fame, a temple like theirs, and without tracing their steps emulate their example and make—while taking care to distinguish themselves from the ancients—what they themselves would make if they lived among us. Let Nature alone, in its endless miracles, be their myth and their gods, and let Nature's laws be their oracles. . . . Let error be banished from the court of Apollo, and finally let Calypso, pupil of Urania, raising her golden lyre to yet a nobler pitch, make Newton speak in the language of the gods.   (pp. 20–21; 1819 edition)

CHATEAUBRIAND

FROM *The Genius of Christianity*

WE HAVE already shown in the preceding books that Christianity, by mingling with the affections of the soul, has increased the resources of the drama. Polytheism did not concern itself about the vices and virtues; it was completely divorced from morality. In this respect, Christianity has an immense advantage over heathenism. But let us see whether, in regard to what is termed the *marvellous,* it be not superior in beauty to mythology itself.

We are well aware that we have here undertaken to attack one of the most inveterate scholastic prejudices. The weight of authority is against us, and many lines might be quoted from Racine's poem on the *Poetic Art* in our condemnation.

However this may be, it is not impossible to maintain that mythology, though so highly extolled, instead of embellishing nature destroys her real charms; and we believe that several eminent characters in the literary world are at present of this opinion.

The first and greatest imperfection of mythology was that it circumscribed the limits of nature and banished truth from her domain. An incontestable proof of this fact is that the poetry which we term *descriptive* was unknown throughout all antiquity; so that the very poets who celebrated the works of nature did not enter into the *descriptive* in the sense which we attach to the word. They have certainly left us admirable delineations of the employments, the manners, and the pleasures, of rural life; but as to those pictures of scenery, of the seasons, and of the variations of the sky and weather, which have enriched the modern Muse, scarcely any traits of this kind are to be found in their compositions.

The few that they contain are indeed excellent, like the rest of their works. Homer, when describing the cavern of the Cyclop, does not line it with *lilacs and roses;* like Theocritus, he has planted laurels and tall pines before it. He embellishes the gardens of Alcinöus with flowing fountains and useful trees; in another place he mentions the hill *assaulted by the winds and covered with fig-trees,* and he represents the smoke of Circe's palace ascending above a forest of oaks. . . .

The philosophic age of antiquity produced no alteration in this manner. Olympus, whose existence was no longer believed, now sought refuge among the poets, who in their turn protected the gods that had once protected them. Statius and Silius Italicus advanced no further than Homer and Virgil; Lucan alone made some progress in this species of composition, and in his Pharsalia we find the description of a forest and a desert, which remind us of the colors of modern artists. . . .

It can scarcely be supposed that men endued with such sensibility as the ancients could have wanted eyes to perceive the charms of nature and talents for depicting them, had they not been blinded by some powerful cause. Now, this cause was their established mythology, which, peopling the universe with elegant phantoms, banished from the creation its solemnity, its grandeur, and its solitude. It was necessary that Christianity should expel the whole hosts of fauns, of satyrs, and of nymphs, to restore to the grottos their silence and to the woods their scope for uninterrupted contemplation. Under our religion the deserts have assumed a character more pensive, more vague, and more sublime; the forests have attained a loftier pitch; the rivers have broken their petty urns, that in future they may only pour the waters of the abyss from the summit of the mountains; and the true God, in returning to his works, has imparted his immensity to nature.

The prospect of the universe could not excite in the bosoms of the Greeks and Romans those emotions which it produces in our souls. Instead of that setting sun, whose lengthened rays sometimes light up the forest, at others form a golden tangent on the rolling arch of the seas,—instead of those beautiful accidents of light which every morning remind us of the miracle of the creation,—the ancients beheld around them naught but a uniform system, which reminds us of the machinery of an opera.

If the poet wandered in the vales of the Taygetus, on the banks of the Sperchius, on the Maenalus, beloved of Orpheus, or in the plains of the Elorus, whatever may have been the charm of this Grecian geography, he met with nothing but fauns, he heard no sounds but those of the dryads. Apollo and the Muses were there, and Vertumnus with the Zephyrs led eternal dances. Sylvans and Naiads may strike the imagination in an agreeable manner, pro-

vided they be not incessantly brought forward. We would not

——Expel the Tritons from the watery waste,
Destroy Pan's pipe, snatch from the Fates their shears.

But then what impression does all this leave on the soul? What results from it for the heart? What moral benefit can the mind thence derive? Oh, how far more highly is the Christian poet favored! Free from that multitude of absurd deities which circumscribed them on all sides, the woods are filled with the immensity of the Divinity; and the gift of prophecy and wisdom, mystery and religion, seem to have fixed their eternal abode in their awful recesses.

Penetrate into those forests of America coeval with the world. What profound silence pervades these retreats when the winds are hushed! What unknown voices when they begin to rise! Stand still, and every thing is mute; take but a step, and all nature sighs. Night approaches: the shades thicken; you hear herds of wild beasts passing in the dark; the ground murmurs under your feet; the pealing thunder roars in the deserts; the forest bows; the trees fall; an unknown river rolls before you. The moon at length bursts forth in the east; as you proceed at the foot of the trees, she seems to move before you at their tops, and solemnly to accompany your steps. The wanderer seats himself on the trunk of an oak to await the return of day; he looks alternately at the nocturnal luminary, the darkness, and the river: he feels restless, agitated, and in expectation of something extraordinary. A pleasure never felt before, an unusual fear, cause his heart to throb, as if he were about to be admitted to some secret of the Divinity; he is alone in the depths of the forests, but the mind of man is equal to the expanse of nature, and all the solitudes of the earth are less vast than one single thought of his heart. Even did he reject the ideal of a Deity, the intellectual being, alone and unbeheld, would be more august in the midst of a solitary world than if surrounded by the ridiculous divinities of fabulous times. The barren desert itself would have some congeniality with his discursive thoughts, his melancholy feelings, and even his disgust for a life equally devoid of illusion and of hope.

There is in man an instinctive melancholy, which makes him harmonize with the scenery of nature. Who has not spent whole hours seated on the bank of a river contemplating its passing waves? Who has not found pleasure on the sea-shore in viewing the distant rock whitened by the billows? How much are the ancients to be pitied, who discovered in the ocean naught but the palace of Neptune and the cavern of Proteus! It was hard that they should perceive only the adventures of the Tritons and the Nereids in the immensity of the seas, which seems to give an indistinct measure of the greatness of our souls, and which excites a vague desire to quit this life, that we may embrace all nature and taste the fulness of joy in the presence of its Author.

(Part Two, Book IV, Chap. 1)

BALZAC

FROM *Seraphita*

THIS LAST hymn was not uttered in words, nor expressed by gestures, nor by any of the signs which serve men as a means of communicating their thoughts, but as the soul speaks to itself; for, at the moment when Seraphita was revealed in her true nature, her ideas were no longer enslaved to human language. The vehemence of her last prayer had broken the bonds. Like a white dove, the soul hovered for a moment above this body, of which the exhausted materials were about to dissever.

The aspiration of this soul to heaven was so infectious, that Wilfrid and Minna failed to discern death as they saw the radiant spark of life.

They had fallen on their knees when Seraphitus had turned to the dawn, and they were inspired by his ecstasy.

The fear of the Lord, who creates man anew and purges him of his dross, consumed their hearts. Their eyes were closed to the things of the earth, and opened to the glories of heaven.

Though surprised by the trembling before God which overcame some of those seers known to men as prophets, they still trembled, like them, when they found themselves within the circle where the glory of the Spirit was shining.

Then the veil of the flesh, which had hitherto hidden him from them, insensibly faded away, revealing the divine substance.

They were left in the twilight of the dawn, whose pale light prepared them to see the true light, and to hear the living word without dying of it.

In this condition they both began to understand the immeasurable distances that divide the things of earth from the things of heaven.

The life on whose brink they stood, trembling and dazzled in a close embrace, as two children take refuge side by side to gaze at a conflagration—that Life gave no hold to the senses. The Spirit was above them; it shed fragrance without odor, and melody without the help of sound; here, where they knelt, there were neither surfaces, nor angles, nor atmosphere. They dared no longer question him nor gaze on him, but remained under his shadow, as under the burning rays of the tropical sun we dare not raise our eyes for fear of being blinded.

They felt themselves near to him, though they could not tell by what means they thus found themselves, as in a dream, on the border line of the visible and the invisible, nor how they had ceased to see the visible and perceived the invisible.

They said to themselves, "If he should touch us, we shall die!" But the Spirit was in the infinite, and they did not know that in the infinite time and space are not, that they were divided from him by gulfs, though apparently so near. Their souls not being prepared to receive a complete knowledge of the faculties of that life, they only perceived it darkly, apprehending it according to their weakness.

Otherwise, when the Living Word rang forth, of which the distant sound fell on their ear, its meaning entering into their soul as life enters into a body, a single tone of that Word would have swept them away, as a whirl of fire seizes a straw.

Thus they beheld only what their na-ture, upheld by the power of the Spirit, allowed them to see; they heard only so much as they were able to hear.

Still, in spite of these mitigations, they shuddered as they heard the voice of the suffering soul, the hymn of the Spirit awaiting life, and crying out for it. That cry froze the very marrow in their bones.

The Spirit knocked at the sacred gate.

"What wilt thou?" asked a choir, whose voice rang through all the worlds.

"To go to God."

"Hast thou conquered?"

"I have conquered the flesh by abstinence; I have vanquished false speech by silence; I have vanquished false knowledge by humility; I have vanquished pride by charity; I have vanquished the earth by love; I have paid my tribute of suffering; I am purified by burning for the faith; I have striven for life by prayer; I wait adoring, and I am resigned."

But no reply came.

"The Lord be praised!" said the Spirit, believing himself rejected. His tears flowed, and fell in dew on the kneeling witnesses, who shuddered at the judgments of God.

On a sudden, the trumpets sounded for the victory of the Angel in this last test; their music filled space, like a sound met by an echo; it rang through it, making the universe tremble. Wilfrid and Minna felt the world shrink under their feet. They shivered, shaken by the terrors of apprehending the mystery that was to be accomplished. . . .

Wilfrid and Minna now understood some of the mysterious words of the being who on earth had appeared to them under the form which was intelligible to each— Seraphitus to one, Seraphita to the other— seeing that here all was homogeneous. Light gave birth to melody, and melody to light; colors were both light and melody; motion was number endowed by the Word;

in short, everything was at once sonorous, diaphanous, and mobile; so that, everything existing in everything else, extension knew no limits, and the angels could traverse it everywhere to the utmost depths of the infinite.

They saw then how puerile were the human sciences of which they had heard. Before them lay a view without any horizon, an abyss into which ardent craving invited them to plunge; but burdened with their hapless bodies, they had the desire without the power.

The seraph lightly spread his wings to take his flight, and did not look back at them—he had nothing now in common with the earth.

He sprang upwards; the vast span of his dazzling pinions covered the two seers like a beneficent shade, allowing them to raise their eyes and see him borne away in his glory escorted by the rejoicing archangel. He mounted like a beaming sun rising from the bosom of the waters; but, more happy he than the day star, and destined to more glorious ends, he was not bound, like inferior creatures, to a circular orbit; he followed the direct line of the infinite, tending undeviatingly to the central one, to be lost there in life eternal, and to absorb into his faculties and into his essence the power of rejoicing through love and the gift of comprehending through wisdom.

The spectacle that was then suddenly unveiled to the eyes of the two seers overpowered them by its vastness, for they felt like atoms whose smallness was comparable only to the minutest fraction which infinite divisibility allows man to conceive of, brought face to face with the infinitely numerous which God alone can contemplate as He contemplates Himself.

What humiliation and what greatness in those two points, strength and love, which

the seraph's first desire had placed as two links uniting the immensity of the inferior universe to the immensity of the superior universe! They understood the invisible bonds by which material worlds are attached to the spiritual worlds. As they recalled the stupendous efforts of the greatest human minds, they discerned the principle of melody as they heard the songs of heaven which gave them all the sensations of color, perfume, and thought, and reminded them of the innumerable details of all the creations, as an earthly song can revive the slenderest memories of love.

Strung by the excessive exaltation of their faculties to a pitch for which there is no word in any language, for a moment they were suffered to glance into the divine sphere. There all was gladness. Myriads of angels winged their way with one consent and without confusion, all alike but all different, as simple as the wild rose, as vast as worlds.

Wilfrid and Minna did not see them come nor go; they suddenly pervaded the infinite with their presence, as stars appear in the unfathomable ether. The blaze of all their diadems flashed into light in space, as the heavenly fire is lighted when the day rises among mountains. Waves of light fell from their hair, and their movements gave rise to undulating throbs like the dancing waves of a phosphorescent sea.

The two seers could discern the seraph as a darker object amid deathless legions, whose wings were as the mighty plumage of a forest swept by the breeze. And then, as though all the arrows of a quiver were shot off at once, the spirits dispelled with a breath every vestige of his former shape; as the seraph mounted higher he was purified, and ere long he was no more than a filmy image of what they had seen when he was first transfigured—lines of fire with no shadow. Up and up, receiving a fresh gift at each circle, while the sign of his election was transmitted to the highest heaven, whither he mounted purer and purer. . . .

As they resumed the bondage of the flesh from which their spirit had for a moment been released by a sublime trance, the two mortals felt as on awakening in the morning from a night of splendid dreams, of which reminiscences float in the brain, though the senses have no knowledge of them, and human language would fail to express them. The blackness of the limbo into which they fell was the sphere where the sun of visible worlds shines.

"We must go down again," said Wilfrid to Minna.

"We will do as he bids us," replied she. "Having seen the worlds moving on towards God, we know the right way.— Our starry diadems are above!"

They fell into the abyss, into the dust of the lower worlds, and suddenly saw the earth as it were a crypt, of which the prospect was made clear to them by the light they brought back in their souls, for it still wrapped them in a halo, and through it they still vaguely heard the vanishing harmonies of heaven. This was the spectacle which of old fell on the mind's eye of the prophets. Ministers of various religions, all calling themselves true, kings consecrated by force and fear, warriors and conquerors sharing the nations, learned men and rich lording it over a refractory and suffering populace whom they trampled under foot,—these were all attended by their followers and their women, all were clad in robes of gold, silver and azure, covered with pearls and gems torn from the bowels of the earth or from the depths of the sea by the perennial toil of sweating and blaspheming humanity. But in the eyes of the exiles this wealth and splendor, harvested with blood, were but filthy rags.

"What do ye here in motionless ranks?" asked Wilfrid.

They made no answer.

"What do ye here in motionless ranks?"

But they made no answer.

Wilfrid laid his hands on them and shouted:

"What do ye here in motionless ranks?"

By a common impulse they all opened their robes and showed him their bodies, dried up, eaten by worms, corrupt, falling to dust, and consumed by horrible diseases. "Ye lead the nations to death," said Wilfrid; "ye have defiled the earth, perverted the Word, prostituted justice. Ye have eaten the herb of the field, and now ye would kill the lambs! Do ye think that there is justification in showing your wounds? I shall warn those of my brethren who still can hear the Voice, that they may slake their thirst at the springs that you have hidden."

"Let us save our strength for prayer," said Minna. "It is not your mission to be a prophet, nor a redeemer, nor an evangelist. We are as yet only on the margin of the lowest sphere; let us strive to cleave through space on the pinions of prayer."

"You are my sole love!"

"You are my sole strength!"

"We have had a glimpse of the higher mysteries; we are, each to the other, the only creatures here below with whom joy and grief are conceivable. Come then, we will pray; we know the road, we will walk in it."

"Give me your hand," said the girl. "If we always walk together, the path will seem less rough and not so long."

"Only with you," said the young man, "could I traverse that vast desert without allowing myself to repine."

"And we will go to heaven together!" said she.

The clouds fell, forming a dark canopy.

Suddenly the lovers found themselves kneeling by a dead body, which old David was protecting from prying curiosity, and insisted on burying with his own hands.

Outside, the first summer of the nineteenth century was in all its glory; the lovers fancied they could hear a voice in the sunbeams. They breathed heavenly perfume from the newborn flowers, and said as they took each other by the hand:

"The vast ocean that gleams out there is an image of that we saw above!"

"Whither are you going?" asked Pastor Becker.

"We mean to go to God," said they. "Come with us, father."

(from Chap. VII)

NERVAL

"El Desdichado"

I AM the dark, the widowed, the discon-
  solate.
I am the prince of Aquitaine whose tower
  is down.
My only star is dead, and star-configurate
my lute wears Melancholy's mark, a
  blackened sun.
Here is the midnight of the grave, give
  back, of late
my consolation, Pausilippe, the Italian
sea, with that flower so sweet once to my
  desolate
heart, and the trellis where the vine and
  rose are one.

Am I Love? Am I Phoebus, Biron,
  Lusignan?
Crimson the queen's kiss blazes still upon
  my face.
The siren's naked cave has been my
  dreaming place.
Twice have I forced the crossing of the
  Acheron
and played on Orpheus' lyre in alternate
  complaint
Mélusine's cries against the moaning of
  the Saint.

HUGO

FROM *The Satyr*

THE SATYR stopped a moment, breathing like a man who cools his forehead in a stream, while another creature seemed to form behind and through his face. The

Gods sat turned, uneasy, towards the master, and thoughtful, gazed at Jupiter astounded. The Satyr then went on:

"Beneath the fearful weight oppressing it, Reality will be reborn, conqueror of ancient evil. You deities know little of the earth and all its ways. You deities have conquered, but you have not understood. You have above you other spirits who, in fire and cloud, in ocean waves and in the small rain, now are dreaming, while they wait upon your massive fall. But what is that to me, wide-eyed with fear at the bottom of vast darkness? You know, you gods, there are other sphinxes than that one old sphinx of Thebes. You had best know, you tyrants both of men and Erebus, you gods who spill blood, gods we all see through, that we have all become outlaws together on this great mountain where land and sea hang in equipoise. But you are here as kings, while I come to be free. While you sow hate and fraud and death and leave no crime undone, I dream. I am an eye fixed in the deep; I see all. Blue of heaven, shade of hell. Temples and charnel houses, forests and cities, eagle and kingfisher are all the same vision in my sight. Divinities and drones, present and to come, all cross my gaze and are of the same flight. I am a witness that all things pass away. But Something does exist, though what or who it is mankind will never know. Mankind guesses, proposes, approaches and tries; he shapes a block of marble, hacks a stone and fashions thence a statue saying 'this is He.' Man sits entranced before the stone, and all the hangers-on, whatever else they are, are priests. So go on being the Immortals; grind down all forms of life; heap up a great pile of trembling, living creatures; go on reigning. And when you have in oh so short a time, bloodied all the now blue heaven, then, oh conqueror, when

you have filled your own cup to the brim, it will be well, when all is said and done, because you'll be replaced by that dark and final god men call Enough. Delphi and Pisa are as winged chariots, and the things that seemed eternal fall to pieces, and all before one can take the time to count to twenty."

As he spoke the Satyr grew enormous; greater at first than Polyphemus, then larger than Typhon who howls and blasphemes and swings his fists like hammers. Then he grew greater than Titan, greater even than Athos. Vast reaches of space were swept up into that dark form, and as the sailor sees the headland grow, so the startled gods watched the fearful thing increase. Upon his forehead burned a strange and eastern light. His hair became a forest. Rivers, streams, and lakes poured from the hollows of his thighs. His two horns seemed like Caucasus and Atlas. Lightning played around him; thunder boomed and crashed; his sides heaved with meadows and fields; his deformities seemed mountains. The beasts, drawn by his sublime music, fallow-deer and tigers, ranged along his frame, and springtime all in flowers grew green along his limbs. The hollows of his armpits shielded bleak Decembers. And wandering peoples asked their way, lost in the crossroads of the fingers of his hand. Eagles wheeled in his vast open mouth. His lyre, when touched, became like him gigantic; it sang and wept, rumbled and crashed, pealed forth loud cries; hurricanes were caught among its seven strings like tiny flies caught fast within a web. His terrible great chest was now a field of stars. He cried:

"The Future, as the skies will make it, will be expansion into endless timeless space. Spirit will penetrate into all aspects of all things. Spirit will manifest itself in everything. We cripple effect by limiting cause. Oh World, the form of the gods is the beginning of all evil. We fashion shadows out of rays of light. Why put phantoms higher than Being? Bright ethereal things are not kingdoms. Make room then in the eternal swarming of the dark heavens for blue skies, noontimes, dawning, twilight. Room for the in-streaming of the universal soul. Wars made kings and darkness breeds the gods. Give way now to Liberty, Life, and Faith. Dogma shall be destroyed. Everywhere light, everywhere genius. Love itself! And all things shall be understood, all things being in harmony. The blue of heaven will still the wolves. Make room for the All! It is I, Pan. Jupiter, fall on your knees."

(Part IV, "Apotheosis")

MICHELET

FROM *Historical View of the French Revolution*

ANOTHER thing which this history will render most conspicuous, and which is true of every party, is, that the people were generally much better than their leaders. The further I have searched, the more generally have I found that the more deserving class was ever underneath, buried among the utterly obscure. I have also found that those brilliant, powerful speakers, who expressed the thoughts of the masses, are usually but wrongfully considered as the sole actors. The fact is, that they rather received than communicated the impulse. The chief actor is the people. In order to find and restore the latter to its proper position, I have been obliged to reduce to their proportions those ambitious puppets whom they had set in motion, and in whom, till now, people fancied they saw, and have sought for, the secret transactions of history.

This sight, I must confess, struck me with astonishment. In proportion as I entered more deeply into this study, I observed that the mere party leaders, those heroes of the prepared scene, neither foresaw nor prepared anything, that they were never the first proposers of any grand measure,—more particularly of those which were the unanimous work of the people in the outset of the Revolution.

Left to themselves, at those decisive moments, by their pretended leaders, they found out what was necessary to be done, and did it.

Great, astonishing results! But how much greater was the heart which conceived them! The deeds themselves are as nothing in comparison. So astonishing, indeed, was that greatness of heart, that the future may draw upon it for ever, without fearing to exhaust its resources. No one can approach its contemplation, without retiring a better man. Every soul dejected, or crushed with grief, every human or national heart has but to look there in order to find comfort: it is a mirror wherein humanity, in beholding itself, becomes once more heroic, magnanimous, disinterested; a singular purity, shrinking from the contamination of lucre as from filth, appears to be the characteristic glory of all.

I am endeavouring to describe to-day that epoch of unanimity, that holy period, when a whole nation, free from all party distinction, as yet a comparative stranger to the opposition of classes, marched together under a flag of brotherly love. Nobody can behold that marvellous unanimity, in which the self-same heart beat together in the breasts of twenty millions of men, without returning thanks to God. These are the sacred days of the world—thrice happy days for history. For my part, I have had my reward, in the mere narration of them. Never, since the composition of my Maid of Orleans, have I received such a ray from above, such a vivid inspiration from Heaven.   (from Preface)

THOMAS KEIGHTLEY

[1789–1872]

GERMAN IDEAS about myth were widely current in England and France during the first half of the nineteenth century: the work of Thomas Keightley will serve here to suggest how German approaches to myth were selected, adopted, and altered in England. Keightley's work also shows how the study of folklore branched off from the study of mythology, and, perhaps most importantly, Keightley's work shows us one last glimpse of the subject of mythology taken as a whole, before it was subdivided into more modern but less inclusive fields of study.

Keightley was born in Ireland. As his numerous sulky prefaces inform us, he took up literature for want of anything better to do, and spent a good deal of his life writing textbooks for school use. His serious interest in myth and his contributions to the study of myth began when he helped Thomas Crofton Croker with the latter's *Fairy Legends and Traditions of the South of Ireland* (1825). Keightley went on to write *The Fairy Mythology* (1828), a collection of fairy stories that was praised by Jacob Grimm and frequently reissued. Keightley was, to some extent, doing in England what the Grimms were doing in Germany, that is, localizing and nationalizing mythology. As Grimm argued in the preface to the second edition of the *Teutonic Mythology* (1844) and as Keightley argued in his *Tales and popular Fictions; their resemblance, and transmission from country to country* (1834), the crucial question in myth study was the relation of a given national mythology to the religion and mythology of other countries. Both Grimm and Keightley agreed that it was foolish to try to "derive all languages from the far-off Hebrew" and equally silly to try to derive all myths and religious systems from a single source. Both the Grimms and Keightley moved away from a concern with international connections, or universal systems of belief, or ideas about primitive or natural religion, toward the idea that myths were essentially a local phenomenon. As Grimm wrote, "every nation seems instigated by nature to isolate itself, to keep itself untouched by foreign ingredients." Similarly Keightley dismisses the idea that myths have been diffused from a single primal source by falling back on the enlightenment idea that since human nature is uniform, imaginative responses to nature, to men, and to events will be similar, and so the resulting myths and legends will be similar. This idea is now reinvoked as a way of sidestepping problems of diffusion and degeneration, and it leaves the student of myth free to concentrate on a local or a national mythology without having to connect it to a large ambitious scheme tracing it back to Indic, Pelasgic, Hebrew, or Egyptian origins.

From this localizing and nationalizing of myth study sprang the field of folklore. Richard Dorson has placed Keightley near the start of this field of study, and it may be remarked here that folklore could become a clearly defined field only during the romantic era, and is, perhaps, a predictable preoccupation of romantic scholarship. Folklore derives some of its leading assumptions from democratic movements and the new emphasis on the common man. Folklore is also connected with the new interest in oral tradition and in the early folkways of English, Irish, German, and other peoples. Rising from romantic concerns and premises, folklore in effect narrows and localizes mythology, separates it from theology and philosophy and classics, and moves it further away from the theoretical and speculative aspects of myth study.

Keightley's next book undertook the *Mythology of Ancient Greece and Italy* (1831). Here he adopts the scrupulously historical point of view advocated by K. O. Müller (and of course, by Lobeck and others), and, as the excerpt below shows, Keightley even refers to mythology as a "science." He presents the sophisticated many-sided interpretation Müller had put forward in his *Introduction to a Scientific System of Mythology,* and at the same time comes out very clearly against what he calls the theological interpretation of myth, which he associates with Vossius, Creuzer, Görres, and Schelling. Keightley claims that these last-named men regard mythology as "the theology of polytheistic religion," and that they seek "to reduce it to harmony with the original monotheism of mankind." Keightley goes on to make a sweeping indictment:

Vossius endeavours to show that the fables of heathenism were only a distortion of the revelations made to man by the true God, and,

at the present day, Görres, Creuzer and others, assigning a common source to the systems of India, Egypt, Greece and other countries, and regarding the East as the original birthplace of mythology, employ themselves in tracing the imagined channels of communication. . . . These men are justly denominated *mystics.*

Thus Keightley comes out in favor of the historical or pluralist approach to myth against any monistic or mystic or theological views. Keightley is still interested in the origins of myth, he still finds it necessary to be up on the scholarship, and while his book is essentially a handbook for university use, it is a scholarly piece of work. Handbooks having this scholarly tone and the historical bias were soon to be superceded by the general Victorian storybooks of Kingsley, Hawthorne, and Bulfinch, leaving scholarship exclusively to the classical dictionaries, while ideas about myth will soon have to be sought in anthropological, philosophical, or literary works. Keightley's is one of the last handbooks on mythology which functions as handbook, as scholarly reference book, and as a theoretical treatment all at the same time.

R.R.

REFERENCES Our texts are from Thomas Keightley, *The Fairy Mythology* (London, 1833), *Tales and Popular Fictions . . .* (London, 1834), and *The Mythology of Ancient Greece and Italy* (London, 1838). Keightley is discussed in Richard Dorson, *The British Folklorists, a History* (Chicago: University of Chicago Press, 1968), and excerpted and discussed in Richard Dorson, *Peasant Customs and Savage Myths, Selections from the British Folklorists* (Chicago: University of Chicago Press, 1968) vol. I.

KEIGHTLEY

FROM *The Fairy Mythology*

Origins of the Belief in Fairies

ACCORDING to a well known law of our nature, effects suggest causes; and another law, perhaps equally general, impels us to ascribe to the actual and efficient cause the attribute of intelligence. The mind of the deepest philosopher is thus acted upon equally with that of the peasant or the savage; the only difference lies in the nature of the intelligent cause at which they respectively stop. The one pursues the chain of cause and effect, and traces out its various links till he arrives at the great intelligent cause of all, however he may designate him; the other, when unusual phenomena excite his attention, ascribes their production to the immediate agency of some of the inferior beings recognised by his legendary creed.

The action of this latter principle must forcibly strike the minds of those who disdain not to bestow a portion of their attention on the popular legends and traditions of different countries. Every extraordinary appearance is found to have its extraordinary cause assigned; a cause always connected with the history or religion, ancient or modern, of the country, and not unfrequently varying with a change of faith.

The noises and eruptions of Aetna and Stromboli were, in ancient times, ascribed to Typhon or Vulcan, and at this day the popular belief connects them with the infernal regions. The noises resembling the clanking of chains, hammering of iron, and blowing of bellows, once to be heard in the island of Barrie, were made by the fiends whom Merlin had set to work to form the wall of brass designed to surround Caermarthen. The marks which natural causes have impressed on the solid and unyielding granite rock were produced, according to the popular creed, by the contact of the hero, the saint, or the god: masses of stone, resembling domestic implements in form, were the toys, or the corresponding implements of the heroes and giants of old. Grecian imagination ascribed to the galaxy or milky way an origin in the teeming breast of the queen of heaven: marks appeared in the petals of flowers on the occasion of a youth's or a hero's untimely death. The rose derived its present hue from the blood of Venus, as she hurried barefoot through the woods and lawns; while the professors of Islam, less fancifully, refer the origin of this flower to the moisture that exuded from the sacred person of their prophet. Under a purer form of religion, the cruciform stripes which mark the back and shoulders of the patient ass first appeared, according to the popular tradition, when the Son of God condescended to enter the Holy City, mounted on that animal; and a fish only to be found in the sea still bears the impress of the finger and thumb of the apostle, who drew him out of the waters of Lake Tiberias to take the tribute money that lay in his mouth. The repetition of the voice among the hills is in Norway and Sweden ascribed to the Dwarfs mocking the human speaker, while the more elegant fancy of Greece gave birth to Echo, a nymph who pined for love, and who still fondly repeats the accents that she hears. The magic scenery occasionally presented on the waters of the Straits of Messina is produced by the power of the Fata Morgana; the gossamers that float through the haze of an autumnal morning are woven by the ingenious dwarfs; the verdant circlets in the mead are traced beneath the light steps of the dancing elves; and St. Cuthbert forges and fashions the beads that bear his name, and that lie scattered along the shore of Lindisfarne.

In accordance with these laws, we find in every country a popular belief in different classes of beings distinct from men, and from the higher orders of divinities. These beings are believed to inhabit, in the caverns of earth, or the depths of the waters, a region of their own. They gradually excel mankind in power and in knowledge, and like them are subject to the inevitable laws of death, though after a more prolonged period of existence.

How these classes were first called into existence it is not easy to say; but as all the ancient systems of heathen religion were devised by philosophers for the instruction of rude tribes by appeals to their senses, we may suppose that the minds that peopled the skies with their thousands and tens of thousands of divinities gave birth also to the inhabitants of the field and flood, and that the numerous tales of their exploits and adventures are the production of poetic fiction or rude invention. It may farther be observed, that not unfrequently a change of religious faith has invested with dark and malignant attributes beings once the objects of love, confidence, and veneration.

It is not our intention in the following pages to treat of the awful or lovely deities of Olympus, Valhalla, or Merû. Our subject is less aspiring; and we confine ourselves to those beings who are our fellow inhabitants of earth, whose manners we aim to describe, and whose deeds we propose to record. We write of Fairies, Fays, Elves, *aut alio quo nomine gaudent* [or in whatever other name they rejoice].

(from Introduction)

FROM *Tales and Popular Fictions, Their Resemblance and Transmission*

CHAPTER I

MANY YEARS ago I chanced to read in a newspaper an interesting account of the loss of a ship; but in what part of the world it occurred, I am now unable to recollect. The narrative stated, that the crew and passengers saved themselves on two desert islets at some distance from each other. They remained for some time separate; at length they joined, and made their way to a friendly port. To their no small surprise, they found that during their state of separation they had fallen on precisely the same expedients for the supply of their wants. As they had been in a state of nearly total destitution, the vessel having gone down, these expedients were necessarily various and numerous, and many of them were remarkably ingenious.

This little narrative made a strong impression on my mind. I often reflected on it: I compared with it other phenomena as they presented themselves, and insensibly fell into the habit of viewing man as an inventive and independent, rather than a merely imitative being.

Aristotle—and his authority is high with me—asserts, in his Politics, that "forms of government, and most other things, have been invented over and over again, or rather an infinite number of times, in the long course of ages; for necessity would of itself teach such as were indispensable, and those relating to comfort and elegance would then follow of course." Of the truth, to a certain extent, of these words of the philosopher, I am firmly convinced; and I will freely confess, that I see little strength in the arguments for the original unity of mankind, founded on a similarity of manners, customs and social institutions; and am also inclined to reject these arguments, when brought forward in proof of migrations and colonisation. I know no proof of the former but the testimony of Scripture and physical characters; I admit no evidence of the latter but language and a constant and credible tradition.

Examples are always agreeable, and sometimes convincing; I will therefore give a few of the cases in which I am sceptical.

The similarity of form between the brazen casque of the Hellenic warrior and the featherhelm of the Polynesian chief, is to me no proof of the common origin of the Greeks and the South Sea islanders. A branch of olive might be the symbol of peace among the one people, and a branch of plantain among the other, and nought be proved thereby. The universal employment of the bow, the spear and the shield, affects me not. I see not why every tribe who dwelt on the shores of the sea or of lakes, or on the banks of rivers, may not have discovered the mode of constructing boats. The Egyptians, we are told, were brewers of beer; so also were the ancient Scandinavians; and it follows not that they borrowed from each other, or from a common instructor. Almost every people of the circle of the earth in which the vine is indigenous, appears to have discovered the art of making wine. Mining and the art of smelting metals may have been practised by tribes as remote in origin as in position. Alphabets, I suspect, are an invention to which more than one people may lay claim. . . . The mariner's compass may have been invented at Amalfi, though familiar to the Chinese from the most remote times. Finally, I cannot discern in the pyramidal form of the Pyramids of Egypt, the temple of Belus at Babylon, and the temples at Cholulu and elsewhere in Mexico, a proof of anything but of the common perception of the stability and convenience of that form.

The same is the case with religious and political institutions. Attic laws occur in the institutes of the Hindoo Menoo; and I do not thence infer any communication between Attica and Hindoostan. Ancient Egypt had its Feasts of Lamps, and China has its Feasts of Lanterns; yet I see no connexion between them. There were Vestals at Rome, and Virgins of the Sun at Cuzco, bound to chastity; yet it does not follow from thence that Peru derived its religion from Asia, or that, as I have seen it asserted, Rome was founded by a colony of gypsies from India. I could cite many more cases, but these may suffice.

A practice, which has been carried to a most ludicrous extent, is that of supposing that where two or more peoples have the same or a similar name, the one is a colony from the other. The Albanians of Epirus, and the Iberians of Spain, are confidently deduced from Mount Caucasus. Scoti happening to resemble Scythi, and Hiberni Iberi, what is called the ancient history of Ireland favours us with an account of the Scythic and Spanish origin of the Celts of that island, perfectly heedless of their community of language, manners and religion with those of Britain and Gaul.

(from pp. 1–5)

FROM *The Mythology of Ancient Greece and Italy*

CHAPTER I

Of Mythology in General

MYTHOLOGY is the science which treats of the *mythes,* or various popular traditions and legendary tales, current among a people and objects of general belief.

These mythes are usually the fabulous adventures of the imaginary beings whom the people worship; the exploits of the ancient heroes of the nation; the traditions of its early migrations, wars, and revolutions; the marvellous tales of distant lands brought home by mariners and travellers; and the moral or physical allegories of its sages and instructors.

The legends which compose a nation's mythology may be divided into two classes. The first will contain the true or fabulous EVENTS which are believed to have occurred either among the people itself, as its own adventures, or those of its princes and heroes, and which may therefore be called *domestic;* or those of ancient or distant nations, handed down by tradition or brought home by voyagers, and these we may entitle *foreign.* The second class will consist of DOCTRINES or articles of popular belief, and will comprise the earliest attempts of man to account for the various phenomena of the heavens and the earth, and the changes which appear to have taken place among them. These last are however, in the popular mode of viewing them, as much events as the former, as they were propounded by their inventors in the historic or narrative form.

The wonderful is usually a component part of mythology. The deities of popular belief are very frequent actors in its legends, which differ from ordinary tales and fables in this circumstance, and in that of their having been at one time matters of actual belief.

Mythology may therefore be regarded as the depository of the early religion of the people. It also stands at the head of their history, for the early history of every people, with whom it is of domestic origin, is mythic, its first personages and actions are chiefly imaginary. It is only gradually that the mist clears away, and real men and deeds similar to those of later times begin to appear; and the mythic period is frequently of long duration, the stream of history having to run a considerable way, before it can completely work off the marvellous and the incredible.

(from pp. 1, 2)

DAVID FRIEDRICH STRAUSS

[1808–1874]

DAVID FRIEDRICH STRAUSS'S *Life of Jesus* was published in 1835, and immediately became and remained perhaps the most famous (or notorious) example of the Higher Criticism of the Bible in the nineteenth century. Strauss's work may indeed be the first to spread the new ideas about "myth" in a popular way, beyond a small preserve of scholars, critics, and poets to a broad cultural audience. For Strauss used the "mythic" method to accomplish what seemed to this large, and at least nominally Christian, audience a shocking effort: the destruction of the historical reality underlying the stories of Christ. Jesus, for Strauss, was indeed still a historical person; but he claimed now that the historical testimony surrounding and supporting the Christ was not real history at all, but only myth—that is, the messianic prophecies, hopes, and legends the Hebrews had transferred easily, unthinkingly, and enthusiastically to the person of Jesus. Strauss's intention was not impious. He sought, as he said, to save the sacred truth in Christianity by separating it from the mythic encrustations it had gathered in the course of history. Such an approach, of course, was familiar since the eighteenth century. But Strauss's study had a tumultuous reception. The eminent Oxford religious scholar, Farrar, writing in 1862, said the effect of the *Life* in Germany (but through Europe as well) made the year 1835 in theology as memorable as the year 1848 in politics. Religious and phil-osophic thinkers, clergy and laymen of all persuasions took sides; translations, denunciations, and praise flooded into publication. But if Strauss's mythic deflation of Scripture seemed like a new bombshell to most, those more versed in the recent history of mythic thought saw it—as Edgar Quinet did—as less a beginning than a culmination of seventy years' mythologizing. Not a little of the clamor about Strauss's book came because for the first time the dangerous implications of the new mythicizing had publicly and aggressively moved beyond paganism and the Old Testament to invade the New Testament. But though in Strauss's treatment myth could seem to become a touchstone of religious authenticity, his work indeed accomplished considerable derogation of myth.

In the first part of the *Life,* Strauss explicitly describes his own approach as deriving from a long line of similar efforts. All of these began with the basic problem that religious authority is always a transmitted authority, which comes into conflict with skepticism as civilization progresses. Sooner or later, the earliest religious accounts begin to seem incompatible with a higher, purer conception of divinity, and attempts are made to reconcile these discrepancies. Strauss names Plato, Anaxagoras, the Stoics, and Euhemerus among the reinterpreters of the often barbarous or inadequate Greek religious myths; Philo's allegorizing is a similar purifying of the Old Testament by a Hebrew, as is Origen's allegorizing for Christianity. But while allegory reigned triumphant in medieval times, the Reformation and deism reopened the problem. In different ways, both sought to defend the spirit against the letter of Christianity. With deism, in fact, the truly modern period of biblical criticism begins; but obsessed with Scripture as disgracefully fabulous, and with religion as the work of priestcraft, deism remains only "barren."

But another approach, which Strauss sees as the root of his own, begins in eighteenth-century Germany. This new approach seeks a more sophisticated, more reliable understanding of the historical origins and truth of the Bible. And the leading method and guide here is derived from the new methods and information appearing in the new mythic studies. The first great pioneer Strauss names here is Johann G. Eichhorn (1752–1827), whose landmark mythic-historic exegetical work, *Urgeschichte* (1775), is—as Strauss notes—specifically an application to biblical religion of Heyne's mythic theories. Eichhorn studied with Heyne at Göttingen. The force of Heyne's teaching for his young pupil was that all primitive histories—pagan, Hebrew, or, with reservations, Christian—must be treated as a whole: what is admitted or denied of one applies to all. For Heyne, and for Eichhorn in his early work, this meant too that the religious truths of any early people are necessarily set forth in the sensuous imagery and poetic style of such "infant and unscientific" ages. But according to Strauss, Eichhorn arrived only at a halfway house about religion and myth. Eichhorn saw pagan and biblical religion as neither right nor wrong, but rather only as religion expressed "naturally": that is, naively, but in good faith. In this way, Eichhorn preserved the reality of historical "fact" embedded in myth and religion, but, according to Strauss, so emphasized history as the key that he lost

the "idea" more importantly dwelling there. This tendency appears with Paulus's *Commentary on the New Testament* (1800), where anything divine in the New Testament or in Jesus' life tended to disappear, with only historical raw matter remaining. But Eichhorn nevertheless went on—in his studies of the Old Testament (1780–1783) and the New (1804–1827)—to broach what Strauss sees as a more adequate approach, close to Strauss's own. Eichhorn now does not preserve the historic reality at the expense of the idea, but the opposite. Myth now embodies a crude but ultimate truth: Genesis 2 and 3, for example, are not ultimately stories about the effect of poison, but intuitive explanations of the coming of evil into the world.

After Eichhorn, myth becomes increasingly a central, but according to Strauss, a confusing key to the exegesis of Scripture. Gabler and the youthful Schelling continued Eichhorn's work; Semler saw myths in the stories of Samson and Esther; G. L. Bauer applied Heynean ideas comprehensively in his *Hebraic Mythology of the Old and New Testament* (1802), arguing that biblical narratives, like those of pagan myth, express legendary occurrences conveyed orally or in symbolic language. One difficulty for Strauss was that these and other mythic exegeses of the Bible made biblical history more homogeneous than it really was, and in another way found it hard to distinguish between purely symbolic myth and myth which only clothed events in historical form.

Before Strauss, Vater and more thoroughly De Wette try to clarify these problems, working especially with how inwardly coherent and consistent the biblical texts are. De Wette's approach goes back clearly to Astruc's study of Genesis (1753). Astruc emphasized how Genesis sometimes spoke of God as "Elohim," sometimes as "Jehovah"—often in the same text, as in Job. Astruc deduced from this internal evidence that Moses used different documents for his sources in the books attributed to him. Eichhorn later noted other discrepancies, and De Wette (a onetime pupil of Herder) in 1805 published a study arguing that the Pentateuch was compiled from three different sources, the "Elohist" as base, with the "Jehovist" and with Deuteronomy (itself a compilation) added later. De Wette was thus arguing that to rely on the biblical narrative as reliable history was misguided, for the historical "facts" of Scripture can be approached only through the documents. How then reconcile the textual discrepancies in language or chronologies? In his *Introduction to the New Testament* (1806–1807), De Wette proposed that the "history" of the Old Testament be seen as falling wholly into the domain of poetry and myth: indeed, the Pentateuch is a kind of Hebrew epic, mostly composed by the priests as a series of separate myths. If De Wette tended to turn Scripture into mythic poetry, he at least usefully demonstrated (in Strauss's view) the arbitrariness and inconsistency in seeing Scripture as now myth, now history, now poetry, now philosophy, now revelation.

Strauss takes up the mythic-religious interpretation of Scripture at this point. The problem facing him generally centered around the dubiousness of Christian "external" evidences, particularly as in the four Gospels. These Gospels resembled each other, suggesting to the orthodox, of course, that they were thus mutually corroborative—but suggesting to others more skeptical, however, that all the Gospels perhaps descended from some obscure original source, or else were compilations of earlier fragmentary writings or oral traditions, or that one or another Gospel gave rise to the rest. Moreover, Strauss was deeply influenced by the various German transcendental philosophies; and these, arguing that Spirit gave rise to all historic reality, offered a transcending solution to the problem of historical discrepancies. As Strauss ceaselessly stated, his effort was to give up history, if necessary, to save the Idea. A study of myth in Scripture becomes a way of accomplishing just this; myth now becomes the realm only of the *historically* religious, not the religious in its perfection.

Strauss thus seeks to separate what is only mythic from what is quintessentially religious. This needs to be done because all religion is at first necessarily permeated by mythic elements and modes of thought. Pagan religion—but also the Old and New Testament—can perceive the truth only indirectly, through imagery, not directly as idea. Myth is then religion in its early, incomplete stage, dependent on and confined to imagery, finiteness of understanding and expression. This is typical of the Jews as well. Impelled by their own messianic traditions, impelled further by an agonized historical moment in which they fervently desired to see this messianic hope fulfilled, they transferred all this to the figure of Jesus. This was not done fraudulently, either by the Jews or Jesus. It was, as Eichhorn had earlier said, only "natural" to a people in that stage of development.

In Strauss's view, myth becomes comprehensively, consistently "natural." Earlier mythologists had sometimes seen myth involved mainly in the miraculous birth and resurrection of Christ. But Strauss sees myth in a Herderian way, as always a communal expression rising from the continuing life of a *Volk*. Myth, a mythic people's religion, is therefore a necessary preparation for higher religion. For Strauss, all religious evolution begins in myth. The gods are at first formless, as for example with the Eskimo; then, the gods are assigned to the moon, stars, and so forth—a clear step forward and upward; then, the divine is made analogous to humanity; then, the mind rises still further to conceive the divine oneness; and finally, a philosophic conception of Spirit, wholly free of mythic crudeness, is achieved. In holding this view, of course, Strauss is conventional, for it is in one way or another the staple of both Schelling's and Hegel's idealist ascent to religious truth. What Strauss seems to mean by holding to "internal" evidences against "external" also seems a familiar part of the transcendental approach to Christianity. Only this internal evidence can suffice, can resist destructive criticism, can yield an unassailable philosophic conception of Spirit. Strauss was a self-declared disciple of Hegel, and Hegel's influence seems undeniable—though some serious students of Strauss see him as in fact opposed to Hegel. At any rate, the *Life of Jesus* ends with Strauss seeking to reconstitute Christian truth on an idealist basis.

Most of the *Life*—the long second part —is devoted to a formidable scholarly discussion of Jesus' life and teachings, with an eye to their source in Hebrew "myth." Strauss saw three kinds of myths clustering around Jesus: evangelical myths, those narratives dealing directly or otherwise with Jesus seen primarily as an "idea" of his disciples; pure myths, in which Jesus embodies Hebrew traditions; and historical myths, in which some distinct event or fact takes mythic form with the idea of the Christ in mind.

The uproar over Strauss's book has a later history. Strauss seemed to sink historical religion into myth, with myth as the poetic-spiritual expression of a *Volk,* but the "humanizing" of religion by tracing it back to myth would be carried further after Strauss. Ludwig Feuerbach, in his *Essence of Christianity* (1841) and *Essence of Religion* (1851), advanced a much more radical view of all religion as indeed finally only a human construction. Myth expressed not God's coming into this world, but man's making himself God; myth thus portrays not God or the gods, but is a self-portrayal of man's deepest, freest understanding of himself. Bruno Bauer extends and revises these ideas in Germany. In England, George Eliot became the first important translator of both Strauss and Feuerbach, linking them to the radical (but nonmythic) biblical criticism of Hennell in the same period.

Later still in the century with Nietzsche, Strauss could become a symbol less for bold anti-Christian criticism than for not going far enough to an "honest" atheism. In *Antichrist, Ecce Homo,* and *Untimely Meditations,* Nietzsche attacked Strauss along these lines, though an immediate cause was Strauss's later book, *The Old Faith and the New,* in which Strauss preached the "higher" criticism along with a kind of Darwinism and yet also piously hoped that belief is possible. By then, it might be said too that what Strauss had hoped to preserve of a "truer" Christianity by divesting it of myth, had become reversed. With thinkers like Nietzsche, myth now openly begins, in a quite modern voice, to argue itself higher than, but also poisoned by, "religion."

B.F.

REFERENCES   Our text is from *The Life of Jesus,* translated from 4th German edition (by Marian Evans), 3 vols. (London, 1846); an earlier translation is *Life of Jesus,* 4 vols. (Birmingham, 1842–44). For Strauss's account of the controversy, see his *Streitschriften zur Verteidigung meiner Schrift über das Leben Jesu* . . . Bd. I, Hefte 1–3 (Tübingen, 1838). For collected writings, *Gesammelte Schriften,* 12 Bde. (Bonn, 1876–78).

For commentary, see: Christian Hartlich and Walter Sachs, *Der Ursprung des Mythosbegriffes in der modernen Bibelwissenschaft* (Tübingen: Mohr, 1952) which is the most penetrating and exhaustive discussion of Strauss's relation to the mythologic tradition before him and his place in modern "demythologizing"; A. S. Farrar, *A Critical History of Free Thought* (New York: Appleton, 1882), especially Lecture VI on German mythic-theological criticism up to Strauss, and

Lecture VII on Strauss; Albert Schweitzer, *The Quest of the Historical Jesus* (London: Black, 1910); for selection of early response to *Das Leben Jesu,* see *Voices of the Church in reply to Dr. D. F. Strauss,* collected and composed by J. R. Beard (London, 1845), with excellent essays by Quinet and Julius Müller; Basil Willey, *Nineteenth Century Studies* (New York: Columbia University Press, 1949), Chap. 8 on George Eliot, Charles Hennell, Strauss, and Feuerbach. John Cairns, *Unbelief in the Eighteenth Century as contrasted with its earlier and later histories* (Edinburgh, 1881), for section on Strauss.

Strauss

FROM *The Life of Jesus*

Whilst the reality of the biblical revelation, together with the divine origin and supernatural character of the Jewish and Christian histories, were tenaciously maintained in opposition to the English deists by numerous English apologists, and in opposition to the Wolfenbüttel Fragmentist by the great majority of German theologians, there arose a distinct class of theologians in Germany, who struck into a new path. . . .

Eichhorn, in his critical examination of the Wolfenbüttel Fragments, directly opposes this rationalistic view to that maintained by the Naturalist. He agrees with the Fragmentist in refusing to recognize an immediate divine agency, at all events in the narratives of early date. The mythological researches of a Heyne had so far enlarged his circle of vision as to lead Eichhorn to perceive that divine interpositions must be alike admitted, or alike denied, in the primitive histories of all people. . . .

The flame and smoke which ascended from Mount Sinai, at the giving of the law, was merely a fire which Moses kindled in order to make a deeper impression upon the imagination of the people, together with an accidental thunderstorm which arose at that particular moment. . . .

Eichhorn was more reserved in his application of this mode of interpretation to the New Testament. Indeed, it was only to a few of the narratives in the Acts of the Apostles, such as the miracle of the day of Pentecost, the conversion of the Apostle Paul, and the many apparitions of angels, that he allowed himself to apply it. . . .

Later, however, Eichhorn himself declared that he had changed his opinion with regard to the second and third chapters of Genesis. He no longer saw in them an historical account of the effects of poison, but rather the mythical embodying of a philosophical thought; namely, that the desire for a better condition than that in which man actually is, is the source of all the evil in the world. Thus, in this point at least, Eichhorn preferred to give up the history in order to hold fast the idea, rather than to cling to the history with the sacrifice of every more elevated conception. For the rest, he agreed with Paulus and others in considering the miraculous in the sacred history as a drapery which needs only to be drawn aside, in order to disclose the pure historic form.

(from Intro., Sec. 6)

These biblical critics [Eichhorn and others] gave the following general definition of the mythus. It is the representation of an event or of an idea in a form which is historical, but, at the same time characterized by the rich pictorial and imaginative mode of thought and expression of the primitive ages. They also distinguished several kinds of mythi.

1st. *Historical mythi:* narratives of real events coloured by the light of antiquity, which confounded the divine and the human, the natural and the supernatural.

2nd. *Philosophical mythi:* such as clothe in the garb of historical narrative a simple thought, a precept, or an idea of the time.

3rd. *Political mythi:* historical and philosophical mythi partly blended together, and partly embellished by the creations of the imagination, in which the original fact or idea is almost obscured by the veil which the fancy of the poet has woven around it.

To classify the biblical mythi according to these several distinctions is a difficult task, since the mythus which is purely symbolical wears the semblance of history equally with the mythus which represents an actual occurrence. These critics however laid down rules by which the different mythi might be distinguished. The first essential is, they say, to determine whether the narrative have a distinct object, and what that object is. Where no object, for the sake of which the legend might have been invented, is discoverable, every one would pronounce the mythus

to be *historical*. But if all the principal circumstances of the narrative concur to symbolize a particular truth, this undoubtedly was the object of the narrative, and the mythus is *philosophical*. The blending of the historical and philosophical mythus is particularly to be recognised when we can detect in the narrative an attempt to derive events from their causes. In many instances the existence of an historical foundation is proved also by independent testimony; sometimes certain particulars in the mythus are intimately connected with known genuine history or bear in themselves undeniable and inherent characteristics of probability: so that the critic, while he rejects the external form, may yet retain the groundwork as historical. The *poetical* mythus is the most difficult to distinguish, and Bauer gives only a negative criterion. When the narrative is so wonderful on the one hand as to exclude the possibility of its being a detail of facts, and when on the other it discovers no attempt to symbolize a particular thought, it may be suspected that the entire narrative owes its birth to the imagination of the poet. Schelling particularly remarks on the unartificial and spontaneous origin of mythi in general.

(from Intro., Sec. 8)

Thus the mythical mode of interpretation was adopted not only in relation to the Old Testament, but also to the New; now, however, without its being felt necessary to justify such a step. Gabler has objected to the Commentary of Paulus, that it concedes too little to the mythical point of view, which must be adopted for certain New Testament narratives. For many of these narratives present not only those mistaken views of things which might have been taken by eye-witnesses, and by the rectification of which a natural course of events may be made out; but frequently, also, false facts and impossible consequences which no eye-witness could have related, and which could only have been the product of tradition, and must therefore be mythically understood.

The chief difficulty which opposed the transference of the mythical point of view from the Old Testament to the New, was this:—it was customary to look for mythi in the fabulous primitive ages only, in which no written records of events as yet existed; whereas, in the time of Jesus, the mythical age had long since passed away, and writing had become common among the Jews. Schelling had however conceded (at least in a note) that the term mythi, in a more extended sense, was appropriate to those narratives which, though originating in an age when it was usual to preserve documentary records, were nevertheless transmitted by the mouth of the people. Bauer in like manner asserted, that though a connected series of mythi, —a history which should be altogether mythical,—was not to be sought in the New Testament, yet there might occur in it single myths, either transferred from the Old Testament to the New, or having originally sprung up in the latter.

(from Intro., Sec. 9)

Thus, indeed, did the mythical view gain application to the biblical history: still the notion of the mythus was for a long time neither clearly apprehended nor applied to a due extent.

Not clearly apprehended. The characteristic which had been recognised as constituting the distinction between historical and philosophical mythi, however just that distinction might in itself be, was a kind which easily betrayed the critic back again into the scarcely abandoned

natural explanation. His task, with regard to historical mythi, was still to separate the natural fact—the nucleus of historical reality—from its unhistorical and miraculous embellishments. An essential difference indeed existed: the natural explanation attributed the embellishments to the opinion of the actors concerned, or of the narrator; the mythical interpretation derived them from tradition; but the mode of proceeding was left too little determined. If the Rationalist could point out historical mythi in the Bible, without materially changing his mode of explanation; so the Supernaturalist on his part felt himself less offended by the admission of historical mythi, which still preserved to the sacred narratives a basis of fact, than by the supposition of philosophical mythi, which seemed completely to annihilate every trace of historical foundation. It is not surprising, therefore, that the interpreters who advocated the mythical theory spoke almost exclusively of historical mythi; that Bauer, amongst a considerable number of mythi which he cites from the New Testament, finds but one philosophical mythus; and that a mixed mode of interpretation, partly mythical and partly natural, (a medley far more contradictory than the pure natural explanation, from the difficulties of which these critics sought to escape,) should have been adopted. Thus Bauer thought that he was explaining Jehovah's promise to Abraham as an historical mythus, when he admitted as the fundamental fact of the narrative, that Abraham's hopes of a numerous posterity were re-awakened by the contemplation of the star-sown heavens.

(from Intro., Sec. 10)

In adopting the mythical point of view as hitherto applied to Biblical history, our theologians had again approximated to the ancient allegorical interpretation. For as both the natural explanations of the Rationalists, and the jesting expositions of the Deists, belong to that form of opinion which, whilst it sacrifices all divine meaning in the sacred record, still upholds its historical character; the mythical mode of interpretation agrees with the allegorical, in relinquishing the historical reality of the sacred narratives in order to preserve to them an absolute inherent truth. The mythical and the allegorical view (as also the moral) equally allow that the historian apparently relates that which is historical, but they suppose him, under the influence of a higher inspiration known or unknown to himself, to have made use of this historical semblance merely as the shell of an *idea*—of a religious conception. The only essential distinction therefore between these two modes of explanation is, that according to the allegorical this higher intelligence is the immediate divine agency; according to the mythical, it is the spirit of a people or a community. (According to the moral view it is generally the mind of the interpreter which suggests the interpretation.) Thus the allegorical view attributes the narrative to a supernatural source, whilst the mythical view ascribes it to that *natural* process by which legends are originated and developed. To which it should be added, that the allegorical interpreter (as well as the moral) may with the most unrestrained arbitrariness separate from the history every thought he deems to be worthy of God, as constituting its inherent meaning; whilst the mythical interpreter, on the contrary, in searching out the ideas which are embodied in the narrative, is controlled by regard to conformity with the spirit and modes of thought of the people and of the age.

This new view of the sacred Scriptures was opposed alike by the orthodox and by the rationalistic party.

(from Intro., Sec. 12)

Seeing from what has already been said that the external testimony respecting the composition of our Gospels, far from forcing upon us the conclusion that they proceeded from eye-witnesses or well-informed contemporaries, leaves the decision to be determined wholly by internal grounds of evidence, that is, by the nature of the Gospel narratives themselves: we might immediately proceed from this introduction to the peculiar object of the present work, which is an examination of those narratives in detail. It may however appear useful, before entering upon this special inquiry, to consider the general question, how far it is consistent with the character of the Christian religion that mythi should be found in it, and how far the general construction of the Gospel narratives authorizes us to treat them as mythi. Although, indeed, if the following critical examination of the details be successful in proving the actual existence of mythi in the New Testament, this preliminary demonstration of their possibility becomes superfluous.

If with this view we compare the acknowledged mythical religions of antiquity with Hebrew and Christian, it is true that we are struck by many differences between the sacred histories existing in these religious forms and those in the former. Above all, it is commonly alleged that the sacred histories of the Bible are distinguished from the legends of the Indians, Greeks, Romans, &c., by their moral character and excellence. . . .

"But that which is incredible and inconceivable forms the staple of the heathen fables; whilst in the biblical history, if we only presuppose the immediate intervention of the Deity, there is nothing of the kind." Exactly, if this be presupposed. Otherwise, we might very likely find the miracles in the life of Moses, Elias, or Jesus, the Theophany and Angelophany of the Old and New Testament, just as incredible as the fables of Jupiter, Hercules, or Bacchus: presuppose the divinity or divine descent of these individuals, and their actions and fate become as credible as those of the biblical personages with the like presupposition. Yet not quite so, it may be returned. Vishnu appearing in his three first avatars as a fish, a tortoise, and a boar; Saturn devouring his children; Jupiter turning himself into a bull, a swan, &c.—these are incredibilities of quite another kind from Jehovah appearing to Abraham in a human form under the terebinth tree, or to Moses in the burning bush. This extravagant love of the marvellous is the character of the heathen mythology. A similar accusation might indeed be brought against many parts of the Bible, such as the tales of Balaam, Joshua, and Samson; but still it is here less glaring, and does not form as in the Indian religion and in certain parts of the Grecian, the prevailing character. What however does this prove? Only that the biblical history *might* be true, sooner than the Indian or Grecian fables; not in the least that on this account it *must* be true, and can contain nothing fictitious.

"But the subjects of the heathen mythology are for the most part such, as to convince us beforehand that they are mere inventions: those of the Bible such as at once to establish their own reality. A Brahma, an Ormusd, a Jupiter, without doubt never existed; but there still is a God, a Christ, and there have been an Adam, a Noah, an Abraham, a Moses."

Whether an Adam or a Noah, however, were such as they are represented, has already been doubted, and may still be doubted. Just so, on the other side, there may have been something historical about Hercules, Theseus, Achilles, and other heroes of Grecian story. Here, again, we come to the decision that the biblical history *might* be true sooner than the heathen mythology, but is not necessarily so. This decision however, together with the two distinctions already made, brings us to an important observation. How do the Grecian divinities approve themselves immediately to us as non-existing beings, if not because things are ascribed to them which we cannot reconcile with our idea of the divine? whilst the God of the Bible is a reality to us just in so far as he corresponds with the idea we have formed of him in our own minds. Besides the contradiction to our notion of the divine involved in the plurality of heathen gods, and the intimate description of their motives and actions, we are at once revolted to find that the gods themselves have a history; that they are born, grow up, marry, have children, work out their purposes, suffer difficulties and weariness, conquer and are conquered. It is irreconcilable with our idea of the Absolute to suppose it subjected to time and change, to opposition and suffering; and therefore where we meet with a narrative in which these are attributed to a divine being, by this test we recognize it as unhistorical or mythical.

It is in this sense that the Bible, and even the Old Testament, is said to contain no mythi. The story of the creation with its succession of each day's labour ending in a rest after the completion of the task; the expression often recurring in the farther course of the narrative, God repented of having done so and so;—these and similar representations cannot indeed be entirely vindicated from the charge of making finite the nature of the Deity, and this is the ground which has been taken by mythical interpreters of the history of the creation. And in every other instance where God is said to reveal himself exclusively at any definite place or time, by celestial apparition, or by miracle wrought immediately by himself, it is to be presumed that the Deity has become finite and descended to human modes of operation. It may however be said in general, that in the Old Testament the divine nature does not appear to be essentially affected by the temporal character of its operation, but that the temporal shows itself rather as a mere form, an unavoidable appearance, arising out of the necessary limitation of human, and especially of uncultivated powers of representation. It is obvious to every one, that there is something quite different in the Old Testament declarations, that God made an alliance with Noah, and Abraham, led his people out of Egypt, gave them laws, brought them into the promised land, raised up for them judges, kings, and prophets, and punished them at last for their disobedience by exile;—from the tales concerning Jupiter, that he was born of Rhea in Crete, and hidden from his father Saturn in a cave; that afterwards he made war upon his father, freed the Uranides, and with their help and that of the lightning with which they furnished him, overcame the rebellious Titans, and at last divided the world amongst his brothers and children. The essential difference between the two representations is, that in the latter, the Deity himself is the subject of progression, becomes another being at the end of the process from what he was at the beginning, something being effected in himself and for

his own sake: whilst in the former, change takes place only on the side of the world; God remains fixed in his own identity as the I AM, and the temporal is only a superficial reflection cast back upon his acting energy by that course of mundane events which he both originated and guides. In the heathen mythology the gods have a history: in the Old Testament, God himself has none, but only his people: and if the proper meaning of mythology be the history of gods, then the Hebrew religion has no mythology.

From the Hebrew religion, this recognition of the divine unity and immutability was transmitted to the Christian. The birth, growth, miracles, sufferings, death, and resurrection of Christ, are circumstances belonging to the destiny of the Messiah, above which God remains unaffected in his own changeless identity. The New Testament therefore knows nothing of mythology in the above sense. The state of the question is however somewhat changed from that which it assumed in the Old Testament: for Jesus is called the Son of God, not merely in the same sense as kings under the theocracy were so called, but as actually begotten by the divine spirit, or from the incarnation in his person of the divine *logos*. Inasmuch as he is one with the Father, and in him the whole fullness of the godhead dwells bodily, he is more than Moses. The actions and sufferings of such a being are not external to the Deity: though we are not allowed to suppose a *theopaschitic* union with the divine nature, yet still, even in the New Testament, and more in the later doctrine of the Church, it is a divine being that here lives and suffers, and what befalls him has an absolute worth and significance. Thus according to the above accepted notion of the mythus, the New Testament has more of a mythical character than the Old. But to call the history of Jesus mythical in this sense, is as unimportant with regard to the historical question as it is unexceptionable; for the idea of God is in no way opposed to such an intervention in human affairs as does not affect his own immutability; so that as far as regards this point, the gospel history, notwithstanding its mythical designation, might be at the same time throughout historically true. . . .

The result, then, however surprising, of a general examination of the biblical history, is that the Hebrew and Christian religions, like all others, have their mythi. And this result is confirmed, if we consider the inherent nature of religion, what essentially belongs to it and therefore must be common to all religions, and what on the other hand is peculiar and may differ in each. If religion be defined as the perception of truth, not in the form of an idea, which is the philosophic perception, but invested with imagery; it is easy to see that the mythical element can be wanting only when religion either falls short of, or goes beyond, its peculiar province, and that in the proper religious sphere it must necessarily exist.

It is only amongst the lowest and most barbarous people, such as the Esquimaux, that we find religion not yet fashioned into an objective form, but still confined to a subjective feeling. They know nothing of gods, of superior spirits and powers, and their whole piety consists in an undefined sentiment excited by the hurricane, the eclipse, or the magician. As it progresses however, the religious principle loses more and more of this indefiniteness, and ceasing to be subjective, becomes objective. In the sun, moon, mountains, animals, and other objects of the sensible world, higher powers are discovered and revered; and in proportion as the significance given to these

objects is remote from their actual nature, a new world of mere imagination is created, a sphere of divine existences whose relations to one another, actions, and influences, can be represented only after human analogy, and therefore as temporal and historical. Even when the mind has raised itself to the conception of the Divine unity, still the energy and activity of God are considered only under the form of a series of acts: and on the other hand, natural events and human actions can be raised to a religious significance only by the admission of divine interpositions and miracles. It is only from the philosophic point of view that the world of imagination is seen again to coincide with the actual, because the thought of God is comprehended to be his essence, and in the regular course itself of nature and of history, the revelation of the divine idea is acknowledged.

It is certainly difficult to conceive, how narratives which thus speak of imagination as reality can have been formed without intentional deceit, and believed without unexampled credulity; and this difficulty has been held an invincible objection to the mythical interpretation of many of the narratives of the Old and New Testament. If this were the case, it would apply equally to the Heathen legends; and on the other hand, if profane Mythology have steered clear of the difficulty, neither will that of the Bible founder upon it. I shall here quote at length the words of an experienced inquirer into Grecian mythology and primitive history, Otfried Müller, since it is evident that this preliminary knowledge of the subject which must be derived from general mythology, and which is necessary for the understanding of the following examination of the evangelic mythus, is not yet familiar to all theologians. "How," says

Müller, "shall we reconcile this combination of the true and the false, the real and ideal, in mythi, with the fact of their being believed and received as truth? The ideal, it may be said, is nothing else than poetry and fiction clothed in the form of narration. But a fiction of this kind cannot be invented at the same time by many different persons without a miracle, requiring, as it does, a peculiar coincidence of intention, imagination, and expression. . . . Hence an inventor of the mythus in the proper sense of the word is inconceivable. This reasoning brings us to the conclusion, that the idea of a deliberate and intentional fabrication, in which the author clothes that which he knows to be false in the appearance of truth, must be entirely set aside as insufficient to account for the origin of the mythus. Or in other words, that there is a certain necessity in this connexion between the ideal and the real, which constitutes the mythus; that the mythical images were formed by the influence of sentiments common to all mankind; and that the different elements grew together without the author's being himself conscious of their incongruity. . . ."

Perhaps it may be admitted that there is a possibility of unconscious fiction, even when an individual author is assigned to it, provided that the mythical consists only in the filling up and adorning some historical event with imaginary circumstances: but that where the whole story is invented, and not any historical nucleus is to be found, this unconscious fiction is impossible. Whatever view may be taken of the heathen mythology, it is easy to show with regard to the New Testament, that there was the greatest antecedent probability of this very kind of fiction having arisen respecting Jesus without any fraudulent intention. The expectation of a Messiah had grown up amongst the Israelitish people long before the time of Jesus, and just then had ripened to full maturity. . . . How could less be expected of the Messiah? Was it not necessary beforehand, that his life should be adorned with that which was most glorious and important in the lives of the prophets? Must not the popular expectation give him a share in the bright portion of their history, as subsequently the sufferings of himself and his disciples were attributed by Jesus when he appeared as the Messiah, to a participation in the dark side of the fate of the prophets (Matt. xxiii, 29 ff.; Luke xiii, 33 ff.; compare Matt. v. 12.)? Believing that Moses and all the prophets had prophesied of the Messiah (John v. 46; Luke iv. 21; xxiv. 27), it was as natural for the Jews, with their allegorizing tendency, to consider their actions and destiny as types of the Messiah, as to take their sayings for predictions. In general the whole Messianic era was expected to be full of signs and wonders.   (from Intro., Sec. 14)

The precise sense in which we use the expression *mythus,* applied to certain parts of the gospel history, is evident from all that has already been said; at the same time the different kinds and gradations of the mythi which we shall meet with in this history may here by way of anticipation be pointed out.

We distinguish by the name *evangelical mythus* a narrative relating directly or indirectly to Jesus, which may be considered not as the expression of a fact, but as the product of an idea of his earliest followers: such a narrative being mythical in proportion as it exhibits this character. The mythus in this sense of the term meets us, in the Gospel as elsewhere, sometimes in its pure form, constituting the substance of the narrative, and sometimes as an accidental adjunct to the actual history.

The pure mythus in the Gospel will be found to have two sources, which in most cases contributed simultaneously, though in different proportions, to form the mythus. The one source is, as already stated, the Messianic ideas and expectations existing according to their several forms in the Jewish mind before Jesus, and independently of him; the other is that particular impression which was left by the personal character, actions, and fate of Jesus, and which served to modify the Messianic idea in the minds of his people. The account of the Transfiguration, for example, is derived almost exclusively from the former source; the only amplification taken from the latter source being—that they who appeared with Jesus on the Mount spake of his decease. On the other hand, the narrative of the rending of the veil of the temple at the death of Jesus seems to have had its origin in the hostile position which Jesus, and his church after him, sustained in relation to the Jewish temple worship. Here already we have something historical, though consisting merely of certain general features of character, position &c.; we are thus at once brought upon the ground of the historical mythus.

The historical mythus has for its groundwork a definite individual fact which has been seized upon by religious enthusiasm, and twined around with mythical conceptions culled from the idea of the Christ. This fact is perhaps a saying of Jesus such as that concerning "fishers of men" or the barren figtree, which now appear in the Gospels transmuted into marvellous histories: or, it is perhaps a real transaction or event taken from his life; for instance, the mythical traits in the account of the baptism were built upon such a reality. Certain of the miraculous histories may likewise have had some foundation in natural occurrences, which the narrative has either exhibited in a supernatural light, or enriched with miraculous incidents.

(from Intro., Sec. 15)

Strauss's footnotes, often copiously referring to Scripture or to other biblical critics, have been omitted here.—Ed.

JOSEPH-ARTHUR, COMTE DE GOBINEAU

[1816–1882]

ARTHUR DE GOBINEAU is remembered mainly as one of the important early theorists of racism, and as the author of at least one superb novel, *Les Pléiades*. He is not usually considered an important mythic thinker or artist, and his explicit work on myth or early religion is indeed negligible. But in another and indirect way, Gobineau moves myth into some new and important involvements with modern political problems and movements. He helps instigate some recent and dangerous ties between race, myth, and politics. But in turn—and it is Gobineau's interest here—this makes painfully clear certain real implications of mythic thought in the early modern period.

The family history of Joseph-Arthur, Comte de Gobineau, is singularly important to his ideas. He was early influenced by his father's aristocratic pretensions and ultra–royalist and reactionary politics during the Bourbon Restoration. In 1830, when the Revolution in effect ruined his father's prospects, his mother moved to Switzerland, where the young Gobineau began to absorb a Germanized education and a quite romantic atmosphere. He was unusually studious, especially drawn to Oriental languages such as Sanskrit, Persian, and Arabic. In 1849, he became an assistant to his older friend Tocqueville during the latter's brief appointment as Foreign Minister. Thereafter to his death, Gobineau's career was in the French diplomatic corps, in Switzerland, Germany, Brazil, Greece, Persia, and else-

where. Two motifs mark Gobineau the private man: an overweening vanity about his aristocratic descent, and ambitions for scholarly and literary recognition. His writings run to more than thirty volumes, including long epic poems, essays, learned treatises, travels, romances, and histories. Among these is a book on Persian cuneiforms in 1864, attacking Grotefend and Rawlinson, but Gobineau's book was in turn contemptuously reviewed by competent philologians as mystic nonsense. He wrote on *Les Religions et les Philosophies dans l'Asie Centrale* (1865), a *Histoire des Perses* (1869), and several Oriental romances besides. His most important—and most influential—theoretical work bearing on myth is also his earliest, the *Essai sur l'Inégalité des Races Humaines* (2 volumes, 1853 and 1855).

The *Essay* is Gobineau's most explicit formulation of his racial ideas, and remains the basis for his later thought on the subject, as well as for his ostensibly historic work. Underneath a superficial systematic analysis and scholarly demonstration, Gobineau's racist theories are fairly simple. There are three primary races, the white, yellow, and black. Against any monogenetic theory, biblical or otherwise, Gobineau sees these as separate species. Not only does each race have absolutely different origins, but each had naturally different and unchangeable capacities. The white is wholly superior, while the black is irredeemably inferior and incapable indeed of any real advance into a civilized state. All human civilization results entirely from these innate abilities, just as all decline results from ignoring the inequality of racial gifts. The white race is destined to be the strongest, wisest, most superior, and dominant; the other races proportionately less. All decline is due then to diluting or tainting racial purity by permitting intermarriage or intrusion of alien racial culture and so on. Gobineau strictly denies that any external cause matters: neither environment, good or bad morality or government, nor finally even war or other accidents and misfortunes. In the course of history, this mixing of bloods has gone so far that none of the original racial stocks has preserved itself: even the highest, the Aryan-Teutonic, has virtually vanished since about 1000 A.D.

Gobineau's racial absolutism is a solution to a problem increasingly familiar and urgent since the early eighteenth century, when the vast variety of peoples, races, customs, and religions began to be widely known. But previously, race was not really ever fastened on as the right explanation. Christians looked to the authority of Genesis to support the unity of human species. Even those who held to multiple natural origins of man—the Pre-Adamite La Peyrère, or perhaps Voltaire or Hume—wrote with heterodox or anti-Christian motives, rather than in support of racism. The main line of rationalist theorizing on human differences stressed perfectibility or progress and the effect of environmental differences in causing differences of skin color or civilized progress. Reaction to the liberalizing movements after the French Revolution led in part to more intransigent racial ideas. This is particularly true as the movement to abolish slavery spread. Antiabolitionists often held deterministic ideas about race—indeed, the first translation of Gobineau's *Essay* was in 1856, by two southern American defenders of slavery, Josiah Nott and H. Hotz.

Gobineau locates himself explicitly in this general opposition to the spreading enthusiasm for what he considered degenerate democracy, modern softness, and self-interest. Such an angry and wounded awareness of modern decadence always feeds Gobineau's racist theories. His theory of superior and inferior races is paralleled by a theory of natural aristocrats and natural inferiors—also on the basis of blood alone, aside from achievement or lack of it. Gobineau's own fanciful ancestral history, worked on for years, *Histoire d'Ottar Jarl* (1879), shows his own descent from an ebullient ninth-century Viking and no less a personage finally than Odin. His Persian history is similarly a genealogy of that people, seen as a losing struggle of its white against its worse racial elements. If Gobineau's scholarship was arbitrary and his theories simplistic, his employment of myth was prophetic in a sinister way. Racism became one of the new explanations of the ever-widely discussed problem of modern decadence, and more attractive as modern political and social problems changed and spread bewilderingly.

Myth enters Gobineau's thought in two ways at least. First, most simply, there is his seemingly hard-headed scholarship on ancient religion, history, and culture, partly drawn from his own firsthand travel observations, from some linguistic knowledge, and from any other learning that seemed to apply, all yielding a scientific aura to his cranky theories. But these theories, too, found support in the already widespread enthusiasm for myth. And just as a Christian-romantic mythologist, such as Friedrich Schlegel or Görres, could appeal back beyond orthodox Christian teachings to some primordial truth that could be grasped only poetically, intuitively, or mystically, so Gobineau appeals back beyond mere politics, history, or environment to primordial race and blood as a higher truth. This is Gobineau's version of the ultimate mythologic primal moment or energy. The direct influence of mythologists on Gobineau is not the issue here, but rather the whole atmosphere, availability, and persuasiveness of the new mythic thinking. Gobineau's ideas can be seen as one more drastic narrowing of the Herderian-romantic exaltation of nation and *Volk* as the vessel for modern spiritual revival through myth. Gobineau directly applies this to immediate historical needs and problems.

Gobineau's racism brings sharply to sight the irrationalism always implicit—if by no means dominant—in German mythic thought. For racial determinism in fact largely denies the possibility of rational political, moral, or educational hopes in human life. Gobineau's friend and correspondent, Tocqueville, saw this with his usual penetration: after so much political tumult, so many exaggeratedly awakened and disappointed hopes, Tocqueville said, we think we can do nothing, that struggle and effort are useless, and that "our blood, muscles and nerves will always be stronger than our will and courage." Gobineau's racism, said Tocqueville, was only disguised fatality, "a vast limitation, if not complete abolition, of human liberty." That indictment perhaps always haunted fervent romantic appeals to mythic forces and causes, but never more so than after Gobineau and others made the appeal explicit.

Gobineau never gained the academic recognition he sought, but he became widely successful in another way. Wagner was one of his admirers (dedicating an edition of his complete work to Gobineau). In 1894, a German disciple, Ludwig Schemann, founded the *Gobineau-Vereinigung*. No French edition of the *Essay* appeared between 1884 and 1968, but five German editions appeared between 1933 and 1940. How accurately these German exaltations reflected Gobineau's own complex motives and his not infrequent protests against racial arrogance—he after all thought no modern nation was other than mongrelized—may be left aside here. He certainly did not by any means go so far as his admirers; but his admirers, like Wagner, found him a rich resource in further wedding myth to race for political purposes.

B.F.

REFERENCES   Our text is from *The Inequality of Human Races,* translated by Adrian Collins, Introduction by Oscar Levy (London: Heinemann, 1915). For commentary, see: Arnold H. Rowbotham, *The Literary Works of Count de Gobineau* (Paris: Champion, 1929); Ludwig Schemann's books on Gobineau include: *Gobineau: Eine Biographie* (Strasbourg, 1913), *Gobineau und die deutsche Kultur* (Leipzig, 1910), *Gobineaus Rassenwerk* (Stuttgart, 1910); Ernest Seillière, *Le Comte de Gobineau et l'Aryanisme Historique* (Paris: Plon, 1903); Maurice Lange, *Le Comte de Gobineau, Études biographiques et critiques,* 2 vols. (Strasbourg, 1913); Raymond Schwab, *La Renaissance orientale* (Paris: Payot, 1950), especially pp. 450–458; Janine Buenzel, *La formation de la pensée de Gobineau* (Paris, 1968); *Correspondance entre Alexis de Tocqueville et Arthur de Gobineau, 1843–1859,* publiée par L. Schemann (Paris: Plon, 1908); Jean Gaulmier, *Spectre du Gobineau* (Paris: Pauvert, 1965); and see *Études gobiniennes,* a collection of studies whose first number appeared in 1966; Michael D. Biddiss, *Gobineau. Selected Political Writings* (London: Jonathan Cape, 1970), with insightful Introduction.

GOBINEAU

FROM *The Inequality of Human Races*

THIS WAS a hope I myself cherished for a brief moment, and I should like to have at once flung back in the teeth of History its accusations and gloomy forebodings, had I not been suddenly struck with the devastating thought, that in my hurry I was putting forward something that was absolutely without proof. I began to look about for proofs, and so, in my sympathy for the living, was more and more driven to plumb to their depths the secrets of the dead.

Then, passing from one induction to another, I was gradually penetrated by the conviction that the racial question overshadows all other problems of history, that it holds the key to them all, and that the inequality of the races from whose fusion a people is formed is enough to explain the whole course of its destiny. . . .

Recognizing that both strong and weak races exist, I preferred to examine the former, to analyse their qualities, and especially to follow them back to their origins. By this method I convinced myself at last that everything great, noble, and fruitful in the works of man on this earth, in science, art, and civilization, derive from a single starting-point, is the development of a single germ and the result of a single thought; it belongs to one family alone, the different branches of which have reigned in all the civilized countries of the universe.

(from Author's Dedication—1854)

In face of the difficulties offered by the most liberal interpretation of the Biblical text, and the objection founded on the law regulating the generation of hybrids, it is impossible to pronounce categorically in favour of a multiplicity of origins for the human species.

We must therefore be content to assign a lower cause to those clear-cut varieties of which the main quality is undoubtedly their permanence, a permanence that can only be lost by a crossing of blood. We can identify this cause with the amount of climatic energy possessed by the earth at a time when the human race had just appeared on its surface. There is no doubt that the forces that inorganic nature could bring into play were far greater then than anything we have known since, and under their pressure racial modifications were accomplished which would now be impossible. Probably, too, the creatures exposed to these tremendous forces were more liable to be affected by them than existing types would be. Man, in his earliest stages, assumed many unstable forms; he did not perhaps belong, in any definite manner, to the white, red, or yellow variety. The deviations that transformed the primitive characteristics of the species into the types established to-day were probably much smaller than those that would now be required for the black race, for example, to become assimilated to the white, or the yellow to the black. On this hypothesis, we should have to regard Adamite man as equally different from all the existing human groups; these would have radiated all around him, the distance between him and any group being double that between one group and another. How much of the primitive type would the peoples of the different races have subsequently retained? Merely the most general characteristics of our species, the vague resemblances of shape common to the most distant groups, and the possibility of expressing their wants by articulate sounds —but nothing more. The remaining features peculiar to primitive man would have been completely lost, by the black as well as the non-black races; and although we are all originally descended from him, we should have owed to outside influences everything that gave us our distinctive and special character. Henceforth the human races, the product of cosmic forces as well as of the primitive Adamic stock, would be very slightly, if at all, related to each other. The power of giving birth to fertile hybrids would certainly be a perpetual proof of original connexion; but it would be the only one. As soon as the primal differences of environment had given each group its isolated character, as a possession for ever—its shape, features, and colour—from that moment the link of primal unity would have been suddenly snapped; the unity, so far as influence on racial development went, would be actually sterile. The strict and unassailable permanence of form and feature to which the earliest historical documents bear wit-

ness would be the charter and sign-manual of the eternal separation of races.

(from pp. 138–140)

Such is the lesson of history. It shows us that all civilizations derive from the white race, that none can exist without its help, and that a society is great and brilliant only so far as it preserves the blood of the noble group that created it, provided that this group itself belongs to the most illustrious branch of our species.

Of the multitude of peoples which live or have lived on the earth, ten alone have risen to the position of complete societies. The remainder have gravitated round these more or less independently, like planets round their suns. If there is any element of life in these ten civilizations that is not due to the impulse of the white races, any seed of death that does not come from the inferior stocks that mingled with them, then the whole theory on which this book rests is false. On the other hand, if the facts are as I say, then we have an irrefragable proof of the nobility of our own species. Only the actual details can set the final seal of truth on my system, and they alone can show with sufficient exactness the full implications of my main thesis, that peoples degenerate only in consequence of the various admixtures of blood which they undergo; that their degeneration corresponds exactly to the quantity and quality of the new blood, and that the rudest possible shock to the vitality of a civilization is given when the ruling elements in a society and those developed by racial change have become so numerous that they are clearly moving away from the homogeneity necessary to their life, and it therefore becomes impossible for them to be brought into harmony and so acquire the common instincts and interests, the common logic of existence, which is the sole justification for any social bond whatever. There is no greater curse than such disorder, for however bad it may have made the present state of things, it promises still worse for the future.

NOTE.—The "ten civilizations" mentioned in the last paragraph are as follows. . . .

I. The Indian civilization, which reached its highest point round the Indian Ocean, and in the north and east of the Indian Continent, south-east of the Brahmaputra. It arose from a branch of a white people, the Aryans.

II. The Egyptians, round whom collected the Ethiopians, the Nubians, and a few smaller peoples to the west of the oasis of Ammon. This society was created by an Aryan colony from India, that settled in the upper valley of the Nile.

III. The Assyrians, with whom may be classed the Jews, the Phoenicians, the Lydians, the Carthaginians, and the Hymiarites. They owed their civilizing qualities to the great white invasions which may be grouped under the name of the descendants of Shem and Ham. The Zoroastrian Iranians who ruled part of Central Asia under the names of Medes, Persians, and Bactrians, were a branch of the Aryan family.

IV. The Greeks, who came from the same Aryan stock, as modified by Semitic elements.

V. The Chinese civilization, arising from a cause similar to that operating in Egypt. An Aryan colony from India brought the light of civilization to China also. Instead however of becoming mixed with black peoples, as on the Nile, the colony became absorbed in Malay and yellow races, and was reinforced, from the north-west, by a number of white elements, equally Aryan but no longer Hindu.

VI. The ancient civilization of the Italian peninsula, the cradle of Roman culture. This was produced by a mixture of Celts, Iberians, Aryans, and Semites.

VII. The Germanic races, which in the fifth century transformed the Western mind. These were Aryans.

VIII–X. The three civilizations of America, the Alleghanian, the Mexican, and the Peruvian.

Of the first seven civilizations, which are those of the Old World, six belong, at least in part, to the Aryan race, and the seventh, that of Assyria, owes to this race the Iranian Renaissance, which is, historically, its best title to fame. Almost the whole of the Continent of Europe is inhabited at the present time by groups of which the basis is white, but in which the non-Aryan elements are the most numerous. There is no true civilization among the European peoples, where the Aryan branch is not predominant.

In the above list no negro race is seen as the initiator of a civilization. Only when it is mixed with some other can it even be initiated into one.

Similarly, no spontaneous civilization is to be founded among the yellow races; and when the Aryan blood is exhausted stagnation supervenes. (from pp. 210–212)

RICHARD WAGNER

[1813–1883]

WITH WAGNER, the romantic epoch of myth may be said to reach an ending and a new beginning. In obvious ways Wagner descends from romantic views linking myth and art: for him, too, true art must rise from primordial and communal depths, from the *Volk,* and all true art will strive to regain mythic unity and totality; for him also, modern attempts to create myth cannot naively go back to Greece or India, but must re-create myth on a totally modern and an explicitly national basis. But Wagner uses these and other romantic commonplaces with quite new emphases. Wagner is thus not merely a profoundly original composer who simply happened to use Germanic or other mythic themes. On the contrary, it is perhaps more true to say that the *idea* of myth helped him understand and reconceive what musical drama might newly accomplish. Wagner's view of opera as the supreme and all-embracing dramatic-musical-mythic form was one fulfillment of the universalizing mythopoetic visions of romantic theorists such as Friedrich Schlegel. And Wagnerian music fulfilled other romantic longings for a language beyond language. Wagner also spectacularly accomplished romantic hopes to create a powerful *public* art of myth. Wagner rightly saw his operatic mythmaking always as also a political act—at once destructively and regeneratively revolutionary. The performance of his *Ring of the Nibelungs* in 1876 has often been cited as the first great expression of the recently unified German nation. With Wagner, mythic art ceases to be aesthetically or philosophically esoteric or special, and gains its first truly popular spread and influence. Nietzsche called Wagner the supreme artist of a mass democratic age.

In his early career, Wagner was musically and culturally cosmopolitan, admiring Beethoven but also French opera, and sympathetic to the antipatriotic ideals of Heine and the "Young Germany" political group; and he was much influenced by Feuerbachian atheism. About 1843, his position changed: he became an ardent nationalist and began to plan an ambitious new kind of opera. Between 1843 and 1848, he sketched and largely completed *Tannhäuser* and *Lohengrin,* conceived *Der Meistersinger* and *Parsifal,* and wrote the poem for *Siegfried's Death.* His subsequent career is famous: his part in the 1848 Revolution, and then in the 1849 Dresden Revolution, followed by an enforced eleven-year exile during which he finished much of the *Ring* cycle and also *Tristan und Isolde;* the dogged fight to have his work performed; and his final apotheosis in Bayreuth, where he died.

Wagner wrote prolifically (and repetitiously) about music, myth, and their necessary relation. His most important essays on these subjects were written in the first years of exile, 1849–1850: *Art and Revolution, The Art-Work of the Future,* and *Opera and Drama.* In these works he makes clear his enormous disgust with what he sees as the mob-ridden, commercialized, sterile, and modish art and culture of his time. A revolution is needed, but one going far beyond such direct but finally futile political acts as those of 1848 and 1849. Art alone can save us from our civilized barbarism; modern spiritual decadence has advanced so far that significant change must go far deeper than surface reform. What is needed then is a genuinely ennobling public art, but to be this, art must rise from the people, rather than be imposed on them. Throughout his life, in essay after essay, Wagner expatiates on the holiness and primordial creativity of the *Volk*. The *Volk* is in fact the true artist of the future, as it was in the past.

Like others earlier, Wagner exalts the organic and national against all social artifice, abstraction, and rootlessness; but he stresses something else as well. He declares the *Volk* to be genuine only as it yields to "Necessity." Necessity here is shorthand for several related ideas—for example, the implacable claims of Fate, or the unconscious, or Will, or nirvana. The *Volk* is the "vice-regent" of Necessity, a classless, blissful communality bathed in selfless fellowship and oneness. A true mythic art will make us again "knowers of the unconscious, willers of the unwilfull. . . ." Wagner preaches the end of "unit-man" by renunciation, by the dissolving of selfhood into some universal ocean of love or death. And he welcomes the possible apocalyptic breakdown of modern culture as an unparalleled opportunity to strip away superficial external causes and regain a mythic condition. Certainly it is part of Wagner's daring and originality to stress what other admirers of Nordic myth usually bypassed—the extraordinary pessimism of Germanic mythology: the slaughter predicted at the end of things, the death of the gods. Here too is at least one important reason for Wagner's enthusiasm for Buddhism, as he first learned of it through

reading Schopenhauer in 1854. What must especially have attracted Wagner was Schopenhauer's "negation of will," the "absolute cessation of personal consciousness," which Wagner soon claimed was "most purely and significantly expressed in the most sacred and oldest religion of the human race, the doctrine of the Brahmins and . . . Buddhism." One direct result of reading Schopenhauer on Buddhist myth was the conception of *Tristan und Isolde,* which blends Christian and Buddhist longing and renunciation. Indeed, as Wagner put it, Christianity is only "pure and unalloyed Buddhism." Schopenhauer (and Burnouf) also gave Wagner the idea for an opera based directly on Buddhist myths, *The Conquerors,* sketched in 1856, but never finished.

The greatest artistic expression of mythic truth for Wagner is in Greek tragedy. Greek drama is a total art-work (such as he conceived his own), placing myth at the center and giving expression at once to all of life through music, dance, speech, and gesture. Even the greatest modern tragedy, as in Shakespeare, had accepted fragmentation and thus limitation. Opera, newly conceived according to the "spirit of music," will realize the total spirit of myth modernity needs. But to do this, Wagner sees himself fighting against two sides: against the claim that the arts must remain apart, and against the scholarly claim to explain myth through history or mere reason. As an art, the Wagnerian opera will not represent, but embody; it will render its ideas in an autonomous and untranslatable emotional language, a magical, nonlogical "enchantment." His aesthetic views help anticipate and prepare later symbolism, and help show again how romantic mythopoesis—as was already clear in Goethe or Moritz—quickly led to symbolist theories.

In his unceasing polemic against historical schools of mythology, Wagner is similarly fighting to preserve mythic autonomy and power, and also the artist's claim to interpret myth on a higher intuitive level. Wagner's composing of his own poetic versions of myth for his operas is one sign of this. His *Tannhäuser* poem is made of two historically distinct legends, one dealing with the visit to Venusberg, the other with medieval song-competitions. Thus, too, he says he learned to understand the purer, truer myth of *Lohengrin,* beyond what medieval Catholic distortions represented. Thus he equates the Nibelungen "Hoard" with the Christian Grail, and draws the *Ring* cycle as much from the primitive *Edda* as from the more historically defined medieval *Nibelungenlied.*

Beyond earlier ardent but vague plans to regenerate a nation through its own myths, Wagner treats his operatic mythologizing as if it were indeed an act of political revolution—and in the most sinister way, later German consequences have often seemed to justify Wagner's hopes. Indeed, it is perhaps fair to say that after Wagner mythopoesis is not only a possible cure for modern problems, but an important cause of those problems. At the same time, needless to say, beyond the simplistic shrillness of his theories, and their often derivative quality, Wagner's music preserves its high artistic stature and force, and transforms his mythic formulas into art with incomparable subtlety and richness.

B.F.

REFERENCES Our texts are from *Richard Wagner's Prose Works,* translated by W. A. Ellis, 8 vols. (New York: Broude, 1966, reprinted from the London: Routledge & Kegan Paul 1893–1899 edition). For Wagner's account of his introduction to Buddhism through Schopenhauer, see *My Life,* 2 vols. (New York: Dodd, Mead, 1911), II, 614–616, and *Wagner on Music and Drama,* edited by A. Goldman and E. Sprinchorn (New York: E. P. Dutton, 1964), pp. 271–278.

For commentary, see: Fritz Strich, *Die Mythologie in der deutschen Literatur von Klopstock bis Wagner,* 2 vols. (Halle, 1910), especially II, 450–478; Charles Baudelaire, "Richard Wagner and Tannhauser in Paris," in *Baudelaire as a Literary Critic,* introduced and translated by L. B. Hyslop and F. E. Hyslop, Jr. (University Park: Pennsylvania State University, 1964), originally published April 1, 1861; Guy R. Welbon, *The Buddhist Nirvana and its Western Interpreters* (Chicago: University of Chicago, 1968), pp. 171–184 for an excellent, concise account; R. Donington, *Wagner's "Ring" and its Symbols; the Music and the Myth* (New York: St. Martin's Press, 1963); Leon Stein, *The Racial Thinking of Richard Wagner* (New York: Philosophical Library, 1950); K. Hildbrandt, *Wagner and Nietzsche im Kampf gegen das 19. Jahrhundert* (Breslau, 1924); *The Volsunga Saga, Translated from the Icelandic by Eiriker Magnusson and William Morris . . . Supplemented with Legends of the Wagner Trilogy by Jessie L. Weston, and Old Norse Sagas Kindred to the Volsung and Nibelung Tales* (London and New York: Norroena Society, 1905); Elliott Zuckerman, *The First Hundred Years of Wagner's Tristan* (New York: Columbia University Press, 1964), esp. Chap. 1, "Schopenhauer, the Myth, and the Music"; Johannes Bertram, *Mythos, Symbol, Idee in Richard Wagners Musikdramen* (Hamburg, 1956); Houston Stewart Chamberlain, *Richard Wagner* (Munich, 1896), for Wagner interpretation by later admirer of Nazism.

WAGNER

FROM *Art and Revolution*

WHEN, in the feverish excitement of the year 1849, I gave vent to an appeal such as that contained in the immediately succeeding essay: *"Art and Revolution,"* I believe that I was in complete accord with the last words of this summons of the grey-headed historian. I believed in the Revolution, and in its unrestrainable necessity, with certainly no greater immoderation than Carlyle: only, I also felt that I was called to point out to it the way of rescue. Far though it was from my intent to define the New, which should grow from the ruins of a sham-filled world, as a fresh *political* ordering: I felt the rather animated to draw the outlines of the *Artwork* which should rise from the ruins of a sham-bred *Art*. To hold this Art-work up to Life itself, as the prophetic mirror of its Future, appeared to me a weightiest contribution toward the work of damming the flood of Revolution within the channel of the peaceful-flowing stream of Manhood. I was bold enough to prefix the following motto to the little pamphlet: "When Art erst held her peace, State-wisdom and Philosophy began: when now both Statesman and Philosopher have breathed their last, let the Artist's voice again be heard."

(I, 24)

But only *Revolution,* not slavish *Restoration,* can give us back that highest Artwork. The task we have before us is im-measurably greater than that already accomplished in days of old. If the Grecian Art-work embraced the spirit of a fair and noble nation, the Art-work of the Future must embrace the spirit of a free mankind, delivered from every shackle of hampering nationality; its racial imprint must be no more than an embellishment, the individual charm of manifold diversity, and not a cramping barrier. We have thus quite other work to do, than to tinker at the resuscitation of old Greece. Indeed, the foolish restoration of a sham Greek mode of art has been attempted already,—for what will our artist not attempt, to order? . . .

It is for Art therefore, and Art above all else, to teach this social impulse its noblest meaning, and guide it toward its true direction. Only on the shoulders of this great social movement can true Art lift itself from its present state of civilised barbarism, and take its post of honour. Each has a common goal, and the twain can only reach it when they recognise it jointly. This goal is *the strong fair Man,* to whom *Revolution* shall give his *Strength,* and *Art* his *Beauty!* . . .

. . . And as the Knowledge of all men will find at last its religious utterance in the one effective Knowledge of free united manhood: so will all these rich developments of Art find their profoundest focus in the Drama, in the glorious Tragedy of Man. The Tragedy will be the feast of all mankind; in it,—set free from each conventional etiquette,—free, strong, and beauteous man will celebrate the dolour and delight of all his love, and consecrate in lofty worth the great Love-offering of his Death. (I, 53–58)

FROM *The Art-Work of the Future*

THE GREAT instinctive errors of the People—which found their earliest utterance in Religion, and then became the starting-points of arbitrary speculation and system-making, in Theology and Philosophy—have reared themselves, in these Sciences and their coadjutrix and adopted sister, Statecraft, to powers which make no less a claim than to govern and ordain the world and life by virtue of their innate and divine infallibility. Irrevocably, then, would Error reign in destructive triumph throughout eternity: did not the same life-force which blindly bore it, once more effectually annihilate it, by virtue of its innate, natural Necessity; and that so decisively and palpably, that Intellect, with all its arrogant divorce from Life, can see at last no other refuge from actual insanity, than in the unconditional acknowledgment of this only definite and visible force. And this vital force is—The Folk (*das Volk*).—

Who is then the Folk?—It is absolutely necessary that, before proceeding further, we should agree upon the answer to this weightiest of questions.

"The Folk," was from of old the inclusive term of *all the units* which made up the total of a *commonality*. In the beginning, it was the family and the tribe; next, the tribes united by like speech into a nation. Practically, by the Roman world-dominion which engulfed the nations, and theoretically, by the Christian religion which admitted of naught but men, *i.e.* no racial, but only *Christian* men—the idea of "the People" has so far broadened out, or even evaporated, that we may either include in it mankind in general, or, upon the arbitrary political hypothesis, a certain, and generally the propertyless portion of the Commonwealth. But beyond a frivolous, this term has also acquired an ineradicable *moral* meaning; and on account of this it is, that in times of stir and trouble all men are eager to number themselves among the People. . . .

The "Folk" is the epitome of all those men *who feel a common and collective Want*. To it belong, then, all of those who recognise their individual want as a collective want, or find it based thereon; ergo, all those who can hope for the stilling of their want in nothing but the stilling of a common want, and therefore spend their whole life's strength upon the stilling of their thus acknowledged common want. For only that want which urges to the uttermost, is genuine Want; but this Want alone is the force of true Need (*"Bedürfniss"*); but a common and collective need is the only true Need; but only he who feels within him a true Need, has a right to its assuagement; but only the assuagement of a genuine Need is Necessity; and it is *the Folk alone that acts according to Necessity's behests,* and therefore irresistibly, victoriously, and right as none besides.

Who now are they who belong *not* to this People, and who are its sworn foes?

All those *who feel no Want;* whose lifespring therefore consists in a need which rises not to the potence of a Want, and thus is artificial, untrue, and egoistic; and not only is not embraced within a common Need, but as the empty need of preserving superfluity—as which alone can one conceive of need without the force of want—is diametrically opposed to the collective Need. . . .

Want will cut short the hell of Luxury; it will teach the tortured, Need-lacking spirits whom this hell embraces in its bounds the simple, homely need of sheer human, physical hunger and thirst; but in fellowship will it point us to the health-giving bread, the clear sweet springs of Nature; in fellowship shall we taste their genuine joys, and grow up in communion to veritable men. In common, too, shall we close the last link in the bond of holy Necessity; and the brother-kiss that seals this bond, will be the *mutual Art-work of the Future.* But in this, also, our great redeemer and well-doer, Necessity's vice-regent in the flesh,—*the Folk,* will no longer be a severed and peculiar class; for in this Art-work we shall be *one,*—heralds and supporters of Necessity, knowers of the unconscious, willers of the unwilful, betokeners of Nature,—*blissful men.* . . .

Not ye wise men, therefore, are the true inventors, but the Folk; for Want it was, that drove it to invention. All great inventions are the People's deed; whereas the devisings of the intellect are but the exploitations, the derivatives, nay, the splinterings and disfigurements of the great inventions of the Folk. Not ye, invented *Speech,* but the Folk; ye could but spoil its physical beauty, break its force, mislay its inner understanding, and painfully explore the loss. Not ye, were the inventors of *Religion,* but the Folk; ye could but mutilate its inner meaning, turn the heaven that lay within it to a hell, and its outbreathing truth to lies. Not ye are the inventors of the *State;* ye have but made from out the natural alliance of like-needing men a natureless and forced allegiance of unlike-needing.   (I, 74–80)

Yet this unveiling was alike the final annihilation of the collective Art-work: for its bond of union had been that very garment of Religion. While the contents of the common mythical religion, the traditional subject of Dramatic art, were employed to point the poet's moral, developed to fit his purpose, and finally disfigured by his selfwilled fancy, the religious belief had already disappeared completely from the life of the Folk-fellowship, now only linked by political interests. This belief however, the honour paid to national Gods, the sure assumption of the truth of primal race-traditions, had formed the bond of all community. Was this now rent and hooted as a heresy, at least the core of that religion had come to light as unconditioned, actual, naked *Man;* but this Man was no longer the associate man, united by the bond of racial fellowship: only the *absolute, egoistic, solitary unit,*—man beautiful and naked, but loosed from the beauteous bond of brotherhood.

From here on, from the shattering of the Greek religion, from the wreck of the Grecian Nature-State, and its resolution into the Political State,—from the splintering of the common Tragic Art-work,—the manhood of world-history begins with measured tread its new gigantic march of evolution, from the fallen *natural kinsmanship of national community* to the *universal fellowship of all mankind.* The band which the full-fledged Man, coming to consciousness in the national Hellenian, disrupted as a cramping fetter—*with* this awakened consciousness—must now expand into a universal girdle embracing *all* mankind. The period from that point of time down to our own to-day is, therefore, the history of *absolute Egoism;* and the end of this period will be its redemption into *Communism.*   (I, 166–167)

Only that action is completely truthful— and can thoroughly convince us of its plain necessity—on whose fulfillment a man had set the whole strength of his being, and which was to him so imperative a necessity that he needs must pass over into it with the whole force of his character. But hereof he conclusively persuades us by this alone: that, in the effectuation of his personal force, he literally *went under,* he veritably threw overboard his personal existence, for sake of bringing to the outer world the inner Necessity which ruled his being. He proves to us the verity of his nature, not only in his actions—which might still appear capricious so long as he yet were doing—but by the consummated sacrifice of his personality to this necessary course of action. The last, completest renunciation (Entäusserung) of his personal egoism, the demonstration of his full ascension into universalism, a man can only show us by his *Death;* and that not by his accidental, but by his *necessary* death, the logical sequel to his actions, the last fulfillment of his being.

The celebration of such a Death is the noblest thing that men can enter on. It reveals to us in the nature of this one man, laid bare by death, the whole content of universal human nature. But we fix this revelation in surest hold of memory by the conscious *representation* of that Death itself and, in order to make its purport clear to us, by the representation of those actions which found their necessary conclusion in that death. Not in the repulsive funeral rites which, in our neo-christian mode of life, we solemnise by meaningless hymns and churchyard platitudes; but by the artistic re-animation of the lost one, by life-glad reproduction and portrayal of his actions and his death, in the dramatic Art-work, shall we celebrate that festival which lifts us living to the highest bliss of love for the departed, and turns his nature to our own.   (pp. 198–199)

FROM *A Communication to My Friends*

. . . I MUST HERE attest that at the time when I first learnt the story of Lohengrin, in connection with that of Tannhäuser, the tale indeed affected me, but in no wise prompted me to store the 'stuff' for future working-up. Not only because I was then completely saturated with Tannhäuser, but also because the form in which Lohengrin first stepped before me made an almost disagreeable impression upon my feeling, did I not at that time keep a sharper eye upon him. The medieval poem presented Lohengrin in a mystic twilight, that filled me with suspicion and that haunting feeling of repugnance with which we look upon the carved and painted saints and martyrs on the highways, or in the churches, of Catholic lands. Only when the immediate impression of this reading had faded, did the shape of Lohengrin rise repeatedly, and with growing power of attraction, before my soul; and this power gathered fresh force to itself from outside, chiefly by reason that I learnt to know the myth of Lohengrin in its simpler traits, and like its deeper meaning, as the genuine poem of the Folk, such as it has been laid bare to us by the discoveries of the newer searchers into Saga lore. . . . This "Lohengrin" is no mere outcome of Christian meditation, but one of man's earliest poetic ideals; just as, for the matter of that, it is a fundamental error of our modern superficialism, to consider the specific Christian legends as by any means original creations. . . . To purge them of this heterogenous influence, and thus enable us to look straight into the pure humanity of the eternal poem: such was the task of the more recent inquirer [Feuerbach], a task which it must necessarily remain for the poet to complete.

Just as the main feature of the mythos of the "Flying Dutchman" may be clearly traced to an earlier setting in the Hellenic Odyssey; just as this same Ulysses in his wrench from the arms of Calypso, in his flight from the charms of Circe, and in his yearning for the earthly wife of cherished home, embodied the Hellenic prototype of a longing such as we find in "Tannhäuser" immeasurably enhanced and widened in its meaning: so do we already meet in the Grecian mythos—nor is even this by any means its oldest form—the outlines of the myth of "Lohengrin." Who does not know the story of "Zeus and Semele"? The god loves a mortal woman, and for sake of this love, approaches her in human shape; but the mortal learns that she does not know her lover in his true estate, and, urged by Love's own ardour, demands that her spouse shall show himself to physical sense in the full substance of his being. Zeus knows that she can never grasp him, that the unveiling of his godhead must destroy her; himself, he suffers by this knowledge, beneath the stern compulsion to fulfill his loved one's dreaded wish: he signs his own death-warrant, when the fatal splendour of his godlike presence

strikes Semele dead.—Was it, forsooth, some priestly fraud that shaped this myth? How insensate, to attempt to argue from the selfish state-religious, caste-like exploitation of the noblest human longing, back to the origin and the genuine meaning of ideals which blossomed from a human fancy that stamped man first as Man! 'Twas no *God,* that sang the meeting of Zeus and Semele; but *Man,* in his humanest of yearnings. . . . (I, 333–335)

Once again, and that the last time, did Myth and History stand before me with opposing claims; this while, as good as forcing me to decide whether it was a musical drama, or a spoken play, that I had to write. A closer narration of the conflict that lay behind this question, I have purposely reserved until this stage, because it was *here* first that I arrived at its definite answer, and thus at a full consciousness of its true nature.

Since my return to Germany from Paris, my favourite study had been that of ancient German lore. I have already dwelt on the deep longing for my native home that filled me then. This Home, however, in its actual reality, could nowise satisfy my longing; thus I felt that a deeper instinct lay behind my impulse, and one that needs must have its source in some other yearning than merely for the modern homeland. As though to get down to its root, I sank myself into the primal element of Home, that meets us in the legends of a Past which attracts us the more warmly as the Present repels us with its hostile chill. To all our wishes and warm impulses, which in truth transport us to the *Future,* we seek to give a physical token by means of pictures from the Past, and thus to win for them a form the modern Present never can provide. In the struggle to give the wishes of my heart artistic shape, and in the ardour to discover *what* thing it was that drew me so resistlessly to the primal source of old home Sagas, I drove step by step into the deeper regions of antiquity, where at last to my delight, and truly in the *utmost* reaches of old time, I was to light upon the fair young form of *Man,* in all the freshness of his force. My studies thus bore me, through the legends of the Middle Ages, right down to their foundation in the old-Germanic Mythos; one swathing after another, which the later legendary lore had bound around it, I was able to unloose, and thus at last to gaze upon it in its chastest beauty. What here I saw, was no longer the Figure of conventional history, whose garment claims our interest more than does the actual shape inside; but the real naked Man, in whom I might spy each throbbing of his pulses, each stir within his mighty muscles, in uncramped, freest motion: the type of the true *human being.*

At like time I had sought this human being *in History too.* Here offered themselves *relations,* and nothing but relations; the *human being* I could only see in so far as the relations ordered him: and not as he had power to order *them.* To get to the bottom of these 'relations,' whose coercive force compelled the strongest man to squander all his powers on objectless and never-compassed aims, I turned afresh to the soil of Greek antiquity, and here, again, was pointed at the last *to Mythos,* in which alone I could touch the ground of even these *relations:* but in that Mythos, these social relations were drawn in lines as simple, plastic and distinct as I had earlier recognised therein the human shape itself. From this side, also, did Mythos lead me to this Man alone, as to the involuntary *creator* of those relations, which, in their documento-monumental perversion, as the excrescences of History, as traditional fictions and established rights, have at last usurped dominion over Man and ground to dust his freedom.

(I, 357–358)

FROM *The Nibelungen*

THE CEASELESS strain of men and races toward never-compassed goals will mostly find a clearer explanation in their Ur- and Stem-sagas than can be gathered from their entrance into naked History, which tells us but the consequences of their essential attributes. If we read the Stem-saga of the Frankish royal race aright, we find therein an explanation of its historic deeds past anything obtainable on other paths of scrutiny.

Unquestionably the *Saga of the Nibelungen* is the birthright of the Frankish stem. Research has shewn the basis of this saga, too, to be of religio-mythic nature: its deepest meaning was the ur-conscience of the Frankish stem, the soul of its royal race, under whatsoever name the primal Asiatic highlands may first have seen that race arise.——

For the moment we will neglect the oldest meaning of the myth, in which we shall recognise *Siegfried* as God of Light or Sun-god: to prepare ourselves for its connection with history, we now will merely take the saga where it clothes itself with the more human garb of ancient herodom. Here we find Siegfried as the winner of the *Nibelung's Hoard* and with it might unmeasurable. This Hoard, and the might in it residing, becomes the immovable centre round which all further shaping of the saga now revolves: the whole strife and struggle is aimed at this Hoard of the Nibelungen, as the epitome of earthly power, and he who owns it, who governs by it, either is or becomes a Nibelung.

Now the Franks, whom we first meet in history in the region of the Lower Rhine, have a royal race in which appears the name "Nibelung"; especially among its

purest scions, who even before the time of Chlodwig were ousted by a kinsman, Merwig, but regained the kingship later as Pipingen or Karlingen [Pepins or Carlovingians]. Let this suffice for the present, to shew, if not the genealogic, at least the mythical identity of the Frankish royal family with those Nibelungen of the saga; which has adopted unmistakable features from the history of this stem into its later more historical development, where the focus still remains possession of that Hoard, the cynosure of earthly rule.—

(VII, 262–263)

FROM *"Origin and Evolution of the Nibelungen-myth"*

MAN RECEIVES his first impressions from surrounding Nature, and none of her phenomena will have reacted on him so forcibly from the beginning, as that which seemed to him to form the first condition of the existence, or at least of his knowledge, of everything contained in Creation: and this is *Light, the Day, the Sun*. Thanks, and finally worship, would be paid this element the first; the more so, as its opposite, Darkness, Night, seemed joyless, hence unfriendly and fear-compelling. Now, as man drew all his joy and animation from the light, it soon would come to mean the very fount of Being: it became the begetter, the father, the god; the breaking of day out of night at last appeared to him the victory of Light over Darkness, of Warmth over Cold and so forth; and this idea may have been the first to breed in man a moral consciousness and lead him to distinction of the useful and the harmful, the friendly and hostile, Good and Bad.

So far, at any rate, this earliest nature-

impression must be regarded as the common basis of all Religions of every people. In the individualising of these general ideas derived from physical observation, however, is to be sought the gradually-conspicuous cleavage of religions according to the character of different nations. Now the stem-saga of the Franks has the high pre-eminence that, in keeping with the stem's peculiarity, it developed more and more from this beginning to historic life, whereas a similar growth of the religious myth into a genealogic saga is nowhere to be found among the other German stems; in exact degree as these lagged behind in active influence on history, did their stem-sagas stop short at the religious myth (superlatively the case with the Scandinavians), or get lost in wholly undeveloped fragments at the first shock with historic nations more alive.

At the farthest point to which we can trace it, the Frank stem-saga shews the individualised Light or Sun-god, who conquers and lays low the monster of the ur-

Chaotic night:—this is the original meaning of *Siegfried's fight with the Dragon,* a fight like that Apollo fought against the dragon Python. Yet, as Day succumbs to Night again, as Summer in the end must yield to Winter, Siegfried too is slain at last: so the god became man, and as a mortal man he fills our soul with fresh and stronger sympathy; for, a sacrifice to his deed of blessing us, he wakes the moral motive of Revenge, i.e. the longing to avenge his death upon his murderer, and thus renew his deed. The ur-old fight is now continued by ourselves, and its changeful issue is just the same as that eternal alternation of day and night, summer and winter, —and lastly of the human race itself, in ceaseless sway from life to death, from triumph to defeat, from joy to grief, and thus perennially rejuvenating in itself the active consciousness of the immortal fund of Man and Nature. The quintessence of this constant motion, thus of Life, at last in *"Wuotan"* (Zeus) found expression as the chiefest God, the Father and Pervader of the All. Though his nature marked him as the highest god, and as such he needs must take the place of father to the other deities, yet was he nowise an historically older god, but sprang into existence from man's later, higher consciousness of self; consequently he is more abstract than the older Nature-god, whilst the latter is more corporeal and, so to phrase it, more personally inborn in man.

(VII, 274–275)

FRIEDRICH MAX MÜLLER

[1823–1900]

F. MAX MÜLLER dominated the study of myth during the third quarter of the nineteenth century, and has thus become a convenient starting place for accounts of modern mythography. The unlikely combination in his work of hard-headed, complex, erudite philology and the dreamy, rhapsodic reduction of all myth to silly locutions for sunrise and sunset ("Another magnificent sunset looms in the myth of the death of Her-acles") made Müller an easy target, for he could be seen as a mighty scholar-fool, an example of how benighted myth study was in the mid-nineteenth century. The great Victorian solar mythologist is, however, more interesting than that, and Müller's work explains a great deal about what has happened to the study of myth since the 1850s.

Müller was first a student at Leipzig, where he heard Hermann and Brockhaus, then at Berlin, where he heard Bopp and Schelling. He took his doctorate at nineteen and published a translation of the *Hitopadésa* at twenty. He went to Paris to work under Eugène Burnouf in 1845, came to England during the Revolution of 1848, was appointed Taylorian Professor of Modern Languages at Oxford in 1850, and spent the rest of his life in England. His career rolled on, checked only by his losing the election to the Chair of Sanskrit in 1860 to Sir Monier Monier-Williams. One of Müller's friends, A. A. Macdonnell, claims that the loss of this chair was such a great disappoint-ment that it deflected Müller from solid Sanskrit scholarship into other fields, such as comparative mythology, and that Müller's writings in those fields won him much acclaim, but at the expense of solid scholarly achievement. However this may have been, Müller did introduce, advance, and popularize in England the newly re-lated fields of comparative philology and comparative mythology, in addition to editing the multivolume *Sacred Books of the East*. Müller's writings on mythology are very numerous, though his approach is already fully expressed in the celebrated book-length essay *Comparative Mythol-ogy*, published in 1856. Other works range from an essay on "Bellerophon" (1855), which is a showpiece of the philological method, to the *Introduction to the Science of Religion* (1873), to the final gathering up of his work on myth in *Contributions to the Science of My-thology* (1897) and many other essays and books.

F. Max Müller's work on myth has been discussed both recently and well. Richard Dorson, in *The British Folklor-ists*, has placed Müller with reference to Tylor, Lang, and the rise of anthropology and folklore; Jan de Vries, in *The Study of Religion*, has discussed Müller's works in the light of subsequent developments in philology and linguistics; and Richard Chase, in *The Quest for Myth*, has fo-cussed on the one-sidedness of the genteel solar explanation of myth. What follows then is only intended as a supplementary account of Müller's approach to myth.

Comparative philology gave rise to the idea that, just as there was a common language—Latin—lying behind and explaining many of the peculiarities of romance languages, so there was a common language—Aryan—lying behind Greek, Latin, Sanskrit, Zend, Celtic, and Gothic. Aryan was the mother tongue of the human race, "a living language," wrote Müller, "spoken in Asia by a small tribe, nay, originally by a small family living under one and the same roof." This language, Müller argued, was incapable of abstractions, so, at an early period, the Aryans took to naming things as best they could. This, for Müller, is the mythopoeic age. The Aryans were more impressed by the dawn and the sun and the darkness than they were with anything else in nature, and they turned their awkward language to describing dawns and sunsets. "Where we speak of the sun following the dawn, the ancient poets could only speak and think of the Sun loving and embracing the dawn. What is with us a sunset, was to them the Sun growing old, decaying or dying. Our sunrise was to them the Night giving birth to a brilliant child." In this early mythopoeic era, then, all language was myth; "every one of these common Aryan words is, in a certain sense, a myth," and the great majority of the Aryan words that Müller identified had to do with solar events.

After the mythopoeic era, the Aryan people split into nations, dispersed, and evolved new languages. The old words describing dawns and sunsets remained, but were no longer understood. So new and often wild or ugly stories (myths) were invented to explain the old names, and we thus have myths piled on myths. Comparative mythology undertook to work back from the Greek or Latin or Indian myths to their supposed Aryan roots, and from the Aryan roots tried to identify the solar event originally sig-

nified. Müller found the Vedas, particularly the *Rig-Veda,* to be the oldest and best clues to this Aryan mythology and myth-language, and he could trace most Greek myths to one or another Aryan root for sun or dawn or night.

As Müller worked it out then, myth was, in his famous phrase, a "disease of language." The original Aryan myth-word was a clumsy and misleading attempt to name a natural event. When later the name and the event had become separated, and a story was made up by, for example, the Greeks, to explain a name, this only compounded the problem. This slippage between words and things is inherent in all language to some degree, Müller claims. We are always in the process of mythmaking, and the only corrective is comparative philology, conceived of as a sort of scientific etymology or as the archaeology of language.

From the nature-filled language of the Vedas, and from the sort of Victorian sensibility one can see in Müller's novel *Deutsche Liebe* (a much read and widely translated romance about a studious youth and a lovely but ill princess and their ideal and hopeless love), came impulses that only reinforced Müller's tendency toward an excessively genteel set of mind. And the idea of the Absolute, or the Ideal, which had played so important a part in German mythic theory, became, in Müller's hands, only a pale wishfulness, an ethereal unworldliness.

Little of this was new, except perhaps the tone; Müller's vast philological erudition was largely in the service of old ideas. The disease of language theory had been touched on by Fontenelle and had been advanced by many eighteenth-century writers on myth. The Aryan hypothesis too is only a late and secular version of the Christian and deist theories that spoke of an early period of truth and simplicity followed by a period of dispersal and degeneration. The celestial or solar explanation was advanced not only by Pluche, but by Dupuis, while the philological method was borrowed from Grimm. Müller's counterpart in Germany, Adelbert Kuhn, whose *Die Herabkunft des Feuers* appeared in 1859, had worked out an approach similar to Müller's (just whose work came first is not clear) in all respects except that thunder and lightning lie at the heart of the explanation instead of sunrise and sunset.

Müller's influence was very great, despite the lack of originality. Cox took up Müller's ideas, and instead of philology, simply used plot analogies to connect similar stories until he emerged with the discovery that all myths are the same myth and tell the same story. Tylor adopted Müller's theories about myth, and Robert Brown applied Müller's approach to uncovering Semitic origins, rather than Aryan. Angelo de Gubernatis's *Zoological Mythology* (1872) makes use of Müller, as does the work of Ignaz Goldzieher. Richard Dorson has treated most of these figures in *The British Folklorists* and he has argued that Müller's greatest antagonist was Andrew Lang. Müller defended a degeneration theory, while Lang espoused a theory based on evolutionary anthropology. To Lang, myths were vestiges of savage totemism. Both arguments work to belittle myth, and neither argument includes any serious religious element. Müller seemed to have lost the battle to Lang, but Dorson claims that it was Lang who gave ground in the end.

Today, Müller's work seems suspect just on the face of it. It strains credulity to find a supposedly disinterested and scientific philological method leading again and again only to new ways of saying the sun kisses the dawn. And to say that Niobe is the snow, and that her tears express the sun melting the snow, no longer seems a full account of the myth. Indeed such reductionist extravagances led others to parody Müller's method; one such is R. F. Littledale's "The Ox-

ford Solar Myth," printed by A. Smythe Palmer in his 1909 edition of Müller's *Comparative Mythology*. Littledale proves conclusively, in the manner of the day, that F. Max Müller is himself the sun.

Müller substituted nature rhapsodies for religious emotion, he substituted a wan ideal for ideas of Divinity, and he substituted a theory of linguistic debasement and degeneration for history. And if the results seem today pale and insubstantial, it should be remembered that in his emphasis on nature and on wonder, in his conviction that kinship names were of the utmost importance, and in his adherence to a linguistic method, he was a harbinger of the future. Nor is his work all narrow. He could write, in "On the Philosophy of Mythology" (1871), "Mythology, in the highest sense, is the power exercized by language on thought in every possible sphere of mental activity; and I do not hesitate to call the whole history of Philosophy, from Thales down to Hegel, an uninterrupted battle against mythology, a constant protest of thought against language."

Müller's work is then an integrative effort, but an unfortunate one, for when he was done with mythology it was stripped of belief, separated from religion, and divested of narrative, poetic, and imaginative interest. Müller's lack of interest in archaeology, in history, and in the fine arts, and his exclusive reliance on language, which even he at last distrusted, narrowed his work disastrously and he was left crying up the study of mythology while he trivialized myth itself.

R.R.

REFERENCES   The text is from F. Max Müller, *Comparative Mythology,* ed. A. Smythe Palmer (New York: Dutton [1909]). See also *Chips from a German Workshop* (New York, 1885) Vol. 2. In addition to the works cited above, see Müller's *Collected Works* (London, 1898, etc.) and *The Sacred Books of the East* (Oxford: Clarendon Press, 1879–1910) 50 vols. translated by various Oriental scholars and edited by F. Max Müller. See also *The Life and Letters of the Right Honourable Friedrich Max Müller* (London, 1902) 2 vols., edited by his wife.

Recent work on Müller includes Jan de Vries, *The Study of Religion* (New York, 1967) and Richard Chase, *The Quest for Myth* (Baton Rouge, 1949). See especially Richard Dorson, *The British Folklorists* (Chicago, 1968), "The Mythological Folklorists." Dorson has also reprinted a large excerpt from "Comparative Mythology" in his *Peasant Customs and Savage Myths* (Chicago, 1968) and has described the conflict between Lang and Müller in "The Eclipse of Solar Mythology" in Thomas Sebeok, *Myth, a Symposium* (Bloomington: Indiana University Press, 1958).

F. Max Müller

FROM *Comparative Mythology*

IN THESE legends the Greek language supplies almost all that is necessary in order to render these strange stories intelligible and rational, through the later Greeks —I mean Homer and Hesiod, had certainly in most cases no suspicion of the original import of their own traditions. But as there are Greek words which find no explanation in Greek, and which, without a reference to Sanskrit and the other cognate dialects, would have for ever remained to the philologist mere sounds with a conventional meaning, there are also names of gods and heroes inexplicable, from a Greek point of view, and which cannot be made to disclose their primitive character, unless confronted with contemporary witnesses from India, Persia, Italy, or Germany. Another myth of the dawn will best explain this:—

Ahan in Sanskrit is a name of the day, and is said to stand for dahan, like a*s*ru, tear, for da*s*ru, δάκρυ. Whether we have to admit an actual loss of this initial d, or whether the d is to be considered rather as a secondary letter, by which the root ah was individualised to dah, is a question which does not concern us at present. In Sanskrit we have the root dah, which means, to burn, and from which a name of the day might have been formed in the same manner as dyu—day, is formed from dyu, to be brilliant. Nor does it concern us here, whether the Gothic *dags*, day, is the same word or not. According to Grimm's law, *daha,* in Sanskrit, should in Gothic appear as *taga,* and not as *daga.* However, there are several of the old common Aryan names in which Grimm's law is violated, and Bopp seems inclined to consider daga and daha identical in origin. Certain it is that the same root from which the Teutonic words for *day* are formed, has also given rise to the name for dawn. In German we say 'der Morgen *tagt*,' and in Old English day was *dawe,* while to dawn was in Anglo-Saxon *dagian.* Now, in the *Veda,* one of the names of the dawn is Ahanâ. It occurs only once, *Rv.* i. 123, 4.

Grihám *grih*am Ahanâ′ yâti *ákkh*a
Divédive ádhi nâ′ma dádhânâ
Sísâsantí Dyotanâ′ *sás*vat â′ agât
A′gram agram ít bha*g*ate vásûnâm.

'Ahanâ (the dawn) comes near to every house—she who makes every day to be known.

'Dyotanâ (the dawn), the active maiden, comes back for evermore—she enjoys always the first of all goods.'

We have already seen the Dawn in various relations to the Sun, but not yet as the beloved of the Sun, flying before her lover, and destroyed by his embrace. This, however, was a very familiar expression in the old mythological language of the Aryans. The Dawn has died in the arms of the Sun, or the Dawn is flying before the Sun, or the Sun has shattered the car of the Dawn, were expressions meaning simply the sun has risen—the dawn is gone. Thus, we read in the *Rv.* iv. 30, in a hymn celebrating the achievements of Indra, the chief solar diety of the Veda—

'And this strong and manly deed also thou has performed. O Indra, that thou struckest the daughter of Dyaus (the Dawn), a woman difficult to vanquish.

'Yes, even the daughter of Dyaus, the magnified, the Dawn, thou, O Indra, a great hero, hast ground to pieces.

'The Dawn rushed off from her crushed car, fearing that Indra, the bull, might strike her.

'This her car lay there well ground to pieces; she went far away.'

In this case, Indra behaves rather unceremoniously to the daughter of the sky; but, in other places, she is loved by all the bright gods of heaven, not excluding her own father. The Sun, it is said, *Rv.* i. 115, 2, follows her from behind, as a man follows a woman. 'She, the Dawn, whose cart is drawn by white horses, is carried away in triumph by the two A*s*vins,'—as the Leukippides are carried off by Dioskuroi.

If now we translate, or rather transliterate, *Dahanâ* into Greek, Daphne stands before us, and her whole history is intelligible. Daphne is 'young, and beautiful—Apollo loves her—she flies before him, and dies as he embraces her with his brilliant rays.' Or, as another poet of the *Veda* (x. 189), expresses it, 'The Dawn comes near to him—she expires as soon as he begins to breathe—the mighty one irradiates the sky.' Any one who has eyes to see and a heart to feel with nature like the poets of old, may still see Daphne and Apollo—the dawn rushing and trembling through the sky, and fading away at the sudden approach of the bright sun. The metamorphosis of Daphne into a laurel-tree is a continuation of the myth of peculiarly Greek growth. Daphne, in Greek, meant no longer the dawn, but it had become the name of the laurel. Hence the tree Daphne was considered sacred to the lover of Daphne, the dawn, and Daphne herself was fabled to have been changed into a tree when praying to her mother to protect her from the violence of Apollo.

Without the help of the *Veda,* the name of Daphne and the legend attached to her, would have remained unintelligible, for the later Sanskrit supplies no key to this name. This shows the value of the *Veda* for the purpose of comparative mythology, a science which, without the *Veda,* would have remained mere guesswork, without fixed principles and without a safe basis.

In order to show in how many different ways the same idea may be expressed mythologically, I have confined myself to the names of the Dawn. The dawn is really one of the richest sources of Aryan mythology; and another class of legends, embodying the strife between winter and summer, the return of spring, the revival of nature, is in most languages but a reflection and amplification of the more ancient stories telling of the strife between night and day, the return of the morn, and the revival of the whole world. The stories, again, of solar heroes fighting through a thunderstorm against the powers of darkness, are borrowed from the same source; and the cows, so frequently alluded to in the *Veda*, as carried off by V*ri*tra and brought back by Indra, are in reality the same bright cows which the Dawn drives out every morning to their pasture-ground—the clouds—which, from their heavy udders, send down refreshing and fertilising rain or dew upon the parched earth. There is no sight in nature more elevating than the dawn even to us, whom philosophy has taught that 'nil admirari' is the highest wisdom. Yet in ancient times the power of admiring was the greatest blessing bestowed on mankind; and when could man have admired more intensely, when could his heart have been more gladdened and overpowered with joy than at the approach of

'the Lord of light,
Of life, of love, and gladness!'

The darkness of night fills the human heart with despondency and awe, and a feeling of fear and anguish sets every nerve trembling. There is man like a forlorn child fixing his eye with breathless anxiety upon the East, the womb of day, where the light of the world has flamed up so many times before. As the father waits the birth of his child, so the poet watches the dark heaving night who is to bring forth her bright son, the sun of the day. The doors of heaven seem slowly to open, and what are called the bright flocks of the Dawn step out of the dark stable, returning to their wonted pastures. Who has not seen the gradual advance of this radiant procession—the heaven like a distant sea tossing its golden waves—when the first rays shoot forth like

brilliant horses racing round the whole course of the horizon—when the clouds begin to colour up, each shedding her own radiance over her more distant sisters! Not only the East, but the West, and the South, and the North, the whole temple of heaven is illuminated, and the pious worshipper lights in response his own small light on the altar of the hearth, and stammers words which express but faintly the joy that is in nature and in the human heart—

'Rise! our life, our spirit is come back! the darkness is gone, the light approaches!'

If the people of antiquity called these eternal lights of heaven their gods, their bright ones (deva), the Dawn was the first-born among all the gods—Protogeneia—dearest to man, and always young and fresh. But if not raised to an immortal state, if only admired as a kind being, awakening every morning the children of man, her life would seem to be short. She soon fades away, and dies when the fountain-head of light rises in naked splendour, and sends his first swift glance through the vault of heaven. We cannot realise that sentiment with which the eye of antiquity dwelt on these sights of nature. To us all is law, order, necessity. We calculate the refractory power of the atmosphere, we measure the possible length of the dawn in every climate, and the rising of the sun is to us no greater surprise than that two and two make four. But if we could believe again, that there was in the sun a being like our own, that in the dawn there was a soul open to human sympathy—if we could bring ourselves to look for a moment upon these powers as personal, free, and adorable, how different would be our feelings at the blush of day! That Titanic assurance with which we say, the sun *must* rise, was unknown to the early worshippers of nature, or if they also began to feel the regularity with which the sun and the other stars perform their daily labour, they still thought of free beings kept in temporary servitude, chained for a time, and bound to obey a higher will, but sure to rise, like Herakles, to a higher glory at the end of their labours. It seems to us childish when we read in the *Veda* such expressions as, 'Will the Sun rise?' 'Will our old friend, the Dawn, come back again?' 'Will the powers of darkness be conquered by the God of Light?' And when the Sun rose, they wondered how, but just born, he was so mighty, and strangled, as it were, in his cradle, the serpents of the night. They asked how he could walk along the sky? why there was no dust on his road? why he did not fall backward? But at last they greeted him like a poet of our own time—

'Hail, orient Conqueror of gloomy Night!'

and the human eye felt that it could not bear the brilliant majesty of Him whom they call 'the Life, the breath, the brilliant Lord and Father.'

Thus sunrise was the revelation of nature, awakening in the human mind that feeling of dependence, of helplessness, of hope, of joy and faith in higher powers, which is the source of all wisdom, the spring of all religion. But if sunrise inspired the first prayers, called forth the first sacrificial flames, sunset was the other time when, again, the whole frame of man would tremble. The shadows of night approach, the irresistible power of sleep grasps man in the midst of his pleasures, his friends depart, and in his loneliness his thoughts turn again to higher powers. When the day departs, the poet bewails the untimely death of his bright friend, nay, he sees in his short career the likeness of his own life. Perhaps, when he has fallen asleep, his sun may never rise again, and thus the place to which the setting sun

withdraws in the far West rises before his mind as the abode where he himself would go after death, where 'his fathers went before him,' and where all the wise and the pious rejoice in a 'new life with Yama and Varuna.' Or he might look upon the sun, not as a short-lived hero, but as young, unchanging, and always the same, while generations after generations of mortal men were passing away. And hence, by the mere force of contrast, the first intimation of beings which do not wither and decay—of immortals, of immortality! Then the poet would implore the immortal sun to come again, to vouchsafe to the sleeper a new morning. The god of day would become the god of time, of life and death. Again, the evening twilight, the sister of the dawn, repeating, though with a more sombre light, the wonders of the morning, how many feelings must it have roused in the musing poets—how many poems must it have elicited in the living language of ancient times! Was it the dawn that came again to give a last embrace to him who had parted from her in the morning? Was she the immortal, the always returning goddess, and he the mortal, the daily dying sun? Or was she the mortal, bidding a last farewell to her immortal lover, burnt, as it were, on the same pile which would consume her, while he would rise to the seat of the gods?

Let us express these simple scenes in ancient language, and we shall find ourselves surrounded on every side by mythology full of contradictions and incongruities, the same being represented as mortal or immortal, as man or woman, as the poetical eye of man shifts its point of view, and gives its own colour to the mysterious play of nature.   (pp. 116–126)

If Hegel calls the discovery of the common origin of Greek and Sanskrit the discovery of a new world, the same may be said with regard to the common origin of Greek and Sanskrit mythology. The discovery is made, and the science of comparative mythology will soon rise to the same importance as comparative philology. I have here explained but a few myths, but they all belong to one small cycle, and many more names might have been added. I may refer those who take an interest in the geology of language to the *Journal of Comparative Philology,* published by my learned friend, Dr. Kuhn, at Berlin, who, in his periodical, has very properly admitted comparative mythology as an integral part of comparative philology, and who has himself discovered some striking parallelisms between the traditions of the *Veda* and the mythological names of the other Aryan nations. The very 'Hippokentaurs and the Chimera, the Gorgons and Pegasos, and other monstrous creatures,' have been set right; and though I do not hold Dr. Kuhn's views on many points, and particularly with regard to the elementary character of the gods, which he, like Lauer, the lamented author of the *System of Greek Mythology,* connects too exclusively with the fleeting phenomena of clouds, and storms, and thunder, while I believe their original conception to have been almost always solar, yet there is much to be learnt from both, even where we cannot agree with their conclusions. Much, no doubt, remains to be done, and even with the assistance of the *Veda,* the whole of Greek mythology will never be deciphered and translated. But can this be urged as an objection? There are many Greek words of which we cannot find a satisfactory etymology, even by the help of Sanskrit. Are we therefore to say that the whole Greek language has no etymological organisation? If we find a rational principle in the formation of but a small portion of Greek words, we are justified in inferring that the same principle which manifests itself in part governed the organic growth of the whole; and though we cannot explain the etymological origin of all words, we should never say that language had not etymological origin, or that etymology 'treats of a past which was never present.' That the later Greeks, such as Homer and Hesiod, ignored the λόγος of their μύθοι I fully admit, but they equally ignored the real origin (τὸ ἔτυμον) of their words. What applies to etymology, therefore, applies with equal force to mythology. It has been proved by comparative philology that there is nothing irregular in language, and what was formerly considered as irregular in declension and conjugation is now recognised as the most regular and primitive formation of grammar. The same, we hope, may be accomplished in mythology. . . . Mythology is only a dialect, an ancient form of language. Mythology, though chiefly concerned with nature, and here again mostly with those manifestations which bear the character of law, order, power, and wisdom impressed on them, was applicable to all things. Nothing is excluded from mythological expressions; neither morals nor philosophy, neither history nor religion, have escaped the spell of that ancient sibyl.   (pp. 89–97, 139–140)

Karl Marx [1818–1883]

Ludwig Feuerbach [1804–1872]

Measured against many of his contemporaries' absorbed study and vast knowledge of myth, Marx's own direct interest could seem either casual or merely derisively hostile. Yet Marx became and remains a mythologist of much originality and extraordinary importance. For it is his work and influence that most powerfully moves myth toward its wide modern usage as a near-synonym of "ideology." From at least 1845, as Marx worked out his theories of history and society, he so broadened and deepened the meaning of "ideology" as to make it include not only politics and political thought but also philosophy, religion, art, or myth as well. All of these must now be explained in a new way:

Upon the several forms of property, upon the social conditions of existence, a whole superstructure is raised of various and peculiarly shaped feelings, illusions, habits of thought and conceptions of life. The whole class shapes these out of its material conditions. . . . The individual unit to whom they flow through tradition and education may fancy they constitute the true reasons for and premises of his conduct.
(*The Eighteenth Brumaire of Louis Napoleon*)

But in fact these seemingly "true" reasons and premises constitute only ideologies, only the commanding "illusions of the epoch." These superstructures reflect but also obscure the true hidden reasons and premises of history—class tension, economic structure, material production, or, underlying these, the deeper rational-

ity by which historical process moves through its necessary phases.

Marx's mythologizing is thus patently in the rationalist tradition. This is so obvious that what needs emphasizing is how his mythology remains independent of positions otherwise similar. Both in his ambition for constructing an ultimate system and for accomplishing an ultimate iconoclasm, Marx's mythology looks back more to systematizers like Spinoza than to critics like Bayle or Voltaire. If Marx attacks the naivete and infamies of religion much in the spirit of those materialist and skeptical *philosophes* he admired, he aims also at a far more thorough-going destruction and philosophic reconstitution. His iconoclasm indeed goes beyond most, if not all, of his predecessors. With his formulation of ideology, myth becomes only one more "definite form of social consciousness." Left at that, Voltaire or Toland could have agreed. But Marx is also intent on demolishing the presuppositions about "nature" which supported the whole basis of their mythology (not to mention their politics or religion). In a similar way he partly agrees and vastly differs with those who, like himself, seated myth or religion in an ever-developing historical process, but who nonetheless affirmed Providence (like Vico or Herder) or Christianity (Hegel). Seeking to strip history of every vestige of religious meaning, Marx dissolves myth into an historical movement itself wholly temporalized, secularized, "material." Like the historical movement from which it rises, myth has no divine origin or meaning or essence, no natural form or meaning. The force of Marx's approach is to treat all "legal, political, religious, aesthetic, or philosophic" forms as if they were merely social dogmas, social superstitions, and idolatries. Marx's analysis thus cuts two ways at once: besides diminishing all myth to "social reflex," he goes on to impugn all earlier mythology (rationalist included) as itself only more ideology. He is therefore the last rationalist critic of rationalist mythology, its conscious end-point more than its continuator: his analysis aims at being ultimate, a final iconoclasm and a final system.

The history of various conceptions of ideology before and after Marx is complex, and at all times implies a new view of myth. In important part, the wider history of the "idea" of ideology is the history of the entire ambitious modern effort to penetrate what Marx called the transient "forms" of historical consciousness, so as to understand them anew on an ultimately rational basis. One strand here derives from the enlightenment effort to reinterpret psychology, religion, politics, history, or thought itself on a variously mixed basis of sensationism, materialism, and religious free-thought: this line runs at least from Condillac and Helvétius through French Revolutionary Ideologues like Dupuis, Cabanis, Volney, Destutt de Tracy (whose *Élémens d'Idéologie* in 1803 coined and popularized the word), and on to Comte. Another strand descends from Kant's critiques, through Hegel's critique of history in terms of the "false consciousness" of those who are the "unconscious" but real agents of historical movement, to Feuerbach's analysis of religion as a disguised "anthropology," and on to Marx. Still another strand runs from Schopenhauer's "pessimistic" analysis of life in terms of will, to Nietzsche's proclamation of life-

affirming myths. The full later history of ideology, with myth often indistinguishable from ideology, falls completely outside our period—as in analyses by Max Weber, Mannheim or Lukacs, or in usages such as George Sorel's "myth of the general strike" or Cassirer's "myth of the State."

Still, of all the theories offered in our period, Marx's formulation of ideology —and ideologic myth—may be said to have remained dominant; not a small reason for this is the carrying force of Marxism in our century's politics and intellectual concerns. Several studies have traced Marx's development among the post-Hegelian and early socialist schools. Here, we may confine ourselves to matters relating particularly to Marx's theory of ideology as the continuation and consummation of certain eighteenth and early nineteenth century radical analyses of myth and religion. For Marx's views begin in and remain deeply indebted to the ceaseless debate about myth, religion, and theology current in his formative years.

Marx is of course among the great derogators of that "opium of the people," religion. Such a position is however a commonplace of the socialist-utopian thought of his youth. What Marx wrote in 1844 (when he was twenty-six), that "communism thus begins . . . in atheism," could (defining "communism" broadly) have been subscribed to by other social prophets such as Condorcet, Comte, Saint-Simon, Feuerbach, Bruno Bauer, or Bakunin. In Germany especially—where religion had been subjected to Kantian and idealist critique, to Lessing's and Herder's historizing, to endless mythological speculations and research into religious origins and parallels, to the "higher" biblical criticism—nothing could have seemed more natural than Marx's confident statement in 1844: "For Germany, the criticism of religion is in the main complete, and criticism of religion is the premise of all criticism." This points directly toward a possibly revolutionary politics as well, since "the basis of irreligious criticism is: man makes religion, religion does not make man. . . . Man is the world of men, the state, society." From this last statement, it is clear that the completion of religious criticism for Marx means the destruction of religion and theology attempted by Marx's early masters and associates— Ludwig Feuerbach, Bruno Bauer, D. F. Strauss, Arnold Ruge, and others.

Following Hegel's death in 1831, these post-Hegelians were at first mainly involved in developing a theology "in opposition," and by the early eighteen forties, especially with Marx, in moving ahead to a politics "in opposition." This revision of theology is provoked but also supported by Hegel's thought, still triumphant in the period. As Karl Löwith has noted, "the questions which were the bones of contention in the thirties had nothing to do with Hegel's attitude toward the state and history, but rather toward religion"—"religion" here meant mainly Christianity.

In his *Lectures on the Philosophy of Religion* (1832), Hegel equated "natural" or primitive "savage" religions with "magic" religions. He thus treated myth merely as a primitive phase in the historical emergence of the true religion, Christianity. But he seemed to treat Christianity as finally not more important than the emergence of true philosophy: "The substance of the Christian religion, the highest developmental stage of any and all true religion, coincides completely with the substance of the true philosophy." The more conservative of Hegel's followers were therefore beset by the possibility that Hegel had destroyed the revealed content of Christianity precisely because he could "raise" it to genuine conceptual status in the form of philosophy. On the other side, the disbelieving Left Hegelians, though welcoming such

a possibility, resisted Hegel's preserving of religion, in whatever philosophic "form" and however ambiguously. The first major provocation here is David Friedrich Strauss's controversial *Life of Jesus* in 1835. For it was under Hegel's alleged aegis that Strauss claimed to interpret the New Testament stories of Jesus as historical myths. And in all the disputes and factionalism starting to swirl about religion, myth continued to be appealed to as a crucial negative weapon.

Strauss had retained Christian truth at least as an "idea," by divesting it of those myths which sought to embody this idea in the historical Jesus. Bruno Bauer and Ludwig Feuerbach develop the position further. In his *The Trumpet of Last Judgment on Hegel the Atheist and Antichrist* (1841), *Hegel's Teaching on Religion and Art* (1842), and *Christianity Revealed . . .* (1843), Bauer argued that Strauss did not go far enough in demythologizing the Bible. Bauer rejected Strauss's division of myths into "pure" and "historical," and portrayed the entire New Testament Jesus as fictitious, and the New Testament itself as an "invention." At the same time, Feuerbach undertook as radical a critique as Bauer's, but also one far more systematic and effective, in his *Essence of Christianity* (1841), *The Philosophy of the Future* (1843), his *Theses* of the same year, the *Essence of Religion* (given as lectures in 1848–49, published in 1851), and his analysis of Greek religion, the *Theogony* (1857).

The youthful Marx was intimately associated with all these men, and between entering the university in 1835 and about 1843 passed successively under the influence of Hegel, Bauer, and Feuerbach —the last most importantly. After transferring to Berlin in 1836, Marx joined the *Doktorklub,* whose leading member was Bauer, then teaching theology at the university. Bauer and Marx remained close friends for several years (some scholars believe Marx may have helped write Bauer's *The Trumpet*); a full rupture occurred with Marx's scathing attacks on Bauer's theological and political position in *The Holy Family* of 1844. In 1838, meanwhile, Bauer together with Strauss and Feuerbach began the *Hallische Jahrbücher,* which became the *Deutsche Jahrbücher* in 1841 when Marx became associated with it. By 1843, Marx had moved decisively into Feuerbach's orbit: punning on Feuerbach's name, he declared that theologians and philosophers now had no road to truth except through the "stream of fire"; Feuerbach is the "purgatory of the present age."

Indeed, Feuerbach may be considered the theologian for Marx's political philosophy. In his own time, Feuerbach was celebrated as an intransigent atheist and destroyer of Christianity and of religion in general; in our time, Karl Barth has declared him one of the most significant nineteenth-century theologians, a scourge of all liberal Protestant theology and even a radical conclusion to Luther's Christology. Feuerbach's general aim was to show that man's religions are not about God at all, but rather entirely about man. The history of the concept of "image of God" is in fact a history of man's coming to know his own powers, qualities, and hopes. Feuerbach divided history into a religious and a post-religious (or Feuerbachian) stage. The first and earliest religious phase is polytheism: man then naively externalizes his own powers and feelings into any natural object around. The next phase is monotheistic: now God moves beyond nature, and becomes supernatural. Christianity moves further forward by conceiving God as a Person, i.e., man (albeit indirectly) conceives himself as a "self-sufficient whole," an "unlimited being," with a free, universal, and unified essence. But, by embodying all this in an external, perfect, aloof "God," man remains self-alienated. All myth thus speaks truth about man, but

only obliquely, thus misleadingly, and finally harmfully. And "higher" religion only keeps man fastened to the raw beginnings of nature-worship. "Religion is nothing else but man's primitive and therefore childish, popular, but unprejudiced, unemancipated consciousness of himself and nature."

Feuerbach saw religious man as not fully self-consciousness, still alienated from himself, still grossly dependent. One of the "Theses on Feuerbach," which the young Marx wrote in 1845, succinctly described Feuerbach's intention:

Feuerbach starts out from the fact of religious self-alienation, the duplication of the world into a religious and a secular one. His work consists in resolving the religious world into its secular basis.

"Resolving the religious world into its secular basis" in an important way meant resolving all religion back into myth, and then arguing that Christianity or any religion is only this earliest mythic moment extended and elaborated but unchanged. Correspondingly, myth is now reduced to simplistic primitive crudity, and loses all richness or variety of dimension or possibility. All myth is naive. Thus, "the Homeric Gods eat and drink —that implies eating and drinking is a divine pleasure" in men's imaginations. Or, if Zeus is the strongest god, this is because men cherish physical strength. An extended example is useful:

Water, as a universal element of life, reminds us of our origin from Nature, an origin which we have in common with plants and animals. In Baptism we bow to the power of a pure Nature-force; water is the element of natural equality and freedom, the mirror of the golden age. But we men are distinguished from the plants and animals which together with the inorganic kingdom we comprehend under the common name of Nature; —we are distinguished from Nature. Hence we must celebrate our distinction, our specific difference. The symbols of this difference are bread and wine . . . if in water we declare:

Man can do nothing without Nature; by bread and wine we declare: Nature needs man. . . .

Feuerbach thus supplements the older theory that religion and myth begin in psychological fear and dependence: if man worships powers, it is really his own powers he is worshipping. Marx summed up Feuerbach's teaching: "man is the highest being for man." In Feuerbach's formula: "Anthropology is the secret of theology." Such anthropology—or "Anthropotheism"—is intended to be the final explanation also of all mythology.

Marx is more intransigently antireligious even than Feuerbach. He criticizes Feuerbach for insisting that religion or myth or theology have objectified the "essence" of man, even if only indirectly. Still, Marx acknowledges Feuerbach's absolute humanizing of religion as providing a basis for Marx's own further translating of religion and myth into wholly social-material terms. At least by 1845, Marx proceeds to plunge that human "essence" radically into social process, and to root all human self-alienation in social alienation and cleavage.

The mature Marx never undertook an extended critique of religion or myth himself (though in 1840 he planned writing a *Philosophy of Religion*). As a university student he became a Hegelian, and much like any other idealist mythologist, wrote a dialogue, that he described as "a philosophical-dialectical discussion of the godhead manifested in a concept per se, as religion, as nature, and as history." But his doctoral dissertation already shows the impact of the "atheist" Hegelian school: *The Differences between the Democritean and Epicurean Philosophy of Nature* is partly an attack on Christianity and all religion through the vehicle of ancient impious thought. In the "Notes" to his dissertation, while ostensibly attacking Plato's philosophic

use of myth, Marx provides a broad but informed parody of the contemporary style of harmonizing all mythology, philosophy, and religion in a transcendental way—and as Marx's repeated satiric use of the term "positive" suggests, the target is doubtless Schelling's later "positive" philosophy of mythology, then being lectured on by Schelling at Berlin.

By 1846, in the unfinished *German Ideology* (with Engels as coauthor), myth and religion are derived systematically from man's social existence. In earliest religion, man is aware of nature as an alien, immense power, and man is overawed "like the beasts." At this primal moment, man looks in opposite ways at once: at nature, as yet unmodified by history; but also toward human history itself. For now, overawed by nature, with a "purely animal consciousness of nature (natural religion)," man becomes conscious of being animalistic, a "member of a flock"; he knows he can respond to nature only with a sheeplike or tribal consciousness—and knowing this, he knows too the start of social life. "Social being . . . determines consciousness." From this decisive primal moment, Marx proceeds to unravel the necessary phases in man's historical development, and his self-alienation as well. New needs, new productivity, and new population begin to increase. But labor now divides into physical and mental labor, and—Marx adds parenthetically—this means the rise of " 'priests', the first form of ideologists." Human alienation begins with this cleavage into material and mental labor, for consciousness now imagines something other than what exists in reality. "Pure" theories arise, such as theology, which come into conflict with social relations as they indeed exist; and as these social relations change, they conflict further with existing forces of production. Consciousness emancipates itself from this world, expands itself in "faith," "higher beings," "specters." What man makes now begins to acquire a "reality" and status outside the maker. Marx borrowed mythic terminology to describe this process of economic alienation in *Capital*: the whole world of capitalist commerce and production stands over against and indeed dominates the worker who has created this world. There is a "fetishism of commodities," in which commodities and property take on an idolatrous aura and power. Ideologic analysis becomes the weapon for unmasking such fetishistic propensities, false social forms and ideals: "We know only one science, the science of history . . . almost all ideology is a distorted interpretation or abstraction from history."

Certain points relating to Marx's formulation of myth and ideology may be emphasized here. Marx's aim to unmask ideology-myth, "the illusions of the epoch," does not lead to his endorsing strict historical relativism or nihilism, though he does help prepare the way for such interpretations by reducing all philosophic, religious, and other forms to social forms. But for Marx, ideologic myths cannot be adequately described finally in terms of class interest or social consensus: these ideologic myths must be understood also as the dimension within which the deepest "real" and "rational" conflicts of human history appear and are fought out. Marx always makes clear that ideologic myths still carry their perverse power to set men against other men and against themselves—and thus, these myths must be denounced and battled. Even now, despite so much effort to destroy religion, the same problem can be seen reemerging in modern man's bourgeois world of work and commerce. Property and money are the modern fetishes. And, as the world grows more technologized, the human capacity for self-deception is gravely accelerated:

Up to now, it was supposed that the growth of the Christian myth under the Roman empire was possible only because printing had not yet been invented. The reverse is in fact true. The daily newspaper and telegraph, which spreads its inventions in a moment over the entire surface of the earth, fabricate more myths . . . in a day than could formerly be invented in a year.

Marx thus helps preserve the view that myth is significantly true. If no longer embodying "religious" truth, myths still embody the kind of power that religion once possessed and commanded: ideology expresses the deepest social faiths, the passionately-held sacrosanct ideals of a class or epoch. Though such illusions may be unmasked by looking to the real underlying material causes, these illusory beliefs have nevertheless been the necessary forms by which history achieved its rational goals. The coming of communism might thus be defined as the end of all ideologies, of all myths. Until then, myth-ideology is a problem never to be ignored as merely irrational: with Marx, myth becomes ambiguously false, ambiguously true, and remains a gravely moral problem.

In an obvious sense, the scathing treatment of myth and religion by Marx and Feuerbach recalls the Euhemerist attack on myth: that the "gods" are only historical men and events writ cosmically large. But Marx's transposing of myth to ideology goes beyond this. A sentence from his dissertation, citing Epicurus, epitomizes the older Euhemerism: "Impiety does not consist in destroying the gods of the crowd but rather in subscribing to the gods the ideas of the crowd." Marx proceeds to dissolve the "ideas of the crowd" further into a progressive, wholly temporalized historical dimension. Marx's Euhemerism argues that men deify not other men, but ideas themselves. In this way, Feuerbach and especially Marx move beyond earlier rationalist derogations of myth as savage error, idolatry, or Jewish-Christian scandal. Now, myth and religion yield a problem infinitely deeper than that posed by superstition, crude philosophizing, priestcraft, or absurd histories. Religion in all its forms is not primarily irrationalism or human failing occurring alongside men's efforts to reason. Religion is rather reason become perverse, the "spirit of a spiritless condition," reason's inward temptation to split and contradict human life, to set up unreal worlds, fears, and hopes and claim these more worthy than man, his world and life. The problem may be illustrated by Marx's complaint against Feuerbach. Feuerbach, though striving to destroy the power of religion, could still argue that reason is "begotten of the essence of religion." But by such views, Marx claimed, Feuerbach simply perpetuated the error of "essences" he had tried to uproot: Feuerbach tried to "resolve the religious essence into the *human* essence," but wrongly, for there is no human "essence." The radical lesson Marx drew from Feuerbach's effort to get rid of myth and religion by transposing them into human terms can be seen in the young Marx's "Theses on Feuerbach." There he announces that more redefining of the problem is not the answer or cure needed: "The philosophers have only *interpreted* the world in various ways; but the point is to *change* it." Marx's new kind of mythology might be summed up by substituting for "philosophers" the term "mythologists." For Marx, the "true" mythologist will not believe that the degradations or indeed the continued existence of myth and religion can be cured by more reinterpretation or theories. The true mythologist will instead show that he understands the power of myth by a revolutionary move against its social root.

Yet Marx also shows a return to earlier rationalist mythology, especially of the Enlightenment. Though he seats man's ideas about the gods in historic process, he also strips the development of myth or religion of any real historic concreteness,

movement, or variety. The mythic epoch of both Marx and Feuerbach is historical only in the sense that the great movement of human consciousness is about to be launched—once and for all, one might say. For the rest, almost like any deist, Marx disdains differentiating between particular mythic histories or moments: myths for him emerge in a universalized dimension the same everywhere. (The modern historian of religion, Wilhelm Schmidt, also accuses Hegel of just such an error.) This tendency to divest myth of its specific historicity can be seen in another way: Marx preserves something of Herder's view that each folk or nation has its special spirit with special, even unique, expression. Ideology might be considered the lore of the class or epoch rather than the lore of the folk. But still the thrust of Marx's ideology is to cut across all national spheres and local particulars: class transcends nation—not the nation but the class is the integer of history. It might be added that Marx subsumes the individual into class as patriotic Herderians would subsume the individual into the folk.

It would be tempting to argue further that Marx remains akin to certain extreme sides of romantic mythology. In the *German Ideology,* he indeed describes the final coming of communism in language fully as exalted as that used by such romantic mythologists as Friedrich Schlegel or Schelling to prophesy the final synthesis and unity to be expected from the attainment of the mythic condition. Communism is

the genuine resolution of the antagonism between men and nature and between man and man; it is the true resolution of the conflict between existence and essence, objectification and self-affirmation, freedom and necessity, individual and species. It is the riddle of history solved and knows itself as this solution.   ("Private Property and Communism")

As much but not more was claimed by the romantic Christian mythologists, the enthusiasts for Indic myth, the mythic illuminists of all kinds. In this sense, Marx might be said to have stood not only Hegel but romantic mythology on its head.

B.F.

REFERENCES   Our selections are from: Ludwig Feuerbach, *The Essence of Christianity,* tr. from 2d German edition by Marian Evans [George Eliot] (London, 1854; repr. New York: Harper and Row, 1957); Karl Marx, *The Difference between Democritean and Epicurean Philosophy of Nature* and *German Ideology,* in *Writings of the Young Marx on Philosophy and Society,* ed. and tr. Loyd D. Easton and Kurt H. Guddat (New York: Doubleday, 1967); "Leading Article of No. 179 of Kölnische Zeitung," *German Ideology* (first selection only), *The Critique of Hegel's Philosophy of Right,* and "Theses on Feuerbach" in K. Marx and F. Engels, *On Religion* (Moscow: Foreign Languages Pub. House, 1957). For Feuerbach: *Sämtliche Werke,* Vol. I–XX/XIII (Stuttgart: Verlag Günther Holzboog, 1960–1964) is a standard edition of Feuerbach: Vols. I–X reprint the edition of 1903–1911 from same publisher, and Vol. XI gives complete bibliography to 1961. Feuerbach's main works are in English translation.

For commentary, see: Eugene Kamenka, *The Philosophy of Ludwig Feuerbach* (New York: Praeger, 1970) for useful introductory survey. Friedrich Jodl, *Ludwig Feuerbach* (Stuttgart: Fromanns Verlag, 1921; 2d ed. revised). Karl Löwith, *Von Hegel zu Nietzsche* (Stuttgart: Kohlhammer, 1941), pp. 84–94, 333–335. F. Engels, *Ludwig Feuerbach and the End of Classical German Philosophy* (London, 1888). For Marx's views on Feuerbach, see esp. *German Ideology* (written 1845–1846) and "Theses on Feuerbach" (written 1845).

For Marx: *Historisch-kritische Gesamtausgabe* (Moscow-Berlin, 1926–1935) covers only through 1848 but is useful here, esp. Bd. 1, 2, 5 and Abt. 1, Bd. 6, 7. For commentary, see: David McLellan, *Marx Before Marxism* (New York: Harper and Row, 1970). H. P. Adams, *Karl Marx in his Earlier Writings* (London: 1940); D. McLellan, *The Young Hegelians and Karl Marx* (London, 1969); R. Tucker, *Philosophy and Myth in Karl Marx* (Cambridge, 1961); George Lichtheim, *The Concept of Ideology and Other Essays* (New York: Random House, 1967), esp. the title essay; Ben Halpern, " 'Myth' and 'Ideology' in Modern Usage," *History and Theory,* IV, 2 (1965), pp. 129–149; Hans Barth, *Wahrheit und Ideologie* (Zurich, 1945); F. Grégoire, *Aux sources de la pensée de Marx: Hegel, Feuerbach* (Louvain/Paris, 1947); W. Sens, *Karl Marx. Seine irreligiöse Entwicklung und anti-christliche Einstellung* (Halle, 1935); S. Hook, *From Hegel to Marx* (Ann Arbor: University of Michigan, 1968; orig. 1950).

For general comment: Basil Willey, *Nineteenth Century Studies: Coleridge to Matthew Arnold* (New York: Columbia University Press, 1949), esp. Chap. VII on Comte and Chap. VIII on Feuerbach, G. Eliot, and Hennell; *The Political Philosophy of Bakunin,* ed. G. P. Maximoff (Glencoe: The Free Press, 1953) for Bakunin's texts on religion, and for alliance to Ruge and others; Frank Manuel, *The New World of Henri Saint-Simon* (Cambridge: Harvard University Press, 1964).

FEUERBACH

FROM *The Essence of Christianity*

To PRECLUDE this misconception, it is better to say, religion is man's earliest and also indirect form of self-knowledge. Hence, religion everywhere precedes philosophy, as in the history of the race, so also in that of the individual. Man first of all sees his nature as if *out of* himself, before he finds it in himself. His own nature is in the first instance contemplated by him as that of another being. Religion is the childlike condition of humanity; but the child sees his nature—man—out of himself; in childhood a man is an object to himself, under the form of another man. Hence the historical progress of religion consists in this: that what by an earlier religion was regarded as objective, is now recognised as subjective; that is, what was formerly contemplated and worshipped as God is now perceived to be something *human*. What was at first religion becomes at a later period idolatry; man is seen to have adored his own nature. Man has given objectivity to himself, but has not recognised the object as his own nature: a later religion takes this forward step; every advance in religion is therefore a deeper self-knowledge. But every particular religion, while it pronounces its predecessors idolatrous, excepts itself—and necessarily so, otherwise it would no longer be religion—from the fate, the common nature of all religions: it imputes only to other religions what is the fault, if fault it be, of religion in general. Because it has a different object, a different tenor, because it has transcended the ideas of preceding religions, it erroneously supposes itself exalted above the necessary eternal laws which constitute the essence of religion—it fancies its object, its ideas, to be superhuman. But the essence of religion, thus hidden from the religious, is evident to the thinker, by whom religion is viewed objectively, which it cannot be by its votaries. And it is our task to show that the antithesis of divine and human is altogether illusory, that it is nothing else than the antithesis between the human nature in general and the human individual; that, consequently, the object and contents of the Christian religion are altogether human.   (pp. 13–14)

The identity of the subject and predicate is clearly evidenced by the progressive development of religion, which is identical with the progressive development of human culture. So long as man is in a mere state of nature, so long is his god a mere nature-god—a personification of some natural force. Where man inhabits houses, he also encloses his gods in temples. The temple is only a manifestation of the value which man attaches to beautiful buildings. Temples in honour of religion are in truth temples in honour of architecture. With the emerging of man from a state of savagery and wildness to one of culture, with the distinction between what is fitting for man and what is not fitting, arises simultaneously the distinction between that which is fitting and that which is not fitting for God. God is the idea of majesty, of the highest dignity: the religious sentiment is the sentiment of supreme fitness. The later more cultured artists of Greece were the first to embody in the statues of the gods the ideas of dignity, of spiritual grandeur, of imperturbable repose and serenity. But why were these qualities in their view attributes, predicates of God? Because they were in themselves regarded by the Greeks as divinities. Why did those artists exclude all disgusting and low passions? Because they perceived them to be unbecoming, unworthy, unhuman, and consequently ungodlike. The Homeric gods eat and drink;—that implies eating and drinking is a divine pleasure. Physical strength is an attribute of the Homeric gods: Zeus is the strongest of the gods. Why? Because physical strength, in and by itself, was regarded as something glorious, divine. To the ancient Germans the highest virtues were those of the warrior; therefore their supreme god was the god of war, Odin,—war, "the original or oldest law." Not the attribute of the divinity, but the divineness or deity of the attribute, is the first true Divine Being. Thus what theology and philosophy have held to be God, the Absolute, the Infinite, is not God; but that which they have held not to be God is God; namely, the attribute, the quality, whatever has reality. Hence he alone is the true atheist to whom the predicates of the Divine Being,—for example, love, wisdom, justice,—are nothing; not he to whom merely the subject of these predicates is nothing. (pp. 20–21)

In Christianity, man was concentrated only on himself, he unlinked himself from the chain of sequences in the system of the universe, he made himself a self-sufficing whole, an absolute, extra- and supramundane being. Because he no longer regarded himself as a being immanent in the world, because he severed himself from connection with it, he felt himself an unlimited being—(for the sole limit of subjectivity is the world, is objectivity),—he had no longer any reason to doubt the truth and validity of his subjective wishes and feelings.

The heathens, on the contrary, not shutting out Nature by retreating within themselves, limited their subjectivity by the contemplation of the world. Highly as the ancients estimated the intelligence, the reason, they were yet liberal and objective enough, theoretically as well as practically, to allow that which they distinguished from mind, namely, matter, to live, and even to live eternally; the Christians evinced their theoretical as well as practical intolerance in their belief that they secured the eternity of their subjective life only by annihilating, as in the doctrine of the destruction of the world, the opposite of subjectivity—Nature. The ancients were free from themselves, but their freedom was that of indifference towards themselves; the Christians were free from Nature, but their freedom was not that of reason, not true freedom, which limits itself by the contemplation of the world, by Nature,—it was the freedom of feeling and imagination, the freedom of miracle. The ancients were so enraptured by the cosmos, that they lost sight of themselves, suffered themselves to be merged in the whole; the Christians despised the world;—what is the creature compared with the Creator? what are sun, moon, and earth compared with the human soul? The world passes away, but man, nay, the individual, personal man, is eternal. If the Christians severed man from all community with Nature, and hence fell into the extreme of an arrogant fastidiousness, which stigmatised the remotest comparison of man with the brutes as an impious violation of human dignity; the heathens, on the other hand, fell into the opposite extreme, into that spirit of depreciation which abolishes the distinction between man and the brute, or even, as was the case, for example, with Celsus, the opponent of Christianity, degrades man beneath the brute.

(pp. 150–151)

MARX

FROM *The Difference between the Democritean and Epicurean Philosophy of Nature*

"IN THE tendency to give philosophical truth an [objective] foundation independent of the subjectivity of the individual, lies the reason why Plato, as he develops truths of highest ethico-religious interest, also presents them in mythical form" (p. 94). [D.F.C. Baur, *Christian Element of Platonism,* 1837]

Is anything clarified this way? Doesn't this include in essence the question of the reason for this reason? It is being asked, in effect, why Plato feels the need to give philosophical truth a positive and at first mythical basis. Such an attempt is the most astonishing thing that can be said of a philosopher when he does not find the objective force in his system itself, in the eternal power of the Idea. Hence Aristotle called mythology a gnomology.

Externally, the answer here can be found in the subjective or dialogic form of the Platonic system and in irony. The utterance of the individual which is valid as such in opposition to opinions or individuals needs a purchase whereby subjective uncertainty becomes objective truth.

But it can further be asked why this mythologizing is found in dialogues preeminently developing ethico-religious truths while the purely metaphysical Parmenides is free of it. It can be asked why the positive basis is mythical and depends on myths.

And here we come to the solution. In developing definite ethical and religious questions, or even questions of natural philosophy as in the *Timaeus,* Plato is not satisfied with his negative interpretation of the Absolute. It is not enough to plunge everything into the depths of a night where, as Hegel says, all cows are black. Here Plato avails himself of a positive interpretation of the Absolute. And its essential, self-grounded form is myth and allegory. Where the Absolute stands on one side and limited positive actuality on the other, and the positive is still to be maintained, it becomes the medium of absolute light which bursts into a fabulous display of color. The finite and positive signifies something other than itself. It has a soul in itself for which this transformation is miraculous. The entire world has become a world of myths. Every form is an enigma. And this has reappeared even in our time by virtue of a similar law.

This positive representation of the Absolute with its mythico-allegorical garb is the fountainhead and heartbeat of the philosophy of transcendence, a transcendence that is as essentially related to immanence as it is distinct from it. Here indeed is the affinity of Platonism with every positive religion, particularly with Christianity, which is the completed philosophy of transcendence. Here also is one of the respects in which a deeper connection can be made between historic Christianity and the history of ancient philosophy. With this positive interpretation of the Absolute it would follow that for Plato an individual as such, Socrates, was the mirror and the myth of Wisdom. Plato calls him the philosopher of Death and Love. This is not to say that Plato superseded the historical Socrates. The positive interpretation of the Absolute goes with the subjective character of Greek philosophy, with the concept of the wise man.

Death and Love are myths of the negative dialectic because the dialectic is the simple inner light, the penetrating eye of Love, the inner soul which is not crushed through the material dissolution of life. It is the inner place of the spirit. Thus Love is the myth of the dialectic. But the dialectic is also the torrent which shatters multiplicity and its limits, which overthrows autonomous forms to plunge everything into the one sea of eternity. Hence the myth of the dialectic is Death.

(pp. 58–60)

FROM *"The Leading Article of No. 179 Kölnische Zeitung"*

BEFORE FURTHER pursuing these "silly" explanations of the leading article on "scientific research," let us regale ourselves a while on Mr. H[ermes'] "*philosophy of religion*," his "own science"!

"Religion is the foundation of the state, as it is the most necessary condition for every social association not aimed merely at attaining some ulterior aim."

Proof: "In its crudest form as *childish fetishism* it raises man to a certain extent above sensuous appetites, which, if he lets himself be dominated exclusively by them, *debase him to an animal* and make him incapable of fulfilling any more elevated purpose."

The leading article calls fetishism the "*crudest* form" of religion. It therefore admits something which is recognized as established by all men of "scientific research" even without his consensus, that "*animal worship*" is a *higher* religious form than fetishism, but does not animal worship debase man below the animal, does it not make the animal man's god?

Now this talk about "fetishism"! Real pfenning magazine learning! Fetishism is so far from raising man *above* the appetites that it is on the contrary "the *religion of sensuous appetites*." The fantasy of the appetites tricks the fetish worshipper into believing that an "inanimate object" will give up its natural character to gratify his desires. The crude appetite of the fetish worshipper therefore *smashes* the fetish when the latter ceases to be its most devoted servant. (p. 22)

FROM *Contribution to the Critique of Hegel's Philosophy of Right*

FOR GERMANY the *criticism* of *religion* is in the main complete, and criticism of religion is the premise of all criticism.

The *profane* existence of error is discredited after its *heavenly oratio pro aris et focis* [speech for the altars and hearths] has been rejected. Man, who looked for a superman in the fantastic reality of heaven and found nothing there but the *reflexion* of himself, will no longer be disposed to find but the *semblance* of himself, the non-human (Unmensch) where he seeks and must seek his true reality.

The basis of irreligious criticism is: *Man makes religion,* religion does not make man. In other words, religion is the self-consciousness and self-feeling of man who has either not yet found himself or has already lost himself again. But *man* is no abstract being squatting outside the world. Man is *the world of man,* the state, society. This state, this society, produce religion, a *reversed world-consciousness,* because they are a *reversed world.* Religion is the general theory of that world, its encyclopaedic compendium, its logic in a popular form, its spiritualistic *point d'honneur,* its en-thusiasm, its moral sanction, its solemn completion, its universal ground for consolation and justification. It is *the fantastic realization* of the human essence because the *human essence* has no true reality. The struggle against religion is therefore mediately the fight against the *other world,* of which religion is the spiritual *aroma.*

Religious distress is at the same time the *expression* of real distress and the *protest* against real distress. Religion is the sigh of the oppressed creature, the heart of a heartless world, just as it is the spirit of a spiritless situation. It is the *opium* of the people.

The task of history, therefore, once the *world beyond the truth* has disappeared, is to establish the *truth of this world.* The immediate *task of philosophy,* which is at the service of history, once the *saintly form* of human self-alienation has been unmasked, is to unmask self-alienation in its *unholy forms.* Thus the criticism of heaven turns into the *criticism of right* and the *criticism of theology* into the *criticism of politics.* (pp. 41–42)

FROM *"Theses on Feuerbach"*

IV

FEUERBACH starts out from the fact of religious self-alienation, the duplication of the world into a religious, imaginary world and a real one. His work consists in the dissolution of the religious world into its secular basis. He overlooks the fact that after this work is completed the chief thing still remains to be done. For the fact that the secular foundation detaches itself from itself and establishes itself in the clouds as an independent realm is really only to be explained by the self-cleavage and self-contradictoriness of this secular basis. The latter must itself, therefore, first be understood in its contradiction, and then revolutionized in practice by the removal of the contradiction. Thus, for instance, once the earthly family is discovered to be the secret of the holy family, the former must then itself be criticized in theory and revolutionized in practice.

V

Feuerbach, not satisfied with *abstract thinking,* appeals to *sensuous contemplation;* but he does not conceive sensuousness as *practical,* human-sensuous activity.

VI

Feuerbach resolves the religious essence into the *human* essence. But the human

essence is no abstraction inherent in each single individual. In its reality it is the ensemble of the social relations.

Feuerbach, who does not enter upon a criticism of this real essence, is consequently compelled:

1. To abstract from the historical process and to fix the religious sentiment [Gemüt] as something by itself and to presuppose an abstract—*isolated*—human individual.

2. The human essence, therefore, can with him be comprehended only as "genus," as an internal, dumb generality which merely *naturally* unites the many individuals.

VII

Feuerbach, consequently, does not see that the "religious sentiment" is itself a *social product,* and that the abstract individual whom he analyzes belongs in reality to a particular form of society.

(pp. 70–71)

FROM *German Ideology*

THE PRODUCTION of notions, ideas and consciousness is from the beginning directly interwoven with the material activity and the material intercourse of human beings, the language of real life. The production of men's ideas, thinking, their spiritual intercourse, here appear as the direct efflux of their material condition. The same applies to spiritual production as represented in the language of politics, laws, morals, religion, metaphysics, etc. of a people. The producers of men's ideas, notions, etc., are men, but real active men as determined by a definite development of their productive forces and the intercourse corresponding to those productive

forces up to its remotest form. Consciousness [*das Bewusstsein*] can never be anything else but conscious being [*das bewusste Sein*], and the being of men is their real life-process. If in the whole of ideology men and their relations appear upside down as in a *camera obscura* this is due as much to their historical life-process as the inversion of objects on the retina is due to their immediate physical life-process.

In direct opposition to German philosophy, which comes down from heaven to earth, here there is ascension from earth to heaven. That means that we proceed not from what men say, fancy or imagine, nor from men as they are spoken of, thought, fancied, imagined in order to arrive from them at men of flesh and blood; we proceed from the really active men and see the development of the ideological reflexes and echoes of their real life-process as proceeding from that life-process. Even the nebulous images in the brain of men are necessary sublimates of their material, empirically observable, materially preconditioned, life-process. Thus, morals, religion, metaphysics and other forms of ideology and the forms of consciousness corresponding to them no longer retain their apparent independence. They have no history, they have no development, but men, developing their material production and their material intercourse, with this, their reality, their thinking and the products of their thinking also change. It is not consciousness that determines life, but life that determines consciousness. In the first view one proceeds from consciousness as from the living individual; in the second, in conformity with real life, from the real living individuals themselves, considering consciousness only as *their* consciousness. . . . (pp. 73–75)

We are certainly dealing with an interesting phenomenon: the rotting away of absolute Spirit. Its last spark having failed, the various components of this caput mortuum began to decompose, entered into new compounds, and formed new substances. The industrialists of philosophy, having lived off the exploitation of absolute Spirit, then seized on the new compounds. Each of them retailed his share with all possible zeal. Competition had to arise, and in the beginning it was rather bourgeois and traditional.

(pp. 405–406)

All German philosophical criticism from Strauss to Stirner is confined to criticism of *religious* conceptions. The critics proceeded from real religion and actual theology. As they went on, they determined in various ways what constitutes religious consciousness and religious conceptions. Their progress consisted of their subsuming the allegedly dominant metaphysical, political, juridical, moral, and other concepts under the class of religious or theological concepts. Similarly, they declared political, juridical, and moral consciousness to be religious or theological consciousness, and the political, juridical, and moral man, *"Man"* in the last resort, to be religious. They presupposed the governance of religion. Gradually every dominant relationship was held to be religious and made into a cult, such as the cult of law, the cult of state, etc. Eventually there was nothing but dogmas and belief in dogmas. The world was more and more sanctified until our honorable Saint Max [Stirner] was able to sanctify it en bloc and dismiss it once for all.

The Old Hegelians have *comprehended* everything once they reduced it to a Hegelian logical category. The Young Hegelians *criticized* everything by imputing religious conceptions to it or declaring everything to be theological. The Young Hegelians are in agreement with the Old Hegelians in believing in the governance of religion, concepts, a universal principle in the existing world. But one party attacks this governance as usurpation while the other party praises it as legitimate.   (p. 407)

((We know only one science, the science of history. History can be viewed from two sides: it can be divided into the history of nature and that of man. The two sides, however, are not to be seen as independent entities. As long as man has existed, nature and man have affected each other. The history of nature, so-called natural history, does not concern us here at all.

But we will have to discuss the history of man, since almost all ideology amounts to either a distorted interpretation of this history or a complete abstraction from it. Ideology itself is only one of the sides of this history.))* (p. 408)

It is obvious at the outset that there is a materialistic connection among men determined by their needs and their modes of production and as old as men themselves. This connection is forever assuming new forms and thus presents a "history" even in absence of any political or religious nonsense which might hold men together in addition.

Having considered four moments, four aspects of the primary historical relationships, we now find that man also possesses "consciousness." ⟨⟨Men have history because they must *produce* their life, and . . . in a *certain* way: this is determined by their physical organization; their consciousness is determined in the same way.⟩⟩ But this consciousness is not inherent, not "pure." From the start the "spirit" bears the curse of being "burdened" with matter which makes its appearance in the form of agitated layers of air, sounds, in short, in the form of language. Language is as old as consciousness. It *is* practical consciousness which exists also for other men and hence exists for me personally as well. Language, like consciousness, only arises from the need and necessity of relationships with other men. ((My relationship to my surroundings is my consciousness.)) Where a relationship exists, it exists for me. The animal has no *"relations"* with anything, no relations at all. Its relation to others does not exist as a relation. Consciousness is thus from the very beginning a social

product and will remain so as long as men exist. At first consciousness is concerned only with the *immediate* sensuous environment and a limited relationship with other persons and things outside the individual who is becoming conscious of himself. At the same time it is consciousness of nature which first appears to man as an entirely alien, omnipotent, and unassailable force. Men's relations with this consciousness are purely animal, and they are overawed by it like beasts. Hence it is a purely animal consciousness of nature (natural religion)—for the very reason that nature is not yet modified historically. On the other hand it is consciousness of the necessity to come in contact with other individuals; it is the beginning of man's consciousness of the fact that he lives in a society. This beginning is as animalistic as social life itself at this stage. It is the mere consciousness of being a member of a flock, and the only difference between sheep and man is that man possesses consciousness instead of instinct, or in other words his instinct is more conscious.

⟨⟨We here see immediately that this natural religion or particular relation to nature is determined by the form of society and vice versa. As it is the case everywhere, the identity of nature and man appears in such a way that the restricted behavior of men toward nature determines their restricted behavior to one another, and their restricted behavior to one another determines their restricted behavior to nature.⟩⟩ This sheeplike or tribal consciousness receives further development and formation through increased productivity, the increase of needs, and what is fundamental to both, the increase of population. Along with these, division of labor develops which originally was nothing but the division of labor in the sexual act, then that type of division of labor which comes

---

* Material in double parentheses was crossed out in the manuscript. Double brackets indicate addenda in Marx's handwriting.—Ed.

about spontaneously or "naturally" because of natural predisposition (e.g. physical strength), needs, accidents, etc., etc. The division of labor is a true division only from the moment a division of material and mental labor appears. ⟨⟨The first form of ideologists, *priests,* is concurrent.⟩⟩ From this moment on consciousness can really boast of being something other than consciousness of existing practice, or *really* representing something without representing something real. From this moment on consciousness can emancipate itself from the world and proceed to the formation of "pure" theory, theology, philosophy, ethics, etc. But even if this theory, theology, philosophy, ethics, etc., comes into conflict with existing relations, this can only occur because existing social relations have come into conflict with the existing force of production. Incidentally this can also occur in national relationships through a conflict not within the nation but between a particular national consciousness and the practice of other nations, that is, between the national and the general consciousness of a nation (as we observe now in Germany). ⟨⟨*Religion.* The Germans and *ideology* as such.⟩⟩ Since this contradiction within national consciousness, and since the struggle seems to be limited to this na((tional crap just because this nation is crap in and for itself.))

Moreover, it does not make any difference what consciousness starts to do on its own. The only result we obtain from all such muck is that these three moments—the force of production, the state of society, and consciousness—can and must come into conflict with one another because the *division of labor* implies the possibility, indeed the necessity, that intellectual and material activity ⟨⟨activity and thinking, that is, thoughtless activity and inactive thought [later deleted]⟩⟩—enjoyment and labor, production and consumption—are given to different individuals, and the only possibility of their not coming into conflict lies in again transcending the division of labor. It is self-evident that words such as "specters," "bonds," "higher being," "concept," "scruple," are only the idealistic, spiritual expression, the apparent conception of the isolated individual, the image of very empirical fetters and restrictions within which the mode of production of life and the related form of interaction move.   (pp. 421–423)

Victorian Popular Mythology

CHARLES KINGSLEY [1819–1875]

THOMAS BULFINCH [1796–1867]

THROUGH the first half of the nineteenth century, popular handbooks on mythology proliferated. In the classical dictionaries of Lempriere, Anthon, and Smith, one could find much detailed information and many of the latest scholarly discoveries and theories. Anthon's *Classical Dictionary* of 1841, for example, praises Keightley for having brought German thought into English scholarship; and Anthon treats all of mythology so as to dramatize the then current conflict between the mystics (Creuzer et al.) and the antimystics (Lobeck et al.).

Besides the classical dictionaries, there were endless handbooks that treated mythology grudgingly and with distaste as mere heathen idolatry. William Sheldon's small volume on *The Heathen Gods* (1809) and Mayo's four-volume *A New System of Mythology* (1815–1819) illustrate the range of these. There were also numerous handy reference books for women and school-children. Representative titles include *Mythologie de la jeunesse,* by A. Millin; *A Catechism of Mythology* (1832), by William Darlington; *The New Pantheon* (1809), by W. J. Hort; *Elements of Mythology,* by A. J. Valpy (another *Elements of Mythology* by Eliza Robbins went through thirteen editions); *A Book of Mythology for Youth,* by S. Goodrich (1832); and so on. Most of these are American, but the list could be matched in England, France,

and Germany with ease. They are handbooks boiled out of handbooks that have been boiled out of still earlier handbooks. Many betray the fact that the venerable Pomey (and Tooke) is the ultimate source.

There were also numerous compilations of a more respectable cast. In England William Godwin did a Mythology under the name of Thomas Baldwin, and Keightley's *Mythology of Greece and Italy* (1831) had some vogue. In France polite or catechism-like books such as Demoustier's *Lettres à Émilie sur la Mythologie* (1799) and the Abbé Lionnois's *Traité de la Mythologie* (1795) were popular, while in Germany *Benjamin Hederich's gründliches mythologisches Lexicon,* and the *Griechische Mythologie* (1854) and *Römische Mythologie* (1858) of Ludwig Preller were widely used.

Perhaps the most significant single development in the popular knowledge of mythology, at least in English-speaking countries, may be attributed to the work and subsequent influence of Nathaniel Hawthorne, Charles Kingsley, and Thomas Bulfinch. These men were not students so much as retellers of myth, and they managed, apparently independently of one another, to uniformly recast Greek mythology into a genteel Victorian subject. These writers undertook to renarrate the old myths, rather than to explain them; they cleaned the stories up, and they pitched them for a simple, even a childlike audience. At a time when the brothers Grimm were treating fairy tales as seriously as myths, these writers were treating myths only as so many old Greek fairy tales, full of charm and nonsense.

In 1852 Hawthorne wrote his *Wonder Book for Boys and Girls,* which he describes as follows in a letter to his publisher:

Unless I greatly mistake, these old fictions will work up admirably for the purpose: and I shall aim at substituting a tone in some degree Gothic or Romantic, or any such tone as may best please myself, instead of the classic coldness which is as repellent as the touch of marble . . . and, of course, I shall purge out all the old heathen wickedness, and put in a moral wherever practicable.

The *Wonder Book,* which has had at least thirty editions and which is still in print, presented cleaned-up versions of the myths of Perseus, Atalanta, and others; Hawthorne successfully removed the Greek quality, and treated the myths as modern fairy stories, writing them in a young people's parlor prose and insisting on the universal nature of the old stories. The *Wonder Book* has been very popular, has even been translated into German, and has helped greatly in creating the impression that Greek myths are decorous and gentle.

Charles Kingsley, the English novelist, published in 1855 a book called *The Heroes,* consisting of children's versions of the myths of Perseus, the Argonauts, and Theseus. Kingsley's preface is stiff, Christian, and condescending, but he does offer a bit of explanation of the myths, as the excerpt below shows. If Kingsley's missionary-like preface is not very attractive now, his retelling of the stories themselves is. Full, detailed, and with sombre endings, Kingsley's versions read well even today, though they are shorn of all sex and most violence. *The Heroes* has had at least thirty-five editions, and with

Hawthorne's work, has been a major influence on popular conceptions of mythology.

The mythological handbooks of Thomas Bulfinch, whose *The Age of Fable* appeared in 1855, has had an even wider impact. Written not only for children and schools but for grown-ups as well, and designed not only as a mythological handbook but as a retelling of the myths and a guide to mythology as it appears in English literature, Bulfinch's work was popular at once and has remained in wide general use. Bulfinch, son of the architect Charles Bulfinch, knew little about the repeated and strenuous attempts of the previous hundred and fifty years to explain mythology, as the brief section on the "origins of mythology" in *The Age of Fable* shows, and he was content to call mythology "the handmaid of literature." He made no bones about referring to "the easy learning of this little volume" and was willing to regard myth as a minor, pleasant, and unimportant diversion, a lesser accomplishment for ladies and gentlemen. Indeed, he seems almost to have scorned his subject, calling it a "science of mere fancy" and apologizing for its lack of utility. Like Hawthorne before him, Bulfinch was not interested in the Greek qualities of Greek myth; he used Roman sources and Roman names, and the popularity of his work is one reason for the marked Romanizing of Greek myth, which still persists. Bulfinch also, like Hawthorne and Kingsley, bowdlerized the myths. Anyone seeking information from Bulfinch about the birth of Aphrodite will find only that "Venus (Aphrodite), the goddess of love and beauty, was the daughter of Jupiter and Dione. Others say that Venus sprang from the foam of the sea." Thus the dark and bloody myths are purged into airy nonsense stories.

In the hands of these men and their imitators, Greek myths came to lose, in the popular mind, their aura of power, of dark origins, of religion, of passion, and of high strange truth, and they became instead something charming, graceful, and trivial, to be associated only with *belles lettres.* And if these writers made the myths available, they made them so in a form that belittled them. No one whose knowledge of mythology came from Hawthorne, Kingsley, or Bulfinch would be apt to consider myth a matter for serious concern or actual study. The romantics had seen primordial truth and power in myth, but in place of great dark energies, these writers leave the myths with only a slight genteel flush.

R.R.

REFERENCES Our texts are from Charles Kingsley, *The Heroes* (Boston, 1885), first published in 1855, and Thomas Bulfinch, *The Age of Fable* (Boston, 1856), first published in 1855.

KINGSLEY

FROM *The Heroes*

FOR, LIKE ALL nations who have left anything behind them, beside mere mounds of earth, they [the Greeks] believed at first in the One True God who made all heaven and earth. But after a while, like all other nations, they began to worship other gods, or rather angels and spirits, who (so they fancied) lived about their land. Zeus, the Father of gods and men (who was some dim remembrance of the blessed true God), and Hera his wife, and Phoebus Apollo the Sun-god, and Pallas Athené, who taught men wisdom and useful arts, and Aphrodite the Queen of Beauty, and Poseidon the Ruler of the Sea, and Hephaistos the King of the Fire, who taught men to work in metals. And they honoured the Gods of the Rivers, and the Nymph-maids, who they fancied lived in the caves, and the fountains, and the glens of the forest, and all beautiful wild places. And they honored the Erinyes, the dreadful sisters, who, they thought, haunted guilty men until their sins were purged away. And many other dreams they had, which parted the One God into many; and they said, too, that these gods did things which would be a shame and a sin for any man to do. And when their Philosophers arose, and told them that God was One, they would not listen, but loved their idols, and their wicked idol feasts, till they all came to ruin. But we will talk of such sad things no more.

(from Preface, xiii–xv)

BULFINCH

FROM *The Age of Fable*

IF NO OTHER knowledge deserves to be called useful but that which helps to enlarge our possessions or to raise our station in society, then Mythology has no claim to the appellation. But if that which tends to make us happier and better can be called useful, then we claim that epithet for our subject. For Mythology is the handmaid of literature; and literature is one of the best allies of virtue and promoters of happiness.

Without a knowledge of mythology much of the elegant literature of our own language cannot be understood and appreciated. When Byron calls Rome "the Niobe of nations," or says of Venice, "She looks a Sea-Cybele fresh from Ocean," he calls up to the mind of one familiar with our subject illustrations more vivid and striking than the pencil could furnish, but which are lost to the reader ignorant of mythology. Milton abounds in similar allusions. The short poem "Comus" contains more than thirty such, and the ode "On the Morning of the Nativity" half as many. Through "Paradise Lost" they are scattered profusely. This is one reason why we often hear persons by no means illiterate say that they cannot enjoy Milton. But were these persons to add to their more solid acquirements the easy learning of this little volume, much of the poetry of Milton which has appeared to

them "harsh and crabbed" would be found "musical as is Apollo's lute." Our citations, taken from more than twenty-five poets, from Spenser to Longfellow, will show how general has been the practice of borrowing illustrations from mythology.

The prose writers also avail themselves of the same source of elegant and suggestive illustration. One can hardly take up a number of the Edinburgh or Quarterly Review without meeting with instances. In Macaulay's article on Milton there are twenty such.

But how is mythology to be taught to one who does not learn it through the medium of the languages of Greece and Rome? To devote study to a species of learning which relates wholly to false marvels and obsolete faiths, is not to be expected of the general reader in a practical age like this. The time even of the young is claimed by so many sciences of facts and things, that little can be spared for set treatises on a science of mere fancy.

But may not the requisite knowledge of the subject be acquired by reading the ancient poets in translations? We reply, the field is too extensive for a preparatory course; and these very translations require some previous knowledge of the subject to make them intelligible. Let any one who doubts it read the first page of the

"Aeneid," and see what he can make of "the hatred of Juno," the "decree of the Parcae," the "judgement of Paris," and the "honors of Ganymede," without this knowledge.

Shall we be told that answers to such queries may be found in notes, or by a reference to the Classical Dictionary? We reply, the interruption of one's reading by either process is so annoying that most readers prefer to let an allusion pass unapprehended rather than submit to it. Moreover, such sources give us only the dry facts without any of the charm of the original narrative; and what is a poetical myth when stripped of its poetry? The story of Ceÿx and Halcyone, which fills a chapter in our book, occupies but eight lines in the best (Smith's) Classical Dictionary; and so of others.

Our book is an attempt to solve this problem, by telling the stories of mythology in such a manner as to make them a source of amusement. We have endeavoured to tell them correctly, according to the ancient authorities, so that when the reader finds them referred to he may not be at a loss to recognize the reference. Thus we hope to teach mythology not as a study, but as a relaxation from study; to give our work the charm of a story-book, yet by means of it to impart a knowledge of an important branch of education. The index at the end will adapt it to the purposes of reference, and make it a classical dictionary for the parlor.

Most of the classical legends in this book are derived from Ovid and Virgil. They are not literally translated, for, in the author's opinion, poetry translated into literal prose is very unattractive reading. Neither are they in verse, as well for other reasons as from a conviction that to translate faithfully under all the embarrassments of rhyme and measure is impossible. The

attempt has been made to tell the stories in prose, preserving so much of the poetry as resides in the thoughts and is separable from the language itself, and omitting those amplifications which are not suited to the altered form.

The Northern mythological stories are copied with some abridgement from Mallet's Northern antiquities. These chapters, with those on Oriental and Egyptian mythology, seemed necessary to complete the subject, though it is believed these topics have not usually been presented in the same volume with the classical fables.

The poetical citations so freely introduced are expected to answer several valuable purposes. They will tend to fix in memory the leading fact of each story, they will help to the attainment of a correct pronunciation of the proper names, and they will enrich the memory with many gems of poetry, some of them such as are most frequently quoted or alluded to in reading and conversation.

Having chosen *mythology as connected with literature* for our province, we have endeavoured to omit nothing which the reader of elegant literature is likely to find occasion for. Such stories or parts of stories as are offensive to pure taste and good morals are not given. But such stories are not often referred to, and if they occasionally should be, the English reader need feel no mortification in confessing his ignorance of them.

Our book is not for the learned, nor for the theologian, nor for the philosopher, but for the reader of English literature, of either sex, who wishes to comprehend the allusions so frequently made by public speakers, lecturers, essayists and poets, and those which occur in polite conversation.

We trust our young readers will find it a source of entertainment; those more advanced a useful companion in their reading; those who travel, and visit museums and galleries of art, an interpreter of paintings and sculptures; those who mingle in cultivated society, a key to allusions which are occasionally made; and last of all, those in advanced life, pleasure in retracing a path of literature which leads them back to the days of their childhood, and revives at every step the associations of the morning of life.

The permanency of those associations is beautifully expressed in the well-known lines of Coleridge, in "The Piccolomini," Act ii Scene 4.

The intelligible forms of ancient poets,
The fair humanities of old religion,
The power, the Beauty, and the Majesty
That had their haunts in dale or piny
   mountain,
Or forest, by slow stream, or pebbly spring,
Or chasms and watery depths; all these have
   vanished;
They live no longer in the faith of reason;
But still the heart doth need a language; still
Doth the old instinct bring back the old
   names;
Spirits or gods that used to share this earth
With man as with their friend; and at this day
'Tis Jupiter who brings whate'er is great,
And Venus who brings every thing that's fair.
                                      (Preface)

American Romanticism and Myth

R A L P H   W.   E M E R S O N   [1 8 0 3 – 1 8 8 2]

M A R G A R E T   F U L L E R   [1 8 1 0 – 1 8 5 0]

E D G A R   A L L A N   P O E   [1 8 0 9 – 1 8 4 9]

H E R M A N   M E L V I L L E   [1 8 1 9 – 1 8 9 1]

H E N R Y   D.   T H O R E A U   [1 8 1 7 – 1 8 6 2]

IF NINETEENTH-CENTURY American scholarship made only slight contributions to the study of myth, American writers were intensely interested in the revival of myth, sought continually for new ways to work myth into their writings, and eventually produced, in the 1850s during the period that F. O. Matthiessen called the "American Renaissance," a body of writing which includes *Walden, Moby Dick,* and *Leaves of Grass* and which amounts to a heroic literature for America. Believing that the mid-nineteenth century in America was a new heroic age, and believing deeply in the future of the great democratic experiment, these writers and others forged a new series of myths about the common man, the American, and embodied them in a literature of workaday epic and democratic heroism that still stands as a high point in American writing.

Indeed it has become customary to deal with much nineteenth-century writing in America in terms of myth, and the closing section of Matthiessen's *American Renaissance* still stands as the best of these attempts. Yet modern scholars and critics tend to treat the mythic qualities in nineteenth-century writing from modern vantage points alone, and while this application of hindsight is one of the purposes of criticism, it can also give its subject an unwarrantably modern look. For most modern myth criticism of *Walden, Moby Dick,* or *Leaves of Grass,* based as it is on Freud, Jung, Cassirer, Frye, or others, or upon biblical archetypes such as those of Adam, the garden of Eden, the fortunate Fall, and so on, does not make clear the fact that Poe, Hawthorne, Melville, Emerson, Thoreau, Whitman, and many lesser writers were themselves actively interested in and well versed in current mythological interests and researches. The meaning of mythology, the origins of mythology, the connections suggested by comparative mythology, and above all, the romantic urge to create new myths and whole new mythologies were subjects of central concern to these writers; they were powerfully aware of the importance of myth to their work, and their experiments with myth in literature were conscious, deliberate, and sophisticated.

American interest in myth had been growing since the late eighteenth century. Many English and European books relating to myth were reissued in America, handbooks such as those of Sheldon, Mayo, Goodrich, and of course Bulfinch were numerous, classical dictionaries abounded, and classical scholars such as George Ticknor, Edward Everett, George Bancroft, and Charles Anthon were vitally interested in myth. John Adams became interested in myth studies in his later years; Frank Manuel has described Adams's fascinated reading of Dupuis, Court de Gebelin, and others. Other Americans interested in myth include Joel Barlow, whose mock-heroic "Hasty Pudding" also contains mock-myth elements, and Noah Webster, whose long etymologizing treatise on mythology, "Origin of Mythology," printed in the *Memoirs of the Connecticut Academy of Arts and Sciences* in 1810, considers Jacob Bryant and George Faber to be the great authorities in the field.

William Cullen Bryant's lectures on poetry in 1825 and his still unpublished lectures on mythology mark one sort of serious interest in myth among American writers. In "On Poetry in its Relation to our Age and Country," Bryant ventured to hope that American authors would be able to do without Venus and Cupid, and would be able to bypass myth (which Bryant regarded as a decorative and decadent European vice) to come to real experience itself. But in the lectures on mythology, Bryant shows more interest in the subject and suggests the allegorical and emblematic qualities that classical myths can have for the writer. But Bryant is still interested only in how the modern writer can use the Greek myths and he has no interest in making new myths.

Margaret Fuller gave a series of "conversations" on the general subject of mythology in 1841, one of which is reprinted below. These spirited sessions are a fascinating record of how the new and exciting German ideas about myth were being received by educated people of all sorts in New England. Emerson attended some of these talks; William W. Story the sculptor was there, as were George Ripley (President of the Association at Brook Farm), Elizabeth Peabody and her sister Sophia Peabody (later Hawthorne's wife), James Freeman Clarke, Jones Very, Charles Wheeler the Greek scholar, Bronson Alcott, and others. Miss Fuller drew upon Creuzer, Herder, Goethe, and Novalis, and the recorded conversations show a highly entertaining jumble of the new German mystical allegorism and the old Baconian allegorism, all tempered by New England moral concerns. These conversations show the exciting and confusing impact of the new ideas, and how current and fashionable mythology had become; and the conversations attended by Emerson show the conflict between those who wished, with Miss Fuller, to appreciate the old Greek myths, and those who, with Emerson, were becoming interested in creating new myths for America.

The Americans were also aware of the theological side of myth study; an example is Theodore Parker's attack on Strauss's *Life of Jesus* which appeared in the *Christian Teacher* for April 1844, parodying Strauss's mythic approach:

The story of the Declaration of Independence is liable to many objections if we examine it *a la mode* Strauss. The Congress was held at a mythical town whose very name is suspicious,—Philadelphia, Brotherly Love. The date is suspicious; the *fourth* day of the *fourth* month (reckoning from April as it is probable the Heraclidae and Scandinavians, possible that the aboriginal Americans and certain Hebrews did). . . .

Mythology was then a part of the general intellectual climate in America, and one should not be surprised to find it being put to great uses by the great writers who, beginning with Emerson, began to look to myth to provide the vital force for a new heroic literature. Emerson was deeply influenced by the thought and literature of Germany and of the Orient and he was acquainted with the scholarship that was extending and questioning these subjects. He knew the work of Bayle, Warburton, Blackwell, Lowth, Mallet, Davies, Stukeley, Jacob Bryant, William Jones, Fénelon, Volney, Grimm, Herder, Friedrich Schlegel, K. O. Müller, F. Max Müller, and Ludwig Preller. Early in his journals, Emerson deals lightly with myth, noting, for example, how an "unprincipled bandit in Greece was a hero in the second generation, a giant in the third and a god in the fourth." By 1835 though, in a lecture subsequently called "The Age of Fable," Emerson sought to connect Greek myth with English medieval romance. As the excerpt below shows, Emerson was now taking myth seriously, though he was still reading it pretty much as a species of free or open allegory. By 1841, Emerson is maintaining, against Margaret Fuller, that there is no good reason why we can't make our own mythology, and in much of Emerson's subsequent work this impulse can be seen. His *Representative Men*, for example, is a book of heroes for the new world to emulate; Emerson treats Plato in quasi-mythical fashion as The Philosopher, Goethe as The Writer, and so on.

Henry Thoreau was perhaps more successful than Emerson in applying the idea of a new mythology for a new heroic age to his writing. Both *A Week on the Concord and Merrimack Rivers* and *Walden* are epics of the common man; each is a recommendation that we live heroic lives in the present, and each is underpinned by an almost religious impulse to worship Nature and to weave stories or myths that will capture elusive but important

truths for us. Thoreau's fanciful flights about the bottomlessness of Walden, about its underground connection with White's pond, and so on, are deliberate mythmaking, as are the bean-field heroics and the battle of the ants. Thoreau's use of the seasonal cycle of the year to give his work structure and meaning ties his modern mythmaking to the birth, growth, harvest, and death cycle of the natural world, and makes his best work an excellent example of the possibilities for modern myth. The brief statement on myth from "Walking," reprinted below, will perhaps explain something of what is not so much discussed as practiced and achieved in *Walden*.

Whitman is the third of the group of writers who might be called the optimistic mythmakers of mid-nineteenth century American literature. Like Emerson and Thoreau, he wished to make myths for the great new democracy, myths glorifying the common man and the "heroisms of the concrete" and giving epic utterance to the present moment, rather than to a glorious past. And for Whitman, as for Emerson and Thoreau, modern literature, alive with mythic significance, seemed an excellent substitute for the conventional Christian sects that were increasingly moribund. These men worked to provide America with beliefs, with heroes, with patterns for the heroic life, and with a sense of wonder at the amplitude of nature and the greatness of man in the new world. And it is probably fair to say that the writings of these men have provided educated Americans with patterns or ideals or perhaps myths, some of which are still alive. Emerson's American scholar, and his self-reliant man, the Thoreau of *Walden* and of "Civil Disobedience," the self that Whitman celebrated who wanted to embrace all people and all experiences have become, in certain limited ways, parts of a still vital American mythology.

While Emerson, Thoreau, and Whitman were celebrating the common man and the new heroic age with such great faith and enthusiasm, there was, in the work of Poe, Hawthorne, and Melville, another kind of literature being written. It was darker, less hopeful about democracy and about the future and the nature of man, but its tragic vision was also expressed in mythic terms. Poe, Hawthorne, and Melville wrote, or at least tried to write, tragic myths that dwelt on destruction and catastrophe rather than on creation, on guilt rather than on love, on heroism doomed to defeat rather than to success.

Richard Wilbur has recently argued that most of Poe's work centers on a mythic pattern worked out most fully in the story called "Ligeia." According to this, the world, which was once unified, is now dispersed and scattered. Only the poet's creative imagination can apprehend truth and can reassemble that original oneness. Death and rebirth are thus the key themes not only in "Ligeia" but in much of Poe's poetry, and his mythic themes of "supernal beauty" and inevitable annihilation are still important to what has been called the disaster-haunted American imagination. Poe took up myth in many ways; his *Eureka* is a remarkable attempt, as Auden has noted, to write a modern cosmogony, and such pieces as "The Power of Words" shows Poe working out a mythology for himself that would serve, as Yeats's *A Vision* served him, as a source for metaphors for poetry.

Hawthorne's work seems, as Matthiessen remarked, less concerned with myth than that of the other writers we are dealing with. But even leaving aside his retellings of Greek myth for children, dealt with elsewhere in this volume, Hawthorne's lifelong interest in legend had deepened into a full preoccupation with myth by the time of his last finished romance, *The Marble Faun*. One can even argue that Hawthorne's own work-

ing idea of a romance (as opposed to a novel) as a kind of "poetic precinct" where the real and the ideal can meet and become interfused is almost exactly the definition of myth given by Moritz and widely adopted in Germany. Hawthorne also knew the work of Friedrich Schlegel, that of Fontenelle, Bayle, Voltaire, Fénelon, and Picart. He used publications of the *Académie des Inscriptions,* the *Asiatick Researches,* and Charles Demoustier's *Lettres à Émilie sur la Mythologie,* and numerous other more general books on ancient civilization and religion. *The Marble Faun* (subtitled *The Transformations*) is a kind of modern and tragic Ovid; a series of metamorphoses figure importantly in the novel, while the central figure, Donatello, is treated half as a mythical being, half as a human, somehow descended from gods. Indeed the book is a vast attempt to make sense of the problem of mythology in art and in modern life.

The greatest of the American writers who worked with myth is Herman Melville. In his early and strange allegorical-philosophical romance *Mardi,* Melville worked out hundreds of playful allusions to mythology, made up numerous myths of his own, canvassed and imitated all the currently fashionable approaches to myth, and generally produced what might be called a fantasia on mythology, as has been argued by H. Bruce Franklin in his work on Melville's mythology, *The Wake of the Gods.* In *Pierre,* Melville used the figure of Enceladus to weight his novel with mythic overtones, but this attempt to revivify Greek myth worked less well than his attempt to use Hindu myth in *The Confidence Man.* Melville's long poem, *Clarel,* is almost a textbook on comparative mythology and comparative religion, and indeed, most of Melville's interest in myth has a strong religious pressure behind it. Melville's great book, *Moby Dick,* may even be described as a book in which religious emotion and mythological knowledge flow together much as Melville says that Ahab's gashed body and his torn soul bled together and became interfused. The novel is one of enormous energy; it is Promethean or Faustian, and while it draws heavily on old religion and old mythology, its focus is always on the insistent present. The result is that this book, steeped in old myth, is one of the few modern works of literature that has successfully created a new myth of serious and tragic proportions. Ahab's pursuit of the white whale is now a permanent image in the American imagination, and it operates at a far deeper level than the Davy Crockett, Paul Bunyan, and Johnny Appleseed stories. Perhaps one can say that if Milton wrote the Puritan epic, Melville forged the Puritan tragic myth. The disaster that overtakes Ahab's grand proud chase is a darkly splendid expression of the disaster latent in the Puritan encounter with the wilderness, in the Puritan reliance on self and on strength of will, and in the Puritan impulse to separation and individual isolation. *Moby Dick* has affinities with Shakespeare and with Greek tragedy too, and Melville's ability to invest Ahab and his antagonist with the heroic, oversized dimensions of high mythic significance is one of the clear triumphs of modern mythmaking.

It is clear that myth was central to this entire group of mid-century writers. It is also clear, though perhaps less obvious, that they were well informed about myth, myth theory, and myth criticism, and that they were aware of and enthusiastic about the possibilities of creating new myths for a new people. Just why this concern with myth came to a head when it did and how it became responsible for so much American masterwork is much less clear, though perhaps the progress of the interest in myth which is the subject of this volume will help to explain why myth had such an enormous impact on the literature first of Germany, then of England, then of France, and finally of America.

R.R.

REFERENCES Texts are from *The Early Lectures of Ralph Waldo Emerson* (Cambridge: Harvard University Press, 1959), Vol. I, ed. Stephen E. Whicher and Robert E. Spiller. Caroline Healey Dall, *Margaret and her friends* (Boston, 1895); Edgar Allan Poe, "The Conversation of Eiros and Charmion," in *The Complete Works of Edgar Allan Poe* (New York, 1902), Virginia Edition; Herman Melville, *Mardi* (New York, 1849); Henry D. Thoreau, "Walking," from *Excursions* (Vol. IX of the Riverside Edition of *The Writings of Henry David Thoreau*, Cambridge, Massachusetts, 1894).

Standard bibliographies include Spiller et al., *Literary History of the United States* (New York, 1948) bibliography volume and supplement, ed. R. Ludwig, and the quarterly bibliographies in *American Literature*. The best study of the period and writers dealt with above is still F. O. Matthiessen, *American Renaissance* (New York, 1941). A good, shorter study is Lewis Mumford, *The Golden Day* (New York, 1926). For the impact of India, see the bibliography in Raymond Schwab, *La Renaissance orientale* (Paris, 1950).

Other useful work includes H. A. Pochmann, *German Culture in America* (Madison: University of Wisconsin Press, 1957); H. M. Jones, *America and French Culture, 1750–1848* (Chapel Hill: University of North Carolina Press, 1927); Octavius Frothingham, *Transcendentalism in New England* (New York, 1876); A. E. Christy, *The Orient in American Transcendentalism* (New York, 1932).

For Emerson, see K. W. Cameron, *Emerson the Essayist,* 2 vols. (Raleigh, North Carolina, 1945), and *Emerson's Reading* (New York: Haskell, 1969); F. I. Carpenter, *Emerson and Asia* (Cambridge: Harvard University Press, 1930); Rene Wellek, "Emerson and German Philosophy," *New England Quarterly,* XVI, 1943, pp. 41–62; Joseph R. Reaver, *Emerson as Mythmaker* (Gainesville, Florida, 1954); John Clendinning, "Emerson and Bayle," *Philological Quarterly,* XLIII, Jan. 1964, pp. 79–86; and Maurice Chazin, "Quinet: An Early Discoverer of Emerson," *PMLA,* 1933, pp. 147–163.

For Thoreau, see E. Seybold, *Thoreau, the Quest and the Classics* (New Haven: Yale University Press, 1951); F. E. Eddleman, "The use of Lempriere's Classical Dictionary in Walden," *Emerson Society Quarterly,* no. 43, 1966, pp. 62–65; W. B. Stein, "A Bibliography of Hindu and Buddhist Literature Available to Thoreau through 1854," *Emerson Society Quarterly,* no. 47, 1967, pp. 52–56; E. E. Leisy, "Thoreau and Ossian," *New England Quarterly,* vol. 18, 1945, pp. 96–98.

For Poe, see D. Ramakrishna, "Poe's Eureka and Hindu Philosophy," *Emerson Society Quarterly,* no. 47, 1967, pp. 28–32; Carol H. Maddison, "Poe's Eureka," in *Texas Studies in Literature and Language,* II, 1960, pp. 350–367; and Richard Wilbur's introduction to Poe in Perry Miller's *Major Writers of America* (New York: Harcourt Brace, 1962), Vol. I.

For Melville, see H. Bruce Franklin, *The Wake of the Gods* (Stanford, 1963); Dorothee Finklestein, *Melville's Orienda* (New Haven: Yale University Press, 1961); R. A. Rees, "Melville's Alma and the Book of Mormon," *Emerson Society Quarterly,* no. 43, 1966, pp. 41–46; T. Vargish, "Gnostic Mythos in Moby Dick," *PMLA,* LXXXI, 1966, pp. 272–277; and J. T. Frederick, "Melville's Early Acquaintance with Bayle," *American Literature,* 1968, p. 545.

Little appears to have been done on Margaret Fuller's use of myth. Other figures in the American Renaissance not represented here by excerpts include Whitman and Hawthorne. Much has been done with their uses of myth; see for example, Wm. A. Little, "Walt Whitman and the Nibelungenlied," *PMLA,* LXXX, 1965, pp. 562–570 and C. M. Lombard, "Whitman on French Romanticism," *Walt Whitman Review,* XII, 1966, pp. 41–43, and Hugo McPherson, *Hawthorne as Myth-Maker* (Toronto: University of Toronto Press, 1969).

EMERSON

FROM *"The Age of Fable"*

VAST COLLECTIONS of tales of this character differing from the Arabian tales only in being joined with European manners and the Christian religion, exist in manuscript in the English public libraries of a date prior to the invention of printing and now make the first compositions in the English tongue. Many of them are the work of unknown authors which is the less important as they possess so little peculiarity of character. Many of them or parts of them have been printed by Ellis, Warton, Ritson, Southey but the most vogue they have at the present day is in the abridgments of Morte d'Arthur, Lancelot du Lac, and the Seven Champions of Christendom which have not yet lost all favor with the rising generation. I shall not quote any specimens of these as the language is for the most part too obsolete to be intelligible by the ear, containing many now forgotten Norman and Saxon words. But it seems necessary to make a few remarks in explanation of their nature and use.

Nobody can recall these without being

struck with the immense difference between the Gothic fables and the fables of antiquity. In the beautiful creations of the Grecian muse every fable, though related as religious truth and believed by the multitude as history, is, at the same time a fine allegory conveying a wise and consistent sense. Those are properly creations of the Imagination; these merely of the Fancy. They beside superficial beauty have a deeper beauty to the wise. These only please us as long as they are new or only please the childish part of us. Compare the various incidents which we collect out of different poets respecting one of the Grecian Gods or demigods with the unchosen and miscellaneous prodigies which are related of Merlin and Arthur. Take for example the story of Prometheus.

The ancients relate that man was the work of Prometheus and formed of clay; only the artificer mixed in the mass particles taken from different animals. And being desirous to improve his workmanship and endow as well as create the human race he stole up to heaven with a bundle of birch rods and kindling them at the chariot of the sun thence brought down fire to the earth for the service of men. Prometheus was repaid for this meritorious act by the ingratitude of mankind so that forming a conspiracy they accused both him and his invention to Jupiter. But the matter was otherwise received than they imagined for the accusation proved extremely grateful to Jupiter and the gods; insomuch that they not only indulged mankind with the use of fire, but moreover conferred on them a most acceptable and desireable present, viz. perpetual youth.

But men, foolishly overjoyed hereat, laid this present of the gods upon an ass, who in returning back with it being extremely thirsty and coming to a fountain, the serpent who was the guardian thereof would not suffer him to drink, but upon conditon of receiving the burden he carried, whatever it should be. The silly ass complied; and thus the perpetual renewal of youth was, for a sup of water, transferred from men to the race of serpents.

Jupiter wishing to revenge himself on Prometheus but finding he could not punish him without afflicting the human race, commanded Vulcan to form a beautiful and graceful woman to whom every god presented a certain gift, when[ce] she was called Pandora, i.e. *all gift*. They put into her hands an elegant box containing all sorts of miseries and misfortunes; but hope was placed at the bottom of it. With this box, she first goes to Prometheus to find if she could prevail upon him to receive and open it; but he, being on his guard, warily refused the offer. Upon his refusal she comes to his brother Epimetheus, a man of very different temper, who rashly and inconsiderately opens the box. When finding all kinds of miseries and misfortunes issued out of it, he, with great hurry and struggle, endeavoured to clap on the cover again: but with all his endeavor, could scarce keep in Hope which lay at the bottom.

Jupiter persisting in his wrath against Prometheus caused him to be carried to Mount Caucasus and there fastened to a pillar so firmly that he could not stir. A vulture stood by him which in the daytime gnawed his liver, but in the nighttime the wasted parts were supplied again, whence matter for his pain was never wanting.

This is one of those elegant fables invented by the Greeks which seem rather to have been gradually formed by the additions of successive poets than to have been devised by one for it was accepted by the people as a part of their sacred history. It seems to be a collection of pleasing allegories. Lord Bacon has drawn out of it a consistent sense explaining it of Providence.

Such another is the fable of Orpheus, explained of natural and moral philosophy, of Atalanta and of Proteus, of Pan.

But see how unlike are these fables from those of our Romantic Literature. The meaning of the ancient apologues is so palpable and consistent, that we cannot persuade ourselves but they were made to convey it. Whereas in our Romance the whole object was amusement by the incidents of the story itself, and nothing was farther from the minstrel's intention than the discovery of a hidden sense.

Yet the obligations of our childhood to these excellent knights, fairies, and magicians, are too great to be hastily dismissed. The progress of refinement, Mr. Addison says, has not entirely plucked the old woman out of our hearts. A skilful tale of superstition or faerie has its own claims on us. But beside the charm of gorgeous fiction for the fancy I believe a fairy tale draws some of its power over us from deep and legitimate sources. A fairy tale, a romance has often (I may say, always) a moral in spite of itself. He who constructs a beautiful fable only with the design of making it symmetrical and pleasing, will find that unconsciously he has been writing an allegory. He finds at the end of his task that he has only been holding the pen for a higher hand which has overseen and guided him. Poets, said Plato, utter great and wise things which they do not themselves understand.

When Lucian, quite in the spirit of romance, relates that Pancrates a magician journeying from Memphis to Coptus and wanting a servant, took a door-bar and pronounced over it some magical words and it stood up and brought him water and turned a spit, and carried bundles, doing all the work of a slave. Now we can in an instant make this idle tale an allegory of the progress of art, by reading for "Pancrates" Fulton or Watt, and for "magical word" read *steam*. For these magicians by this spell of steam have made an iron bar and half a dozen wheels do the work not of one but of one thousand skilful servants.

So with the similar fictions of our Arabian and English romance. Without the most remote intention of allegory on the part of the writer they still are such. Magic and all that is ascribed to it is manifestly nothing but a deep presentiment of the powers of science. The power of subduing the elements, of using the secret virtues of minerals, of understanding the voices of birds are only the obscure efforts of the mind in a right direction. Then the preternatural strength and success of the hero, the gift of perpetual youth and the like are only alike the endeavor of the human spirit to bend the shows of things to the desires of the mind. In endeavoring to make his hero agreeable the writer insensibly makes him virtuous. And being virtuous it is agreeable to our constitution to believe him powerful and successful. Many of these fictions are exceedingly beautiful. In Perceforest and Amadis de Gaul a garland and a rose bloom on the head of her who is faithful and fade on the brow of the inconstant.   (pp. 257–260)

MARGARET FULLER

FROM *Margaret and Her Friends*

MARGARET recapitulated the statements she made last week. By thus giving to each fabled Deity its place in the scheme of Mythology, she did not mean to ignore the enfolding ideas, the one thought developed in all—as in Rhea, Bacchus, Pan. She would only imply that each personification was individual, served a particular purpose, and was worshipped in a particular way.

Before proceeding to talk about Ceres, she wished to remind us of the mischief of wandering from our subject. She hoped the ground she offered would be accepted *at least to talk about!* Certainly no one could deny that a mythos was the last and best growth of a national mind, and that in this case the characteristics of the Greek mind were best gathered from this creation.

Ceres, Persephone, and Isis, as well as Rhea, Diana, and so on, seem to be only modifications of one enfolding idea,—a goddess accepted by all nations, and not peculiar to Greece. The pilgrimages of the more prominent of these goddesses, Ceres and Isis, seem to indicate the life which loses what is dear in childhood, to seek in weary pain for what after all can be but half regained. Ceres regained her daughter, but only for half the year. Isis found her husband, but dismembered. This era in Mythology seems to mark the progress from an unconscious to a conscious state.

Persephone's periodical exile shows the impossibility of resuming an unconsciousness from which we have been once aroused, the need thought has, having once felt the influence of the Seasons, to retire into itself.

CHARLES WHEELER reminded Margaret that she had said that the predominant goddesses, without reference to Greece, enfolded only one idea, that of the female *Will* or *Genius,—the bounteous giver.* He had asked her if she could sustain herself by etymological facts, and she replied that her knowledge of the Greek was not critical enough. Since then he had inquired into the origin of the proper names of the Greek deities, and found that it confirmed her impression. The names of Rhea, Tellus, Isis, and Diana were resolvable into one, and the difference in their etymology was only a common and permissible change in the position of the letters of which they are composed, or a mere provincial dialectic change. Diana is the same as Dione, also one of the names of Juno.

E. P. P. asked if Homer ever confounded the last two? MARGARET thought not. Homer was purely objective. He knew little and cared less about the primitive creation of the myths.

R. W. EMERSON thought it would be very difficult to detect this secret. Jupiter, for instance, might have been a man who was the exponent of Will to his race.

MARGARET said, "No; they could have deduced him just as easily from Nature herself, or from a single exhibition of will power."

R. W. EMERSON said that a man like Napoleon would easily have suggested it.

"What a God-send is a Napoleon!" exclaimed CHARLES WHEELER; "let us pray for scores of such, that a new and superior mythos may arise for us!" Is it malicious to suspect a subtle irony turned against the sacred person of R. W. E. in this speech?

MARGARET retorted indignantly that if they came, *we* should do nothing better than write memoirs of their hats, coats, and swords, as we had done already, without thinking of any lesson they might teach. She could not see why we were not content to take the beautiful Greek mythi as they were, without troubling ourselves about those which might arise for us!

R. W. E. acknowledged that the Greeks had a quicker perception of the beautiful than we. Their genius lay in the material expression of it. If we knew the real meaning of the names of their Deities, the story would take to flight. We should have only the working of abstract ideas as we might adjust them for ourselves.

MARGARET said that a fable was more than a mere word. It was a word of the purest kind rather, the passing of thought into form. R. W. E. had made no allowance for time or space or climate, and there was a want of truth in that. The age of the Greeks was the age of Poetry; ours was the age of Analysis. *We* could not create a Mythology.

EMERSON asked, "Why not? We had still better material."

MARGARET said, irrelevantly as it seemed to me, that Carlyle had attempted to deduce new principles from present history,

and that was the reason he did not *respect* the *respectable*.

EMERSON said Carlyle was unfortunate in his figures, but we might have mythology as beautiful as the Greek.

MARGARET thought each age of the world had its own work to do. The transition of thought into form marked the Greek period. It was most easily done through fable, on account of their intense perception of beauty.

EMERSON pursued his own train of thought. He seemed to forget that we had come together to pursue MARGARET's. He said it was impossible that men or events should *stand out* in a population of twenty millions as they could from a population of a single million, to which the whole population of the ancient world could hardly have amounted. As Hercules stood to Greece, no modern man could ever stand in relation to his own world.

MARGARET thought Hercules and Jupiter quite different creations. The first *might* have been a deified life. The second could not.

CHARLES WHEELER said that R. W. E.'s view carried no historical obligation of belief with it. We could not deny the heroic origin of the Greek demi-gods, but the highest dynasty was the exponent of translated thought.

SOPHIA RIPLEY asked if the life of an individual fitly interwoven with her experience was not as fine a Poem as the story of Ceres, her wanderings and her tears? Did not Margaret know such lives?

R. W. E. thought every man had probably met his Jupiter, Juno, Minerva, Venus, or Ceres in society!

MARGARET was sure she never had!

R. W. E. explained: "Not in the world, but each on his own platform."

WILLIAM STORY objected. The life of an individual was not universal. (!)

SOPHIA RIPLEY repeated, "The inner life."

WILLIAM STORY claimed to be an individual, and did not think individual experience could ever meet all minds,—like the story of Ceres, for example.

SOPHIA said all experience was universal. . . .

STORY said every face had its own beauty. No act that was natural could be ungraceful.

EMERSON said that we all did sundry graceful acts, in our caps and tunics, which we never could do again, which we never wanted to do again.

MARGARET said, at last we had touched the point. We could not restore the childhood of the world, but could we not admire this simple plastic period, and gather from it some notion of the Greek genius?

R. W. E. thought this legitimate. He would have it that we could not determine the origin of a mythos, but we might fulfil Miss Fuller's intention.

MARGARET said history reconciled us to life, by showing that man had redeemed himself. Genius needed that encouragement.

Not *Genius,* SOPHIA RIPLEY thought; common natures needed it, but Genius was self-supported.

MARGARET said it might be the consolation of Genius.

MRS. RUSSELL asked why Miss Fuller found so much fault with the present.

MARGARET *had* no fault to find with it. She took facts as they were. Every age did something toward fulfilling the cycle of the mind. The work of the Greeks was not ours.

SOPHIA RIPLEY asked if the mythology had been a prophecy of the Greek mind to itself, or if the nation had experienced life in any wide or deep sense.

MARGARET seemed a little out of patience, and no wonder! She said it did not matter which. The question was, what could *we find* in the mythi, and what did the Greeks mean that we should find there. Coleridge once said that certain people were continually saying of Shakespeare, that he did not mean to impart certain spiritual meanings to some of his sketches of life and character; but if Shakespeare did not mean it his Genius did: so if the Greeks meant not this or that, the Greek genius meant it.

In relation to the progress of the ages, JAMES F. CLARKE said that the story of Persephone concealed in the bowels of the earth for half the year seemed to him to indicate something of their comparative states. Persephone was the seed which must return to earth before it could fructify. Thought must retire into itself before it can be regenerate.

MARGARET was pleased with this, more especially as in the story of the Goddess it is eating the pomegranate, whose seed is longest in germinating, which dooms her to the realm of Pluto.

GEORGE RIPLEY remarked that we saw this need of withdrawal in the slothful ages when mind seemed to be imbibing energy for future action. The world sometimes forsook a quest and returned to it. We had forsaken Beauty, but we might return to it.

Certainly, MARGARET assented. A perfect mind would detect all beauty in the hearth-rug at her feet: the meanest part of creation contained the whole; but the labor we were now at to appreciate the Greek proved conclusively that *we* were not Greek. A simple plastic nature would take it all in with delight, without doubt or question.

Or rather, amended EMERSON, would take it up and go forward with it.

It makes no difference, said MARGARET, for we live in a circle.

I did not think it pleasant to track and retrack the same arc, and preferred to go forward with R. W. E., so I asked if there was to be no *higher* poetry.

MARGARET acknowledged that there was something beyond the aspiration of the Egyptian or the poetry of the Greek.

GEORGE RIPLEY thought we had not lost all reverence for these abstract forces. The Eleusinian mysteries might be forgotten, but not Ceres. We did not worship in ignorance. The mysteries led back to the Infinite. The processes of vegetation were actually heart-rending!

Here, *I* thought, was a basis for my higher poetry.

GEORGE RIPLEY acknowledged that it was so. He seemed to be more conscious of the movement of the world than any of our party. He said we must not measure creation by Boston and Washington, as we were too apt to do. There was still France, Germany, and Prussia,—perhaps Russia! The work of this generation was not religious nor poetic; still, there was a tendency to go back to both. There were to be ultraisms, but also, he hoped, consistent development.

CHARLES WHEELER then related the story of Isis, of her hovering in the form of a swallow round the tree in which the sarcophagus of Osiris had been enclosed by Typhon; of her being allowed to fell the tree; of the odor emitted by the royal maidens whom she touched, which revealed her Divinity to the Queen; of the second loss of the body, as she returned home, and its final dismemberment.

There was little success in spiritualizing more of this story than the pilgrimage, and R. W. E. seemed to feel this; for when MARGARET had remarked that even a divine force must become as the birds of the air to compass its ends, and that it was in the carelessness of conscious success that the second loss occurred, he said that it was impossible to detect an inner sense in all these stories.

MARGARET replied, that she had not attempted that, but she could see it in all the prominent points. . . .

The Eleusinian mysteries were now alluded to. Although it has been said that only moral precepts were inculcated through these, WHEELER urged that a whole school of Continental authors now acknowledged that the higher doctrines of philosophy were taught.

R. W. E. added, that as initiation became more easy such instruction must have degenerated into a mere matter of form, and many of the *un*initiated surpass the initiated in wisdom.

MARGARET admitted this. Socrates was one of the uninitiated. The crowd seldom felt the full force of beauty in Art or Literature. To prove it, it was only necessary to walk once through the Hall of Sculpture at the Athenaeum, and catch the remarks of any half-dozen on Michael Angelo's "Day and Night." He would be fortunate who heard a single observer comment on its power.

MRS. RUSSELL asked why the images of the sun and moon were introduced into these mysterious celebrations.

MARGARET asked impatiently why they had always been invoked by every child who could string two rhymes together.

I said that if Ceres was the simple *agricultural* productive energy, of course the sun was her first minister, its genial influence being as manifest as the energy itself.

In regard to the etymology of the proper names, it seemed reasonable to me that this energy should have gained attributes as it did names. Any nation devoted to the chase would learn to call the lunar deity Diana; any devoted to the cultivation of grain would project her as Ceres. The reproductive powers of flocks and herds would suggest Rhea or Juno, and philosophy or art would invoke Persephone.

When we were talking about beauty, J. F. C. quoted Goethe, and said that the spirit sometimes made a mistake and clothed itself in the wrong garment.

(from Conversation 2, pp. 40–59)

POE

FROM *"The Conversation of Eiros and Charmion"*

THE INDIVIDUAL calamity was, as you say, entirely unanticipated; but analogous misfortunes had been long a subject of discussion with astronomers. I need scarce tell you, my friend, that, even when you left us, men had agreed to understand those passages in the most holy writings which speak of the final destruction of all things by fire, as having reference to the orb of the earth alone. But in regard to the immediate agency of the ruin, speculation had been at fault from that epoch in astronomical knowledge in which the comets were divested of the terrors of flame. The very moderate density of these bodies had been well established. They had been observed to pass among the satellites of Jupiter, without bringing about any sensible alteration either in the masses or in the orbits of these secondary planets. We had long regarded the wanderers as vapory creations of inconceivable tenuity, and as altogether incapable of doing injury to our substantial globe, even in the event of contact. But contact was not in any degree dreaded; for the elements of all the comets were accurately known. That among *them* we should look for the agency of the threatened fiery destruction had been for many years considered an inadmissible idea. But wonders and wild fancies had been, of late days, strangely rife among mankind; and, although it was only with a few of the ignorant that actual apprehension prevailed, upon the announcement by astronomers of a *new* comet, yet this announcement was generally received with I know not what of agitation and mistrust.

The elements of the strange orb were immediately calculated, and it was at once conceded by all observers, that its path, at perihelion, would bring it into very close proximity with the earth. There were two or three astronomers, of secondary note, who resolutely maintained that a contact was inevitable. I cannot very well express to you the effect of this intelligence upon the people. For a few short days they would not believe an assertion which their intellect, so long employed among worldly considerations, could not in any manner grasp. But the truth of a vitally important fact soon makes its way into the understanding of even the most stolid. Finally, all men saw that astronomical knowledge lied not, and they awaited the comet. Its approach was not, at first, seemingly rapid; nor was its appearance of very unusual character. It was of a dull red, and had little perceptible train. For seven or eight days we saw no material increase in its apparent diameter, and but a partial alteration in its color. Meantime, the ordinary affairs of men were discarded, and all interest absorbed in a growing discussion, instituted by the philosophic, in respect to the cometary nature. Even the grossly ignorant aroused their sluggish capacities to such considerations. The learned *now* gave their intellect—their soul—to no such points as the allaying of fear, or to the sustenance of loved theory. They sought—they panted for right views. They groaned for perfected knowledge. *Truth* arose in the purity of her strength and exceeding majesty, and the wise bowed down and adored.

That material injury to our globe or to its inhabitants would result from the apprehended contact, was an opinion which hourly lost ground among the wise; and the wise were now freely permitted to rule the reason and the fancy of the crowd. It was demonstrated, that the density of the comet's *nucleus* was far less than that of our rarest gas; and the harmless passage of a similar visitor among the satellites of Jupiter was a point strongly insisted upon, and which served greatly to allay terror. Theologists, with an earnestness fear-enkindled, dwelt upon the biblical prophecies, and expounded them to the people with a directness and simplicity of which no previous instance had been known. That the final destruction of the earth must be brought about by the agency of fire, was urged with a spirit that enforced every where conviction; and that the comets were

of no fiery nature (as all men now knew) was a truth which relieved all, in a great measure, from the apprehension of the great calamity foretold. It is noticeable that the popular prejudices and vulgar errors in regard to pestilences and wars—errors which were wont to prevail upon every appearance of a comet—were now altogether unknown. As if by some sudden convulsive exertion, reason had at once hurled superstition from her throne. The feeblest intellect had derived vigor from excessive interest.

What minor evils might arise from the contact were points of elaborate question. The learned spoke of slight geological disturbances, of probable alterations in climate, and consequently in vegetation; of possible magnetic and electric influences. Many held that no visible or perceptible effect would in any manner be produced. While such discussions were going on, their subject gradually approached, growing larger in apparent diameter, and of a more brilliant lustre. Mankind grew paler as it came. All human operations were suspended.

There was an epoch in the course of the general sentiment when the comet had attained, at length, a size surpassing that of any previously recorded visitation. The people now, dismissing any lingering hope that the astronomers were wrong, experienced all the certainty of evil. The chimerical aspect of their terror was gone. The hearts of the stoutest of our race beat violently within their bosoms. A very few days sufficed, however, to merge even such feelings in sentiments more unendurable. We could no longer apply to the strange orb any *accustomed* thoughts. Its *historical* attributes had disappeared. It oppressed us with a hideous *novelty* of emotion. We saw it not as an astronomical phenomenon in the heavens, but as an incubus upon our hearts, and a shadow upon our brains. It had taken, with inconceivable rapidity, the character of a gigantic mantle of rare flame, extending from horizon to horizon.

Yet a day, and men breathed with greater freedom. It was clear that we were already within the influence of the comet; yet we lived. We even felt an unusual elasticity of frame and vivacity of mind. The exceeding tenuity of the object of our dread was apparent; for all heavenly objects were plainly visible through it. Meantime, our vegetation had perceptibly altered; and we gained faith, from this predicted circumstance, in the foresight of the wise. A wild luxuriance of foliage, utterly unknown before, burst out upon every vegetable thing.

Yet another day—and the evil was not altogether upon us. It was now evident that its nucleus would first reach us. A wild change had come over all men; and the first sense of *pain* was the wild signal for general lamentation and horror. This first sense of pain lay in a rigorous constriction of the breast and lungs, and an insufferable dryness of the skin. It could not be denied that our atmosphere was radically affected; the conformation of this atmosphere and the possible modifications to which it might be subjected, were now the topics of discussion. The result of investigation sent an electric thrill of the intensest terror through the universal heart of man.

It had been long known that the air which encircled us was a compound of oxygen and nitrogen gases in the proportion of twenty-one measures of oxygen, and seventy-nine of nitrogen, in every one hundred of the atmosphere. Oxygen, which was the principle of combustion, and the vehicle of heat, was absolutely necessary to the support of animal life, and was the most powerful and energetic agent in nature. Nitrogen, on the contrary, was incapable of supporting either animal life or

flame. An unnatural excess of oxygen would result, it had been ascertained, in just such an elevation of the animal spirits as we had latterly experienced. It was the pursuit, the extension of the idea, which had engendered awe. What would be the result of a total extraction of the nitrogen? A combustion irresistible, all-devouring, omni-prevalent, immediate;—the entire fulfilment, in all their minute and terrible details, of the fiery and horror-inspiring denunciations of the prophecies of the Holy Book.

Why need I paint, Charmion, the now disenchained frenzy of mankind? That tenuity in the comet which had previously inspired us with hope, was now the source of the bitterness of despair. In its impalpable gaseous character we clearly perceived the consummation of Fate. Meantime a day again passed—bearing away with it the last shadow of Hope. We gasped in the rapid modification of the air. The red blood bounded tumultuously through its strict channels. A furious delirium possessed all men; and, with arms rigidly outstretched toward the threatening heavens, they trembled and shrieked aloud. But the nucleus of the destroyer was now upon us; —even here in Aidenn, I shudder while I speak. Let me be brief—brief as the ruin that overwhelmed. For a moment there was a wild lurid light alone, visiting and penetrating all things. Then—let us bow down, Charmion, before the excessive majesty of the great God!—then, there came a shouting and pervading sound, as if from the mouth itself of HIM; while the whole incumbent mass of ether in which we existed, burst at once into a species of intense flame, for whose surpassing brilliancy and all-fervid heat even the angels in the high Heaven of pure knowledge have no name. Thus ended all.

_____

MELVILLE

FROM *Mardi*

"The Centre of Many Circumferences"

[The following one-page chapter from Melville's early philosophical romance shows him at his satirically high-spirited best. In the manner of Swift's *Tale of a Tub,* Melville is writing both in earnest and in fun, and his satire is working on many levels. In one page he plays with pyramids and labyrinths, and with great rhetorical relish delivers a Euhemerist interpretation of the "holy of holies" or the innermost secret realm which is at last seen to contain only a man, and a foolish man at that. The passage also comments on how divinities may be formed.]

LIKE DONJALOLO himself, we hie to and fro; for back must now we pace to the House of the Morning.

In its rear, there diverged three separate arbours, leading to less public apartments.

Traversing the central arbour, and fancying it will soon lead you to open ground, you suddenly come upon the most private retreat of the prince: a square structure; plain as a pyramid; and without, as inscrutable. Down to the very ground, its walls are thatched; but on the farther side a passage way opens, which you enter. But not yet are you within. Scarce a yard distant, stands an inner thatched wall, blank as the first. Passing along the intervening corridor, lighted by narrow apertures, you reach the opposite side, and a second open-

ing is revealed. This entering, another corridor; lighted as the first, but more dim, and a third blank wall. And thus, three times three, you worm round and round, the twilight lessening as you proceed; until at last, you enter the citadel itself; the innermost arbour of a nest; wherof, each has its roof, distinct from the rest.

The heart of the place is but small; illuminated by a range of open skylights, downward contracting.

Innumerable as the leaves of an endless folio, multitudinous mats cover the floor; whereon reclining by night, like Pharoah on the top of his patrimonial pile, the inmate looks heavenward, and heavenward only; gazing at the torchlight processions in the skies, when, in state, the suns march to be crowned.

And here, in this impenetrable retreat, centrally slumbered the universe-rounded, zodiac-belted, horizon-zoned, sea-girt, reef-sashed, mountain-locked, arbour-nested, royalty-girdled, arm-clasped, self-hugged, indivisible Donjalolo, absolute monarch of Juam:—the husk-inhusked meat in a nut; the innermost spark in a ruby; the juice-nested seed in a golden-rinded orange; the red royal stone in an effeminate peach; the insphered sphere of spheres.

(Chap. lxxix)

THOREAU

FROM *"Walking"*

WHERE IS the literature which gives expression to Nature? He would be a poet who could impress the winds and streams into his service, to speak for him; who nailed words to their primitive senses, as farmers drive down stakes in the spring, which the frost has heaved; who derived his words as often as he used them—transplanted them to his page with earth adhering to their roots; whose words were so true and fresh and natural that they would appear to expand like the buds at the approach of spring, though they lay half-smothered between two musty leaves in a library—aye, to bloom and bear fruit there, after their kind, annually, for the faithful reader, in sympathy with surrounding Nature.

I do not know of any poetry to quote which adequately expresses this yearning for the Wild. Approached from this side, the best poetry is tame. I do not know where to find in any literature, ancient or modern, any account which contents me of that Nature with which even I am acquainted. You will perceive that I demand something which no Augustan nor Elizabethan age, which no *culture,* in short, can give. Mythology comes nearer to it than anything. How much more fertile a Nature, at least, has Grecian mythology its root in than English Literature! Mythology is the crop which the Old World bore before its soil was exhausted, before the fancy and imagination were affected with blight; and which it still bears, wherever its pristine vigor is unabated. All other literatures endure only as the elms which overshadow our houses; but this is like the great dragon-tree of the Western Isles, as old as mankind, and, whether that does or not, will endure as long; for the decay of other literatures makes the soil in which it thrives.

The West is preparing to add its fables to those of the East. The valleys of the Ganges, the Nile, and the Rhine having yielded their crop, it remains to be seen what the valleys of the Amazon, the Plate, the Orinoco, the St. Lawrence, and the Mississippi will produce. Perchance, when, in the course of ages, American liberty has become a fiction of the past—as it is to some extent a fiction of the present—the poets of the world will be inspired by American mythology.

BIBLIOGRAPHY OF WORKS
ON MYTH, 1680–1860

This is a bibliography of primary works written about myth between 1680 and 1860. (For secondary works written since 1860, see the checklist at the end of the General Introduction.) No adequate bibliography of this subject in this period exists in English; and even the best earlier compilations, in German and French, are far from satisfactory. We hope to provide here mainly an adequate bibliographical *introduction* to the complexity and richness of early modern interest in myth.

Our bibliography admits to being selective, for our listings could have been much more inclusive. But in some obvious ways, a really ambitious inclusiveness here is more an ideal than a possibility. In this period, mythology reached out into nearly every field of scholarly, speculative, and creative interest. A major and fundamental problem in studying myth in this time is that pertinent material constantly emerged (or became submerged) under such rubrics as theology, history, philosophy, religion, science (such as biology, astronomy, geology), travels, philology, literary and art criticism, and politics, or in fields such as "popular antiquities" (the older term for folklore) or "sacred geography" (currently subsumed under biblical archaeology). We have selected those works that could claim a fairly direct focus on myth, all the while keeping a broad but distinct sense of limits. Assuredly, the limits of our own scholarly and imaginative competence have in part dictated those limits; we have missed much unwittingly. Sometimes we have missed much knowingly but unavailingly: our titles in minor European languages are scanty, and worse, they are scantier in major languages such as Italian or Russian.

In part, the chronology of our study has set natural limits. We have waived all titles appearing after 1860, no matter how interesting or close to our upper time limit—Bachofen's *Das Mutterrecht* of 1861 is an example, not to mention only slightly later and crucial work by Tylor or Nietzsche or others. Similarly, the great flourishing of work on Egyptian myth, on totemism, or on the impact of Darwin's theories falls beyond our period. As much is of course true of works before 1680: we have not generally listed works written before our period even though these were reprinted within it. For the sake of brevity, too, we have also listed almost no translations or later editions of works.

Further, we have chosen deliberately to exclude certain kinds of works that might otherwise claim inclusion. Thus we have excluded from this listing almost all works of imaginative literature. One reason is that a mere survey of these alone would require another volume; moreover, some individual studies—such as by Douglas Bush—have already surveyed parts of this field, and we have indicated some of these in our secondary checklist. In addition, the separate bibliographic sections of the text give more detailed guides to some important works of literature involving myth. For the same reasons, we have excluded listings of paintings, music, sculpture, drama, or opera—again, listing in our secondary bibliography works such as that by Herbert Hunger, who surveys operatic, dramatic, and plastic uses of myth. Thus too, although we have listed some indispensable essays from the periodical literature, we have hardly tried to itemize the hundreds of brief reviews, articles, and notes on myth and related subjects that appeared in scores of journals. In some fields crucial to the study of myth, such as philology, we have sifted vigorously and hopefully. Certain prolific writers, such as Herder or Voltaire, have only been partially represented in this primary listing, with fuller bibliography confined to the appropriate sections in the text. Other writers crucial to our subject but rarely writing on myth directly or extensively, such as Rousseau or Hegel, have either been omitted here or most briefly cited. Finally, we have listed here again only the most important titles cited in the separate bibliographical sections of the text.

We have annotated, but at a minimum. Asterisks mark important titles. For the sake of brevity, we have employed certain useful formulaic descriptions in our annotations. Most of these are self-evident, but some may need a word of explanation. Thus, "chronology" means the Bible is stressed as strict source of all historical dating. "Euhemerist" means that myth is reduced to historical events or figures. "Rationalist" means the work stresses a rational skepticism about claims that myth teaches or conveys deep or wise teaching or has divine or transcendent origin. "Allegorist" on the contrary means the author stresses myth as conveying allegorical wisdom. "Symbolist" refers mainly to the school around Creuzer, which saw myth as conveying esoteric religious wisdom in symbolic form. "Historical school" (or variants) means the author stresses the study of myth through a dominantly historical approach—often the author is influenced by Karl Otfried Müller, and is so described. "Nature mythology" means the work sees myth mainly as expressing a primitive response to some natural phenomenon—dawns, moon, suns, and so forth. "Handbook" means the work is one or another kind of dictionary or guide.

Abbreviations: *A.I.B.L.* means: *L'Académie des Inscriptions et Belles-Lettres; Comm. Soc. Reg. Gott.* means: *Commentationes Societatis Regiae Scientarum Gottingensis.*

Adelung, F. von, *Versuch einer Literatur der Sanskrit-Sprache* (St. Petersburg, 1830).

Akenside, Mark, *The Pleasures of Imagina-tion* (London, 1743). Discusses myth and Orphism in notes.

Albold, H., *Dissertatio de Saturnides* (Greifswald, 1706).

Alison, Archibald, *Essays on the Nature and Principles of Taste* (London and Edinburgh, 1790). Preromantic literary interest in myth.

Ambrosch, J. A., *Studien und Andeutungen im Gebiet des altrömischen Bodens und Cultur* (Breslau, 1839). Comparative history of mythic ritual.

Andersen, Hans Christian, *Eventyr, fortalte for Børn* (Copenhagen, 1835–44). The famous fairy-tale book.

Andres, le P. Juan, *Dell' origine, progressi e stato attuale d'ogni letteratura . . .* (Parma, 1782–1822). Volume two in 1785 has first appraisal of the Eddas in literary history.

Anon., *A Dictionary of Polite literature: or Fabulous History of the Heathen Gods and illustrious heros* (London, 1804). Handbook.

Anon., "Edda doctrine and its origins," in *Foreign Quarterly,* Vol. 2, 1827, p. 210.

Anon., *Mythology made easy, a new History of the Heathen gods, goddesses . . . the whole reconciled to scripture* (London, 1790). Handbook.

Anquetil-Duperron, A. H., *Oupnek'hat* (1801). Translates selections from Upanishads; unreliable but influential.

Anquetil-Duperron, A. H., *Recherches historiques et chronologiques sur l'Inde* (Paris, 1786). Volume two contains first translation of (four) authentic Upanishads.

* Anquetil-Duperron, A. H., *Zend-Avesta, ouvrage de Zoroastre* (Paris, 1771). First translation.

* Anthon, Charles, *A Classical Dictionary* (New York, 1841). A standard work.

* Arnim, L. A. von and Brentano, C., *Des Knaben Wunderhorn* (Heidelberg and Frankfurt, 1806–08). Most important German romantic literary folksong collection.

* *Asiatick Researches,* Vols. 1–20 (Calcutta, 1784–1839). First most important journal giving scholarly translations, history, etc. of India and East.

Ast, F., *Ideen zu einer allgemeinen Mythologie der alten Welt* (1808).

Astruc, Jean, *Conjectures sur les mémoires originaux . . . que Moyse s'est servi pour composer le livre de la Genèse . . .* (1753). Historico-textual biblical criticism.

Bachofen, Johann Jacob, *Versuch über die Gräbersymbolik der Alten* (Basel, 1859). Mythic grave objects as symbolic expressions.

Baehr, C. C., *Symbolik des mosaischen Kultes* (Heidelberg, 1837–39). Follows Creuzer.

Bailly, Jean-Sylvain, *Essai sur les fables, et sur leur histoire* (Paris, 1799).

Bailly, Jean-Sylvain, *Histoire de l'astronomie ancienne, depuis son origine, jusqu'à l'établissement de l'école d'Alexandrie, jusqu'à l'epoque de 1730,* 3 vols. (Paris, 1779–82). Scientific critique of earlier chronologies.

Bailly, Jean-Sylvain, *Lettres sur l'Atlantide de Platon et sur l'ancienne histoire de l'Asie* (London and Paris, 1779).

Bailly, Jean-Sylvain, *Lettres sur l'origine des sciences, et sur celles des peuples de l'Asie; addressées a M. Voltaire . . .* (London [Paris], 1777). Argues Indic origins for Greeks and common origin for Chinese, Persians, and Indians.

Bakewell, Robert, *An Introduction to Geology,* 2d ed. (London, 1832). Gives table by Benjamin Silliman giving comparative table of geology and Genesis. Originally published in 1812.

Baltus, J. F., *Réponse à l'Histoire des oracles de M. de Fontenelle . . .* (Strasbourg, 1707). Refutation of Fontenelle and Van Dale.

* Banier, Antoine, *Explication historique des fables, où l'on decouvre leur origine et leur conformité avec l'histoire ancienne,* 2 vols. (Paris, 1711). Early version of important 1738 work.

Banier, Antoine, *Histoire du culte d'Adonis* (Mém. A.I.B.L. III, 98 ff., Dec. 14, 1717).

* Banier, Antoine, *La Mythologie et les fables expliquées par l'histoire,* 3 vols. (Paris, 1738–40). Advances sixteen theories for origin of myth, but emphasizes Euhemerist.

Banier, Antoine, *Sur l'origine de culte que les Égyptiens rendoient aux animaux* (Mém. A.I.B.L. III, 84 ff., April 21, 1716).

Banier, Antoine, *Sur Typhon* (Mém. A.I.B.L. III, 116 ff., Feb. 19, 1717).

Barlow, Joel, *The Vision of Columbus* (Hartford, 1787). Includes "a dissertation on the genius and institutions of Manco Capec."

Barrett, Francis, *The Magus, or Celestial*

Intelligencer (London, 1801). Cabalism, astrology, occultism and other arcana.

Barth, Christian Carl, *Die Kabiren in Teutschland* (Erlangen, 1832).

Barth, Christian Carl, *Hertha und über die Religion der Weltmutter in alten Teutschland* (Augsburg, 1828). On role of earth-mother in Germanic myth.

Barth, Christian Carl, *Ueber die Druiden der Kelten und die Priester der alten Teutschen als Einleitung in die altteutsche Religionslehre* (Erlangen, 1826).

* Barthélemy, Jean-Jacques, *Voyage du jeune Anarcharsis en Grèce dans le milieu du 4ᵉ siècle avant l'ere vulgaire,* 5 vols. (Paris, 1788). Popular didactic fiction.

Barthélemy Saint-Hilaire, Jules, *Des Vedas* (Paris, 1854). Popularization of Langlois's translation of *Rig Veda.*

* Barthélemy Saint-Hilaire, Jules, *Du Bouddhisme* (Paris, 1855).

Barthélemy Saint-Hilaire, Jules, *Le Bouddha et sa religion* (Paris, 1860).

Bartholinus, Thomas, *Antiquitatem Danicarum de causis contemptae a Danis ad huc gentilibus mortis libri tres* (Copenhagen, 1689). Early work on Scandinavian paganism.

Le Batteux, Abbé Charles, *Histoire des causes premières* (Paris, 1769). Forerunner of Dupuis.

Baudeau, Nicholas, *Mémoire à consulter pour les anciens druides Gaulois* (n.p., 1777). Reply to Bailly 1777; argues Druids as native Celts.

Baudry, Frederic, *Étude sur les Vêdas* (Paris, 1855). Comparative philology, myth expresses nature feeling.

* Bauer, Bruno, *Das Entdeckte Christentum* (Zurich and Winterthur, 1843). Post-Hegelian "atheist" attack on religion as myth.

Anon. [Bauer, Bruno], *Die Posaune des jungsten Gerichts über Hegel . . .* (Leipzig, 1841).

Anon. [Bauer, Bruno], *Hegels Lehre von der Religion und Kunst . . .* (Leipzig, 1842). Post-Hegelian "atheist" antimythicizing.

Bauer, G. L., *Entwurf einer Hermeneutik des alten und neuen Testamentes* (Leipzig, 1799).

Bauer, G. L., *Hebräische Mythologie des Alten und Neuen Testaments, mit Parallelen aus der Mythologie anderer Völker, vor-*

nehmlich der Griechen und Römer (Leipzig, 1802). Biblical criticism.

Baur, F. C., *Die christliche Gnosis* (Tübingen, 1835).

* Bayle, Pierre, *Dictionaire historique et critique,* 4 vols. (Rotterdam, 1697). A major source of later skeptical attitudes toward myth and religion.

Beaumarchais, Antoine de la Barre de, *Le Temple des Muses* (Amsterdam, 1733). Picture-book: engravings by Picart et al.

Beaumont, John, *Gleanings of Antiquity . . .* (London, 1724). Part I relates paganism to Flood. Part II on oracles.

Beausobre, Isaac de, *Histoire critique de Manichée et du Manicheïsme,* 2 vols. (Amsterdam, 1734–39). Defends Manicheism against Christian charges.

Becchetti, Filippo, *La filosofia degli antichi popoli . . .* (Perugia, 1812). Anti-Dupuis.

Bekker, Balthasar, *De betoverde Weereld* (Leuwarden, 1691–93).

Bell, John, *New Pantheon; or, Historical dictionary of the gods, demi-gods, heroes, and fabulous personages of antiquity . . . ,* 2 vols. (London, 1790). Handbook.

Bellamy, John, *The History of all Religions* (London, 1812).

* Bergier, N.-S., *L'Origine des dieux du paganisme et le sens des fables découvert par un explication . . .* (Paris, 1767). Christian defense of myth as allegoric wisdom.

Bergmann, Frédéric, *Les Amazones dans l'histoire et dans la fable* (Paris, 1852).

Berisch, Heinrich W., *Einleitung zur allgemeinen Harmonie der Gotterlehren aller Völker und Zeiten* (Leipzig, 1776).

Binet, Benjamin, *Traité historique des dieux et des demons du paganisme* (Delft, 1696).

Bingham, Joseph, *Origines ecclesiasticae, Antiquities of the Christian Church,* 10 vols. (London, 1708–22).

Björner, Erik Julius, *Inledning til de Yfwerborna Göters gamla Häfder . . . Introductio in antiquitates hyperboreogothicas . . .* (Stockholm, 1738). On Nordic myth.

Björner, Erik Julius, *Nordiska Kåmpaldater* (Stockholm, 1737). Saga texts in Latin.

* Blackwell, Thomas, *An Enquiry into the Life and Writings of Homer* (1735). First influential treatment of Homer in historical context; precursor of romantic views.

* Blackwell, Thomas, *Letters concerning My-*

thology (London, 1748). Derives Homer's mythology from Egypt and allegoric tradition.

Blair, Hugh, *A Critical Dissertation on the Poems of Ossian, the Son of Fingal* (London, 1763). Influential defense of authenticity of Ossian.

Blome, Richard, *The Present state of his Majestie's Isles and Territories in America* (London, 1687). Travel book; New World religious customs.

Blount, Charles, *Great is Diana of the Ephesians, or the Original of Idolatry . . .* (1680).

Blumenbach, Johann, *De generis humani varietate nativa* (Göttingen, 1775). Early anthropological theory of degeneration from "primitive" races due to climate, racial mixing, etc.

Bode, G. H., *Scriptores rerum mythicarum latini tres Romae nuper reperti* (Cellis, 1834).

Boner, U., *Fabeln aus den Zeiten der Minnesinger,* ed. J. J. Breitinger and J. J. Bodmer (1757).

* Bopp, Franz, *Über das Conjugationssystem der Sanskritsprache in Vergleichung mit jenem der griechischen, persischen und germanischen Sprache . . .* (Frankfurt, 1816). Early important comparative philology.

Bos, Lambert, *Antiquitatum graecarum . . .* (1714).

* Bosman, Willem, *Voyage de Guinée, contenant une description nouvelle . . .* (Utrecht, 1704). First influential account of fetishism.

Bötticher, Karl, *Andeutungen über das Heilige und Profane in der Baukunst der Hellenen . . .* (Berlin, 1846). Role of temples in myth.

Bötticher, Karl, *Der Baumkultus der Hellenen . . .* (Berlin, 1856). Role of architecture in mythology.

Böttiger, K. A. (ed.), *Amalthea, oder Museum der Kunst-Mythologie* (Leipzig, 1820–25). Early important period for study of mythic art.

* Böttiger, K. A., *Ideen zur Kunst-Mythologie,* 2 vols. (Dresden and Leipzig, 1826–36). Lectures given in 1808; partly Creuzerian, mainly eclectic study of mythic art of antiquity and pre-Homeric age.

Boucher de Perthes, Jacques, *Antiquités celtiques et antédiluviennes, Mémoire sur l'in-* *dustrie primitive et les arts à leur origine* (Paris, 1847–64). Archaeology of "pleistocene," modifying Genesis.

Boucher de Perthes, Jacques, *De l'homme antédiluvien et de ses oeuvres* (Paris, 1860). Important work in paleontology; great antiquity of earth.

* Boulanger, Nicolas-A., *L'antiquité dévoilée par ses usages, où Examen critique des principales opinions, cérémonies et institutions religieuses et politiques des differens peuples de la Terre* (Amsterdam, 1766). Derives all myth from traditions after the Flood.

Bouterweck, Friedrich, *Parallelen vom griechischen und modernen Genius* (Göttingen, 1791).

Brand, John, *Observations on Popular Antiquities,* ed. Sir Henry Ellis, 2 vol. (London, 1813). Famous early folklore collection; first published in 1777.

Braun, Emil August, *Griechische Götterlehre* (Hamburg and Gotha, 1850, 1854).

Braun, Emil August, *Vorschule der Kunstmythologie* (Gotha, 1854). Handbook.

Breitinger, J. J., *Critische Abhandlung von der Natur, den Absichten und dem Gebrauche der Gleichnisse . . .* (Zurich, 1740). Concerns Aesopian fables.

Brewster, David, *Letters on Natural Magic* (London, 1822). Connects myth and magic.

Broughton, Thomas, *An Historical Dictionary of All Religions* (London, 1742). Handbook.

Brouwer, P. van Limbourg, *Histoire de la civilisation morale et religieuse des Grecs,* 8 vols. (Groningen, 1833–42). Early "history of religions" approach—Brouwer perhaps coined the phrase.

Brown, Thomas, *A Short Dissertation about the Mona of Caesar and Tacitus . . . with a short account of the . . . Druids, etc.,* in W. Sacheverell, *An Account of the Isle of Man . . .* (1702).

* Bryant, Jacob, *A New System, or an Analysis of ancient mythology: wherein an attempt is made to divest tradition of fable, and to reduce the truth to its original purity . . . ,* 3 vols. (London, 1774). Traces myth to descendents of Ham.

Buddeus, Johann, *Historia ecclesiastica Veteris Testamenti . . .* (Halle, 1715). Etymologically connects sacrifice of Isaac and Iphigenia.

Buddingh, D., *Verhandeling over de noordsche godenleer* (1836).

Buffon, Georges, *Les époques de la nature* (Paris, 1778).

* Bulfinch, Thomas, *The Age of Fable . . .* (Boston, 1855). Influential Victorian handbook.

Bunsen, C. von, *Aegyptens Stelle in der Weltgeschichte* (Hamburg, 1845–57).

Burkhardt, G. E., *Handbuch klassischen Mythologie* (Leipzig, 1844).

Burnet, Thomas, *Archaeologiae Philosophicae . . .* (London, 1692).

Burnet, Thomas, *Telluris theoria sacra . . .* (London, 1681).

* Burnouf, Eugène, *Commentaire sur le Yaçna . . . contenant le texte zend . . .* (Paris, 1833). Seminal philologic study.

* Burnouf, Eugène, *Essai sur le pali . . .* (Paris, 1826). Crucial first great philological study of Pali.

* Burnouf, Eugène, *Introduction à l'histoire buddhisme indien* (Paris, 1844). Indispensable, first great scholarly history of subject.

Butler, Charles, *Horae Biblicae, being a connected series of miscellaneous notes on the original text, early versions, and printed editions of the Old and New Testament* (London, 1797).

Buttmann, P. C., *Älteste Erdkunde des Morgenländers. Ein biblisch-philologischer Versuch* (Berlin, 1803). Influenced by Herder; oldest myth from India.

* Buttmann, Philipp K., *Mythologus, oder gesammelte Abhandlungen über die Sagen des Alterthums,* 2 vols. (Berlin, 1828–29).

Buttmann, Philipp K., *Über den Mythen von der ältesten Menschengeschlechtern* (1814–15).

Buttman, Phillip K., *Über den Mythos der Sundflut . . .* (Berlin, 1819).

Caesar, Karl J., *Ein Beitrag zur Charakteristik Otfried Müller's als Mytholog . . .* (Marburg, 1859).

Calmet, Dom Augustin, *Commentaire littéral sur tous les livres de l'Ancien et du Nouveau Testament* (Paris, 1707–16).

Calmet, Dom Augustin, *Dissertations sur les apparitions des anges, des démons, et des esprits. Et sur les revenants et vampires. De Hongrie, de Bohème, de Moravie et de Silesie* (Paris, 1746).

Calmet, Dom Augustin, *Trésor d'antiquités sacrées et profanes . . .* (Amsterdam, 1723). Translated into English 1727.

Carlyle, Thomas, *Sartor Resartus* (London, 1834).

Carr, T. S., *A Manual of Classical Mythology, or a Companion to the Greek and Latin poets* (London, 1846). Handbook.

Carus, Carl Gustav, *Psyche. Zur Entwicklungsgeschichte der Seele* (Pforzheim, 1846).

* Caylus, Comte de, *Receuil d'antiquités égyptiennes, étrusques, grecques et romaines,* 7 vols. (Paris, 1752–67). Important art collection.

Chambers, Ephraim, *Cyclopedia, or Universal Dictionary of Arts and Sciences* (London, 1728). Treats myth extensively as "fable," literary plot, etc.

Chambers, Robert, *Vestiges of Natural History of Creation* (London, 1844). Important in controversy between Genesis and geology.

* Champollion, J. F., *De l'écriture hiératique des anciens Égyptiens* (Grenoble, 1821).

Champollion, J. F., *Lettres écrite d'Égypte et du Nubie en 1828 et 1829* (Paris, 1833).

Champollion, J. F., *Pantheon égyptien, collection des personnages mythologiques de l'ancienne Égypte . . .* (Paris, 1823–25).

Champollion, J. F., *Précis du Système Hiéroglyphique des anciens Égyptiens,* 2 vols. (Paris, 1824).

* Chateaubriand, René de, *Le Génie du Christianisme* (Paris, 1802).

Choiseul-Gouffier, M. G., *Voyage pittoresque de la Grèce,* 2 vols. (Paris, 1782).

Chompré, Pierre, *Dictionnaire abbregé de la fable, pour l'intelligence des poètes . . .* (Paris, 1727). Handbook.

Christmas, Henry, *Universal Mythology: an account of the most important systems . . .* (London, 1838). Handbook.

Chwolson, D. A., *Die Ssabier und der Ssabismus,* 2 vols. (St. Petersbourg, 1856). Russian orientalist—follower of Creuzer.

Claustre, André de, *Dictionnaire de mythologie* (Paris, 1745). Handbook.

Clayton, Robert, *A Journal from Grand Cairo to Mount Sinai and back again* (London, 1753).

Cleveland, H. R., "Classic Mythology," in *The North American Review,* Vol. 41 (1835) p. 327.

Clingius, Fr. Michael, *Natales Saturni in historia primi parentis Adami investigati*

(Greifswald, 1703). Myth as degenerate biblical history; etymological method.

* Colebrook, H. T., "On the Philosophy of the Hindus," in *Transactions of the Royal Asiatic Society* (1823–27). His essays collected in *Misc. Essays* 1873.

* Colebrook, H. T., "On the Religious Ceremonies of the Hindous and Brahmans especially," in *Asiatick Researches* V (1799). Important early studies of Vedas.

Coleman, Charles, *The Mythology of the Hindus with notices of various mountain and island tribes inhabiting the two peninsulas of India and the neighboring islands: and an appendix comprising the minor avatars and the mythological and religious terms etc. of the Hindus* (London, 1832).

Coleridge, Hartley, "On Poetical Use of Heathen Mythology" (1822), in *Essays and Marginalia,* ed. D. Coleridge (London, 1851).

Colonia, Dominique de, *La Religion chrétienne autorisée par le témoignage des anciens auteurs payens,* 2 vols. (Lyon, 1718).

* Comte, Auguste, *Cours de philosophie positive,* 6 vols. (Paris, 1830–42). History has a theological phase which is successively fetishist, polytheist, monotheist.

Condillac, Abbé Étienne, "De l'ancienne mythologie," chap. XXIII of *Histoire ancienne,* in *Cours d'études* (Parma, 1775).

Condillac, Abbé Étienne, *Essai sur l'origine des connoisances humaines . . .* 2 vols. (Paris, 1746). Psychological origins of myth.

* Condorcet, Marquis de, *Esquisse d'un tableau historique des progrès de l'esprit humain* (1793). Myth as first phase in theory of historical perfectability.

* Constant, Benjamin, *De la religion considérée dans sa source, ses formes et ses développements,* 5 vols. (Paris, 1824–31). French eclectic school.

Constant, Benjamin, *Du Polythéisme romain considéré dans ses rapports avec la philosophie grecque et la religion chrétienne,* 2 vols. (Paris, 1833). French eclectic school.

Conti, Abate (Antonio), *Réponse aux observations sur la chronologie de M. Newton* (1726).

Cooke, William, *An Enquiry into the Patriarchal and Druidical Religion* (London, 1754). Ties Druids to Bible.

Cory, Isaac Preston, *Ancient fragments of the Phoenician, Chaldean, Egyptian, Tyrian, Carthaginian, Indian, Persian and other writers; with an introductory dissertation and an inquiry into the philosophy and trinity of the ancients . . . ,* 2d ed. (London, 1832). Myth derived from corrupt legends of Noah and Ark; follows G. S. Faber; first edition, 1828.

Cory, Isaac Preston, *Mythological Inquiry into the recondite Theology of the heathens* (London, 1837).

Couplet, Père Philippus, *Confucius, Sinarum philosophus, sive Scientia Sinensis Latinè exposita . . .* (Paris, 1687). "Connects" Chinese and biblical history.

* Court de Gebelin, Antoine, *Monde primitif analysé et comparé avec le monde moderne* (Paris, 1773).

Crabb, George, *New Pantheon; or Mythology of all nations . . . for the use of schools and young persons* (London, 1840). Handbook.

Craufurd, Quintin, *Researches concerning the Laws, Theology, Learning, Commerce, etc. of Ancient and Modern India* (London, 1817).

Creuzer, F. and Hermann, G., *Briefe über Homer und Hesiodus, vorzüglich über die Theogonie . . .* (Heidelberg, 1818). Debates Creuzer's *Symbolik.*

Creuzer, F., "Commentatio de causis rerum Bacchicarum et Orphicarum" (Heidelberg, 1807).

Creuzer, F., "Dionysus s. Commentationes academicae de rerum Bacchicarum Orphicarumque originibus et causis" (Heidelberg, 1809).

Creuzer, F., "Idee und Probe alter Symbolik" (Heidelberg, 1806).

Creuzer F., "Philologie und Mythologie in ihrem Stufengang und wechselseitigen Verhalten" (Heidelberg, 1807).

* Creuzer, F., *Symbolik und Mythologie der alten Völker . . .* (Heidelberg, 1810). German romantic *cause célèbre;* India as source of Greek myth and mystery religions.

Creuzer, F., "Über Philologie und Mythologie," in *Heidelberg Jahrbücher* I, 1808.

Croese, Gerhard, *OMEROS EBRAIOS . . .* (Vol. 1 only) (Dordrecht, 1704). Etymologically proves fall of Troy really corrupt version of Jericho.

Croker, Thomas C., *Fairy Legends of the South of Ireland* (London, 1825). Folklore.

Csoma, Alexander, "The Life and Teachings of Buddha," in *Asiatick Researches,* XX, 1836.

Cumberland, Richard, *Origines Gentium Antiquissimae; or, Attempts for discovering the times of the first planting of nations* (London, 1724). Chronology.

Cumberland, Richard, *Sanchoniatho's Phoenician History,* translated from the first book of Eusebius . . . (London, 1720). Christian Euhemerist interpretation of Phoenician myth.

Dalin, Olof, *Histoire de Suède depuis les origines jusqu'à notre temps* (Stockholm, 1747–62). Describes ancient Swedish religion.

Damm, C. T., *Einleitung in die Götter-Lehre und Fabel-Geschichte der alten griechischen und römischen Welt* (1763). Handbook.

Darlington, William, *A Catechism of Mythology* (Baltimore, 1832). Handbook.

* Davies, Edward, *Celtic Researches* (London, 1804). Celts descended from Patriarchs.

Davies, Edward, *The Mythology and Rites of the British Druids* (London, 1809).

* De Brosses, Charles, *Du culte des dieux fétiches, ou Parallèle de l'ancienne religion de l'Égypte avec la religion actuelle de Nigritie* (1760). First claim for fetishism as first stage in all religions.

De Guignes, J., *Histoire Générale des Huns, des Turcs, des Mongols* . . . (Paris, 1756–58). Early Indic history.

De la Barre, Louis, *Mémoires pour servir à l'histoire de la Religion de la Grèce (Mém. A.I.B.L.* XVI-XVIII, 1 ff., Nov. 1737).

Demeunier, Jean Nicolas, Count, *L'Esprit des Usages et des Coutumes des Différents Peuples* . . . , 3 vols. (London, 1776). Ethnography.

Demoustier, Charles A., *Lettres à Émilee, sur la mythologie* (Paris, 1790–99). Children's handbook.

Denis, Michael, *Die Lieder Sineds des Barden* . . . (Vienna, 1772). Early interest in national poetry.

Dennis, John, *Advancement and Reformation of Modern Poetry* (London, 1701). Chapters 11–13 on Greek poetry flourishing and failing with their religion.

De Paw, Corneille, *Recherches Philosophiques sur les Égyptiens et les Chinoises* (Berlin, 1773).

Destutt de Tracy, A. L. L., *Analyse raisonée de l'origine de tous les cultes où religion universelle* (Paris, 1804). Abridgment of Dupuis.

* De Wette, W. M. L., *Beiträge zur Einleitung in das Alte Testament* (Halle, 1806–07). "Higher" biblical criticism.

De Wette, W. M. L., *Lehrbuch der christlichen Dogmatik, in ihrer historischen Entwicklung* . . . (Berlin, 1813–16). "Higher" biblical criticism.

De Wette, W. M. L., *Lehrbuch der hebräisch-jüdischen Archäologie, nebst einem Grundriss der hebräisch-jüdischen Geschichte* (Leipzig, 1814). "Higher" biblical criticism.

Dirckinck-Holmfeld, Constant, *Ueber den geistigen Gehalt der alten Religionen und Mythen . . . der nordischen Mythen* (Copenhagen, 1828).

Dornedden, K. F., *Erläuterung der aegyptischen Götterlehre durch die griechische in besonderer Rücksicht auf den Ursprung der Mosaischen Kosmogonie und des Mosaischen Gottes,* in *Allgemeine Bibliothek der biblischen Literatur X* (1800). Hieroglyphs symbolize higher mysteries; myths derive from astronomy.

Dornedden, K. F., *Neue Theorie zur Erklärung der griechischen Mythologie* . . . (Göttingen, 1802).

Dornedden, K. F., *Phamenophis, oder Versuch einer neuen Theorie über den Ursprung der Kunst und Mythologie* (Göttingen, 1797). Philological approach, influenced by Heyne.

Dornedden, K. F., *Über die Dämonen und Geniusse der Alten* (Göttingen, 1793). Philological approach, influenced by Heyne.

Dow, Alexander, *The History of Hindostan . . . translated from the Persian* (1768). With Dow's prefatory "Dissertation on Customs, Manners, Languages, Religion and Philosophy of the Hindoos"—early unreliable account.

Dulaure, J. A., *Des cultes qui ont précédé et amené l'idolatrie où l'adoration des figures humaines* (Paris, 1805). Fertility interpretation of myth and religion.

Dumesnil, Alexis, *De l'esprit des religions,* 2d ed. (Paris, 1811).

Dupuis, Charles, *Mémoire explicatif du zodiaque chronologique et mythologique* (Paris, 1806). Extends thesis of Dupuis's 1795 work.

* Dupuis, Charles, *Origine de tous les cultes, où religion universelle,* 7 vols. (Paris, 1795). Rationalist derivation of myth from zodiac and sun worship.

Dusch, Johann J., *Betrachtungen über die Mythologie* (Leipzig, 1776).

Dussieux, Louis-Étienne, *Essai sur l'histoire de l'érudition orientale* (Paris, 1842). Best early account of Oriental scholarship.

Dwight, Mary Ann, *Grecian and Roman Mythology, with an introductory notice by . . . T. Lewis . . .* (New York, 1849). Handbook.

Dyer, George, *Poetics: or a series of Poems and disquisitions on Poetry,* 2 vols. (London, 1812). Preromantic literary interest in myth.

Eckermann, Karl, *Lehrbuch der Religionsgeschichte und Mythologie der vorzüglichsten Völker des Altertums* (Halle, 1845–46). Scholarly handbook of K. O. Müller school.

Edwards, Charles, *Hebraismorum Cambro Britannicorum Specimen* (London, 1675), in Myles Davies, *Athenae Britannicae* (1716), Vol. 1.

* Eichhorn, J. G., *Einleitung in das Alte Testament* (1780–82). Seminal work in "Higher" biblical criticism.

Eichhorn, J. G., *Einleitung in das Neue Testament,* 5 vols. (Leipzig, 1804–27). "Higher" biblical criticism.

* Eichhorn, J. G., *J. G. E.'s Urgeschichte,* ed. J. P. Gabler, (Altdorf and Nürnberg, 1790–93). Important early work in "Higher" biblical criticism written in 1775.

Ellies-Du Pin, Louis, *Bibliothèque universelle des historiens: contenant leurs vies, l'abregé, la chronologie, la géographie, et la critique de leurs histoires . . .* (Paris, 1706).

Ellis, William, *Polynesian Researches . . . ,* 2 vols. (London, 1829). Early standard work.

* Émeric-David, T. B., *Introduction a l'étude de la mythologie où essai sur l'esprit de la religion Grecque* (Paris, 1833). Stresses mythic art and its symbolism.

Émeric-David, T. B., *Jupiter. Recherches sur ce Dieu, sur son culte, et sur les monumens qui le représentent* (Paris, 1833).

Émeric-David, T. B., *Neptune, Recherches sur ce Dieu* (Paris, 1839).

Émeric-David, T. B., *Vulcain. Recherches sur ce Dieu* (Paris, 1838).

"Mythology," in *Encyclopaedia Britannica,* 1st ed., Vol. III (Edinburgh 1771).

"Mythology," in *Encyclopaedia Britannica,* 3d ed., Vol. XII (1797). Substantially different from first edition.

* "Mythologie," in *Encyclopédie, où Dictionnaire raisonné des sciences, des arts et des métiers* (Paris, 1751–65). Fréret's work, adapted by Jaucourt, myth as key to Greek mind.

Evans, Evan, *Some Specimens of the Poetry of the Antient Welsh Bards* (London, 1764). Alludes to Druids and Cabala.

Evans, T. S., *Mathematogonia, The Mythological birth of the nymph Mathesis* (Cambridge, 1839). Without parallel.

L'Ezour Vedam ou Ancien Commentaire du Vedam contenant l'exposition des opinions religieuses et philosophiques des Indiens, traduit de Samscretan par un Brame (Yverdon, 1778). Spurious but influential Indic work.

* Faber, G. S., *A Dissertation on the Mysteries of the Cabiri; or, the Great Gods of Phenicia, Samothrace, Egypt, Troas, Greece, Italy, and Crete . . .* (Oxford, 1803). Traces all myth to Noah and ark.

Faber, G. S., *Horae Mosaicae, or a view of the Mosaical Records with Respect to their coincidence with profane antiquity . . . and their connection with Christianity* (Oxford, 1801).

* Faber, G. S., *The Origin of Pagan Idolatry . . . ,* 3 vols. (London, 1816). Myth as debased types of Noah and ark.

Fairbairn, Patrick, *The Typology of Scripture* (Edinburgh, 1845). Revival of Christian "type" interpretation.

Farmer, Hugh, *A dissertation on Miracles . . .* (London, 1771).

Farmer, Hugh. *An Essay on the Demoniacs of the New Testament* (London, 1775). Anachronistic explanation of madness as demonology.

Farmer, Hugh, *The general Prevalence of the worship of human spirits in the antient heathen nations, asserted and proved* (London, 1783).

Fell, John, *Daemoniacs. An Enquiry into the Heathen and the Scripture Doctrines of*

Daemons (London, 1779). Christian demonology.

Fell, John, *The Idolatry of Greece and Rome* (1785). Christian demonology.

* Feuerbach, Ludwig, *Das Wesen des Christenthums* (Leipzig, 1841). Post-Hegelian materialist transforming of theology to "anthropology," myth as nature worship.

* Feuerbach, Ludwig, *Das Wesen der Religion* (Leipzig, 1846).

Feuerbach, Ludwig, *Theogonie nach den Quellen des klassischen, hebräischen und christlichen Altertums* (Leipzig, 1857).

Feuerbach, Ludwig, *Vorlesungen über das Wesen der Religion* . . . (Leipzig, 1851).

* Fontenelle, Bernard de, *De l'origine des Fables* (1724). Brief, sophisticated, many-sided rationalist overview of myth.

* Fontenelle, Bernard de, *Histoire des Oracles* (Paris, 1686). Exposé of pagan oracles as fraudulent priestcraft; translated into English 1688.

Forchhammer, P. W., *Hellenika. Griechenland im Neuen das Alte* (Berlin, 1837). Greek myth based on maritime phenomena.

Forster, Johann Georg, *A voyage round the world . . . 1772, 3, 4, & 5*, 2 vols. (London, 1777).

Forster, George, *Sketches of the Mythology and Customs of the Hindoos* (London, 1785).

Forster, Reinhold and Sprengel, Matthias C., *Neue Beiträge zur Völker—und Länderkunde* (Leipzig, 1790–93). Contains articles and translations on India.

Foucher, Abbé, "Recherches sur l'origine et la nature de l'Héllenisme," (*Mém. A.I.B.L.* XXXIV-XXXVI, 435 ff., 1762).

Fourmont, Étienne, *Linguae Sinarum Mandarinicae, Hieroglyphicae, grammatica duplex, Latine, et cum characteribus Sinensium* (Paris, 1742). Philology.

Fourmont, Étienne, *Meditationes Sinicae* (Paris, 1737).

Fourmont, Étienne, *Réflexions critiques sur les histoires des anciens peuples, Chaldéens, Hébreux, Phénicians, Égyptiens, Grec, etc* . . . (Paris, 1735). Gods as debased patriarchs, etymological method.

Fréret, Nicolas, *Défense de la chronologie, fondée sur les monumens de l'histoire ancienne* . . . (Paris, 1758). Attacks Newton's chronology.

Fréret, Nicolas, *Oeuvres philosophiques* (London [Paris], 1776) (actually written by Holbach, et al.). Antireligious, antimythical tracts.

* Fréret, Nicolas, "Réflexions générales sur la nature de la Religion des Grecs et sur l'idée qu'on doit se former de leur Mythologie . . . ," in *Hist. A.I.B.L.*, XXIII, 19 ff. (1756).

* Fréret, Nicolas, "Réflexions sur l'étude des anciennes histoires, et sur le degré de certitude de leurs preuves" (1724), in *Hist. A.I.B.L.*, VI, 146–189 ff. (1718–25). Important appeal for scholarly historical approach to myth.

Fuller, Margaret, *Margaret and her Friends, or Ten Conversations with Margaret Fuller upon the Mythology of the Greeks* . . . reported by Caroline W. Healy Dall (Boston, 1895). Conversations held in 1841.

Ganander, Christfrid, *Mythologia Fennica, . . . De Nomina Propria Deastrorum, Idolorum, Locorum* . . . (Abo, 1789). On Finnish myth.

Gayley, Charles M., *Classic Myths of English Literature and Art* (Boston, 1855). Handbook.

Gedike, Friedrich, *Über die mannigfaltigen Hypothesen zur Erklärung der Mythologie* (1791), in *Vermischte Schriften* (Berlin, 1801). Philological approach, influenced by Heyne.

Gedike, F., *Über die Verschliessung des Ianustempels als Symbol des Friedens* (1795), in *Vermischte Schriften* (Berlin, 1801).

* Gérando, Joseph Marie de, *Histoire comparée des systèmes de philosophie* (Paris, 1804). New edition 1822 shows strong influence of Creuzer; influenced Emerson.

Gerhard, E., *Griechische Mythologie* (Berlin, 1854). Follower of Creuzer.

Gerstenberg, Heinrich, *Gedicht eines Skalden* (1766). Nordic Renaissance.

Gibbon, Edward, *Essai sur l'étude de la littérature* (London, 1761). Includes rationalist account of mythic origins.

Gilbert, E. A., *A compendium of Heathen Mythology; for the use of young ladies* (London, 1849). Handbook.

Gillies, John, *The History of Ancient Greece* . . . , 2 vols. (London, 1786).

Giorgi, Antonio Agostino, *Alphabetum Tibetanum* (Rome, 1762).

Girardet, P. A., *Nouveau système sur la mythologie* (1788). Handbook.

Gladstone, William Ewart, *Studies on Homer and the Homeric Age,* 3 vols. (Oxford, 1858). Pagan myth as degenerate version of Revelation.

Gluckselig, Anton T. [pseud. Gustav Thormod Legis], *Alkuna. Nordische und Nord-Slawische mythologie* (Leipzig, 1831).

* Gobineau, Arthur de, *Essai sur l'Inegalité des Races Humaines,* 2 vols. (Paris, 1853–55). Argument for racism partly appeals to theories of primal "blood" and nation.

Gobineau, Arthur de, *Lectures des Textes Cunéiformes* (Paris, 1858).

Gobineau, Arthur de, *Trois Ans en Asie, de 1855 à 1858* (Paris, 1859).

[Godwin, William], *The Pantheon: or Ancient History of the Gods of Greece and Rome* by Edward Baldwin [pseud.] (London, 1806). Handbook.

Goguet, Antoine-Yves, *De l'origine des loix, des arts, et des sciences, et de leur progrès chez les anciens peuples* (Paris, 1758).

Goodrich, S., *A Book of Mythology for Youth* (Boston, 1832). Handbook.

Göransson, Johan, *De yfverborna Atlingars eller Svio-gôthars . . . patriarkaliska lära . . .* (Stockholm, 1750). One of Mallet's sources.

Göransson, Johan, *Is Atlinga; det âr : De Forna Göters, hår uti Svea Rike, Bokstâfver ok Salighets Lâra, Tvåtusend Tvåhundrad år fôre Christum. . .* (Stockholm, 1747).

Görres, J. J. von, *Altteutsche Volks—und Meisterlieder . . .* (Frankfurt, 1817). Collection.

Görres, J. J. von, *Die teutschen Volkbücher* (Heidelberg, 1807). Folksong collection.

* Görres, J. J. von, *Mythengeschichte der asiatischen Welt* (Heidelberg, 1810). Extreme romantic exaltation of India as primal fatherland.

Gräter, F. and Böckh, C. G., start publication of *Bragur* (Leipzig, 1791–1802). First journal for study of Old German—runs 1791–1802, also titled *Braga und Hermada,* from 1796.

Gräter, F. D., *Briefe über den Geist der nördischen Mythologie und Dichtkunst* (Ulm, 1823).

Gräter, Friedrich, *Nordische Blumen . . .* zur näheren Kenntnis der nordischen Dichtkunst und Mythologie (Leipzig, 1789).

Gräter, F. D., "Übersicht und Classification der Nordischen Götter und Göttinen" (1790), "Darstellung der Nordischen Kosmogonie und Theogonie" (1792), in *Zerstreute Blätter* (Ulm, 1824).

Gräter, F. D., *Versuch einer Einleitung in die Nördische Alterthumskunde . . . ,* 2 vols. (1829–31).

Gravelot, H.-F. B., *Almanach iconologique ou des arts . . . orné de figures avec leurs explications* (Paris, 1765–73).

Grey, Sir George, *Polynesian Mythology and ancient traditional History of the New Zealand race . . .* (London, 1855).

* Grimm, J., *Deutsche Mythologie* (Göttingen, 1835). Folklore as key to "Germanic," i.e., non-Nordic, myth.

Grimm, J. and W., *Deutsche Sagen,* 2 vols. (Berlin, 1816–18).

* Grimm, W. and J., *Kinder—und Hausmärchen* (Berlin, 1812–15).

Grimm, W., *Altdanischen Heldenlieder, Balladen und Märchen . . .* (Heidelberg, 1811). Collection.

Grimm, W., *Die deutschen Heldensage* (Göttingen, 1829). Collection and annotation.

Grimm, Wilhelm, *Über deutschen Runen* (Göttingen, 1821).

Grose, Francis, *The Antiquities of England and Wales* (London, 1773–87).

Grose, Francis, ed., *The Antiquarian Repertory, A Miscellany intended to preserve and illustrate several valuable Remains of old times . . .* (1775–85). Early folklore.

* Grote, George, *A History of Greece,* 12 vols. (London, 1846–56). See esp. Vol. I, "Grecian mythical vein compared with . . . modern Europe." Standard work; views on myth influenced by Lobeck.

Gruber, Johann Gottfried, *Wörterbuch der altklassischen Mythologie und Religion* (Weimar, 1810–14). Dictionary.

Grundtvig, Nicolai, *Brage-Snak om Graeske og Nordiske Myther og Oldsagn for Damer og Herrer* (Copenhagen, 1844).

Grundtvig, Nicolai, *Nordens Mythologie eller Udsigt over Eddalaeren* (Copenhagen, 1808).

Guigniaut, J. D., *Le dieu Sérapis, et son origine . . .* (Paris, 1828). Creuzerian school.

Guthrie, Matthew, *Dissertations on Russian Antiquities; containing ancient mythology* (St. Petersburg, 1795).

Hager, Johann G., *Einleitung in die Göttergeschichte der alten Griechen und Römer* (Chemnitz, 1762). Handbook.

Hager, Joseph, *Panthéon chinois, où Parallèle entre le Culte Religieuse des Grecs et celui des Chinois* (Paris, 1806). Rationalist handbook.

* Hales, William, *A New Analysis of Chronology in which an attempt is made to explain the History and Antiquities of the primitive Nations of the world . . .* (London, 1809–12). Reviews over a hundred ancient and modern chronologies.

Hamann, J. G., *Aesthetica in Nuce* (1762). Pietistic work influencing Herder.

Hamann, J. G. (the elder), *Nutzlich und brauchbarer Vorrath von allerhand poetischen Redens-Arten . . . nebst einer Kurtzen Erklarung der mythologischen Nahmen* (Leipzig, 1725).

Hammer-Purgstall, Josef von, *Encyklopädische Übersicht der Wissenschaft des Orients . . .* (Leipzig, 1804).

Hammer-Purgstall, Josef von, *Mithraica où les Mithraiques . . .* (Caen and Paris, 1833).

* d'Hancarville, Pierre (Hugues), *Recherches sur l'origine, l'esprit, et les progrès des arts de la Grèce* (1785). Pornography and symbolism of mythic art.

Hartung, J. A., *Die Religion der Römer* (Erlangen, 1836). Handbook, follower of K. O. Müller.

Hatfield, S. [Miss], *The Theology and mythology of the antient pagans* (London, 1815).

Haupt, K. G., *Tabellarischer Abriss der vorzüglichsten Religionen und Religionsparteien der jetzigen Erdebewohner . . .* (Leipzig, 1821). Charts tabulating Jews, Christians, but also Confucianists, Hindus, Arabs, Persians, Buddhists, Fetishists, etc.

Hawthorne, N., *A Wonder-Book for Girls and Boys* (Boston, 1852). Myth for children.

Hawthorne, N., *Tanglewood Tales . . . a second Wonder-Book* (London, 1853).

Hederich, Benjamin, *Grundliches Lexicon Mythologicum* (Leipzig, 1741).

Hederich, Benjamin, *Lexicon Mythologicum* (Leipzig, 1724). Handbook.

Heffter, M. W., *Die Religion der Griechen und Römer . . . für Lehrer und Lernende . . .* (Brandenburg, 1845). Handbook.

* Hegel, G. W. F., *Vorlesungen über die Philosophie der Geschichte*, ed. E. Gans (1837). Deals in passim with Chinese, Hindu, Buddhist, Persian, Egyptian, fetishist myth, etc.

* Hegel, G. W. F., *Vorlesungen über die Philosophie der Religion . . .* (Berlin, 1832).

Heiberg, J. L., *Nordische Mythologie. Aus der Edda und Oehlenschlägers mythischen Dichtungen . . .* (Schleswig, 1827).

Heine, Heinrich, *Die Götter im Exil* (Hamburg, 1854). On pagan *vs.* Christian.

Hennell, Charles C., *An Inquiry Concerning the Origins of Christianity* (London, 1838). "Higher" biblical criticism.

* Barthélemy d'Herbelot, *Bibliothèque Orientale* (Paris, 1697). Useful index to contemporaneous knowledge of Orient.

Herbert, Algernon, *An Essay on The Neo-Druidic Theory in Britannia* (1828). Follower of Faber: myth as debased legends of Noah and ark.

Herbert, Algernon, *Cyclops Christianus* (London, 1849). All myth as debased legends of Noah and ark.

Herder, J. G., *Abhandlung über den Ursprung der Sprache . . .* (Berlin, 1772).

Herder, J. G., *Älteste Urkunde des Menschengeschlechts*, 2 vols. (Riga, 1774–76). Claims "hieroglyphic" in Genesis 1: 2–3 explains Egyptian theogony.

Herder, J. G., *Archäologie des Morgenlandes* (written 1769). Genesis to be understood as primitive history and poetry.

* Herder, J. G., *Auch eine Philosophie der Geschichte* (1774). Seminal work on national, temporal, and individual basis of culture. Nordic myth and art highly exalted.

Herder, J. G., *Briefe zur Beförderung der Humanität* (1793–97). History as movement toward *Humanität*.

Herder, J. G., *Das Lied von der Schöpfung der Dinge* (written c. 1768, pub. post.). Genesis as folk song.

Herder, J. G., *Homer, ein Günstling der Zeit* (1795). Homer as folk-oral-ballad poetry.

Herder, J. G., *Homer und Ossian* (1795). Ossian praised as genuine and near rival of Homer; Nordic-Ossian expresses inwardness, Homer outwardness.

* Herder, J. G., *Ideen zur Philosophie der Geschichte der Menschheit* (Riga and Leipzig,

1784–91). Seminal work; mankind's cultural-spiritual development from beginnings; morphologic and biologic view of history and culture; myth and religion as "proofs" and keys.

Herder, J. G., *Iduma* (1796). Praises artistic-cultural claims of Nordic myth against classic.

* Herder, J. G., *Journal meiner Reise im Jahre 1769* (written 1769). Myth best understood if "relived" or re-experienced.

* Herder, J. G., *Kritische Wälder* (Riga, 1769). The historicity of myth, religion, poetry, nations; Homer as Greek, Ossian as Nordic.

* Herder, J. G., *Über die neuere deutsche Litteratur. Fragmente.* (1766–77). His first extended characteristic work: myth and literature derive from specific rational contexts. Myth must be seen in its historic context.

Herder, J. G., *Über die Wirkung der Dichtkunst auf die Sitten der Völker in alten und neuen Zeiten* (1781).

Herder, J. G., *Volkslieder* (Leipzig, 1778–79). Collection.

* Herder, J. G., *Vom Geist der Ebraischen Poesie* (Dessau, 1782–83). Important preromantic document: Bible as "sublime" poetry, myth and poetry as "symbols" of truth.

* Herder, J. G., *Von Ähnlichkeit der mittleren englischen und deutschen Dichtkunst* (Leipzig, 1777). Promotes worth of medieval English and German poetry against dominance by classic or French.

* Herder, J. G., *Von deutscher Art und Kunst* (Hamburg, 1773). Contains two essays by Herder, esp. *Auszug aus einem Briefwechsel über Ossian und die Lieder alter Völker,* which urges collection of German national songs to inspire moderns, and praises vitality of "songs of people"; Goethe's *Von deutscher Baukunst,* praising native German Gothic style; Justus Moser's *Osnabrückische Geschichte* urging history to emphasize regional peoples.

Herder, J. G., *Zerstreute Blätter,* 3 vols. (Gotha, 1785–87). On origin of poetry, problem of fables; gives translations, and H's "imitations" of myths, "paramyths."

Hermann, B., *Detecta mythologia Graecorum in decantato Pygmaeorum, Gruum et Perdicum bello* (Leipzig, 1714).

Hermann, Gottfried, *De Mythologia Graecorum Antiquissima dissertatio* (Leipzig,

1817). Mainly history and philology; also critique of Creuzer.

* Hermann, Gottfried, *Über das Wesen und die Behandlung der Mythologie. Ein Brief an Herrn Hofrath Creuzer* (Leipzig, 1819).

Hermann, M. G., *Handbuch der mythologie aus Homer und Hesiod . . .* 3 vols. (Berlin, 1787–95). Popular semi-scholarly handbook; preface by Heyne.

Heyne, C. G., "De fide historica aetatis mythicae"; "Historiae scribendae inter Graecos primordia"; "De opinionibus per mythos traditis"; "De Mythorum poeticorum natura et causis," in *Comm. Soc. Reg. Gott.* Vol. VI, 1798.

Heyne, C. G., "De origine et causis fabularum Homericarum," in *Comm. Soc. Reg. Gott.* Neue Folge, Vol. VIII (1777).

Heyne, C. G., *Opuscula Academica collecta . . . ,* 6 vols. (Göttingen, 1785–1812).

* Heyne, C. G., "Quaestio de causis fabularum seu mythorum veterum physicis" (1764), in *Opuscula Academica* I (1785).

Heyne, C. G., *Sammlung antiquarischer Aufsätze* (Leipzig, 1778–79).

* Heyne, C. G., "Sermonis mythici sive symbolici interpretatio ad causas et rationes ductasque inde regulas revocate," in *Comm. Soc. Reg. Gott.* Vol. XVI, 1807.

Heyne, C. G., "Temporum mythicorum memoria a corruptelis nonnullis vindicata," in *Comm. Soc. Reg. Gott.* Vol. VIII (1763).

Heynig, J. G., *Theorie der sämmtlichen Religionsarten, des Fetichismus, des Uranotheismus . . .* (Leipzig, 1799).

Hickes, George, *Linguarum Veterum Septentrionalium Theasaurus Grammatico-Criticus et Archaeologicus,* 2 vols. (Oxford, 1705). An early philological treatise giving texts of Nordic sagas.

Higgins, Godfrey, *Anacalypsis: An attempt to draw aside the veil of the Saitic Isis: or, an inquiry into the origin of languages etc.* 2 vols. (London, 1836). Derives from Faber: myth from corrupt legends of Noah and ark.

Higgins, Godfrey, *The Celtic Druids . . .* (London, 1829). Druids came from India, built Stonehenge.

Hodgson, Francis, *Mythology for Versification or, a brief sketch of the fables of the ancients, prepared to be rendered into Latin verse . . .* (London, 1831). Handbook.

Hoelty, Arnold, *Zoroaster und seine Zeitalter* (Luneburg, 1836).

Holbach, Paul Henri, Baron d', *La Contagion sacrée, où Histoire naturelle de la superstition, ouvrage traduit de l'Anglois* (London, 1768). Terror as origin of religious superstition.

Holbach, Paul Henri, Baron d', *L'Enfer détruit, où Examen raisonné du dogme de l'éternité des peines* (London [Paris] 1769). Anticlerical and antimythic rationalist tract.

* Holbach, Paul Henri, Baron d', *Système de la Nature* (London, 1770). Rationalist-pantheist nature mythology.

Holwell, J. Z., *Interesting historical events . . . of Bengal and . . . Indostan . . . also the Mythology and Cosmogony . . .* (London, 1765).

Holwell, J. Z., *A Review of the Original Principles . . . of the ancient Brahmins: comprehending an account of the mythology . . . of the Gentoos* (London, 1779).

Holwell, William, *A mythological . . . Dictionary; extracted from the Analysis of Ancient Mythology* [of Bryant] (1793). Handbook.

Homberg, Tinette, *Mythologie der Griechen und Römer . . . Nebst einem Anhänge über des Ägyptische Mythensystem* (Leipzig, 1839).

Hort, William Jillard, *The New Pantheon* (Boston, 1809). Handbook.

Hottinger, J. J., *Versuch einer Vergleichung der Deutschen Dichter mit den Griechen und Römern* (Mannheim, 1789).

Houtteville, Charles François, *La Religion Chrétienne prouvée par les faits. Avec un discours historique et critique, sur la méthode des principaux Auteurs qui ont écrit pour et contre le Christianisme depuis son origine* (Paris, 1722).

Howe, E. D., *Mormonism unveiled* (Painesville, Ohio, 1834).

Huerta, F. M., *Sobre si la mitologie es parte de la historia,* in *Memorias de la Real Academia de la Historia,* I (1796) pp. 1–34.

Humbert, J., *Mythologie classique elementaire* (1835). Handbook.

Humboldt, Alexander von, *Researches concerning the Institutions and Monuments of the ancient inhabitants of America* (written in French by A. de H. and translated into English by H. M. Williams), 2 vols. (London, 1814).

Humboldt, W. von, *Über die Verschiedenheit desmenschlichen Sprachbaues und ihren Einfluss auf die geistige Entwickelung des menschengeschlechts* (Berlin, 1836).

* Humboldt, W. von, *W. v. Humboldt's Briefe an F. G. Welcker,* ed. R. Haym (Berlin, 1859). Authors discuss myth and various mythologic approaches.

Hume, David, *Dialogues Concerning Natural Religion* (London, 1779).

* Hume, David, *The Natural History of Religion* (London, 1757). Derives primitive monotheism; myth born from fear.

Hunt, Leigh, "Spirit of the Ancient Mythology," in *A Day By The Fire,* ed. J. E. B. (London, Cambridge, 1870). Originally published in 1832?

Hurd, William, D. D., *A New Universal History of the Religious Rites, Ceremonies, and Customs of the whole world* (Newcastle-upon-Tyne, 1811).

Hutton, James, *The Theory of the Earth, from the transactions of the Royal Society of Edinburg* (Edinburgh, 1785). Expands historical period needed for Genesis.

* Hyde, Thomas, *Historia Religionis Veterum Persarum* (Oxford, 1700). Early account of Zoroastrianism.

Ingemann, B. S., *Grundtrack lil en nordslavik og vendisk gudeaere* (1824).

Jablonski, Paul, *Pantheon Aegyptiorum . . .* (Frankfurt, 1750–52).

Jacobi, E., *Handwörterbuch der Griechischen und Römischen Mythologie* (1835). Handbook.

Jahn, F. L., *Deutsches Volkstum* (1810). Myth used for nationalism.

James, D., *Patriarchal Religion of Britain* (1836).

Jennings, David, *Jewish Antiquities: or a course of lectures on the three first books of Godwin's Moses and Aaron* (London, 1766).

Johnes, Arthur James, *Philological proofs of the original unity and recent origin of the human race* (London, 1843).

Jones, Rowland, *Hieroglyfic: or a grammatical introduction to an universal hieroglyfic language . . .* (London, 1768).

Jones, Rowland, *The Circles of Gomer, or an essay . . . of English as an universal language . . .* (London, 1771).

Jones, Rowland, *The Io-Triads; or the tenth Muse, wherein the origin, nature, and con-*

nection of the sacred symbols . . . are discovered . . . (London, 1773). Druidism.

Jones, Rowland, *The Origin of Language and
Nations* (London, 1764).

* Jones, Sir William, "On the Gods of Greece,
Italy and India," written 1785, pub. in *Asiatick Researches* (1799). Implies common
origin for these mythologies.

Jones, Sir William, *Poeseos Asiaticae* . . .
(1774). Modelled on Lowth's *Sacred poetry
of the Hebrews.*

* Jones, Sir William (tr.), *Sacontalá* . . .
(Calcutta, 1789). First translation.

Jourdain, J. P. P., *De la Mythologie indienne
de la côte de Malabar et de la peninsule
de l'Inde* (Paris, 1845).

Jurieu, Pierre, *Histoire critique des dogmes
et des cultes, bon et mauvais . . . où l'on
trouve l'origine de toutes les idolatries
de l'ancien Paganisme* . . . (Amsterdam,
1704).

Kanne, J. A., *Neue Darstellung der Mythologie
der Griechen und Römer* (Leipzig, 1805).
Myths express "mystery"-teaching symbolically.

* Kanne, J. A., *Erste Urkunden der Geschichte oder allgemeine Mythologie* (Bayreuth, 1808). Greek and Nordic gods derive
from India.

* Kanne, J. A., *Pantheon der ältesten Naturphilosophie, die Religion aller Völker* (Tübingen, 1811). Oldest myth is primal pantheism, most purely from India.

Kanne, J. A., *System der indischen Mythe,
oder Chronus und die Geschichte des Gott-
menschen in der Periode des Vorruckens*
. . . (Leipzig, 1813).

Kavanaugh, Morgan, *Myths traced to their
primary source through language,* 2 vols.
(London, 1856).

Keightley, Thomas, *Tales and Popular Fictions: their resemblance, and transmission
from country to country* (London, 1834).
Folklore and theory.

* Keightley, Thomas, *The Fairy Mythology*
(London, 1828). Grimm's folklore theories
applied to fairy tales.

* Keightley, Thomas, *The Mythology of An-
cient Greece and Italy* . . . (London, 1831).
Standard history modelled on methods of
German historical mythic school, K. O.
Müller, et al.

Kennedy, John, *A new Method of stating and*

explaining the Scripture Chronology (London, 1751).

Kennedy, Lt. Col. Vans, *Researches into the
nature and Affinity of ancient and Hindu
Mythology* (London, 1831).

Keyssler, Johann Georg, *Antiquites selectae
septentrionales et celticae* (Hanover, 1720).
Nordic myth.

King, Edward (Viscount Kingsborough), ed.,
Antiquities of Mexico (London, 1830–48).

King, William, *An Historical Account of the
Heathen Gods and Heroes* (London, 1710).
Handbook.

Kingsley, Charles, *The Heroes: or Greek Fairy
Tales* (Cambridge, 1855). Myths for Victorian children.

Klaproth, H. J., *Aperçu du l'origine des diverses Écritures de l'ancienne Monde* (Paris,
1832).

Klaproth, H. J., *Archiv für Asiatische Litteratur, Geschichte und Sprachkunde* (St.
Petersburg, 1810).

Klaproth, H. J., *Asia Polyglotta* (Paris, 1823).

Klaproth, H. J. (ed.), *Asiatisches Magazin,*
2 vols. (Weimar, 1802). Periodical translations and articles on Indic myth.

Klaproth, H. J., *Briefe über den Fortgang der
asiatischen Studien in Paris* . . . (Ulm,
1828).

Klaproth, H. J., *Examen Critique des travaux
de feu M. Champollion, sur les hiéroglyphes*
(Paris, 1832).

Klaproth, H. J., *Lettre . . . sur la découverte
des Hiéroglyphes acrologiques* . . . (Paris,
1827).

Klaproth, H. J., *Mémoires relatifs a
l'Asia* . . . , 3 vols. (Paris, 1824–28).

Klotz, C. A., *Epistolae Homericae* (Alten-
burg, 1764). Rationalist derogation of use
of pagan myth in Christian poems.

* Knight, R. P., *A discourse on the Worship
of Priapus* (London, 1786). Traces myth
and religion to phallic worship.

* Knight, R. P., *An Inquiry into the symbolical
Language of Ancient Art and Mythology*
(London, 1818). Rewrite of 1786 work now
emphasizing myth as artistic symbolism.

Köppen, Carl Friedrich, *Crata repoa, Oder
Einweihungen in der alten geheimen Gesell-
schaft der Egyptischer Priester* (1778).

Köppen, C. F., *Literarische Einleitung in die
Nordische Mythologie* (Berlin, 1837).

Kröger, Johann C., *Abriss einer vergleichenden Darstellung der Indisch-Persisch und*

Chinesischen Religionssysteme mit . . . auf die späteren Religionsformen und den Ursprung religiöser Ideen (Eisleben, 1842). Myth as "symbol."

* Kuhn, A., *Die Herabkunft des Feuers und des Göttertränks. Ein Beitrag zur vergleichenden Mythologie der Indogermanen* (Berlin, 1859). Myth derived from fire.

Kuhn, A., *Sagen, Gebräuche und Märchen aus Westfalen und einigen anderen . . .* (Leipzig, 1859).

Kuhn, A. and Schwartz, F. L. W., *Norddeutsche Sagen Märchen und Gebräuche* (Leipzig, 1848). Folklore, "nature mythology."

Lachmann, Karl, "Kritik der Sage von Nibelungen," in *Rheinisches Museum für Philologie,* No. 249–250 (1829). Nibelungenlied originated as Nordic myth.

La Créquinière, M. de, *Conformité des coutumes des Indiens Orientaux avec celles des Juifs . . .* (1704). Typical "conformities" approach, translated 1705 by John Toland.

* Lafitau, Joseph, *Moeurs des Sauvages Ameriquains comparées aux moeurs des premiers temps,* 2 vols. (Paris, 1724). Influential comparison of Iroquois to ancient pagans.

Lajard, J. B. F., *Introduction à l'étude du culte publique et des mystères de Mithra en Orient et Occident* (Paris, 1847).

Lajard, J. B. F., *Nouvelles Observations sur le grand Bas-Relief Mithraique . . .* (Paris, 1828).

Lajard, J. B. F., *Recherches sur le culte, les symboles, les attributs . . . de Vénus, en Orient et en Occident . . .* (Paris, 1837).

Länder und Völkerkunde, 18 vols. (Prague and Dresbach, 1807–23).

Langlès, Louis M., *Fables et contes indiens . . . avec un discours préliminaire et des notes sur la religion, la littérature . . . des Hindous* (Paris, 1790). Handbook.

Lassen, Christian, *Indische Altertumskunde,* 4 vols. (Leipzig, 1847–62).

Lavaur, Guillaume de, *Histoire de la fable conférée avec l'histoire sainte, où l'on voit que les grandes fables, le culte et les mystères du Paganisme ne sont que copies altérées des histoires, des usages, et des traditions des Hébreux,* 2 vols. (Amsterdam, 1731). Pagans as corrupt descendants of Noah.

Layard, Sir Austin H., *Nineveh and its Remains* (London, New York, 1849).

Leblanc, Prosper, *Les religions et leur interpretation chrétienne* (Paris, 1852–54). Allegorical view of myth.

* Le Clerc, Jean, *Bibliothèque Universelle et Historique . . .* (Amsterdam, 1700). Anti-allegorist and Euhemerist; myth as political history; important antiquarian.

* Le Gobien, Charles, *Lettres édifiantes et curieuses écrites de la Chine . . .* (1702). Influential reports by Jesuit missionaries, partly on heathen religions.

* Lempriere, John, *Bibliotheca Classica; or, a Classical Dictionary . . .* (Reading, England, 1788). Most popular scholarly handbook.

Lepsius, Karl R., *Das Todtenbuch der Aegypter nach dem hieroglyphischen Papyrus in Turin* (Leipzig, 1842). First edition of "Book of Dead."

Lepsius, Karl R., *Denkmäler aus Ægypten und Aethiopien,* 12 vols. (Berlin, 1849–58). Early great collection of Egyptian antiquities.

Le Roy, Julien D., *Les Ruines des plus beaux monumens de la Grèce* (Paris, 1758).

* Lessing, G. E., *Die Erziehung des Menschengeschlechts . . .* (Berlin, 1780). Religion and rationality realized through history.

Lessing, G. E., *Briefe, antiquarischen Inhalts* (Berlin, 1768).

Lessing, G. E., *Fabeln* (Berlin, 1759). Fables as moral lessons.

Lessing, G. E., *Laokoön . . .* (Berlin, 1766).

Levesque de Burigny, Jean, *Histoire de la Philosophie Payenne . . .* (The Hague, 1724). Skeptical rationalist.

Lindemann, Johann Gottlieb, *Geschichte der Meinungen älterer und neuerer Völker . . .* (Stendal, 1784–95).

Lindemann, J. G., *Historischer und philosophischer Überblick über die Religionsbegriffe und Gebraüche kultivirter und roher Völker* (Braunschweig, 1820).

Lionnois, J. J. B., *Traité de la Mythologie,* 2 vols. (Paris, 1795). Handbook.

* Lobeck, C. A., *Aglaophamus: sive, de theologiae mysticae Graecorum causis . . .* (1829). Massive rebuttal of Creuzer's *Symbolik;* unsympathetic to romantic mythology.

Locke, John, *The Reasonableness of Christianity, as delivered in the Scriptures* (London, 1695). Influential deist tract.

Loen, J. M., *Neue Sammlung der Merkwürdigsten Reisegeschichten,* Vol. VI (Frankfurt a.M., 1753). Travel and explorations.

* Lowth, Robert, *De sacra poesi Hebraeorum* (Oxford, 1753). Latin, original version of 1787 work.

* Lowth, Robert, *The Sacred Poetry of the Hebrews* (London, 1787). English version of 1753 work; first treatment of Scripture as nonclassic "higher" poetry.

Lucas, Charles, *A Descriptive Account, in blank verse of the Old Serpentine Temple of the Druids, at Avebury,* 2d ed. (Marlborough, 1801).

Macpherson, James, *Fingal: an Ancient Epic Poem in Six books . . . composed by Ossian the son of Fingal* (London, 1762).

* Macpherson, James, *Fragments of Antient Poetry collected in the Highlands of Scotland and translated from the Gaelic or Erse Language* (1760). Dubious mythic Celtic epic.

Magnússon, Finnur, *Eddalaeren . . . ,* 4 vols. (Copenhagen, 1824–26).

Magnússon, Finnur, *Lexicon Mythologicum in vetusta Septentrionalium carmina, quae in Edda . . .* (Hafniae, 1828).

Magnússon, Finnur, *Priscae veterum Borealium Mythologiae Lexicon . . .* (Hafniae, 1828).

Maius, Johann H., *Observationes sacrae* (Frankfurt a.M., 1713–14). Etymologically derives Greek ritual from Bible.

Maius, Johann H., *De mutus ebraicarum et graecarum antiquitatum convenienta* (Greifswald, 1709). Etymologically connects sacrifice of Isaac and Iphigenia.

Majer, Friedrich, *Brahma, oder die Religion der Indier als Brahmaismus* (Leipzig, 1818). German romantic interpretation.

* Majer, Friedrich, *Allgemeines Mythologisches Lexicon . . .* (A to Izeds) (Weimar, 1803). Widely-used German romantic myth encyclopedia.

Malaspina di Sannazaro, Luigi, *Cenni sulla Mitologia Egizia* (Milan, 1826).

* Mallet, Paul Henri, *Introduction à l'Histoire du Danemarc où l'on traite de la religion, des loix, des moeurs et des usages des anciens Danois,* 2 vols. (Copenhagen, 1755–56). Second volume is first widely-read account of Nordic mythology.

Mannhardt, W., *Die Götterwelt der deutschen und nordischen Völker* (Berlin, 1860). Exponent of "lower" mythology.

* Mannhardt, W., *Germanischen Mythen* (Berlin, 1858). Exponent of "lower" mythology.

Manso, J. C. F., *Versuche über einige Gegenstände aus der Mythologie der Griechen und Römer* (Leipzig, 1794).

Marangoni, Giovanni, *Delle cose gentilesche e profane, trasportate ad uso e adornamento delle chiese* (Rome, 1744).

Martin, Jacques, *La religion des Gaulois* (Paris, 1727).

* Marx, Karl, *Die Deutsche Ideologie* (1845–46). Co–author, F. Engels, posthumous publication; myth subsumed into ideology.

Masch, Andreas G., *Abhandlung von der Religion der Heiden und der Christen* (Halle, 1748–53).

Maurice, Thomas, *Brahminical Fraud detected; or, the attempts of the Sacerdotal Tribes of India to invest their fabulous deities and heroes with the honors and attributes of the Christian Messiah . . .* (London, 1812).

Maurice, Thomas, *The History of Hindostan* (London, 1795–98).

Maurice, Thomas, *Indian antiquities . . . ,* 7 vols. (London, 1794–1800). Reduced Indic myth to Christian Trinity.

Maury, Alfred, *Essai historique sur la religion des Aryas pour servir à éclairer les origines des religions hellénique, latine, Gaulois, Germaine et Slave* (Paris, 1853). Indic myth related to nature myth.

Maury, Alfred, *Essai sur les légendes pieuses du moyen-âge . . .* (Paris, 1843). Applies Creuzerian mythic view to medieval legends.

Maury, Alfred, *Histoire des Religions de la Grèce antique . . . Tome I: La religion hellénique depuis les temps primitifs . . . Tome II: Les institutions religieuses de la Grèce* (Paris, 1857). Connects nature mythology to India.

Maury, Alfred, *Les Fées du moyen-âge . . . de la mythologie gauloise* (Paris, 1843). Applies Creuzerian mythic view to medieval legends.

Mayo, R., *A New System of Mythology,* 3 vols. (Philadelphia, 1815–19). Handbook.

Meiners, Christoph, *Allgemeine Kritische Geschichte der Religionen* (Hanover, 1806–07). With useful bibliography.

Meiners, Christoph, *Grundriss der Geschichte alter Religion* (Lemgo, 1787).

Meiners, Christoph, *Versuch über der Reli-*

gionsgeschichte der ältesten Völker, besonders der Egyptier (Göttingen, 1775). Mainly rationalist approach, though influenced by Herder.

Menzel, Wolfgang, Mythologische Forschungen und Sammlungen (Stuttgart and Tübingen, 1842). Study of nature symbolism in myth and literature—rainbows, bees, etc.

Menzel, Wolfgang, Zur Deutschen Mythologie (Stuttgart, 1855).

Meridas-Poullé (Mariya-Das Pillaio), Bagavadam où doctrine divine . . . (Paris, 1788). Translation of Bhagavatpurana from Tamil with preface on Hinduism.

Meyer, Leo, Bemerkungen zur ältesten Geschichte der griechischen Mythologie (Göttingen, 1857). Comparative Indogermanic philology and Greek myth.

Meyern, Wilhelm F., Dya-Na-Sore, oder die Wanderer, 3 vols. (Leipzig, 1787–91). Fiction presented as authentic translation, influenced Jean Paul.

Michaelis, Johann David, Mosaisches Recht (Frankfurt a.M., 1770). Early important work on Hebrew antiquities.

Michaelis, Johann Georg, De Abrahamo et Isaaco a Graecis in Hyrieum et Orionem conversis (Frankfurt a.O., 1721). Christian etymological derivation.

Michel, Francisque, Le Chanson de Roland où de Roncevaux, du XIIᵉ siècle: publiée pour la premier fois d'après le manuscrit de la Bibliothèque Bodléienne à Oxford (Paris, 1837). Two hundred copies printed.

Mickle, W. J., "Inquiry into the religious tenets and philosophy of the Brahmins," in The Lusiad . . . (1776). Influential popular treatment.

Middleton, Conyers, Letter from Rome, Shewing an exact conformity between Popery and Paganism (London, 1729). Attacks Catholicism for retaining pagan myth and rituals.

Millin de Grandmaison, Aubin L., La mythologie mise à la portée de tout le monde (1797). Handbook.

Mitchell, Logan, The Christian Mythology Unveiled (London, 1842). All fables as astronomical allegories.

Mitford, William, The History of Greece, 5 vols. (London, 1784–1818). A standard history.

Mohl, Jules, ed., Confucii Chi-King, sive Liber carminum. Ex Latina P. Lacharme interpretatione edidit (n.p., 1830).

Mohl, Jules, Fragments relatifs à la religion Zoroastre (1829). Oriental philology.

Mone, F. J., Celtische Forschungen zur Geschichte Mitteleuropas (Freiburg, 1857).

Mone, F. J., Geschichte des Heidenthums im nördlichen Europa, 2 vols. (Leipzig and Darmstadt, 1822–23). Applies Creuzer's views to Nordic myth.

Mone, F. J., Untersuchungen zur Geschichte der teutschen Heldensage (Quedlinburgh and Leipzig, 1836). Applies Creuzer's views to Nordic myth.

Moneta, M. Johannes, Problema mythologicum: utrum immolatio Phrixi eadem sit ac Isaaci necne? (Wittenberg, 1721). Christian etymological derivation.

Monsigny, Mary, Mythology: or, a history of the fabulous deities of the ancients (London, 1780). Handbook.

* Montfaucon, Bernard de, L'Antiquité expliquée et representée en figures . . . , 10 vols. (Paris, 1719). Famous illustrated antiquarian collection.

Moor, Edward, The Hindu Pantheon (London, 1810).

Moor, Edward, Oriental Fragments (London, 1834).

Morgan, R., Letters on Mythology (London, 1807).

Moritz, K. P., Lehrbuch der Mythologie (1789). Handbook.

* Moritz, K. P., Götterlehre oder mythologische Dichtungen der Alten (Vienna, 1792). Gods as aesthetic symbolic expressions of nature; possibly co–authored by Goethe.

Moritz, K. P., Mythologischen Almanach für Damen (1792). Handbook.

Moritz, K. P., Die symbolische Weisheit der Aegypter (n.p., 1793).

Mosheim, J. L. von, Dissertationum ad Historiam Ecclesiasticum . . . (2d ed., 1743).

* Müller, F. Max, Comparative Mythology (London, 1856). Epochal argument for "nature" mythology, "disease of language" theory and comparative philologic method.

Müller, F. Max, On the Comparative Philology of the Indo-European languages in its bearing on the Early Civilizations of Mankind (1849). Early memoir presaging his later position.

Müller, Julius, "On the Theory of Myth," in

Voices of the Church against Strauss (1845). In volume of essays by several critics, with useful article by Quinet.

* Müller, Karl Otfried, *Prologemena zu einer wissenschaftlichen Mythologie . . .* (Göttingen, 1825). Key figure in classical historical school; stresses mutual integrity and origins of Greek myth.

* Müller, Karl Otfried, *A History of the Literature of Ancient Greece* (orig. pub. in English) (London, 1840). Influential standard work, myth as tool for study of early Greek history.

Munckerus, Thomas, *Mythographi Latini* (Amsterdam, 1681).

* Muratori, Lodovico Antonio, *Delle Antichità Estensi ed Italiane,* 2 vols. (Modena, 1717–40). Antiquarian history.

Murgeaud, F. L., *Instruction sur l'Histoire, comprenant l'histoire ancienne, l'histoire grecque, l'histoire romaine, et la Mythologie* (London, 1847). Handbook.

Musgrave, Samuel, *Two Dissertations. I. On the Graecian Mythology . . .* (London, 1782).

Mushet, R. (the younger), *The Book of Symbols* (1844).

Mushet, R. (the younger), *The Trinities of the ancients, or the mythology of the first ages, and writings of some of the Pythagorean and other schools examined, with reference to the knowledge of the Trinity ascribed to Plato and other ancient Philosophers* (London, 1837).

Nash, David William, *Taliesin, or the Bards and Druids of Britain* (London, 1858). Scholarly study of Celtic myth, discredits Davies.

Natalis, Alexander (Alexandre, Noël), *Conformité des cérémonies chinoises avec l'idolatrie grecque et romaine* (Cologne, 1700).

Neale, John Mason, *Stories from Heathen Mythology and Greek History for the use of Christian Children* (London, 1845). Handbook.

Newton, Isaac, *Observations upon the Prophecies of Daniel and the Apocalypse of St. John* (London, 1733). Christian Euhemerist chronology.

* Newton, Isaac, *The Chronology of the Ancient Kingdoms Amended . . .* (London, 1728). Christian Euhemerist chronology.

Nicolas, A. de, *Études philosophiques sur le Christianisme* (Paris, 1843–45). Catholic viewpoint: pagan myth preserves Revelation.

Niebuhr, Barthold Georg, *Griechische Heroengeschichten von B. G. Niebuhr an seinen Sohn erzählt* (Hamburg, 1842).

Nitzsch, Paul, *Beschreibung des häuslichen, gottesdienstlichen, sittlichen . . . Zustandes der Griechen . . . Zum Schulgebrauch . . . ,* 2 vols. (Erfurt, 1791, 1795). Handbook.

Noël, J. M., *Cours de mythologie, où histoire des divinités et des héros les plus célèbres du paganisme . . .* (Paris, 1830). Handbook. Twenty-first edition by 1873.

Noël, J. M., *Dictionnaire de la fable où Mythologie Grecque, Latine, Égyptienne, Celtique, Persane, Syriaque, Indienne, Chinoise, Scandinave, Africaine, Américaine, Iconologique etc.* (Paris, 1801, 2 vols. 1823). Handbook.

Nork, F. [F. Korn], *Andeutungen eines Systems der Mythologie . . . aus der . . . Mysteriosophie und Hierologie des alten Orients* (Leipzig, 1850).

Nork, F. [F. Korn], *Biblische Mythologie des Alten und Neuen Testamentes . . .* (Stuttgart, 1842). Popularizer of neo-Creuzerian comparative mythology.

Nork, F. [F. Korn], *Etymologisch-symbolisch-mythologisches Realwörterbuch zum Handgebrauch für Bibelforscher, Archäologen . . . ,* 4 vols. (Stuttgart, 1843–45). Popularizer of neo-Creuzerian comparative mythology.

Nork, F. [F. Korn], *Populäre Mythologie, oder Götterlehre aller Völker . . .* (Stuttgart, 1845). Handbook.

Nork, F. [F. Korn], *Vergleichende Mythologie . . .* (Leipzig, 1836). Popularizer of neo-Creuzerian comparative mythology.

Novalis, "Die Christenheit oder Europa" (1799). Essay urging new Christian mythology.

Nyerup, Rasmus, *Wörterbuch der Scandinavischen Mythologie* (Copenhagen, 1816). Translated from Danish.

Oegger, G., *Le Vrai Messie* (Paris, 1829). Swedenborgian; Christianity has replaced myth as language of nature.

Palgrave, Sir Francis, "Antiquities of Nursery Literature," in *Quarterly Review* XXI (1819), pp. 91–112.

Palgrave, Sir Francis, "Popular Mythology of the Middle Ages," in *Quarterly Review* XXII (1820), pp. 348–380.

Pastoret, Claude, *Zoroastre, Confucius, et Mahomet* . . . (Paris, 1787).

Paulinus a Sancto Barthelomaeo, *De veteribus Indis dissertatio . . . Alphabeti Tibetani* (Rome, 1795).

Paulinus a Sancto Barthelomaeo, *Sidharubam seu Grammatica Samscrdamica* . . . (Rome, 1790).

Paulinus a Sancto Barthelomaeo, *Systeme Brahmanicum Liturgicum, Mythologicum* . . . (Rome, 1791). Catholic missionary account of Hindu myth and ritual.

Pelloutier, Simon, *Histoire des Celtes, et . . . des Gaulois et des Germains* . . . (Paris, 1741).

Percy, Thomas (tr.), *Five Pieces of Runic Poetry from the Islandic Language* (London, 1763). Translation influenced by Lowth and Mallet.

* Percy, Thomas, *Reliques of Ancient English Poetry* (1765). Most popular collection of ballads and early English poetry.

Pérès, Jean-Baptiste, *Comme quoi Napoleon n'a jamais existé, où grand erratum,* . . . (Agen, 1835). Parody on Dupuis's mythology.

Pernety, A. J., *Dictionnaire Mytho-hermétique . . . des philosophes hermétiques expliqués* (Paris, 1787). Myth as alchemical code.

* Pernety, A. J., *Les Fables Égyptiennes et Grecques devoilées et réduites au même principe* . . . (Paris, 1758). Myth as code for alchemical secrets.

Petersen, N. M., *Nordisk mythologi* (Copenhagen, 1849).

Petit-Radel, F. L. C., *Examen analytique tableau comparatif des synchronismes de l'histoires des temps héroiques de la Grèce* (Paris, 1827). Mainly Euhemerist viewpoint.

Pezron, Paul-Yves, *Antiquité de la Nation et de la langue des Celtes autrement appellez Gaulois* (Paris, 1703).

* Picart, Bernard, *Cérémonies et Coutumes religieuses de tous les peuples du monde* . . . (n.p., 1723), Mythic art history.

* Pictet, Adolphe, *De l'affinité des Langues Celtiques avec la Sanscrit* (Paris, 1837).

* Pictet, Adolphe, *Du Culte des Cabires chez les anciens Irlandais* (Geneva, 1824). Relates Celtic myth to Indic myth using comparative philology.

* Pictet, Adolphe, *Les Origines Indo-Européenes, où les Aryas primitifs: essai de paleontologie linguistique* (Paris and Geneva, 1859–63).

Pigott, Grenville, *A Manual of Scandinavian Mythology, containing a popular account of the two Eddas and of the religion of Odin, illustrated by translations from Oehlenschlager's Danish poem The Gods of the North* (London, 1839).

Piper, F., *Mythologie und Symbolik der Christlichen Kunst* (Weimar, 1847–51).

Plessing, Friedrich Victor, *Memnonium oder Versuche zur Enthüllung der Geheimnisse des Alterthums,* 2 vols. (Leipzig, 1787). Pietist; myth as symbolic allegoric expression of mysteries.

Plessing, Johann Friedrich, *Versuch vom Ursprung der Abgötterey* (Leipzig, 1757), Etymological method; myth derives from debased biblical history.

* Pluche, Abbé Noël, *Histoire du Ciel, considéré selon des idées des poètes, des Philosophes et de Moïse,* 2 vols. (Paris, 1739–41). Derives myth from astronomy and agricultural calendar.

Pococke, Edward, *India in Greece: or, Truth in Mythology. Containing the sources of the Hellenic race, the colonization of Egypt and Palestine, the wars of the grand Lama, and the Bud'histic propaganda in Greece* etc. (London, 1852).

Polier, Marie Elizabeth de, *Mythologie des Indous travaillée par Mme de Polier sur des manuscrits authentiques apportés de l'Inde par feu M. de Polier* (Rudolstadt and Paris, 1809). Early unreliable pro-Christian work on Vedas.

Pomey, François A., *Pantheum Mythicum; seu fabulosa Deorum historia* (1697). Popular handbook.

* Pott, A. F., *Etymologische Forschungen, auf dem Gebiete der Indogermanischen Sprachen* (Lemgo, 1833–36). Comparative philology.

Potter, John, *Archaeologiae Graecae, or the Antiquities of Greece* (Oxford, 1697–99).

* Preller, L., *Griechische Mythologie,* 2 vols. (Leipzig, 1854). Famous scholarly dictionary.

Preller, L., *Römische Mythologie,* 2 vols. (Berlin, 1858). Scholarly handbook.

Prichard, J. C., *An Analysis of the Egyptian mythology* . . . (London, 1819). Influenced by Creuzer, Egyptian myth traced to India.

Prichard, J. C., *The Natural History of Man* (London, 1848). Early important anthropology on evolution, race selection.

Prideaux, Humphrey, *The Old and New Testaments connected in the history of the Jews and neighboring nations* . . . 2 vols. (London, 1716–18). Conventional chronology; harmonizes biblical, pagan history.

Priest, Josiah, *American Antiquities, and discoveries in the West* (Albany, 1833). American Christian antiquarianism; ark built in Ohio, etc.

Priestley, Joseph, *A Comparison of the Institutions of Moses with those of the Hindoos and other ancient nations: with remarks on Mr. Dupuis's Origin of all Religions* . . . (Northumberland [Penn.], 1799). Unitarian defense of Old Testament against Indic superstition.

Priestley, Joseph, *The Doctrines of Heathen philosophy compared with those of Revelation* (Northumberland [Penn.], 1804).

Prinsep, Henry Thoby, *Essays on Indian Antiquities* (1858). Indic archaeology.

Pustkuchen, Friedrich W., *Die Urgeschichte der Menschheit in ihrem vollen Umfänge* (Lemgo, 1821). Mainly texts: Phoenician, Old Persian, Indic, etc.

* Quinet, Edgar, *De l'Origine des Dieux* (1828).

* Quinet, Edgar, *Du Génie des Religions* (Paris, 1842). Inspired by Creuzer.

Rahnaeus, Joh. Friedrich, *De Hecate* (Griefswald, 1703). Etymologically derives Isis from Eve.

Ramler, Carl W., *Mythologie* . . . (Berlin, 1790). Handbook.

* Ramsay, Andrew M., *The Travels of Cyrus* . . . *To which is annex'd, a discourse upon the theology and mythology of the ancients* (London, 1727). All myth and religions share three-stage cycle.

Regis, F., "Le mitologia come maestra di morale e di politica," in *Turin Ac. d. Sci. Mem.,* Vol. XIII (Turin, 1803).

Reinhard, Philipp C., *Abriss einer Geschichte der Entstehung und Ausbildung der religiösen Ideen* (Jena, 1794). Fetishism as origin of all myth and religion.

Rémusat, Abel, "Discours sur le genie des peuples orientaux," in *Mélanges posthumes d'Histoire et de Littérature Orientales* (Paris, 1843). Oriental scholar and translator.

Renan, Ernest, *Histoire générale et système comparé des langues sémitiques* (Paris, 1855). Hebrew language as key to Jewish monotheism.

Renan, Ernest, "Les religions de l'antiquité" (originally published May 15, 1853 in *Revue des Deux Mondes*) reprinted in *Études l'histoire religieuse* (Paris, 2d ed., 1857). Review-essay of Creuzer, rationalist critique of modern mythology.

Renneville, Sophie de, *Nouvelle Mythologie du jeune age* (Paris, 1824). Handbook.

Reynaud, Jean, *Philosophie Religieuse. Terre et Ciel* (Paris, 1854). Neoplatonic-esoteric.

Richardson, John, *A Dissertation on the Languages, Literature, and Manners of Eastern Nations* . . . (Oxford, 1777).

Richter, Jean Paul, *Vorschule der Aesthetik* . . . (Hamburg, 1804). Has chapter on myth.

Ritter, Karl, *Die Erdkunde in Verhältnis zur Natur und zur Geschichte des Menschen* (Berlin, 1822–59). Important studies of primitive national migrations.

Robbins, Eliza, *Elements of Mythology,* 13th ed. (Philadelphia, 1830). Handbook.

Robertson, William, *An Historical Disquisition concerning the knowledge which the Ancients had of India* . . . (London, 1791). Crucial for spread of enthusiasm for India.

Rolle, P. N., *Recherches sur le Culte de Bacchus,* 3 vols. (Paris, 1824). Neo-Creuzerian view.

Rolle, P. N., *Religions de la Grèce* (Chatillon-sur-Seine, 1828). Neo-Creuzerian.

Rowlands, Henry, *Mona Antiqua Restaurata, an archaeological discourse on the antiquities* . . . *of the Isles of Anglesey* . . . *with* . . . *a comparative table of primitive words, and the derivatures of them* . . . (Dublin, 1723). English Druidic speculation.

Rückert, Emil, *Trojas Ursprung, Bluthe, Untergang* . . . *in Latium, Eine mythologisch chronologische und ethnographische Untersuchung der trojanisch-römischen Stamm-*

sage (Hamburg and Gotha, 1846). Follower of K. O. Müller.

Rückert, Friedrich, *Die Weisheit des Brahmanen* (Leipzig, 1836). Follower of K. O. Müller.

Sabatier, Antoine de Castres, *Les Siècles Païens, où Dictionnaire Mythologique* . . . (Paris, 1784). Handbook.

* Sainte-Croix Guillaume, Baron de, *Memoires pour servir à l'Histoire de la religion secrète des anciens peuples; où recherches historiques et critiques sur les mystères du paganisme* (Paris, 1784). Influenced by Herder; Egypt as origin of mystery religions.

Sale, George, *The Koran* . . . Tr. into English . . . with explanatory notes . . . (London, 1734). Extensive historical introduction.

Sanchez, Juan Antonio, *Colección de Poesías Castellanas Anteriores al Siglo XV* (1779). First modern edition of The Cid.

Von Sarn, Peter, *Specimen dissertationis historico-philologico-theologica de cognominibus quibusdam Jovis vero Jehovae quam verissima congruentibus* (1732). Etymological method; pagan myth as debased Bible history.

Savary, Claude-Étienne, *Lettres sur l'Égypte,* 2d ed. (Paris, 1786). Letters 40–74 treat Egyptian religion and antiquities.

Schelling, F. W. J., *Bruno, oder uber das göttliche und naturliche Prinzip der Dinge* (Berlin, 1802).

Schelling, F. W. J., *De prima malorum humanorum origine* (1792). School-thesis on Genesis and myth.

* Schelling, F. W. J., *Philosophie der Mythologie* (Stuttgart, 1856). Most important philosophic exposition of idealist view of myth.

* Schelling, F. W. J., *System des transcendentalen Idealismus* (Tübingen, 1800). Reinterprets myth in terms of German Idealist philosophy.

* Schelling, F. W. J., *Über die Gottheiten von Samothrace* . . . (Stuttgart and Tübingen, 1815).

Schelling, F. W. J., *Über Mythen, historische Sagen und Philosopheme der ältesten Welt* (1793). Influenced by Heyne: myth as primitive history and philosophy.

Schiller, J. C. F. von, *Briefe über die ästhetische Erziehung des Menschen* (1795).

* Schiller, J. C. F. von, "Der Götter Griechenlands" (1788). Controversial poem contrasting paganism favorably to Christianity.

Schiller, J. C. F. von, *Über naive und sentimentalische Dichtung* (1796).

Schlegel, A. W., "De l'origine des Hindous," in *Essais littéraires et historiques* (Bonn, 1842).

Schlegel, A. W., *Réflexions sur l'étude des langues asiatiques* . . . (Bonn, 1832). Comparative philology.

* Schlegel, A. W., *Vorlesungen über dramatische Kunst und Litteratur* (Heidelberg, 1809–11). Utilizes myth for history and criticism of tragedy.

* Schlegel, A. W., *Vorlesungen über schöne Literatur und Kunst* (1801–04). Incorporates German romantic myth and views into literary and artistic criticism.

Schlegel, F., *Geschichte der alten und neuen Litteratur* (Vienna, 1814).

Schlegel, F., *Geschichte der Poesie der Griechen und Römer* (1798).

Schlegel, F. *Kritik der Philosophischen Systeme,* lectures given 1804–06 (Bonn, 1836–37).

* Schlegel, F., "Rede über Mythologie," in *Athenäum* (Berlin, 1800). Calls for modern mythopoesis.

* Schlegel, F., *Über die Sprache und Weisheit der Indier* (Heidelberg, 1808). First extensive German interpretation of Indian religion based on philologic competence; influential—finally unsympathetic.

* Schlegel, F. and A. (eds.), *Athenäum* (Berlin, 1798). Periodical promoting German romantic interest in myth.

Schlegel, Johann K. F., *Über den Geist der Religiosität aller Zeiten und Völker* (Hanover, 1819). Discusses pluralist *vs.* monist origins of myth.

Schleiermacher, Friedrich, *Über die Religion. Reden an die Gebildeten unter ihren Verächtern* (Berlin, 1799).

Schmidt, Friedrich S. von, *Opuscula, quibus res antiquae praecipue Aegyptiacae explanantur* (Karlsruhe, 1765). Etymological method; myth as debased biblical history.

Schmidt, Isaac J., *Über die Verwandtschaft der gnostisch-theosophisch Lehren mit den Religionssysteme des Orients, vorzüglich dem Buddhismus* (Leipzig, 1828). Gnostics derive from East.

Schmitt, H. J., *Grundideen des Mythus . . .* (Frankfurt, 1826). Pro-Catholic interpretation.

* Schoolcraft, H. R., *Algic Researches, comprising inquiries respecting the mental characteristics of the North American Indians. First Series. Indian Tales and legends* (New York, 1839). Includes sections on American Indian myth.

Schoolcraft, H. R., *The Indian Fairy Book* (New York, 1856).

Schoolcraft, H. R., *The Myth of Hiawatha, and other oral legends, mythologic and allegoric, of the North American Indians* (Philadelphia, 1856).

* Schopenhauer, Arthur, *Die Welt als Wille und Vorstellung . . . ,* 1st ed. (Leipzig, 1819). Second expanded edition, 1844; crucial interpretation of myth and Western philosophy in Indic terms, stressing Hinduism first, then Buddhism in 1844.

Schubert, Gotthilf, *Die Symbolik des Traumes* (Bamberg, 1814).

Schütze, Gottfried, *Der Lehrbegrif der alten deutschen und nordischen Völker von dem Zustande der Selen nach dem Tode . . .* (Leipzig, 1750).

Schütze, Gottfried, *Drei kleine Schutzschiften für die alten Deutschen* (Leipzig, 1746–47). Vulgarizes Nordic myth.

Schwartz, F. L. W., *Der heutige Volksglaube und das alte Heidenthum . . . auf Norddeutschland* (Berlin, 1856). Folk legends give birth to ancient myth.

Schwartz, F. L. W., *Der Ursprung der Mythologie dargelegt an griechischer und deutscher Sage* (Berlin, 1860). Higher religions derive from popular beliefs in fairies, etc., and coins "lower mythology."

Schweigger, J., *Einleitung in die Mythologie auf dem Standpunkte der Naturwissenschaft . . .* (Halle, 1836). Myth from viewpoint of romantic *Naturphilosophie.*

Schwenk, Conrad, *Die Mythologie der asiatischen Völker, der Aegypter, Griechen, Römer, Germanen und Slaven,* 7 vols. (Frankfurt a.M., 1843–53). Myth as symbolic expressions of natural forces such as sun, moon.

Schwenk, Conrad, *Etymologisch—mythologische Andeutungen . . .* (Elberfeld, 1823). Comparative philologic approach.

Anon. [Leclerc de Septchênes], *Essai sur la religion des anciens Grecs* (Lausanne, 1787.) Follower of Dupuis, anti-allegoric; gods express national-religious conditions.

Seybold, D. C., *Einleitung in die Griechische und Römische Mythologie . . . für Jünglinge* (Leipzig, 1779). Handbook.

Seyffarth, G., *Die Grundsätze der Mythologie und der alten Religionsgeschichte sowie der hieroglyphischen Systeme de Sacy's, Palin's, Young's, Spohn's, Champollion's, Janelli's . . .* (Leipzig, 1843).

Sheldon, William, *History of the Heathen Gods, and Heroes of Antiquity* (Boston, 1810). Handbook.

Shuckford, Samuel, *The Sacred and Profane History of the World connected . . . ,* 2 vols. (London, 1728–30). Continuation of Prideaux 1716, Christian chronology.

Sickler, F. *Die Hieroglyphen in dem Mythus des Aesculapius . . .* (Meinigen, 1819).

Sickler, F., *Homers Hymnus an Demeter . . . nebst einem Brief an Hrn Creuzer . . .* (Hildburgshausen, 1820).

Sickler, F. *Kadmus oder Forschungen in den Dialekten des semitischen Sprachstammes, zur Entwicklung des Elementes der ältesten Sprache und Mythologie der Hellenen* (Hildburghausen, 1818).

Sickler, F., *Thot oder die Hieroglyphen der Athiopen und Ägypter . . .* (Hildburghausen, 1819). Influenced by Creuzer.

Sillig, K. J., *Dictionary of the Artists of Antiquity,* tr. H. W. Williams (London, 1836). Handbook; originally in Latin, published 1827.

Silvestre de Sacy, A. I., *Exposé de la religion des Druzes,* 2 vols. (Paris, 1838). Sacy occupied first French chair of Sanskrit, 1814.

Simon, Richard, *Critical Enquiries into the various editions of the Bible . . . concerning the oracles of the Sibylls* (London, 1684).

Simon, Richard, *A Critical History of the Old Testament . . .* (London, 1682).

* Simon, Richard, *Histoire critique du Texte du Nouveau Testament* (Rotterdam, 1689). Textual-historical biblical criticism.

Simrock, K. J., *Handbuch der deutschen Mythologie, mit Einschluss der nordischen* (Bonn, 1855). Handbook; solar interpretation.

Smith, Joseph, *The Book of Mormon* (Palmyra, New York, 1830).

* Smith, Sir William, *Dictionary of Greek and Roman Biography and Mythology*, 3 vols. (London, 1844–49). Among best nineteenth century classical dictionaries.

Solger, K. W. F., "Über die ältesten Ansichten der Griechen von der Welt," "Über die Religion der Griechen und einiger anderer Völker . . . ," "Über den Ursprung der Lehre von Dämonen und Schutzgeistern," in *Solgers Nachgelassen Schriften*, 2 vols. (Leipzig, 1826).

Sonnerat, Pierre, *Voyage aux Indes Orientales et à la Chine . . .* , 2 vols. (Paris, 1782). Egyptian and Greek religion derive from India.

Souverain, N., *Le Platonisme dévoilé ou Essai touchant le Verbe Platonicien* (Cologne and Amsterdam, 1700). Attacks Neoplatonism as origin of Christian beliefs.

Spearman, Robert, *Letters to a Friend Concerning the Septuagint Translation etc. and the Heathen Mythology* (Edinburgh, 1759). Pagan myth as debased Christianity.

* Spence, Joseph, *Polymetis; or, An Enquiry concerning the Agreement between the Works of the Roman Poets and the Remains of the Antient Artists* (London, 1747). Chiefly on Roman mythology.

Spencer, John, *De legibus Hebraeorum ritualibus et earum rationibus libri tres* (Cambridge, 1685).

* Staël, Madame de, *De l'Allemagne* (London, 1813).

Stalhös, *Dissertation De Danao* (Upsala, 1721). Christian Euhemerism.

Starck, Johann August von, *Hephästion* (Königsberg, 1775). Paganism was esoteric mystery religion.

Stark, Karl B., *Forschungen zur Geschichte und Alterthumsk. des hellenistischen Orients . . .* (Jena, 1852).

Staveren, A. von, *Auctores mythographi Latini* (Amsterdam, 1742).

Stillingfleet, Edward, *Originae Britannicae, or the Antiquities of the British Churches* (London, 1685).

* Strauss, D. F., *Das Leben Jesu* (Tübingen, 1835). Landmark of "higher" biblical criticism.

Stuhr, P. F., *Allgemeine Geschichte der Religionsformen der heidnischen Völker* (Berlin, 1838). Myth as spiritual symbols.

Stuhr, P. F., *Die Religionssysteme der heidnische Völker des Orients* (Berlin, 1836).

Stukeley, William, *Abury, a temple of the British Druids* (London, 1743).

* Stukeley, William, *Stonehenge, A temple restor'd to the British Druids* (London, 1740). Druidism as primitive, undefiled Christianity.

Suhm, P. F. von, *P. F. von S.'s Geschichte der Dänen* (Leipzig, 1782). Oriental origins of Scandinavian deities; originally published in Danish, 1782.

* Swedenborg, Emanuel, *Arcana Caelestia* (n.p., 1749–56).

Sykes, A. A., *An essay on the nature . . . of sacrifice* (1748).

* Taylor, Thomas, *A Dissertation on the Eleusinian and Bacchic Mysteries* (London, 1790). Neoplatonic, Orphic viewpoint.

Taylor, Thomas (tr.), *Jamblichus on the Mysteries of the Egyptians* (1821). Neoplatonic and Orphic viewpoint.

Taylor, Thomas, *Select Works of Porphyry . . . tr. from the Greek by T. Taylor with an appendix explaining the allegory of the Wanderings of Ulysses, by the translator* (1823). Neoplatonic and Orphic viewpoint.

Temple, Sir William, "Of Heroic Virtue," in *Miscellanea: the second part, in Four Essays* (London, 1692). First important notice of Nordic myth.

Terrasson, Jean, *Dissertation critique sur l'Iliade d'Homère*, 2 vols. (Paris, 1715). Takes up Ancients-Moderns controversy.

Thorkelin, G. J., *De Danorum rebus gestis secul III & IV. Poëma danicum dialecto anglosaxonica* (1815). First printing of Beowulf, in Anglo-Saxon and Latin.

Thormodus, Torfaeus, *Orcades, seu Rerum Orcadensium historiae libri tres* (Hafniae, 1697). Serves later Nordic Renaissance.

Thormodus, Torfaeus, *Series dynastarum et regum Daniae* (Copenhagen, 1702).

Thorpe, Benjamin, *Northern mythology*, 3 vols. (London, 1851). Handbook.

Toland, John, *A Critical History of the Celtic religion and learning; containing an account of the Druids . . .* (London, n.d. [1718]).

Toland, John, *Christianity not Mysterious* (London, 1696). Early influential deist tract.

* Toland, John, *Letters to Serena . . .* (London, 1704). Myth originates in worship of dead; Letter III concerns origins of myth.

Toland, John, *Pantheisticon cosmopoli* (1720).

Program for new rationalist religious society.

Tooke, Andrew, *The Pantheon: representing the fabulous histories of the heathen Gods* (London, 1698). Translation of Pomey.

Tournemine, René, "Projet d'un ouvrage sur l'origine des fables," in *Mémoires de Trévoux* (December 1702 and January 1703).

* Trenchard, John, *The Natural History of Superstition* (London, 1709). Religious fanaticism as psychopathology.

Tressan, Abbé M.-E., *La mythologie comparée avec l'histoire* (Paris and Amsterdam, 1803). Popular Euhemerism.

* Turgot, Baron de l'Aulne, *Tableau philosophique des progrès successifs de l'esprit humain* (Paris, 1750). Religion as phase of progress.

Uhland, J. L., *Alte hoch—und niederdeutsche Volkslieder* (Stuttgart and Tübingen, 1844, 1845).

Uhland, J. L., *Der Mythus von Thôr nach nordischen Quellen* (Stuttgart and Augsburg, 1836).

Ullmann, Carl, *Historisch oder Mythisch!* (Hamburg, 1838).

Uvarov, Sergei, *Essai sur les mystères d'Eleusis* (Paris, 1812). Influenced by Creuzer; translated into English by J. D. Price, 1817.

Uvarov, Sergei, *Examen critique de la fable d'Hercule commentée par Dupuis* (Paris, 1818).

Valpy, A. J., *Elements of Mythology,* 4th ed. (Philadelphia, 1821). Handbook.

Van Amringe, William, *An Investigation of the Theories of the Natural History of Man* (New York, 1848). Anthropology.

Van Dale, Antonius, *De Oraculis Ethnicorum dissertationes duae* (Amsterdam, 1683). Adapted by Fontenelle in *Histoire des Oracles,* in turn translated by Aphra Behn.

Van Dale, Antonius, *Dissertationes de origine ac progressu idololatriae et superstitionum* (Amsterdam, 1696).

Vico, Giambattista, *De nostri temporis studiorum ratione* . . . (Naples, 1709).

* Vico, Giambattista, *Principi di una Scienza Nuova* (Naples, 1725). Seminal, indispensable revaluation; third edition, 1744, must also be consulted.

Völcker, K. H. W., *Die Mythologie des Japetischen Geschlechtes, oder der Sündenfall des Menschen, nach Griechischen Mythen* (Giessen, 1824). In "historical" school of K. O. Müller.

Völcker, K. H. W., *Mythische Geographie der Griechen und Römer* (Leipzig and Giessen, 1832). Follower of K. O. Müller.

* Volney, Comte de, *Les Ruines où Méditation sur les révolutions des empires* (Paris, 1791). Rationalist derivation of myth from astronomy.

Volney, Comte de, *Recherches nouvelles sur l'Histoire Ancienne* . . . (Paris, 1814). Non-Christian chronology.

* Voltaire, F. M. A. de, *Essai sur les moeurs* . . . (Paris, 1769). Anti-Christian philosophy of history; diminishes place of classical myth and Bible in world history.

Von der Hagen, F. H., *Minnesinger,* 4 vols. (Leipzig, 1838).

Von der Hardt, H., *Celebris Graecorum mythus Pyramus et Thisbe* . . . (Helmstadt, 1736). Allegoric-mystic view of myth.

Von der Hardt, H., *Aenigmata prisci orbis* . . . *Homeri, Hesiodi, Orphei* . . . *Hercules* . . . *Thetis* . . . *Arion* . . . (Helmstadt, 1723).

Von der Hardt, H., *Tres Graecorum Mythi apud Ovidium.* . . (Helmstadt, 1736).

* Voss, J. H., *Antisymbolik* (Stuttgart, 1824–26). Polemic against Creuzer.

Voss, J. H., *Mythologische Briefe,* 2 vols. (Königsberg, 1794). Eclectic, rambling, polemic, mainly rationalistic.

Wagner, J. J., *Ideen zu einer allgemeinen Mythologie der alten Welt* (Frankfurt a.M., 1808).

* Wagner, Richard, *Das Kunstwerk der Zukunft* (Leipzig, 1850). Art and myth.

* Wagner, Richard, *Die Kunst und die Revolution* (Leipzig, 1849). Myth as revolutionary artistic and social force.

Wagner, Richard, *Oper und Drama* (Leipzig, 1852). Myth and opera.

Wagner, Richard, *Tannhäuser und der Sängerkrieg auf Wartburg* (Dresden, 1845).

* Waitz, Theodor, *Anthropologie der Naturvölker* (Leipzig, 1859–72). Early modern anthropological approach.

* Warburton, William, *The Divine Legation of Moses demonstrated* . . . , 2 vols. (Lon-

don, 1737–41). Derives Greek religion from Egypt, influential treatment of hieroglyphics and animal worship as historic records.

Ward, William, *Account of the writings religion and manners of the Hindoos . . .* , 4 vols. (Serampore, 1811).

Warton, Thomas, "On the Origin of the Romantic fiction in Europe," in *The History of English Poetry* (London, 1774–81). Preromantic, influenced by Nordic Renaissance.

Watson, David, *A Clear and Compendious History of the Gods and Goddesses and their Contemporaries* (London, 1752). Handbook.

Weber, Albrecht, *Indische Skizzen* (Berlin, 1857). Rationalist, "social" Buddhism.

Weber, Henry W., *Illustrations of Northern Antiquities, from the earlier Teutonic and Scandinavian Romances; being an abstract of the Book of Heroes, and Nibelungen Lay; with translations of Metrical Tales, from the Old German, Danish, Swedish and Icelandic languages. With notes and dissertations [by H. Weber and R. Jamieson]* (Edinburgh, 1814).

Weber, Henry W., *Tales of the East: comprising the most popular Romances of Oriental origin . . .* , 3 vols. (Edinburgh, 1812).

Webster, Noah, "The Origin of Mythology," in *Memoirs of the Connecticut Academy of Arts and Sciences*, Vol. I (New Haven, 1810), pp. 175–216. Reduces all myth to Celtic place-names.

Weisse, C. H., *Darstellung der Griechischen Mythologie*, Vol. I (Leipzig, 1828). Handbook.

Welcker, Friedrich, *Alte Denkmäler erklärt*, 5 vols. (Göttingen, 1849–64). Mythic art studies, influenced by K. O. Müller.

Welcker, Friedrich, *Die griechischen Tragödien mit Rücksicht auf den epischen Cyclus geordnet* (Bonn, 1827). Myth as allegorical expression of hierarchical nature.

* Welcker, F. G., *Griechische Götterlehre*, 3 vols. (Göttingen, 1857–63). Early modern "history of religions."

Whiston, William, *An essay towards restoring the true text of the Old Testament* (London, 1722). Orthodox Christian chronology.

Whiston, William, *A New Theory of the earth* (London, 1696).

Wieland, Christoph, *Musarion, oder die Philosophie der Grazien* (Leipzig, 1769).

* Wilford, Capt. Francis, "An Essay on the Sacred Isles in the West," in *Asiatick Researches*, Vol. 8–11 (1805–10). Identified Britain as Sacred Isles of Hindus.

Wilkie, William, *The Epigoniad*, 2d ed. (London, 1769). Has interesting preface on myth.

* Wilkins, Charles (tr.), *Bhagvat-Geeta . . .* (London, 1785). First direct complete translation of a major Sanskrit text.

Wilkins, Charles (tr.), *The Heetopades . . .* (1787). First translation.

Wilkinson, Sir J. G., *Manners and Customs of the ancient Egyptians*, 2d series (London, 1837–41).

* Wilkinson, Sir J. G., *Materia Hieroglyphia. Containing the Egyptian Pantheon . . .* (Malta, 1828).

Williams, Rowland, *Paraméswara-juyána-góshthí, A Dialogue . . . in which are compared the claims of Christianity and Hinduism* (Cambridge, 1856).

* Wilson, H. H., *The Vishńu Puráńa, a System of Hindu Mythology* (Bombay, 1840). Wilson held first English chair of Sanskrit.

Wilson, John, *The Parsi Religion, as contained in the Zand-Avasta . . . unfolded, refuted, and contrasted with Christianity* (Bombay, 1843).

Winckelmann, J. J., *Anmerkungen über die Baukunst der alten* (Leipzig, 1762).

Winckelmann, J. J., *Anmerkungen über die Geschichte der Kunst des Alterthums* (Dresden, 1767).

Winckelmann, J. J., *Gedanken über die Nachahmung der griechischen Werke . . .* (Friedrichstadt, 1755). Classical revival and romantic Hellenism; imitation of Greek art and spirit.

* Winckelmann, J. J., *Geschichte der Kunst des Alterthums* (Dresden, 1764). "Apollonian" qualities of Greek art.

Winckelmann, J. J., *Monumenti antichi inediti spiegati ed illustrati* (Rome, 1767).

Winckelmann, J. J., *Versuch einer Allegorie, besonders für die Kunst* (1766). Myth as allegories, but as useful for modern artists.

Windischmann, F. H., *Über den Sonnenkultus der Aryer* (Munich, 1846). Nature myth.

* Wolf, F. A., *Prolegomena ad Homerum . . .* (Halle, 1795). Standard work on "Homeric" problem, explains Homer as folk-oral epic.

Wollheim da Fonseca, A. E., *Kurzgefasste Mythologie aller Völker der Erde* (Hamburg and New York, 1849).

Wood, John, *Choir Gaure, vulgarly called Stonehenge* . . . (Oxford, 1747).

* Wood, Robert, *A Comparative View of the antient and present state of the Troade. To which is prefixed an essay on the original genius of Homer* (London, 1767). Reissued 1769 as *Essay on the Original Genius of Homer.*

Wood, Robert, *The Ruins of Balbec, otherwise Heliopolis, in Coelosyria* (London, 1757).

Wood, Robert, *The Ruins of Palmyra, otherwise Tedmor, in the Desert* (London, 1753). Influential early firsthand travel account of ruins.

Woodward, John, *An Essay toward a Natural History of the Earth* (London, 1695). Flood caused all geologic strata and fossils.

Woolston, Thomas, *A Discourse on the Miracles of our Saviour* (1727–29). Neoplatonic allegorizing.

Wright, Thomas, *Essays on subjects connected with the literature, popular superstitions, and history of England in the Middle Ages,* 2 vols. (London, 1846). Folklore antiquarian school.

Wuttke, Karl F., *Geschichte des Heidenthums* (Breslau, 1852–53). On fetish cults and nature worship.

Zampi, Giuseppi, *Relation de la Religion des Mingreliens,* in Chardin, *Voyages en Perse etc.,* Vol. I (1711).

Zeitschrift für Völkerpsychologie (founded by Steinthal and Lazarus), 1860.

Zobelius, Nikolaus, *Dissertatio inauguralis de lapsu primorum humani generis parentum a paganis adumbrata* (Altdorf, 1730). Derives Greek myth from debased Bible history; etymological method.

Zoega, Georg, *De origine et usu obeliscorum* . . . (Rome, 1797). Elaborates Hindu folkmyth and Goethean symbol.

Zoega, Georg, *Li Bassirilievi antichi di Roma* . . . , 2 vols. (Rome, 1808).

* Zoega, Georg, *Vorlesungen über die Griechische Mythologie,* ed. G. Welcker (Göttingen, 1817).

INDEX

Page numbers of primary introductory material to each figure are set in italics.